The Carol Burnett Show Companion:

So Glad We Had This Time

by Wesley Hyatt

The Carol Burnett Show Companion: So Glad We Had This Time

Published in the USA by:
BearManor Media
P O Box 71426
Albany, Georgia 31708
www.bearmanormedia.com

Printed in the United States of America
ISBN 978-1-59393-179-7 (paperback)

Book & cover design and layout by Darlene Swanson • www.van-garde.com

Contents

Dedication

To Todd Day, a friend who kept me sane throughout
more than two years of research on a project I'm sure he wondered
would ever become a reality. Here's your answer.

Acknowledgments

In much the same way Carol Burnett began her exceptional variety series by announcing her regulars and guests at the top, I want to start this book by thanking those who contributed their precious time and memories about participating in her series. In alphabetical order followed by their interview date, they are Bill Angelos (June 24, 2014), Kaye Ballard (June 18, 2014), Bobbie Bates (Sept. 24, 2013), Roger Beatty (email March 11, 2014), Joe Blasco (Sept. 18, 2014), Julie Budd (June 23, 2014), John Byner (email Sept. 23, 2013), Dyan Cannon (Sept. 23, 2014), Vikki Carr (July 22, 2014), Pat Carroll (May 31, 2013), Charo (July 23, 2014), Kathy Clements (Aug. 11, 2013), Kay Cole (May 18, 2013), Mike Dann (April 20, 2013), Jerry Davis (Oct. 18, 2013), Rudy De Luca (July 12, 2014), Dick DeBenedictis (Aug. 5, 2014), Randy Doney (Sept. 18, 2013), Barbara Feldon (Aug. 27, 2013), Stan Hart (June 23, 2014), David Hartman (Oct. 14, 2014), Bob Illes (July 2, 2013), Carl Jablonski (June 21, 2014), Sande Johnson (Oct. 22, 2013), Bo Kaprall (May 23, 2013), Lainie Kazan (May 27, 2013), Arnie Kogen (Feb. 19, 2014), Buz Kohan (July 26, 2013), Chris Korman (Aug. 10, 2014), Michele Lee (email March 14, 2014), Barry Levinson (Aug. 25, 2014), Trini Lopez (Aug. 4, 2014), Gloria Loring (May 21, 2013), Stan Mazin (June 9, 2013), Nick Meglin (June 26, 2014), Jack Mendelsohn (Feb. 22, 2014), Gene Merlino (June 20, 2014), Heather North (July 14, 2014), Cubby O'Brien (May 14, 2014), Gail Parent and Kenny Solms (July 13, 2013), Gene Perret (June 24, 2013), Anita Pointer (July 10, 2014), Pat Proft (Aug. 13, 2013), Carl Reiner (Aug. 7, 2014), Chita Rivera (Oct. 16, 2013), Wayne Rogers (Sept. 4, 2014), Paul Sand (Aug. 31, 2013), Ronnie Schell (June 23, 2014), Larry Siegel (Aug. 5, 2013), Franelle Silver (June 29, 2014), Fred Silverman (July 15, 2014), Saul Turteltaub (Sept. 23, 2014), Violette Verdy (Aug. 17, 2013), Shani Wallis (Aug. 20, 2013), Ken Welch (Sept. 16, 2014) and Karen Wyman (June 22, 2014).

I am equally indebted if not more so to the kindness and dedication of Mark Quigley, manager of the Archive Research and Study Center in the UCLA Film and Television Archive, as well as Martin Gostanian, supervisor of visitor services for the Paley Center for Media in Los Angeles, and Richard Holbrook and Jane Klein, the library supervisor and manager of research services respectively for the Paley Center for Media in New York City. All of these individuals were instrumental—make that essential—in allowing me exclusive access to many key classic episodes of *The Carol Burnett Show* and related TV programs I otherwise would have been unable to view during multiple visits to their offices. This book would be sorely lacking without their gracious assistance and input. I encourage everyone to support financially the wonderful work done by their organizations in preserving America's pop culture history.

Also helping me immensely were trades I made with fellow video collectors Todd Brost (a/k/a "Professor Video") and Richard Sackley. Phil Gries, leader of Archival Television Audio, Inc., allowed me access to audiotapes of some shows otherwise unavailable in video form. For additional video assistance and advice on this project, I graciously thank Chris Buhler and Norman "Van" Vanhorne.

Another nod of appreciation goes out to Ashley Dumazer with Getty Images, who patiently endured countless months of me trying to narrow down the right pictures to illustrate each chapter. Getty Images was the best resource by far in providing unique classic images connected to *The Carol Burnett Show*, and I highly recommend the firm to other authors seeking great photos to illustrate their books.

I am also indebted to fellow TV enthusiasts Stu Shostak, Ed Robertson and Bob Leszczak (a/k/a "Bob O'Brien") for their connections in finding several of the key personnel listed previously for me to interview. For moral support, I must thank Steve Beverly and Tom Kennedy, my favorite game show host of all time, who loved the idea of this book when I first shared it with him.

Last and never least, I want to thank the help and endurance of my family, friends and colleagues who understood when I told them I could not join them for a function due to work on this book (for some, it was a phrase they had heard from me previously). To Gayle Willard Hyatt, Art Callahan, LuAnn Hyatt Martinson, Skip Martinson, Bennett Martinson, Brynn Martinson, GerShun Avilez, John Bowser, Rodney Carroll, Marion Carter, Todd Day, Renee Duncan, Julie Ellis, Ed Emory, Anthony Evans, Kevin Grady, David Guinnup, Corey Harris, Jeff Johnson, Jimmy Lancaster, Drew McNeil, Reggie Shuford and Joe Watkins, I sincerely appreciate your love and support, and I hope you enjoy what I have created during my absence from you.

Finally, the absence of direct interviews in this book with Tim Conway, Vicki Lawrence, Lyle Waggoner, Bob Mackie, Bernadette Peters, Steve Lawrence, Ken Berry, Jim Nabors and of course Carol Burnett herself is not intentional. I contacted them or their representatives, and for whatever individual reasons they had, they declined to participate, as did several others with less consequential connections to the series. I have done my best to portray their contributions to *The Carol Burnett Show* fairly given the circumstances, and I hope my immense respect for the talents comes through as I attempt to summarize and analyze what they added to this classic TV series.

Prologue: Let's Bump Up the Lights

When participants of *The Carol Burnett Show* discuss their memories of what many critics and historians regard as a great TV series, one word comes up often—family.

The term makes sense in several ways. When creating the show with her then-husband, Joe Hamilton, Carol wanted a family of regulars. The series' first recurring sketch was "Carol & Sis," detailing the adventures of Carol, her husband and her younger sister and based somewhat on Carol's own life. It was later supplanted by a Southern clan where Carol played a character based on her mother. Appropriately, the segment's original name was simply "The Family."

At the same time, it was the show's ability to appeal to all members of any family that made it such a success for eleven seasons. In particular, its sketches offered comedy ranging from silly slapstick to sophisticated satire—sometimes all within the same skit. There were moments that were bawdy and made sense mainly to adults, but the series never wallowed in off-color or mean humor. That made it an easy hour for everyone to enjoy, from children to senior citizens.

"My feeling is the reason everyone liked it is because they would watch it with their family," says Bill Angelos, a writer for the series from the start to 1973.

A principal guest turned regular on *The Carol Burnett Show* concurs. As Tim Conway recalled on the 2004 DVD commentary, "We never said anything nasty about anybody. There was no language or nudity, outside of you (gesturing comically at fellow regular Harvey Korman). But no, seriously, it was nice. Wonderful family shows. You could all get around and enjoy them."

Along the same lines, members of *The Carol Burnett Show* consider themselves part of a unique clan. Many of the crew that joined the series stayed for years, often until the end of its run. It had a remarkably stable record with on-air regulars as well, losing just two (one just a year before it ended), and adding one who had virtually been a regular due to his frequent guest roles on the series. The atmosphere was one of familiarity and friendliness throughout the show, with Carol acting as the wacky but solid mother in charge of it all.

"It was a family," agrees Bob Illes, who wrote for the series' last season. "Everybody, even the camera guys, had been there ten years. All friendly people."

"It was a family show, and it starts with the lead," says dancer/choreographer Carl Jablonski. "Carol was so kind and polite with the company. She was such fun."

"She was the nicest person in the world," recalls Bobbie Bates, a dancer on the series. "She was great. Every time a new person came on the show, she came across the stage and said, 'Hi, I'm Carol.'"

The camaraderie extended beyond working hours, a relative rarity among TV series. As Jablonski recalls, "Carol and Joe Hamilton (Carol's husband at the time and the series' executive producer) would always throw a great Christmas party. They would rent the Los Angeles Yacht Club. It was an old school party, first class, for everyone. They were very generous about that."

Even the personnel not on camera felt clannish. "They used to give jackets to crew members saying 'Burnett's Bums,'" notes Chris Korman, Harvey's son.

Like any other families, though, there were some stresses. Among the regulars, Harvey Korman, Vicki Lawrence and Tim Conway all witnessed their marriages dissolve during the series' run. (Tim later married Charlene Beatty, a production assistant on the show.) Carol and Joe would divorce after the show's run as well. Even so, these negative personal situations never came to the forefront, allowing the show to maintain its reputation for being family friendly for eleven years.

Part of its favorable standing had to do with the titular star, who began each show coming across as warm and endearing talking with members of her studio audience. Thereafter, Carol could and did indulge in mugging, belting and dancing up a storm, along with occasional dramatic acting, to offer viewers a multidimensional performer who had few peers in entertainment, male or female. She made you think that being part a comedy variety series was the best fun you could have in the world, and her engaging presence won over even the most cynical of viewers.

Though her humor and approach often reminded people of Lucille Ball, four-time guest star Pat Carroll points out a crucial difference between the women. "Lucy could not step outside of herself," she says, meaning Ball would have had a difficult time slipping in and out of character plus introduce acts and do numbers the way Carol did. Simply put, Carol was one of a kind.

Carol also emphasized having fun in her production and treating everyone fairly, no matter what his or her position was. As a result, there were mostly minor conflicts that emerged regarding the series, and none resulted in negative news coverage. In the same vein, network officials loved how little drama came from *The Carol Burnett Show*, which only enhanced its renewal chances every year—not that it was really in jeopardy (it finished in the top 30 rated series every year apart from its last two seasons).

"We never had a problem with the show," former CBS programming head Fred Silverman says. "They delivered a quality show week in and week out."

Given all these elements, it is not surprising *The Carol Burnett Show* is one of those increasingly rare TV series enjoyed by a large swath of viewers across all demographics. No matter your age, gender, race, religion, sexuality or income, chances are the series will appeal to you.

This accessible image has been a double-edged sword for the series from the start, however. As it became part of the pop culture landscape when it debuted in 1967, *The Carol Burnett Show* has largely been taken for granted, as shown by this book being the first devoted solely to telling its story. Dozens of tomes have popped up praising many lesser series in terms of quality, length and cultural impact. An assessment of this series is sorely overdue.

Consider this: *The Carol Burnett Show* still remains among the top 1 percent of all TV series to win an Emmy for best in its genre, the top ten nighttime entertainment series with the most Emmy wins, and the top 100 longest-running nighttime entertainment series as well. Given those distinctions, its coverage by the media has been sparse in comparison to its accomplishments, even during its years in production.

As a reporter with the Associated Press wrote in 1972, "Carol Burnett has become such a familiar light in the television firmament that neither she nor her CBS series receives the attention it deserves (sic)." That same year, *The Carol Burnett Show* finally won the Emmy for outstanding variety series after five years, an inordinately long wait for a series to win American TV's top honor.

More Emmys would come its way, along with a raft of other awards, all chronicled in the following pages. Yet overall, the series and its legacy in the industry have largely and strangely been ignored, even among TV historians who should know better.

For example, the fine season-by-season review of the industry, *Watching TV*, makes no mention of the series at all, while devoting paragraphs to other series that have had lesser popular and critical impact of the medium's history. It took Tim Brooks and Earle Marsh two updates in *The Complete Directory to Prime Time Network TV Shows 1946-Present* to straighten out its summaries of some of the recurring sketches while missing others. *TV Guide Guide to TV* in 2004 devoted just a single paragraph to the series despite its having finished at Number Sixteen in the publication's list of the 50 greatest shows of all time a year earlier. (*The Carol Burnett Show* remained just as strong a decade later, finishing at Number Seventeen in *TV Guide's* list of 60 best series of all time in 2013.)

These are just some of the most glaring oversights that this book intends to correct. By talking with its personnel, guest stars and others connected intimately to the series, and covering the series from its inception to its aftermath, readers will find the most complete picture of how and why *The Carol Burnett Show* became such a critical and commercial success for more than a decade.

Overviews and summaries of key changes, highlights and occasional lowlights for each season occur in each chapter, along with a capsule description of each of the series' 276 shows and comments on them. A single asterisk (*) means the episode was available for partial viewing in the syndicated half-hour version or in segments included in DVDs, archive or online collections, or in a few cases had the script available for review. A double asterisk (**) next to a summary means that episode was a rare one unavailable for personal viewing. All told, the author watched 213 full episodes and 26 partial ones, providing the most extensive coverage of the series anywhere prior to this publication.

This book fulfills the need to recognize *The Carol Burnett Show* as part of the family of excellent entertainment. As a critical appreciation, it is meant to recount, recognize and celebrate its accomplishments, while fully acknowledging the series' occasional flaws and lapses of judgment.

It is fully admitted up front that compared to other series awarded Emmys for best variety show, *The Carol Burnett Show* can be found to come up short in some respects. *Your Show of Shows* was more groundbreaking and, at 90 minutes, more expansive. *The Red Skelton Show* had better pantomimes. *Caesar's Hour* had more manic energy from its lead. *The Ed Sullivan Show* presented more guest stars, often in segments that showcased their talents better than Carol's show. *The Dinah Shore Show* and *The Andy Williams Show* presented more diverse musical numbers and talent. *Rowan and Martin's Laugh-In* was more irreverent and often better paced. And *Saturday Night Live* had more of a contemporary edge, not to mention a more stinging and raunchy presentation than Carol's show, which arguably is more of a drawback.

Yet *The Carol Burnett Show* still shines brightly simply because it typically is so very good in all departments that it easily compensates in not being as outstanding in the individual categories just mentioned. For maintaining a consistently high average of presenting a tight hour show with quality comedy and music, *The Carol Burnett Show* has no peers.

This book's purpose is to reflect the show in all its glory without deifying it. While some may disagree with some of the conclusions and comments presented, the intent is to provide a multifaceted evaluation designed to serve as a starting point for discussion and not the final word of this great work of art.

With that in mind, to paraphrase how Carol would start every show, let's bump up the lights and tell the story of *The Carol Burnett Show*!

Garry Moore and Carol Burnett celebrate their wins at the fourteenth annual Emmy Awards ceremony presented May 22, 1962, Moore for Outstanding Variety Program as star of ***The Garry Moore Show*** and Burnett for Outstanding Performance in a Variety or Music Program or Series on that series. Having already announced she was leaving after three seasons as a regular on ***The Garry Moore Show***, Burnett's departure spurred CBS to keep under contract the comic talent many considered the next Lucille Ball, with a provision that led to the creation of ***The Carol Burnett Show***. Courtesy of Getty Images.

Chapter 1

Setting the Groundwork, or Pushing the Button

Thanks for going to Hollywood, even though that show is going to bomb."—A long-forgotten CBS executive talking to writers Buz Kohan and Bill Angelos before they left New York City to work on *The Carol Burnett Show* in the summer of 1967.

Imagine being the leader of the top medium of the twentieth century, on the verge of being even more successful, yet being intimidated by a talent who you consider a friend.

That was what CBS head of programming Mike Dann faced in the summer of 1962 to determine his network's future relationship with Carol Burnett. She had just won an Emmy for her regular supporting role as an actress, singer and dancer on *The Garry Moore Show*, a hit Tuesday night variety series that helped the network stay at Number One overall. Now Burnett wanted to do more on her own, and Dann had to determine what new working relationship would exist with her.

"It was the first major contract I was involved in," Dann notes. His boss, CBS President William Paley, favored exclusive deals with name performers like Burnett to retain their services. "He was anxious that I build a stable of stars as much as I could," Dann says.

Complicating matters was his own relationship with Burnett. He had first met her back in the mid-1950s when he was a programming executive for NBC and she was a fresh newcomer to New York City who impressed him with her work away from the stage.

"She helped children with physical problems to use the pool as rehabilitation," Dann recalls. "She was very confident on what to make kids secure in that situation."

Carol went on to appear on many NBC series, including regular stints on two shows, but she really became a star on *The Garry Moore Show* from 1959-1962 on CBS. Coincidentally, Dann switched from working at NBC to CBS at that time, and he adored Carol as both a talent and a human being.

With that, he reluctantly hammered out a settlement. By August, Dann had helped negotiate an exclusive contract for $1.1 million which guaranteed Carol a one-hour special and two guest appearances annually on any of the network's series through 1972.

Also included was an odd option of doing 30 one-hour shows guaranteed for CBS at any time by Carol's request. "Just push the button!" Dann told Carol. He quickly forgot that statement. After all, no one had thought of a comedy variety series starring a woman.

Dann had absolutely no idea that he had put into motion what would turn out to be the longest-running series on CBS installed during his presidency (except for *Hawaii Five-0*, whose twelve years from 1968-1980 beat out Carol's residency by just one season), or that it would be the biggest Emmy-winning series during his tenure as well. Both are incredible achievements, and they all stem from the talent and input of the series' leading lady.

Carol's Backstory

Carol has given her biography so many times that this will just be a condensed summary of her pre-TV series years. Born in San Antonio, Texas, on April 26, 1933, she moved to Los Angeles with her family at a young age. As her parents were alcoholics, her grandmother raised her and her younger sister, Chrissy (also known as Chris).

Although Carol found an escape going to the movies constantly in the 1940s—even becoming a movie theater usher at one point—she planned to be a cartoonist or journalist when she entered UCLA in the early 1950s. Passing time on campus, she appeared on stage as a hillbilly woman as a lark, and people laughed heartily. Suddenly, Carol realized she really wanted a career in show business and went into acting in earnest.

Performing with her boyfriend, Don Saroyan (who became her husband in 1955), she attracted the attention of a wealthy arts patron at a party in 1954. Impressed with her talent, he loaned her $1,000 to fly to New York City, with the agreement that she would repay him fully five years later and never reveal his identity. She did both, and he remains a mysterious investor to this day, as Carol has remained mum about his identity.

Moving to Manhattan in 1955, Carol made the rounds as a starving actress to audition. One of them involved a gentleman who was essential in getting her early work.

"I was a young coach and accompanist in New York," recalls Ken Welch. "An agent there had sent me people, and in return, I offered to accompany their auditions for him." The agent was Gus Schirmer Jr., "who had a lock on booking musical talent during the summer in the East."

One of Schirmer's suggestions was Carol Burnett, who already has her own accompanist, Peter Daniels. "She sang, 'How About You,' and I thought she was terrific, but Gus wasn't impressed, felt she was wrong, but I didn't," relates Welch.

Welch congratulated Carol as she left to do a job at a different summer theater called Green Mansions, where she worked with a choreographer named Frank Wagner. At the end of her tour there, she asked him if she should work with a vocal coach. He said yes and told her to try Kenny Welch. "I think I met him!" Carol exclaimed.

"She didn't have any money, so I spoke to an agent about what to do, and he said, 'Go to the stationery store and get promissory notes and have her sign them each time you work,'" Welch recalls about her paying him. That worked, but after several auditions Carol received no job offers. The answer hit Welch, and he shared it with Carol.

"I don't think people realize you are a comedienne," he said. "We need to write comic material for you." Welch did so, and soon, Carol found substantial work, including one relatively new medium of entertainment—television.

TV Time

TV in New York was booming in the mid-1950s, with plenty of opportunities for those ready to work hard. Carol got bit parts on shows such as *The Colgate Comedy Hour* before securing a thirteen-week gig starting in December 1955 on *Paul Winchell and Jerry Mahoney*, a children's show seen Saturday mornings on NBC. Winchell was a ventriloquist, Mahoney was his wisecracking dummy, and Burnett played the latter's girlfriend. It was not prestigious, but it did pay the bills.

The stint also marked the beginning of Carol tugging her left earlobe, something she will do at the end of every *Carol Burnett Show*. She did this initially because her grandmother wanted her to say hi to her on TV and tell her everything was fine in New York. Knowing this was impossible, Carol developed this technique as a way to indicate both to her nana with a deft maneuver.

A higher profile part came in the fall of 1956 with *Stanley*, a live NBC sitcom starring Buddy Hackett in the title role and Carol as his girlfriend. She bonded on the series with Paul Lynde as Stanley's heard-but-not-seen boss and Jane Connell as her friend, and both would later guest star on *The Carol Burnett Show*. Alas, *Stanley* could not overcome running against the popular *Arthur Godfrey's Talent Scouts* on CBS, and within six months, Carol was out of a job.

Carol's real future in TV laid in variety series. It was a form that was perfect for her, since it has its roots in stage performances, according to one expert in the genre.

"It was Max Liebman who brought Broadway reviews to television," says Carl Reiner. He ought to know, as he was a performer and a writer for *Your Show of Shows*, a variety series that dominated Saturday nights on NBC from 1950 through 1954 the way Carol's program would do in the 1970s. Liebman developed much of the talent he would later use as producer for *Your Show of Shows* at Tamiment, a theatrical training ground in New York's Poconos Mountains that will prove important to Carol later as well.

"When we first started, sketches were to run five, six, seven minutes," Reiner continues. "Under Sid [Caesar], the sketches became like playlets, longer." Reiner worked as a reliable, versatile support to Caesar—the same role Harvey Korman will have on *The Carol Burnett Show* later—on *Your Show of Shows* and then *Caesar's Hour* from 1954 to 1957, also on NBC.

Reiner asserts that comedy variety prospered until the advent of westerns on television in the late 1950s. "After that, the genre disappeared. A girl named Carol Burnett brought it back. If it weren't for Carol, the revue wouldn't have come back."

He notes that while she was doing *Paul Winchell and Jerry Mahoney* and then *Stanley*, Carol made time to experience the creation of the top comedy variety work of Caesar and Reiner in person thanks to a crucial professional friendship.

"In the second year of *Caesar's Hour*, I found a guy named Milt Kamen to serve as Sid's stand-in," says Reiner. "Sid wanted to go watch the show being rehearsed in the director's booth, and Milt would take his place on stage then. Milt Kamen told me about this girl he met, Carol Burnett, and he invited her to sit with us during rehearsal and the day of shooting. Carol would go home to watch the show and see what changes we made."

Reiner adds that Carol was so intrigued with the development and presentation of TV sketch comedy that she turned down a free ticket to see *My Fair Lady*, the hottest musical on Broadway at the time, to watch the latest installment of *Caesar's Hour*. "I have to see what changes they made on Saturday night," she informed her surprised friends.

Carol would repay all of what she learned by having Caesar and Reiner on her own series as guests years later. This generosity to those who inspired her made Carol beloved among the entertainment community in later years.

The Star-Making Song

After *Caesar's Hour* ended in 1957, Carol finally broke big professionally on TV later that year with "I Made a Fool of Myself Over John Foster Dulles." Written in honor of the secretary of state at the time whose persona lived up to the first syllable of his surname, it was a number that took Ken Welch months to write while doing musical reviews with Carol in Tamiment in the Poconos. Just a few months earlier he married the former Mitzie Cottle, a fellow performer at Tamiment with Carol.

Ken had been trying to complete a comic number he called "Destroy Me." He wanted it to be a send-up of the frenzy young women were making over rock stars such as Elvis Presley at the time, but he could not think of an unlikely object for such intense desire. "Then it occurred to me to make it about John Foster Dulles," Welch says. Mitzie reviewed it and told him he needed to explain more why the woman was in jail for her ardor for Dulles. He made the change, and the two became lifelong writing collaborators.

Carol introduced the tune at the Blue Angel nightclub, and audiences went wild. She performed it next on *The Tonight Show* starring Jack Paar, and he loved it so much, he has Carol do it again the following night. That results in a booking on *The Ed Sullivan Show* that following Sunday. Carol became a hot property briefly.

One temporarily popular novelty number does not make a career, however, and Carol went back to auditioning as well as appearing often on *The Garry Moore Show*, a morning series on CBS that has a slot for little-known and upcoming talent to perform. Its host was an affable, diminutive star with a crew cut and bow tie who had previously his own morning TV series of the same name on CBS from 1950, assisted by tall Durward Kirby. Carol started on the series in October 1956 and continued with it until Garry ended it in the summer of 1958. That fall, he started his own live show Tuesday nights, but that version of *The Garry Moore Show* was an unexpected flop. It would take the intervention of several men to save it, all of them key in the story of *The Carol Burnett Show*.

Moore and More

When Mike Dann joined CBS in its programming department in 1958, coming straight from NBC, one of his first duties was to salvage *The Garry Moore Show*. To fulfill that mission, he recruited two producers he knew were already doing successful work to turn it around, Bob Banner and Joe Hamilton.

Born Joseph Hamilton Jr. on Jan. 6, 1929 in Los Angeles, the latter made inroads into the entertainment field as a member of the Skylarks, a vocal quintet of three men and two women that backed Russ Morgan's orchestra in the late 1940s. They recorded on their own but managed only one minor pop chart entry, 1953's "I Had the Craziest Dream."

Nonetheless, they were energetic and photogenic, qualities that made them ideal for many TV appearances, including regular stints provided musical accompaniment for the disastrous *Judge for Yourself* game show, hosted by an ill-at-ease Fred Allen in 1954, and then *The Dinah Shore Show* in 1955, which aired twice a week for fifteen minutes. When the titular star got her own hour-long weekly series in 1956, *The Dinah Shore Chevy Show*, the Skylarks followed her on that program as well for a year before disappearing.

What dissolved the Skylarks was that Joe began arranging music for guests appearing on *The Dinah Shore Chevy Show* as well as his group, and his success there led him to become a producer under Bob Banner, the series' executive producer and director. Banner previously held those titles on *The Dinah Shore Show* in its fifteen-minute incarnation, and together with Hamilton, the two men helped *The Dinah Shore Chevy Show* win multiple Emmys through its first three seasons, including three for Dinah as hostess, two for best music, variety, audience participation or quiz series, and one for Banner as best director for a series of one hour or more in length.

Their strong reputation behind the scenes led to Mike Dann's offer to revamp *The Garry Moore Show*, and both men bit. They emphasized a better mix of comedy and music along with Garry and Durward Kirby that brought up the ratings in early 1959, as did a serendipitous bit of guest casting.

When guest star Martha Raye was too sick to perform on one show, she told Garry he should replace her with Carol. Carol filled in on *The Garry Moore Show* on Feb. 17, 1959, and got a huge ovation at the end when the audience learned she did all the sketches and singing within just two days. This appearance "kind of put the bug" into being a regular, as Carol recalled the time on her own series on Nov. 20, 1967.

Indeed, when Dann saw Carol's guest spot, he recommended that she became a regular. "I had a meeting with Garry," he says. "She was comedy, and comedy, unlike singers and dancers, is the most successful ingredient for a variety show." A cautious Moore allowed Carol to appear occasionally until she was added permanently on Nov. 19, 1959.

By that time, the series was taped Fridays from 7-8 p.m. to allow many guests to make their 8:30 p.m. stage calls. This included Carol herself, as in 1959 she had her own Broadway hit starring in *Once Upon a Mattress*.

With Carol in place, *The Garry Moore Show* rose in the ratings every year, culminating at Number Twelve in 1961-1962, the same season it won an Emmy for best variety series and Carol won her first statuette. Her comic chops were evident in sketches tailored to her strengths of being brassy and man hungry, and she wrung out laughs constantly. She felt at home with the personnel involved, including the arrival of an old friend.

"She was hired for *The Garry Moore Show*, and there were two men who'd been writing special musical material, and one of them left," says Ken Welch. "A choreographer I had worked with remembered my name." That choreographer was Ernest "Ernie" Flatt, who like Welch will later be part of *The Carol Burnett Show*.

For *The Garry Moore Show* every other week, Welch says, "I either chose numbers for people to sing on the show or wrote numbers, put together medleys." When Barbra Streisand came on the series to debut her memorable slow, impassioned version of "Happy Days Are Here Again," "I came up with that notion," he says.

The series' acclaim made Carol a household name, and she taped a special with Julie Andrews called *Julie and Carol at Carnegie Hall*. By the time it aired as a critical and popular hit in the summer of 1962, Carol announced she was leaving *The Garry Moore Show*, feeling she had done all she could there. She did a couple of guest shots on it through 1964 while Dorothy Loudon replaced her. A talented comic actress and singer, Loudon unfortunately received often unfavorable comparisons to Carol by critics and viewers. Amid declining ratings, Garry ended his series in 1964 after just two years with Loudon. (Ironically, Burnett later assumed the right to recreate Loudon's Tony-winning role in the motion picture version of the musical *Annie* in 1982.)

Carol's decision led to her exclusive contract with CBS that included the "push the button" option for her own variety series. At that same time, it became know that she was seeing Joe Hamilton, who remained a producer on *The Garry Moore Show*. Seven years Carol's senior, he had been separated from his wife (where he already had eight children) a year before dating Carol, who was divorcing Don Saroyan. Both Joe and Carol were still technically married, as Carol's divorce from Saroyan had not been finalized, and Carol received some backlash about being a home wrecker.

Overcoming the controversy, Carol and Joe married in 1963. Joe would produce most of Carol's specials after she left *The Garry Moore Show* and a few other efforts. Carol's initial focus was starring in her first Broadway musical, which would prove to be a big professional disaster and indirectly lead to the creation of *The Carol Burnett Show*.

The Big *Fade*

On Feb. 16, 1964, Carol discussed her upcoming musical while appearing as the mystery guest on *What's My Line?* Carol mentioned how the show would start rehearsing in five weeks, but the title remained up in the air.

"Well, they've changed it so many times, I read in the paper, you know," she told the panel after Buddy Hackett successfully identified his former costar on *Stanley*. "I don't know. As of late, it was *A Girl to Remember*, then they changed it to *A Name to Remember*, then they changed it to *One, Two, Three, Five*, then they changed it *Idol of Millions*. And I think they should keep that, but put a question mark after it."

The final title was *Fade Out—Fade In*. Featuring Carol as an usherette who becomes an unlikely star (a supposedly original concept that sounds like it was lifted from Burnett's life), the production's failure appeared foredoomed from the start. It was to open on Nov. 23, 1963, which if it had followed that schedule meant it would have been postponed in the wake of the assassination of President John F. Kennedy the previous day.

Rehearsals began before Burnett announced she was pregnant in June. When Harvey Sabinson, press agent to the show, learned this news from co-producer Lester Osterman, he callously wondered why she could not have an abortion so the show could proceed as scheduled. Burnett gave birth to her first daughter, Carrie Hamilton, on Dec. 5, 1963, before returning to rehearsals in March. *Fade Out—Fade In* opened three months later to mixed reviews but solid business. Shortly thereafter, things went sour for the show's star.

On July 10, 1964, a taxicab accident caused a neck and back injury to Carol that led to her to miss several performances for surgery and recovery. Since she was the basic reason to see the musical, the box office fell off greatly during the summer. More upsetting to Osterman, Sabinson and others connected to the show was the announcement that Burnett would co-host a new variety series for CBS, *The Entertainers*, with comedian Bob Newhart and singer Caterina Valente. Supporting regulars were future *Carol Burnett Show* guest stars Ruth Buzzi, John Davidson and Dom DeLuise.

"We worked together first on *The Entertainers*, and it was so much fun!" recalls Buzzi. "Dom and I were comedy partners back then. He played a bumbling magician called Dominic the Great, and I was his silent sidekick and even more bumbling magician's assistant, Shakuntala. We got an amazing reaction to the audience, and it was a wonderful springboard for both of us." But while Ruth and Don received great notices for their work, the rest of the show's content was not as sparkling with viewers.

Although the repertory format of *The Entertainers* meant that Carol would not have to be on every show (and thus kept the program from qualifying as her own series under her 1962 CBS contract), joining it indicated what Burnett later confirmed, that she was disappointed by *Fade Out—Fade In*. In fact, her manager offered a $500,000 settlement for her to leave the show, but its co-authors Betty Comden and Adolph Green rejected the deal, thinking that they had a potential hit with her as the lead.

The atmosphere worsened when Carol went to the hospital for traction in October 1964, forcing her to miss both *The Entertainers* and *Fade Out—Fade In*. The former was bombing, with negative reviews about its disjointed format and poor ratings opposite *The Addams Family* on ABC Friday nights, while the latter was forced to close on Nov. 14 without Burnett performing. Osterman and his co-producer, composer Jule Styne, filed suit against Carol with Actors Equity Association, charging that the performer had to fulfill her contract to do their show before accepting any other work.

The association surprised some observers by siding with the producers and forcing Carol to resume doing the musical. *Fade Out—Fade In* reopened on Feb. 15, 1965, but the controversies surrounding it and lack of strong word of mouth led it to fade out totally two months later. Carol would not appear on Broadway again until nearly 30 years later.

To compound Burnett's frustration, *The Entertainers* ended on March 27, 1965. The other stars had already viewed it as a lost cause. Newhart had quit the show in December, and Valente taped her spots in advance for a concert tour. Even moving the series to Saturday nights, where CBS had been doing well, failed to improve the ratings. The only consolation for Carol over the last year was that many of the series' principals—Don Crichton, producer Bob Banner, choreographer Ernie Flatt, orchestra leader Harry Zimmerman—would work for her two years later on *The Carol Burnett Show*.

Pushing the Button

Stung by professional defeats and seeking a change of scenery, Carol and Joe moved to Hollywood in October 1965. After a year, however, offers for work for both were scarce outside of Carol's bare minimum of TV specials and a handful of guest shots on *Gomer Pyle—USMC*, *The Lucy Show* and *Get Smart!* To complicate matters, Carol was pregnant with her second daughter (Jody would be born on Jan. 18, 1967). In the wake of Christmas 1966, the Hamiltons realized they were in dire straits.

"We were kind of broke," Carol recalled in 2012. Then they remembered that they could "push the button" and automatically get a series on the air guaranteeing Carol 30 shows. As the contract's deadline neared expiration, Carol called Mike Dann immediately.

Caught off guard about a provision he had forgotten, Dann tried to change Carol's mind. "We established and hoped that we could do a situation comedy with her," he says. But Carol had no intention to play the same character every week.

Dann had reason to be cautious about a variety series with Carol. Her star power had dimmed following *The Entertainers*, and her most recent special, *Carol and Company*, on Oct. 9, 1966, was a far cry from the raves her specials had generated previously. Additionally Garry Moore, on whose series Carol had flourished, was now bombing badly in the ratings with a new series opposite the western *Bonanza* on NBC that would go off in January 1967. This all indicated Carol's show would be a shaky proposition.

Being the Number One network meant Dann had few available slots to put Carol, particularly since she was doing an hour series. His decision became more complicated when finalizing his schedule in the late winter of 1967 because the show that replaced Garry Moore, *The Smothers Brothers Comedy Hour*, was an unexpected hit that cut into the ratings of *Bonanza*, ruling that option out. He gave Carol arguably the toughest slot on CBS: Monday nights from 10-11 p.m. Eastern and Pacific, 9-10 p.m. Central.

"It was the only thing I could put it in," Dann says. In fact, he believes Carol's agent was so desperate to secure a regular series order that he could have put the show on Saturday mornings and it would have been accepted there.

There will be more about the slot later. Suffice it to say that Carol is correct when she said in 2012 that "They (CBS executives) did not have any faith in us at all." That included Mike Dann. Shortly after the show's debut, Joe Hamilton met with Dann in the latter's office in CBS's New York City headquarters. Dann had the network's schedule printed out behind him, and when Dann stepped out briefly, Hamilton opened a folding door in *The Carol Burnett Show* time slot with a top card reading "Sept-Feb Burnett Show." Underneath it was a question mark, indicating Dann thought he had to replace the show with something in midseason.

Hamilton pointed it out to Dann, who sheepishly apologized. The damage was done, however, and Hamilton knew he had his work cut out if he was to make his wife's series a hit in the eyes of the leaders of CBS.

Getting the Production Together

With the series approved by CBS, Carol decided to use Bob Banner and Joe Hamilton as her co-executive producers. The title was a boost for the latter, who now was equal in title with the man who had been his boss on *The Dinah Shore Chevy Show* and *The Garry Moore Show*. Given his marital status with his star, some people felt privately felt he was not up to the job, but Carol was never one of them.

"It's tough being married to your producer," she acknowledged to *TV Guide's* Dwight Whitney in 1972. "But it is Joe who makes the show. I depend on his judgment. He would be my producer even if he weren't my husband."

According to writer Buz Kohan, Joe Hamilton was the real powerhouse behind producing the series. "Bob Banner was not there at all," he asserts.

Kohan's writing partner, Bill Angelos, has a slightly different perspective on Banner. "He was around, but he wasn't there. I don't recall saying anything of substance with him."

In essence, Banner was a co-executive producer in name only, and Hamilton called the shots for everything. While some found Joe demanding, particularly several writers, many other staff members give him credit for establishing and cultivating a conducive work atmosphere and solid output overall for *The Carol Burnett Show*.

"He was very efficient as a producer on the show," recalls singer Gene Merlino.

"Joe was like an older brother to me," says Angelos.

"He never stinted on costumes and production numbers," says writer Stan Hart. "He gave Carol want she wanted. He set the bar very high."

It was Hamilton who typically told the cast and crew that something had been changed or dropped for a show. Oftentimes he did it on behalf of Carol, who would inform him quietly away from everyone else if something was occurring she did not like and have him deliver the news. Some personnel thought he was mean in transmitting that information, while others just saw it as Joe trying to make the show as good as possible and satisfy the wishes of its star as well.

"I know Joe was a very tough guy and knew how to say no, and Carol didn't," says writer Jack Mendelsohn. "She was always afraid to hurt anyone's feelings. As someone said, 'She's too nice to be in show business!'"

Helping out Hamilton as associate producer was Bob Wright. "A great unsung hero," says Angelos. Like Hamilton, Wright was a transplant from *The Garry Moore Show*.

Along Came Jones (to Direct)

Clark Jones directed the first season only as a favor to Joe because he didn't want to move to the West Coast. A veteran in his field, Clark earned the first of his nine Emmy nominations in 1954 for *Your Hit Parade*, followed by the acclaimed live version of "Peter Pan" on *Producers' Showcase* in 1955, *The Patrice Munsel Show* in 1957, *The Perry Como Show* in 1959 and *The Bell Telephone Hour* in 1964.

Jones' direction of the *Carol & Company* special and the failed *Sammy Davis Jr. Show*, both in 1966, impressed Hamilton, who was executive producer for each. Joining Clark as assistant director was Dave Powers, who would assume Jones' role from the fall of 1968 until the series ended.

The Carol Burnett Show would tape in Studio 33 in a huge soundstage known as CBS Television City located in Hollywood, the same spot where *The Price is Right* continues to hold court as of this writing. Carol loved working in the studio on her previous specials because it allowed most audience members to see the stage during taping rather than have to look at monitors as was (and is) the case in most other cramped TV studios where audiences are seated on bleachers.

Jones directed four cameras. Camera One was on stage right and Camera Four was on stage left. "Camera Two typically was on a crane situated center on the back of the house ramp," says Roger Beatty, who was the series' stage manager and later assistant director and writer. "This crane could rise to about sixteen feet and allowed [the director] to get high shots for the production numbers. Next to Camera Two was Camera Three's position. Also on stage were two mobile boom platforms with their operators and pushers."

While it helps to have top professional directors and producers for a variety series, the truth is that great writing is crucial for a program in the genre to succeed. Joe wisely selected a head writer who crafted sturdy scripts from his staff from the start.

A Rosen in Bloom

Arnie Rosen began writing and producing shows while in the Marine Corps in the 1940s. After writing nearly twenty sample shows, he was hired to write for the CBS radio show of comedian Robert Q. Lewis by 1949. Rosen then teamed with Coleman Jacoby, and they became head writers for the first year (1950-1951) of *Cavalcade of Stars*, a variety series on the DuMont network that made Jackie Gleason a star (he left for CBS in 1952).

The duo went on to write for several other variety series, including interestingly two short-lived ones hosted by females, *Take It From Me* with comedienne Jean Carroll (ABC, 1953-1954) and *The NBC Comedy Hour* with Gale Storm (1956). Their biggest professional success occurred when they did scripts for *The Phil Silvers Show* and won three consecutive Emmys for their work on it from 1955-1957.

The next stop for Rosen-Jacoby was *The Garry Moore Show*, where they arrived in 1959 along with Bob Banner and Joe Hamilton as the new producers. The duo wrote for the program until it ended in 1964.

After co-writing the pilot for the NBC sitcom *Hank* in 1965 (the series ran until 1966), Rosen split with Jacoby when the latter stayed in New York City while Rosen moved to California. Rosen wrote and served as a producer of the acclaimed NBC sitcom *Get Smart!* from 1966-1967. But variety writing held the biggest appeal to him, and when the chance to assume leadership of a team on Carol's show came to him, he took it.

By all recorded accounts from co-workers and others, Rosen did a stellar job as head writer of *The Carol Burnett Show*. "I never worked with him, but I knew people who had, and that opinion was unanimous," says writer Gene Perret.

As far as his leadership style. Rosen stressed that his writers work collectively as a group to overcome any problems they may have while developing sketches on their own. He sought scribes who were compatible in working with him as much as having good ideas. His initial group included a pair of newcomers to TV writing, Kenny Solms and Gail Parent.

"The Kids"

Talking to Solms and Parent jointly nearly 50 years after they connected, they still have a bubbly interplay between themselves in describing their story. "We met in college, New York University," Kenny says. "We were living in the same dorm," Gail says.

One day by chance Gail caught Kenny doing show business routines of the top comedy duo of the early 1960s. "We realized we had both memorized everything (Mike) Nichols and (Elaine) May said," she notes. "They came to my high school," Kenny adds.

With that kinship established, both wanted to do a similar act, but as Kenny puts it, "We were laughing and lazy." Instead, they took the advice Kenny received from the drama club he attended to sell the jokes he was creating to other comedians. Most rejected their efforts, but the tide turned with a notable exception.

"We finally got our groove with Joan Rivers," says Kenny, mentioning a future guest star on *The Carol Burnett Show*. Soon they were connected with and supplying material to other up-and-coming funny ladies who would later do the series as well, including Lily Tomlin and Madeline Kahn. "They'd pay you $10 for a sketch," Kenny says.

The pair understood they needed representation to get more money in the business, and they somehow secured agents and managers despite their admittedly odd joint working style. As Gail puts it, "I was always shy, and Kenny was aggressive in a good way."

By 1966 they had established themselves enough in the New York comedy writing community to secure a deal to record a comedy album in five days using twelve routines making fun of the recent marriage of the president's daughter, Lucy Baines Johnson. *Our Wedding Album or the Great Society Affair* made the *Billboard* LP chart for fourteen weeks in the fall and attracted some new fans for Parent and Solms. Their business manager, Marty Bregman, informed them in early 1967 that one admirer was Carol Burnett. She asked Bregman to let her meet the duo to talk about writing for her new series.

"We were the first ones signed," Gail says. "She made such a fuss over us, and we loved Carol," Kenny interjects. "She was adorable and charming and made us feel invaluable for that show," says Gail.

The two specialized in pop culture parodies during their tenure with the series. Among their best were two in 1970—"Slippery When Wet," a takeoff on Esther Williams films, and "Golda," a roasting of *Gilda* so well done that its star, Rita Hayworth, made a rare TV acting appearance on the series afterward in appreciation of their work.

Gail created one send-up so strong that it became the longest recurring sketch, appearing every season on the show. Its inspiration came a few years before the series ran.

"I was watching a soap opera, and they were having a last episode and winding up twenty years of plots, which was funny to me," she says. Though she cannot recall the title, it was likely *Young Dr. Malone*, which ran on radio and then television from 1939 to 1963.

In any event, the stilted dialogue and conventions of serialized daytime drama was a ripe source for comedy, and when Gail's initial installment of "As the Stomach Turns" debuted on Feb. 12, 1968, it received such huge laughs that Carol insisted it become a recurring sketch. The title was a play on *As the World Turns*, the top soap opera on TV at the time (it ran on CBS from 1956-2009). Over the years, Carol's character, Marian, would be depicted as a desperately horny, much widowed woman with weird guests, a wayward daughter and a sound effects crew that always let her down.

Solms and Parent appreciated how much Carol could add to the humor of their skits while sticking to the script exactly as written. "She would bring so much to everything," Kenny says. "In 'Mildred Fierce' (the show's first spoof of *Mildred Pierce* in 1970), she worked those shoulder pads like Joan Crawford."

There was at least one instance where Carol rejected one of their scripts simply because she could not find the character. When Lee Radziwill, sister to Jacqueline Kennedy Onassis, received pans from the critics for her deadly star performance in the 1968 ABC special *Laura*, Gail seized the opportunity for laughs. "She was a model who got a part in a movie, but she couldn't act, only did model stuff," Gail recalls. She had Carol practicing posing stiffly, but Carol never felt confident enough that she was conveying the character effectively, even with Gail showing her how to make the rigid motions.

The other main memory they have of the series' early years was a little bit of a culture shock in the writers room regarding their youth. "We were like 22 or 24 years old," Kenny says. "Everybody seemed older to us." The two did bond with Bill Angelos and Buz Kohan, both approximately ten years their senior.

Angelos and Kohan

The one defining element that many people associate with *The Carol Burnett Show* throughout its run is the elaborate parodies of old films. The first of those was "The Fun Family of Broadway" on Dec. 11, 1967, and its authors were Bill Angelos and Buz Kohan, who had been collaborating since they were teenagers.

"Bill and I went to Bronx High School of Science together," notes Kohan. Its alumni include Stokely Carmichael, Bobby Darin and seven Nobel prize winners.

"It was a very prestigious school. Bill and I got in by mistake," jokes Kohan. "I was a musician then. I had a band called the Blue Notes, and Bill was my vocalist."

"I was also an emcee for a lot of high school performances," adds Angelos. "The first thing we wrote together was a commercial for the sophomore hop. And we'd put it on stage."

When they graduated, Kohan went to Eastman School of Music through the assistance of Angelos, who attended Syracuse. They stayed in touch and watched each other's productions whenever possible. After college, Kohan wrote a musical revue called *Once Over Nightly* at the University of Rochester for his master's degree that was so well promoted, it earned him a review by *The New York Post* critic Leonard Lyons.

Kohan's streak of success faced a curve ball when he was drafted in 1956, where he met actor Bob Dishy. "We formed a little team and entered what was known as the All-Army Contest," he recalls. Winning the specialty group category, Kohan and Dishy toured a year as the act and got on *The Ed Sullivan Show* on Aug. 9, 1957.

"One guest on Ed Sullivan was Carol Burnett for that show," Kohan says. "She was singing 'I Made a Fool of Myself Over John Foster Dulles.'" Dishy knew Carol previously from her work in Tamiment as well.

As Angelos served in the Air Force for four years, Kohan went back to civilian life and served as music director five mornings a week on a local New York City series starring ventriloquist Shari Lewis called *Hi, Mom!* He remained unfulfilled professionally, however, and when Angelos finished his tour of duty, Kohan came calling.

"I was never really determined to go into show business, but Buz showed up on my doorway literally," laughs Angelos. He rejoined Kohan, and they performed a summer show in the Adirondacks. Two agents with William Morris saw their act. "They hired us on the spot."

Kohan and Angelos started writing musical material for a variety of acts, starting with Arthur Godfrey. Their work eventually secured them a regular job on *The Keefe Brasselle Show*, a 1963 night-time summer variety series on CBS.

"After Keefe, we auditioned for Perry Como, who was no longer doing a regular show, but specials," Kohan says. They won the job, and their special music material earned notice by those in the know. "From Como, we got to do *The Sammy Davis Jr. Show* [on NBC in 1966, executive produced by Joe Hamilton] and *The Steve Lawrence Show* [on CBS in 1965, in what would later be the first time slot for *The Carol Burnett Show*]."

In the summer of 1966, Carol Burnett contacted Kohan and Angelos to come out to Hollywood and write a special she was doing with Rock Hudson, Frank Gorshin and Jim Berry called *Carol and Company*, which aired on CBS Oct. 9, 1966. A few months after that, Burnett and Hamilton revealed to the duo the plans for the series and its 30 weeks of guaranteed payments writing for it. Still, it was not an easy decision for the men to make.

"It was very difficult in that our original plan was to write for musical theater, and the contempt for writing for Hollywood was known," Angelos says. "But everything was moving to Hollywood."

"You could see everything was drying up in New York," Kohan says. "We saw the writing on the wall for a fair amount of money, and with kids, well."

Viewing themselves as "nicely pigeonholed—we could do funny, we could do music, we could do serious," as Kohan puts it, the duo made an impression on the series with "The Fun Family of Broadway," an extended send-up of theatrical clan musical biographies based largely on the movie *There's No Business Like Show Business* (1954).

"That was the best one we did," opines Angelos. "That whole thing was written straight. That's why it's so funny."

"Carol always loved to make fun of the movies," Kohan recalls. "She loved it and did a great job. It was a fun sketch to do."

Thereafter, Kohan and Angelos did many specialty musical numbers for the series' first four seasons, alternating with Artie Malvin. (Ken and Mitzie Welch, who had performed the same role for Carol on *The Garry Moore Show* and several of her specials, were already were signed to do *The Kraft Music Hall* variety series for NBC in 1967.)

"My gift was primarily conceptual," Angelos says of their partnership. "I could hear music and hum it to him." Otherwise, their ideas just grew out of mutual admiration and determination.

"There were no rewrites," Angelos adds of their work. "We were good." At the same time, they appreciated the contributions and talents of everyone else involved in the series. It became a second family to both men.

Kohan has only one regret regarding *The Carol Burnett Show*. "When we first came out, Joe said, 'You got any ideas for a theme song?' And I didn't," he says. That led Hamilton toward creating the familiar "It's Time to Say So Long" theme associated with the series and Burnett ever since. It was about the only missed opportunity he and Angelos had on the series.

The Rest of the Original Writers

The remaining surviving writer of the first season as of this writing is Saul Turteltaub, who will earn his third Emmy nomination for his work on *The Carol Burnett Show*. He previously earned Emmy nods in 1964 and 1965 writing for *That Was the Week That Was* on NBC, then worked on a rather unlikely project prior to joining Carol and crew.

"I was writing for a show called *The Pat Boone Show*, a daytime talk show," says Turteltaub, referring to an NBC series from 1966-1967 starring the squeaky clean singer. "Arnie Rosen, the head writer, was looking for a sketch for Carol and her sister." Turteltaub had the notion of Carol struggling to stay awake while facing a college recruiter for her sister, and that served as the basis for the audition piece Vicki Lawrence undertook and won for a regular role on the series.

Turteltaub's piece was strong enough to earn a spot to run on the second installment of *The Carol Burnett Show*. More importantly, it secured Turteltaub a regular job on the series writing just by himself, a rarity for the series.

"I came up with the sketches myself," Turteltaub says. "They went to Arnie, who put them in the script." He remembers one other skit he created was Harvey playing Carol's superhero husband who had trouble controlling his strength around her, which appeared on the Oct. 2, 1967 show.

Turteltaub liked working with everyone on the show. So did other scribes, who credited it to the supportive work atmosphere created by Carol, Joe Hamilton and Arnie Rosen.

"Carol had a great trust in Arnie," notes Buz Kohan. "A lot of faith in him. Between Joe and Arnie, they had a very entertaining group of people."

"It was truly an eclectic group," agrees Bill Angelos.

Besides the aforementioned Kenny Solms and Gail Parent ("The kids. Kenny was the court jester even then."), Kohan assesses some of them as follows: Don Hinkley was "A little offbeat. He did the 'Comedy Shots' on Steve Allen [the blackouts on *The Steve Allen Show* in the 1950s when the host played the piano and short comic bits interrupted the activity]. He had a wonderfully bizarre, macabre sense of humor."

In Kohan's opinion, the writing team of Stan Burns and Mike Marmer was the most reliable contributors for the series. "They were just so solid," he says. "They could come up with anything anywhere, and it would be so funny."

Angelos terms Hinkley, Burns and Marmer as "old school joke writers." All had Emmy nominations apiece prior to *The Carol Burnett Show*—Marmer for *The Ernie Kovacs Show* in 1956, Burns and Hinkley for *The Steve Allen Show* in 1959 and Hinkley again for *The Bob Newhart Show* (the variety series, not the sitcom) in 1962. Together with Angelos, Kohan, Solms, Parent, Turteltaub and Rosen, they established in the first season the knockabout yet at the same time witty setups that would define *The Carol Burnett Show* throughout its run, as well as the general tone for camaraderie backstage.

"It was a whole bunch of wonderful writers," concludes Turteltaub. "They were all nice, and it was fun watching the show the night of the taping."

Working Together

The first thing a solo writer usually did when arriving on *The Carol Burnett Show* was to pair up with another scribe because of the economic conditions dictated by the Writers Guild of America. Under the union's rules, it actually cost a variety series more to employ two individual writers than if they were designated as a working duo. Jack Mendelsohn got to enjoy both statuses during his tenure in 1970-1971.

"There were a lot of forced marriages," he notes of the pairings. "At least you got to work together. When I was on the Burnett show, Paul Wayne was my partner. Paul had problems, and he was fired halfway during the season because he had migraine headaches and couldn't work. So I was on my own, and it didn't bother me."

From there, the standard working process each week for Rosen and his writers was to meet Monday mornings to hear him say what kind of sketches were needed for upcoming shows. He was always open to suggestions as well. "We have a session in which we all pitch ideas, most of which we reject amongst ourselves, fastening onto the good ones, and developing them," he told William F. Fray and Melanie Allen in *Life Stories of Comedy Writers*. "In other words, we explore it, develop it, and so on."

If those concepts appeared viable from the discussions, Rosen would assign specific writers to handle the assignment, depending on their strengths. Some excelled with one-liners, others with character development or pantomime.

Mendelsohn, who wrote under Rosen, confirms this approach and adds that "It was kind of a group thing, like someone would say, 'Carol's a klutzy waitress,' and we'd go around the table and everybody would make a contribution. After an hour of this, Arnie offered who wanted to do what concept for a sketch."

"We'd have the meeting and pitch, and it was so well organized," says Buz Kohan.

Rosen himself preferred to write late at night. Sometimes the staff had to stay late as well. But those occasions were rare.

"We weren't there until 2 a.m. in the morning," notes Gail Parent.

Stan Hart recalls of his schedule on the show from 1970-1973 that "We worked from 10 to 5:30 for Carol, and we were free to do what we wanted to do thereafter."

"When you hear these horror stories of writers staying up all night—I think we had to stay only till 7 one night," says Franelle Silver. "It was like a well-oiled machine."

"I think there was one night we had to stay until 12 o'clock," says Rudy DeLuca. "Lev [Barry Levinson, his partner] and I had a sketch with no punch line. We never got it."

"It was great writing for her," says Larry Siegel. "They [the producers] were real human beings when it came to working conditions. We had free weekends."

The pattern for such leisurely hours started under the original head writer, who received high praise from several writers who worked under him. "Arnie Rosen was the best," says Mendelsohn. "He was a brilliant writer, and a very mild mannered guy. Soft spoken. Didn't have an attitude."

Another hallmark of the series was a surprising lack of rewriting, especially compared to today's sitcoms where most scripts undergo several revisions. "There was a great deal of respect for the writing," noted Bob Illes, who contributed to the series in its last season. He says there were few line changes if any to anyone's work.

"Those writers didn't need help, certainly not from me," says Saul Turteltaub of rewriting others' work. If so, Rosen did rely on one writing team to help out if he felt a sketch submitted came up short with what he wanted to include in his draft script.

"He enjoyed us and knew we could punch up things," Gail Parent says of what she and Kenny Solms did beyond their own sketches along with Arnie. However, she says, "Arnie had an iron hand in doing the script." "Joe (Hamilton) had an even hand," adds Solms.

"You had a full week to write your sketch, seven to eight minutes long, three jokes per page, lots of reaction," Mendelsohn recalls of his working conditions. At the end of the week, he would submit his work to Rosen, who would tell him of any changes needed or give the sketch to others to rewrite before deciding if and when it went into a final script.

Unlike some shows, the writers could mingle with the talent on the series, and they often were in awe of meeting their idols, much less writing for them. "We couldn't believe the guest stars," says Gail Parent. "Lucille Ball—oh my God!" Some of the relationships even generated work as a result, such as Tim Conway being so impressed by Gail and Kenny Solms that he had them write for his act outside the series. (They later created for him *The Tim Conway Show*, a sitcom which unfortunately bombed in 1970.)

Most of the scribes agree the series' hardest challenge was finding inspiration for writing material that would be both humorous and unique. "Writer's block" was an unnerving frustration they often faced and feared. "There were weeks when it was pretty dry," admits Kenny Solms.

Sometimes what alleged comedy made it to the page seemed desperate to those who did not have to perform it. "Ernie [Flatt, the show's choreographer] knew me so well that I could look at next week's script and think, 'What will she do with this?'" dancer Carl Jablonski says. "It didn't seem so funny. But they found humor in it."

Indeed, Burnett sympathized with the plight of her comedy writers to come up with scripts, even when she and/or others thought what they submitted fell short. Talking to Dick Cavett on his Feb. 21, 1974 show, she explained that "Each week, our writers have to sit down to a blank sheet of paper that says, 'Be funny,' and it's a whole new sketch. Well, you can't win 'em all. And consequently, there are many times when we have to go out and do something none of us are really in love with, just to really fill up the time. So you just gird yourself and try to fool yourself into 'You love it a whole lot.'"

Carol quickly followed by clarifying to Cavett that "When I do love it a whole lot, I never want to quit. It's just great fun."

As for the writers themselves, they credit the star for enhancing what they put on the page. "You work with someone like Carol, she makes your good stuff great," Stan Hart says. "She had respect for good writing."

The same applies to her other regulars, starting with the show's reliable leading man.

"With Harvey Korman"

He convincingly played more than a dozen Oscar-winning actors, from Emil Jannings and Clark Gable to John Wayne and Rod Steiger, not to mention Porky Pig and Mickey Mouse. Accents ranging from Irish to French to German easily rolled off his tongue. He could go from prompting hysterical laughter dressed in drag to effectively emoting a love song in a smooth baritone with fine footwork, all in one show.

In short, Harvey Korman was the key versatile actor needed for *The Carol Burnett Show*. He complemented Carol beautifully as he easily adapted from one segment to the next, creating distinctive characters and giving 100 percent of his efforts on sketches that sometimes did not merit his hard work. He was equally facile as a straight man and a buffoon, and the series' episodes without him often suffer greatly with his absence.

"He really was the anchor that the show revolved around," contends writer Gene Perret. Calling him the real actor in the troupe, Perret notes that "our zany cast of characters could get as zany as all get out because they had a strong character to antagonize—Harvey Korman. To me, that was a major part of the show's success."

Even so, for a man who was essential to the appeal and popularity of *The Carol Burnett Show*, it is stunning the relative lack of appreciation shown to him in his lifetime. While he earned four Emmys from 1969-1974, his wins in 1971 and 1972 were not given on the air. In 1975, he received his Golden Globe for Best Supporting Actor in a Television Series during a commercial break for the ceremony.

Thankfully, people on *The Carol Burnett Show* realized his true worth. Bill Angelos, who worked with Harvey for five years, succinctly states that "Harvey Korman was brilliant."

Harvey's talents may have been taken for granted by others because he fulfilled a role as a comic supporting player. It is a deceivingly tough assignment usually described by a phrase that unfortunately connotes it as being trivial—the "second banana."

"The second banana is the one who quietly sets up the first banana. It's the person you want to pitch to you to score," says Carl Reiner, using a baseball analogy to explain the importance of the position. He himself was considered a great "second banana" to Sid Caesar in the 1950s, and along with Korman and Art Carney, who worked opposite Jackie Gleason in the 1960s, they formed a triumvirate of the greatest supporting comic actors ever seen on TV variety series. The difference for Harvey was that he had a tougher time getting to the top than Reiner or Carney.

Born in Chicago on Feb. 15, 1927, Harvey spent four years in the Windy City studying and training to be an actor after World War II ended. "His background is the Goodman Theatre in Chicago," says his son, Chris Korman. "He was a student along with Geraldine Page and Shelley Berman."

Harvey credits learning where the jokes were in rehearsals for plays in this period as a crucial development in mastering comic acting. "It was rare for my father talking over a laugh," notes Chris. His father realized having a basis in reality helps spark the humor.

"I don't look for gags. I look for characters," Harvey told Peter Andrews of his acting philosophy in *The New York Times*. "Even in the broadest sketch, I try to find out what kind of person I'm playing, what his problems are and what he's trying to do."

Making his way to New York City in 1950, Harvey scored bit parts in two plays that year, *The Tower Beyond Tragedy*, a Greek drama that starred Judith Anderson and ran less than a month before closing two days before Christmas, and George Bernard Shaw's *Captain Brassbound's Conversion*, a production where he faded in the background almost as quickly as the show burned through sixteen performances from Dec. 27, 1950 through Jan. 7, 1951. Work became scarce after that.

"My dad didn't know that you needed an agent at the time," Chris Korman explains. So despite studying with acclaimed acting teacher Stella Adler, all else Harvey could amass in New York City the next five years were meager stage roles and a one-line part on *Philco TV Playhouse*. Chris says his father got the latter because Harvey's mother knew an executive who in turn knew someone else connected to the series and leveraged those associations to help out her son. While it did earn him his actor union card, it failed to prompt much major work for him.

"He and Tom Bosley were roommates in the 1950s," says Chris. While his dad auditioned constantly and often fruitlessly, his roommate got increasingly larger parts that eventually led to a starring role in the hit musical *Fiorello!* in 1959. Meanwhile, Harvey had to content himself by selling candy at Radio City Music Hall between the few jobs he got off-Broadway and in stock productions in theaters near Manhattan.

In 1956 Harvey appeared in out-of-town tryouts with the play *Uncle Willie* before being fired just before Christmas prior to its opening on Broadway (no big loss—the show ran only for four months). Frustrated, he went back to Chicago to act more, along with work in stock companies and occasional visits to Los Angeles to try to break through in that market, but little seemed to click for him the rest of the 1950s.

What finally turned the tide was his supporting role in the 1960 Chicago production of *Mr. and Mrs.*, a comedy written by Sherwood Schwartz, later the creator of *Gilligan's Island* and *The Brady Bunch*. At the time, Schwartz was the head writer for *The Red Skelton Show*, and the director of that program, Seymour Berns, filled the same role with the stage show. He was impressed with Korman in the production and encouraged him to give Hollywood a shot one more time, which Harvey did.

This time, Harvey earned a few guest shots on TV, starting with *The Donna Reed Show* on Dec. 6, 1960. It was only three lines, but he maximized them and soon found himself returning to that show two more times as well as become a busy guest star on *Hazel*, *Route 66* and more the next three years. (Incidentally, *Mr. and Mrs.* became an hour TV comedy special starring Lucille Ball on April 18, 1964, with Harvey nowhere in sight.)

With Berns' encouragement, Harvey won a spot on *The Red Skelton Show* on Dec. 26, 1961. Unfortunately, its star hated sharing his comic spotlight with anyone, and as Red noticed how Harvey's excellent delivery attracted laughs and attention, he stopped the actor's appearances almost as soon as they started. Berns appreciated the actor's talent despite Red's attitude and recommended him to Perry Lafferty, the producer of *The Danny Kaye Show*, to use as a regular on that CBS comedy variety series when it started in the fall of 1963.

"He had suggested to Perry Lafferty that 'Harvey's tall enough, he can play older and bigger than Danny, and do the snobbery,'" notes Chris Korman. Kaye was skeptical until he saw Harvey audition and wring big laughs out of a few lines. Still, the two had a rocky working relationship thanks in part to similar personalities but different work ethics.

"He was a very abrasive man," Chris says of Kaye. "He did not like to rehearse—which made him like Dean Martin—but my dad did. He was very emotional and surly like my father. One day, they would be getting along great, the next day they weren't talking."

Despite the clashes, Harvey's well-regarded work with Danny Kaye won him many other TV guest shots. He appeared twice on *The Lucy Show* and supplied a recurring vocal role as the Great Gazoo, a finicky alien, on the cartoon *The Flintstones* in 1965-1966.

Carol Burnett and Joe Hamilton were among many in the industry who realized he would be a great second banana for their variety series through all his work. When organizing Carol's series in early 1967, however, Harvey was still committed to *The Danny Kaye Show*. The series' cancellation would occur a few months later, after which Harvey immersed himself in staging the sketches for *The Steve Allen Comedy Hour*, which would serve as the summer replacement for *The Danny Kaye Show*.

Believing Harvey to be out of pocket, Carol and Joe auditioned more than 50 actors considered to be a "Harvey Korman type," including Bernie Kopell. (Ironically, Kopell would star ten years later in *The Love Boat*, the first series on ABC to beat *The Carol Burnett Show* in the ratings.) Carol was dissatisfied with their choices, and as luck would have it, she ran into Harvey in the parking lot at CBS Television Studio as he finished his work on *The Steve Allen Comedy Hour* one day. She pleaded that he join the series, and he agreed. It was as simple as that, apart from negotiating the deals of his contract.

"He knew Carol, he didn't know her well," Chris says of his father's working relationship with the star at the outset of the series. Chris contends that some CBS executives were uneasy about using a person already identified with a previous hit series as a regular, but they let it slide. As for his dad, Harvey was happy to be on a series where the atmosphere was much more pleasant than that of *The Danny Kaye Show*.

"Their whole thing was, 'Let's have fun, let's get along,'" Chris says.

When he joined the series, Harvey was invaluable for providing acting lessons for the other cast members as well as perform on air himself. That included even providing insights for the show's star, according to one observer. "I think Carol Burnett learned a lot of from Harvey Korman," opines Kaye Ballard. "He was a great teacher."

Given all this, coupled with his genuine talent, it is odd that Harvey became known as the moodiest regular. "He could be difficult with the cast," notes writer Kenny Solms. He says Harvey convinced Carol and the other regulars not to do new comedy bits for the anniversary shows, feeling they were not up to snuff with what the show did previously.

"There were times he thought the writing wasn't great, and he became surly," Chris acknowledges. "As he once told me, 'I knew I was troublesome. It was because I cared.'"

He also felt a certain insecurity regarding his performing capabilities (he would take a pill to calm down before every show). "Harvey was great," says writer Larry Siegel. "He's the best variety or sketch performer. But he couldn't take compliments."

Money worried him as well. "You could always tell when he was negotiating his contract," dancer Stan Mazin recalls. "He wouldn't say anything to anybody."

"He would quit at the end of every season," quips Chris. In actuality, Harvey loved the series, and when his backstage behavior once threatened to get him fired by Carol on the Nov. 10, 1973 show, he apologized and fell in line. He stayed with the show until the opportunity to star in his own sitcom made him leave after ten years, producing disastrous results for both him and *The Carol Burnett Show* in 1977-1978.

Though it might sound like hyperbole, it is hard to overstate the symbiotic chemistry between Harvey and Carol in the sketches and singing and how that fed into making *The Carol Burnett Show* such a satisfying program to watch. Chris Korman put it best when he told Carol after his father's funeral that "My dad had a love for you that would not be held in his heart by anybody else. If it weren't for you, he wouldn't be known."

The Rock Hudson Type—Lyle Waggoner

Carl Reiner takes credit for adding Lyle Waggoner to the series—or at least his role on it. "I remember when Carol was going to go on the air, her husband asked me if I would be interested to help produce the show," he says. Reiner demurred, due to his already heavy schedule in movies and television, but he did make a suggestion to enhance the series.

"I said, 'She really needs a handsome guy to play opposite for comedy,'" Reiner recalls. Hamilton took his advice, and he and Bob Banner advertised in the show business trade papers for a "Rock Hudson type" to play her announcer. (Obviously they could not afford Hudson himself.)

What they received were dozens of applicants of guys struggling for work. That included Lyle, whose thin resume since coming to Hollywood in 1965 included small parts in commercials, a handful of TV shows and movies (including a horrible flick filmed in Georgia called *Swamp Country* in 1966) and consideration for the lead in *Batman* (Adam West earned the job instead when the series debuted on ABC in early 1966).

Lyle was the second-to-last to audition for his part on *The Carol Burnett Show* on Aug. 17, 1967. He met with Joe Hamilton and Arnie Rosen and thought he might amuse them by stuttering when saying he wanted the job. They gave him a blank response, and Lyle thought he had blown his opportunity with the failed joke until his agent informed him Carol wanted to meet him the next day. She faked a faint in front of him to see how he would react, and his assistance and small talk were enough to win Lyle the job that day.

According to Carol, another factor was at play in hiring Lyle. The CBS secretaries stared at his muscular 6-foot-4 frame and winning smile when he arrived, and that sort of attention combined with his talent got him the thumbs up to join the series.

Waggoner was handsome and funny in a tongue-in-cheek, happy-go-lucky way, and he soon graduated from just being the announcer to doing sketches and even musical numbers. This was beneficial for the series as well as his status on it, as the bits where Carol attempted to seduce him or became jealous when he won the affections of a female guest star wore thin before the end of the first season and forced him to be used in better capacities. He lacked the versatility that Harvey possessed, however, and he was usually relegated to minor parts in every show except in rare cases.

Nevertheless, Lyle was a popular attraction, particularly for many women who wanted to kiss him on the show during the Q&A. He appreciated the work during his seven years on it—even if he often did little more on screen than smile and appear shirtless.

Finding a Little Sister—Vicki Lawrence, or Heather North?

In early 1967, even though she had grown up in Los Angeles, teenager Vicki Lawrence planned to be a dental assistant and avoid participating in the surrounding entertainment industry. But her mom encouraged her to take piano, ballet, jazz, and tap lessons and sing at least since the third grade, and the experiences did encourage her to broaden her horizons somewhat in extracurricular activities.

As a freshman in high school, Vicki discovered the Young Americans, a nonprofit, integrated vocal group of 60 or so Southern California high school students and graduates ages fifteen to twenty-one. She met the qualifications (you needed to have at least a B average and to pass an audition to qualify) and became an active member. Half of them would be on tour (about thirty members), while the rest would be on backup at various times.

As luck would have it, a movie documentary crew covered the group's 1966 summer tour, and she was very noticeable saying a few lines that appeared to be scripted. The resulting movie, *Young Americans,* won the Oscar for Best Documentary Feature in 1969, which the Academy of Motion Pictures Arts and Sciences rescinded once the organization learned it had been playing in some theaters two years earlier, outside its eligibility period. Incidentally, Vicki's next movie was 30 years later, in *Elvis is Alive!*

Following filming of the documentary, Vicki entered the Miss Fireball contest in 1966, her senior year in high school. A newspaper profiled the eight women contestants and noted how Vicki looked like Carol Burnett (a fact her classmates had already noticed). Vicki wrote a fan letter accompanying the article to Carol and said she wanted to meet the actress some day.

Carol's cousin, who read the star's fan mail, forwarded the letter to Carol, who in turn called Vicki and told her she wanted to see her in the Miss Fireball contest, to Vicki's astonishment. Carol request that Vicki keep her appearance there quiet, but the producers of the event found out, and at the show they brought up a very pregnant Carol to crown Vicki. Carol then promised her she'd call Vicki have lunch and discuss her career.

Coincidentally, Carol was looking for someone to play her sister in the "Carol & Sis" segment when Vicki contacted her. Vicki first saw Carol again after she gave birth in January 1967 (Vicki heard the news on the radio and fooled the nurses into thinking she was Carol's sister, Chris). A few weeks later, Joe Hamilton called her to meet with him and Arnie Rosen to Television City at CBS to gauge her interest in auditioning for the series in June, playing Carol's little sister in a regular feature on the show.

This was not an easy decision for her to make, as it meant she would have to leave the Young Americans while the group was gaining more exposure nationally. Vicki appeared with them on *The Andy Williams Show* a week after the Miss Fireball contest and also when they performed the nominated song "Born Free" on the 1967 Oscar telecast.

There was also no guarantee that Vicki would win the role. Auditions were open to other actresses. Even given these concerns, Vicki decide to try out to be Carol's sister, Chris.

Among the actresses who unsuccessfully read for the role were Joyce Bulifant and Sherri Alberoni. The producers whittled the finalists down to Vicki and Heather North.

Heather was far more experienced as an actress than Vicki, with a continuing role in the NBC soap opera *Paradise Bay* already on her resume. She had a trial by fire on that show, as the original lead, Keith Andes, was unable to remember his lines and left, forcing Heather and Marion Ross, who played her mother, to learn more dialogue to compensate for his departure. It ended in July 1966 after nine months on the air.

"I had been acting since eleven," Heather recalls. "All these things went through my agent's office. They got a call looking for people, and my agent thought I was right for it. The original audition, I do remember seeing Joe Hamilton, and he was a really nice guy."

Hamilton told Heather they needed her to audition on a test taping of the series, to give sponsors an idea of what the show would be like. She rehearsed for a week, never knowing what her competition looked or sounded like for four days.

"During the day of the show, the 'other gal' came in," she says. "They told me it's down to us two. It was until I saw her that I realized she had to be really bad not to get it, because she looked liked Carol." Vicki dyed her mousy brown hair red to heighten her similarities to Carol, and though both women received the same mild reaction from test audiences, Vicki's looks gave her the edge in being selected.

Heather has no regrets about losing the part. "It was a really nice experience," she says of her audition. "My attitude is that things happen for a reason. Right after that, I got *Days of Our Lives*, which I did not want to do." Heather gritted her teeth and stayed on that NBC soap opera from 1967 to 1971, and she found romance with its producer and director, H. Wesley Kenney, with whom she was married until his death in 2015.

"He thought I'd become a big star," she notes. "I really wanted to be married and have a child." She acted for a few more years after the soap, most notably as the voice of Daphne on the long-running *Scooby-Doo, Where Are You?* cartoon, before retiring. "I said, 'That's it,' and I wasn't doing anything except the voice of Daphne, because it didn't matter what you looked like to record it."

She would watch *The Carol Burnett Show* occasionally without any envy. As she puts it, "I don't see myself as Mama," referring to Vicki's most famous character. But there is an amusing postscript to her story that occurred in 1993.

"I was in my bathroom, and I was watching Vicki's talk show," she recounts. "And she had Harvey Korman and Tim Conway on. Harvey started to tell Vicki about me during my audition, and he said, 'That was a terrific actress.' He was sure I would get it. It definitely took me back."

During rehearsals for the first "Carol & Sis" to go on the air, Danny Simon, the show's sketch director, was appalled at how raw and naive Vicki was in her acting, but not Carol. She sent Vicki a telegram on Sept. 2, 1967 that said, "I hope you will be my sister for at least 30 years."

Still, Vicki knew she had a lot to learn, and as she appeared sparingly in the first season (sometimes not at all in several shows), she diligently studied acting principles under Harvey and developed humorous voices. Vicki improved to the point where she received substantial parts fairly regularly by the third season—and she did it while taking morning classes at UCLA, just to be safe in case her role fell through! Ironically, despite being the least experienced among the supporting players, Vicki wound lasting longer than all of them and appeared on the most number of shows only behind Carol herself.

And Then There's Tim

He was not a regular when the series began—heck, he did not even become a permanent weekly fixture until its eighth season. Yet for many viewers of *The Carol Burnett Show,* Tim Conway was a big factor in its appeal. Few others made low-key humor so hysterical, whether he was sporting a white wig and shuffling along as "the Old Man," murmuring wisecracks at his zaftig secretary as Mr. Tudball, stumbling along as Mickey Hart to the irritation of Mama in "The Family" or playing dozens of other characters.

Tim appeared in many sketches with Harvey Korman alone, where audiences reveled in their interaction, particularly because Tim insisted on ad libbing comic bits that left audiences in stitches as Harvey often laughed uncontrollably in response. Everyone connected to the series swears Tim's actions were unrehearsed, including Korman's son Chris, who notes that "My father was a very serious actor. He rarely broke character." The contrasts in their height (Harvey was eight inches taller) and general approach to acting (Harvey exuded passion and quick delivery of lines, while Tim's demeanor could be laidback, slow and methodical) only added to the humor.

For someone who seemed natural as a professional comedian, it is rather surprising that he basically was forced into becoming one. Born Tom Conway in Willoughby, Ohio, on Dec. 15, 1933, he grew up in Chagrin Falls, Ohio. Compact in stature (he stood 5-foot-8), he wanted to be a jockey but was too heavy to ride the horses. Instead, he attended Bowling Green University, where he did some comedy on a local radio station, then volunteered for the Army two years after that and came out unemployed in 1958, uncertain where he wanted to go in life.

What turned the corner for him was an old friend who recommended that he apply to be an assistant on a morning radio at KYW in Cleveland. Three months after working there, a spot came open as a copywriter for KYW's TV division, and he took it. While there, he connected with Ernie Anderson, a wild local entertainer, and they somehow sold the station manager on having a two-hour morning show with Ernie hosting a movie series and Tim directing it—even though Tim had never directed a TV show before! (For more on Anderson, see the opening of the 1968-1969 chapter.)

Tim never knew how to time a movie properly, so often there were dead spots on air left to fill the running time. In those cases, Tim drafted himself to play a guest that Ernie would interview spontaneously. The results were riotous to watch.

One who saw them was Rose Marie when she was in Cleveland in the late summer in 1961 to promote her new TV series, *The Dick Van Dyke Show*. Impressed, she asked for a couple of tapes of Tim and Ernie's work that she could show comedian Steve Allen, who was known in Hollywood for wanting to showcase new comic talent. Allen found the submissions amusing and wanted Tim alone to come out to do Steve's TV series. He did so, and the material he offered to do on the show impressed Allen to have his newcomer write his own skit for his guest shot, a rarity on TV then and now.

Steve Allen also encouraged his new entry to rename himself Tim Conway, in order to avoid confusion with the actor Tom Conway. Thus dubbed, the new attraction on *The Steve Allen Show* scored so well that its star drafted him to become a regular on the series. Tim was reluctant to leave home, but Ernie encouraged him to make the move, and he did. Although *The Steve Allen Show* went off the air on Dec. 27, 1961, Tim gained an agent who successfully got his client more work. Two jobs were especially pivotal.

Tim guest starred on *The Garry Moore Show* on June 12, 1962. Although he did not work directly with Carol on stage, the two bonded during the taping and appreciated each other's comic timing. Carol would remember to include Tim on her series as a result.

Another crucial offer was securing a regular supporting role on *McHale's Navy*, a sitcom set in World

War II starring Ernest Borgnine that ran on ABC from 1962-1966. It firmly established Tim as a leading comic presence, along with several concurrent TV guest shots including *The Hollywood Palace*, where he once sparkled in a routine with none other than hostess Joan Crawford acting as his straight man. His reputation was so strong that ABC gave him his own sitcom, *Rango*, in early 1967, but it bombed.

Then came the offer to be on *The Carol Burnett Show* on its fourth episode, and from there Tim was indelibly linked to the series. There will be more to his story with the series told in the upcoming pages, particularly when he becomes a regular in the 1975-1976 season. For now, let's just say that based on ratings and letters to the show, Tim Conway was by far the most popular recurring guest star the series had in its early years.

The Choreographer

Born Oct. 30, 1918 in Denver, Colorado, as Ernest Flatt but known by everyone on *The Carol Burnett Show* as simply Ernie, the series' resident choreographer unsurprisingly began as a hoofer. He took his talents as a tap dancer to Hollywood to break into movies.

"Most of the choreographers today don't have a tap background," says dancer Bobbie Bates. "Ernie was famous for it."

Ernie's excellence as a tap dancer became so renowned at MGM that Gene Kelly asked for his assistance in doing routines for the classic *Singin' in the Rain* (1952). Kelly got Flatt his union card as well, and from there, he never lacked for work in movies or television, where he joined *Your Hit Parade* in 1955 to take over staging of dance numbers from Tony Charmoli. Flatt stayed with that series until NBC canceled it in 1958.

A year later, Ernie joined *The Garry Moore Show*, which established much of the working pattern his dancers would later have on *The Carol Burnett Show*. For one thing, like Carol's show, "Garry Moore included his dancers in all the sketches," says Randy Doney. Ernie left the series to do *The Judy Garland Show* in 1963, reunited with Carol on the ill-fated *The Entertainers* in 1964 and then worked on *The Steve Lawrence Show* in 1965 before being available and agreeing to join *The Carol Burnett Show*.

For this assignment, Ernie brought Don Crichton and several other dancers from *The Garry Moore Show* with him, but he kept an eye out for new talent. He tended to go through female dancers, none of whom lasted as long as Crichton, Stan Mazin or Randy Doney. All knew that they were never assured of having a job beyond more than a year if Flatt or possibly the production crew decided not to renew an option.

Ernie's routines stood out as much for their athleticism as their showmanship, with dancers constantly in motion leaping, lifting and being lifted across the stage, all while trying to look as graceful as possible in Bob Mackie's elaborate costumes.

"They could be very exhausting," says Doney of Flatt's moves.

"There was so much to know so quickly," says Carl Jablonski.

"He could be a taskmaster," says Bobbie Bates. "A lot of people didn't like him, but I did. The only thing that was hard for me personally was that he never said anything after the numbers." She only learned later from his surviving longtime companion that Ernie considered her one of his favorite dancers.

"He could definitely be a taskmaster," agrees Sande Johnson, who danced on the series the last two seasons. "He worked fast. But he had a great sense of humor."

"He had to be tough and strong to get it done," notes drummer Cubby O'Brien, who worked intensely with Flatt to rehearse choreography for shows each week from 1969-1972. O'Brien credits Ernie for teaching him to remember everything he was supposed to be doing for each show and write it down to secure it.

Stan Mazin, a compact, dark-haired dynamo who joined the show in the middle of its first season and stayed through the end, enjoyed Flatt immensely, especially given his personal style of showing how he wanted members of his troupe to move. "Working with Ernie was incredible," Mazin says. "If he wanted a girl to jump off a platform, he would just dive off the platform himself, just like that!"

"Ernie loved to do lifts," remembers Johnson. "We did lots of taps, and he would prerecord a small group of us doing the taps to be used on air." Johnson also served as Carol's stand-in during rehearsals for numbers on Mondays and Tuesdays.

"Ernie was very good at using props," says Jablonski. "I did jumping rope, and tumbling I learned in acrobat class."

Even though some shows had musical numbers that took up the bulk of air time, and they presented dancers in multiple presentations, amazingly there are no reports of serious injuries from anyone involved in the series. It is a tribute to the quality of the dancers, especially given all of the moves they had to learn.

"His dances were fun to do, even though they some of them were incredibly challenging," Mazin says. In fact, he remembers one routine Flatt presented was so complex that no dancer could get it, forcing him to come up with other moves.

Despite what Vicki Lawrence's memoirs imply, Mazin confirms that at least one terpsichorean in the troupe, Birl Johns, was straight. Still, he allows, "It's safe to say most of the male dancers are gay. With women, it's harder to tell."

Regardless of their sexual orientation, there was overall a lot of love and respect among the gypsies and with their leader, who had their undying attention. "Ernie was a true mentor to me," says Jablonski. "He taught me about cameras and blocking."

Indeed, *The Carol Burnett Show* used Flatt's dancers in sketches far more elaborately than did *The Garry Moore Show* or any other variety series for that matter. Carol's acknowledgment of the dancers getting to bow at the end of most shows was the exception to the rule in the industry too, and it made her all the more beloved by those individuals. It's also another reason why the show is considered among the greatest ever.

Guest Starring

Nearly 200 guest stars appeared on *The Carol Burnett Show*, most if not all at the behest of the host and her producers. The talent booked was diverse and composed largely of entertainment award winners that reflected the series' emphasis on presenting the best.

Almost all who Carol requested to appear did so. "I think Carol got just about everybody she asked for," notes Roger Beatty, who was with the series for its entire run.

The overwhelming majority of guests came back at least one other time, both for the material as well as a backstage atmosphere that was one of happiness and enjoyment.

"Everybody loves her," says Paul Sand, who guest starred four times. Another four-timer, Michele Lee, concurs with that opinion. "Carol was easygoing and made everyone feel comfortable, so it was easy to learn anything. She was always laughing with the guys and never acted as producer on the set or rehearsal hall."

Carol often drew inspiration for inviting guests after seeing their work on stage, screen or television. She first fell in love with Jim Nabors when she saw him sing a folk song on a porch swing to his girlfriend on *Gomer Pyle—USMC*. He became her good luck charm and guest starred on the first episode of every show each season.

Ken Berry was familiar to Carol when she went to a testimonial dinner at UCLA in the early 1960s and attended the Billy Barnes Revue afterward, where he was a featured dancer. She loved his work and made a note to have him as a guest on her show, which was helped by the fact that in 1968, he was being groomed to take over *The Andy Griffith Show* as the lead of *Mayberry R.F.D.*

Carol also had a soft spot for New York stage performers who were not known by the general public at the time, such as Bernadette Peters in 1969. "What was so cool about Carol, she used to fight for Broadway show people to come on," recalls Julie Budd.

Of course, not all actors are created equal, especially when it comes to the demands of singing and dancing. Carol and her crew did their best to compensate for those shortcomings wherever possible. "Some of the stars had several left feet, but it all worked out," says dancer Randy Doney. "Ernie had the dancers go around to disguise that."

"He was brilliant at that," concurs Bobbie Bates of how Flatt choreographed those individuals. "He just had to bring the star in and plug him in."

Carol's protective nature to her visitors even affected the writers to a degree in crafting material for them. "She loved it if you did a great thing for the guest star," notes Arnie Kogen, who wrote for the series from 1972-1976.

The guest stars were by and large friendly to the cast and crew. "The big ones were always the nicest," contends writer Bill Angelos. "Always." He recalls when a woman in a mink coat approached him and said, "Hi, I'm Lana Turner," and he was speechless.

For stage veterans especially, doing the show was a breeze. "When you have a great cast and great material, all you have to do is to do it," says Chita Rivera. "Her show just enabled us to turn ourselves inside out. It was a great and a happy, happy experience with everyone involved."

Most of the shows the first eight years included two guests, sometimes three, usually one of them being a singer. The latter sometimes appeared in skits too if they had the training to do so (and sometimes even if they did not!). When Tim Conway became a regular in 1975, the show almost always used one guest star who had to sing, dance and act, which limited the guest pool somewhat but arguably produced better shows overall.

Although Carol and the producers made the final selections, she did listen to fans when they let Carol know who they enjoyed most and would like to see often. Usually they concurred with Carol. For example, Kathy Clements, a fixture at tapings of the series in the 1970s, has two favorite guests. "Steve (Lawrence) and Eydie (Gorme)," she says. "They seemed like they were always there. They were very nice. When Steve and Eydie were on the show, that was the highlight."

The show's warmth and appreciation toward its guests would bear out at the end, when Carol would have them sign their names to her personal book and join her and the regulars in doing a kick line (most other shows just simply said good night without them). Some guests wrote more than their names, making sure to share their feelings of appreciation for doing her series.

"I probably wrote something like, 'I love you madly,'" says Julie Budd. "She was a very easy person to work with."

The 2012 *Ultimate Collection* DVD includes images from the tenth season's guestbook that confirms that at least Betty White, Madeline Kahn and Ken Berry all wrote "I love you" under their signatures. The most poignant entry, however, comes not to a guest star but a regular. When Harvey departed at the end of that season, he wrote: "Carol dear, it's not good night or goodbye. You will always be in my heart. I love you."

Making Music—Harry Zimmerman and Others

While always presented beautifully, the music on *The Carol Burnett Show* often came off as old-fashioned. In fact, if anything dates the series the most, it is the musical selections, as most songs typically were hits at least ten years older than when the shows were first taped (and often much older than that). The cumulative effect often makes viewers feel if the series knew of no songs made beyond the 1950s, sometimes to its detriment.

Consider the Jan. 22, 1977 show, where Carol played a gal desperate for a party. This was indicated by the radio playing "Saturday Night is the Loneliest Night of the Week," a hit in 1945. The show chose that 32-year-old song even though the thematically similar "Another Saturday Night" had been a hit in the interim twice, including a version by Cat Stevens that was less than two years old.

Presumably because Carol felt more at home with songs she knew from her childhood, those became part of the show over current popular music as a result. Combine that with long sketches of old movies, and the show could give off a distinctive vibe of being something more out of the 1930s and 1940s rather than the 1960s and 1970s.

To be fair, Carol and/or her guests did sometime take on contemporary tunes. When they did so, however, the results could be so aggravating to endure that one wishes they never took the chance, such as Dinah Shore plodding her way through Paul Simon's "50 Ways to Leave Your Lover" while missing how important the phrasing is to convey the song's message. Even Carol herself failed with Anthony Newley in capturing even a hint of the soulful romantic mood Roberta Flack and Donny Hathaway provided in the latter duo's hit version of "Where is the Love." By and large, only artists performing their original hits on the series have withstood the test of time well.

Leaving this aside, *The Carol Burnett Show* did attract a fair amount of excellent tuneful talent support, and much of that stemmed from its first conductor. Born Aug. 27, 1905, in West Virginia, Harry Zimmerman came to national prominence in the 1940s as a chorus leader and then conductor for several radio series, including *Maisie* (1949-1953). Moving to TV, he was the orchestra leader for Dinah Shore from 1954-1963 before doing *The Entertainers* from 1964-1965. Since the latter starred Carol Burnett, it was only natural that he was asked to join the series and accepted.

For his orchestra on *The Carol Burnett Show*, Zimmerman included some musicians from *The Danny Kaye Show*, such as Buddy Collette on lead alto and Red Callender on tuba and bass. "Harry was a good guy and he knew who he wanted: 'I've got to have you and you,'" Collette recalled in his autobiography. "We had a good band and we got along."

The name in the orchestra most familiar to TV viewers during Zimmerman's tenure was drummer Cubby O'Brien, since he had been a member of *The Mickey Mouse Club*, seen on ABC daytime from 1955-1959 and in reruns in the 1960s. At age 23, he joined the series in 1969 after being a rehearsal drummer on *The Jim Nabors Hour*. That role required him and a pianist to play the numbers for dancers and guest stars to practice their routines on the show Mondays through Wednesdays prior to taping. He and the pianist would sketch the accents out from these rehearsals and present them for the Paul Weston Orchestra to use for the final show. His work was appreciated, and when Zimmerman felt the drummer he had in his orchestra was inadequate, he tapped O'Brien to replace him.

"We got along fabulously," O'Brien says of working with Zimmerman. "It was a big thrill for me to be on the show."

O'Brien says the orchestra numbered between sixteen to eighteen pieces, including a drummer, guitarist, pianist, three trumpets and five saxophonists. "It was a big band," he notes.

Bringing in Zimmerman and his later replacement, Peter Matz, to orchestrate the numbers during rehearsals was a little-heralded asset in making the show pleasurable when watching dance routines. As choreographer Carl Jablonski says, "If we did funny, kooky things, they would score it that way."

For vocals, it was a little-heralded fact that George Becker arranged a group of between eight to twelve male and female singers to provide choral backing for virtually every mini-musical finale as well as several solos, duos and group numbers needing an extra bit of support. The dancers, regulars and guests typically lip-synced to the previously recorded vocals during tapings, and unless you followed the credits and realized Becker being the series' choral director meant there were singers offstage, you were none the wiser. (There is a credit for the George Becker Singers for the shows aired from 1968-1970.)

"We were rarely on camera," notes Gene Merlino, who sang as part of the chorale for at least eight years on *The Carol Burnett Show*. "There was a bunch of singers who were kind of a clique doing these things." Merlino joined Becker prior to doing vocals on *The Danny Kaye Show* with the Earl Brown Singers as well as some other productions for NBC. Like Becker, Earl Brown was a member of the Skylarks along with Joe Hamilton in the 1950s, and both moved into arranging for TV series after the group disbanded.

Becker directed the singers on *The Garry Moore Show* from 1959 to 1964. His reputation there led to an offer to join other veterans of that series to work on *The Carol Burnett Show*, only this time his group would be virtually confined from appearing on the show.

The singers would tape their parts for each week's show on Thursdays, a day ahead of the tapings. "Most of the time, we would just come in and pre-record," notes Merlino. Because of their professionalism in learning swiftly and delivering quickly on pitch, sessions with Becker and his singers usually were finished within a short period of time. They could stick around to watch the rehearsals that day, and as Merlino notes, on infrequent occasions, such as the May 13, 1968 show where they backed Vicki Lawrence, they would appear on camera.

Despite the limited exposure, Merlino loved his experience with *The Carol Burnett Show.* "That was really a wonderful show," he says. "Carol couldn't have been sweeter to me."

Getting back to memorable guest musical performances, only eight acts sang their current top 40 hits on the series, an embarrassingly puny tally for such a long-running national television program. They were Sonny and Cher, Dionne Warwick, the Carpenters, Helen Reddy, the Jackson 5, the Pointer Sisters, Glen Campbell and Natalie Cole. If you count regulars, the total is nine, with Vicki with "The Night the Lights Went Out in Georgia."

Industry observers felt this lack of contemporary pop music performers was a drawback. In 1974 a reviewer for *Variety* praised the series' use of the Pointer Sisters on a program while bemoaning "the show's reliance on guest stars who draw only rheumatic demographics." It was during this time onward that the show did in fact have the bulk of its hit artists appear through the rest of its run, to its (minor) credit.

Nevertheless, it is a shame that one would be hard pressed to make the case that the musical moments on *The Carol Burnett Show* were as equally memorable and effective as the comic ones—especially since they could have reached that peak with a little more thought and care.

The Costumer

Bob Mackie was a 28-year-old costume designer who had worked professionally for four years when he interviewed for the series with Carol. Ernie Flatt recommended him based on the work he had done with Mitzi Gaynor's stage show. Mackie already had one Emmy nomination in 1966 for his collaboration with Ray Aghayan for *Wonderful World of Burlesque,* a Danny Thomas variety special, and an Emmy win in 1967, again with Aghayan, for the live action version of *Alice Through the Looking Glass*. Aghayan also became Mackie's longtime companion following the latter's divorce.

Mackie was familiar with Carol via *The Garry Moore Show*, and he enjoyed learning that her series was to work in the same way, with an emphasis on comedy along with some musical numbers. As he recalled in the 2012 *Ultimate Collection* DVD, "I'd had a lot to do with sort of musical variety kind of people—singers and dancers—but I wanted to do something because I loved doing funny, and I loved doing the other too, the glamorous, the funny, the whole thing. It kind of fulfilled me."

His vision was perfect for the series, so much so that it became a staple for audience members to ask who created the show's costumes during the Q&A. Mackie did more than just put performers in showy or funny clothes—he brought out aspects of the roles they played, often in ways that pleasantly surprised the actors and increased the laughs.

For example, he suggested to Carol that rather than play Mrs. Wiggins as an old woman, she should be a blonde bimbo instead. He had her put her knees into a baggy black skirt when walking, which in the process made her posterior stand out and created the "Wiggins walk" that created hilarious commentary by Mr. Tudball (Tim Conway).

Some have even gone so far as to designate Mackie as a writer in a certain sense for the series, a claim with which he strongly disagrees. "I didn't create a character, I just enhanced a character," he said. Likewise, not all of the ideas with costumes originated with him—Tim for one came up with the idea of the loose-fitting toupee for Mr. Tudball that would flop off his head every time he banged it against a wall, for example.

Having said that, Mackie's work consistently dazzled everyone on the series, particularly the dancers, where he made them shine in production numbers.

"It was a thrill to be dressed by Bob Mackie every week," says Bobbie Bates. "The costumes were made just for us."

"The jumpsuits were always fabulous," notes Stan Mazin.

Sande Johnson calls Bob Mackie a genius. She is proud to have received two sketches of costumes he designed for her.

The process for envisioning the costumes was much easier than producing them. Mackie would get a copy every weekend of the script for next week's show to review and think what would work best to convey the message of each sketch and musical number. Oftentimes the characters had no description of what they were wearing, allowing him to determine if they should appear in regular workday clothes or something special.

From there, time was the enemy. "We had four days to do the entire show, from Monday through Thursday, because Friday they were wearing the costumes and performing in them for the dress rehearsal," Mackie notes.

His seamstresses had to create around 60 costumes a week on average. Sometimes they made even more costumes, up to 100, particularly in shows with blackouts (short comic bits that lasted less than a minute, like most of the commercial spoofs). Approximately 45 seamstresses sewed clothes for the show's eleven-season run.

On Fridays during tapings, Mackie had the advantage that the show had to set up scenery between numbers and sketches, which allowed him time to get the costumes styled properly for everyone's entrance rather than rush on the air. He accomplished this with a skeleton staff. "I only had a couple of assistants, and then the day of the show, we had dressers and all those kind of people and a sewer on hand," he says. Despite that limitation, the shows always came in town with no hitch in the costumes.

Of course, there was much more to getting the show ready than just outfits. Here is what all was involved in a typical week producing *The Carol Burnett Show*.

Putting It All Together

"People can't believe we did it in one week," says dancer Randy Doney. But they did, and though the process was intense, it was one of the smoothest ever for a TV series.

Each workday for Carol began at 8 a.m. with regular yoga exercise classes for an hour. This would be followed on Mondays and Tuesdays by rehearsals from 10 a.m. to 5 p.m., except for the dancers, where workdays lasted much longer starting promptly at 9 a.m. "By 9:01 you were late," notes Carl Jablonski.

"If we did a heavy duty dance number, they would call us in a day early, on Sunday," adds Stan Mazin. Dancers would rehearse in costumes on Tuesdays and work in time with a guest star practicing, should he or she be performing a number with the gypsies.

For the cast and guests, Mondays involved a table reading of the script followed a half hour of rehearsals for the sketches. Those who were singing would meet with Artie Malvin, Buz Kohan and Bill Angelos (in the 1960s), Ken and Mitzie Welch (in the 1970s), and any others involved in special musical materials for discussion and rehearsal for a half hour. Writers would work on any changes if needed as well as create sketches for future shows, while Bob Mackie's staff sewed costumes he designed for this week's show. Guests would take home a recorded tape to learn the lyrics for production numbers.

Tuesdays were similar to Mondays, with the addition that Carol would meet with Joe, the director and the head writer for a production meeting to review the first draft of the following week's show. Based on notes from those meetings, the script of next week's show would be printed by Friday evening for everyone to review over the weekend.

On Wednesdays rehearsals continued in the morning, while the director marked the sets. This was when Carol and the guests started working with the dancers, as well as when Carol saw what outfits Bob Mackie designed for her to wear for that week's show. The production crew including

Carol had lunch in Joe's office. After more sketch rehearsals in the afternoon, there was a run-through for the show for the cast in the rehearsal hall, with the writers and staff present for any changes needed for the next day.

"It was always reasonably orderly," remembers Barry Levinson of the Wednesday run-through. "If a sketch didn't work, you'd drop it." That meant either a last-minute substitution or, in a few cases, simply remaking a previous sketch.

A production meeting followed thereafter. As Cubby O'Brien notes, "A lot of work had to be done on the first three days."

Writer Gene Perret believes Dave Powers' work as a director during these first three days merits special mention. "He worked hard with the cast during rehearsals to keep the sketches moving smoothly and to enhance the comedy," says Perret.

Camera blocking occurred Thursdays from 11 a.m. to 6 p.m., with an hour break for lunch, along with the dress rehearsal and recording music and singing. "We had a three-hour period to do everything we had to do," Cubby O'Brien says regarding recording the Thursday evening orchestrations, typically done for the dance numbers and other sketches with lots of songs within them for playback during Friday tapings.

"By the time they came to work Friday, they pretty much had it down," says Jerry Davis, who was the videotape editor of the series. Some pretaping of numbers and sketches, particularly the short spoofs of commercials, typically occurred Friday mornings for insertion during tapings. Otherwise, it was run-throughs with the cameras from 11 a.m. to 2:15 p.m. followed by a half hour on technical changes including lighting. During this time, CBS employees could and did watch the rehearsal in the audience. Everyone would break for lunch for an hour, then the cast would receive notes prior to taping.

The first taping, also known as the dress taping, would occur from 4:15 p.m. to approximately 5:45 p.m. After a meal break, there would be another half hour of notes about any changes before the second taping, also known as the air taping, at 7:15 p.m. For both tapings, seating time was a half hour in advance. Officially, tickets were only for those ages sixteen and up, but enforcement of that rules was lax, since a fair amount of youth in their early teens and younger proved to be enthusiastic fans in the audience.

Super fan Kathy Clements says celebrities in the audience usually appeared only in the dress taping. Tickets never revealed who the guest stars were, which confirms that the audience's excited reactions were genuine when Carol announced names at the top.

The shows usually ran without stopping during shooting except in rare cases, with some additional promos for the show or the station(s) carrying the series recorded at the end of the final taping if needed. "If you lost your costume, too bad," notes Carl Jablonski. "And when they did that in Carol's show, they kept the cameras going." Bobbie Bates recalls there were a lot of times the dancers fell down off camera that thankfully missed showing up on air. However, some gaffes did make it to air, simply because Joe Hamilton found the rest of the main action to be of higher quality.

There were breaks only to stop and change the sets. Although a good amount of music was recorded the night prior to taping, "In and out of the sketches was pretty much live music [from the orchestra]," O'Brien says.

The breaks also provided a little bonus for the studio audience to enjoy humor that never made it to air. "When Carol had something on funny, like padding, she would come out to show us," recalls Kathy Clements. "She was real big on not keeping us there any longer than necessary."

"If they got something really good the first time, they'd bank it," says dancer Bobbie Bates. That meant the piece was considered fine from the first (dress) taping, and viewers in the second one (air) would watch a playback of it in the monitors, particularly if it was a messy sketch to depict or involved a difficult change in wardrobe or scenery.

Just about everyone on the show would watch the tapings, including writers and dancers in sketches without them. "We would go in the back of the audience and watch what was going on," Randy Doney recalled. "We enjoyed it as much as the audience."

After second taping ended around 9 p.m., the cast and crew left with next week's scripts and had dinner at a restaurant. Typically it was Chassen's, where Carol could still come up with quality comic moments on her own. Charo remembers that after she did the show in 1973, Carol played around with silverware in front of her at the restaurant before proudly announcing that "Finally! I've found a spoon big enough to fit my mouth!"

That would be it for everyone on the show except for the producer and the editing team. "Joe got a VHS copy [of both tapings] that he looked at over the weekend," recalls Jerry Davis, videotape editor on the series during the mid-1970s. "He would call [assistant director] Roger Beatty Sunday night and give him selections of what parts to include."

Since the series ran before computer programs existed, the editors had to slice by hand the videotape copies for each show in post production. "It was probably one of the last network shows to have a physical edit in it every week," says Davis. "We actually had to cut the tape and put it back together."

As one might surmise, one cut came between the end of the question and answers Carol had with audience members before the main animated titles and the scripted portion of the series. Questions and answers—to be known henceforth as the way most on the series called the segment, Q&A—basically served as the adjustment for timing the rest of the show in post production.

Roger Beatty, who served as stage manager the first season and then assistant director on the series thereafter, explains the process. "Carol would do about ten or fifteen minutes of Q&A on both shows. In the booth during those segments, the writers' secretary, Becky Mann, would make note of the questions and also time them. At the end of the air taping, Maggie [Scott, designated as the "script girl" at the time] would give Joe the whole show's overall timing and tell him we need, for example, six minutes and 40 seconds to bring the whole show to the correct time. Joe would look for the best questions from both shows and select the ones that would time out closest to 6:40."

Beatty would take that list of questions along with notes from Joe and directors Clark Jones and Dave Powers of what sketches from the dress and air tapings should go into the final edited series. Sometimes that would involve inserting something as minor as one line from a taping into a sketch otherwise taken from the other one. From those notes, Beatty would convene with his team to edit and combine the selected portions from both taping into a final show for airing.

"We had the Burnett show together on Monday mornings, usually in four hours," Davis says. There were never any difficulties arising in post production under this setup. "I could always find an edit when needed," asserts Beatty.

Davis added that before any show aired, "There was a sweetening session (to add to the aural track) on Tuesday. It also was brief. But almost everything you heard on the air was the original laughs." He denied the show added a laugh track or canned laughter, as some call it, only improvements to make the soundtrack crisp and clear on the air.

Beatty concurs. "We actually did very little of it, because the laughs were pretty much always there. The audience in Studio 33 numbered a little over 300 and was always receptive. Sweetening for us usually consisted of putting in applause for pre-taped production numbers, or covering an edit or maybe adding a laugh on top of a laugh that wasn't quite big enough. But the laughs were mostly already there."

Despite this precise procedure, some technical glitches made it on air. Boom mikes can be seen at the top on several shows simply because there was no feasible way at the time to electronically edit them out, either because Joe Hamilton liked the other aspects of a scene to include it, or it was just the best shot from both the dress and air tapings.

"There were folks watching the show for continuity errors, and they called about it," Davis says. The worst he remembers was a dinner scene on the Dec. 21, 1974 show with Alan Alda. A stagehand forgot to light the candles for the second taping, so in some shots the wicks would be burning, and other times they would not.

Still, most viewers focused more on content than continuity goofs when the programs finally appeared, and everyone involved was proud of the results overall. "It was the smoothest show," concludes Davis. "It was the best run show I've ever worked on."

Overture to the Opening

Before going into production for the series, Rock Hudson threw Carol a big Hollywood party with Princess Grace, Henry Fonda and other luminaries coming to wish her the best. Within parts of the industry, however, there were doubts the series would last.

Mike Dann had placed *The Carol Burnett Show* on Mondays smack dab opposite two established programs on competing networks heading into their third year, *I Spy* on NBC and *The Big Valley* on

ABC. *I Spy* had finished in the top 30 in the prior season, knocking off its CBS competition, *The Danny Kaye Show*, after four years on the air (the same series where Harvey Korman previously worked). Though less successful than *I Spy*, *The Big Valley* had held its own Monday nights, surpassing *The Jean Arthur Show*, *I've Got a Secret*, *To Tell the Truth* and *Password* on CBS during 1966-1967 alone.

Indeed, Monday nights from 10 p.m. to 11 p.m. had been a sore spot on the CBS schedule throughout the 1960s. The only series to run more than one season there was the sitcom *Hennessey*, which ran in the first half hour from 1959 through 1962. Otherwise, a slew of losers populated the slot, among them *The New Loretta Young Show*, *Stump the Stars*, *East Side/West Side*, *Slattery's People* and *The Steve Lawrence Show*. The host of the latter became a mainstay on *The Carol Burnett Show* in the 1970s.

With the competition and history it encountered, it would be understandable if the personnel on the series worried that they were part of a losing enterprise, but few had that feeling due to Carol and Joe emphasizing their mantra of having fun above all else.

"We never even thought about that," maintains writer Bill Angelos about the series' viability. Instead, what the series accomplished at the start was its template for long-term success. As Angelos puts it, "It set its tone the first year, and it stayed there."

On that note, let's see what the cast and crew of *The Carol Burnett Show* created after they began taping their first set of programs in the late summer of 1967.

And the beat doesn't go on: Harvey and Carol fail to impress Sonny and Cher as being just as "mod" and happening as the latter duo visits the series on the Nov. 6, 1967 episode of ***The Carol Burnett Show***. During her visit, Cher envied the colorful outfits Bob Mackie made for Carol and wished he could do the same for her. He wound up doing that when ***The Sonny and Cher Comedy Hour*** debuted on CBS in 1971. Courtesy of Getty Images.

Chapter 2

1967–1968: "Don't Go Away, We'll Be Right Back!"

Audience member: "How do you account for your girlish figure?"
Carol (after laughter): "Our costume designer is a master of deception!"—From the Dec. 25, 1967 show

The Carol Burnett Show opened with the following crew this season:
Director: Clark Jones
Writers: Arnie Rosen (head writer), Stan Burns, Mike Marmer, Don Hinkley, Saul Turteltaub, Kenny Solms, Gail Parent, Bill Angelos, Buz Kohan, Barry E. Blitzer (Oct. 16, 1967, Jan. 22, 1968, and Feb. 5, 1968)
Comedy Sequences Staged By: Danny Simon
Special Musical Material: Art(ie) Malvin
Choreographer: Ernie Flatt
Music Conductor: Harry Zimmerman
Music Coordinator: Nat Farber
Choral Director: George Becker
Assistant to Producer: Patricia Lillie
Production Coordinator: Don Mitchell
Production Assistant: Charlene Del Sardo
Assistant Director: Dave Powers
Technical Director: Dick Hall
Audio: Bud Lindquist
Videotape Editor: Buzz Felty

Art Director: Paul Barnes
Lighting Director: Dick Holbrook
Set Director: Richard Harvey, Donald J. Guild
Makeup: Lou Phillipi
Hair Stylist: Edie Panda Jevtic
Stage Managers: Buddy Borgen, Roger Beatty
Camera Operator: Marty Wagner
Video Animation: Elizabeth Savel and Jean DeJoux

A commonly held belief is that *The Carol Burnett Show* began with Jim Nabors as its premiere guest, and Carol made him her first guest every season thereafter thanks to kicking it off well. The second part is true, but the first needs some correcting.

The first two shows taped opened with a big, artificial production number that did not set the right tone. As a result, Joe Hamilton and Bob Banner insisted that Carol take questions from the studio audience to start future shows. She had done this on *The Garry Moore Show* during breaks between taping to keep the audience interested, and her ad libbed answers were very entertaining. Joe and Bob also thought it would connect viewers personally with Carol right from the start. Carol worried that people might think questions were planted, and that she would lack snappy responses. Nevertheless, she went ahead and did "Q&A" starting with the Nabors show. And it worked well.

So, the series delayed its Mike Douglas-Lynn Redgrave and Martha Raye-Juliet Prowse shows till later in the season. For more, see the Nov. 17, 1967 and Jan. 1, 1968 entries.

Reviewers were mixed about the debut. George Gent of *The New York Times* praised Burnett effusively, saying that she "has more stops in her comic lute than most of the high-priced funny men around," but added that the star "got only minimal help from her writers." Only the Q&A and the Shirley Temple spoof impressed him. Gent concluded that "The show depends on Miss Burnett's multiple talents, and that may not be enough if she doesn't get some help from her writers."

Variety was less enthusiastic, remarking that "this slant is painfully boondock with lumpish sketch humor and square turning." The reviewer disliked the Temple bit in particular. However, the publication reassessed the series two shows later (Sept. 25, 1967) and proclaimed that "the femme has found her best TV métier to date with an hour variety spread that deserves to be the indicated hit it is so far."

A major reviewer who hated the series was Cleveland Amory of *TV Guide*, a publication whose coverage was strangely guarded during the production of *The Carol Burnett Show*. "Miss Burnett is an odd choice for an emcee," he said. "In the first place, a little of her goes a long way, and a lot of her mugging, tongue-outs, etc., often goes the wrong way.

"In the second place she's not a standup comedienne—perilous enough for an emcee choice; she's an outright outrageous clown." These comments reeked of sexism and ignorance. The same criticism could have been made about Red Skelton, who had the top variety series when Carol's show debuted. Amory apparently forgot Carol's success hosting variety specials, or that Dinah Shore or Ed Sullivan weren't comics either.

Of course, the ultimate arbiter for any commercial series is not reviews but ratings, and there was where Carol shined. Even though about 40 CBS affiliates did not air the series initially, *The Carol Burnett Show* handily beat *I Spy* and *The Big Valley* in its initial outing and became the only new series on CBS to crack the top twenty. The series stayed in the top 30 ahead of its competitors thereafter. *Variety* termed *The Carol Burnett Show* "the season's sleeper" by late October, and holdout stations added it. Mike Dann and other CBS executives found themselves pleasantly surprised with a hit on their hands.

With that in mind, let's review how all this success started. To imagine you are there as it happened on TV in 1967, visualize the letters C, B and S being dropped onto the screen in that order, then having the company's corporate eye symbol run through those black letters to add hues while an announcer says, "This program is presented in living color." The following summaries and their commentaries are designed to give you an impression of what unfolded, what worked (and what did not), and what matters about each show.

Sept. 11, 1967: Jim Nabors

Q&A; Harvey plays interviewer F. Lee Korman in "V.I.P." talking with child actress Shirley Dimple (Carol); Jim sings "You Don't Have to Say You Love Me" in Italian and English; Carol and Jim make a connection while wearing casts in "Ski Lodge"; Jim and Carol perform a Broadway medley; the boy next door is taking Chrissy (Vicki) out on a date amid the watchful eye of her sister, Carol, and the general indifference of her brother-in-law, Roger (Harvey); the Charwoman (Carol) sweeps up to "Soul Finger" at a discotheque that comes to life with dancers and lights.

Comments: The first image viewers see is Carol addressing her audience in a haircut that resembles Mia Farrow's in *Rosemary's Baby*. (Gail Parent said the stylist cut so much more than Carol expected that she wore wigs for two months after seeing how bad it looked on air.) With no fanfare, Carol tells everyone they looked gorgeous as she tries to egg them into asking her questions, like who is on the show tonight. One man does that, so she talks about the "Carol & Sis" sketch with Vicki as her sister, mentions Harvey Korman (who gets some applause) and her guest star and godfather of her new baby, Jim Nabors (who receives "ooos" thanks to his recognition as a top TV star at the time with *Gomer Pyle—USMC*). "Do I get nervous?" she restates another question. "No," as she drops to the ground. When asked when the series will air, she jokes 3 a.m. and reveals its competition. Noting that she wanted Bill Cosby and Robert Culp as guests until learning she would be running against them thanks to NBC running *I Spy* opposite her series, Carol says she will get Pearl Bailey on and do a spoof of the series instead. (Bailey would not do the show until Oct. 25, 1972, but Carol did mock *I Spy* on May 6, 1968.) She liked when one person guessed she was 26 years old and was stunned when someone asked if *Stanley*, her flop live series on NBC from 1956-1957, would ever be rerun.

Carol interrupts the questions to bring out a smiling Lyle. She melts into his arms and quips, "Did you hear those shoulders?" There is more snuggling involved by Carol as Lyle teaches her to breathe with her abs, and as she seems overcome with lust for him, she informs the audience jokingly that they nearly hired Harry Von Zell, the heavyset announcer from *The George Burns and Gracie Allen Show* of the 1950s.

Lyle introduces Harvey as host of "V.I.P.," and Harvey ad libs, "Can you hear those shoulders?" before launching into a fairly lame send-up of 1930s child actress Shirley Temple, an impersonation which Carol would have more success later on the series with better material. Here, there is little to enjoy except her tap dancing to "On the Good Ship Lollipop" and remarking that "Jane Withers said something in a movie that wasn't very nice. . . . My fairy godmother changed her into a plumber!" (Withers was playing Josephine the Plumber in a series of commercials for a cleanser at the time.)

Jim's number features him in a tux walking among panels and columns on a set. He is in good voice and follows this with some effective interplay in his first sketch with Carol, with her having a broken left arm and him having an injured right foot, both from skiing. She is accident prone, so her crutches hit him, her pen gets stuck in the palm in his hand, and so on. It is unplanned when Carol knocks the glasses off Jim's face, however, judging from his reaction. The two become attracted to each other during their interaction, and they share addresses so they can stay in touch, with Carol telling Jim to ask any ambulance to find her. This is moderately funny and cute.

In a pink dress, Carol joins Jim back in a tux for duets on numbers such as "If My Friends Could See Me Now" and "The Rain in Spain," the latter with Jim employing his Gomer Pyle characterization as his "before" voice and Carol joining him in a similar Southern twang. This segment has some enjoyment, but at nearly ten minutes, it is overlong.

The first "Carol & Sis" installment has Carol offering advice to Chrissy's date (Cliff Marcus), a nerd with glasses who wears elevator shoes since he stands only 5′5″. Carol encourages Chrissy to slump to help eliminate their height difference as they go out. She remains overprotective and concerned about what might happen, to Roger's general disinterest. ("She's sixteen and never been arrested," Carol notes wistfully.) Chris returns from the disastrous date and attempts to console herself with food. As she enters the living room, the kitchen door hits Carol. That ending will be the trademark of later "Carol & Sis" sketches. This effort holds more promise than actual accomplishment in laughter.

The Charwoman joins the dancers as lights and a mod background come up while they boogie to a recent soul hit by the Bar-Kays. Carol follows it with a solo slow vamp of "Georgy Girl" and then says good night. Overall, the presentation's strengths outweighed its notable flaws, a summation that will apply to many of the shows this season.

Sept. 18, 1967: Sid Caesar, Liza Minnelli

Q&A; Carol sings "Cabaret"; F. Lee Korman (Harvey) interviews Lucy Braines (Carol), the president's daughter, on "V.I.P."; Liza performs "The Debutante's Ball"; Caesar does a monologue of a father worried about his son's future; a mouthwash commercial spoof; a *Star Trek* takeoff with Harvey as Capt. Quirk, Sid as Lt. Cmdr. Spook and Carol as a robot; Carol and Liza duet on a medley of songs about time; Carol tries to stay awake while talking to a representative from a college Chris wants to attend in "Carol & Sis"; a Ziegfeld Follies finale with Carol, Sid and the women dancers.

Contents: Few could have imagined that less than five years after this show ran, Liza would be singing the first song Carol performs here as the lead in the movie adaptation of the Broadway hit *Cabaret*. This curiosity stands out in an episode that starts relatively strong, sags in the middle and comes back to par by the end. In a floral dress, Carol announces her guests are Liza ("I don't know where she got all that talent," she jokes about Judy Garland's daughter) and Sid, who gallivants on stage to say he has lost 43 pounds by eating no bread and just one potato in a year in a half. The main questions are for the hostess. "Is Carol Burnett your real name?" "My real name is Ben Gazzara," goes one memorable round. It is revealed that Lyle's height is 6-foot-4 and Carol's is 5-foot-7— "I'm the same exact height as Sophia Loren!"

Carol's rendition of "Cabaret" is no show stopper, but seeing her tackle the tune in a white floral dress, accompanied by the female dancers in green waitress outfits and the male ones in chefs' garb, is certainly not boring. She fares better as a bright parody of LBJ's spawn, trilling at the outset to Harvey that "The eyes of Texas is (sic) upon you, all the live long day!" and claiming that she lives in an integrated Texas neighborhood—"40 percent Republican." She sprays her puffy black hairdo and says that Phyllis Diller is her stylist. Showing off her newborn, who wakes up at 2 a.m. ("We nicknamed him Early Bird"), Carol reveals Vice President Hubert Humphrey likes to entertain the baby, and if her son is not smart, "He can go into politics." A few final jabs at the 36th president and the First Family come at the end, when Carol picks up the red phone to speak with the ruler of the country—her mother—and asks that the president quit picking the baby up by his ears (an act Lyndon Johnson did to his pet dog, to the dismay of many observers).

Wearing a black dress and standing among empty chairs and risers on the set, Liza effectively conveys pathos with her solo number. To lighten the mood, Carol introduces Sid and says how she went to watch his TV series *Caesar's Hour* in the audience in 1956 rather than see the original *My Fair Lady* on Broadway. His lengthy monologue fantasizing about how his soon-to-be-born son will grow up and cause him problems has spotty laughter, but it does have a kicker of an ending when he learns his wife has given birth to the boy, and a girl, and another boy, and another.

The commercial quickie is light and tight. Carol plays a woman whose breath is so pungent it makes flowers droop. She takes "Golcate 200" to combat her halitosis, then emerges on stage looking disheveled from a make-out session and leers, "It works!"

The same cannot be said of "Star Trip: Who's Afraid of Virginia Robot?" which only vaguely refers to the classic science fiction show it jests. While Sid is wearing big ears a la Spock, the set little resembles the deck of the *USS Enterprise*, neither Harvey nor Sid sound like William Shatner or Leonard Nimoy respectively, and Carol's robot beamed aboard from another ship is a generic character. Some fun comes as Sid asks Carol if he can open her control panel (to program her to love him) and she responds, "Only if you respect me." Harvey informs Sid it was a bad idea to inspire feelings in Carol, for she is actually a walking bomb. For reasons too belabored to explain, the sketch ends with Carol leaving, exploding and coming back as a lamp. Chalk this up as a fizzle.

The pace picks up some when Carol and Liza wear red dresses and tights to dance to bits of numbers like "Just in Time" and "Bidin' My Time," and when Carol enacts great physical shtick of having her body sag while Harvey walks her to keep her conscious in "Carol & Sis." Carol has taken a sleeping pill just before an interviewer from Chris's prospective college (Reta Shaw) visits to see if the home environment is ideal for studying. Struggling to keep her eyes open, Carol spills coffee on Harvey and accidentally drugs the interviewer with another sleeping pill. She and Carol both pass out, and when the interviewer wakes up, Harvey takes advantage of the situation by insisting she had accepted Chris to the school. The fairly funny segment ends with Harvey hitting Carol with the kitchen door and knocking her out again.

The frantic finale has "Sid Ziegfeld" bedeviled when singing and dancing by a clumsy showgirl (Carol), who gets hooked onto his jacket and rips his arm sleeve off to free herself, damages his shoe and has her headdress fall off as part of her unintentional mayhem on stage while in the female chorus line. Carol immediately segues at the end of this into "It's Time to Say So Long" for a rather abrupt finish.

Both Sid and Liza will return to the series, Sid on Dec. 25, 1967 and Liza on Feb. 5, 1968. Liza's *Cabaret* movie costar, Joel Grey, will do the series too, on Oct. 18, 1972.

Sept. 25, 1967: Jonathan Winters, Eddie Albert

Q&A; an obese actress (Carol) emerges from retirement to rehearse a dance with a choreographer (Harvey) in "Comeback"; Eddie sings "Like Animals"; Carol and Roger are visited by a couple whose names they have forgotten in "Carol & Sis"; a comic bit between Carol and Lyle; Carol and Eddie perform a medley of songs about roads; Harvey interviews Gerald Cufflinker (Jonathan), a shy college student, followed by Goo Goo Gabor (Carol), Zsa Zsa and Eva's sister, and a tough cop (Jonathan), all at an international airport; Carol sings "For Once in My Life"; a "Talk to the Animals" finale.

Comments: With some surprise appearances by familiar TV faces and great comedy from Jonathan Winters, this outing provides more consistent enjoyment than the previous two, even if does waste Eddie Albert in just musical numbers. Carol describes Lyle as "the one who's got shoulders like Joan Crawford" and Jonathan as "a true nut" before noting that Elizabeth Montgomery and Ken Berry are in the audience and both have shows on ABC (Carol whispers the network's call letters). She mentions that the 1963 movie in which she and Liz co-starred with Dean Martin, *Who's Been Sleeping in My Bed?*, was on TV the other night (actually two weeks ago by the time this show airs) and says she thought about calling Liz to tell her. Liz jokes about the movie's poor quality by referencing it with her husband, Bill Asher: "We saw it on an airplane and had seventeen walkouts!" The movie mention inspires an audience member to ask, "What about Dean Martin? When are you going to have him on your show?" Carol said she spoke to him when he was passed out on the floor, so no go. Jonathan comes out to answer questions about his movie *It's a Mad, Mad, Mad, Mad World* (it took six months to shoot and was a lot of fun), what party he would affiliate with if he ran for senator (he said he would skip that office to go for president instead) and his military experience. "I was in the Marines. . . . I killed a Japanese gardener. Didn't mean to," he deadpans. He and Carol wind up Q&A with an improvised sketch as a husband and wife, whereupon he tells her to let out their fifteen children from the attic, caresses her body and leers, "I may not go after all!"

Harvey directs dancers in "Give My Regards to Poland" when Carol arrives as a stout starlet. She breaks a folding chair in which she sits, causes a bench with Harvey on it to tumble over, knocks over scenery and gets stuck in a wall as she attempts to perform her routine. If you can overlook politically incorrect fat jokes, then this segment is a howl.

Carol emerges still wearing the fat suit and saying how she would love to go into a restaurant clad in the outfit and order a cow. After describing her getup some more ("First time I ever had a bosom. It's a like a whatnot shelf!"), she introduces Eddie, "a complete delight," to vocalize "Like Animals" with giraffe heads in the background. This mild interlude makes way for Carol and Roger to try and recall the identities of a husband and wife who drop by. The couple (played by Jackie Joseph, Ken Berry's then-wife, and Dave Ketchum, then on *Get Smart!*) reveal their names through careful prodding by Roger and Carol. This is a solid if rather standard "Carol & Sis" piece.

When Carol tells Lyle she has a stiff neck, he massages her and naturally prompts Carol to make passes at him before leaving. "I wonder if he makes house calls," she muses. A better laugh comes when the second half of the show starts and Jonathan says in a sissy voice, "And away we go!" mimicking the catch phrase used by Jackie Gleason.

Carol's teaming with Eddie to sing tunes such as "King of the Road" is fine, but Harvey's interviews are even better. Jonathan's first character is a wallflower who says his parents are in their 90s and his dad enjoys shuffleboard. Carol's Gabor sister, replete with jewelry and tall dogs, claims to have been wed 25 times. Best is Jonathan as a nightstick-wielding cop. "You'll never know who you'll meet in a peace protest!" he booms in explaining his demeanor to Harvey. He even mock clubs Harvey a few times.

The pace slows as Carol sits on stage at an angle where the audience can be seen to sing Stevie Wonder's recent hit, then perks up again as the dancers are dressed as creatures while Carol, Harvey,

Eddie, Jonathan, Lyle and Vicki sing and dance to the Oscar-winning Best Song of 1967. It's a lively end to a fairly upbeat show. Still, Jonathan and Eddie will be put to even better use on later episodes this season.

Oct. 2, 1967: Lucille Ball, Tim Conway, Gloria Loring

Q&A; Lucy and Carol are uneasy patrons at "Café Argentine," where the maitre d' (Harvey) appears to be a Nazi; Carol is a housewife besieged by TV commercial events; Carol and Vicki perform "I Dig Rock 'n' Roll Music"; Tim plays a TV anchor who lacks news to read; Lucy, Carol and Lyle do a skit; Gloria sings two pop hits; car rental agents Lucy and Carol compete for Tim as a customer; Carol is inadvertently hurt by the power of her husband, Super Guy (Harvey); Carol and Lucy present "See What the Boys in the Back Room Will Have."

Comments: This key episode sets in place Tim's status as favorite guest and launches four years of crossovers between Carol and her mentor, Lucille Ball, on their respective series. It shakes off a weak opening sketch to rally as a winner. Additionally, it is the first of three appearances by Gloria Loring, which will be discussed in more detail shortly.

Carol introduces her guests distinctively at the start of Q&A. For Tim, "Y'all know him from *McHale's Navy* and *Rango*," she notes, oddly citing the latter ABC sitcom which bombed earlier in 1967. Loring is "a lovely new lady" and Lucy (Carol calls her just that, no last name) is "my favorite redhead." She eagerly runs to embrace and kiss Durward Kirby in the audience and is thrilled to learn he is moving to Los Angeles. For the inquiry "What are your measurements?" Carol replies, "38, 26 and 30, and I won't say in what order!" She brings out Lyle, who apparently is unprepared and needs Carol to help him put on his tie. After that, Carol asks if anyone has questions for Lyle, and a wiseacre cameraman says, "What are your measurements?" With that, the show commences.

The opening sketch is the show's worst by far, probably the season's nadir. Carol and Lucy enter a restaurant run by Harvey, wearing a monocle and talking with a German accent. Tired Nazi "jokes" such as Harvey forcing the ladies to march in a goose step single file behind him fall flat as do several lines. Carol cackles a lot to try to bolster the segment, and Harvey and Lucy pump as much pep as they can into their roles. This supposed comic routine concludes badly by having the ladies demand to see the manager and getting a man who resembles Hitler, causing Lucy and Carol to scream and flee.

Recovering from this, the show introduces what will become an occasional feature—Carol as a housewife beset by scenarios from TV ads. In a quick and well-executed piece of pantomime, she first is hit in the face from a punch coming from her washer, followed by clothes being thrown back at her from the machine as it rises to burst through her ceiling. A flock of doves enters her kitchen window when she uses dishwashing liquid. After putting butter on a slice of bread, she sticks her head in a refrigerator and emerges with an oversized crown on her head, a la a margarine ad. It ends when she goes outside and is gored by the White Knight's sword. This bit excels as a well-paced comic allegory about the pernicious effects of commercialism in our lives.

Another great comic segment emerges between two lesser entries—Carol and Vicki's forced "mod" song-and-dance routine to a contemporary Peter, Paul and Mary hit, complete with miniskirt outfits and jump cuts that make it scream 1967, and Lucy meeting Lyle and kissing him a long time while Carol thinks her fellow redhead is being rejected by her announcer. Towering over both is Tim Conway as a newscaster awkwardly coping with faulty reports, a missing weathercaster and filmed commercials that fail to run. Begging viewers to call and ask questions, only to get just his wife and her grocery orders, pouring out his jug to clear his throat and seeing his cup has been filled with cigarette butts—all this and more bring solid guffaws. Tim based this routine on an actual event that happened on live TV in Cleveland when he was working there, and even *TV Guide's* staid Cleveland Amory admired his contributions here.

Tim is in another strong sketch as Lucy (with Gertz) and Carol (with Mavis) each want him to rent a car only from her company. Harvey shows up briefly as Carol's dad, who reluctantly goes with Gertz after her badgering, while Tim tries to placate both women. Carol hooks him by the neck. Lucy gives him a massage. Their battle escalates to where they are pulling on his tie at both ends. Both women lose when a female model cozies up to Tim, says, "Why not go by bus and leave the driving to us?" and departs with her. All the actors play their roles to a T, and the setup and jokes are perfect for the show.

Next, introducing the show's guest singer, Carol says that she watched Gloria Loring on Merv Griffin's syndicated talk show and wanted her to come on. Loring confirms that *The Merv Griffin Show* kept her busy early in her career. "I did about 26 of those shows in a year," she says, "My agent and manager were thrilled with the offer."

When going over with Burnett's producers what material to include, Loring sold them on "Try to Remember" from the musical *The Fantasticks*. "I had kind of a jazzed-up version of it," she says. She sings it seated after doing the slower "Going Out of My Head" first.

The final sketch is just slightly less satisfying than preceding ones. Carol mugs amid many props as her superhero husband Harvey cannot control his strength. It ends with her going to bed in a suit of armor instead of pajamas to protect herself when sleeping.

The show satisfyingly closes with Lucy and Carol looking beautiful as showgirls in a saloon singing and dancing to a number Marlene Dietrich popularized in the 1939 movie *Destry Rides Again*. They do the can-can while joined by the dancers. This outing is so lively that Carol includes it as a clip in her one-woman shows.

Loring recalls taking what was happening for granted. "The excitement of being around Lucille Ball and Carol and all those people, I don't think I appreciated them fully and the really hard work that goes into putting on a show," she says. Interestingly, she was the first of this show's guest stars to return to the series—see Nov. 13, 1967 for her next shot.

Oct. 9, 1967: Imogene Coca, Lainie Kazan

Q&A; "V.I.P." has Harvey interviewing a vapid Miss America (Carol); Harvey is a director who convinces two ordinary ladies (Imogene and Carol) to star in a coffee commercial; Lainie sings a medley of "Sunnyside" and "Silver Lining" and duets with Carol on "Watch What Happens"; Carol and Imogene are wallflowers at a fancy party in a production number with the dancers; Harvey and Carol portray the title characters in a *Bonnie & Clyde* takeoff; Carol, Lainie, Harvey, Lyle, Imogene and the dancers sing and play "Nola" on toy pianos; the Charwoman imagines she is a hit stripper on stage.

Comments: In the first of several shows this season without Vicki, Carol gets her initial opportunity to work with Imogene Coca. "I'm a big fan," she gushes. Unfortunately, Imogene is not shown to best advantage, nor did the show let Lainie Kazan flex her comic chops either. "I don't think I knew I was funny then," Lainie recalls about this singing-only appearance. "Even though I had come out of *Funny Girl* [on Broadway, where she replaced Barbra Streisand], I considered myself more of a chanteuse."

Lainie said getting this booking was simple. "My agent just called and asked if I would come in at that time. I had some heat on me." She was an Imogene fan like Carol too. Recalling working with her, she said, "I was flabbergasted. I watched her every single week on *Your Show of Shows*."

Before Imogene or Lainie appear, Carol's Q&A is pretty nice. She says one of her funniest moments on stage was when she did summer stock and her dressing room lights went out, prompting her to put her panties on wrong for the next scene. A few more questions lead to bringing out Lyle, who Carol says has been practicing riding a unicycle and will teach her how do it tonight. "I'll hold you," he says. "All right!" she enthuses. A skeptical Harvey emerges to try too ("You sure this is the way you become tall, dark and handsome?"), and the unicycle gets out from under him in a fun bit.

After that, a Miss America (Carol) with a Southern twang and stilted talking pattern twirls her scepter like a baton that she drops a lot, even though that was her talent for the competition, and notes that pageant losers get two albums of Bert Parks (the longtime host of Miss America specials) singing "There She Is." Carol mugs a lot to prod the sketch along, and it has a killer ending: She tells Harvey that she plans to follow in the footsteps of previous Miss Americas and thus will never be heard from again.

The show's only sketch with Imogene has her and Carol praising the coffee they are drinking at a table when a director (Harvey) who has surreptitiously watched them offers both to star in a commercial for the product. The two fight over who should say the first lines, with Carol freezing up on her attempts and Imogene mangling her efforts so badly that Carol laughs heartily. That prompts Imogene to hit Carol with a pie, then vice versa and finally both hit Harvey with one. This is more raucous than humorous but passable.

The show improves with Lainie singing with gusto in a gown showing considerable cleavage. Regarding her solo numbers, Lainie calls the piece "A very clever arrangement that my conductor put together, Peter Daniels. It was like an interpolation." Lainie suggested the number for the show. "I brought my musical book to them. I gave them a choice of several songs, and they chose that." Before her duet with Carol, the latter praised Lainie's work in *Funny Girl*, but Lainie recalled she had known Carol professionally before that when Carol starred in *Once Upon a Mattress* on Broadway.

Unfortunately, the show sags as Imogene and Carol wish via song for a man to dance with them and then fantasize about that with the male dancers. Solemnity is not expected when teaming these comediennes, but that is what happens before this mercifully ends.

The "Bonnie and Clod" spoof is an improvement, but there is little verisimilitude in approximating the movie. Harvey's Clod complains about a tough day at work—turns out it was Sunday and he only got money from backing up into a parking meter. Carol's Bonnie swarms over him to convince him he still is tough, and she lets him squeeze a grapefruit in her face, slug her and finally kill her to prove it. Before she dies, she kills Clyde after hearing him say he will hook up with a chorus girl he will spoil. This intermittently amusing bit will be surpassed by another send-up seen on April 15, 1968.

"Nola" is clever, especially with Carol, her male regulars and guests being pushed by the male dancers around the stage to play miniature pianos in specially designed chairs. The show's best part follows when the Charwoman hears a drum roll while cleaning on stage, joined by the string section sounding as she manipulates her fingers. This encourages her to do a mock bump-and-grind pantomime to "Let Me Entertain You," ending with her going offstage to real applause from the studio audience. She returns to sit on the bucket and do a strong, slow version of "There's No Business Like Show Business."

This was Lainie's sole appearance on the series. "At the time, I was busy touring and doing *The Dean Martin Show* a lot," she says of her unavailability. Lainie stresses she enjoyed her time on this episode and wished she could have done more shows. "She was a most wonderful person to work with. She was incredible. I was such a fan." Apparently so was Imogene, who returned to Carol's show later in the season—see March 4, 1968.

Oct. 16, 1967: Phyllis Diller, Gwen Verdon, Bobbie Gentry, William Schallert

Q&A; William is Dr. Jekyll and Carol is his frustrated wife, attracted to a debonair playboy dentist (Harvey); Phyllis performs a comic monologue; Gwen sings and dances to "Feelin' Groovy" with Ernie Flatt's regulars; Carol and Chrissy try to learn Swedish for an exchange student coming to live with them in "Carol & Sis"; Bobbie sings "Bugs" and "The Look of Love"; a murder trial has Lyle as the defendant, Harvey as his lawyer, Carol as the prosecutor, William as the bailiff and Phyllis as the judge; Carol, Phyllis, Gwen and Bobbie portray the Beatles in a "Sgt. Pepper's" salute.

Comments: Stuffed with top talents in comedy (Phyllis), dancing (Gwen), singing (Bobbie) and acting (William), this show thankfully avoids suffering from overkill, with enough room for everyone to show off here. Carol takes queries without mentioning her guests in the Q&A, which suggests this part was taped after the rest of the show to make it like the preceding ones. After revealing that she wore a retainer at age 25, she brings out Vicki, who is so shy facing the audience that she holds Carol's hand. When a man asks, "How old are you?" she nervously shoots back with "I don't know!" Carol proves that Vicki is not her sister by showing her real-life sibling, Chris, in the audience.

In 1910 London, Carol tells her husband home from work that "Now you can relax in the bosom of the family—such that it is" while looking at her chest. Dr. Jekyll cannot resist old habits and has a drink that makes him cross his eyes, grab his throat and change into a werewolf that Carol treats as a dog. Harvey arrives to see her husband, but he notices her frustration and tries to woo her unsuccessfully. Carol realizes she has only one solution to her problem. She drinks a potion to transform herself into a cackling Phyllis, who eagerly goes after the werewolf. It is a great finish to what is only an average sketch otherwise.

Up next, Carol says that "I've known her for many years, we used to make the rounds together in New York. . . . My dear friend, Miss Phyllis Diller!" Sporting a coat with mink tails, Phyllis jests that her skin is named after an old TV show—*Rawhide*—and that Fang, her husband, has a sister so thin she fell through a bed of nails. Jokes about her looks predominate. "Most women have a vanity table. With me, it's a humility counter!" she quips, adding that Fang was arrested for leaving the scene of an accident when he was separated from her. The size of Fang's mother draws laughs too—Phyllis says she is so big she has her own zip code and that Navy planes identified her as Cuba in the water. This is a solid set by Phyllis.

Carol calls Gwen "the sweetest and the best dancer I think in the whole wide world," and indeed Gwen's moves are tight. Her part is oddly augmented by the male dancers dressed in troubadour outfits, while Gwen wears flowers and a pantsuit in a mod set with musical instruments shaped out of something from a Dr. Seuss book. Well, this was 1967.

In "Carol & Sis," Roger's objections to having a Swedish foreign exchange student vanish when of course she turns out to be a hot blonde (Barbara Hedstrum). Asked her age by Chrissy, the blonde says "39" and points to her chest to indicate its size in inches. "She won't live to see 40," cracks an irritated Carol, who is thrilled to learn they got a Swedish maid instead of a student by mistake. The real student arrives in the form of Randy Doney, to Harvey's dismay. This is pretty good by "Carol & Sis" standards this season.

After Bobbie contributes nicely with her songs (alas, no "Ode to Billie Joe"), Phyllis mugs it up as a judge enamored with murder suspect Rodney Harrison (Lyle—his character is the same name as Ryan O'Neal's on the TV series *Peyton Place*, whose storyline this is spoofing). He is represented by famed attorney Clarence Sparrow (Harvey), who generates laughs when Phyllis tells him, "Your opening remarks" and he glances to see if his zipper is open. What he says makes little impression on Phyllis, who falls off her chair when Lyle stares at her. She squeezes his bicep and a honking sound emerges. Her lust is so intense that when Carol attempts to get her attention by addressing her formally, Phyllis snarls back, "Stop talking about my honor!" Phyllis flexes her gams, shows her bejeweled shoes and sits on Lyle's lap as he claims that the killer was a one-armed man, a la *The Fugitive* TV series. Phyllis finally rules that Lyle must serve 30 days for his crime—in her chamber. This riotously funny bit is one of the season's best.

In the finale, all the women except Vicki wear dark wigs to resemble the Beatles performing "Sgt. Pepper's Lonely Hearts Club Band," with a mustachioed Bobbie doing a fine job as lead singer. As Billie Shears, Phyllis offers a surprisingly commendable take on "With a Little Help from My Friends," while Carol and Gwen achieve the same results with "When I'm 64" before all four reprise the first number, with the dancers moving around them at all times. After the quartet stroll out to the audience to finish the number, Carol races back on stage to sing "It's Time to Say So Long" before going back into the aisles to have Phyllis, Gwen and Bobbie sign her book and hugging William and the regulars. It is a rousing contemporary finish to a generally satisfying outing.

Oct. 23, 1967: The Smothers Brothers, Diahann Carroll, Richard Kiley

Q&A; Tom and Dick Smothers sing "John Henry" followed by Carol joining them on "Pretoria"; Kiley sings "The Impossible Dream"; Diahann performs "Rules of the Road" and "Where Am I Going?"; a deodorant commercial spoof; a sketch with Carol and the Smothers Brothers about the Maharishi (played by Tom); Richard and Diahann duet on a song from *No Strings*, followed by Carol accompanying them on "Happiness"; "Carol & Sis" has Carol worried about Roger's day based on his horoscope; Carol and Diahann are pigtailed trick-or-treaters facing a scary Halloween night, joined by the dancers.

Comments: With lots of music and only one sketch with Harvey and Vicki, this feels more like *The Smothers Brothers Comedy Hour* with Carol as a guest. The humor is more appropriate to that show, with the usual shtick of Tom interrupting Dick's introduction of "John Henry" and calling him "a big high school dropout," followed by Tom continually messing up the song. When Carol appears and Tom says, "She just can't come on our show and take over!" it seems more a statement of fact than a joke.

Nonetheless, there are some pleasures to be savored, even if you are not a Smothers Brothers fan. Carol and Tom doing a fast series of tongue twisters prior to their song is amusing, and Carol holds her own despite bobbling one phrase. In the Maharishi Yogi sketch, Dick meets the mystic on a mountaintop and learns that the spot on the Yogi's forehead is just his bubblegum. Tom is able to get off a good variant of his standard joke, saying "Mohammad always liked you best!" before Dick leaves. Carol appears as film star Pepper Grinder, a blonde bimbo, who visits the Yogi seeking redemption from the falseness of Hollywood. The best line here comes when Tom puts her into the lotus position, asks Carol what she feels and she responds, "Pain!" The sketch ends with Tom deciding to choose his lust for Carol over spiritualism and take her back to his lair.

"Carol & Sis" is little more than Carol doing everything to prevent Roger from going outside their home, as the newspaper's write-up for his astrological sign indicates he faces danger. Naturally, Roger gets hurt by her efforts. It ends with Chrissy hitting him with the kitchen door as he attempts to sneak out the back. Apart from doing his Porky Pig impersonation, this skit—and this program—is a waste of Harvey Korman's time.

Otherwise, this show is just music. Seeing Richard in his *Man of La Mancha* makeup and outfit to perform his Broadway hit's signature song is interesting. Diahann ("one of my favorite singers and one of my buddies," according to Carol) looks great in a glittering white gown during her solo. Richard and Diahann's duet from *No Strings* is marred by the use of stringed instruments, something their Broadway hit explicitly avoided, and that they cannot be intimate due to the TV standards of the time—the interracial duo vocalizes facing away from each other without touching. The choice to do "Happiness" from *You're a Good Man, Charlie Brown* along with Carol is a tenuous one, but all three carry it off, with Richard dapper in his tux and Diahann beautiful in a sheer black gown.

In the Q&A, Carol tells the audience she is sporting her own hair ("I wouldn't wear this one if it was a wig"), says she likes mod clothes and mentions tongue in cheek that she thought about having Ann-Margret as a guest but "We're too much alike." Her bit with Lyle has him saying his exercise program consists mainly of running, with Carol chirping in "With me chasing him!" He encourages Carol to do a few movements before she asks him, "Can you pick up 125 pounds?" "Sure," Lyle responds. "Good, pick me up after the show!" she shoots back. Like most of the show itself, this portion is not as satisfying as what had happened previously on the series. Luckily, better efforts would follow.

Oct. 30, 1967: Pre-empted by a special NFL football game

Nov. 6, 1967: Nanette Fabray, Sonny and Cher

Q&A; F. Lee Korman in "V.I.P." interviews a resident of the Sunnydale Nudist Camp (Carol); an office worker (Carol) is envious of her colleague (Nanette) sucks up to her boss (Harvey) and attempts to get even with her; Carol and Nanette sing "Bosom Buddies"; a coffee commercial spoof with Harvey and Carol; Cher sings "You Better Sit Down Kids," then duets with Sonny on "Living for You," followed by Harvey and Carol doing a song for them; an extended sketch with Nanette and the cast on the differences between foreign airlines (French, Japanese and Russian); a finale with tambourines.

Comments: This is the first professional work Carol does with Nanette and Sonny and Cher. Both associations are fruitful, with Nanette becoming a frequent guest through 1972 and Carol making a cameo on Sonny and Cher's series in 1972 as well as Cher's show later (for more on that, see Sept. 27, 1975). In fact, Cher is so impressed by Bob Mackie's outfits that he becomes her designer when *The Sonny and Cher Comedy Hour* launches in 1971 and retains his services as she continues to perform 40 years later.

Nanette is the only guest who does Q&A with Carol. She talks about her decision to shorten her dress before leaving Carol solo to answer a battery of questions—if she is a native Californian (sort of—she was born in Texas but raised in the Golden State), how long she rehearses and what are her measurements. Carol does the Tarzan yell and her cameraman shakes the shot to indicate its impact. Afterward, she points out her cousin Janet in the audience and notes she always played Jane to Carol's Tarzan when they were children. When asked "How do you enjoy being TV's new sex symbol?" her cameraman (Pat Kenny) precludes her answer with "Male or female?" This sparks another audience member to pipe up to Carol about the cameraman that "If he has such a smart mouth, why don't you fire him?" Carol and company laugh it off, and she gets in one last good line with "I love to cook, but nobody likes to eat it."

"V.I.P." has one of the series' first and most notoriously bizarre instances of censorship. As Carol recounted on the tenth anniversary show (April 2, 1977), Harvey was to ask Carol, "How do nudists dance?" and she was to say, "Very carefully." The censors thought that was too suggestive of sexual activity, so the producers asked for a replacement. The censors came back with "Cheek to cheek." That answer cracked up Carol and the staff, as apparently the censors did not realize "cheek" is slang for buttocks. It went in, along with a few other sly comments. "I have nothing to hide," Carol tells Harvey as she stands behind carefully positioned shrubbery. Regarding her boyfriend at the camp, she says, "We see a lot of each other," and she reveals the camp song is "On a Clear Day You Can See Forever." This is cute and effective.

In the so-so office sketch, Harvey overworks Carol while Nanette uses her feminine wiles to impress him. She wears a tiger dress, wiggles while she walks and rotates her butt when sharpening pencils (a routine that will appear as part of Carol's Mrs. Wiggins character in 1975). Carol's attempts to win over Harvey at the same time are futile, such as having her contact lens fall out as she bats her eyes. When Harvey invites Nanette into his office for some lovemaking, all appears lost for Carol until Harvey's wife (an unidentified actress) arrives and Carol directs her to what is happening. The wife hauls Nanette out on her ear while Harvey emerges disheveled. Ready to take the opportunity with her competition gone, Carol plans to join Harvey in his office, but her vanity in losing her contact lens leads her to walk through and fall out an open window instead.

After Carol and Nanette do a tune from *Mame* at a bus stop where they paint makeup on each other's faces, a good blackout follows where Harvey plays a husband who hates his wife's coffee. In the original commercial, she switches to another brand, but in this spoof, she poisons him for complaining.

Sonny and Cher finally appear in the second half hour, with Cher performing on a stylized home set what will soon be a top ten solo hit for her. Sonny joins her to do their duet, which barely scraped the Hot 100 in 1966. Carol and Harvey follow them in an attempt to appear hip (Harvey is wearing a turtleneck) and sing their own nondescript teenybopper tune, which prompts Sonny and Cher to leave in mock disgust.

The last sketch presents Nanette first as a French stewardess promising a nude revue on the flight and matchmaking couples on board, including pairing Lyle with herself. Harvey is a dancing and drinking pilot. Fade to black, and Nanette now is a Geisha flight attendant who wears a parachute with her kimono in case of a crash. "As for you, rotsa ruck!" she tells passengers. Her fellow flight attendant (Carol) makes moves on Lyle, then slurs and spits out the menu selections. She says they have fresh octopus and makes the point by having a tentacle wrapped around her. Carol and Nanette strip Lyle of his shirt to give him a Japanese bath on board before this ends. On Slavik Airlines, Carol has a strewn outfit as she tells first class passengers they can expect crashes and the plane has no bolts. Noting this is a champagne flight, she pops open a bottle of beer. Harvey's delivery of lines as a pilot is wild enough to crack up Don Crichton as a passenger. This politically incorrect segment nevertheless has a fair share of laughs.

The final number features Carol, Nanette, Sonny and Cher, Harvey and Lyle singing in Dapper Dan costumers with the dancers. There is no Vicki in this show.

TV Guide critic Cleveland Amory hated virtually every sketch here, as well as those on the following week. He did like Cher, and in 1972 he wrote how much more he enjoyed *The Sonny and Cher Comedy Hour* over *The Carol Burnett Show*. As it turned out, Carol's series surpassed Amory's tenure at *TV Guide*. He left the publication in 1976.

Nov. 13, 1967: Richard Chamberlain, Gloria Loring

Q&A; Harvey interviews Carol as the Mother of the Year with seven children; Carol does a number with Don Crichton and the other dancers to "Everybody Gotta Be Someplace"; a bit between Carol and Lyle where she takes a picture with him; Richard sings "Lazy Day"; a takeoff on *Gone With the Wind*; Gloria sings "A Taste of Honey" and "I've Gotta Be Me; Roger's sister Mimi (Kay Medford) visits the family to help out while Roger recovers from a broken foot in "Carol & Sis"; a finale with Carol learning how to do the boogaloo from Vicki.

Comments: When Carol went to Hollywood in 1962 to film an episode of *The Twilight Zone*, she met Richard Chamberlain at the MGM Studios, then starring on NBC's *Dr. Kildare* series. Her interest spurred the New York *World Telegram and Sun* to write the two were in love, to which Dorothy Kilgallen at the New York *Journal American* retorted that "Carol and Richard are about as much in love as Martha Raye and Rock Hudson," mocking another friendship between a comedienne and handsome gay actor. In any event, Richard displays his charm and good looks well here. Calling him a "good buddy" with whom she had never worked professionally, Carol brings out Richard during Q&A. A woman hates his longer hairstyle, which he says he had to do for a film role in England (not stated but presumably *Petulia*, released in 1968). When asked "Are you a playboy?" Richard slyly replies, "From time to time." Carol has Richard make moves on her to make Lyle jealous, but the latter just laughs it off. Nonetheless, Carol tells Richard to keep hugging and kissing her to make Harvey jealous before the introductory credits roll.

Additionally during the Q&A, Carol provides some good insights. She discusses being an usherette in the 1940s and says she likes miniskirts. For an inquiry as to whether Robert Goulet might appear, Carol relays that he was booked but dropped when he received an opportunity to star in a Broadway show (Carol did not say, but it was *The Happy Time*). Goulet will guest on April 7, 1969. Carol does confirm that Garry Moore and Durward Kirby will do her show, which will occur on the Feb. 26, 1968 installment.

A roughly equal split of good comedy sketches with somewhat awkward contemporary musical numbers begins with Harvey talking to Carol about how she raises septuplets, or as she calls it, "Getting Seven the Hard Way." The moderately enjoyable bit is followed by a dance number and a one-joke effort where Lyle learns that a camera's timer for a picture Carol is trying to take with him is set to go off in an hour and a half. This is unimpressive, as is Richard's take on a current hit for Spanky and Our Gang, although the visuals of him in a turtleneck sweater with co-ed dancers are easy to take.

The show's featured presentation is "Gone with the Breeze," which starts spoofing the intro (here it is a Metro Gold Mouth presentation with Carol doing her Tarzan yell in place of Leo the Lion) and informs us that the producers thank the Civil War, without which this picture could never have been made. Richard plays Rat Butler (without resembling Clark Gable—no mustache or other major physical adjustments), who upon his arrival at the plantation Ta-Ra-Ra-Ra-Ra is informed by old Uncle Ben (Harvey) that Scarlett is delusional and does not realize the war is over. Carol's Scarlett sounds more like Prissy in the original film as she thinks Rat has killed Ashley and mugs about her situation, singing "Swing Low Sweet Chariot" at one point. This rather aimless parody livens up as it proceeds thanks to the regulars, such as Harvey tripping and ad libbing, "I blew the table bit" and Carol having trouble lifting her hoop skirt and preventing it from popping up on the sofa. The sketch ends with Rat leaving and pillars tumbling down as the mansion collapses from him slamming the door. Despite its weaknesses, no less than *Variety* cites the sketch as "brief and bright" in a special article.

Gloria sings "A Taste of Honey" slowly in a spotlight before doing "I've Gotta Be Me" bathed in more illumination. Regarding these tunes, she says, "I performed them and they liked them." She knew the producers wanted one ballad and one up-tempo number from her previous show (see Oct. 2, 1967), so these songs made the cut. Gloria also keeps her long, straight blonde hairstyle. "I was coming out of the Peter, Paul and Mary era," she laughs. (The trio's Mary Travers was known for her shoulder-length tresses.)

Backstage, Gloria's role was as limited as it was on screen. "I wasn't around all the time they did the sketches," she says. "I stayed across the street at the Farmer's Daughter hotel. You took an elevator to the second floor at CBS Television City, and you went to a rehearsal hall." She says the rehearsals and show itself went fine for her.

Kay Medford appears in "Carol & Sis" as Harvey's smothering sister, treating him like a child during his recuperation to the point that she wants to call his pediatrician. During the skit, Carol amusingly mocks Harvey when he blows a line. It ends with Harvey being hit with the kitchen door. For her masterful work, Kay signs Carol's guest book and participates in the end kick line, following another strained "mod" dance routine.

With this episode, Loring has the distinction of becoming the first repeat guest on *The Carol Burnett Show*. She will appear twice more (see Feb. 19, 1968 and March 25, 1968). This was Richard Chamberlain's swan song on the series.

Nov. 20, 1967: Juliet Prowse, Martha Raye

Q&A; a production number with the cast, guests and dancers featuring Carol as Sleeping Beauty; Carol is a cruise ship passenger whose efforts to relax are interrupted by a rowdy suite mate (Martha); Juliet dances and banters some with Carol and Lyle; Carol is a psychic who can see into the future so vividly she answers Harvey's questions before he asks them; Martha sings; "V.I.P." interviews Lynda Bird Johnson (Carol) as she plans to get married; "A Dame is a Dame is a Dame" spotlights Carol, Martha and Juliet singing and dancing together; the Charwoman has a football fantasy.

Comments: This Vicki-free entry is notable for prompting the series' first *TV Guide* article. The short, shallow story frothed over the gams of Carol and her guests in their production number where they "give thanks for their shanks," as the writer put it. Otherwise, this spotty affair—actually the second show taped—has a production number of Carol awakening Martha, Juliet, Harvey and Lyle before she sings and moves with the dancers dressed as European courtiers. It follows a fascinating Q&A taped later.

Carol says she likes contemporary music but wants the male singers to have shorter hair, then lets loose a torrent of jokes. When asked how she got her start, she responds, "My mother met my father." An audience member guesses her age as twenty-six, and she points to her bust line and says, "Right up here!" She claims that one of the female dancers measured her and Martha's famed big mouths and found out that they are "Exactly the same. Juliet Prowse's mouth is bigger!" Finally, a twelve-year-old named Cindy Cohen is invited onstage by Carol after asking how to get on TV. Carol asks her what she can do, and when Cindy nervously says she cannot sing or dance, Carol tells her, "You'll make it!"

After the production number, Martha wears a mod outfit and makes passes at Harvey, the purser, as she disrupts the solitude Carol sought on a cruise. Martha throws out Carol's clothes to put hers in the closet while deadpanning that "I'm a topless waitress." Ready to swing, Martha noisily puts her bunk bed down while Carol tries to sleep, among other business. Fed up, Carol threatens to use karate on Martha before the latter changes cabins. This sketch starts strong but unfortunately peters out by the end.

After Carol does a labored bit where she tells Lyle she needs his measurements to knit a sweater for him, she introduces Juliet as "one of the nicest and sexiest girls I know." Dressed as a genie, Juliet sparkles with her singing and shaking moves while working with the male dancers clad in sailors outfits. When it ends, Juliet tells Carol she wants to meet Lyle, which our hostess reluctantly allows, and the two of them make out in the shadows unwittingly to Carol, who screams when she finally sees what is happening. The forced routine of treating Lyle as a sex object has already run its course, and this is so irritating that it almost makes one forget how good Juliet's solo number was.

A man studying ESP (Dick Wilson) tells Harvey, his colleague, that he has found a girl with an uncanny knack of seeing into the future. Carol starts reacting before anyone says or does anything, such as telling Dick to answer the phone before it rings and even telling him it is a woman. It culminates with Carol telling Harvey they will be married. This is a good comic premise that produces iffy results despite the cast's best efforts.

Carol recounts how Martha's absence on *The Garry Moore Show* in 1959 opened the door for her to become a regular there and calls her guest "a truly great lady" before Martha sings and then banters briefly with Carol, both rather inconsequential except for when Martha gets laughs for claiming she once replaced Ernest Borgnine. Better humor occurs in "V.I.P." as Carol speaks in a Texas twang licking envelopes and wearing a ten-gallon hat under her veil as Harvey interviews her. This has some surprisingly pointed barbs for this series. For example, the First Daughter says she will be going to Europe on her honeymoon as part of the Beautify America campaign and jokes that her father had Gov. George Romney brainwashed into being a Democrat.

In "A Dame is a Dame is a Dame," Carol, Martha and Juliet all have great harmonies and solo singing bits, with Carol doing a nice mini-monologue about legs during the number. All look and sound fine, as does Carol on the closing number, which is filmed on location at night in a football field as the Charwoman imagines hearing nonexistent fans cheer her on as she cleans up the gridiron. She takes the opportunity to pretend to kick her bucket, return it downfield, acts as a quarterback and throws to herself before she sings a number.

Harvey and Lyle sign Carol's book along with Martha and Juliet at the end. That's how early in production this show was. Martha will return on Feb. 12, 1968 and Juliet on Nov. 9, 1970.

Nov. 27, 1967: Don Adams, Lesley Ann Warren

Q&A; Harvey and Carol play a married couple, with Carol meeting a Venusian (Lyle) after watching science fiction movies while Lyle sleeps; Lesley performs with three male dancers; Don, Harvey and Carol spoof *The Joey Bishop Show*; Harvey and Don commiserate on a bench while waiting to pick up their kids; Carol and Harvey mock a commercial; Carol sings "Enter Laughing"; "The Lost Purse" finds Carol plotting how to tell her husband (Don) that she has lost her pocketbook containing papers he needs for his taxes; Carol and Lesley Ann duet on "All God's Children" with the dancers.

Summary: As Arnie Rosen wrote and produced *Get Smart!*, it is unsurprising that Don Adams, the star of that series on NBC at this time, joins Carol this week. So does Lesley Ann Warren, who when this first appears is in the movie *The Happiest Millionaire,* which Carol plugs during the Q&A. After joking that they put gauze on Camera Four to handle her close-ups and promoting her new album, *Carol Burnett Sings*, with "If you buy it, you'll be the first one," the hostess brings out Don. He reveals he has a 2-year-old daughter who loves fashion shows and has gained confidence from doing his TV series. He denies that he is tired of people saying the show's many catch phrases to him, then riffs on his golf experience before the segment ends.

The show launches decently with Lyle in his first real acting role on the show, appearing outside Carol's apartment window as an alien who kisses her and then informs her that he is invisible and inaudible to men. Intrigued by this specimen, she decides to cheat on Harvey and obeys Lyle's command that she fly away with him. She ends up falling to the ground, followed by Harvey thanking Lyle for pretending to be a Venusian and conning his wife. If not really clever, the regulars at least maximize the fun out of this sketch.

Lesley's song features quick cuts and a set using low ceiling fans, which generates mild enjoyment. Better is the rowdy talk show takeoff with Harvey as Regis McMahon (combining the first name of Joey Bishop's then-co-host on his ABC late night show with the last of Johnny Carson's sidekick, Ed McMahon, on *The Tonight Show*) and Don as Donny Bishop. Supposedly taping during a technical crew strike (which actually had occurred and affected TV production in the spring of 1967), the duo endure feedback from microphones, bad shots, missing props and the revelation that Don has no pants on. Carol arrives as a blonde bimbo in a miniskirt who is hit on the head with a lowered boom mike and has the curtain drop on her when she sings. This is amusing comic chaos.

The kicker in the Harvey-Don sketch is that after all their grousing about waiting for their children, Don reveals he is a marriage counselor. That is satisfactory, but bigger laughs come when an avalanche of fake snow drowns Carol and Harvey when she consumes a soft drink. The original commercial promoted how cool and refreshing the beverage tastes—Carol and company just did what they do best and took it to the logical extreme.

Unfortunately, the momentum flags thereafter, first with Carol sitting on the lip of the stage to sing the title song of Carl Reiner's autobiographical movie and then doing an overlong, tiresome sketch with Don. After telling her friend (an unidentified actress—Vicki does not appear in this show) that she fears her husband's reaction to losing crucial information contained her purse, she eventually confesses her oversight to Don. Perturbed, he forces her to re-enact her activities during the day to recall where she might have left it, and she does so in excruciating detail. Don yells much of his part to try to energize the effort as he plays people Carol encountered along the way. In what seems like an eternity, Carol retrieves her purse from a visiting grocery store employee (an unidentified actor), then gets the upper hand as Don announces he will reward the man before discovering he has lost his wallet. At least the activity mercifully ends the sketch.

The show winds up with Carol and Lesley Ann singing and dancing in flapper outfits. It is adequate but nothing special. This episode airing after Thanksgiving reflects that time period by offering plenty of unexceptional leftovers and not much else to recommend.

Dec. 4, 1967: Jonathan Winters, Barbara Eden

Q&A; F. Lee Korman interviews Santa (Jonathan) in "V.I.P."; Carol has to hide guests when Rogers comes home earlier than expected for his surprise party in "Carol & Sis"; Barbara performs with the dancers; Carol is a wife coping with having a husband who is invisible (voice of Harvey); Barbara and Carol sing about magic and display a few feats of illusion at the same time; Jonathan, Harvey, Carol and Lyle participate in a multipart documentary on "The Wonderful World of Prisons"; and the Charwoman cleans up a playground and rides the equipment before singing "I Believed It All."

Comments: Jonathan Winters' brand of lunacy dominates this installment, although there is room to shine for Barbara Eden. Coincidentally or not, she will be Jonathan's guest star when his series launches a few weeks later (see Dec. 25, 1967 for more info on that). Carol describes Barbara as "lovely and cute" and Jonathan as "the nuttiest man I know" before taking questions. She says she and Lucille Ball have talked about doing a movie together ("Beauty and the beast!" interjects cameraman Pat Kenny). When a little girl wonders why Carol lists different numbers for her measurements on every show, the hostess cleverly responds that it varies depending on what she has had to eat. She brings out Jonathan and Barbara for brief chit-chat, with Carol doing a bit with Barbara when she discovers her guest has the same supernatural powers as she does on the concurrently airing *I Dream of Jeannie* on NBC. Carol asks for three wishes involving Lyle, and first she gets a compliment from him, then a hug from him, and then . . . he hugs Barbara.

"V.I.P." gets things rolling with Jonathan as a lively St. Nick, making puns (he unveils a life-sized wife doll he calls Pat Pending), cracking wise (he says booze is what makes him go "ho ho ho") and even doing satire (he shows dolls based on several politicians, including one of George Romney, "Brain is completely washable," in reference to the GOP presidential candidate whose aspirations dissolved when he claimed he was brainwashed into supporting the Vietnam War). "Carol & Sis" after it is enjoyable if a little predictable, as Carol engages in extensive physical comedy to sequester her guests while putting Roger in a hammerlock at one point to prevent him discovering others in the house. Roger winds up being hit by the kitchen door as the guests finally can emerge.

Barbara sings a forgettable tune, then comes a sketch with several otherworldly touches. As "Mrs. Invisible Man," Carol earns compliments from her aunt (Barbara Morrison) for the way she treats her husband without being able to see him. Carol's physical skills are on fine display as she pretends to dance and be kissed and felt up by Harvey (speaking offstage). More complications ensue as she reveals they have an invisible baby. Finally, Harvey takes a potion to correct his condition, and he emerges from the back as Leonard Nimoy in his Spock costume from *Star Trek*. Carol thanks Nimoy for the surprise cameo at the show's end, but neither he nor Morrison appear in the guest kick line.

The theme continues with the next musical number, as Carol and Barbara sing about prestidigitation while trying to do tricks simultaneously. Naturally, a couple fail to come off, but nonetheless they provide a cute variation on the standard musical presentation on this show. At the very least, it provides a solid warm-up to the big remaining skit.

"The Wonderful World of Prisons" begins with reporter Walter Crankcase (Harvey) interviewing a bellowing Southern warden (Jonathan), an ex-inmate. "These boys love me like a father," he insists to Harvey. "In fact, I'm a father of one of them!" The laughs keep flowing as Carol hits on prisoner Lyle to allow Jonathan to dress up as his old woman character of Maudie Frickert. Spunky as ever, Maudie says one tooth is from her dog. Jonathan's ad libs such as "Be nice to me, or I'll cold cock you!" constantly crack up Harvey as well as viewers throughout the segment, which succeeds masterfully.

The wrap-up with the Charwoman features yet another unmemorable song, but the strong comedy previously presented compensates for that and makes this an overall top entry for the season. This was Eden's only appearance on the show.

Dec. 11, 1967: Mickey Rooney, John Davidson

Q&A; Carol, Harvey, Lyle and Mickey star in "Heil Chaparral," a German western; John sings "There's a Kind of Hush" as well as "Somewhere" from *West Side Story*; a spoof of *The Dating Game* with Harvey as the host, Carol as a wallflower contestant and Mickey, John and Lyle as her three pathetic potential suitors; "The Fun Family of Broadway" presents a 53-year musical comedy odyssey of the travails encountered by a vaudeville clan with Mickey as the father, Carol the mother, John and Vicki their children, Harvey as theatrical producer Ziggy Flofeld and Lyle as a Walter Winchell-like reporter.

Comments: "I think we have one of my favorite shows we've done," Carol announces up front, and a good chunk of that is due to the spirited performance of Mickey Rooney, whose name draws cries of "Wow!" from the studio audience. That contrasts with the lower profile of her other guest—in fact, when Carol brings John Davidson out for the Q&A, one boy wanted to know what show he was on. Carol mentioned his guest shots on *The Kraft Music Hall* and appearance in *The Happiest Millionaire*, which did not help. Even stranger, one woman propositions him for a date, and someone else asks if John knew Roy Rogers. There must have been something in the water for the audience in this show, as one youngster wonders, "How does a boy get to be an actress?" and generates waves of laughter for his mistake. Carol quips back, "That's not too hard nowadays!"

After Harvey references how more movie westerns are being shot overseas, we see a saloon showgirl (Carol) singing "See What the Boys in the Back Room Will Have" until Mickey arrives as the marshal. He snarls at Lyle, a bad guy, and makes an in-joke about his personal life by saying, "You don't scare me! Three of my wives are bigger than you!" Mickey throws Lyle out, only to have Carol announce that Wilhelm the Kid (Harvey dressed in black with a monocle) has pledged to kill him. "I'm going to cut you in half!" Harvey tells Mickey. "Someone beat you to it," snaps Carol in reference to Mickey's height. Mickey and Harvey duel and end up shooting Carol, who keeps singing until she dies. The spoof is a bit ragged but a winner nonetheless.

John comes out in an orange turtleneck and pale green suit for two numbers. The first he does amid a twinkling background, and the second is done downstage with bongos played loudly and more rapidly than his vocals, which are fine but bland.

He appears again next in "The Rat Race," with Harvey as Larry Rat, who presents three eligible bachelors for Carol to choose. John is Tab Tyler, an aspiring actor from Paris, Texas, and 37-time loser on the show, Lyle is the dumb star of the TV series "Run from Your Wife," and Mickey is a playboy. Mickey's suave responses impress Carol, a frigid type with big glasses and disheveled hair, more than John's hick attitude and Lyle's denseness. In fact, Carol clamors to climb over the wall to meet Mickey immediately. When the game ends, she is amazed by how handsome John and Lyle are and says she wants them instead. But she is stuck with Mickey, and she throws her wig off because he is the same bad date she had previously. This bit is raucously amusing.

The second half of the show is "The Fun Family of Broadway," which provides Vicki with her meatiest role to date and one that she carries off with aplomb along with the rest of the cast. In 1917 Carol, Mickey, John and Vicki's struggling song-and-dance family tries to write a hit patriotic song. Harvey's Ziggy Flofeld hears them singing it and is intrigued, but his Broadway revue has room for only a trio, so Mickey nobly lets the rest go on without him. "I'll be back when I'm a success," he vows. "I guess we'll never see him again," Vicki ripostes, to laughter. Lyle's radio reporter informs us that the trio is a hit in vaudeville, and we see the dancers perform as well as a duet by John and Vicki.

It's now 1927, and Mickey has disguised himself as an old stagehand over the years to stay near his family. Harvey discusses plans for his next show when John says he is quitting to run for president, causing Carol to belt him and exclaim, "Where did I go wrong?!" Vicki announces she has something to say, and as Harvey looks nervous, implying that she slept with him, she adds, "Not that, Ziggy!" She wants to pursue a career in medicine, and she and John leave. Ziggy professes his love for Carol but she demurs, saying she still pines for Mickey, and settles for a solo spot in the show. That leads us to 1970 (three years ahead of when this show was taped), where an aging Lyle says this will be Carol's farewell performance. In a cane, blue gown and white frills surrounded by mod dancers, Carol tells the audience that she attributes her success to one man. Harvey thinks she means him, then moves on when learning he is wrong. Joined by her son, who is the president, and her daughter, who has discovered a cure for hickeys, they are stunned when Mickey emerges from backstage to reveal who he is. Expecting a warm embrace, Mickey instead has Carol upset with him deceiving her for so long. Among the series' innumerable show business movie parodies, this is one of its best.

At the end, Carol sings "It's Time to Say So Long" in her old lady voice first. The show's good vibes are reflected by John falling when they all lean in one direction and knocking everyone down like a series of dominoes. It is a fun and funny moment in a show loaded with more of them than most of the previous entries.

Dec. 18, 1967: Pre-empted by special *Flanders and Swann*

Dec. 25, 1967: Sid Caesar, Ella Fitzgerald

Q&A; Professor Ludvig von Stranglehold (Sid) provides self-defense instruction to Carol; Ella sings "A Foggy Day" and "Always True to You in My Fashion"; Carol and three costumed characters from the movie *The Jungle Book* perform "The Bare Necessities"; Sid and Carol play a couple bickering on Christmas Eve; Carol and Ella sing a medley; Sid, Harvey, Lyle and Carol appear in a spoof of ancient Roman spectacles titled "Fiddler on the Forum"; the Charwoman decorates her own Christmas tree with discarded ornaments in an abandoned lot.

Comments: The first image on this show is Jonathan Winters, telling the audience that "I just didn't have anything to do, just running out there in the parking lot" as he takes over the Q&A. Asked, "What's your age?" he responds, "Physically, forty-two. Mentally, six." Carol interrupts Jonathan to tell him, "You're on Wednesday, John." (*The Jonathan Winters Show* debuts on CBS Dec. 27, 1967.) After he leaves, Carol's repartee included answering "What were your first words when you made *Los Angeles Times'* Women of the Year?" with "That I was going to subscribe!"

This episode places a lot on Sid Caesar to deliver comedy, sometimes lacking enough strong material to support him. As the professor, his uneven routine with Carol tellingly has one of its biggest laughs when she bobbles a line about not feeling pain when drunk. Their interplay pays off when Sid tells Carol to hit him as hard as she can to show how he can resist her power, and his facial expressions in repressing his hurt is priceless. It ends strong when Sid has Carol pretend to strangle him to show how to avoid an attacker, and he faints. As a terrified Carol releases him, Sid pipes up with "See how I got out?"

Next, Ella sings two songs, the first with a chandelier in the background with flowers and the second upstage. This was followed by Carol in pigtails and a girl's dress doing an Oscar nominee for Best Song that featured three dancers, one each in a bear, orangutan and elephant costume. The outfits came courtesy of Disneyland to promote Disney's cartoon movie *The Jungle Book*. The studio will make a similar publicity move on the show a few years later (see Dec. 29, 1971).

In a living room with a tree and presents, Carol tells her husband (Sid) how she dislikes how his mother dresses up like Santa and treats him like a child on Christmas. This escalates until they even disagree about how much they argue during the Yuletide season. "My Christmas from now on will be the Fourth of July!" says a disgusted Sid as Carol fights with him over everything including when to take the tree down—she says it will stay up until April. The two naturally reconcile by the end of the sputtering sketch.

After that, Carol and Ella (in pretty purple/pink and aqua gowns) perform "What Good is a Gal Without a Guy," "Happiness is a Thing Called Joe," "Won't You Come Home, Bill Bailey," Ella's old hit "Mack the Knife" (with Carol exclaiming, "Henry's dead?!" at one point), and more. The great ending has Ella belting out "Deck the halls with lots of fellas!" Incidentally, that is the only lyric indicating the time of the season.

A ragged but generally good sketch follows, with Carol doing a Tarzan yell in place of the MGM lion for the opening of "Fiddler on the Forum" ("This picture is recommended for Victor Mature audiences only," Lyle announces). Harvey plays Emperor Lascivious opposite Carol's Princess Passionata, who has the hots for a traitor who amusingly introduces himself with "My name is Caesar." ("All right then, call me Sidney," he says as the laughter subsides.) After some other wordplay (e.g., "And where are you from?" "Serf City"), the sketch ends with Sid accidentally killing Harvey and Carol—and the boom mike inadvertently appearing on camera as well.

The show ends with a sentimental pantomime by the Charwoman that could have easily been done by Red Skelton on his show's "Silent Spot" instead. As the closing credits run, Vicki appears at the end, even though she had nothing to do during the episode. Overall this show alternately embraces and avoids its Christmas airing date, making it a rather disjointed affair throughout. The highs outnumbered the lows in the end, however.

Jan. 1, 1968: Lynn Redgrave, Mike Douglas

Q&A; an Aztec production number; Mike sings "On a Clear Day You Can See Forever" and "Born Free"; Harvey and Carol, back from a whirlwind international tour, are interviewed at an airport by Mike; Carol and Lyle banter before she introduces Lynn, who does a routine with the dancers; "Carol & Sis" features a stray dog found by Carol who babies it back to health and wants to keep it despite Roger's allergies to animals; Mike and Carol duet; Lynn, Harvey and Carol star in "A Dirty English Movie"; Carol and Lynn sing about springtime joined by the dancers.

Comments: Originally planned to be the opener, this was held back. That was wise, as much of this is flat and unfunny, with a large number of quiet moments from the audience. That does not apply to the added Q&A however, where Carol says "Happy new year" and reveals her resolution for 1968 is not to paw Lyle too much. She says they would love to have Herb Alpert (he never does the series), reveals Lyle is married and recounts how she did a Q&A when she recently attended her class reunion at Hollywood High. Regarding an embarrassing incident, Carol relates how a moth flew into her mouth when she did *Calamity Jane* at an outdoor theatre in Kansas City. She laughs when someone asks, "Why aren't you wearing a miniskirt?" as well as how long it takes her to put her makeup on. Then it is mostly downhill from there.

The planned introductory number announces the arrival of Mike, Harvey, Vicki, "special guest star" Lynn and Lyle dressed up before the dancers launch into an Aztec number offering people as sacrifices. The supposed humor is that Harvey appears to volunteer to be killed once he sees Carol. This is not a good start.

Carol calls Mike "my talented and good friend" and says she is glad to return the favor of having him here after she has appeared several times on his talk show. He does well with his two numbers. However, Mike's charm cannot save the next skit, where he plays himself talking to two travelers fresh off a plane after having seen 23 countries in five days. Chomping on a cigar, Harvey is upbeat while Carol is exhausted and weighed down by cameras wrapped around her neck. Harvey brags about their trips while Carol grudgingly tolerates him, which ticks him off. He even threatens her with a catch phrase from *The Honeymooners*, saying "One of these days, right to the moon!" She decks Harvey and takes a picture of him on the floor as this forced entry mercifully ends.

The requisite suggestive banter between Carol and Lyle occurs next, with Carol sliding her face into his chest as he gives her a golf lesson, before he leaves and Carol introduces Lynn, who receives praise in Carol for her Oscar-nominated title role in *Georgy Girl*. Lynn sings and dances a "mod" number with Ernie Flatt's crew that is unremarkable.

The energy continues to flag in "Carol & Sis," where Carol attempts to hide an adorable puppy she finds from Roger as the veterinarian (Jim Milhollin) arrives to check on it. Carol implores the vet to pretend she is his patient, so naturally he treats her like a dog to Roger's confusion. When Roger leaves the living room, the vet tells Carol the pooch is fine but needs care, so when Roger learns the truth, Carol begs him to let the pup stay, but as it turns out, the dog is allergic to Roger. It plays as poorly as it reads.

The show slogs along with two forgettable songs by Mike and Carol about marriage and honeymoons before the last skit. Subtitled "A Man and a Woman and Another Man and Another Woman and Another Man and a Lot of Fooling Around," this parody is nowhere nearly as provocative or enjoyable as that phrase. Lynn lives in an underground flat with Harvey, and the pipes overhead are so low that Harvey keeps hitting his head on them—that is the tiresome recurring joke. Carol is an upper-class woman who comes to visit (hitting her head several times, of course) and incorrectly thinks Lynn is Harvey's mother rather than his wife after some inconsequential dialogue and physical comedy. Both women end up hitting Harvey at the end of what is a waste of everyone's time.

The none-too-soon finale is acceptable, with Lynn and Carol joining the dancers for a number designed to sound like it was coming from a lute. The ending has Carol thanking her regulars and guests (including Jim Milhollin), but there is no book to sign, and Carol does not sing "It's Time to Say So Long." Instead, the credits roll with the cartoon Charwoman character in various poses near each of them. Regular viewers must have wondered if this was a new approach the show was taking without explanation.

When this episode aired, *TV Guide* did a cover story on the series and noted how the British movie sketch bombed. "We learned an awful lot," Carol said about the taping of this series. The same article informed readers that the series' renewal was "apparently assured" based on ratings. That was good news for the crew and staff, who had to take a breath because this show marked the season's midpoint—fifteen shows down, fifteen left to go. That might not have been the case if this misfire had kicked the series off.

Jan. 8, 1968: Lana Turner, Frank Gorshin

Q&A; F. Lee Korman interviews chef Julia Wild (Carol) in "V.I.P."; Frank sings "I Love You How Many Different Ways to Say" and impersonates nine stars; Lana performs a dramatic monologue with "Greensleeves" that segues into a dance number; in "Carol & Sis" Carol and Roger audition at their house as lovebird contestants for the Happily Married game show; "The Sound of Murder" has Frank as Bluebeard, Carol as his new wife and Lana as Frank's conspirator to try to kill Carol; Carol and Frank sing "By the Beautiful Sea" in scuba wear accompanied by the dancers in similar outfits.

Comments: Lana Turner is the first classic movie star parodied on Carol's shows who guest stars as well. It is a coup, as her TV appearances were rare up to 1968. She does not appear in the Q&A, but Lyle wants to meet her, and Carol shoos him away by saying Lana only likes goofy looking men. Looks are a big topic in this week's questions. A woman brings Carol a red girdle from Duncanville, Texas, and another person inquires about how Carol fits into her costumes. "There's a lot of pudding," she deadpans. After she goes into the audience to autograph a gentleman's book, another fellow asks "Are those your own teeth?" (They are.) The segment ends with Lyle coming out wearing "beagle puss" glasses to meet Lana, because she likes homely guys. Ho ho.

Moving on, Carol samples lots of wine while being interviewed in "V.I.P.," but unfortunately this poky sketch's drunk humor is nowhere near as funny as, say, the Vitameatavegamin routine Lucille Ball did on *I Love Lucy*. Carol does squeeze some laughs fiddling with a rubber chicken before "passing out" at the end of the bit.

The guest stars have back-to-back solo turns. After Carol notes Frank's fame for playing the Riddler on *Batman* (which would end on ABC in 1968), the gray tuxedoed impressionist displays his versatility by following a tune sung at a small table with an array of impressive mimicry. With a different woman dancer standing opposite him for some interaction, Frank portrays Howard Duff, Joseph Cotten, Anthony Newley, James Cagney, Bela Lugosi, Richard Burton (as Anthony to a Cleopatra), Clark Gable (as Rhett Butler to a Scarlett O'Hara), Cary Grant and Anthony Quinn as Zorba. He omits arguably his best impersonation, of Kirk Douglas. In fact, the show blows a great chance to satirize 1952's *The Bad and the Beautiful* with Gorshin doing Douglas opposite Turner, who appeared in the original. This show has a lot of such missed opportunities.

Lana lip syncs part of her monologue before she dances with Don Crichton, the other male dancers and finally the whole troupe. Carol appears at the end to applaud the star with Lyle, still wearing the false nose. Lana removes it and leaves with him, but Carol is fine, saying "What the heck is she going to do with an unemployed announcer?"

At the outset of "Carol & Sis," the Bradfords argue about Roger hitting a parked car when Harvey blows one of his lines. Vicki shows she has been studying up her acting skills and wisely waits for the laughs to die down and Harvey to recover before responding. She leaves while a game show producer (Dick Wilson) interrupts Carol and Roger's quarrel to see if they are as content and compatible as they said on their submission. The couple strain to be pleasant until Wilson leaves, when they go back to attacking each other, even making fun of their chests. In a none-too-surprising finale, Wilson returns to get his briefcase he "unintentionally" left behind and reveals it has a tape recorder. This so-so effort was the first sketch for the show written by Roger Beatty.

"The Sound of Murder" is an overlong melodrama spoof set in London in 1900 with Harvey as a butler amid Frank and Lana's machinations to knock off Carol. Three efforts fail, although Harvey gets injured in the process. Lana has a few good lines through the drawn-out scenarios, telling Frank that "You are the finest rotten person I know!" and saying after their second attempt bombs, "Number two—we've got to try harder!" to paraphrase a rental car company's ad campaign at the time. Frank is amusing during his death throes, falling on scenery several times before coming to a halt on the ground. But all this, along with the revelation that Lana and Carol are ending up dead too, cannot overcome an overextended premise. The musical finale afterward is similarly uninspired—seeing dancers make ballet moves with fins on their feet is just weird.

Overall, the writers clearly failed to match the talents of the guests for this show. That could explain why neither Turner nor Gorshin appeared on this series again.

Jan. 15, 1968: Trini Lopez, Ken Berry

Q&A; "V.I.P." has Harvey interviewing Carol as the harried wife of the Jolly Green Giant; Trini has backup musicians and the dancers accompany him as he performs "Sally Was a Good Old Girl," "Sunny" and "Land of 1,000 Dances"; a parody of *The Jackie Gleason Show* as a newscast features Harvey as the titular star, Carol as a gossip columnist and weather girl, and Lyle and Ken as song-and-dance reporters; Ken sings and tap dances to "Mack the Knife"; a send-up of *Show Boat* features Trini as the captain, Carol and Ken as lovebirds, and Harvey as a villain.

Summary: After two consecutive disappointing entries, the series rallies with some excellent moments featuring "two of the most absolutely nicest people in show biz," as Carol describes her guests in the Q&A. She thanks the Canadian Broadcasting Company for adding her show before answering rather mundane, familiar queries about how long she has been in show business and her favorite performer. More of interest is Jim Nabors and Minnie Pearl appearing in her audience, with Carol telling the latter, "I've been wanting to meet you!" (Minnie will guest star on April 15, 1968.) Ken comes out to say he will be starring in *Mayberry, R.F.D.* in the fall on CBS and show how to tumble and fall on stage without getting hurt, then it is off to the main festivities.

"We met on *The Dating Game*. I had my choice between him and King Kong," Carol tells Harvey in "V.I.P." about how she became Mrs. Jolly Green Giant. She resignedly talks about the hassles of their relationship, like how her husband drank Niagara Falls during their honeymoon and it took her three days to give birth to their son. The interview ends with the giant sneezing so strongly that Carol is pushed onto a couch that collapses through a wall in her house—a good visual joke ending to a spotty bit overall.

The show unexpectedly revs up as Trini performs three peppy numbers (well, as peppy as you can make "Sunny"). The energetic feeling continues as Lyle introduces "The Swinging Six O'clock News," an elaborate spoof of *The Jackie Gleason Show* down to mocking the overhead shots of that series' June Taylor Dancers before Harvey appears in a fat business suit as anchor Jackie Cronkite. "There's good booze tonight!" Harvey intones before introducing Carol as Rona Rumor (a dead-on nasal impersonation of gossip columnist Rona Barrett) and Lyle and Ken doing "Tea for News" with jokes about current events inserted between their dance routine, including another George Romney brainwashing crack. Carol reappears as Sunny Storm, a blonde stripper doing the weather who suggestively removes her gloves as she announces temperatures are rising. Carol stumbles a little bit singing new lyrics for "Let Me Entertain You," but she survives and joins everyone at the end as Harvey runs past them in this spirited skit.

Tap dancing on a street corner set with female dancers, Ken provides an acceptable "Mack the Knife" before "Showdown at the Showboat," a two-parter where Trini inserts some Spanish before introducing Carol as the Mouth of the Mississippi. Trini says there is a line he says in this skit— "OK, who gets the enchiladas?"—that Carol finds so amusing that whenever she now sees him in a social setting such as a restaurant, she repeats that exact question back to him. Here, Carol cracks up Trini by imitating his dialect before striking a romance with Ken, who is willing to help Carol and Trini pay off Harvey, a bad guy intent on closing down the boat. Harvey ties Carol to the paddle wheel and activates it to torture her before Ken arrives, beats up Harvey and promises to marry Carol. The jaw-dropping set (the paddle wheel actually works) plus some strong jokes makes this a pleasant diversion.

The end confirms the show's only glaring drawback—no Vicki. Luckily she will return the following week. Ken and Trini will reappear next season.

Jan. 22, 1968: Shirley Jones, George Chakiris

Q&A; "V.I.P." has Carol interviewing Charles De Gaulle (Harvey); Shirley sings "When Did I Fall in Love?"; Harvey and Carol are a married couple intent on showing each other that their luxurious trappings mean nothing to them; a commercial spoof with Carol as a housewife; an international star (Harvey) tries to rest in a hospital while a nurse (Carol) fawns over him; George dances to "Never on Sunday"; an attractive secretary (Shirley) assisting Roger irks Carol in "Carol & Sis"; the Charwoman fantasies about a rich woman's wardrobe she is cleaning and sings "If My Friends Could See Me Now."

Comments: "We have two Academy Award winners with us this evening!" Carol exclaims at the start, referring to the Oscars won by Shirley for *Elmer Gantry* (1960) and George for *West Side Story* (1961). With that talent, it is puzzling that the show limits them to a song and two skits for Shirley and a dance number for George. Leaving that aside, this is an above-average installment for this season, although the Q&A is rather blah. Carol gives a boy an autograph, receives a flower made by a girl, says she never has a tight throat and relates the embarrassing summer stock story she told on the Oct. 9, 1967 show. George comes out for queries and gives bland answers. He forgot what it was like winning the Oscar apart from receiving it from Shirley, says that he has been making movies in Europe and declines to give his age. Carol introduces Capt. Barney Barnum and Jack Cassidy (Shirley's husband) in the audience before the Q&A concludes.

For "V.I.P.," Carol appears Ms. F. Lee Korman, saying that her husband who normally hosts the show has taken ill after seeing its ratings (interestingly, the series that inspired this segment, *Good Company*, had ended its run by this airing). Wearing a putty noise with a good French dialect, Harvey's imperious De Gaulle implies that he thinks he is God, can walk on water and will live forever in his discussion with Carol. The best and strongest exchange here comes when Carol says, "There are people all over the world who compare you to Adolf Hitler," and Harvey immediately responds, "Thank you!"

Carol mentions the advantage of having a series is having the opportunity to pay back favors but neglects to say what those are regarding her singing guest star. Nonetheless, Shirley is impressive in her number, even starting it out a capella. That leads to Carol playing a wife upset that Harvey is in a hurry talking into his dictating machine while ignoring her. He says he has to work hard in order to afford all the pricey items she wants. Carol denies she is materialistic and proves it by throwing out everything from the apartment, which Harvey does in kind. Carol tosses their maid (a stuffed doll) and her wig out the window, and Harvey matches her by doing the same with his mustache and stripping to his underwear. A cop (an unidentified actor) arrests them both for dropping materials onto the street, but Carol is happy that she finally has won back Harvey's attention. Both Carol and Harvey acquit themselves well with the slapstick here.

An uproarious advertising parody follows, as Carol is bedeviled by indigestion and other problems as her perky friend offers products while pushing their irritating slogans. Hysterical laughter occurs when Carol announces, "My living bra died! It starved to death!" More chuckles occur next when Harvey is ordered by his doctor (Brad Trumbull) to be hospitalized for two weeks. He encounters Carol, a nurse and an obsessed fan. She mistreats Harvey's roommate and paws him so much that he attempts to leave and accidentally dangles outside his window. His calls for help prompt his roommate to pull the bandages off his faces, and it is Lyle. Carol sees this and goes for him, causing Harvey to drop. Once again, the regulars smoothly deliver this broad comedy.

George's dance number is spectacular. Joining the male dancers in a kick line, he then sings "Never on Sunday" with its lyrics in Greek before making more incredible spinning and leaping moves. He certainly maximizes his only moment in the show.

Carol and Chrissy halt going to a movie when Shirley appears at the house in a miniskirt and long blonde wig as Roger's secretary. Her looks cause Carol to put a blanket over Shirley's legs when sitting, among other actions. Sensing Carol's discomfort, Shirley leaves—but not before giving Roger a big, long hug, making one think Carol's instincts about Shirley's intentions were right. Finally, the Charwoman puts up clothes in the closet of a rich lady out on the town and fantasizes about looking gussied up in a mirror. Carol's pantomiming and singing of a tune from the musical *Sweet Charity* are on the mark.

This episode ends with two firsts, a pitch to donate blood and a mention of next week's guests. While George never returns to the series, Shirley does—see Feb. 17, 1969.

Jan. 29, 1968: Jonathan Winters, Dionne Warwick

Q&A; Jonathan and Carol are a couple who speak like the commercials they watch on TV; Dionne presents "(Theme from) Valley of the Dolls" and "Children Go Where I Send Thee" with the dancers and duets with Carol on "T'Morra, T'Morra"; Roger tries to help preserve Carol's fancy new hairdo in "Carol & Sis"; a commercial blackout; Carol sings "Come Rain or Come Shine" with a twist; Lyle, Harvey, Carol and Jonathan contribute to a comic look at "The Wonderful World of Hospitals"; Carol and the dancers present a Spanish-flavored "You Don't Have to Say You Love Me."

Comments: Great comic moments and splendid singing make this a classic. The eleven-minute Q&A (!) has common queries such as the Tarzan yell and the designer of her clothes mixed with a few odd ones. A twelve-year-old boy who says he has admired Carol for years asks her to go to dinner with him (she offers to eat a candy bar with him after the show instead). Asked if she'll play Sophia Loren, she says no, she'll actually portray Sophia's husband, film producer Carlo Ponti. She brings out Jonathan, with whom she appeared on *The Jonathan Winters Show* on Jan. 10, 1968. His visits with Carol led CBS to give him that series, which ended in 1969. "I'm trying to get through to April!" Jonathan says to one audience member who wanted to know who Jonathan's summer replacement would be. He does brief impressions of his familiar characterizations and some lesser-known ones, including a slot machine and most hilariously Walter Brennan.

Jonathan and Carol sparkle in the first skit as a couple who watch TV for sixteen hours a day and bicker in clichés they have seen on the tube. Their great rapport and fine slapstick compensate for most of the references being arcane to today's viewers.

Carol introduces her musical guest by saying, "I think she's a marvelous singer, one of the best to come along in a long time." Regarding Dionne's numbers, her duet with Carol comes from the 1944 Broadway musical *Bloomer Girl*, and "Children Go Where I Send Thee" is an unusually spiritual number for the series to present. "(Theme from) Valley of the Dolls" is just the second time on the show since Nov. 6, 1967, that an artist is presenting his or her own current top 40 hit (it's the Number Two song in America this week, a coup for the show). This will not occur again until the Carpenters on Sept. 22, 1971. Incidentally, the series will spoof the *Valley of the Dolls* movie on Feb. 19, 1968.

"Carol & Sis" finally allows Chris to do more than go see her friend Marsha as another pal, Willy (Flip Mark), show up with her dressed in matching outer space transparent helmets. He leaves as Carol plans to stay up the entire night to maintain her bouffant for a wedding in the morning with the help of Chris. Roger reluctantly decides to let his sister-in-law get some sleep while he assists his wife, but she keeps getting drowsy and nearly crushes her follicles while propped in several positions. Finally, Roger gets the idea to put on Chris's helmet, but it locks unexpectedly. He goes to get tools to open it when Carol manages to pull it off. She runs to tell him the good news, only to have him smack her accidentally with the kitchen door and of course cause her hairdo to collapse. This moves nimbly with plenty of laughs throughout.

"Kiss of Death" has Harvey smooch Lyle on the lips for a brief, funny ad spoof, and the laughs unexpectedly keep coming when Carol's straight version of "Come Rain or Come Shine" is interrupted by drops and later buckets of water thrown at her to get her thoroughly soaked. The audience applauds her work in this tickling bit.

In the last skit, reporter Walter Crankcase (Harvey) interviews a doctor (Jonathan) who knows the problem people in his industry are physicians who work weekends or hate money. Jonathan has great fun improvising with his outfit and equipment as he solidly delivers some great quips. A cut to an operating scene finds a surgeon (Lyle) is attracted to a nurse (Carol) until she removes her mask. Then it's back to Crankcase interviewing Maudie Frickert (Jonathan), an 83-year-old mother of a newborn who said she came to the hospital originally for a rabies shot. She makes a few moves on Crankcase before this hysterical segment ends.

The humor keeps flowing in the finale, as flamenco dancers perform at a cantina before a senorita (Carol) sings a 1966 hit for Dusty Springfield. Like Carol's previous number, it appears to be a regular rendition until a man with a whiplash uses the device to knock off her wig and outfit to leave her in her underwear. The problem is that he did it too quick, leaving Carol to laugh her way on the last set of lyrics while standing semi-exposed as a great way to end a wonderful show.

Sadly, this is the last of three great visits by Jonathan on the series. Dionne will return, but not until Dec. 15, 1971.

Feb. 5, 1968: Liza Minnelli, Jack Palance

Q&A; "Carol & Sis" finds Carol and Roger worried about Chrissy's new boyfriend; Liza performs "Butterfly McHart" and "Remember the Happy Time" accompanied with the dancers; a Chicago gangland wars sketch features Jack as the boss and Carol as his secretary; a quick Old West send-up; Carol sings "Wait Till the Sun Shines Nelly"; Jack, Lyle, Harvey and Carol appear in the playlet "Svengali and the Milkmaid, or the Eyes Have It"; Carol and Liza dress up as clowns to do a duet, followed by a hula hoop routine with the dancers.

Comments: As Carol says in the Q&A, Jack Palance is "one of my favorite actors" and acquits himself rather well despite being better known as a screen villain than a comic performer. He has a good line in the gangland sketch. Glancing at his henchman Lyle, he exclaims, "I'm getting sick of you, jealous of my looks!" Jack's faithful secretary (Carol) tells him that his mother called from Alcatraz and records the responses of a man beaten up by Jack. Harvey is a rival mobster who engages in a shootout that kills everyone. A dying Jack dictates his will to Carol, then shoots her because "You know too much!" This is followed by Harvey as a bartender who has hired a new saloon singer (Carol) whose rendition of "I Got Rhythm" is so shatteringly off-key that it collapses a chandelier.

In a longer and uneven sketch, Jack is Svengali, Harvey his British partner and Lyle a "nice guy but a dummy" accompanying them when they discover Carol, as the milkmaid Trilby. Sporting a decent British accent, Jack actually sings well along with Harvey and Lyle as they attempt to refine Trilby, who does the Tarzan yell as part of her audition before being trained on how to sing. The male trio performs an operetta spoofing several old songs before putting Trilby on stage, where she assumes her old habits and does the yell. In desperation, Jack looks at Lyle and the latter suddenly starts singing operatic with a high pitch, leading Jack to draft him as Carol's replacement.

The other main skit has Carol and Roger anxious to meet Chrissy's new crush, Stanley Hinkle. As Chrissy prepares for her date, a flower child hippie (Neil Elliot) visits. He stands on his head, announces that he and Chris will go to a love-in, and attempts to light up a banana peel when Carol grabs it and declares, "No smoking!" After a petrified Carol and Roger attempt appeasement by meditating with him, they are relieved when Chris says the guy is a classmate she despises, and Roger throws him out. He and Carol's comfort disappears when the real Stanley arrives and he is a biker in black leather.

For the Q&A, when asked if Vicki was her sister in real life, Carol responds, "My real sister looks like Sophia Loren, and that's sad—for me!" She misidentifies a boy as a girl in the audience, to everyone's amusement, and debuts what will become a standard response to a frequently asked question. When a gentleman queried, "What are you doing after the show?" she leeringly shot back, "What do you have in mind?" She is caught off guard, however, when one man asks "Is it true all you need to get on television is a pretty face?" which cracks her up and makes her say yes in response.

Best of all, we have a somewhat spontaneous interplay between Carol and Lyle. Noting that this is the first show where he sings, Carol coaxes Sue, a redhead from the audience, to appear onstage as Lyle serenades her. She giggles from embarrassment, and when asked what she thought of his vocalizing, she responds, "It isn't bad." Indeed it was not, and the show overall was serviceable as well, if somewhat bumpy.

Feb. 12, 1968: Betty Grable, Martha Raye

Q&A; "V.I.P" features F. Lee Korman interviewing Queen Elizabeth II; Betty performs "Hello, Dolly" with the dancers; Carol and Martha duet on "Flings"; Lyle presides over an audience vote to see who among the performers hidden from the top has the best legs; "As the Stomach Turns" is a soap opera ending its nineteen-year run on TV and its star, Marian (Carol), must summarize the action quickly with the help of two other long-suffering characters (Martha and Betty); a musical finale has Carol and her guests playing gun molls of mobsters opposite the male dancers as police officers.

Comments: Everything sparkles in this great show that includes the debut of "As the Stomach Turns," the only recurring sketch to last all eleven seasons. The Q&A is bright (a sample Carol response: "Was I up for any part in *Valley of the Dolls*? Yeah, but Paul Burke got it!"), and Martha prompts amusement from the outset by pulling down on her skirt, pretending that it is too revealing.

One highlight is Betty's reprise of the title tune of the Broadway musical she recently headlined after Carol Channing left the role. Another is having the curtain block the tops of Carol, Martha and Betty and letting the audience applaud as to which one they felt had the shapeliest gams. The winner is a dark horse fourth contestant—Harvey in stockings!

Best of all is the hilarious debut of "As the Stomach Turns," which brilliantly mocks the convention of daytime serial dramas, from the overheated dialogue to botched sound effects, such as Martha being drowned out by an organ while doing a dramatic delivery, forcing her to go out of character and yell for it to end. This setup generates laughs so easily that it becomes a staple of the series with even more outlandish episodes to come.

In the finale, Carol, Betty and Martha ride in on a motorcycle with a sidecar in white berets and beaded gray and black striped outfits that show off their legs. Each male dancer solos while the ladies sing "That Old Gang of Mine," with strobe effect edits to speed up the action. That is dated and distracting, but overall the number is a winner.

This show marks the only appearance of Carol's idol, Betty Grable, on the series. Martha will continue to be a frequent guest over the next three years.

Feb. 19, 1968: Art Carney, Nanette Fabray

Q&A; a spoof of *Valley of the Dolls*; Harvey shocks his parents (Art and Carol) when he introduces them to his latest flame—a mermaid (Nanette)—in a parody of *Guess Who's Coming to Dinner?*; "The 1936 Academy Awards" has child presenters Shirley Dimple (Carol) and Janie Dithers (Nanette) arguing during a routine; Carol and Lyle do an improvisation; Vicki and the dancers present "Bend Me, Shape Me"; "Passion on Tenth Ave." has Carol as an insanely jealous wife of a trash collector (Art) who is suspicious of Nanette; Carol, her guests and the dancers do a roller derby finale.

Comments: It is a tribute to the series' reputation at this point that Art Carney takes time off from his regular role on *The Jackie Gleason Show* to do a rare guest shot during that period here. The superb dialectician and comic actor helps make this episode a classic. After saying this was her first time meeting Art, she reveals she is double jointed and displaces her hip and says she has no beauty secrets to share. On doing movies, she muses, "I would really love to, but Rod Steiger gets all my roles." She cracks up as she answers, "Is my mouth insured? There's not enough money!" Then in a turn of mood, Carol brings out Nanette, who beautifully renders "Somewhere Over the Rainbow" in sign language while singing it a cappella. The shots of some children in the audience mesmerized by the presentation add to it being a magical moment.

But comedy is not forgotten as Lyle introduces "Valley of the Dollars," with Carol, Vicki and an unbilled Gloria Loring looking eerily close to the way Barbara Parkins, Patty Duke and Sharon Tate respectively looked in a promotional still for the movie. This is flat out hilarious throughout. For example, Vicki moans, "I made $3 million last year, and did it buy me happiness?!" Carol: "Did it?" Vicki: "A little." It ends wonderfully with Carol saying she's leaving Hollywood and its lying and cheating to go back home to Peyton Place (Barbara Parkins starred in that TV series before doing the movie).

"I was so thrilled to be involved in the sketch for *Valley of the Dolls*," recalls Gloria. "It was good to have the experience, because I didn't have any acting chops at all." She worried she might laugh during airtime because rehearsals were funny.

"It was so hard not to crack up," she says. "All I had to do was keep a straight face." It was up to Carol, Vicki and the rest of the actors to do deliver the lines. Somehow, Gloria maintained a poker face throughout the experience.

The laughs keep rolling with "Guess What's Coming to Dinner?" Carol does a bang-up job as Katharine Hepburn and Art comes close with his Spencer Tracy as they awkwardly cope with the arrival Nanette, seen in a stunning green body outfit down to her tail. "Holy mackerel!" Art says and Carol covers his mouth. Nanette explains that she lured Harvey by singing "Indian Love Call," then splashes water from a goldfish bowl to stay cool. Her name is Ethel Mermaid, and regarding children, she says, "I just swim upstream and spawn!" After Art's monologue of acceptance for the couple, they all head to the living room, where it's fish for dinner and hopefully no one Annette knows. Sure it's silly, but it's funny, wacky and brisk in the manner of the best skits on this series.

More humorous fun occurs as Shirley Dimple mocks her rival, Jane Dithers, during the latter's award acceptance speech. The nervous host (Harvey) requests that they re-enact their musical number from the film "Babes in Armenia," and as they sing and dance, their animosity emerges, and they bite and hit each other with toys. It ends in a pillow fight where Harvey tries to save himself from the mayhem. This is motivated slapstick well presented and carried out to the fullest degree, another example of what people consider typical comedy on *The Carol Burnett Show*.

An "improvisation" that really is not one can be irritating, but not on this show. When Lyle says he studied that style of acting in St. Louis, Carol takes advantage of the situation and has him play the notion that they are two people in love with each other who reunite after five long years. He does so and says to here, "Oh, I'm so glad to see you, Mother!" This is another winning payoff.

Art invokes a look and sound reminiscent of his Ed Norton character on *The Honeymooners* as the disheveled husband of Carol, wearing curlers and a tacky flower house dress. She clings to him constantly and adores him so much that she is in ecstasy when he opens a can of beer. But her possessiveness makes her think that her slovenly pal (Nanette in a hairnet) desires him just as much, and her feelings lead to their friendship being dissolved. Although a little long, this is strong overall and does include a great mistake when Carol's headpiece fall off, prompting Art to crack, "The very first time a woman flipped her wig over me!"

Sporting wild hair and blacked out teeth, Carol and Nanette roller skate around a rink singing "I Enjoy Being a Girl" with the dancers as their fellow roller derby players. Art comes out as the referee moving smoothly too, but the best dance routines on wheels come from Don Crichton, Randy Doney and two other male dancers. This is an inventive and rousing finale, and it's even topped in the closing by everybody in the kick line coming out with blacked out teeth as well!

Art will return to the series on Jan. 4, 1971. Fabray will reappear on Oct. 7, 1968.

Feb. 26, 1968: Garry Moore, Durward Kirby, John Gary

Q&A; John sings "The Most Beautiful Girl in the World" and "That's My Desire"; two Martians (Carol and Durward) base their behavior on Earth on TV shows they have watched; Durward, Carol and Lyle engage in comic banter; a drunk Carol nearly destroys efforts by Chris to impress a teacher for a scholarship in "Carol & Sis"; Garry narrates "That Wonderful Year" spotlighting 1937, where the cast make fun of married couple morning radio shows, the musical *Golden Boy*, the movie *Lost Horizon*, exotic island dramas with Carol spoofing Dorothy Lamour and a salute to music from Tin Pan Alley.

Comments: The less said about this outing, the better for all involved. It is an awkward reprise of *The Garry Moore Show* that attempts to graft elements of that show such as the "That Wonderful Year" and a Martians sketch previously done on that series along with a redo of the "Carol & Sis" segment from the Sept. 18, 1967 segment, here substituting intoxication in place of sleep deprivation for Carol to cause havoc for Chris and Roger. Combine that with unexciting numbers from bland vocalist John Gary, and you have a show that does no one any favors. The only good news is that at least Garry and Durward fare better in their next outing on the series (see Nov. 25, 1968).

March 4, 1968: Mel Torme, Imogene Coca

** Harvey is a TV personality whose quips get on the nerves of two congressional wives (Carol and Imogene); the male American and Russian athletes at the Olympics offer contrasting views on life; Imogene and Carol are two female astronauts; Carol is the long-suffering spouse of Dracula (Harvey); Mel sings "That's All," performs a jazz waltz medley with Carol and does a number with the dancers.

Comments: With nine appearances from 1968-1971, Mel Torme was this series' most frequent male guest during this period after Tim Conway, thanks to smooth vocals and assured comic delivery. Torme appreciated the work as an effort to establish himself as more than a singer after his tenure as musical advisor on *The Judy Garland Show* in 1963-1964, where he denounced that star's behavior in a book, *The Other Side of the Rainbow*. (Others on that series have denied what Torme claimed happened there.)

"After the madness of the ill-fated Judy Garland series, working with Carol, Harvey Korman, Vicki Lawrence and Lyle Waggoner was pure pleasure," he noted in his autobiography *It Wasn't All Velvet*. "Rarely, if ever, was there a more professional, talented company assembled under the roof of CBS Television City." Besides acting and singing, Mel also contributed some arranging to the nine shows on which he appeared.

March 11, 1968: Rerun of previous show

March 18, 1968: Tim Conway, Jack Jones

Q&A; Roger's attempts to compile his taxes are complicated by Chrissy's girlfriend (Ruth Buzzi) having a crush on him in "Carol & Sis"; Jack sings "I Got So Much Love in Me"; Tim plays an unconventional bullfighter discussing his techniques with Harvey; Carol and Tim are survivors of a sunken cruise ship alone on an island; brief movie genre takeoffs on explorer sagas, prison dramas and Italian romantic triangles; Carol sings "I Can't Get Started With You"; Jack and Carol participate in a number with the dancers dressed as cowboys on an oilfield.

Comments: Although not billed at the top, Ruth Buzzi adds a lot to this show's sizable humor. "They wanted me to be a surprise for the audience, so I got my credit at the end of the show," she relates. "My bosses on *Laugh-In* were very generous about allowing me to work on any other shows. All I had to do was ask, and (executive producer) George Schlatter, (hosts) Dick (Martin) and Dan (Rowan) would say to go right on and do it!"

As Chrissy's gal pal who stares at Roger intently, Ruth generates many laughs when his efforts to mention how much he loves his wife backfire by making Ruth loathe Carol. Ruth stays devoted to him even as he claims to be a sick, 56-year-old Lawrence Welk fan with false teeth—until his accountant (Jack) arrives and she switches swooning to him. She also chases Jack after his solo numbers and participates in a movie parody.

Otherwise, this installment is fairly balanced in showcasing Tim and, as Carol puts it at the start of Q&A, "just about the best singer to come down the pike in ages, Jack Jones." In the opening, Carol receives a caricature from a girl and kisses a bearded man for the first time ("I love it!" she yells) before inviting Tim out for queries. After one audience member rather rudely inquires, "Where'd you get the bald head?" Tim nicely deadpans, "I don't know, just kind of crept up on me." After seriously responding that he may do another TV series, the rest of his answers generate laughter, claiming that movie scripts are "pouring in like crazy," that the jokes on *McHale's Navy* "were written in the sand" and that he has been happily married three out of six years.

After the aforementioned "Carol & Sis" sketch and Jack's songs, Tim is a matador telling Harvey that he is drunk going into the ring, so he always sees two bulls in action. He breaks up Harvey when he brings up possibly dating bulls before accidentally injecting himself with a barbed dart. As Tim-Harvey routines go, this is mild but effective.

Tim is back next as a fellow castaway with Carol, who worries that he will pursue her. Instead, he unintentionally hurts her while searching for supplies, like breaking her foot with a rock. Their precise comic rapport is fine here as the sketch ends with them awkwardly beginning a romance. "You busy tonight?" Tim says as a come-on line.

The movie send-ups are "The Jungle Kook," "Sing Sing Ding-a-ling" and "Shut Uppa Your Face" (where Carol cheats on Harvey with Lyle). The first two are the best. Jack and Lyle encounter Carol, a wild jungle girl in an animal skin outfit. They determine that Carol needs to be kissed to be tamed before leaving. Then Ruth comes out from hiding and Carol tells here "Hey, here comes two more!" as they attempt to con more kisses out of male visitors. In the second, Tim is a gangster asking a priest for help, and his troubles closing a door produce hysterical ad libs along with good scripted material.

Carol's solo and the finale are inconsequential and somewhat drag down an otherwise lively show. Ruth signs Carol's book along with Jack and Tim, and the camaraderie is reflected by everyone wrapping their arms together during the kick line. "Jack Jones was terrific to work with, and of course, Tim Conway was the best!" Buzzi notes.

March 25, 1968: Soupy Sales, Gloria Loring

** A shy young couple (Soupy and Carol) check into their honeymoon suite; Gloria sings "Little Girl Blue" and "Don't Tie Me Down"; Carol and Soupy portray child students taking an etiquette class; Roger's too-enthusiastic greeting of the latest boyfriend for Chris (because he hopes the latter will marry her and make her leave the house) complicates the young lovers' relationship in "Carol & Sis"; Soupy stars in a musical comedy production of "Real Live Girl" with the dancers.

Comments: After two billed appearances and one unbilled (see Feb. 19, 1968), this guest shot marks Gloria Loring's last appearance on the series. Gloria speculates that the producers may have wanted to find more new talent but appreciated the exposure.

Loring notes that working on Burnett's series was one of her happiest professional experiences. "She was so gracious, so kind, always in a good mood. It was incredible, and just to know her and see her was a great joy," she says.

April 1, 1968: Rerun of previous show

April 8, 1968: Rerun of Jan. 15, 1968 show

April 15, 1968: Peter Lawford, Minnie Pearl

Q&A; Carol and Chrissy watch a horror movie that leads them to be scared when they discover a man (William Schallert) Roger brought home in secret in "Carol & Sis"; Minnie performs a monologue; Carol and Minnie are Americans visiting Paris who meet Charles de Gaulle (Harvey); Harvey, Carol, Minnie and Peter pose as the principals depicted in the movie poster for *Bonnie & Clyde*; Peter, Minnie and Carol sing "Country Girl, City Man"; "Mail Order Bride" has Carol as the title character delivered to Peter in the Amazon in 1908; a musical medley with the cast, guests and dancers.

Comments: It is a little odd given its popularity with middle America, Carol's roots in Texas and the rural slant of 1960s CBS programming that *The Carol Burnett Show* rarely presented country-based humor or singing beyond this stint by Minnie Pearl. Both she and Peter Lawford draw "oooos" from the studio audience when Carol mentions them. Minnie acquits herself well as an actress here. Likewise, Lawford handles the Q&A with pluck despite a weird query of if he knew and liked David Janssen. He has lost weight and notes that "I was getting a little heavy, so I quit booze"—while at the same time he smokes a cigarette. The bulk of the segment had Carol surprising Peter by saying his hip clothes had inspired Lyle and Harvey and brought them out to model their new looks. Describing them as if they were in a fashion show, Carol notes Lyle wears green boots, striped green trousers and a velvet blouse with white lace (and poofy sleeves to match), while Harvey sports a guava-orange muumuu with bells around the neck. Both men wear beads, which Carol adds, "They go with anything, and so do they!" The implied gay humor is done without meanness, and all including Peter have a good laugh about it.

Carol is serious in mentioning how her show had been renewed and the regulars will return and how she avoids solos because "I'm kind of chicken singing by myself." There are laughs, such as Carol claiming she was named Miss Community Chest when attending UCLA and shrieking when a young boy guesses her age is 40.

Thanks to seeing a thriller on late night TV, Carol and Chrissy are susceptible to fright. As luck would have it, as they head to bed, Roger arrives with a drunk pal who needs to sleep off his condition. Roger tells the man to be quiet so as not to "awaken" Carol and Chrissy as he goes to make coffee in the kitchen. Naturally, Carol snoops downstairs, spots the man lying on the couch and hits him on the head with a skillet as he attempts to rise up. The incident prompts Roger to look for a possible intruder in the house, and each time he goes, Carol comes back to knock the man in the head. William Schallert's reactions to these three additional times are golden, and when this ends with Roger being hit by the door as he rushes into the kitchen having figured out what has happened, the comic momentum built here makes this a winning part of the show.

Carol first met Minnie when Jim Nabors brought her to the Jan. 15, 1968 taping, and she invited the "living doll" to do her routine. Minnie jokes about her date's eligibility ("He was breathing") and wearing a muumuu that made her resemble "a mama kangaroo with everybody at home." She references her fictional hometown of Grinder's Switch as well as her kin and friends there, then yodels and dances a jig accompanied by the orchestra before she skips off stage. This monologue is quite enjoyable.

Minnie appears next with Carol as two lively ladies at a cafe in the City of Lights. They buy absinthe to give to and seduce the handsome Lyle, but he leaves with another woman. Next, they see Charles de Gaulle (Harvey), who when learning they are from the United States greets them with "I hate you." He has no qualms about comparing himself to Julius Caesar and Napoleon and even one bigger figure in history, saying that "I will walk on water!" Minnie does her part in making this a fairly lively sketch.

The "Bonnie and Clod" spoof is much better than the Oct. 9, 1967 effort, first starting visually—Minnie with her hair down in a modern dress looks eerily close to Estelle Parsons from the movie, and Harvey definitely is closer in appearance to Gene Hackman than Warren Beatty. They are joined by an unidentified and non-speaking actor standing next to the quartet as Michael Pollard's character, all posed like the film's main production still. Wisely short and sweet, this bit with plenty of quips is highlighted by Minnie's deadpan but urgent appeal to be able to walk away and go to the bathroom.

Wearing a white turtleneck, Peter joins Carol and Minnie in vocalizing what they all have in common. Minnie steals the show, simply by shimmying and saying, "Groovy!"

In the final skit, an explorer (Harvey) presents an entrepreneur (Peter) with a mail order bride for the latter's home in the jungle. She costs more than he expected because, as Carol puts it, "I've put on a few more pounds since I came over." A picture of Peter's ex-wife has her huge breasts pointing eye level at Carol, prompting the latter to do bust exercises in response. As Peter rhapsodizes about what his former companion did, Carol tries to mimic the activities, such as gathering wood and running out of breath doing so, but he tells her she fails. As Carol plans to leave, Peter contracts a disease that makes him be her slave and do her chores instead. This decent entry gets funnier as it goes along.

The finale starts hilariously when Carol cracks up as the cue card guy is late in hitting his spot. She and Peter resume their bit, which she sings about the hats he wore in his old films before they start wearing various caps as they perform such tunes as "A Couple of Swells" and "The Varsity Rag." Minnie joins them for a reprise of "A Couple of Swells" along with the dancers, and Harvey and Vicki by the end. It is nice but not spectacular.

At the end, William Schallert signs the guest book, even though he was not introduced as a guest star by Carol at the show's start, just was the case with his Oct. 16, 1967 appearance. No other actor can make that same dubious claim for this series.

April 22, 1968: Rerun of Nov. 27, 1967 show

April 29, 1968: Tim Conway, Shani Wallis

** F. Lee Korman (Harvey) interviews America's first native American president (Tim) in "V.I.P"; an engagement dinner for a couple (Tim and Carol) is a debacle; Roger is upset with the way Carol has rearranged the Bradfords' living room in "Carol & Sis"; Shani sings "It Had to Be You" and joins Carol and the dancers in presenting "What Takes My Fancy"; Carol performs "Meantime"; Lyle vocalizes on "All of Me."

Comments: This originally was to have aired on March 11, 1968, but was pushed back. When this show first ran, Shani Wallis was months away from her most famous role as the prostitute in the movie version of *Oliver!* However, she had established a relationship with Carol Burnett that led to her guest shot here.

"I first met Carol through *The Garry Moore Show*," Wallis says. Coming to America in the early 1960s after good stage roles in her native United Kingdom dried up, Shani leveraged her association with English dancer Roy Castle, "a brilliant, talented man," to appear on that series, and Garry liked her talent enough to invite her back again. She continued her connection with Carol by appearing on the June 3, 1964 TV version of *Once Upon a Mattress*. Even though she had returned to England by 1968, when she got a call to appear on *The Carol Burnett Show*, she willingly flew back to the States.

"It was wonderful for me," Wallis says of her experience on the series. "I loved doing it. She was just an incredible partner."

Regarding her fellow co-star, Shani acknowledged that Tim Conway was a "cut-up," but others were entertaining to her as well. "Everybody on that show was a character, and they were all brilliant," she says.

Asked to describe what made Carol's show so successful, Shani quips, "She was a great adapter. Sounds like something out of a socket, doesn't it? (laughs) But she was electric. She is a labor of love itself." Although this was her sole appearance on the series, Shani said she would have done another one if asked.

May 6, 1968: Sid Caesar, Barbara McNair

** A series of romantic, political and family complications enmesh Sid, Carol and Harvey; Carol and Barbara star in a spoof of *I Spy*; "V.I.P." features F. Lee Korman interviewing the silent movie couple Pico and Rivera (Carol and Sid); two soap opera stars (Harvey and Carol) are beset by challenges prompted by a drunken sound effects man during a live show; Barbara sings "I've Grown Accustomed to Your Face" and "The Second Time Around" and duets with Carol on "Up Above My Head"; the Charwoman visits the United Nations building and sings "If I Ruled the World."

Comments: Like its predecessor, this episode was originally set to air earlier, on April 1, 1968. It marks the first of three appearances by Barbara McNair, the first guest star to wear an Afro on the show. She went to UCLA together with Carol in the 1950s. Her gender bending take on *I Spy* with Carol fulfilled what the hostess vowed to do on the season opener, albeit without Pearl Bailey as promised (see Sept. 11, 1967 for more).

By the time this show aired, Stan Mazin had joined the Ernie Flatt Dancers and would become a prominent featured member over the next decade. He had been a successful dancer in New York City for four years prior to moving to Los Angeles in 1967. "I was doing a Broadway show, *Walking Happy*, and we were touring out here," he recalls. During that stopover, Mitzi Gaynor and her husband, Jack

Bean, were auditioning men to perform as support in her live show, but unlike others in the chorus, he was reluctant to try for the job when asked about it by Jack.

"I told him, 'I'm a dancer who sings, and you want a singer who dances,'" Mazin says. But Jack implored Stan to show him and Mitzi what he could do. "Let's let us turn you down," Jack says. The "us" included Ernie Flatt, who was hiring the men for Mitzi's show. Ernie ended up selecting Stan along with Randy Doney and Lee Roy Reams for Mitzi's stage show in Lake Tahoe, Calif., and remembered the dancer for future work.

"As soon as there was an opening, I got on Carol's show," Mazin says. "There were about six shows left to do that season."

He came to work on a Monday and headed to the second floor to the huge rehearsal room to join the other dancers. "The second day, I got on the elevator, and Carol joins me on it," he said, "She looks at me and puts out her hand and says, 'How are you doing, Stan?' She's a wonderfully warm person."

Mazin soon became a recognizable face to viewers in dance segments, often being featured as much as Don Crichton and Randy Doney. He credits Flatt for doing that and noted with pride that the latter once said, "If I had one dancer to hire, it would be Stan."

"It was because I had a lot of different styles," Mazin elaborates on that statement. "I really enjoyed everything." He also enjoyed acting, and he will be seen frequently in small parts on the show over the next ten seasons.

Incidentally, the sound effects sketch on this show will be remade on Nov. 10, 1971.

May 13, 1968: Family Show

Q&A; Carol gushes over a visiting recording star (Lyle) to Roger's chagrin in "Carol & Sis"; the dancers perform to a stylized minuet; Vicki vocalizes "Best of Both Worlds" with the George Becker Singers; five mature ladies in Harvey's fan club attack him in his dressing room and even his fantasies; Carol is a housewife assaulted by products behaving the way they do in commercials; the male dancers play a rock group; "The Old Folks" ruminate about their lives; the Charwoman waves goodbye to the cast and recalls the season's highlights.

Comments: Setting the template for all future season-ending episodes—and saving the show from having to pay guests—this "family" entry runs from great to grating, which pretty well reflects the quality of shows presented during 1967-1968. It starts promisingly with Carol first thinking that a big toothbrush a girl has for her is a bra. She brings out Harvey, Lyle and Vicki and sits on a chair on stage facing them to ask questions like a member of the studio audience. All watch the series at home ("That way, I get the illusion I truly exist," cracks Harvey). When Carol asks Lyle, "What are your measurements?" he responds, "I don't know." One man tells Vicki she is good in the dance numbers and she shines by saying back, "I know!" It ends with five senior females coming on stage supposedly playing Harvey's fan club, which unfortunately is just as awkwardly scripted as had been most of the Carol-Lyle interactions during the Q&A this season.

For "Carol & Sis," Lyle makes his first appearance in the segment as a smooth singer who knows Roger. The latter warns Chrissy not to make a fool of herself over him, but it turns out Carol is unhinged by Lyle's good looks. She sits on his lap and giggles over him, lights up two cigarettes in her mouth and offers him one (even though she does not smoke), and unexpectedly joins in when Lyle suggests to Chrissy that they duet on "Strangers in the Night." It ends with Carol smacked in the face by Chrissy opening the kitchen door this time. This "Carol & Sis" is better than usual.

Carol introduces her dancers—Ellen Graff, Stan Mazin, Suzy Edmunds, Birl Johns, Jackie Gregory, Randy Doney, April Nevins, Don Crichton, Patty Tribble and Eddie Pfeiffer—plus the "marvelously talented" Ernie Flatt all by name next to her before the dancers launch into a number featuring Elizabethan-era outfits and an instrumental styled in that period's music. It has a nice surprise comic ending with Randy reaching for his hat and unexpectedly knocking down the rest of the troupe.

The show unwisely followed it with another musical number that put the previously unseen George Becker Singers in the background as Vicki provides the lead vocal for a top 40 entry by Lulu in 1968. Although performed well, the slow number and unimpressive visual presentation causes the show to slacken its momentum.

The senior citizen fan club for Harvey reappears as he retreats to his dressing room. He extricates himself from their clutches, looks at a centerfold in a men's magazine and imagines being a playboy in a dinner jacket, singing and romancing women coming out of the mirrors surrounding his bed. The fantasy vanishes when the elderly lady fans interrupt it to sing and strip him of his clothes. This is a good bit.

Even better is Carol as a housewife terrorized by slogans from popular ads. She hears "Ring around the collar!" as she puts up shirts and the Jolly Green Giant theme as she opens a can of vegetables, and most uproariously she sees a "living bra" floating in her kitchen and stomps on it. Harried by it all, she leaves her house quickly with a suitcase, only to be gored by the White Knight. Apart from stealing the ending from a similar sketch on the Oct. 2, 1967 show, this segment is a stellar one.

However, the excitement subsides as Carol introduces the Banana Wristwatch, a takeoff in name at least of the Strawberry Alarm Clock, with the male dancers clad in loud pants and beads. Their moves are tight, but as a rock parody, this contrived effort flops badly.

Hopes recuperate with an amusing "Old Folks" sketch with some choice ad libs by Harvey (or at least lines seemingly spontaneous). When Bert grabs Molly's leg, she puts his hand on the chair's arm, prompting him to say, "That feels even better!" That plus his "Why don't we have another kid?" line crack up Carol, as does her repartee in telling Harvey, "Let's go inside and turn on Lawrence Welk" with his response of "I don't think that's possible." For more on these characters, see the 1968-1969 introduction.

With all this show's ups and downs, it figures the last cast segment is just so-so. Lyle strums a guitar and sings "By the Time I Get to Phoenix" in the back of a pickup truck before he joins the other regulars sitting in wooden chairs and having mock arguments about how talented they are and the roles they fulfill on the show. This stilted conversation leads into a song about this is not the right way to end the season, followed by all singing "Together, Wherever We Go" from the musical *Gypsy* in unison.

The Charwoman watches the end of the show backstage as the dancers walk by, then waves bye to Harvey, Lyle and Vicki and turns over a placard on an easel saying "Closed for the Summer." She visits the sets of "Carol & Sis," "The Old Folks" and the Q&A out front, remembering bits from each during the season, and reads the autograph book. The Charwoman sings all of "It's Time to Say So Long" and then exits through the empty audience seats. This ending would remain the same except for a few tweaks for the next decade.

Final Notes for the Season

The Carol Burnett Show debuted when viewers showed relatively little enthusiasm for newcomers. No new series finished in the top fifteen highest-rated shows for the 1967-1968 season, a first in the 1960s. Critics were unimpressed too. Jack Gould in *The New York Times* called the new offerings "electronic baloney sliced with a minimum of imagination and innovation." Of 31 new shows introduced, only eight survived more than two years.

Amid these circumstances, *The Carol Burnett Show* shone as an exception to the rule and performed well. It won its time slot over *I Spy*, which NBC cancelled after three years in favor of movies, and *The Big Valley* on ABC, which nevertheless renewed the show for the same time slot for 1968-1969. The series' average rating of 20.1 put it at Number Twenty-Seven for the season. Only three other freshman series surpassed that—*Gentle Ben* at Number Nineteen (whose rating dropped dramatically the following year, leading CBS to can it in 1969), *Rowan and Martin's Laugh-In* at Number Twenty-One and *Ironside* at Number Twenty-Six. The latter two aired on NBC.

Laugh-In became both a spoiler and an inspiration to *The Carol Burnett Show*. At the Emmy awards presented May 19, 1968, *Rowan and Martin's Laugh-In* beat *The Carol Burnett Show* for Outstanding Musical or Variety Series and for writing (both were the series' only nominations). *Laugh-In's* quick edits and pacing revolutionized TV comedy variety, and Carol's production team aped it somewhat in 1968-1969, with mixed results. As previously mentioned, Carol won a Golden Globe as Best TV Star—Female, which her series was nominated for Best Show (and lost to *Mission: Impossible*).

After May 13, *The Carol Burnett Show* ran in repeats through June 17. After a *CBS News Special* the following week, on July 1 the network unveiled *Premiere*, a series of failed drama pilots. It ran until Sept. 9, but only seven episodes aired due to preemptions by the Republican and Democratic national conventions, pro football and another *CBS News Special*. Pro football popped up again on Sept. 16 before the series finally returned.

In three years, football would be more problematic for *The Carol Burnett Show*. But that was far from the minds of its principals, who were just happy to have survived their longest season ever and thrilled to know their jobs were secure for at least another year.

Harvey and Carol play Bert and Molly, "The Old Folks," in a recurring sketch that flourished this season and popped up occasionally in the next six ones. They typically appeared in rocking chairs where Molly asked her husband to get hers pushing before she sat down and mused about their lives. This is one of several portrayals of "crotchety" senior citizens that generated some criticism of the series in later years. Courtesy of Getty Images.

Chapter 3

1968–1969: No Sophomore Slump Here

Audience member:	"Who's Ernie Anderson?"
Carol:	"He's a friend of ours, and we're going to make him a star!"—From the Dec. 2, 1968 show

Crew Additions This Season
Writers: Hal Goodman, Al Gordon
Casting: Marilyn Budgen
Assistant Choreographer: George Foster
Set Decorator: Donn Gibson, Bruce Kay (1969)
Hairstylist: Enid
Stage Managers: Willie Dahl

When *The Carol Burnett Show* returned for its sophomore season, there were a couple of changes in store. The main one noticed by viewers involved the presentation of material.

The success of *Laugh-In* led to a recurring segment of blackouts built around the theme of signs of the horoscope. "What's in the Stars?" led off with Carol's own sign of Taurus on Sept. 30, 1968, followed by Leo (Nov. 4, 1968) and Aquarius (Jan. 20, 1969). While tying together jokes related to the same premise sounds clever, *Laugh-In* already did that, so the move appeared to be a basic steal from that series. Making matters worse, many of the gags were neither as funny or as tightly executed as tightly as on *Laugh-In*. Response to the segment was lukewarm at best, and the series discontinued "What's in the Stars?" before all twelve astrological signs were covered.

A more fruitful addition this season is the increasing use of Carol and Harvey playing Bert and Molly respectively as "The Old Folks," first introduced last season (see May 13, 1968). In this segment, the sprightly couple make wise comments about their age and sex life while in rocking chairs outside their home, and sometimes end with a song. They will remain recurring characters through 1975. Chris Korman notes that Carol's print dress and orthopedic shoes her character wears in this sketch will later be handed down to Vicki when she begins Mama in "The Family" sketches in 1974.

The tail end of this season's shows brings two more enduring characters. Alice Portnoy the Fireside Girl had Carol trying to blackmail men to buy more of her fundraiser cookies. The pushy child is rather one-dimensional both in characterization and plotting, but somehow the basic setup will pop up with lessening frequency through 1975.

Also occasionally featured is a gentle needling of President Nixon and his family, with Harvey playing the chief executive, Carol as his wife and Vicki as their daughter. Their efforts to appear to be tolerant and "with it" will be mocked for the next two seasons. As they did with Alice Portnoy, Gail Parent and Kenny Solms created these recurring bits.

Best of all is the send-up by Carol and Harvey as stage professionals attempting to deal with all sorts of mishaps. It will not be until the 1970s that they will get a name, Funt and Mundane, a play on the last name of theatrical greats Alfred Lunt and his wife, Lynn Fontanne. The germ of this concept will appear in the March 31, 1969 episode.

Another alteration was a decrease in shows produced from thirty in 1967-1968 to twenty-six. Network executives realized it made little economic sense to produce more than they would be able to repeat, so they contracted for fewer episodes. With twenty-six shows, theoretically every program during one season would be rerun for a full fifty-two weeks before starting the next season. Of course, since *The Carol Burnett Show* went off every summer for repeats of other shows or summer series, this rule did not apply well, but nonetheless it taped twenty-six shows each season through 1970-1971. The shortened schedule was most advantageous for Vicki, as she was still studying at UCLA through 1969 while doing the series, uncertain where she wanted to take her career! (She wisely chose the show.)

The major switch in personnel occurred in the director's chair. Even after earning a Directors Guild of America nomination as best television director for the series (he lost to George Schaefer for *CBS Playhouse*), Clark Jones held firm to his promise of helming only its first season. Joe Hamilton decided to promote Dave Powers, the series' assistant director, to fill Jones' old post. Powers agreed to do so only if Roger Beatty, the series' stage manager, would be promoted to assistant director as well.

"So Dave, who had never directed a show, and myself, who had no experience as an AD, kicked off the second season of *The Carol Burnett Show* in 1968," Beatty notes. "Needless to say, we were a couple of very nervous guys in the control booth that night. In fact, I think everybody was a bit apprehensive on the opening show.

"To prove this point, outside the big back stage door in the hallway behind Studio 33, they always had a sign saying which show was currently in production, but that night, somebody had taken it down and replaced it with 'The HMS Titanic.' (I personally think it was one of the cameramen on the show who did it, but I never found out who.) Anyway, the show went off without a hitch, and everybody was happy."

Beatty had spent more than a decade working his way up at the network. "I began my career at CBS in the cue card department in 1956," he says. "In those days, it was pretty much policy to be promoted to stage manager from the cue card department." Beatty claims this is what happened to Dave Powers as well as Beatty's successor as stage manager on *The Carol Burnett Show* this year, Willie Dahl. Dahl previously was stage manager for *The Red Skelton Hour*, where Beatty had worked as well.

"It took nine years in the cue card department before I was finally promoted to stage manager," adds Beatty. "My first assignment was on *The Danny Kaye Show* in 1965. Dave Powers had been promoted to associate director that year, which left a stage manager position open."

Beatty's duties as assistant director was to watch the full run-through in the rehearsal hall each Wednesday along with the crew and writers, then participate in a production meeting with final notes that he gave to Maggie Scott, the script girl (that was the title at the time), to add for the next day's final version. At the same time, Dave Powers had noted every camera shot he wanted for the week's show on his copy of the old script.

"Then I would meet Dave about 5:30 a.m. on Thursday morning, camera blocking day, where we would pick up copies of the final version of the script, and he would transfer all of his shots into my script," Beatty continues. He then would meet with each of the show's four camera operators about which shots they would have for blocking.

This process became streamlined after the series taped an episode in London (see Nov. 9, 1970 for more info on that). The production crew learned that the British Broadcasting Corporation numbered their shots per camera operator for blocking, which made it easier to make changes during rehearsal, and *The Carol Burnett Show*—and other CBS series—adopted that practice because it saved time.

As Beatty explains, "Each cameraman had a 'shot card,' a small index card that they would attach to their camera just below their viewfinder. During our meeting, say for a 'Carol & Sis' sketch for example, I would say 'Camera two, shot one, wide establishing shot,' and cameraman two would write this on his shot card." With this method, every camera operator knew what shots he or she had to take during the show in exact order, and any changes would just need to reference the shot number to have the operator make a quick adjustment.

While Powers talked to the cameramen during blocking Thursdays, Beatty would assume the duty during the Friday tapings. He, Powers and Harry Tatarian, the technical director who switched shots between cameras during tapings, all wore headsets allowing them to hear and talk to the stage managers and sound personnel as well as the camera operators. It was Beatty's responsibility to review the preview monitor in the booth to make sure the upcoming camera shot was in proper place.

"I would say, 'Shot Sixteen this, ready four and hold the sit,'" Beatty recalls. "This" meant the camera operator has the correct shot, in this case Number Sixteen, and it is on Camera Four. "Hold the sit" would remind the operator that the person will sit down during the shot. When that shot went onto the monitor recording the activity on videotape, Beatty already was looking at the next shot to go on the air and checking if it was correct.

If all this activity was not enough, Beatty also began writing on spec for the series the previous season, starting with a "Carol & Sis" sketch on the Jan. 8, 1968 episode. He will provide further bits for the show to use this season for that segment, which will culminate in him becoming a regular writer for the series in 1970 as well as its assistant director.

"Maybe because of that 'Carol & Sis' sketch I wrote back in 1968, I was pretty much delegated to writing dozens more of those sketches in the next few seasons," Beatty says. "I wrote so many that sometimes, watching them on the syndicated series [*Carol Burnett and Friends*, the half-hour reruns], I knew I wrote them, but couldn't wait to see how they ended, because I couldn't remember!"

The contributions by Beatty were not the only changes connected to the writing staff. Saul Turteltaub received a lucrative offer from Bernie Orenstein, a former writing partner, to produce and contribute scripts to *The Beautiful Phyllis Diller Show*, a variety series starring the comedian airing on NBC in the fall of 1968. He had to break the news to his executive producer and head writer, and both had different reactions.

"Joe Hamilton said, 'Go ahead,'" he recalls. "Arnie Rosen said, 'I'm releasing you to a fate worse than death.'" Rosen was kidding of course. *The Beautiful Phyllis Diller Show* ended up flopping by the end of 1968, but Turteltaub and Orenstein would experience more success producing several sitcoms in the 1970s and 1980s, including *That Girl*, *The New Dick Van Dyke Show*, *Sanford and Son*, *What's Happening* and *Kate & Allie*.

Replacing Turteltaub were Hal Goodman, a writer for *The Jack Benny Program* from 1954-1965 who rejoined Stan Burns and Mike Marmer on *The Carol Burnett Show* following their joint stint together on the failed *Milton Berle Show* on ABC in 1966-1967, and Al Gordon, who previously worked with Goodman as a partner on *The Smothers Brothers Comedy Hour*. Both lasted only this season with the series, but they continued to stay busy writing for other sitcoms and specials into the late 1980s before retiring.

The show faced one odd challenge two months into production when a musicians strike prevented Harry Zimmerman and his orchestra from performing. For a series so dependent on songs, this could have been lethal. The production staff wisely decided to use recorded music where possible, such as with the dancers; use lip syncing when needed, such as with Ella Fitzgerald on the Nov. 18, 1968 show, the first one affected; and hum or sing a capella as a last resort. There was another option: The Nov. 25, 1968 show had the animated opening titles accompanied by sound effects added in post production.

By the start of 1969 the strike ended, and the show resumed its regular activities, including usually beating its new competition of the second hour of movies on NBC and the return of *The Big Valley* on ABC. The latter fared so poorly that ABC ended its four-season run in May 1969, before *The Carol Burnett Show* finishes its rerun cycle. The network replaced it with *The Dick Cavett Show*, trying the talk show host in one of three nighttime slots before moving him to late night in the fall of 1969. Ironically, Carol will be a guest star on his ABC series several times, and he will serve as host of a summer series replacement for *The Carol Burnett Show* in 1976 as well.

All this matters little to Carol's fans, who this season see Carol emerge to applause from stage left in front of a yellow panel background set behind to start the show. She retains Jim Nabors as her opening guest, as she will in future seasons, and brings back a considerable number of stars from 1967-1968, including Tim Conway, whose four guest shots here will cement him as a series favorite—especially his hysterical work in the classic dentist sketch. That will be examined more in depth in the March 3, 1969 episode.

And to answer the question at the outset of this chapter, Ernie Anderson was Tim's on-air partner on TV in Cleveland from 1959-1961. He relocated to Los Angeles by 1967 to work more with Tim, and Carol will introduce him a lot in the audience during Q&A this season. In 1974 Anderson will become the series' announcer, replacing Lyle Waggoner.

Sept. 23, 1968: Jim Nabors, Alice Ghostley

Q&A; "Candidates at Home" profiles a desperate political family with Harvey running for office joined by Carol, his nervous wife and Vicki, their daughter; Jim sings "There's a Kind of Hush" and "To Give (The Reason I Live)"; Roger's possessive sister, Mimi (Alice), brings Carol much grief in "Carol & Sis"; a commercial blackout with Lyle and the dancers; Carol and Jim put the blind in blind date when they remove their glasses beforehand and pretend to have normal vision; members of the Canoga Falls High School graduating class display their questionable talents; the Charwoman explores a photography studio.

Comments: "It's marvelous to be back," Carol greets her audience in this season opener that really clicks. Our hostess is glad to have Alice Ghostley as a guest along with Jim and says she has been a fan of the actress ever since seeing her in the Broadway revue *New Faces of 1952*. The main query interaction comes from Carol saying the secret she uses to develop her fabulous figure is "Silicone. And in all the wrong places!" She brings out Vicki, Lyle and Harvey and notes that the latter broke his toe playing hide and seek plus eighteen rounds of golf. After acknowledging Tim Conway and Ernie Anderson in the audience, Carol compliments the looks of Vicki and Lyle—but not Harvey, yuk yuk. Luckily, there is better scripted comedy ahead.

For "Candidates at Home," Carol and Vicki sport similar poofy hair and bland blue outfits as they along with Harvey strain to connect with voters. To that end, they bring out the family dog and a senior citizen that one assumes is the grandmother who sleeps through most of their pitch. Carol starts by talking how she likes to cook apple pies, tacos, chow mein, lasagna and matzo balls. "In fact, we had all of them tonight," she adds. Vicki pipes in with "I've applied to college in all 50 states!" Don Crichton plays Vicki's fiancé, who makes sure to salute the flag, and best of all, Isabel Sanford is the family's maid who is shocked to hear them call her "sweetheart" and let her sit on the same couch with them. Her amazed reaction to Carol claiming to make her own clothes prompts Carol to quip, "You're a riot," then quickly apologize for implying a connection with the recent uprisings in black neighborhoods. Isabel gets her own good one back when Carol says the maid is like one of the family and Isabel interjects, "Except I sleep in the basement!" Finally, grandma awakens as everyone sings "My Country, 'Tis of Thee" in unison. This is quite a hilarious piece of campaign comedy.

In a curled hairstyle she would laugh at heartily when repeated in the series finale, Carol talks about enjoying her time with Jim on his *Girlfriends and Nabors* special. His takes on two contemporary hits are fine. "Carol & Sis" follows, with Roger's visiting sister treating Carol condescendingly at every turn. Alice is at her animated best here, shining as she implies that the house is dusty while she babies Roger and gives Carol a gift of linen napkins taken from the airplane she rode to get to Los Angeles. "There are two dates I'll never forget—your anniversary and Pearl Harbor!" she snarls. After irritating Carol, Alice leaves, but Chrissy accidentally knocks her out when opening the door. This solid entry surpasses most of the previous season's "Carol & Sis" skits.

After a quick and dated joke about a deodorant commercial, another very good sketch has Carol and Jim letting vanity get the best of both of them as they take off their glasses. That results in them missing and hitting each other, Jim walking over Carol's couch and falling over twice trying to grab her, and Carol struggling to get a cigarette lit, among other things. There is an element of irony present, as Carol is an interior decorator and Jim unintentionally destroys her furniture. Both have their glasses broken but claim they do not need them, then bond by talking and learning what they have in common. Although a little long, this is generally funny and sweet.

Belly laughs are plentiful as Alice does her trademark nervous fidgeting as a principal presenting her dubious graduating class. Lyle gets an award for arithmetic obviously based on his looks. And poor Carol is forced to sing "The Whiffenpoof Song" as a duet while her partner is absent, an event that once happened to Carol in real life. She runs off ashamed and gets applause for her bit. To top it off, the class valedictorian (Jim, in his Gomer Pyle voice) provides a stilted reading of the school's history where presentations meant to illustrate certain events go awry, such as losing the turkey for the Thanksgiving pageant and watching dancers fall. Finally, everyone collapses in the big number at the end, to Alice's chagrin. (Everyone but Harvey, that is, since his toe injury prevented him from participating in this engaging slapstick.) The school's name is an in-joke—Canoga Falls is the same fictional location for "As the Stomach Turns."

The show concludes with the Charwoman imagining herself in pictures as a glamour girl in an empty photography studio before sitting on her bucket to sing "I'm Always Chasing Rainbows," first popularized by Judy Garland. It is a little anticlimactic after all the good humor and energy on display, but it is endurable if not very original.

This assured launch for the show's second season has Isabel Sanford signing the guest book along with Jim and Alice at the end. Strangely, Alice never guest starred on the series again despite her stellar work here, though she did appear in the audience a few times.

Sept. 30, 1968: Carol Channing

Q&A; a presidential candidate (Harvey) informs his weary wife (Carol B.) that she must act alert and happy for his upcoming appearance; Carol C. dresses as a 1920s flapper and performs "Homesick Blues" from *Gentlemen Prefer Blondes*; Roger mistakenly believes he has forgotten his anniversary in "Carol & Sis"; "I Love You, Alfred B. Tomkins" has Harvey as an old man, Carol C. as his nurse and Carol B. as his scheming adopted niece; "What's in the Stars?" combines blackouts centered around celebrities born under the sign of Taurus with a matchmaking finale featuring Carol C., the cast and the dancers.

Comments: The *TV Guide* listing wrongly promoted *Mission: Impossible* stars Barbara Bain and Martin Landau as guests for this installment. In reality, the effervescent Ms. Channing dominates the proceedings so much that it is hard to imagine anyone else with her on the stage. Too bad this is a flawed show. Carol invites her guest out for the Q&A after a couple of interesting conversations, such as whether she ever has butterflies in her stomach ("No," then Carol mock faints onto the floor), if she has a business card ("What business?! No!"), if she is wearing a wig ("I wouldn't buy this" she says of her hair) and if Burnett is her real name (yes, in fact the family had a cowboy relative named Black Bart Burnett). This show is the first time the two Carols worked together professionally, and the hostess praised her guest's personality ("She's an absolute nut!") and looks ("She's got the greatest face. I want to dive into those eyes!"). Channing says she was never nervous doing *Hello, Dolly!* on Broadway, where she made 1,273 performances, and she believes in wearing false eyelashes, as she is doing for tonight's show.

The Q&A ends with the hostess noting that since Channing has the reputation of making every performance no matter how she feels, the cast and crew were surprised she was a no-show earlier in the week. "She was ill Tuesday when we were rehearsing, and she had ptomaine poisoning," the hostess relates. Channing blamed her condition on elk meat she had shipped to consume that defrosted too fast, and she warned Burnett to avoid eating any old elk, advice which Burnett says she observes to this day, with a wink and a smile.

The first skit places Carol B. next to Harvey on a table next to the podium where he is speaking for his campaign. Worn out by the grind, she nods and mouths along to his speech, then falls asleep, prompting Harvey to smack her to keep her awake. Other mischief follows—Carol gets her hand stuck in a glass, leans on the emcee, falls asleep again and so on. This is amusing enough but has no real ending. Better is what follows, as Carol C. rousingly reprises a number she did on Broadway in the 1950s (and as with *Hello, Dolly!* she did not get to appear in the musical's movie version).

The moment slows again with a lesser "Carol & Sis," as Roger arrives home with a golfing buddy (Lyle), discovers a watch with today's date engraved on it and assumes it is an anniversary gift from Carol (it actually is the watch of a friend). This leads Roger to hurriedly surprise Carol with a pearl necklace. Confused by her husband's sudden extravagant gift and indications from him that this is a special day, Carol voices her concerns to Chrissy in the kitchen, and they determine what happened.

Crafty Carol decides to leverage the misunderstanding by telling Roger she needs earrings to go with her new necklace as well. This skit has a premise so familiar and obvious that it garners only sparse laughter during its execution.

Next is a better but not great sketch when nurse Carol C. can tell how Carol B. is trying to milk the fortune of the latter's ill uncle (Harvey). She fakes injecting a shot into Carol B.'s butt to show her exasperation at one point. Never fear—Carol C. is so devoted that when she drops Harvey out of his wheelchair and out through the window, she follows him there to her own death. This at least is brightened by Carol C.'s comic antics.

Carol C. also appears in the salute to Taurus. As Carol B. says at the outset, the zoological sign was chosen as the first one to cover out of twelve possibilities because "It's my sign, and this is my show!" Harvey describes the traits of those born a Taurus and notes one is being stubborn, which leads to Carol playing a bank teller insistent that a robber (Lyle) fill out forms and show identification before he steals money, only to learn that the bank is now closed. Another characteristic is gluttony, leading to Vicki and Carol B. singing an ode to suppertime. Next comes a Taurus Hall of Fame song by Carol noting famous folk born under the sign such as Sigmund Freud (Harvey), Dr. Spock (Harvey), Fred Astaire (Lyle), General Grant (Harvey), Mickey Mouse (an unidentified actor) and William Shakespeare (Harvey). Apart from Lyle forgetting to put on his pants along with his top hat as Astaire, most of the blackouts are mediocre at best. The amusement level does pick up some as we get to Salvador Dali (Don Crichton), who is painting until Carol C. enters and starts singing "Well, hell-o, Dali!" Also, Catherine the Great (Carol B.) shows that she got her nickname by having an enormous pair of breasts.

Carol C. speaks with a whistle about the compatibility of Taureans, which leads into the musical finale of "Matchmaker" from *Fiddler on the Roof* sung by Carol B. and Vicki as they attempt to pair themselves with the men. Vicki has Lyle and Carol has Harvey, but Carol outwits Vicki to get Lyle instead. Vicki goes to Don Crichton instead of Harvey, who dancers with an unbilled female, and all six sing "The Two of Us." The dancers then appear—the men in tuxes with the Taurus sign on their backs, the women in golden gowns—to perform to "Matchmaker," then join the rest of the cast and Carol C. in reprising "The Two of Us" at the end. It is obvious from his moves and facial expressions that Harvey remains in pain while recovering from his broken toe.

As the show closes, Carol is caught behind the beat as she starts to sing "It's Time to Say So Long." It is an apt sign for a show that never quite gets its comic rhythm together.

Oct. 7, 1968: Nanette Fabray, Trini Lopez

Q&A; Carol and Nanette play two nonchalant girls on a bench; Trini sings two numbers and joins Carol to perform "Gonna Get Along Without You Now"; Nanette plays Marian's sister with only six months to live in "As the Stomach Turns"; a potato chip commercial send-up; Nanette mocks opera divas as "special guest Patrice Callas"; Carol is a housewife with no date until a hoodlum (Harvey) arrives and she tries to seduce him, to his surprise; "The Old Wrangler" (Trini) narrates a tale of saloon gals led by Nanette trying to make it in the wild west.

Comments: This up-and-down affair, where segments basically either score quickly or drag slowly, is highlighted by a classic Q&A moment when a woman admits she needs to go to the ladies room and Carol invites her on stage to show her where it is located near the dressing room. She scurries off and returns a few minutes later to a chorus of the audience saying, "We know where you've been!" instigated by Carol. Amid this situation, Carol accepts a present of a doll that resembles herself, denies that she is going to run for political office like Shirley Temple and jokes that her favorite song is "Flight of the Bumblebee." She introduces in the audience actor John Ericson, her kid sister, Chrissy, Lyle's parents (visiting from St. Louis) and Lyle's wife, Sharon. Asked by an aspiring dancer for some career advice, Carol says to practice and gets Don Crichton to contribute—he agrees with Carol and says to study hard. Repeating the question of "How old was I when I had my first date and what did I do?" a slightly flustered Carol says, "That's all the time we have for questions!" and segues to the program's titles.

The Carol-Nanette segment is a strange, spottily paced affair, notably only in that both women act and sound like Lily Tomlin's Edith Ann character before that characterization is popularized. One of its few outstanding lines has Carol saying her family has a French maid who turns on her father. The less said about this, the better for all involved.

Trini, who Carol introduces as a "marvelous entertainer," fares better, wearing a white turtleneck as he strums his guitar and sings "She's Walking Through My Memory" and "Mountain Dew." The dancers accompany Trini with a hoedown for the latter. Carol teams up with him for a lively duet before Trini disappears until near the end of the show.

In "As the Stomach Turns," Nanette tells her sister, Marian, she has contracted malaria from a pile of *National Geographic* magazines at the library and that the terminal disease is contagious after encountering Marian's daughter (and thereby her niece). Marian summons for help from an old doctor (Harvey), who says he finally is going to medical school and that Lyle will replace him. Marian naturally lusts after Lyle, who reveals that Nanette does not have malaria. For her real condition, tune in tomorrow, when Marian will have a brain transplant. This is a satisfactory installment.

In the commercial blackout, Carol offers Harvey a bag of potato chips and says "Bet you can't eat just one!" He chews one chip and dies, whereupon Carol quips, "Guess I was wrong." This bull's-eye bit unfortunately follows Nanette trilling "On the Sunny Side of the Street" whose enjoyment ends far after the two-plus minutes it takes to perform.

After grousing about her lack of male companionship to a friend (Kate Montgomery), Carol pounces on Harvey when he comes to rob her, offering to polish his gun and so on. Appalled by her smothering advances, Harvey demands that a cop (Lyle) arrest him to save himself. Carol learns Lyle is single, so she starts wooing him instead, and the sketch ends pretty much as a waste of time for all involved.

The show recovers in the finale, as Trini whittles while recounting how some ladies came to work at a deserted outpost and found Indian Princess Moon River (Carol), who is so named because like the song, she is wider than a mile. The princess wants to hide for her safety, so Nanette makes her into one of her saloon gals as another Native American (Harvey) looks for her and shows his mean tendencies by whipping out Col. Custer's scalp. "Not true blonds have more fun," he says. The wig gets caught in his crotch, causing some laughter, and Carol hides her face when Harvey ad libs he is looking for someone wearing an 8 1/2—"Shoe, that is." When a medicine man (Lyle) recognizes who the princess is yet rejects her as unfit, she is free to join the dancers in celebration.

While this show has some deficiencies, none can be blamed on its guests' spirited efforts. The series will reprise the Nanette-Trini combo on the March 9, 1970 episode.

Oct. 14, 1968: George Gobel, Bobbie Gentry

** Harvey interviews a duke and duchess (Carol and George) for "V.I.P."; Carol is an average housewife chatting with her black counterpart (Vivian Bonnell) in "The Neighbors"; George and Carol star in an imagination of what television might have been like if it existed in 1776; Bobbie sings "Sweet Peony" and joins George for a duet on "Little Green Apples."

Comments: This show as well as next week's one has a five-minute political ad following its conclusion. For this show, it is for the Democrats—the Republicans get equal time next week. Vivian Bonnell will reappear as Carol's neighbor on the Dec. 2, 1968 episode.

Oct. 21, 1968: Tim Conway, Edie Adams

* A nervous robber (Tim) fumbles his first holdup and a bank teller (Harvey) pities him; Tim and Carol play a Southern governor and his wife who uneasily work on impressing a presidential nominee and his wife (Harvey and Edie) for the Number Two slot on the party ticket; Edie sings a tune; two teachers, one a spinster (Carol) and the other an awkward bachelor (Tim), find they must share a hotel room; Carol and Edie play themselves planning a wedding for their children in the year 1988; Vic ki, Edie, Carol and the dancers present "Those Were the Good Old Days."

Comments: Though Edie appears more throughout the show, this pretty solid entry really allows Tim to shine best. First he fails hilariously in trying to rob Harvey. He blows delivering his demands and has to give Harvey the written statement he used for rehearsal to explain his motives. Tim says he has no set amount of money he wants and confesses he left his gun on the bus because his wife's family is visiting and needed the getaway car. Harvey knows he is dealing with an amateur and puts no dollars in Tim's bag. This upsets Tim, who cries about how Harvey is teasing him on his first robbery attempt, leading Harvey to apologize in a good round of comic dialogue interrupted by a call from Tim's wife, complaining about problems with their car. Discouraged about the proceedings, Tim takes solace in Harvey suggesting that he come back tomorrow to steal—but not before Tim deposits $10 for his wife to join the bank's Christmas club.

After Edie sings, Harvey and his wife with a forced smile (Edie) take a break from campaigning to interview an overfed Southern governor (Tim) and his blowsy wife (Carol) for their worthiness as running mates for the White House. Harvey's maid (Isabel Sanford) disdains the governor's racist reputation and crushes Tim's hat when he gives it to her. Tim does himself no favors by seeing a painting of Gainsborough's "Blue Boy" and asking if this depicted one of Harvey's "hippie" sons, as well as admitting that he belongs to the KKK, but insists it is only the South's take on the AAA for car trouble. Meanwhile, Carol asks for orange juice and pulls out a flask to add liquor and give it some kick. Displeased by what he witnesses, Harvey tells the couple he has dropped them from consideration. As they leave, Isabel gives Tim his crushed hat and tells Harvey he is making a mistake. Harvey asks why, and Isabel says she wants him to lose and he would have done so with Tim on the ticket. This political skit crackles.

Carol and Tim played stumbling potential lovers on the March 18, 1968 show and do the same this time, meeting each other during confusion of booking rooms for a convention due to their characters having the same last name. Carol checks in first and goes to the bathroom while Tim enters and prepares himself for about a half-minute before they both scream and realize their predicament. Since the hotel is booked, they nervously agree to share the room, but Tim is uncomfortable trying to sleep on two chairs, and a phone call by his mother that forces Carol to pretend to be a male roommate does not help matters either. To get their minds off their situation, they try to watch TV, but the only options are the movies *It Happened One Night* and *Sex and the Single Girl*. The two gradually become turned on as they look for other activities to pursue when a bellhop tells Tim there is a room opening for him. A horny Carol informs Tim she will follow him to his room to watch a movie. This is sweet and cute.

The concluding sketch is the oddest one, with Carol and Edie making references to their actual daughter and son (Erin Hamilton and Joshua Adams, respectively) being married now, twenty years in the future. Edie wants an extravagant ceremony with hundreds of guests and worries that Carol will dress as the Charwoman, while Carol shoots back about how it takes gumption from the woman playing Muriel the fine cigar lady in commercials to fret about her appearance. Both plan to join their children on the honeymoon before agreeing that the important thing now is to make Erin and Joshua happy, without worrying about the cost of the wedding. They then argue about the cost of their desserts at a restaurant. Bizarre and a little unsettling in imagining the two women considering their kids as potential mates before they are adolescents, this is a so-so way to lead into the finale.

Incidentally, Carol beat Edie Adams for an Emmy two years consecutively (1963 and 1964) for performance in a variety or musical program or series. It is a nice, classy move to have her on the series, even if just for this one time. For additional information on the rerun of this episode, see the Final Notes for the Season at the end of this chapter.

Oct. 28, 1968: Pre-empted by a special NFL football game

Nov. 4, 1968: Lucille Ball, Eddie Albert, Nancy Wilson

Q&A; a segment with "The Old Folks" culminating in a number about showing love while your body matures; Nancy sings "The Folks Who Live on a Hill"; "Carol & Sis" has Carol and Roger worried because Roger's visiting new boss (Eddie) is obsessed with his employees being fit and they are out of shape; Eddie sings "The Father of Girls"; "As the Stomach Turns" has Lucy and Carol returning from a funeral to encounter a widower (Eddie) and "The first Negro we've had in Canoga Falls" (Nancy); and a finale honoring celebrities born under the sign of Leo.

Commentary: Of Carol's four shows with Lucille Ball, this presents her comic idol at her most consistently funny and glamorous, even though Lucille does relatively little compared to Eddie and Nancy. She shines when she does appear, and it is telling about their relationship and her esteemed TV status when Carol introduces her in the Q&A simply as Lucy and bows down when she joins her for a few audience inquiries. One girl asks if Lucy can do a Tarzan yell like Carol, and Lucy cracks, "I'm lucky to talk!" As with the tapings at her own sitcoms, Lucy's mother is in the studio audience, and she stands up. Lucy acknowledges that the light blue Rolls Royce parked outside is hers and says that she worried needlessly about her children working with her on *Here's Lucy*, as they are loving the work. The two end with a great bit of repartee when Ball inquires about one potential guest, "Did you get Dean [Martin] this season?" and Carol shoots back, "I've never had Dean any season!"

Prior to Lucy's appearance in the Q&A, Carol tells audience members there are no plans to have Richard Burton as a guest, that she has known Don Crichton since they worked together on *The Garry Moore Show*, and that the Mickey Mouse watch she is wearing is a vintage gift she received earlier in the year from Soupy Sales (see March 25, 1968). Ernie Anderson is introduced in the audience again, as well as Peggy Lennon of the Lennon Sisters with her son and daughter. This is a busy Q&A indeed.

Apart from a semi-song with a few cracks like "How do you expect to get sparks when the flint's gone," the humorous meditation on the challenges of loving as a senior citizen by "The Old Folks" is rather unremarkable. The same can be said about Nancy and Eddie's songs, but they are broken up by one of the better "Carol & Sis" segments. Showing off impressive flexibility at age 62, Eddie jogs with his knees high in the air as he enters Carol and Roger's apartment, while the couple attempt to show they are as committed to exercise as he is. As misfortunate would have it, Carol's back goes out, forcing her into doing some solid physical shtick. Harvey participates in great slapstick as well when he crushes his hand hitting Eddie's rock-hard stomach. The sketch ends with Carol being hit by Roger at the door while she is bent over in pain.

Even better is "As the Stomach Turns," which oddly has Harvey rather than Lyle as its narrator. Lucy and Carol come back unimpressed from a funeral (Lucy: "There was no place to dance") and adopt perfect cardboard serious faces as they mock many conventional soap opera devices—Carol announcing a call before the phone rings, tells Lucy to sit down when the latter is already seated, etc. After Vicki does her part as Carol's daughter, returning with a baby after flunking out of the convent, Eddie arrives and announces, "I'm just passing through." "Why don't you stay here?" Carol says. "OK," he nonchalantly answers. Next, Nancy claims to have come to integrate the town. Learning that Nancy also lost her husband, Carol quips, "Oh, a black widow." Nancy gets in a good one as well, telling Eddie that he is a credit to his race before he suddenly dies. Lucy was going to wed Eddie but forgets that when Lyle arrives, only for the episode ending with one of the questions being whether Lyle would be fathering Lucy's baby, prompting considerable laughter.

Nancy and Carol launch the salute to famous Leos by singing "The Other Man's Grass is Always Greener" before a series of blackouts, the best one being Lyle as Henry Ford. "I'm going into mass production," he says, to which a pregnant Carol responds, "Count me out." A montage of other Leos leads into Vicki playing a hippie minstrel introducing Nancy as Cleopatra, Eddie as Marc Anthony, Carol as Queen Elizabeth I with Harvey as her husband, and Lucy as Russia's Catherine the Great. Wearing a stunning white outfit, Lucy shows off strong dance moves as the mini-musical closes the show.

Carol said in Nancy's solo introduction that she hoped to have back on the show, and that does happen, along with Lucy in separate episodes. This marks Eddie's last time on the show, however.

Nov. 11, 1968: Don Rickles, Nanette Fabray, Mel Torme

Q&A; Carol and Nanette playing two expecting women trying to impress Lyle, a hunky doctor's assistant; Mel sings "Take a Letter Miss Jones"; Don is a beleaguered shoe salesman who must be nice to a haughty customer (Nanette) in order to impress his demanding boss (Harvey); and a two-act musical comedy has Don as Harry Familiar, a music promoter on Tin Pan Alley in 1910 who narrates the story of two aspiring songwriters (Carol and Mel) who encounter various successes and failures amid their efforts with a big star (Nanette) and Broadway impresario Ziggy Flofeld (Harvey).

Comments: Vicki is absent here, perhaps due to the overwhelming presence of Don Rickles, who dominates pretty much every scene he is in, including the Q&A. After pointing out Ernie Anderson in the audience, Carol brings out "Mr. Warmth himself," as she describes him, and notes that he was recently voted one of the three best-dressed men in Hollywood along with Frank Sinatra and Don Adams. Despite this shared accolade with two close friends, Don is ready to pounce when Carol introduces Lyle as a man she thought should have made the list as well. "I'm fed up with you, Lyle," Don says amid chuckles from his subject and Carol. "I mean that. You've got a perfect body, but I've seen you in the shower and the soap walked away." That crack leaves everyone in hysterics. Don has more to say about Lyle ("Who does your hair, Geronimo?"), and an audience member who makes the mistake of revealing he was from Norway prompts Don to respond, "Let me see your papers!" Sensing that perhaps she was losing control of the show, Carol ends the segment by blurting out "Don't go away, we'll be right back!"

The first sketch is not much more than its description, with Harvey shuffling in and out as 92-year-old Dr. Zaslow while Carol and Nanette vie for hunky Lyle's attention. The song by Mel, who Carol calls "charming, sweet," is similarly mild, although the scenario of him playing an executive with graphs and charts behind him is at least visually appealing.

What really revs up the show is Don grousing about having to fit a small shoe on a stout customer ("She couldn't get a 4 1/2 on her big toe!") before his effeminate boss (Harvey) upbraids him for losing business and tells him he has to make a sale with their next client. That turns out to be Nanette, whose comments such as how she was getting a glare from Don's bald pate riles him as he tries to stay calm and placate her. As typical for Don on variety shows, he ad libs frequently here, which only adds to the humor as he melts down against Nanette. The best part is when he blows his line and tells Nanette, "You got me so upset, you got my gums locked!" Nanette leaves in a huff and Harvey fires Don as he calls the latter a savage, which prompts Don to respond, "Where does it say his line says, 'Savage?'" More spontaneous insults generate chuckling from Harvey as the sketch ends.

The rest of the show keeps Don more in check following the script for the two-part musical spoof, as he rejects the solo efforts of songwriters Carol and Mel but loves their collaboration. The latter duo's partnership goes awry as Nanette has the hots for Mel and recruits him to help her while leaving Carol by the wayside. In Act Two, nightclub emcee Lyle introduces Nanette singing songs she claims only Mel wrote while Carol gets drunk. But when Carol gets an opportunity to sing, she becomes the toast of the town, while Mel struggles on a new musical without her help. She loves him, but her commitment to Harvey and Don is more important to her career. Mel's downward spiral continues, and at the end, he comes up to the group as a beggar. In a refreshing, amusing avoidance of sentimentality, Carol looks at Mel's face, says "No, it's not him" and the group leaves.

Don will return to this series one more time, oddly with Mel again—see Dec. 7, 1970.

Nov. 18, 1968: Sid Caesar, Ella Fitzgerald

Q&A; F. Lee Korman interviews two Japanese film stars (Sid and Carol) in "V.I.P."; Ella sings "Day In—Day Out" and "Skylark"; Roger dresses in drag to perform at a PTA show with his wife and sister-in-law in "Carol & Sis"; the dancers perform a 1920s jazz number; "Classic Movie Theater" presents a send-up of *Mrs. Miniver* with Carol as the title character, Harvey as her son and Sid as her husband; Carol lip syncs to her recording of "The Trolley Song" while her director speeds up and slows it down randomly; Carol and Ella duet.

Comments: This show has moments of great amusement, but sadly few involve Sid, who is mostly wasted as he has been in previous visits. He does shine in the Q&A, doing impressions of planes in World War movies and spy films, following a rather lengthy Q&A between Carol and her audience. Asked whether she prefers kissing Lyle or Harvey, she smartly replies "Yes!" to both. A girl presents her with a gift in a brown paper bag (not alcohol) before some strange queries emerge about whether Carol will make a movie with Lyle, bring back Fanny Brice's Baby Snooks character on her show or is related to Spiro Agnew. The answer is no to all. For what she thought of the presidential election results, Carol quips, "I wanted Pat Paulsen" to applause. She draws laughs when she claims that she has signed to play the lead in a movie about Sophia Loren. Lyle pops up as a topic too—a woman says she wants him for her birthday and her husband approved the idea, while someone else wonders if Lyle's wife has given birth yet. A man finds Carol very sexy and wants to know when she will wear a mini dress, and the answer is on this show during the "Carol & Sis" segment. She also points out that Ernie Anderson and the "talented, wonderful" Ross Martin are in the audience.

Carol also cautions everyone about the effects of the musicians strike at the outset. "So tonight, it's going to sound strange, because we're humming a lot," she says. Indeed, after Carol hums her theme to her opening titles, Harvey hilariously does the same for the usual musical accompaniment at the top of "V.I.P." This segment disappointingly uses some dated, unfunny humor about Japanese pronunciations (Carol does "On the Good Ship Lollipop" with the L's in it replaced with R's, for example), and Carol and Sid's efforts to look ethnic worsen matters. Some bits do work, such as Carol ordering a drink from Lyle, her house servant, saying "Saki to me!" in reference to the popular "Sock it to me!" catch phrase on *Laugh-In*. And Carol's behavior bothers Sid so much that he commits hari kari to avoid more of it. When one of your biggest laughs comes from a mock suicide, though, you know a sketch is in trouble.

"The fabulous Ella Fitzgerald," as Carol introduces her, unfortunately must lip sync to two numbers due to the strike, but does so effortlessly. Recorded music also figures into "Carol & Sis," where Roger dresses up at his office in the same outfit with Carol and Chrissy in a wig, silver earrings, a sparkling necklace, a black dress, stockings and high heels for a PTA charity benefit. He thinks doing it late at night will allow him to avoid any problems, but he failed to count out a cleaning lady (Isabel Sanford) who arrives, witnesses the getup and state, "I got a cousin like you. It didn't work out though, he got drafted anyway!" Compounding matters, Roger's new partner (Dick Patterson) appears and insists on treating Roger like a lady by lighting a cigarette for him and so on. Isabel and Dick finally tell an embarrassed Roger that they knew about his predicament from Carol and Chrissy talking to them about it on the elevator. The two women join Roger to run though a lip sync of the Andrews Sisters' 1938 hit "Bei Mir Bist Du Schoen." Afterward, Carol breaks out of character to have Harvey take a special bow, during which Lyle presents the actor with flowers and kisses him to everyone's delight.

Following a dance number is an uninspired parody where Carol does a Tarzan yell to introduce Metro-Goldwyn-Mouth's "Mrs. Magnificent," starring her as a London lass cheerfully cleaning up her house despite explosions near and inside it from Germans during World War II. She focuses her flowers and ignores her son (Harvey) as he goes to the front line, as well as her husband (Sid), who wants to leave immediately. When one bomb lands on their dining table, Carol insists upon eating. Her obliviousness troubles Sid, who takes action and removes it so that it detonates outsides instead. All the while, Carol is more concerned about how her mums are growing. This so-so spoof never ignites humorously the way the explosives in it do.

There is great laughter when Carol lip syncs to her 1960 recording of "The Trolley Song" while director Dave Powers instructs his team to adjust its tempo from frenetic to plodding. Carol's facial and body reactions to the changes are priceless, and it ingeniously ends with the last line cut out to throw Carol off before it is finally played.

After singing with Ella, Carol is joined by Harvey playing a harmonica to get on pitch and sing "It's Time to Say So Long" rather speedily. Isabel Sanford and Dick Patterson sign the guest book along with Sid and Ella to conclude this bumpy outing.

Nov. 25, 1968: Garry Moore, Durward Kirby

Q&A; "The Old Folks" get a visit from two old gossiping biddies (Garry and Durward); Vicki and Lyle play guitars and sing "Call Me" as a duet; Garry practices taping a toast with a princess (Carol), who becomes plastered due to constant retakes; a review of the progressive trend on television includes spoofs of *Blondie*, *Julia* and *Supermarket Sweep*; the president of the United Safety Committee (Durward) dictates tips for an article to his secretary (Carol), who ends up being injured unintentionally during their session; Don Crichton leads a dance number based on "Give My Regards to Broadway."

Comments: Garry and Durward are much better here than their appearance on Feb. 12, 1968, as there is more humor that reflects Carol's series rather than trying to be a revival of *The Garry Moore Show*. Introducing them as just "Durward and Garry," Carol intriguingly says what people write in her guest book at the end of the show is "Usually their names, but then there's Martha Raye." Asked if she has always been as beautiful as she is now, Carol jests that "At one time, I was very plain." Regarding when she graduated from UCLA, she interjects, "That's all the time we have!" She does point out her sister, Chrissy, and Ernie Anderson in the audience and gets in a few more zingers. Carol turns down the idea of entering politics "since Pat Paulsen lost," says her plastic surgeon is Phyllis Diller and adds "I'd love to have Julie Andrews on the show, but she's not that talented." However, Carol does crack up when someone asks when she will have Tiny Tim of "Tiptoe Thru the Tulips" fame on as a guest (she never does). She also brings out Garry and Durward for a few questions, including Garry saying he will never do another variety show but Durward saying he would consider it (he never gets one).

"The Old Folks" is pretty spry this time, starting with Molly sitting down and asking Bert if it reminds him of famed stripper Gypsy Rose Lee and he responding it is more like Gen. Robert E. Lee. They are joined by two old ladies (Garry and Durward), who before taking a drink toast it by saying "Tippecanoe and Tyler too!" The amusing line appeared before in the April 15, 1968 show where Carol and Minnie Pearl made the remark in a skit set in Paris. Anyway, with jokes about Garry claiming to be on the pill and Molly thinking Bert is making moves on Durward, this is generally funny, helped by Durward and Garry reprising their old lady characters they had been doing since the 1950s.

Vicki and Lyle's acoustic take on a 1966 Chris Montez hit is a nice, effective diversion before Carol's drunk routine. She is a princess who must record her toast for another dignitary in advance of the event due to her schedule with Garry introducing her. However, the director (Harvey) is dissatisfied with the initial takes and has her redo them, requiring Carol to take a swig each time. There are some twists to the tipsy scenario that make this fun. The bit is a remake from *The Garry Moore Show* on Oct. 10, 1961.

Garry shows up again to host a segment on how TV in 1968 is becoming more diverse, starting with Isabel Sanford playing a black Blondie and Carol as a Native American Julia. This leads into "Shoplift," a game show send-up wherein the host (Harvey) presides over two contestants (Carol and Durward) competing to steal as many items as possible from a store. Carol looks like she might be the winner, but Durward tops her by brandishing a gun and robbing her of what she has already purloined. This is a dandy.

The final sketch has laughs too, but it is more strained. Once it is established that Durward is a safety expert, it follows that Carol will be injured, and of course she is burned in the hand by his cigarette, hit in the head twice by a tray and so on. It culminates with Durward opening a door and knocking Carol out the window. While well handled by Durward and Carol, the setup is predictable and more stale than clever. This is a remake of a sketch Carol and Durward did on *The Garry Moore Show* on June 27, 1961.

Noting that Don Crichton is a featured dancer in Julie Andrews' new movie *Star!* Carol shows a clip of his work from the film before he begins his spotlight number as an aging performer looking back at his glory years. Starting off as a solo, Don's routine becomes a duo with Vicki followed by the other dancers joining them. Crichton is fine, but it is a rather solemn ending to what had been a fairly spirited show.

As with the preceding program, Harvey blows an instrument to put Carol on pitch to sing "It's Time to Say So Long." Garry and Durward will return again on Dec. 15, 1969.

Dec. 2, 1968: Michele Lee, Flip Wilson

Q&A; Harvey interviews retired sex symbol Mae East (Carol) in "V.I.P."; Flip performs a comic monologue; Michele sings "Knowing When to Leave" and "Laugh Clown Laugh"; "The Neighbors" has Carol gossiping through the window of her corner apartment to Vivian Bonnell, followed by their husbands (Harvey and Flip) doing the same; Carol finds herself overshadowed by Michele's beauty in "The Roommates"; Harvey serenades Carol, playing a homely wife; a spoof of *In the Heat of the Night*; Vicki, Carol and Michele sing "Do You Know the Way to San Jose?" before joined by the dancers interpreting "The Mexican Shuffle."

Comments: This is a very 1968 episode, to its benefit and detriment. After joking that Kate Smith is her favorite rock group and introducing Ernie Anderson in the audience, Carol brings out Lyle to show pictures of his baby born Nov. 20. She surprises him with a $1,000 savings bond as a gift. Next, Flip wears a Nehru jacket and joins Carol in answering odd audience questions. Asked if his wife is in show business, he says he is not married, yet someone after that asks about his children! Carol compliments him on looking good, while Flip quips that the show will be seen in living color, to Carol's laughter (and as the first of several indications of what year this show is produced).

In a dazzling silver and gold outfit, Carol is a buxom Mae West parody dropping lots of sex and breast jokes talking to Harvey. Claiming she was well developed at the age of 5, she comments that "Every time I turned around, I erased the blackboard." Age gags appear too—she says she did a movie with Ulysses S. Grant. Before the skit ends, her "adopted son" (Lyle) flexes his muscles and escorts her offstage. This is pretty enjoyable.

Calling him "one of the brightest comedic talents to come down the pike in a long, long time," Carol introduces Flip, who provides an acceptable but not outstanding routine encompassing little old ladies, a talking horse and a boy complaining about his breakfast cereal. He does employ his Geraldine voice effectively as part of his monologue.

Next up, Carol describes Michele Lee as a "very lovely, very talented" woman from the movie version of *How to Succeed in Business Without Really Trying* that she hopes will be back on her show (and she will, for three other times). This show marks Michele and Carol's initial meeting, according to Michele. Looking stunning in a red dress, Michele powerfully lip syncs her two tunes—the musicians strike is still in effect.

In "The Neighbors," Carol and Vivian Bonnell exchange some jokes based on race and obesity before Harvey and Flip assume their positions in a dialogue that reflects the time but seem dated and questionable in retrospect. Smoking a cigarette, Flip grouses about how Vivian domineers over him by saying, "I've been overcome twice!" Harvey sympathizes with Flip's situation and notes that he works like a slave before apologizing. He also slips in asking how Flip's "clan" is doing—Flip reacts as if Harvey meant the Ku Klux Klan. If one overlooks the sometimes politically correct humor, this is an OK bit.

Much funnier is Michele playing Carol's roommate who is so sexy she steals all of the latter's boyfriends. Carol tries to prevent this from happening with Harvey, who speaks with a Brooklyn dialect, by making Michele change from a bikini that shows off her stunning figure before he arrives. But Michele emerges in a nightie that arouses Harvey, as does a yellow towel she wears next. Once Michele comes out in a red gown, Carol waves a white flag and allows Harvey to go out with her to the movies instead.

What follows next is a moving moment of Carol exposing her character's emotions. As Michele recalls, "Carol sang 'Wait Till the Sun Shines Nellie' as the door closes. It was so wonderful, I gave her a hug [backstage afterward] and told her it was incredible. She could hardly say thank you, but she knew. She knew. She always just went for it." The skit ends with Carol saying she hopes her prospective new roommate will be more compatible, and it looks like she will—Carol opens the door, and out comes Phyllis Diller! Carol has the comedienne take a bow after her surprise cameo.

Even more hilarious is Harvey crooning "The More I See You" to a slovenly Carol, replete with messy hair in curlers and dingy clothes. As she prepares to go to bed by smearing on goops of cream and popping open a beer, Harvey intensely vocalizes and demonstrates his love for the beauty he sees in her, even dancing a jig. After getting into her dusty bed and using nasal spray, Harvey kisses her and says, "Good night, sweet princess," to her continuing general disinterest. This is a howl from start to finish.

There are laughs too in the following bit, but it is more problematic. Lyle is a dumb cop in the South who arrests Carol for speeding and she pleads for him to frisk her as a result, but instead he turns her over to his boss, a redneck sheriff (Harvey, in a splendid approximation of Rod Steiger's drawl from *In the Heat of the Night*). The sheriff acts as the only judge and lawyer in the town, posing a problem for Carol until Flip arrives in a space suit. He claims he has magic power that can rectify racial injustices whenever he says "Ray Charles!" Flip proves this at the end when Harvey walks off stage and comes back in blackface. This dated ending caps off a moderately amusing skit.

Ethnic insensitivity unfortunately continues in the contemporary finale, where Vicki finally appears with Carol and Michelle doing Dionne Warwick's recent hit. That itself is fine, but doing it while riding in a golf cart with sombreros and other items strapped on top is demeaning to Mexicans, and the dancers wearing ponchos to move to Herb Alpert's instrumental hit only contribute more to a condescending tone.

In the closing, an offstage vocal chorus provides "ooos" that act as solid accompaniment for Carol as she does "It's Time to Say So Long." Vivian Bonnell comes out for the bows to join the others. She, Flip and Michele will return to the show in the next three years.

Dec. 9, 1968: Vic Damone, Imogene Coca

** In order to obtain a "family" rate for a flight, Carol and Imogene pretend to be husband and wife; "The Old Folks" have a discussion after dinner; Imogene and Carol are operators of a diner beset by a motorcycle gang played by Harvey and the dancers; the entire cast participates in a series of commercials for taboo subjects; Vic sings "If You Are But a Dream" and "Time After Time" and joins Carol to perform a medley of classic pop tunes.

Comments: It's hard to judge without seeing the episode whether Vic Damone's medley with Carol included any of his own hits such as "You're Breaking My Heart," "My Heart Cries for You" and "On the Street Where You Live." In any event, this marks his sole time on the series and the second of three for Imogene. For her last one, see the April 7, 1969 entry.

Sharp-eyed viewers by this point may have recognized blond Randy Doney among the male dancers who was a carryover from Carol's days on *The Garry Moore Show*. He danced on that series for three years in the early 1960s under choreographer Ernie Flatt, who asked Randy to join *The Carol Burnett Show* even though he was under contract since 1966 to work in Mitzi Gaynor's stage show. That led to an unusual agreement.

"Ernie would always leave a spot for me while I did Mitzi Gaynor's show for a week or two," Doney says. That flexibility occurred due to Flatt's high respect for Doney's talent, which led to the latter staying with the series all eleven years, including the last two as assistant choreographer as well as dancer. He thoroughly enjoyed the work and vividly appreciated the opportunity to dance with Lucille Ball, Shirley MacLaine, Gwen Verdon and Bernadette Peters in particular on the series.

"Carol's the greatest of all time," Doney says. "Fabulous to work with. If you were a new dancer or just new to the show, she'd say hi."

Dec. 16, 1968: Marilyn Horne, Eileen Farrell

Q&A; members of the new First Family (Carol, Harvey and Vicki) appear with their reluctant maid (Isabel Sanford) in their first fireside chat to the nation; Eileen sings "Kiss Him Now" with the dancers; awkward interviewer Charlene Fusco (Carol) interviews matinee idol Hugh Handsome (Lyle); Marilyn presents "The Page's Aria" from Mayerber's *Les Huguenots*; Marilyn, Eileen and Carol plays the Three Little Pigs to Harvey's Big Bad Wolf in an operatic adaptation of the tale; Carol, Marilyn and Eileen sing "Big Spender" from the musical *Sweet Charity*; the ensemble including Isabel Sanford perform a medley of Christmas carols.

Comments: Even if you hate opera, this is a very engaging show starting with the lively Q&A. After calling divas Eileen and Carol earthy as well as talented, Carol gets a big Christmas card delivered in person by the mother of a friend depicting "A Christmas Carol" inside with a drawing of the Charwoman. The lady is from Chicago, and Carol grudgingly and amusingly says, "Give Mayor Daley my best." (Daley attracted criticism from the way his police beat demonstrators during the 1968 Democratic national convention in the Windy City.) A man from Finland also gives her a gift. Joining Ernie Anderson being recognized in the audience is a physician. Vicki's stint entertaining the troops in Vietnam last summer gets a mention too. A child guesses Carol has been in show business "a long time," and when she says her teeth are so shiny because she brushes six or seven times a day, cameraman Pat Kenny breaks out in a slow clap to audience laughter. She also tells the audience to "Uncross your legs" for some reason at one point, which produces hearty, embarrassed chuckles for her and everyone else.

Richard Nixon and his family found themselves mocked though not by name in the first sketch as the president-elect (Harvey) and his wife (Carol) nervously greet the American public on TV from their home. The youngest daughter (Vicki) is embroidering an American seal and wearing a wedding gown in anticipation of marrying the grandson of a famous president (Don Crichton). The parents essentially pimp out their eldest daughter (an unidentified actress) to get married, and then bring out their maid (Isabel Sanford), who reads from cue cards how happy she is. When Harvey claims she's just one of the family, she blurts, "Then how come you always lock up the liquor?!" They end by singing "Getting to Know You," while the maid grunts, "Doo dah!" This bit of political satire stings without biting too much and is enjoyable overall.

Carol mentions how she knows Eileen from the latter being a frequent guest on *The Garry Moore Show* (Eileen even played a Charwoman along with Carol once on that series) before she performs in front of the dancers clad in tuxes and yellow gowns. Although Eileen sings like a Broadway belter, it's still a pretty stuffy presentation.

The show improves with Carol as a reporter who meets a man ranked as the number one through nine most unbelievably attractive man in the world via his effeminate butler (Harvey). Lyle is so handsome that when he arrives, Harvey quips, "I'm getting a bit woozy myself!" and leaves. Carol constantly faints as she learns more provocative things about Lyle, including a nude statue that he posed for personally, and she finally goes unconscious seeing his bronzed loincloth and is dismissed from the apartment. Lyle goes behind a panel and gives Harvey his elevator shoes, smoking jacket, padding, hairpiece and girdle so he can be himself—and out emerges Bob Hope! The comedian thanks Carol for having appeared on his first special this season while she appreciates him making this cameo before his Christmas tour of Vietnam. He compliments Carol on this sketch and promotes his upcoming show on NBC in three days before adding, "And uncross your legs!" to audience hysteria.

Carol says Jim Nabors introduced her to Marilyn Horne, "my new best friend," and the latter does a good job in her aria. For those who prefer opera with a comic twist, Milton Crass (Lyle) next offers "El Trios Piccolo Piggos," Italian for "The Three Little Pigs," with a boy pretending to be a conductor at the lip of the stage. Carol criticizes her fellow sows (Marilyn and Eileen) for downplaying the threat of the wolf (Harvey). He blows down Marilyn's straw house and does the same at Eileen's wood one before they go to Carol's brick house (and a stagehand can be seen briefly on the right). They defeat the wolf and celebrate by singing, with Eileen and Marilyn's high notes at the end managing to cause the brick house to collapse. This has it all—great sets, staging, music and clever lyrics that are actually funny rather than cute, as can happen sometimes in these bits on the show. Buz Kohan and Bill Angelos wrote this along with Artie Malvin, and Kohan considers it one of their best contributions to the series ever.

For "Big Spender," Carol, Eileen and Marilyn vibrantly sing the tune in long black gowns with umbrellas. The choreography was a little shaky, however. Dancer Stan Mazin recalls that Eileen's talents as a singer did not extend to footwork on this show. "Eileen Farrell, if you told her to take three steps, she would end up on the wrong foot," he says. Indeed, she is off the movements in several places. There will be more on this number shortly.

Buz Kohan, Bill Angelos and Artie Malvin put together the moving finale. It starts with "What Child Is This?" and Carol saying there will be toys donated to several charities cited on screen for Christmas celebrations. Everyone then stands or sits on stage to sing (or pretend to sing) "Here We Come A-Caroling," "Good King Wenceslas," "God Rest Ye Merry Gentlemen" and "Angels We Have Heard on High." And in place of "It's Time to Say So Long," the ensemble does "We Wish You a Merry Christmas." One assumes Eileen and Marilyn signed Carol's guest book offstage in favor of this segment, which is inspirational to all but the most coldhearted.

Eileen says in her memoirs that one of Marilyn's contact lenses dislocated itself briefly and disoriented her temporarily during "Big Spender," and because she wanted a reshoot that Joe Hamilton insisted could not happen with the show's schedule and budget, that argument ended the chance of another show with all three ladies. The fact is that any supposed problems did not show up, and they did reunite on the show one more time—see March 22, 1971.

Dec. 23, 1968: Rerun of Sept. 30, 1968 show

Dec. 30, 1968: Mickey Rooney, Nancy Wilson

** Carol is an outgoing First Lady reluctantly providing a tour of the White House to her successor; Nancy and Carol get their parts confused during an audition; Mickey leads a spoof of his 1938 movie *Boys Town* along with Harvey, Lyle and Carol; Carol sings "The Twelve Days After Christmas"; Nancy presents "The Man That Got Away" and "For Once in My Life"; Mickey performs "Cycles" and joins Nancy and Carol in offering "Hard-Lovin' Loser."

Comments: This episode reportedly includes appearances by Emmaline Henry and Roland Winters along with Mickey Rooney's second and last guest shot. Without it being circulation as of this writing, the claim cannot be confirmed.

"The Twelve Days After Christmas" is a novelty song Carol performs with a pianist in the manner of "I Made a Fool of Myself Over John Foster Dulles." Wearing a green gown, she recounts how on the first day how she cut down the pear tree and shot the partridge, used rubber gloves to wring the necks of the turtles on day two and made chicken soup out of the three French hens the following day. After revelations that the five golden rings were fake, the six geese stopped laying eggs and the seven swans drowned, Carol informs us by the eighth day she had bundled up all the remaining presents (except one of the twelve drummers drumming) and sent them back to her lover, telling him the gifts were for the birds. This is a cute number delivered winningly.

Jan. 6, 1969: Tim Conway

Q&A; Carol interviews fried chicken franchise owner Col. Flanders (Harvey) in "V.I.P."; a nervous Tim asks Carol for help as he attempts to do a standup routine; Chris is out late on a date to Carol's consternation and Roger's indifference in "Carol & Sis"; Vicki performs "American Boys" with the dancers; Tim and Carol are a prospective bride and groom trying to save money by painting their apartment; a burlesque house tribute narrated by Lyle features Harvey as the emcee, Tim as a bumbling magician, a comic dialogue between Carol and Vicki, and a star turn by Carol with Harvey.

Comments: It is a mark of Tim's talents that this episode makes him the series' first solo guest outside of Jim Nabors and Carol Channing earlier this season on Sept. 30, 1968. This will not happen again until Feb. 17, 1973. Tellingly, Carol describes this program at the outset "kind of a family show," underlining Tim's already exalted status on her series. In the Q&A, Carol denies having a nose job and knitting her skirt before Lyle hugs a girl who turns out to be his younger sister. A woman says loves watching Carol on Wednesday nights, prompting audience laughter since the show airs Mondays and causing Carol to pretend to be upset and say "Get her out of here!" Carol also laughs when someone inquires if she gets tired of being a sex symbol. Tim comes out and shows a great rapport with Carol in the segment. "My original name is Betty," he tells everyone, then introduces his wife, mother and mother-in-law in the audience. Carol reveals Tim's wife just had a baby, and Tim interjects, "Oh my Lord, I didn't know that!" He quips that they will name him Encyclical, as he is their fifth child. This is an excellent Q&A.

The segments without Tim on this show are no more than passable. Harvey provides an excellent send-up of Col. Sanders of Kentucky Fried Chicken fame, but he has few truly funny lines to deliver in "V.I.P." The "Carol & Sis" skit is an obvious, somewhat tiresome protracted bit with Carol obsessed about her sister's possible deflowering which of course does not happen during a date, although Chris does suggest she and her boyfriend will move in with Carol and Roger when they wed. Vicki's vocalizing and dancing with Ernie Flatt's troupe is similarly unexceptional.

However, Tim sparkles first as he confesses to Carol he is worried how the audience will react to his first standup routine, so she tells everyone to be quiet. Tim faces the wall rather than the audience, then remains so shy that Carol sends him offstage with a mike to deliver his jokes, which leaves him to call her to ask how they are received. Carol finally forces him to come back on stage, where he compromises by just doing the movements to "Strangers in the Night." As the orchestra plays the number, Tim mocks the way Frank Sinatra typically cocked his hat and held his coat. This was a winner.

Even better is his interaction with Carol in accidentally cutting her finger and causing other damage to her as they try to save money for their wedding by painting on their own. This is expertly played slapstick, albeit a little extended. The same note pretty much applies to the knockabout finale.

At the end, Carol promotes the repeat that will air next week, apparently a first for the show. After a week off, she and her crew return along with Tim, making him the first guest to be seen in consecutive first-run episodes, another distinction in his cap.

Jan. 13, 1969: Rerun of Nov. 11, 1968 show

Jan. 20, 1969: Tim Conway, Perry Como

Q&A; Tim is a prison warden called out from a party to quell an uprising convicts who discusses and implements ineffective solutions, with Harvey as his devoted assistant; Perry sings two solo songs and duets with Carol; Carol is a spinster introducing her boyfriend (Tim) to her father (Harvey) when Tim starts acting like a cat; another installment of jokes and songs regarding astrological signs focuses on individuals born under the sign of Aquarius and features the number of the same name from the Broadway show; the ensemble sings "Brotherhood of Man" in the finale.

Comments: This is a rare disappointing superstar appearance on Carol's series. Perry has great vocal form, but he has little exciting material to do, and his considerable comic talents are virtually wasted—a real surprise, given that writers Bill Angelos and Buz Kohan had worked with him on specials previously. Even Tim's contributions are weaker than usual. However, the Q&A is quite fascinating.

Appearing in a red dress before a green background, Carol generates gasps by telling the audience that Perry is a guest. She provides some insightful commentary when asked "If you had to do it all over, what would you change?" and responding "Nothing." Returning from the show's winter break in taping, she reveals she has a cold she is fighting. Then there is a query about one of her few negative media appearances.

"How do you feel about being on the list of the ten worst dressed women?" a person asks. This refers to designer Mr. Blackwell's annual designation of celebrities that he released from 1960 until his death. Carol answers forthrightly that "First, I was hurt, then I thought it was because I wouldn't let him wear my clothes!" Referring to him mistakenly (or perhaps purposefully) as Mr. Criswell, the surname of a popular TV psychic at the time, Carol adds she was surprised some ladies such as Brigitte Bardot and Jane Fonda were on the same list, since they were more famous for being disrobed in public. The series would wreak revenge on Mr. Blackwell soon (see Feb. 17, 1969), but he would hit back by including Carol again at Number Six in both next year's list and in 1971, and he even put her daughter, Carrie Hamilton, at Number Seven in his rankings for 1988.

Carol is not the show's only recuperating cast member. Harvey comes out in a cast on his arm to say he broke his left pinky when he hit a lead pipe while riding on a disk going down a snow-covered golf course. He exits and Perry enters, clad in a tuxedo like Harvey to talk to the audience. Asked why he is no longer doing a regular TV series (he had one from 1948 through 1963), he says, "My age. I promised myself when I reached the age of 50 I would slow down." His revelation that he has been wed thirty-six years with three children and three grandchildren prompts Carol to joke that "You must've been a little devil!"

Lyle introduces the night's Tim and Harvey routine, with Tim playing a somewhat inebriated warden vowing to control his subjects despite having a megaphone and food thrown at him by them. Learning that the convicts finally have taken over the prison, Tim tells Harvey he has a solution—open the main gate to release them. Although fairly slow and uneven, Steve Allen included this sketch as a representative example of Tim in action for a profile of the latter in his 1982 book *More Funny People*.

Paraphrasing his old series' lyrics to "sing for me," Carol introduces Perry, who sits behind a stand like the way he did on his old series. He lends his vocals to "Sunshine Wine," a track from his upcoming album *Seattle*, followed by "Here's That Rainy Day" before Carol joins him on "My Funny Valentine." While all are presented well, they lack a spark to make them memorable musical moments.

Tim reappears licking his hand, curling up in a chair, shedding hair, coughing up a fur ball and causing other havoc as the feline-influenced fiancé for Carol, who is trying to impress her father (Harvey), who favors her playboy brother in jodhpurs (Lyle). Here Tim cracks up Harvey when the latter plays with his timepiece in a manner that fascinates Tim and makes him grab for it. The so-so sketch ends with a dog going after Tim.

Saying she received favorable reaction in the mail to the first set of astrological-themed blackouts, Carol introduces a third edition for the season following Taurus and Leo. Noting that Harvey is an Aquarian (born Feb. 15), Carol shows the romantic and determined nature ascribed to the sign by playing a woman infatuated by her doctor (Lyle). This is a long bit by blackout standards, and Carol constantly returning to Lyle in different outfits belabors the theme. Other characters appear to varying comic effect, from Charles Lindbergh (Lyle) getting the Legion of Honor from a French official (Harvey) and wondering if he will be kissed twice (a play on a popular TV ad at the time) to John Barrymore (Perry) and even Abe Lincoln (Harvey). A typical example of the shaky humor here is when Galileo (Perry) introduces a telescope and reveals that you need a dime to activate looking through it. But apart from Carol and Lyle's sketch, this segment does at least move fast.

"Aquarius" allows Vicki a chance to finally shine in the show with the dancers, as well as provide the most contemporary music on this episode. Everyone else except Tim appears in the finale to perform a song from *How to Succeed in Business Without Really Trying*.

Before the end credits roll, Carol receives some tissues to blow her nose due to the ongoing effects of her cold. It serves as a representative indicator of how this installment, like its hostess, was not at 100 percent.

Jan. 27, 1969: Martha Raye, Mel Torme

** The ensemble participates in a salute to the year's worst commercials; Martha and Carol pantomime being messy painters; Roger has begun talking in his sleep and Carol wonders what he is trying to communicate in "Carol & Sis"; Mel sings "Ridin' High" and "What's New Pussycat?" and joins Carol in a bossa nova medley; Carol, Martha and the dancers present a tribute to 1930s and 1940s novelty songs including "Chickery Chick," "Mairzy Doats," "Three Little Fishies," "Hut Sut Song," "The Flat Foot Floogie" and more.

Comments: "Martha was funny a lot, but she became a little crazy," notes Kenny Solms of the female guest seen twice a year during the series' first four seasons. Another writer, Jack Mendelsohn, opines of the other featured performer on this show that "Mel Torme was an outstanding guest. He could do sketches and sing."

Mel and Martha will team together again next year on the March 23, 1970 show. They will be the first pair of guests to reappear together on a later show on the series if one discounts the annual appearances Garry Moore and Durward Kirby, Carol's old buddies from the series that boosted her stock, *The Garry Moore Show*.

Feb. 3, 1969: Vince Edwards, Chita Rivera

Q&A; "The Old Folks" muse about rekindling their old romantic ways; Vince sings "I've Got the World to Hold Me Up"; Chita dances to an outer space-themed routine with three male dancers; the principal of Pulaski High School (Harvey) demands that repressed instructor Miss Gooch (Carol) teach botany; an elaborate two-part spoof of 1930s weepers, *To Each Her Own Tears*, features Carol as the unloved sister of Vicki, Chita as their mother, Vince as the playboy Carol loves, Lyle as captain of a ship and Harvey as a crusty old physician; the Charwoman cleans up an old men's club.

Comments: Having had Richard Chamberlain, TV's Dr. Kildare, on last season (see Nov. 13, 1967), Carol evens the score by presenting Vince Edwards, the other big physician on the tube from 1960-1966 as Ben Casey, along with Chita Rivera. Carol describes both as "lovely and talented" in her introduction in the Q&A, where much amour occurs. One girl in the audience says she grades kisses on a one to ten basis and wanted to add Lyle to her research. Carol tells her, "He's an eleven." Whether the lady got to kiss him is not shown. An eighteen-year-old guy inquires about Vicki's status (single and nineteen, Carol says), and another person compliments Carol for being much prettier in person. Carol notes Ernie Anderson in the audience before noting that Lyle has a younger brother, and laughter results when a wimpy gentlemen stands up and claims to be that person.

There is plenty of sharp repartee in "The Old Folks," as Bert asks Molly, "Why don't we go on a second honeymoon while there's still time?" and Molly shoots back, "Time for what?! You give up easy!" She says if they have that experience, she will plan to secure a 40-year-old gigolo to satisfy her needs. "It won't be the same!" Bert warns her. "I hope not!" she responds. Eventually Bert's charm wears Molly down, and she says, "Let's go upstairs." "Then what?" he asks. "Let's see if you survive that," she retorts.

Vince lip syncs to his new song in a blue sports suit. Unfortunately, this single will bomb. Next, noting that Chita had just finished filming the movie version of the Broadway hit *Sweet Charity*, Carol introduces the singer-dancer-actress in an odd number where she plays an alien with a wild headdress who flips pancakes along with trips the light fantastic. The use of freeze frame and sped-up footage enhances the bizarre atmosphere as she appears with Don Crichton, Stan Mazin and Carl Jablonski. "That was a fun number," Carl says, calling it one of his favorite routines.

For her part, Chita recalls nothing about the performance, but she notes that she had a history of doing otherworldly numbers in connection with Carol, stretching back to one they did on *The Entertainers* with Boris Karloff. "It was Caterina Valente, Carol and myself as three vampires," she says. "It was choreographed to a T. And we danced to 'I Enjoy Being a Girl.' Can you believe that? That arrangement was so great." A similarly striking number occurs in her later appearance on this series—see Feb. 22, 1971.

The high school sketch employs the usual "unleash the beast behind the quiet type" approach, with Carol's character so afraid of talking anything remotely about sex that she hides behind a blackboard in her initial try. When told by Harvey that she could go to Hollywood if her delivery on the school's TV system is a success, she loosens up totally, going so far as dancing like a hoochie while describing pollination. This is an OK effort.

Much better overall is the classic movie melodrama send-up, which starts with Carol as an old woman reminiscing about how her mother (Chita, sporting huge breasts) and sister belittled her growing up until she met Vince on a cruise, the SS Mildred Pierce. Vince lights two cigarettes in his mouth, but unlike the memorable scene in *Now Voyager*, he keeps them both to smoke. Nevertheless, the two fall in love, sing their theme song and hold a wedding before he falls overboard. Carol then reads a telegram that says, "My husband is dead" and meets the captain (Lyle) who comforts her before disappearing. "At least I'm carrying his child," Carol notes as the fast-moving first act ends.

In the second part, Vicki becomes successful and gets married with the approval of Chita, whose loss of her personal fortune fails to diminish her favoritism among her daughters. After Carol loses and regains her sight, Chita takes her child and gives the boy to Vicki and her husband to raise. Meanwhile, Carol become rich and is astounded to see that Vince, her presumed deceased husband, is alive ("I swam ashore," he deadpans) but dies again for real. Then Carol sees how her son raised by Vicki looks exactly like Vince and valiantly resists telling him who she is. As these notes indicate, the conventions of the genre are mocked wonderfully, and everyone is pitch perfect in their characterizations.

"That was fun. Kenny Solms wrote that," Chita recalls. She feels her character's haughtiness was an inspiration for Vicki's Mama character in 1973, or as she puts it, "I did my version before they wrote that version for her." Regarding Vince's contribution to the show, Chita says, "He was very stiff, very nice, very actor-y. I don't think he was terribly musical, but Carol made everyone better."

Given how tight and funny as that portion of the show is, it is a letdown to end with the Charwoman pantomiming a routine as the male dancers dressed as old men at their social club wake up and perform with her, followed by the Charwoman sitting on her bucket to sign "Young at Heart" solo. While well done, this part lacks the verve and inventiveness of the sketch that came before it.

Chita will return to the show in two years and secures a good friendship with Burnett in the process. "I feel really blessed for our paths to have crossed," she says.

Feb. 10, 1969: Rerun of Nov. 4, 1968 show

Feb. 17, 1969: Ken Berry, Shirley Jones

Q&A; Carol interviews male fashion designer Mr. Irving (Harvey) in "V.I.P."; Shirley performs "I've Gotta Be Me"; Carol and Ken perform a turn-of-the-century number with the dancers; Carol is hypnotized to be attracted to a man any time she hears the word "February," resulting in plenty of complications when the term is used often by Roger's accountant (Ken) in "Carol & Sis"; Ken and Carol sing a medley of songs about home; Shirley is a mentally imbalanced friend threatening to harm Marian in "As the Stomach Turns"; the cast and guests do a British-based musical finale.

Comments: The audiences for the two tapings of these shows appear to have been the most star-studded affairs ever, based on Carol's introductions. She points out Betty Hutton, Rock Hudson, Jackie Joseph (Ken Berry's wife), Ernie Anderson, Jim Nabors, and Rod Serling and his daughter, Anne, which included promoting Rod's work on the upcoming movie, *The President's Plane is Missing*. The extended Q&A included a couple of insights, such as Carol had never took dancing lessons even though she is a talented hoofer and had not been to India but would love to visit some day. She receives greetings from a tourist from Canada and an old schoolmate from Hollywood High, as well as an offer to have her hair cut for free if she visited one woman's father in Nebraska. Noting that Harvey recently finished working in the film *The April Fools* with Jack Lemmon, Carol praises his thespian talents and says "Harvey outdoes himself every week." The one query that amuses her the most is from a lady who asks, "When are you going to have George Raft on your show?" She responds, "As soon as I can, because you sound like you're going to kill me if I don't!" The vintage longtime movie tough guy indeed might have been an interesting guest, but he never appears.

"I heard through the grapevine that Carol Burnett wasn't at all pleased with my back-handed tribute," wrote Mr. Blackwell in his book *Mr. Blackwell's Worst: 30 Years of Fashion Fiascos*. He ranked Carol Number Two on his 1968 worst-dressed women list (behind Julie Andrews!) and commented "Looks like a tornado hit the bargain basement and Carol collected it all!" Mr. Blackwell either forgot or missed the devastating caricature Harvey provides in this show's "V.I.P." installment. One can surmise the joy Carol and her writers had in paying back the designer by hitting him with every gay stereotype imaginable, starting with Carol describing Mr. Irving as living "just a rhinestone's throw from Hollywood." Harvey plays his role to the hilt. Inhaling a cigarette while sporting a smoking jacket, he tells Carol how he once had to hit a woman with his own handbag and wanted to be a model but high heels made him dizzy. Asked by Carol (not playing herself) why Burnett made his list, he says, "I once saw her in a peek-a-boo dress. I took one peek and said 'Boo!'" "You didn't!" says Carol. "Yes, I did!" Harvey hisses back. "Don't contradict me, Mary! Now I'm in an absolute snit!" He concludes his assessment of her by saying "Tacky, tacky, tacky!" and adds, "If there are no more questions, I must fly." "I'm sure you can!" Carol cracks back. Incidentally, Mr. Blackwell put Carol on his list again at Number Six both in 1969 using the same repetition of "Tacky" in his description and 1971 ("Mass confusion purchased from a Park Avenue garage sale!").

This sketch and the others in the show are funny and strong, which compensate for musical numbers which lack any real sparkle. Shirley looks fine in a red gown standing amid chandeliers and roses, but "I've Gotta Be Me" is a familiar tune that receives no real distinctive treatment by her. Ken and Carol's duets similarly stand out only by their set and costumes—the home medley has them on a porch swing with mailboxes surrounding them as Ken wears a tuxedo and Carol has a spangly pants suit. Even the finale, which has Ken, Shirley and Carol singing "It's a Fine Life" from *Oliver!* dressed up as Victorian ladies and a bobby and later joined by Harvey, Vicki, Lyle and the dancers, is more of interest visually than aurally.

More pleasurable is the "Carol & Sis" bit, where Carol pulls out all her comic tricks to indicate her aggressive lust for Ken every time he says "February" until the sound of a snap breaks the spell. It has an unexpected and clever ending—watching the news on TV, she hears the magic word and unplugs the set and takes it to her bedroom in response.

In "As the Stomach Turns," Marian entertains Shirley, her best friend, who is recuperating from a breakdown that forbids her from handling pineapple or other sharp fruit. Shirley remains unstable and pulls a gun out on Carol, who responds with "Is there something wrong with the coffee?" They are interrupted by Lyle as young progressive Congressman Tom Anderson (a spoof of Tom Hayden). Lyle is so oblivious that he shakes Shirley's gun while campaigning. More havoc ensues as Shirley shoots the offstage organist for drowning out her voice, and a handsome black man shows up and causes problems. "It's such a wonderful thing to meet someone who's not a credit to his race," Carol responds—but only after bobbling the line first by saying "It's such a credit" and stopping. She makes a few more bloopers before Ken arrives as a concerned priest ("I sensed a member of my flock was having trouble with her mouth" he ad-libs wittily) and Harvey shows up as a doctor ("No wonder you can't talk—all those teeth" he pipes in to pile onto Carol's performance woes). Also present is Vicki as Carol's perpetual wayward daughter, who is dating the dean at her college. Like the other comedy bits in this show, this is top material overall, although Shirley's deadpan delivery makes her character appear more creepy than funny, even if she is playing a potential killer.

With all the stars in the audience for this show, it is odd that Jack Cassidy was not one of them, given that he was Shirley's husband and appeared with Carol in *Fade Out—Fade In* on Broadway. He will show up as a guest on the Jan. 6, 1973 show.

This is the last of Shirley's two series appearances—for the other, see Jan. 22, 1968. On the other hand, this is the second guest shot by Ken Berry, who will become a mainstay of the series. "He was as good as (Fred) Astaire, (Gene) Kelly, (Gregory) Hines," Chris Korman assesses of the guest's talent. "But most people see him as a guy from *F Troop* or *Mama's Family*. He was the warmest, most self-deprecating guy."

Feb. 24, 1969: Barbara McNair, Soupy Sales

Q&A; department store salespersons (Harvey and Vicki) bring out the romantic sides of their shy clients (Carol and Soupy); Barbara sings "The Windows of the World"; a ninety-year-old neighbor woos Molly in "The Old Folks"; Carol and Barbara fulfill their fantasies of being showgirls in a number with the dancers; Soupy and Carol are a costumed horse team that may break up due to a job offer from their manager (Harvey); Carol hides her efforts to quit smoking in front of Roger's prospective boss (Harold Gould) in "Carol & Sis"; the cast and guests portray children in a clubhouse.

Comments: Some wonderful elements here unfortunately are negated by a prolonged, dull finale. In the Q&A, Carol promotes a benefit for leukemia research she is doing with Jim Nabors on March 16 and appreciates being named the Harvard Hasty Pudding Women of the Year. Amid a lot of pedestrian inquiries and responses—her favorite color is rust, her favorite food is enchiladas—and another introduction of Ernie Anderson in the audience, a few interactions do click. "When is Dean Martin coming on again?" asks one person. "He's never been on before," Carol gently informs the poor soul. She also speaks the "op" language, where you say the "op" syllable before each sounded vowel.

The festivities begin with an effeminate perfume pusher (Harvey) helping a wallflower determine what to wear, although he cannot guarantee it will win over a man ("I've kind of built up an immunity," he purrs to her about women's smells). A more relaxed Vicki similar assists Soupy in the cologne department. When Carol and Soupy meet, the intoxicating aromas make them so amorous for each other that their body heat causes the store's sprinkler system to activate, capping off a pretty good sketch.

Barbara, "my school buddy," as Carol notes, wears a tie-dyed gown as she sings a top forty hit for Dionne Warwick in 1967. Following it is a solid visit with "The Old Folks," where an elderly hippie type (Bernie Kopell) makes moves on Molly to the dismay of her husband. Quickly done and thankfully with no song at the end, this one is a winner.

Carol teams with Barbara next to appear in three different and stunning outfits as showgirls with the dancers, under the pretext that the woman talked about this fantasy when they were students at UCLA. This is a very elaborate production for the middle of the show, and it works much better than what serves as the finale here.

The show's momentum slows with a choppy segment as Soupy and Carol portray the respective back and front of a costumed horse act on tour. Their manager (Harvey) informs them a booker wants only Carol because Soup has not been holding his end of the act up. After that good line comes sappy dialogue from Carol about how she will stick with Soupy, and the two of them sing a song of devotion that deadens the show's pace.

Interest perks up some with a well-acted if slightly shakily written "Carol & Sis." Carol attempts to avoid showing her craving for a cigarette from Roger and his visiting potential new boss (Harold Gould). The latter smokes, so Carol tries to grab his cigarette, capture his smoke in her sweater and even rub the smell of the ashtray on her neck while coping with ending her addiction. Unable to deny the truth, she hides in the kitchen with Chrissy in embarrassment while the men stand on the other side telling her they understand her predicament. Relieved, she opens the door and knocks out the boss.

The humor and goodwill generated here sadly vanishes as Lyle, Harvey, Vicki, Barbara, Soupy and Carol appear in shabby children's clothes to do banter and songs from a clubhouse shack. This effort emphasis cuteness over cleverness regarding how they bond, and it goes on seemingly interminably—a bad way to end an otherwise pretty good show.

Carol uses her child voice to do "It's Time to Say So Long" while Harold Gould gets to sign her book along with Soupy and Barbara. When Carol grabs Harvey's slingshot from his pants, it accidentally flies offstage to much laughter from everyone. Too bad the sketch from whence it came lacked such humor in it.

March 3, 1969: Tim Conway, Ethel Merman

Q&A; Harvey plays a man with a toothache who seeks relief from a dentist in training (Tim); Ethel sings "Elusive Butterfly"; "Fanny Get Your Gun" has Carol playing an understudy with eyes on injuring stage musical star Lillian Larson (Ethel) backstage so she can assume her place for that night's performance; Vicki does a routine with the dancers; an old lawyer (Harvey) advises Tim and Carol that they must stay alive 24 hours on their late uncle's estate to receive their inheritance, while Vicki and Lyle plan to kill the duo; Carol and Ethel sing a medley of show tunes.

Comments: The appearance of one of the greatest musical comedy performers together with a classic sketch that set the pattern for future Tim-Harvey pairings are just some of the delights of this, one of the series' best episodes. It begins with an unusually long (nearly eight minutes) but fulfilling Q&A, where Carol reveals it is her first time working with Ethel, why she pulls on her ear and what guest shot she wants to do. "I would love to be on *Mission: Impossible*," she says. "That's one of my favorite shows." (It never happens, but her show does mock the series later—see Jan. 19, 1970.) A child gives her a button that says "You can kiss me all you want, I'm non-fattening" and wants her to wear it while smooching Lyle one time. Asked "Are you going to be on next season?" she says, "Yes, unless you know something I don't!" When someone notes that "Sometimes I fall asleep during your show," Carol shoots back, "Sometimes we do!"

Amid this riled-up crowd, Carol brings out Tim, who gets queries on the order of "How old are you?" and "When did you lose your hair? Are you going to get a wig?" Carol defends Tim by announcing that "I think bald men are sexy." She introduces Tim's wife and Tim's old comic partner, Ernie Anderson, in the audience, then Tim says he will have a new series on the network next year, joking that "CBS doesn't know about the contract yet." (*The Tim Conway Show*, a sitcom, runs on CBS for only six months in early 1970.)

Ethel enters in a black gown that nicely contrasts with Carol's yellow one, and thankfully the questions are more respectful. The great lady of stage says she stays young through good habits, loved doing her scenes with Tyrone Power on screen in *Alexander's Ragtime Band* and somewhat surprisingly names Jack Klugman, her co-star in *Gypsy* on Broadway, as her favorite leading man. "We had some very dramatic moments in the show, and it was sort of a challenge playing opposite him," she explains.

When Tim and Harvey did the dentist sketch during the first taping, the results were lukewarm, and the show thought about dropping it. Tim pleaded to give it one more go for the 7 p.m. show, and the result was a comic bonanza due to his improvisations (the outline for the skit came from an actual event that happened to him while getting his teeth cleaned). Starting slow with an unidentified actress playing Harvey's admitting nurse, the sketch blossoms when Tim prepares to administer an anesthetic but ends up accidentally injecting himself in his hand and leg. Watching Tim's body parts go limp and numb cracks up Harvey tremendously, who cannot escape seeing them as he is trapped in a dentist's chair. The physical comedy business includes Tim dragging his deadened leg over to a small stool and swinging it on top of it, and a fly landing on a page, which Tim swats with his sleeping hand. (Tim rigged up that part with the show's sound effects man.) Tim even accidentally injects his forehead. The audience is in hysterics for much of the bit until it finally resolves with Tim somehow removing Harvey's tooth.

Calming down from this moment, the show presents one of its oddest music moments ever: one of the best belters ever inexplicably taking on Bob Lind's ethereal 1966 pop hit in front of an old couch with a farm on an orange-colored background. If that was not enough, Kenny Solms said Ethel did not know the words, so they had to write the lyrics on cue cards near her face when taping it! Still, it works.

Ethel comes off better in her skit with Carol as a scheming upstart wanting to assume Ethel's lead role on stage during a musical's final performance. "Before this show closes tonight, they'll be applauding my Fanny!" Carol tells her backstage buddy (Vicki). But despite sabotaging a throat atomizer and trying to hit Ethel with an iron board and throw her out the window, all of Carol's plots backfire. Then to her surprise, Ethel tells Carol she can take her place tonight anyway. Carol is thrilled, but her pal Vicki heard the news as well, so she locks Carol in a trunk to play the role instead. This well-done effort does have one oddity: the dressing room prominently features a picture of Frances Bavier, who played Aunt Bea on *The Andy Griffith Show*.

After Vicki's routine with the dancers, we go to a house full of cobwebs where Lyle and Vicki are suspected of having killed Carol and Tim's uncle. Harvey informs the latter two they must spend the night there to receive their share of the deceased's wealth, and Tim is grinning at Harvey while he delivers this news. Tim and Carol also break character when she leans on the prop dagger that goes into the back of a victim (Stan Mazin). All end up being killed in a flurry in a rather weak ending for an otherwise decent comic piece.

The evening ends with a simple but effective duet between Carol and Ethel on stools, Carol dressed in orange and red and Ethel in blue. Naturally, it ends with Ethel's theme song, "Everything's Coming Up Roses," where she does some patter with Carol when the latter sings the opening lyrics. It is simply a wonderful meeting of two top musical comedy voices, and it puts a nice final touch on a great show.

March 10, 1969: John Davidson, Ross Martin

* Q&A; John offers his takes on "Both Sides Now" and "I Will Wait For You"; Harvey is a bachelor whose moves on the ladies face their most formidable foe—Fireside Girl Alice Portnoy (Carol); Ross receives musical praise from Carol as she sings "Look at That Face," followed by him performing "The Man in the Looking Glass"; Carol stars as a tippling vocalist in "The Helen Feidelbaum Story," a two-part movie takeoff with John as her dumb baby brother, Ross as her abusive gangster husband and Harvey as her lovestruck accompanist.

Comments: Despite much undistinguished singing and comedy, this show does have a few fascinating elements chiefly involving Ross Martin, who might have made a good substitute for Harvey Korman were it not for the fact he was already on *The Wild Wild West* when Carol's series started in 1967. In fact, this show tapes just as Ross has ended his regular TV role, as his series was canceled after four years. "It was a showoff's dream," Martin comments during the Q&A about playing Artemus Gordon. He estimated he did 120 different characters on his series, prompting Carol to quip, "I think your Mae West was the best." Ross introduces his daughter and son-in-law in the audience, plus Carol hails Ernie Anderson, before he leaves and John Davidson enters. He has been married 58 days to the day of this taping and notes his wife is in the audience.

John's vocals on a contemporary Judy Collins hit and a 1965 Best Song nominee ("I Will Wait for You" is from *The Umbrellas of Cherbourg*) are fine but not dazzling. They precede Harvey's lecherous efforts to seduce Vicki at his residence before Alice Portnoy extorts him to buy more cookies or else she will expose him. There is not really much more to that, nor more that is worth saying.

Praising Ross as a versatile star and dear friend, Carol says, "In my opinion, he's the best young character actors anywhere" before she serenades him with a tune from the musical *The Roar of the Greasepaint—the Smell of the Crowd*. This leads into Ross crooning a number just as sentimental as Carol's. At this point, it is clear this will not be a rollicking installment for the series.

The last half of the show consists of a segment that sends up 1955's *Love Me or Leave Me* as much as the 1957 biographical motion picture *The Helen Morgan Story*. Set in Chicago during the Roaring Twenties—"The good old days, before Mayor Daley," quips Lyle narrating the opening—this spoof has Carol battle the bottle while being abused by Ross (in a good Cagney-esque interpretation). It has a surprise cameo by Dick Martin as a lush at a bar where Helen drowns her sorrows during her career downturn. Ross rediscovers Carol there and puts her back into performing, where she claims to everyone she was gone because of a bad cold. She and Ross accidentally shoot each other, but Helen valiantly musters up strength to sing "Love Me or Beat Me Up" one last time before expiring. This has some laughs to it, but it is overextended when comparing the amount of guffaws to the time it takes to present it.

Both Martin and Davidson will return to the series, Ross first on the Nov. 16, 1970 show, followed by John two weeks later on Nov. 30, 1970. Between that time, curiously *The Wild Wild West* will serve as a summer replacement series for *The Carol Burnett Show* (see Final Notes for the Season in the 1969-1970 chapter for more details on that).

March 17, 1969: Martha Raye, Mike Douglas

** A 1930s dance marathon parody of *They Shoot Horses, Don't They?*; a pair of housewives (Carol and Martha) visit a topless waiter bar; Roger, Carol and Chris are caught stuck in a snowstorm during a mountain trip in "Carol & Sis"; Martha sings "Don't Worry About Me"; Mike solos on "Life is Just a Bowl of Cherries," "This Guy" and "Can't Take My Eyes Off You" and accompanies Carol on a musical salute to the Irish in observance of St. Patrick's Day.

Comments: "I was so happy to appear on that show," Mike Douglas said in an interview with the Archive of American Television in 2005, a year before his death, about his work on *The Carol Burnett Show*. "I was such a fan of hers, and she's an absolute delight. She's the hardest working women I met in show business. Boy, she worked hard.

"And she was so helpful, you know. I don't read music. So I'd sit down, they'd start playing, everybody's singing, she's singing. . . . And she was patient, lovely, helpful about helping me. And it was a great experience."

Mike previously appeared on the series on Jan. 1, 1968, and he will make one more guest shot on it (see March 8, 1971). He and Carol have a good rapport, and she will appear on his syndicated daily talk show, which started in 1960, several times until it nears its end in 1982. Mike acknowledged that there was little comparison between his work schedule and Carol's, adding that "She worked harder to do one show that I did for five!"

March 24, 1969: Larry Hovis, Barrie Chase

*"The Schlumps" (Harvey and Carol) duet on "Goin' Out of My Head" and "Can't Take My Eyes Off You"; Barrie and the dancers interpret "MacArthur Park"; Larry has a comic monologue; a Western Union delivery man (Lyle) meets characters played by Harvey and Carol in bits centered around winners of a $150,000 sweepstakes drawing; "The Marriage Game" has Harvey questioning a blonde bimbo and her square husband (Vicki and Kenny Solms), a gorgeous duo (Lyle and Barrie) and two nervous Midwesterners (Carol and Larry); everyone participates in a hillbilly family's production number of "What Now My Love."

Comments: In her memoirs, Vicki credits this episode as showing her growth as a comic actress and encouraging the writers to develop bigger parts for her when they heard her high-pitched voice get laughs in "The Marriage Game. "It was when Vicki started the dumb character," says Kenny Solms of this segment. He himself wore a Nehru suit to complete the effect of being an out-of-touch nerd husband in the skit. This certainly is a rollicking showcase, as "The Marriage Game" allows her to scream like an idiot even when she lost because she was just following instructions from the producers.

This roasting of *The Newlywed Game* starts with Harvey getting crushed when panels of the couple connect with him being stuck between them. Prying himself lose, the conceited host promises viewers "30 uninterrupted minutes of bad taste" before introducing three distinctive couples—Vicki with teased hair chewing gum opposite boring Kenny; Barrie with equally narcissistic Lyle; and prim and proper Larry and Carol. Telling all that the show wants dirty answers and priding himself on supposed ad libs, Harvey's host asks the six players to guess how many times they kiss each other every day. Vicki and Kenny miss as do Barrie and Lyle, with Barrie guessing 100 times while Lyle responds with just two—"All morning and all night"—prompting more over-affection between the beauties. A frigid Carol thinks Larry is oversexed and passes out before hazarding zero as a guess—which is just what Larry wrote as well. The two win a couch that folds into a double bed, causing a sensitive Carol to faint again.

That segment follows a potpourri of entertainment starting with Carol and Harvey's duet. Originally planned as part of the March 10, 1969 episode, it appears here due to lack of air time for that show. Barrie and Larry then display their talents, followed by a trio of depictions involving a lottery of varying comic success. First and least, Harvey announces to Carol, a countess, that he is leaving her now that all of her inheritance is gone and she is broke. She rides him piggyback to prevent him from leaving, but he is adamant that she is a loser, saying no one else in her family is rich and ready to die. When Lyle tells Carol she was won, she goes into his arms and ignores Harvey.

The other skits are better. Harvey is a stereotypical flaming beauty shop operator treating Carol and another irate customer offstage when Lyle tells him he has won. After holding onto Lyle's hand as a sign of affection, he jams the hair dryer on Carol's head and throws a bucket of water offstage to a woman needing a rinse. Finally, Harvey plays a man so confident he has become rich from a drawing that he throws out and destroys parts of his residence because he can afford replacements. But Lyle's telegram reads, "Happy birthday to you," causing Harvey to faint.

This is the sole installment this season where both guest stars appear on the series just this one time. That same situation had appeared three times the previous season—see Nov. 27, 1967, Jan. 8, 1968 and April 15, 1968—and will happen again at the start of the next year (see Jan. 5, 1970).

March 31, 1969: Ronnie Schell, Vikki Carr

*Harvey is a gambler so compulsive he goes to extremes to place bets that his wife (Carol) attempts to thwart at every instance; Ronnie performs a comic monologue; Vikki sings two compositions; a drunk lawyer (Ronnie) complicates Roger's work on deciding who will be his beneficiaries in his will, as does Carol when she learns some of her husband's decisions in "Carol & Sis"; Carol is an ingénue determined to be a scene stealer opposite Harvey and Lyle in a summer stock production; Carol and Vikki sing a duet on "The Straight Life" with the dancers.

Comments: Actor and comedian Ronnie Schell had met Carol at a party prior to his work here, which airs around the same time she makes her second guest appearance on the series where he played a supporting role, *Gomer Pyle—USMC* on April 18, 1969 (when she last did that series on Sept. 22, 1967, Schell was a regular on *Good Morning World* at that time). On this show, besides having the opportunity to do one of his routines, Schell offers a preview of his recurring drunk character Audie that he would employ as a regular on *The Jim Nabors Hour* from the fall of 1969 through 1971. His inebriate is concerned about staying tipsy because he finds making out wills to be depressing. Meanwhile, his client, Roger, has to deal with Carol's consternation with both Ronnie's condition and her husband's decisions of what he will leave to his sister, Mimi, who Carol loathes. "I'd rather have Richard Nixon driving our car than your sister Mimi!" she yells at one point, adding an unexpected political edge to their debate. As Carol gripes about Roger's proposed allocations, Ronnie becomes more bombed, as indicated by singing "Melancholy Baby," and he ends up being accidentally knocked out by Carol at the end as she opens the kitchen door on him while he goes to get more alcohol. He mentions that that drink punched a wallop before passing out in this better-than-average sketch.

The skit prior to this has Harvey telling Carol in dinner that since he lost $10 at bingo at church, he has sworn off games of chance, yet his actions indicate otherwise. For example, when she asks if he wants more soup, he says, "Hit me again!" Soon he is back to his old habits, planning to bet on a horse called incorrigible when Carol uses the term on him, and Carol has to take evasive actions to stop him. She rips out the phone, smashes a device where he uses Morse code, stops him from waving two semaphore flags and even shoots a carrier pigeon, all to prevent him from contacting a bookie. Carol appears to have stymied Harvey's desire and put him under his control, but then she learns there is a horse named after her in a race, so she takes a spare $8 from her dress to place the money down in its name without Harvey knowing. This is another strong skit.

The last sketch provides the groundwork of what will become Funt and Mundane. Harvey is a haughty actor starring in a play with Lyle playing a blackmailer. Carol is a squeaky-voiced actress upset that she has no lines in the production, so she takes matters in her own hands to gain attention. She plays to the crowd by taking a bow at the start and waving her fingers constantly, and she raises the ire of her fellow actors more by dancing around with Lyle's coat while putting it up and wiping with a feather duster with flair. Her scene-stealing antics continue to ramp up, including animatedly watching Harvey and Lyle's rapid-fire delivery of line, and they culminate with Carol interrupting Lyle when he shoots Harvey to take the "bullet" herself and making an elaborate death scene. This makes it three-for-three among successful sketches in this week's episode.

This episode is the first of two appearances by Ronnie and Vikki, each of whom enjoyed the series immensely and were not strangers to each other prior to the taping. "I worked with Vikki Carr in Lake Tahoe at Harrah's, so I already knew her," says Ronnie.

"When we were touring in Vegas or anywhere, there was always a comedian to warm up the audience," adds Vikki. "I admire the comedians who can do that." She later worked Ronnie Schell again on *The Jim Nabors Hour*.

Vikki attributes securing a spot on the series due to the success of her record "It Must Be Him," which came close to topping the pop chart in late 1967. "Nine times out of ten, if you had a hit record, you would be able to do a variety show in this period," she says. "It was an incredible, beautiful time for artists. It was almost like a golden time for artists."

For Ronnie, the main benefit of this guest shot was establishing a rapport with one of the regulars. "Harvey was one of my best friends," Ronnie says. "Harvey was a little competitive with her." Ronnie thinks that an amiable competition to see who could get more laughs between Harvey and Carol strengthened the show's appeal.

Both Vikki and Ronnie will return to the series in the following season, Vikki on Jan. 19, 1970 and Ronnie on March 16, 1970.

April 7, 1969: Robert Goulet, Imogene Coca

Q&A; Robert croons "On a Clear Day You Can See Forever," "(There's) Always Something There to Remind Me" and "Didn't We?"; Harvey is a man battling both a hangover and efforts to extort money from him by Alice Portnoy the scout (Carol); two school teachers (Carol and Imogene) attempt to find love while sightseeing in Rome, during which Imogene offers her version of "If Love Were All"; Carol portrays the starstruck Swedish maid of Lyle, a matinee idol, to the disgust of his companion (Vicki); the entire cast participates in a burlesque called "Cinderumplewhite" narrated by Vicki.

Comments: This show comes across as a slapdash effort to fulfill nearing the end of the season. The only segment that belies this impression is the lively Q&A, where Carol says she has no interest in going into politics, claims she is lazy and plans to watch Jimmie Rodgers show replacing her this summer. She notes her series plays in Australia, Mexico, South America and will appear as CBS's entry in the Montreal Film Festival. Lyle and Robert come out—the latter startling Carol with a big black spider doll he wields—and says he's growing a beard for a World War II movie called *Underground* (released in 1970). Lyle gets chuckles for brushing Robert's beard with his own face, and the audience generates a few beard jokes as well. Then comes an obviously scripted moment when Lyle and Robert argue who should use one of Carol's extra tickets. They go off stage to debate the issue, and the winner is—Imogene Coca, who comes on stage smiling without a word. That sets the standard for humor on this episode.

Of Bob's three songs, the last, popularized by Richard Harris in 1968, is his best. He does the title tune from the 1965 Broadway musical in a disconcerting "hep cat" style, and he slows down a Burt Bacharach-Hal David standard that demands to be sung faster. His missteps are nothing compared to another irritating visit by Alice Portnoy, who shakes down Harvey for dozens of dollars thanks to having seen his wild party the previous night from her own window. Vicki shows up as her sister at the end of this time killer.

A seriocomic moment follows as Imogene witnesses her American compatriot (Carol) whisked away by an Italian count (Harvey), leaving her alone at a festival at Rome. But Lyle invites her to join the dancers in swaying to "Volare," and she does so with gusto until she learns he expects to be compensated financially. This leads into a plaintive song she handles well to end the bit. But for people who expect Imogene Coca to do humor rather than dance and sing the blues on a comedy variety show, this is a letdown.

Another tiresome sketch has Carol beaming over Lyle and trying to get attention while cleaning his residence while Vicki resists the attention. In desperation, Carol knocks out Lyle's limo driver (Harvey) and replaces him, only to learn that she's been fired. Much ado about nothing here.

The finale has the cast energetically tackling a generic take on fairy tales with Carol as the heroine, Imogene as the witch, and Harvey and Lyle as a two-headed monster in feathers sent by Imogene to attack Robert, the prince who wants to save Carol. Robert cuts the monster in half and knocks both Harvey and Lyle out, prompting Imogene to turn herself into a dragon (the dancers), which Robert also defeats. He embraces Carol and she kisses him, only to see him turn into a frog. The clever ending belies the sluggish nature of the operetta, which should be wilder and funnier to stand out.

This show marks the swan song for Imogene Coca on the series (curiously, her *Your Show of*

Shows co-star, Sid Caesar, also did three episodes of *The Carol Burnett Show*). Robert Goulet, who worked with Carol on *The Garry Moore Show*, will return to this series on the Dec. 28, 1970 show.

April 14, 1969: Rerun of Dec. 2, 1968 show

April 21, 1969: Pre-empted by drama special *Spoon River*

April 28, 1969: Family Show

** Carol recalls when she played Nelson Eddy and her cousin was Jeanette MacDonald in her childhood; Harvey sings while facing adversity in a spoof of TV campaigns for mayor; a sample of how *The Carol Burnett Show* sounds in its Spanish translation; Harvey sings "They Call the Wind Maria," while Vicki offers "And When I Die" and Lyle croons "I'm Just a Country Boy"; the Charwoman says goodbye to the cast as they wrap up the season.

Comments: Harvey's take on a familiar number from the Broadway musical *Paint Your Wagon* (which is on screens during this taping in a horrible movie adaptation) is so hilarious that it will reappear on the show's finale. Taking the wheel of a ship on a set that rocks from side to side, he is pelted by fish, water sprays and other objects thrown at him as everything around him disintegrates.

This appears to be the first episode where Lyle does a solo vocal. "I certainly don't have a singing voice," he acknowledged in an interview in the 2012 *Ultimate Collection* DVD. Nevertheless, he was able to carry a tune to a certain extent, and sound much better than Tim Conway, who admits he can barely hit a note right.

By the 1970s the wrap-up of each final show will include Carol as the Charwoman reviewing the season in some fashion before singing "It's Time to Say So Long" and then walking through the audience. A man is always seen sleeping in one of the seats midway as she walks up the stage left aisle to the exit. That man was George Bye, the head of the series' prop department, according to Roger Beatty, longtime assistant director on the show.

"I think Carol's thought behind this was that the Charwoman finished closing up the season, and as she made her way up the aisle, she passed George, who was exhausted after working the whole season and kind of represented all the others who had worked on the show that year," Beatty adds. "Anyway, that's what I think the reason for him being there was. I could be wrong, but that's my best guess."

Final Notes for the Season

Carol and crew end their second year with about the same average rating as the previous one—20.8—but a higher finish at the end at Number Twenty-Four, tied with another CBS variety series, *The Jackie Gleason Show*. For the first time ever, the network had all of its Monday night series finish in the top twenty-five.

As it did the previous season, *Rowan and Martin's Laugh-In* bested *The Carol Burnett Show* in competition to win Emmys as Outstanding Musical or Variety Program and writing for that category. Bob Mackie also lost for Outstanding Individual Achievements in the Visual Arts (as did his competitors—Emmy rules at the time allowed for no winner in the category if the judges indicated that was their preference).

However, Harvey Korman tied with Arte Johnson of *Rowan and Martin's Laugh-In* for special individual achievement. It was the first Emmy for the series as well as for Korman, who viewed winning his catch-all category with disparagement. As he later jokingly told his son Chris, "I almost lost out to a werewolf and Marlin Perkins (the latter being the host of the *Wild Kingdom* animal documentary series)." *Rowan and Martin's Laugh-In* topped *The Carol Burnett Show* as Best TV Show at the Golden Globes as well.

The Carol Burnett Show also lost in the Emmy writing category to *The Smothers Brothers Comedy Hour*, which CBS cancelled in the spring of 1969 despite finishing at Number Twenty-Seven due to political pressure from the Nixon administration about the series' satirical content. What makes this interesting is that CBS programmer Mike Dann considered moving *The Carol Burnett Show* to Sunday nights from 9-10 p.m. Eastern and Pacific to fill the void, but he ultimately decided to go with *The Leslie Uggams Show* instead. That new variety series bombed and went off after thirteen weeks.

On Mondays, *The Carol Burnett Show* continued in reruns through June 9, 1969, culminating with a repeat of the Oct. 21, 1968 show. There, a newly taped segment was inserted with singer Jimmie Rodgers performing his newest record, "Today" (which failed to crack the pop chart) and introducing his new summer series that would replace *The Carol Burnett Show* the following week. Officially titled *Carol Burnett Presents the Jimmie Rodgers Show*, the program featured Vicki Lawrence, Lyle Waggoner and Don Crichton as regulars, but no appearances by Carol, despite what its name implied.

During one show, Jimmie Rodgers introduces Bobby Russell as a guest, doing his semi-hit "Saturday Morning Confusion" (which Carol's show did later—see Oct. 27, 1971). Vicki, whose main purpose on the series was to dance with Don constantly to make up for a lack of a regular troupe of terpsichoreans, finds Bobby enchanting, leading to both good and bad consequences for her as they embark on a rocky romance.

As for the series itself, Rodgers' heyday with hits like "Honeycomb," "Oh-Oh, I'm Falling in Love Again" and "Secretly" was already on the wane when he did a summer series on NBC in 1959, so it was not surprising that this effort similarly fails to impress CBS to make it a regular fixture, especially when another variety series this summer on the network, *Hee Haw*, becomes a Number One show during its initial run. *Carol Burnett Presents the Jimmie Rodgers Show* ends its run on Sept. 1, 1969. Specials will occupy the slot thereafter before Carol and crew returned two weeks later.

The Carol Burnett Show stays at Mondays 10-11 p.m. Eastern and Pacific for a third consecutive year when it returns in the fall. CBS moves its lead-in, *Family Affair*, to Thursdays at 7:30-8 p.m. Eastern and Pacific, and replaces with *The Doris Day Show*, an even more compatible sitcom given its female lead. This activity all indicates that things looked bright for the series in its third year, and happily the shows bear this out to be true.

Fireside Girl Alice Portnoy shakes down two criminals (Dan Rowan, left, and Dick Martin) in the Nov. 10, 1969 episode that also featured Bing Crosby and Ella Fitzgerald and not surprisingly finished in the top ten that week. Alice would blackmail many others through 1975. As Bob Mackie noted, Carol's recurring characters like this wore the same outfit every appearance to help with audience identification. Courtesy of Getty Images.

Chapter 4

1969-1970: Great Guests + Weak Challengers = Top Ratings

Audience member:	"What do you think of sex education in the schools?"
Carol:	"Depends on the teacher!"—From the Sept. 29, 1969 show

Crew Additions This Season

Writers: Larry Klein, Bob Weiskopf (1970), Bob Schiller (1970), Buz Kohan (1970), Bill Angelos (1970), Kenny Solms (1970), Gail Parent (1970)

Musical Coordinator: Nat Farber

Art Director: Paul Barnes, Bob Sansom

Set Director: Bill Harp

Hair: Gus Le Pre of Paganos

Casual viewers checking out *The Carol Burnett Show* in the fall of 1969 might have noticed that Harvey decided to let his hair go gray rather than color it. That was the most prominent superficial alteration in place, but other major developments do occur that were apparent to more discerning types.

For one, Carol unveils a major new character. Zelda the nudge was a nagging, whiny, homely creation who terrorized her husband, George (Harvey), by making every issue revolve around herself to his neglect. In later seasons he will be seen in various fantasy scenarios where his sex appeal is evident to a shapely lass (usually Vicki) until it dissolves when he hears the call of "George!? George!?" interrupt it. This setup usually generated consistent laughs due to their interplay, but a little of this character goes a long way, and it became overexposed in the next few years, eventually giving Carol as much a headache as Zelda did to George. She stopped portraying Zelda in 1973.

Two other new recurring characters came on the scene this season too, but they proved less durable. Stella and Harry were an apparent effort to emulate *The Honeymooners* with a grungier atmosphere, with Carol and Harvey as a couple with a rundown apartment and shabby outfits to match. Vicki and Lyle played their similarly sleazy kids, and despite several tries on the series this season and next, they never really clicked with the audience and vanished in 1971.

This season also establishes an integrated dance troupe for the series, as tall, muscular Charles Moore joins the other men working with Ernie Flatt. Even so, he will last just this season. Another male black dancer will appear later this season briefly as well, but he will not become a regular until the fall of 1972. For more on him, see the 1972-1973 introductory section for information on Carlton Johnson.

Among visitors to the set, the series debuts one of its most frequently seen guest stars, Bernadette Peters. If there is any relatively unknown talent the series can take credit in popularizing, she is the one. Carol adored the multitalented blonde sprite, and so did the dancers, who knew they always had a number with her when she appeared. "She sang, she danced, she was cute," recalls dancer Carl Jablonski.

There were also a considerable number of unannounced cameos that pop up this season to the delight of audiences. Surprise visits occur by Rock Hudson (Oct. 6), Kay Medford (Oct. 20), Bob Hope (Nov. 10), Merv Griffin, Ruth Buzzi and Arte Johnson (Nov. 17), Alexis Smith (Jan. 5) and producer Ross Hunter (March 2), among others. Whether these occurred due to increasing popularity or the show's willingness to take chances, they by and large worked well for the series.

The main change for the writing team involved Kenny Solms and Gail Parent, who left to devote time to produce and write the ill-fated sitcom *The Tim Conway Show*, which reunited the title comedian with his former *McHale's Navy* star, Joe Flynn, in a venture that never took off. Their replacements included the return of Buz Kohan and Bill Angelos, and the arrival of two veteran comedy writers, Bob Weiskopf and Bob Schiller. The latter duo had a rocky time on the series, but it was not Carol's fault. For a summary of their experience, see the March 9, 1970 entry.

It appeared in the series' first week that there might be trouble ahead, as a *Flip Wilson Show* special beat the season debut of *The Carol Burnett Show* handily. However, the series rallied back, and by early 1970, *Variety* reported *The Carol Burnett Show* finished tied for Number 19 for the first three months of the season and averaged a 37 share of the audience. It got more popular after that, thanks in part to programming errors by NBC and ABC.

What happened with NBC was that since it ran its best feature films on Saturday nights, it left a lesser combination of new TV movies mixed with reruns of older titles such as 1960's *Exodus* for Mondays in hopes that the popularity of *Rowan and Martin's Laugh-In*, still the Number One series in America, would carry over some audiences prior to their airing. That was not effective, and viewers either shut off their sets or switched over to CBS to watch *Mayberry R.F.D.* and *The Doris Day Show* (Number Four and Number Ten for the season respectively).

Meanwhile, ABC's new Monday lineup faltered so horribly that three of the four shows ended in midseason and the remaining one, *Love American Style*, which appeared directly opposite *The Carol Burnett Show*, moved to the safer confines of the network's Friday night schedule, where it lasted until 1974. ABC's replacements included a movie series of some new but mostly repeated theatrical features, some more than a decade old (e.g., 1958's *Teacher's Pet* with Clark Gable and Doris Day), and others of dubious quality such as 1966's *The Oscar*, that concluded its last half hour opposite the first part of *The Carol Burnett Show*. Following it was a documentary series called *Now*.

As one might expect, those movies did little against *Laugh-In* on NBC and *Here's Lucy* on CBS, so by the time *The Carol Burnett Show* aired a little later, there was no incentive to watch the end of a movie and a news show. These moves by default gave Carol a big audience, and her series respectably provided quality entertainment, although the last few shows flagged a little in terms of overall appeal.

The increasing success of *The Carol Burnett Show* this season did not surprise Mike Dann, head of programming at CBS, who credited much of its success to the star. "She was a representation of the average person that anyone would like," he says. "She never did anything in poor taste. She never appeared in sexy clothing. And when you appeared on her show, she always looked in awe, and she never did anything that wouldn't make you look better."

Dann enjoyed working with Carol much more than most of his other 1960s variety series stars such as Danny Kaye, Red Skelton and Jonathan Winters, who struck him as difficult personalities. "She was probably the most cooperative, ethical human being I dealt with," he says. "She was in a Lucy [Lucille Ball] class, who was always my kind. She was the Mother Superior of her staff. She surrounded herself with good people. It was a sheer delight for me to fill a full hour with her show."

The third year was indeed the charm for *The Carol Burnett Show*. Here is what really clicked—and admittedly sometimes misfired—during the season.

Sept. 22, 1969: Jim Nabors

** Q&A; several maximum security devices installed by a love shy lass (Carol) harass Jim as he walks down the hall to her apartment for a date; Jim sings "Turn Around Look at Me"; everyone plays themselves as first graders; "Carol & Sis" finds Roger, Chris and Carol adjusting into living in a new home; Carol performs "There Won't Be Any Trumpets"; Harvey is a passenger on a cruise battling seasickness, a hangover and a pushy child (Carol); Jim, Carol and the dancers do a novelty production number involving chairs.

Comments: Bob Duggan, who resembles a dark-haired version of a young Karl Malden, appears as a phone repairman in this season opener. He will appear regularly as a bit player on the series the following season and occasionally thereafter.

The Bradfords move from their previous address (Maple Drive, for true trivia fanatics) into a new abode, although the set does not appear too radically different from last season. The stairwell previously seen on stage right has been replaced by only a few steps up and a bookcase, apparently for quicker exiting off camera, but there still remains a kitchen door for someone to get smacked on their head at the end of most sketches.

Assessing this effort, *Variety* stated, "The platoon of writers under Arnie Rosen's supervision would be well advised to hypo the pace somewhat, as the linking between skits and numbers was needlessly awkward." Even so, the publication liked the show overall and concluded, "Withal, it should be a vintage year for Miss Burnett." It definitely turned out to be one.

Sept. 29, 1969: Bernadette Peters, Nancy Wilson, the Burgundy Street Singers

Q&A; Harvey interviews classic movie star Mae East (Carol) in "V.I.P."; Nancy performs "Can't Take My Eyes Off You"; "Fireside Chat" has President Richard Nixon (Harvey), First Lady Pat (Carol) and their daughter, Julie (Vicki) addressing the nation while on vacation in their San Clemente residence; Bernadette sings "Poor Butterfly"; the Burgundy Street Singers present their version of "Marrakesh Express"; Carol battles laryngitis as well as a bubbly blonde next-door neighbor in "Carol & Sis"; Carol, Bernadette and Nancy sing "They Don't Make Them Like That Anymore" to set up parodies of *Morocco*, Carmen Miranda and *42nd Street*.

Comments: The show marks the first of many appearances by Bernadette Peters, whose comic chops, booming voice and attractive features make her a popular guest star. Carol tells the audience in her introduction before the guest's solo that she saw Bernadette dazzle as the lead in *Dames at Sea* off-Broadway in May and was grateful to get her on the show before she rehearsed for her first Broadway musical lead in *La Strada* (which closed after one performance on Dec. 14, 1969). Carol is similarly effusive about her cast, referring to "Emmy-winning Harvey Korman" before starting the Q&A. She has a good sense of humor when one man guesses she is forty-three years old when in fact she is thirty-six.

For this "V.I.P." edition, Carol resembles Mae West in her Diamond Lil finery and nails her strut perfectly as the character returns for a visit after being on "V.I.P." in the Dec. 2, 1968 show. She tells Harvey she reclines on a chaise because she is "top heavy," and other double entendres follow, such as "I've been inflated since I was seven" and "Is it hot in here, or am I turning myself on?" Lyle plays her houseboy in this smooth entry.

Nancy sings her new single, "Can't Take My Eyes Off You," in a slow tempo with a hazy background. The song had been a big hit for Frankie Valli just two years earlier, but Nancy's promotion of her version here is not a strong launch—it will crack the pop charts only two months later and fail to break the top fifty.

After Bernadette sings with a butterfly design with her, we have an unprecedented third consecutive musical number by a different act. Carol thanks Jimmie Rodgers for his summer replacement series in her slot and calls his regulars the Burgundy Street Singers a bright spot on that show. The group—seven men and five women—appear in mod-inspired Indian garb to sing "Marrakesh Express" more akin to the bright theme of *Love American Style* (then running opposite Carol on ABC) than to the rocking hit original by Crosby, Stills and Nash still being played on the radio when this show first airs. If nothing else, this bit provides a contemporary air to the series.

Finally taking a break from the tunes, a doctor (Ken Olfson) tells Carol Bradford her voice is shot and she needs to take care of it. Naturally Roger is oblivious to the condition at first. But what really ticks off Carol is a visit by Cindy (Elaine Joyce), a perky divorceé who lives one house over. She drops off tea and manipulates Roger to come by her place to Carol's chagrin. The expert pantomime work by Carol and good contributions by Harvey and Elaine make this sketch work.

Dressed in frilly yellow dresses, Carol and her female guests sing at the outset of several spoofs of 1930s and 1940s films and their personalities. For *Morocco*, Nancy is Little Sheba singing "You Need to be My Flame." Carol's Carmen Miranda impersonation includes Harvey as a bongo player. Bernadette inherits the Ruby Keeler role for *42nd Street* when Vicki's character is injured, and she nails it with a tap routine on silver ramps and platforms with the dancers that beautifully approximates Busby Berkeley's choreography and direction in the 1933 classic. A more elaborate parody of this movie will appear on the Nov. 17, 1971 show.

With its yin and yang between contemporary material and items relevant more than a quarter century earlier, this is a schizophrenic entry that fails to jell as a whole. Nancy and Bernadette will be seen to better advantage on later shows.

Oct. 6, 1969: Steve Lawrence, Edward Villella

Q&A; Steve sings "The Drifter" and "I've Gotta Be Me"; Roger resents Carol hiring an interior decorator for their home, but his homophobia turns into intimidation when he learns that Mr. Bruce is the manly Lyle in "Carol & Sis"; Edward performs a ballet routine; Carol and Steve do a medley of songs with numbers in their titles; a takeoff of *The Postman Always Rings Twice* has Carol in Lana Turner's role, Steve in John Garfield's part and Harvey as their target for murder; the Charwoman dreams on the New York City ballet stage that she dances with Edward.

Comments: This installment offers the first of many guest appearances by Steve Lawrence as well as an ironic critique on conflicting beliefs about masculinity and homosexuality, although the latter's subtext is more apparent in retrospect. The Q&A has Carol give a twist to the standard "What would you do if you were not an actress?" inquiry with the response, "I would like to be a Playmate of the Month. Or a truck driver." She cracks up when someone asks, "How do you remain beautifully unpolished?" When she brings out Steve to say hello, his wife, Eydie Gorme, is in the audience and amusingly and seductively asks him, "What are you doing after the show?"

Wearing a tuxedo and standing in a reflective background with blue and red lights, Steve appears in the first segment lip syncing to his first song. It is his latest single that generates some airplay on easy listening music stations but fails to crack the Hot 100. He then performs a tune he did originally in 1967 in the Broadway musical *Golden Rainbow*. That too was an easy listening success with no pop chart action, although Sammy Davis Jr. had a hit with "I've Gotta Be Me" earlier in 1969.

The "Carol & Sis" sketch appears to be designed to dispel anyone's fears that guest Edward Villella's ballet background should be equated with homosexuality (Villella is straight). Roger complains of Carol's decision to hire a male decorator, saying "I don't want to see any those guys flittering around the house!" But when that man is Lyle, Roger changes his tune and asks Lyle leading questions about his personal life—if he is married, lives with his mother, has a roommate and so on. In the process, Roger sounds like he is coming onto Lyle, who is a former athlete and not interested at all sexually.

This sketch so far attacks swishy stereotypes pretty well, but then the show adds a twist whose implications only a few viewers would get at the time. Carol reveals to Roger she also has hired a plumber, who is played by Rock Hudson. The then-closeted actor showing up in a sketch dealing with people's misconceptions about gayness and masculinity boggles the mind when watching it today, but at the time all it brought was applause and whistles from the audience. Carol calls him out for a bow as the sketch ends and she tells everyone her producers called him for the cameo right when he returned from filming a picture in Italy (not stated, but it was *A Fine Pair*). "He hadn't slept in seventy-two hours," Carol says after she kisses and hugs him and falls into his arms.

The emphasis on masculinity continues as Carol introduces Edward by showing his athletic posing in a swimsuit in a *Life* magazine profile. As he dances to a Cossack-themed number (excerpts from "Prince Igor" which are previously recorded), he performs some truly incredible stage movements to watch, both solo and with the female dancers.

Wearing an orange dress, Carol joins a still tuxedoed Steve for an OK medley of number songs like "Ten Cents a Dance." They then change to do "The Murderer Always Rings Twice" introduced as a Metro Golden Mouth picture with Carol doing the Tarzan yell in place of Leo the Lion. This solid parody has Carol wearing an all-white outfit, and when her husband (Harvey) gets her skirt greasy from his cooking, she peels it off to reveal an identical tight white skirt underneath it. She and Steve are adulterous lovers so intense that he sucks off one of her white earlobes while kissing her. Their plans to run away after killing Harvey are foiled when she ends up being killed accidentally, but before she goes, she confesses having other loves in her life—including Shirley the waitress, keeping with the show's hints of homosexuality. Steve was so effective in this sketch that most of his subsequent appearances had him play Carol's lover in old movie takeoffs.

The Charwoman closes out the show, first by pretending she is a toreador on stage, then nodding off to appear in a comic pas de deux with Edward. At one point she appears to be lifting him rather than vice versa. It ends with the Charwoman alone singing the Frank Sinatra standard "Here's That Rainy Day."

Even though he will become a frequent guest in the 1970s, Lawrence will not reappear until Sept. 28, 1970, while Villella came back on Jan. 25, 1971. Hudson will have the longest wait—he will not be an official guest star until Feb. 15, 1975.

Oct. 13, 1969: Pre-empted by an unknown program, according to Ross Reports TV Index—program listings had Scooey Mitchlll (yes, that's how he spelled his surname) and Bobbie Gentry as guests, but apparently this episode never ran, if it was even taped.

Oct. 20, 1969: Tim Conway, Ken Berry

Q&A; a veteran truck driver (Harvey) trains a meek apprentice (Tim) on the basics of handling a rig; a computer dating system misfires and teams an aggressive female (Carol) with a reserved date (Ken); Carol and Roger's celebration of their marriage renewal vows are dampened by the surprise arrival of his cranky sister, Mimi (Kay Medford), at their home; Marian confronts complications from Gramps (Tim), a teenage temptress (Vicki), her brother (Lyle), a priest (Ken) and a doctor (Harvey) in "As the Stomach Turns"; a tribute to vaudeville with the dancers, cast and guests.

Comments: Were it not for Ken and Carol's computer dating bit, this episode, taped on April 25, 1969, would be a classic. The Q&A is remarkably brief—Carol brings Tim and Ken out for questions, introduces their wives, solicits one question from someone inquiring if Tim was nervous, and that's it. It leads into a Harvey-Tim pairing where Tim is such a novice around trucks that he accidentally slams Harvey's fingers in the door. He puts on glasses that give him googly eyes and cracks up Harvey as the latter drives and Tim rides alongside. As night falls, Tim dons his pajamas, says he needs to go to the bathroom and asks Harvey to sing "Rock-a-bye Baby" to him to go to sleep. This is fairly amusing, although it could have been even more so if it had been written tighter.

Carol and Ken's bit, introduced by Harvey, is a flimsy offering where they alternately sing tunes to express their feelings about their mismatch. So, Carol belts out "Big Spender," "Trouble" and "Shy" from *Once Upon a Mattress* aggressively, while he slowly loosens up to her with "She Touched Me." They end up in a duet doing the Oscar-nominated song "More" as a sign that they have matched up. The back-and-forth numbers grow tedious quickly, making this lengthy and difficult to endure.

Things perk up much better with Kay Medford's stellar underplaying as Roger's sister, Mimi, in "Carol & Sis." After Chrissy leaves to spend the night with a friend, Carol and Roger plan to take off their wedding renewal garb when Mimi enters out of the blue. "I see you married the same girl," she says disgustedly, adding surprise that Carol was wearing a white gown. She likes the new house but wonders where her guest room is located. As Carol kisses her husband, Mimi interjects with "Roger, do you want to get mononucleosis?!" A frustrated Carol heads to her bedroom as Mimi tells Roger she will go to a hotel instead, sounding like a martyr in the process. Relieved, Roger tells Carol what has happened so they can resume their romance, but she already has covered her face in beauty cream to go to bed. This is one of the best "Carol & Sis" installments ever.

Following it is an equally strong "As the Stomach Turns" wherein Tim debuts his slow "old man" character. Shuffling along the floor with his body hunched over to join Marian for tea, he pats down the carpet in the process. "Don't rush on my account," Marian tells him as the audience laughs. Tim milks more amusement with a delayed reaction of dismay in lifting his hands up slowly, then shuffling upstairs slowly as he announces he will run away before going to a rest home. Meanwhile, the arrival of Vicki the slut entices Marian's brother Ralph (Lyle), who announces he wants to divorce his fourth wife for Vicki, who is unimpressed with him. "If only you weren't my brother," Marian says while looking over Lyle's body. He cries about his situation, but Lyle does such a poor job faking it that Carol cracks up. As Ralph leaves, Father Calucci (Ken) enters for brief repartee with Marian, followed by Gramps saying he is sick and Marian calling for a doctor (Harvey). Gramps rolls down the stairs slowly to hit Harvey in the knees and then lifts his leg like a dog peeing on him, prompting laughter from Harvey and Carol. "That's the fastest I've ever come down," Tim adds to top off his situation. Harvey sees Vicki and falls in love with her before the end of this very good sketch.

The finale has Lyle and Harvey trading jokes as bums, Carol and Vicki doing a seriocomic duet that ends with Carol taking Vicki's date (Lyle) that the latter had planned to marry, Tim playing an inept springboard artist (he cannot hold a lady on his shoulders, for example) and Ken doing a song-and-dance routine with the dancers. Everyone joins together at the end to sing about "Two a Day." It is a quite satisfying windup.

Something Tim does at the end cracks up Carol as she sings "It's Time to Say Goodbye." Kay Medford gets to sign the book along with Tim and Ken. It's a shame she does not do any more shows on the series, given her brilliant work on it.

Oct. 27, 1969: Pre-empted by a special NFL football game

Nov. 3, 1969: Pat Boone, Gwen Verdon

Q&A; "The Old Folks" get ready to go to bed while Bert serenades Molly with "Kiss of Fire"; Gwen plays a young girl entertaining neighborhood boys in a song and dance routine; Pat does a solo number followed by a duet with Carol; the cast performs a series of commercial spoofs; a sick stage actress (Carol) insists on performing with Harvey despite intensely sneezing and coughing; "As the Stomach Turns" has Pat as Marian's baby brother who plans to marry the town's naughty lady (Gwen); Carol, Vicki and Gwen play clowns joined by the dancers and men at the end.

Comments: It is jarring to see such a clean-cut personality as Pat Boone among the freewheeling atmosphere of *The Carol Burnett Show*, and while he carries himself well through the proceedings, one wonders how he and others on the show really feel about him being there, given some ribald moments it contains. It starts with Carol answering a query about where she grew up and then bringing out Gwen, who said her favorite Broadway shows were *Redhead* and *Sweet Charity* (Carol saw her on opening night for the latter). Recounting how dancers in New York City are taught how to impersonate objects, Gwen pretends to be a lighthouse, then the audience suggests Carol portray a piece of bacon frying and Gwen a clothes washer, both of which they do beautifully.

The pantomiming continues in "The Old Folks," wherein Bert is turned on by Molly's preparation in going to bed and sings a 1952 hit to indicate his desire. That's about it. This is a limp variation of what Harvey did to Carol when they played lower-class types on the Dec. 2, 1968 show, and it is a weak kickoff to the show.

Gwen and Pat's separate feature numbers are overlong and uninspired as well. For Gwen, she dances wonderfully as always, but the cuteness factor is excessive. Pat, "my new best friend," as Carol calls him, appears in a tux before we transition into a piece taped earlier of him singing a trivial tune as a clown. After it ends, Carol and Pat joke about his "white bucks" image before he mentions a recent appearance on *The Dean Martin Show* as a springboard for another forgettable number he does with Carol as they sit on a hassock.

The show thankfully disrupts its torpid pace with a decent set of commercial spoofs. A child brags to his father (Harvey) that he has only one cavity, and the father tells him to scram and tell his mom while he is cheating on her with another woman. Lyle is a smoker who keeps refusing to let Vicki have one of his cigarettes, so she decks him. Carol lists every bad condition she is enduring in deadpan. The most disorienting and dated one has three of the male dancers dressed as construction workers mocking Pat as a sissy and Lyle picking one in the trio as more manly—it is hard to swallow that setup.

In a dry run to what will become Funt and Mundane, Carol is a flu-stricken diva acting opposite Robert Preston Foster (Harvey) who is determined to appear in their play. Her doctor (Lyle) is likewise as dedicated to giving her a shot while she is acting. On stage, Carol coughs excessively while Lyle attempts to inject her from behind curtains and other scenery. She spits out her cigarette and rubs her nose on Harvey's sleeve before screaming very loudly once Lyle is able to inject her by surprise. Her condition does not disappear immediately, however—she sneezes strong enough to blow off Harvey's toupee, and she still coughs strongly even after being shot by a villain (Don Crichton). This very amusing bit sets the pattern for Carol and Harvey playing a theatrical duo bedeviled by outside problems that will appear occasionally over the next eight seasons.

"As the Stomach Turns" is similarly enjoyable, although the plot and characters are not ones you typically would associate with Pat Boone. As Marian's sibling, he tells her he is ready to shower for the fourth time today before introducing his fiancée (Gwen), a woman he says is almost as pretty as he is. Marian warns Pat not to marry her, but she is interrupted by her daughter (Vicki) delivering her illegitimate child. Next to arrive is Harvey as Canoga Falls' richest man, who discovers Gwen is his sister and gives her $10 million as a gift. That prompts Gwen to dump Pat and leads to the "tune in tomorrow" part for the ending. While this mockery of Pat's image shows he has a sense of humor, one wonders how his more devout and pious followers felt about this racy presentation.

Adding to the spicy atmosphere, Gwen, Carol and Vicki sport clown costumes with ample bosoms during the final dance number. The falsies are so big that Carol balances her arm on her fake right breast during the show closing, while Gwen signs the guest book balanced on top of her inflated mammaries. Pat cracks up at the sight, but given his religious background, the question remains whether he is doing so to be polite and privately objected to it. And, despite Carol saying in her introduction of Pat earlier in the show that this is his first visit and "I certainly hope it won't be the last," he never returns to the series. This turns to out to be Gwen's swan song on *The Carol Burnett Show* as well, though not intentionally—see Dec. 28, 1970 for more details.

Nov. 10, 1969: Bing Crosby, Ella Fitzgerald, Dan Rowan, Dick Martin

Ella performs "Get Ready"; Dan leads a group of motley robbers whose efforts are disrupted by a collection drive from Fireside Girl Alice Portnoy (Carol); Carol and Bing duet on "Flattery"; Bing plays himself being hounded by an admiring waitress (Carol); at the Brown Derby; Carol and Ella sing together; Dick plays Carol's forgetful husband; a salute to Paramount Pictures parodies many of its movies and includes Bing and Ella presenting a medley of the studio's tunes that were nominated for the Academy Awards' best picture; a finale saluting the funny men of the screen.

Comments: Man, what a guest lineup—and that's not even including a cameo by Bob Hope! Bing, Dan and Dick are all appearing in appreciation for Carol appearing on their upcoming NBC specials, the former for *Bing Crosby and Carol Burnett—Together Again for the First Time* (Dec. 17, 1969) and the latter duo for *Rowan and Martin Bite the Hand That Feeds Them* (Jan. 14, 1970). With such standout talent on hand, which prompts audible "ahhhs" from the audience before going into the show without a Q&A, expectations for great comedy and music are high, and the show mostly fulfills it.

The one misstep is the opening number. Watching the great Ella snapping her fingers and scat singing to the soul hit "Get Ready," surrounded with four black dancers in silver lame jumpsuits and fringed vests, is kitschy rather than hip. Thankfully, her contributions to the show are redeemed when she later appears in fine form to join Carol on "I'll Never Fall in Love Again" (which Ella released as a single that bombed, prompting Dionne Warwick to record the hit version of the song from the musical *Promises, Promises*) and with Bing on songs that were hits from Paramount movies. Bing himself does fine with bantering with Carol before their duet in complimenting her dress (a beautiful spangly silver outfit), reminiscing with Carol about his work at Paramount and cracking jokes at old onscreen partner Bob Hope when the latter appears at the end of the restaurant sketch to attract the attention of Carol's waitress character. As Bob describes how and where he obtained a new jacket, Bing muses, "Where were you at the time?" to much laughter.

Otherwise, this entry is dominated by the hosts of the most popular TV series at the time, *Rowan and Martin's Laugh-In*, which airs two hours before Carol's on NBC. As a gang leader lording over a hurt accomplice (Harvey) and other dolts in the first sketch, Dan obviously reads cue cards while trying to get rid of Carol's scout visiting their hideout. Seeing Harvey in distress, Carol senses something fishy is happening. To put her off, Dan pays for all the ticket she is selling for her troop's Mexican fiesta, but she tells Dan she believes it is stolen money and threatens to shake him down. Dick actually gets off a joke comparing Dan and Carol to sounding like (Dean) Martin and (Jerry) Lewis before he and Dan accidentally kill themselves for Carol's triumph.

Later, in a sketch written by David Panich, Dick keeps failing to recall his anniversary, number of children, wife's name and even his own identity. To combat his problem, his wife (Carol) results to pantomiming clues in an excellent exasperated display of physical comedy by the hostess. It ends with the arrival of Dan—another guy suffering from temporary amnesia about his life.

The Paramount Pictures tribute begins amusingly with the studio's logo dropping in front of Carol. She tells how Marlene Dietrich was a big early hit for the studio and performs the star's theme song "Falling in Love Again" by stepping on a chair, only to break the seat. This leads into a series of spoofs, starting with *Samson and Delilah*, where Lyle's character has his hair shorn and becomes a scrawny guy, played by an unidentified actor. Next is *For Whom the Bell Tolls* (misidentified by Bing in his intro as "For Whom the Bells Toll"), where Carol and Dan play Ingrid Bergman and Gary Cooper's roles and pledge that nothing will come between them, followed by Dick showing up between them in the sleeping bag they are sharing to shout, "Will you two shut up?" The studio audience still laughs raucously at that as the actors leave the set, making Bing chuckle too and holding up doing his duet with Ella on "Moon River" and "Call Me Irresponsible."

Following the duet comes a long but solid parody of *A Place in the Sun*. Using elements of her whiny Zelda voice along with some inflections by Shelley Winters from the original, Carol elicits guffaws while Harvey grimaces as he attempts to kill her in the boat. Eventually her belly aching is too much for him to handle, so he jumps overboard to kill himself by drowning instead. The show concludes with a Marx Brothers tribute that features Vicki (nearly overlooked in this show) with a dead-on Harpo impersonation, with the four male black male dancers dressed as Harpo as well!

Having so many luminaries involved near the top of their game gives this episode the feeling more of a special than part of the series, which speaks well of its overall quality. It also proved to be a huge audience attraction—the show finished at Number Ten for the week, the first time the series finished in the top ten. Two of the four guests would return to the show—Crosby (see Nov. 3, 1971) and Martin (see Dec. 29, 1971).

Nov. 17, 1969: Andy Griffith

Q&A; the King Family sisters visit "V.I.P." with Lyle as host; Carol reads a poem and sings "I Believed It All"; a wife (Carol) hates that her policeman husband (Andy) brings his work habits home; Vicki and Don Crichton perform an interpretation of the novelty song "Mah-Na-Mah-Na"; Roger neglects Carol and Chris in favor of a football game, then ignores them both upon the arrival of Cindy (Elaine

Joyce), the pretty neighbor; "Cinderellie" is a countrified take on the fairy tale with Carol as the title character, Andy as a prince and Harvey as the fairy godfather.

Comments: This show has some shining moments, but unfortunately few of them involve the guest star. Interestingly, the other leading TV personality with a surname that sounds close to Andy Griffith's appears in the Q&A. After Carol tells an audience member that "I love Merv (Griffin) very much," he surprises her on stage. She was his first guest earlier in the week as he taped his CBS late night show in Los Angeles (it would later relocate there permanently from New York). Following that, Carol thanks someone for complimenting her Lana Turner impersonation on the Oct. 6, 1969 show, then brings out Andy Griffith. Asked about the format of his series coming to CBS next season (it would be the flop drama *The Headmaster*), Andy replies, "Gee, I don't know." Calling him "one of my very favorite storytellers," Carol implores Andy to narrate a lengthy parable involving animals about how no amount of kindness however small is ever wasted.

From that wobbly start comes a pretty good sketch. In this installment of "V.I.P.," Carol, Vicki, Elaine Joyce and Isabel Sanford join the female dancers to comprise the giggly clan—and Harvey does too. He claims to have been adopted by the family after being left in a fruit basket. As for Isabel's presence, Carol claims that "She's our token sister" due to integration. Isabel gets a good line back regarding her family—"I ain't the only blonde here with black roots!" This is one of the first and best skits to feature Harvey in drag for much of its humor, and it will not be the last.

Likewise, this marks an early installment of Carol reading a letter from a young viewer, in this case an eight-year-old writing about what the color pink means to her, and then singing a song. This segment tends toward being sappy, but it will appear over the next few seasons occasionally.

After crying to Vicki about her difficulties in living with a cop, Carol sees Andy shoot off the lock to their door and frisk her as he comes home. He describes dryly as a suspect and even maces her after an argument. Upset by being treated like a criminal, she holes up in a room and dares him to come get her. Before things worsen, Vicki arrives and tells them she has her own problems with her husband, a firefighter, who breaks a window to join of the rest of them. This is fairly amusing by all involved.

The show's biggest laughs come from Vicki and Don's number, a nonsense ditty popular on TV at the time that became a recurring element on *Sesame Street* during the 1970s. What makes this so amusing is that Ruth Buzzi and Arte Johnson from *Rowan and Martin's Laugh-In* take part as their characters as Gladys Ormphby (a dowdy woman in a hairnet) and Tyrone Horneigh (a dirty old man). Carol has both take a bow after it ends.

The "Carol & Sis" sketch is not much more than what the summary lists. When Cindy leaves, Carol and Vicki imitate her squeaky voice and teasing approach toward Roger, to his disdain before the skit ends. This is much ado about very little.

Andy narrates "Cinderellie," featuring Carol with a Southern accent with a banjo twang played behind her. When she finds a wishbone, she conjures up Harvey, a fairy godfather so effeminate she asks, "What are you?!" After he sings a tune of being fond of his wand (!), he materializes roller skates for her to go to the ball, where she meets Andy. From there, it is a pretty standard take on the classic tale, with a few laughs as Andy hopes the slipper will not fit Harvey's foot. This overlong, corny take suffers greatly in comparison with the superior "Cinderella Gets It On" the series will present six years later (see Nov. 29, 1975). Vicki appears briefly as the evil stepmother.

Andy's leisurely paced humor makes him somewhat of an awkward fit for a series that relies on a rowdier atmosphere. Still, he will return twice, first on Dec. 8, 1971.

Nov. 24, 1969: Lucille Ball, George Carlin

Q&A; George performs a monologue discussing the Emmys and imagining the FBI's top ten list as a talk show; Carol performs a song written for her by an audience member; Lucy and Carol are flight attendants trying to impress a passenger (Harvey) who turns out to be a hijacker; the dancers perform "Try a Little Kindness"; Carol sings "I Say A Little Prayer"; a parody of *Bob & Ted & Carol & Alice*; George is a deejay whose dumb aide (Vicki) books an aging vaudeville act, the Rock Sisters (Lucy and Carol), for his upcoming concert, and complications ensue.

Comments: This guest combination of what will soon be a leading anti-establishment comedian with arguably the most traditional of female comic actresses works pretty well. After introducing her distaff visitor simply as "Lucy," Carol gets down to business in Q&A to discuss a picture an audience member had of Carol's Halloween party, where she dressed up as Vampira along with Harvey's wife, while their husbands were dressed as Dr. Frankenstein's assistant Igor. They had lots of props in the house as well, and it may have been too effective, as Carol said one child ran away scared from the experience. But hardier souls found out, and even as late as 10 p.m., there was a line of twenty trick-or-treaters who wanted to check out the activities.

George's discussion about television is a good opening attraction. He enacts "The J. Edgar Hoover Show" with the FBI director coming across as Johnny Carson to deliver jokes along with details about criminals on the run and Vice President Spiro Agnew as Hoover's announcer/sidekick. Along the way, George makes a good crack about Abe Fortas, Lyndon Johnson's failed nominee for the U.S. Supreme Court.

The first number comes courtesy of Sue Vogelsanger, who three weeks earlier as a guest in the audience presented Carol with songs she had written for the hostess. Carol brings Sue back from out of state for this show to see her perform the number in a flowing white gown accompanied with the dancers. With the song's theme of a housewife who wants to get away from it all, this is a pleasant diversion to watch and hear.

The show is nearly a third done before Lucy first appears, as a dueling stewardess with Carol. With each gunning to win a contest as best on their airline, Lucy advertises on her posterior for passengers to vote for her, prompting Carol to retort, "You sure got the billboard for it!" Sporting Fidel Castro's beard with Peter Lorre's voice, Harvey is smothered by both women for his affections, from fighting over what pillow to give him to brushing his beard. Lucy detects he is a foreigner because of his dialect and notes that "If there's one thing I know, sir, it's a Cuban accent!" Audience members familiar with the in-joke concerning Lucy's relationship with ex-husband Desi Arnaz applaud the line. The sketch ends with the ladies' fighting resulting in accidentally dropping Harvey out the airplane door while in flight.

Two musical numbers follow this, the first a "mod" version of a recent Glen Campbell hit, with the dancers dressed up in late 1960s garb. It is fine, but what follows it is a head scratcher. Carol sings the Burt Bacharach-Hal David standard in a shower mostly straight, then swallows a little incoming water for a few laughs. When it ends, the camera pans and shows some dancers playing musical instruments in the back of the tub to accompany Carol. This interjection of intended comedy is confusing and unsatisfying, yet it would be repeated for some reason on the April 5, 1975 show.

The *Bob & Ted & Carol & Alice* spoof has a couple of surprisingly risqué lines for the time, which seems appropriate given the movie's focus on sexual mores. Carol, Lucy, Harvey and Lyle are in bed together because the one at Lucy and Lyle's residence is malfunctioning. Adjusting to her circumstances, Lucy says, "I sleep anywhere." "So I've heard!" Carol shoots back. Lyle boasts that he sleeps like a log and Lucy adds, "You do everything like a log!" The wrap-up has Lucy's parents getting in bed with the foursome.

The finale has George contacting an ancient agent (Harvey) on the recommendation of his bimbo assistant (Vicki) to book the Rock Sisters—Vicki thinks they sound groovy, even though it has been decades since the ladies were a hot attraction. Gamely, Carol and Lucy try to stay hip by following a rock act called the Frozen Nostrils and singing a tune which is goosed up by members of the previous band joining them. Carol cracks Lucy up during their song with her old woman voice for a few lines. Like most of the show, the number is serviceable but not spectacular.

Lucy will return the series next season (see Oct. 26, 1970). George will as well, but not until nearly nine years later on March 12, 1978.

Dec. 1, 1969: Pre-empted by *CBS Playhouse* special presentation of "Sadbird"

Dec. 8, 1969: Tim Conway, Martha Raye

** A salute to 20th Century Fox includes takeoffs of Shirley Temple, Charlie Chan, *The Fly* and *Doctor Dolittle*; Martha and Carol play respectively downscale and upscale mothers who encounter each other; Tim portrays a slow-moving racing mechanic whose sluggish demeanor irks Harvey; a prince with frog tendencies is after the affections of a sleepy princess (Carol) to save him; Harvey impersonates Tom Jones doing "It's Not Unusual"; Martha sings "Is That All There Is?" and joins Carol to do "Big Beautiful Ball"; the ensemble presents "On The Good Ship Lollipop."

Comments: There is some irony of Martha doing "Is That All There Is?" as the singer who popularized it, Peggy Lee, will be a guest three months later (see March 30, 1970). Tim's Old Man character seen previously on Nov. 20, 1969, has its second appearance here, and by now it is established that he and Harvey will have one sketch wherein Tim will torment Harvey virtually every show the rest of the run with Tim. Carol gets to reprise Shirley Dimple as well.

Also by this point, Carol already was allowing Tim to indulge in new bits in the second taping of each show. "She'd let me do kind of what I wanted to do on the show, and a lot of times I would drift from the script," he acknowledged in an interview in the 2012 *Ultimate Collection* DVD.

In that same DVD, Carol explained how the show would compensate for an extended routine from Tim that ran several minutes beyond what had been planned in rehearsal. "What we would do would be to cut down on something else or save another sketch for another week," she said. "Because what Tim would come up with was gold."

Dec. 15, 1969: Garry Moore, Durward Kirby

** Garry and Durward introduce commercials for Christmas gifts inspired by television programming; Mrs. Peter Piper (Carol) appears before a judge (Harvey) with two attorneys (Garry and Durward) in court; Roger hosts a poker game with his buddy to Carol's chagrin in "Carol & Sis"; Carol sings "Make Your Own Kind of Music" and joins the Bob Mitchell Boys Choir in performing "Do You Know How Christmas Trees Are Grown?"; the Bob Mitchell Boys Choir presents "Sleigh Ride."

Comments: This Yuletide episode has special poignancy because it is the last joint professional appearance of Carol and her two co-stars from *The Garry Moore Show*. Moore is easing himself out from acting as he begins his last regular TV job as host of the syndicated version of *To Tell the Truth*, which he started in the fall of 1969 and continued through December 1976. Durward will appear on this series again next year (see Dec. 14, 1970), then will pretty much retire from acting on TV until his death in 2000.

Carol reunited with Garry Moore two more times on TV before his death in 1993. She came on *To Tell the Truth* as a special guest panelist on an edition taped on March 25, 1976. "He's responsible for whatever career I've got," she told the appreciative audience at the outset.

Three years later, she and Moore presented the Outstanding Comedy Series award at the Emmy on Sept. 9, 1979, and he pointedly criticized the trigger-happy network programming practices of the time. "These days if a show doesn't make it in a couple of weeks, it goes out the alley," he said. "Faith has become too expensive." Moore realized that had such a policy been in place back in 1958, *The Garry Moore Show* would have been toast—and possibly Carol may not have gotten her big break on television as well.

This is fanciful food for thought, of course. As it stands, this episode definitively marks the end of Carol's ties to *The Garry Moore Show* and the establishment of hers as its own entity.

Dec. 22, 1969: Rerun of Oct. 6, 1969 show

Dec. 29, 1969: Donald O'Connor, Nancy Wilson

** A salute to MGM includes spoofs of the movie studio's 1930s hits including *Mutiny on the Bounty*, *San Francisco* (with Carol singing the motion picture's title number), *Red Dust* and the series of Andy Hardy films; another installment of Carol as a housewife bedeviled by characters from TV commercials; Nancy sings "This Girl is a Woman Now" and "Everybody Goes to the Moon" and joins Harvey and Lyle in presenting "Backfield in Motion"; Donald performs "Without a Song."

Comments: This is the first of three appearances Nancy Wilson will have over the next four months. It follows three other guest shots she had in the previous season, giving her a total of six episodes and putting her among the series' top ten most frequently seen guests. Oddly, she will never appear after this season even though she continues to record throughout the 1970s. Part of this could be due to her declining sales and radio airplay—"This Girl is a Woman Now," her featured number here that interpreted the Gary Puckett and the Union Gap hit, will become Nancy's last minor entry on the adult contemporary chart later in 1970.

In a 2010 interview with Marc Myers for the JazzWax website, Nancy claimed she encountered little racism in the entertainment industry and added, "That's what I loved about doing *The Carol Burnett Show.* There was no color involved. I didn't have to play black characters. I could just do comedy, which I loved to do." She said in the interview she had no professional acting training either.

The series will do a longer spoof of *San Francisco* on its Nov. 1, 1977 episode. As for Donald O'Connor, he will return to the series next season on Oct. 12, 1970.

Jan. 5, 1970: Audrey Meadows, Kaye Stevens

* Q&A; Audrey and Carol play old high school chums who snipe at each other while recounting bygone days; Kaye sings "Eli's Coming" and joins Carol in a duet on "Games People Play"; Harry and Stella (Harvey and Carol), a slovenly couple, discuss plans to divorce following an argument; Don Crichton dances to a medley of three songs; Carol reads a twelve-year-old's poem and sings a song; Marian tries to intervene as a friend (Audrey) threatens to commit suicide on "As the Stomach Turns"; Kaye, Audrey, Vicki and Carol sing about being four redheads intersperses with bits of other tunes.

Comments: This flaccid entry is no more than tolerable in any segment except Don's solo. Even the Q&A is brief. A lady says she thinks the questions were planted, which Carol of course denies, and another woman wonders if Carol was called "Big Mouth" as a kid (no to that as well). That leads into an opening sketch with Carol and Audrey spouting tired putdowns of each other when they meet after years of being apart. For example, Audrey snidely recounts how Carol went to the prom with her own brother, while Carol shoots back about Audrey's brother being homecoming queen. After some tiresome repartee, it mercifully ends with Audrey inviting Carol to come to her house and meet her husband's bachelor friend and Carol accepting. This is a time waster.

After being asked to appear several times on the show, according to Carol in the introduction,

Kaye offers a take on a Three Dog Night hit so awkward that it makes one appreciate the artistry of the original more. Her bass-heavy, semi-funky rendition of a recent Joe South smash with Carol similarly misses the mark, as their precise enunciation is at odds with the mood set by the orchestration.

In the first appearance of the dowdy Stella and Harry, following through on Stella's threat to divorce him, Harry splits up their property, with him taking the ironing board to go surfing. Neither wants their children (Vicki and Lyle), both of whom look freakish and are unfazed by their parents splitting. Stella and Harry decide to reunite at the end of this up-and-down effort that fails to spark. The best that can be said here is at least Audrey does not show up here to draw even more comparisons with how Stella and Harry are no Alice and Ralph Kramden. Nonetheless, the characters will reappear on Feb. 2, 1970.

Dancing and singing to "Old Lonesome Me," Don Crichton segues into doing just fancy footwork behind "Everybody's Talking" and "Theme from Midnight Cowboy" in his solo. It is the best part of the show by far, especially considering it comes before the tedious reading of a twelve-year-old's poem on "The Things I Love" by Carol, who sings a ballad that further makes the show sickly sentimental when it should be soaring.

"As the Stomach Turns" improves as it goes along, but it is still a lesser effort. Marian's long-suffering friend (Audrey) is poor and separated from her husband, so she contemplates killing herself. The worn-out words of compassion from Marian fail to impress her, and she plans various ways to commit suicide. After a visit from Marian's daughter (Vicki), who was naked on stage in *Oh, Calcutta!*, a doctor (Harvey) who Marian obtains to treat Audrey turns out to be the latter's first husband. He now has a snooty wife (Alexis Smith) who adds to complications as he attempts to diagnose his ex-spouse. Harvey has some good ad libs, but this intriguing set up really goes nowhere before it putters out. Smith appears to promote her guest shot on *The Governor and J.J.* sitcom on CBS the next night of this show's original air date (Jan. 6, 1970).

The finale has Carol, Vicki, Audrey and Kaye singing an original composition about being redheads, mingled with excerpts from "Cheek to Cheek," "Comin' Through the Rye" and others. It is an unspectacular ending in tune with much of the rest of the show. Unsurprisingly, this episode marked the sole guest appearance of both Audrey and Kaye.

Jan. 12, 1970: Nanette Fabray, Nancy Wilson

Q&A; Bert feels energetic but Molly thinks otherwise in "The Old Folks"; Fireside Girl Alice Portnoy blackmails a teacher (Harvey) for a higher grade in his class; Nancy sings "Spinning Wheel" and joins Carol to perform "Get Together"; Carol's fumbling efforts to practice first aid techniques with a mannequin and hiding what she is doing lead Roger to suspect she is cheating on him in "Carol & Sis"; Marian assists a friend who is a kleptomaniac (Nanette) in "As the Stomach Turns"; Nanette, Nancy and Carol dress "mod" and sing together in a production number on "Mothers of Tomorrow."

Comments: There is so little for Nanette to do here that she doesn't appear until halfway into the show. She didn't miss much, as this is a flaccid entry with weak new installment in the recurring sketches, plus no dancers. And that's with a Q&A running eight minutes, and it's hit or miss. It includes Carol's Tarzan yell, her mention of Bob Mackie, a summary of the talk shows she has visited (Joey Bishop, Johnny Carson and Merv Griffin) and her recollection of the joke pulled on her during her last sketch on *The Garry Moore Show* when Durward Kirby pretended to be drunk. The real highlight is Carol introducing Bernadette Peters in her audience, and they do a little chit chat. The show is then off and stumbling.

The first so-so skit has Bert saying he feels virile to Molly's disbelief. He grabs her knee and asks, "How does that feel?""Compared to what?" she snorts. Saying he can still entice her, she retorts, "Turn on? You're lucky you can find the switch!" Everything is on that level and really goes nowhere. Still, this is more tolerable than watching Alice Portnoy use her well-worn method of escalating threats on a man to go up one grade level every time on a teacher who flunked her, starting with saying she'll blab about him going to a topless restaurant. The final revelation that she has taped one misdeed he thought she missed in a recorder hidden in her lunch box is a steal of how "Carol & Sis" ended on the Jan. 8, 1968 episode.

Carol calls Nancy "kind of a semiregular" in introducing the songstress. Nancy's version of the Blood Sweat and Tears hit is a track on her album *Hurt So Bad*, which was in stores when this episode first ran, and it's more Vegas than rock. She does better when she and Carol harmonize passionately on another recent smash, this time originally done by the Youngbloods.

The most chuckles of the night, albeit intermittent ones, comes on "Carol & Sis" where Carol and Chrissy successfully train on handling an emergency on a life-sized male dummy and celebrate with brandy afterward, some of which spills on Carol's blouse. She gives it to Chrissy to clean while Roger comes home earlier than expected. This forces Carol to hide the mannequin, since she didn't want Roger to know about her class, and greet him at the door wearing her slip on top. Seeing that and the brandy glasses, Roger becomes suspicious and after tearing through the closet discovers the truth. Carol generates some unintentional laughs when she says "hummy dome" instead of "dummy home," and amusement continues at the end when Chrissy accidentally hits Roger with the kitchen door, forcing her and Carol to administer first aid for real this time.

Nanette finally emerges on "As the Stomach Turns," but her role as a demented thief addict does not produce many guffaws, nor does Vicki as Marian's hippie daughter, Lyle as a politician looking for votes and Nancy as a nurse treating Nanette. The only spark comes from Harvey as Gaylord Fontaine, "the civic group's sissy director," as Marian introduces him. Harvey flits and glides across the set as he tells Marian he wants her to star in his next play instead of Nanette, and he gets applause for his work. But it's not enough to save this skit. The finale with Carol, Nancy and Nanette pretending to be younger, hipper versions of themselves to connect with their daughters is a strained, tedious effort that only cements this show as a lesser episode.

Nancy and Nanette will appear once more this season—see March 16, 1970 for Nancy and April 13, 1970 for Nanette. This show's date is noteworthy because it is the final airing of *Love American Style* on ABC Mondays opposite *The Carol Burnett Show*. The rest of this season and next, Carol will face only football, movies and documentaries as her competition, and no other original series.

Jan. 19, 1970: Flip Wilson, Vikki Carr

Q&A; Carol and Harvey are two social outcasts for having halitosis and dandruff respectively; Vikki performs "Go"; Flip does a comic monologue; Carol gets drunk and contemplative as she turns 30 in "Carol & Sis"; Vicki and the dancers present "Raindrops Keep Fallin' on My Head"; "Mission: Improbable" features Lyle as the ringleader, Harvey as the master of disguise, Carol as the female spy, Flip as a engineer, an unnamed actor as a strongman and Vikki as the murderess they attempt to entrap with a fake séance; the cast and guests perform "There's Enough to Go Around" as the finale.

Comments: Except for Flip's dragging monologue, this overall strong episode presents the skills of the guest stars wonderfully. The Q&A includes Carol's thoughts about how UCLA has changed and her opinion of Mr. Blackwell, who ranked her the sixth worst dressed woman of 1969 (she makes a raspberry and jokes that he asked to borrow her clothes, as she quipped when she made the list in 1968). Flip joins her to reveal his stage name came from being flippant in the military and reveals his real first name is Clerow, to Carol's shock. He also gives his age as 35, and then the show commences.

As two nebbishes rejected by others at a party, Carol and Harvey bond over each other as they go into detail about every deficiency they have before leaving happily. This is middling but short. Vikki's solo follows and is effectively conveyed visually and aurally.

Next is Flip's routine, which he at one point admits "It's a long story." It is, and his tale a private ordered by a colonel to go behind enemy lines for a successful mission after complaining about conditions on camp has little to laugh about apart from his Geraldine impersonation at the end. At least he delivers his material confidently.

Better is seeing a tipsy Carol come home from her birthday with Chris, who tries to help her hide her condition from Roger in "Carol & Sis." Of course he finds out, and when he does, Carol does a great job confiding all of her fears about getting older to Roger. This gets funnier as it goes along and ends with Roger accidentally knocking Carol out with the kitchen door.

Vicki presents the Oscar-winning Best Song of 1970 as a bum on a bench while pretending to play a ukulele. The dancers pass by her while carrying umbrellas, but no precipitation ever hits Vicki. This routine is acceptable and not much more than that.

Next comes one of the series' best parodies ever. Series ranging from *Get Smart!* to *Here's Lucy* had already offered their spoofs of *Mission: Impossible*, but this is arguably the best of the bunch, as it brilliantly mocks several conventions of the series while using its theme music. It even makes mincemeat of the opening, where an unseen person attempts to ignite a fuse with a match and a lighter before taking a huge torch to start the sequence of previews. Next, Lyle dons a blond wig to play the Jim Phelps equivalent, and he gets a message in a phone booth to make Vikki confess that she killed her husband, a dictator who was friendly to the United States, or make her commit suicide. The booth explodes on the next unlucky soul to occupy it (Stan Mazin) as the tape self destructs.

Lyle goes to explain his plans to Harvey, Flip, an unidentified tall actor (as the equivalent of the Peter Lupus character) and Carol, who enters a room and postures several times silently with her mink coat before winning an Emmy and applause from Lyle. The moment is clearly meant to ridicule the string of victories for Barbara Bain, who claimed three consecutive awards for her work on *Mission: Impossible* over the more highly regarded Barbara Stanwyck (for *The Big Valley*, which competed unsuccessfully opposite *The Carol Burnett Show*) and Diana Rigg (for *The Avengers*). In fact, after Harvey does a variety of impressions and facial distortions, Lyle congratulates him and gives Carol another Emmy, which she puts on a mantle loaded with several others.

However, the real hoot is Flip disguising himself as Geraldine to fool Vikki, the target of the group's con. It seems that Vikki's maid looks exactly like him, ostensibly prompting Flip to do his drag routine during a séance conducted by Carol with Harvey playing Vikki's dead husband. Wearing a great hot pink print outfit, Flips shows excellent comic timing and performing as he sassily proclaims that Vikki killed her husband, eliciting applause for his work and showing he was more than deserving of his own variety series that debuted on NBC in the fall of 1970. Vikki does a superb job of remaining poker faced during her séance scene as the strongman carries her off in a chair.

Capping it off, the "original team" shows up, and Peter Graves, Leonard Nimoy, Peter Lupus and Greg Morris enter to applause. "How can you thank these guys enough?" Carol tells the audience as saying they agreed to show up on the series at her request, as *Mission: Impossible* was her favorite TV series. If that wasn't enough, Flip as Geraldine flirts with Greg for being the tall, dark and handsome man she wanted to have. It all adds up to a simply magnificent sketch that's a total delight in all aspects.

Similarly enchanting is the finale, where everyone wears fezzes, lattice work shaped like oversized hearts and Arabian outfits in warm, bright colors while playing banjos and singing. Harvey strums his banjo at the end to punctuate Carol doing "It's Time to Say So Long," providing the right notes for a feel-good ending.

Vikki credits the regular cast for making this show a success. "All of the characters were lovable," she says. "Number one was Carol Burnett. Everything was so spontaneous. No matter what you'd read or learn, there was always something that went wrong during the live taping, which always kept everyone from trying to fall apart."

Though her focus was on her vocals, Vikki did appreciate the comedy aspect of the series. "They had a magic that nowadays on TV seems so forced," she says. "It's so reaching for the most vulgar and double entendre lines."

Another interesting item in relation to the series is the confusion some people had at the time between Vikki Carr and Vicki Lawrence. Vikki is able to laugh now about the fact that she received fan mail saying "I love you on *The Carol Burnett Show*!" long after she did this episode. (This was the last appearance by Flip Wilson on it as well as Vikki.)

Even though Vikki guest starred on just two episodes of the series (for the other appearance, see March 31, 1969), she retains fond memories of the experience. "Carol was a love, and it was a joy to work with her and everybody on the show," she says. "They were such an incredible ensemble."

Jan. 26, 1970: Mel Torme, Soupy Sales

Q&A; Soupy plays a fraudulent insurance complainant whose efforts to collect are hampered by the appearance of Alice Portnoy the Fireside Girl (Carol); Mel sings "Hurry On Down"; Carol is on a hunger strike so that she can go with Roger on a trip to Hawaii in "Carol & Sis"; a tribute to Warner Brothers includes Carol as Bugs Bunny and Soupy as Elmer Fudd, followed by a musical salute to the studio by the cast, dancers and guests; Carol stars in the show's first takeoff of *Mildred Pierce*; a drama teacher (Carol) instructs students on how to act mean.

Comments: The installment has several bright spots, including the Q&A's very special guest—Ronald Reagan, California's newly elected governor and future president of the United States. Before he is introduced, there is a memorable moment where a boy in the audience reads Carol a tribute poem that includes the line, "This girl I love, this glorious girl, is old enough to be my mother." Carol cracks up and then tells him to sit down.

After that precious bit, Carol informs the audience that the show has a segment devoted to Warner Brothers and coincidentally a featured player with that studio in the 1940s is here. Reagan receives a warm reception and tells Carol that "I was delighted to come and very excited. . . . Our family sees you every week." Taking questions, one audience member brings up a philosophical foe of Reagan's and asks, "Does [Los Angeles] Mayor [Sam] Yorty know you're in town?" Reagan jests back with "Is he in town?" On a telling question about whether he still harbored ambitions for higher office, he demurs and says "I can't understand anyone who'd want to live any place but California." A person queries if he and Carol were running mates, and he laughs and quips, "I'd win in a walk if she was!" Reagan's appearance occurred because Carol's secretary and cousin, Janice Vance, was a big supporter of his campaign, and he asked if he could come on the show.

The first sketch has rehabilitating patient Soupy angling with his doctor (Lyle), who coincidentally is his brother-in-law, and his nurse (Vicki) to bilk $250,000 from his insurance company. His efforts are destroyed once Alice Portnoy goes from selling goods to saying she witnessed him claiming to be hit by a truck that was not even moving. A flustered Soupy ends up flying out a window. As Alice skits goes, this is pretty good.

For some reason Carol is amused when introducing Mel, lip-syncing to "Hurry On Down" in a tux with five female dancers around him. The tune had briefly appeared on the adult contemporary music chart in 1969 when sung by Claudine Longet, but Mel's version went nowhere apart from this show.

For "Carol & Sis," we see Carol envy Chris eating a deviled egg while trying to abstain, as she does when Roger and his boss (Harold Gould) come home to consume with gusto, while her stomach growls. She is so desperately hungry that when the dip from the celery Roger's boss is chewing is accidentally smeared on her face, she gobbles it up greedily. Recognizing how bad she wants to go, Roger relents and invites Carol to come to Hawaii with him, only she passes—turns out she now has a stomach ache. This is OK.

The Warner Brothers segment begins with Bugs outwitting hunter Elmer Fudd by bending his rifle back to face him. Carol's Bugs is fine, but Soupy's Elmer is weak, particularly a shame coming from someone associated with children's TV. Harvey probably could have done a better job, but at least he does appear as Porky Pig at the end of the skit, saying "Th-th-that's all, folks!" Carol then duets with Mel and they are joined by Harvey to present a ditty called "Makin' Movies" in place of "Makin' Whoopee," followed by Vicki doing "Let's Fall in Love," Soupy imitating Eddie Cantor (better than his Elmer Fudd) and the entire ensemble performing "You're a Grand Old Flag."

In "Mildred Fierce," Carol plays the title character working in a high-rise office, with Soupy as her gay secretary whom she intimidates. She knows she has a bad attitude. "Maybe it's not too late for me to change. After all, I'm only twenty-six," she says, immediately peering out to see if she will be hit by lightning for lying. She talks on the phone to a doctor to see if she hates men until their conversation is drowned out by violins. Lyle enters, and Carol immediately narrates the details of how their date will go before he responds with "Lady, I just came in to check the air conditioner!" Mel enters as her ex-husband with an unidentified juvenile actress dressed as Mildred Jr. "Why didn't you tell me we had a child?!" Carol says when they enter, to much laughter. After reviewing their situation, Carol tells Mel to take an alimony check and leave. Mel's pained reactions to their conversation are wonderful, and the audience applauds as he leaves. Harvey enters as a macho man telling Mildred he wants to take her home when Soupy interrupts them to deliver a telegram. "Here, hold this," she says, and Soupy embraces Harvey. The telegram reveals the final horror for Mildred—"I've been drafted!"

This excellent sketch precedes an acceptable finale continuing the Warner Brothers theme, as Vicki introduces a drama school with Carol singing numbers to teach actors Mel, Soupy, Harvey and Lyle how to be masculine on screen. Her advice does work—by the end, Harvey smashes a grapefruit in Carol's face a la Jimmy Cagney in 1931's *The Public Enemy*. Testosterone is indeed rather heavy throughout this show, which is not the case for next week's episode.

Feb. 2, 1970: Barbara Feldon, Joan Rivers

Q&A; "The Old Folks" contemplate various activities for having fun; Barbara performs "If You've Got the Money" and "Yakety Sax" with the dancers; Joan offers a comic monologue; Harry and Stella (Harvey and Carol) reluctantly prepare to celebrate their twentieth anniversary in their ratty apartment along with their children (Lyle and Vicki); Harvey plays Bert Sparks, emcee of an international beauty pageant featuring Vicki as Miss Holland, Barbara as Miss India, Joan as Miss China and Carol as Miss USA; the Charwoman plays with toys after hours at the Sunshine Nursery School before singing "Where Did My Childhood Go?"

Comments: Carol's first time working with Barbara Feldon and Joan Rivers shines best with the sketch featuring all three together, and well enough in the other departments to give this a passing grade. In the Q&A, Carol says she considers the year when she had her official start in show business to be 1955. "I was twelve," she cracks. A lady says how much she enjoyed the *Mission: Impossible* parody (see Jan. 19, 1970), and Carol agrees. "We loved doing that," she says. Carol says she is always exuberant and does want to do movies before the show commences.

The rambling installment of "The Old Folks" has gags about how Bert may get sterile watching TV and Molly saying she is still on the pill. When Bert grabs her leg this time, she says, "I thought the doctor told you to avoid excitement." "Best way I know!" Bert retorts. It is the best line before the duo sings, ending an unexceptional sketch.

As Barbara recalls for the next bit, "I did a dance number. The beads on my dress on my dress broke, and they were all over the floor. The dress stayed, but the beads went." Luckily, the show taped twice and used the version where there were no bead problems. Her most distinctive element of her costume actually was a feather boa. Barbara does fine in dancing with Don Crichton to "Yakety Sax," which uses the original hit instrumental recording by Boots Randolph from 1963.

In her monologue, Joan complains about her flight out to Los Angeles from New York via the fictional, questionable Trans Jersey airline ("They gave me a rabbit foot and cross"). She claims the flight attendants ignored her requests for help by saying, "It's not my aisle!" Joan contends that several college degrees are useless, such as philosophy (her actual major), calculus and physics. She discusses the drudgery of being a housewife as well, with a frequently repeated line in later years about chores: "You make the bed, you do the dishes, six months later you have to start all over again!" She even references her young daughter Melissa, though not by name. This gets better as it progresses and is fairly funny if much tamer than what Joan will do in her act in the future.

Last seen on the Jan. 5, 1970 episode, Harry and Stella return, with her as an interior decorator and him as a struggling jobseeker. Their biker son (Lyle) beats up Harry even though he loves him, while their bubblegum-chewing daughter with frizzy hair (Vicki) is a slut. Harry and Stella manage to get both out of the house to celebrate two decades of wedded bliss, with Harry putting beer on ice and Stella appearing in a ratty nightgown to seduce him. Despite some potential, this sketch never really catches fire. Nonetheless, the characters will return on the season finale (see April 27, 1970).

The show finally catches its groove with a wild if politically incorrect roasting of beauty pageants. In the semifinalist round, Miss Holland (Vicki) is upset she only earned a scholarship for winning the congeniality award, considering what host Bert Sparks (a wonderfully phony Harvey) promised her she would win last night. Bert then asks each of the finalists a question. Miss USA (Carol in a cowgirl outfit) believes the answer for underdeveloped countries is to work out, and she does bust exercises before Bert stops her. Miss India (Barbara in a sari) says her impression of New York City is similar to her native land—Chicago. Bert then reveals she is Miss India because he found her watching the nudie musical *Oh Calcutta!* Miss China (Joan in stereotypical garb) releases a badly dated and racist joke saying the man of her dreams will be found in the Yellow Pages.

The ladies then compete in the talent section. Miss USA does a strip tease that once again is interrupted by Bert. Miss China provides standup comedy. Her lines include "I am Alan King's sister—Chun King!" and hitting a gong hidden between her legs as emphasis for each. Joan accidentally hits her thighs once, adding to the considerable humor she generates here. For Miss India, she does a "Snakes Alive!" dance, with a hand puppet on Barbara serving as a fake serpent moving to the music. Miss USA attempts to redeem herself by singing "Don't Fence Me In," but her version is off-key and off the beat.

Revealing the winner, Bert first tells Miss China she has lost, prompting her to threaten to reveal their tryst to his wife. Getting her offstage, Bert then announces Miss USA is the new queen. Miss India responds by trying to choke her before being forcibly removed. As Miss USA goes down the runway, Bert croons about how she will have to return the crown the next year and then disappear from the public eye. This is very enjoyable despite a few missteps in retrospect.

The final bit with the Charwoman is inconsequential, just Carol mugging in the mirror, drawing a face, doing the Tarzan yell and other minor things before sitting on a child's chair to sing her number. In the closing, Carol makes a pitch for the Heart Fund and plugs the repeat for next week's show.

Despite working with the star for only one show, Barbara was impressed by Carol. "I remember being absolutely dazzled by her talent. I've been an absolute admirer of hers 100 percent," she says.

Feldon also reunited with one of her ex-producers on *Get Smart!*, head writer Arnie Rosen, "a very nice person." Unfortunately, CBS was canceling *Get Smart!* at the end of this season due to declining ratings (it spent its first four years on NBC before moving). Feldon believes she had already finished filming those shows before doing her Burnett guest shot but had no idea the series was going off the air. Replacing *Get Smart!* on the CBS schedule for a few months in 1970 was *The Tim Conway Show*—funny how these things all seem to connect to each other.

Feb. 9, 1970: Rerun of Oct. 20, 1969 show

Feb. 16, 1970: Family Show

Q&A; two meek teachers (Carol and Harvey) review having to present sex education to their students; drummer Cubby O'Brien plays "The Beat Goes On" and "Think" in a routine with the dancers; a warden (Lyle) tells George (Harvey) his whiny wife Zelda has come to visit him in jail, which George regrets; Vicki sings the Beatles' hit "Something" and dances to it with Don Crichton; Carol and Harvey perform solo numbers; Lyle duets with Carol on "Do Re Mi"; Carol reprises her song "Shy" from *Once Upon a Mattress*; Roger gets drunk at a masquerade party in "Carol & Sis."

Comments: Apparently done to offset the costs of the Nov. 10, 1969 episode with Bing, Ella and Rowan & Martin, this midseason show with just spotlights the talents of the regulars, the orchestra and dancers. With so much to feature, the rather short Q&A includes a woman presenting Carol with a pillow sporting a big smile and Carol's name on it. This transitions swiftly to a teachers' recreational room, where Carol confesses she has problems ("You can tell me, I'm a Republican!" says Harvey). The difficulty is one Harvey shares—a fear of how to instruct their sex ed class. Somewhat predictably, both loosen up and become horny as their unease shifts into excitability about the material, culminating with Carol letting down her hair and shouting, "It's too good for the kids!"

Next, Carol introduces Cubby O'Brien as a member of the Harry Zimmerman Orchestra who viewers might remember as a regular on *The Mickey Mouse Club*. Cubby shows off his skills in a bizarre number involving ropes that allows him to clash cymbals as part of his accompaniment. The inclusion of two well-known recent pop hits helps cover some of the rough spots in this presentation.

O'Brien recalls that his appearance here emerged as a fluke. "Ernie Flatt knew that I was a tap dancer too, and said, 'Do you want to do a show?' I said yes, and so Ernie put together this thing for me to do. It was nerve wracking but fun."

The next sketch has poor George enduring a meeting with Zelda while holed up in San Quentin. She is in top complaining form as always, telling him how she endured a long bus ride and lost $3 in mahjongg and thus is suffering as much as he is in prison. When George informs Zelda he is having his last meal before execution, she critiques his dinner choice. To top it off, she asks, "When do you think I ought to start dating again?" The final blow for George is that he learns he has been pardoned, which means he has to go back to the outside world and be with crappy Zelda again.

Five consecutive music numbers occur next, including Carol as a tomboy in a solo and Harvey as a singer of the "Unrequited Lovers' March," with a Valentine's Day background as the dancers celebrate the season. All are acceptable but unspectacular.

For "Carol & Sis," complications ensue when Carol and Chrissy learn they have brought home the wrong intoxicated man dressed in the same knight's outfit Roger wore with them at a costume party. Roger finally arrives and challenges his double to a mock duel that he wins, but complains as a victor that he should not have to stay with Carol. Roger Beatty says this is his favorite "Carol & Sis" sketch of the dozens he wrote for the series.

The finale starts with the regulars and dancers in casual clothes before dissolving into the participants wearing tuxedos and fancy dresses while doing the polka. Harvey, Vicki and Lyle join Carol in singing "It's Time to Say So Long" as the show ends.

This hodgepodge has variable highs and lows, both musically and humorously. It feels occasionally more like an effort to fill time with leftover or last-minute bits than to present a creative, inspired and cohesive show, and nobody is shown to his or her best advantage overall. Next week's effort is an improvement—although not by much.

Feb. 23, 1970: Jack Jones, Pat Carroll

Q&A; Carol and Pat are actresses auditioning for a foot powder commercial for a lecherous ad exec (Harvey); Jack performs "Get Together" and "God Bless the Child"; Carol and Pat vie for the attention on a golf driving range of a handsome instructor (Lyle); Carol reminisces and re-enacts her early comic routines she did in the mid-1950s; Pat is a friend of Marian's who overeats to compensate for a lack of love in her life, but nevertheless is wooed Lyle and Jack, in "As the Stomach Turns"; Carol and Pat play aspiring showgirls in a saloon for the finale.

Comments: "We're from Canada and we want to know what shtick is" asks a visiting couple at the start of Q&A. Carol explains it by referencing the comic routines Tim Conway does when he visits her show (coincidentally, Tim will be next week's guest). She adds that she will remake her Broadway hit *Once Upon a Mattress* on TV in color (that does happen but does not air until nearly three years from this original broadcast) and that she can wear some of her outfits offstage. Carol autographs one man's leg in a cast before the scripted bits commence.

At the Peabody Advertising Agency, a bimbo secretary (Vicki) gets romantic with her boss before he auditions veteran commercial actresses Carol (who has played a woman with stuffed up nasal passages) and Pat (Miss Dry Underarms) for a foot powder promotion. All is for naught—the two lose out to Vicki. Both women are similarly unlucky competing in their next sketch for Lyle's love, as he ignores them for another woman. Between these bits, Jack Jones sings two songs popularized by other artists.

Carol tells the audience how she started tugging her ear on TV in the 1950s as a sign to her grandmother that things were fine, and for a time added rubbing her nose to say hi to her sister, Chris. The setup leads to Carol doing her old routines on girl singers she did on variety shows, like ones who are over-emotive. While amusing, this feels like filler that is turning the episode into a blah, forced affair, until it is redeemed by the next offering.

A strong "As the Stomach Turns" has Pat wearing a fat suit and eating a layer cake while her friend Marian frets Pat would be svelte if only she accepted romance in her life. Pat jogs and flits about so well in her oversized garb that the audience applauds her physical grace. The skit mocks the unisex look by having Vicki appear bald with her love child, and the wildness continues, with Harvey showing up as a lawyer granting Pat a quickie divorce from her husband (Lyle) before she falls for a man who narrates words from Broadway songs (Jack). The most "out there" moment comes at the end, when it is implied Marian might find amour in her own life with a biker chick!

The end number with the dancers is energetic, maybe too much so, as Carol is short of breath as she announces next week's guests and prepares to sing her theme. This show marks the first professional engagement Pat Carroll and Jack Jones worked together, but Pat mentions that they did come close one time previously. "He was supposed to be the prince in *Cinderella*," she says, referring to the 1965 TV production of the musical in which she played a stepsister. "He was replaced by Stuart Damon. And I don't know what happened. I do know that I thought Jack Jones was dandy, and what a lovely voice." This was his second and last time on the series (for the first, see March 18, 1968), but Pat will return to it three times next season, beginning on Dec. 28, 1970.

March 2, 1970: Jane Connell, Tim Conway

Q&A; "The Old Folks" discuss the doctor's new 21-year-old female assistant and other random topics; Jane sings a song about pollution; Tim is a drunk man trying not to wake up his wife as he arrives home late at night with Harvey; Vicki performs "Leaving on a Jet Plane"; a salute to Universal Studios includes Vicki and Jane as flappers singing the title tune to *Thoroughly Modern Millie*, a spoof of *Pillow Talk* and a send-up of Maria Montez exotic movies including *Arabian Nights* and *Ali Baba and the Forty Thieves* featuring the cast, dancers and guests.

Comments: Carol reunites with her co-star on *Stanley* (1956-1957), Jane Connell, and enjoys her third visit this season by Tim. While both perform well, the outstanding sketch of this show employs neither of them. The Q&A is simply an acknowledgment of producer Ross Hunter in the audience (apparently invited there because of his creating hits for Universal motion pictures since the 1950s) and Carol saying Tim is one of her favorite comedians. She notes that while his sitcom *The Tim Conway Show* will be ending this series, he will have a variety show next fall on CBS (which will bomb too).

It's on to an aimless edition of "The Old Folks," with jokes about President Nixon trying to hide out from gaffe-prone Vice President Spiro Agnew and a come-on from Bert that Molly compares to *Mission: Impossible*. When Bert grabs Molly's leg, she says it reminds her of atheism. "Why?" Bert asks. "You haven't got a prayer!" she shoots back. A remark about Bert saying he saw the pyramids in Egypt as a kid and Molly cracking "They're finished now!" rounds out this time killer.

Carol introduces her female guest as "I've known her for many years" and mentioning her portrayal of Agnes Gooch on Broadway in *Mame*. Jane appears in a dowdy outfit trilling about water and air pollution while dancers dressed as street cleaners remove items off her clothes. This is more preachy than funny.

What appears to be initially another Tim-Harvey combo actually is more of a solo pantomime effort by Tim. Tim is so nervous about waking his wife that he drowns the cuckoo clock in his kitchen's fish tank. A cold can of orange juice gets stuck on his forehead and then his tongue, and to handle the latter situation, Harvey tells him to dunk his head in the tank's warm water to loosen the can. The look he gives to Harvey when he emerges cracks Harvey up before he leaves. On his own, Tim warms up water in a teakettle, but its whistle is so loud he has to put it in the refrigerator. Inserting his hand in a wrapper with a loaf of bread, he puts his hands through all the slices in a great bit. He has difficulty unscrewing a jar of mayonnaise and then putting it onto the few bread crust left when he destroyed the loaf in the wrapper. He cannot open a package of luncheon meat, and he fights so much with plastic wrap that he ties it up into a bow and carries it outside. This skit gets much better as it goes along.

After a decent rendition of Peter, Paul and Mary's recent Number One hit, Vicki fares better joining Jane to do "Thoroughly Modern Millie" with four male dancers. It kicks off the Universal tribute, which Carol introduces with a glittery rotating globe that collapses when she sings the studio theme. That's amusing along with Jane and Vicki's number, but the best was yet to come.

In "Pillow Squawk," Harvey introduces a freckled-face Carol to a penthouse apartment she considers renting that is shared by a man who is out of town. Making fun of Doris Day's goody two shoes reputation as a character called Mary Ellen Janie Sue, Carol says things like "Golly gee!" and smacks Harvey when he says "bed." "Take it easy, miss, I've got diabetes!" he exclaims, and his wonderful disdain of her cutesy behavior earns applause as he exits. She gets ready to go to bed by brushing her teeth to keep "Mr. Tooth Decay" away and recite the Girl Scout pledge in the bathroom.

Meanwhile, the pilot who shares the apartment (Lyle) shoos away two girls accompanying him so he can get a drink in another room. Carol emerges with her teddy bear which she has blindfolded because she forgot the bottom part of her pajamas. She adds freckles to her face and hopscotches to the kitchen while Lyle comes out shirtless in pajama pants with hearts on them and gets in bed. Not noticing him, Carol turns on a nightlight and sings "Que Sera" before finding Lyle in bed with her. Carol has a great hysterical reaction in hiding from Lyle before he promises to marry her if she will come out. She does so in a bridal gown. Lyle suggests that they stay in bed together tonight before they wed, and Carol responds pulling up the rollout bed into the wall with Lyle on it and singing "Que Sera" again.

This send-up is so delicious that the series will include part of it in the 1978 finale. Kenny Solms remembers it as one of his favorite sketches he wrote. While he thinks Doris Day was fine with the spoof and adds that "She would've been great as a guest," the reaction from her son, rock producer Terry Melcher, was strongly negative. "I heard the son wrote a letter saying it was in 'shitty taste,'" notes Kenny.

A comedown from that follows with "The Thief of Arabian Nights," where in ancient Baghdad Ali Ben Gay (Harvey) sees seven new slave girls that include Carol and Jane as Carol's aide. Carol refuses to be tamed by Ali and dances "The Tale of the Veils" with the other slave girls to show her independence. She obtains a ring from Ali that her family lost that grants her three wishes from a 500-year-old genie (Tim), who shuffles slowly before doing her bidding awkwardly. She asks him to make Ali's guards freeze when attacking her, but they end up getting a chill that nevertheless provokes them to leave. Her second wish is to make Ali jump in the snake pit, which does work. Her final request is for the genie to become a handsome prince, so naturally Tim becomes Lyle. This concoction has some pleasure but is too long in the telling to be really successful.

During the closing, Carol introduces Lyle Waggoner's wife as playing one of the women in the harem. The hostess is surprised by Ross Hunter joining her on stage to present her with an award—a pair of blue jeans worn by Debbie Reynolds in the movie *Tammy and the Bachelor* with "Property of Ross Hunter Productions" written on the back of it. Carol guffaws at the gift before singing "It's Time to Say So Long."

Incidentally, Carol will talk with Hunter about a potential collaboration that does not occur—see Nov. 10, 1971 for more on that. She and Jane Connell will work again professionally in 1995 in *Moon Over Broadway* (see the final chapter for details).

March 9, 1970: Nanette Fabray, Trini Lopez

** Bert and Molly observe their 70th anniversary with jokes before singing "I Remember It Well"; Trini sings "Yesterday I Heard the Rain" and joins Carol in a duet of his old hit "Lemon Tree"; a plot of a movie on TV convinces Carol that Roger plans to follow the behavior depicted and leave town with another woman in "Carol & Sis"; a boozer (Nanette) tries to hide her battle with the bottle in "As the Stomach Turns"; the dancers and Nanette present "Good Old Sounds"; Trini stars with Carol and Nanette in "Pata Cum Cum Fiesta," a Latin rock number.

Comments: This is the third consecutive season that Trini Lopez guest stars, and he credits obtaining his appearances to Carol wanting him there. "She is a big fan of mine," he says. "She was so popular and a Texan like me, so I was so proud to do her show."

Lopez recalls that he usually had his musical conductor on the series to play bass with members of the orchestra. He felt very comfortable in the way he was presented in all of Carol's programs, including this one, which unsuccessfully promoted his latest single "Pata Cum Cum" ("It was a little takeoff on 'La Bamba'" is how he describes the tune).

"When she liked talent on the show, she specifically made sure that they got more than the usual treatment," Lopez says. "She was such fun, so down to earth."

This was Trini's second appearance with Nanette Fabray (for the first, see Oct. 7, 1968). "She was very nice," he recalls. He has even more fond memories of Lyle Waggoner and Harvey Korman, both of whom became golf buddies of his. In fact, regarding Harvey, Lopez says, "I played in his celebrity golf tournament in Palm Springs, where I live."

Trini also worked one show with Carol for Texas Gov. John Connally in addition to his work on this program. "It was a thrill doing the series," he concludes.

By this show, Bob Schiller and Bob Weiskopf had joined the series as writers. They appeared to be perfect for the assignment. The two men wrote for Lucille Ball in the last two years of *I Love Lucy* (1955-1957) and the first two years of *The Lucy Show* (1962-1964), followed by three years on *The Red Skelton Show*. They knew clearly knew how to create popular broad humor and variety segments. According to Schiller in an interview in 2000 with the Archive of American Television, the reason why did they not last long on *The Carol Burnett Show* was head writer Arnie Rosen.

"He wanted all of his own stuff on the show," Schiller recounted. "And we kept writing sketches, and he kept putting them in the drawer and not using them. So when *The Flip Wilson Show* was about to go on the air, we sent the abandoned sketches over to the head writer, who bought them. He said, 'Come join the staff.' And we later won an Emmy for one of the sketches that we did that was rejected by this head writer on Carol Burnett."

That victory came in 1971, by which time Schiller and Weiskopf were well established as regular writers on *The Flip Wilson Show*, even though there were a couple of installments of *The Carol Burnett Show* from September to December 1970 that credited them at the end as well, even if their contributions were not used. One can only wonder how Rosen felt losing a third time for writing *The Carol Burnett Show* to the two Bobs he formerly had under his wing. If that was not enough, Hal Goodman and Larry Klein left at the end of this season to go to work at *The Flip Wilson Show* too in 1970-1971, meaning that four recent ex-scribes of *The Carol Burnett Show* beat the latter series for an Emmy win less than a year after they had been on it.

After two seasons on *The Flip Wilson Show*, Schiller and Weiskopf went back to sitcoms with success on *Maude* and later *All in the Family*. It's a shame that their considerable comic acumen was not allowed to flourish on *The Carol Burnett Show*.

March 16, 1970: Ronnie Schell, Nancy Wilson

** A comedian (Ronnie) aggravates his wife (Carol) by his constant need to make wisecracks offstage; Harvey is tormented for money both by Alice Portnoy and her sister (Vicki), a fellow Fireside Girl; Carol sings "Where is Love?" and duets with Vicki on "Second Hand Rose"; Carol accidentally gets a ball-and-chain locked to her body while goofing around at a garage sale and tries to hide what has happened from Roger in "Carol & Sis" ; Nancy solos on "Waitin' for Charlie to Come Home" and joins Carol to present "Follow the Lamb" and "Brother Love's Traveling Salvation Show."

Comments: Regarding the role he plays on this episode, Ronnie Schell quips, "I didn't go far for my character!" As with his prior outing on March 31, 1969, he had worked previously with the other singing guest star and had an enjoyable time on the series.

What Ronnie remembers most is what happened after this episode when he had to open for

Carol at Caesars Palace as an emergency move. "What happened was Jim Nabors, he got 'Vegas throat,' and he was working with Carol, and she said, 'What can I do?'" Ronnie received a request to help out, since he was a known performer on *The Jim Nabors Hour* and obviously had worked with Carol before, and she liked his humor.

In Vegas, Ronnie did a comic bit with Carol along with his monologue, where they put two strings in their mouths as part of being literally blind people on a blind date. "It was a really fun sketch," he recalls, and the audience loved it. "When the first curtain closed, she said 'I love you!'" Ronnie thought their successful albeit limited run meant he would get more guest shots on Carol's show, but that turned out not to be the case. "I would desperately go back for a third and fourth show," he said.

Still, apart from this being his second and last appearance on the series, Ronnie has nothing but praise for Carol. "Everybody loved Carol," he says. "She was so lovable on camera and off. She was a joy to be with. Didn't have an ego. And very, very talented."

Incidentally, "Where is Love?" from the musical *Oliver!* will be performed at least two more times on the show by others—see Dec. 14, 1970 and Oct, 25, 1972.

March 23, 1970: Martha Raye, Mel Torme

Q&A; a classy lady (Carol) encounters an earthy counterpart (Martha) on a park bench; Mel does a medley of two Blood, Sweat and Tears tunes; Martha sings "Just a Little Mad Sometime"; a tribute to the Disney studio includes Harvey and Martha as peacocks being filmed for a True Life Adventure documentary, clips from *Fantasia* interspersed with dancers recreating parts on stage, an imagining of *Sleeping Beauty* as done under three rating levels, Mel and Martha singing hits popularized by the movies, a spoof of *Mary Poppins*, and a finale with Harvey and Carol as Mickey and Minnie Mouse respectively.

Comments: This episode has one of the best long-form themed salutes ever to a great American institution, and what proceeds it is fairly acceptable. The Q&A has Carol reminiscing about her old days, from her first professional jobs on stage ("I did some industrial shows, I went to Chicago") to her love for Garry Moore ("One of the dearest, most marvelous men") and her audition for him on Nov. 9, 1957. She also reveals her favorite pastime is exercise and golf, and she advises an aspiring actress to go to college and study theatre arts for at least two years. "Then save your money, get a part-time job," she adds. Her final announcement is telling everyone her show has been sold to British television, and she will head to London with the cast to tape a show a few weeks later.

Dressed fancy with a poodle, Carol is aghast when frumpy Martha joins her with a big shaggy dog (perhaps foreshadowing the upcoming Disney tribute by referencing a character from the studio's hit 1959 movie) and opens up a beer. Martha is tickled by Carol's upscale habits as the contrasts continue. For example, after Carol coos "Frere Jacques" to her poodle, Martha lets loose with "Beer Barrel Polka." This is a serviceable though not quite sparkling display of the comediennes' talents.

Watching Mel perform "You've Made Me So Very Happy" and then a slow "Spinning Wheel" followed by Martha's number makes one fear the show's momentum is dimming. That gets rectified quickly when the next act launches into the Disney segments and involves Harvey, in an incredible peacock costume, riffing humorously with a similarly feathered Martha as she is about to lay an egg. "Me a father—I never thought it would happen!" he exclaims. "I thought you were the sterile cuckoo!" Martha hits back, paraphrasing the title of a recent movie. She gives birth to a parrot and tells Harvey defensively of how she got pregnant that "I couldn't help it—he was a smooth talker!"

The second half of the show remains Disney focused, first with an excellent selection of clips from *Fantasia* appearing between a live routine of dancers dressed as the alligators, ostriches and hippos seen in the film's "Dance of the Hours" segment. Next is *Sleeping Beauty*, with a snippet of the movie appearing before doing modern retellings. The G version has Lyle as the prince with a Dudley Do-Right voice awakening Vicki as the princess, who blows bubblegum and tells Lyle that "You're even better looking that I am!" before they honeymoon in Disneyland. For mature audiences (the M rating at the time, which would be PG today), Harvey and Martha play the prince and princess with Italian dialects, and Martha calls for the police when she hears how Harvey awoke her with a kiss, only to then go after him. The X version is pretty wild for 1970 network TV—Lyle kisses Mel, who wakens and smiles as he says in a mincing voice, "Well, hi there!"

After stills of cartoons are on display while Mel and Martha perform standards like "When You Wish Upon a Star," we have Lyle introduce "Perry Poppins," with Carol as the title character, Martha as the tippling mother of the family, Vicki as the maid, Harvey as an old man and Mel as Martha's son in a Little Lord Fauntleroy getup. This odd but effective takeoff has Carol come down with an umbrella promising magic but then telling everyone she needed help taking off the wires that dropped her. Her tricks fail miserably, first as she tries to tidy the house but instead breaks items. When Harvey needs help for a condition, she gives him medicine and mentions "A Spoonful of Sugar," but he is diabetic and dies as a result. Her results are similarly awful for Mel—she tells him he can fly by saying "SupercalifraglisticexpialiPOcious," but he falls out the window instead. "It was docious," she recalls of the spell's true two last syllables after Mel splats offstage. "Oh well, he is all over London!" With two men dead, Perry decides it is time for her to leave, but Martha pleads for her to stay. "Where's another nanny who can fly?" she moans. At that point, an unidentified actress zooms down as the Flying Nun.

Lyle introduces Mickey Mouse (Harvey) and Minnie (Carol, both dressed as the characters with big ears and gloved hands) to sing a number and then lead everyone in the "Mickey Mouse Cheer" at the end. The regulars, dancers and guests come out wearing big ears in this segment. Carol keeps the theme going at the end, singing "It's Time to Say So Long" in Minnie's high-pitched voice. It ends a clever appreciation for a great part of Americana that only the most rabid Disney hater would dislike.

March 30, 1970: Peggy Lee, Tim Conway

Q&A; Lyle interviews a pregnant Miss Vicki (Carol) and her husband, Tiny Tim (Harvey), in "V.I.P."; Peggy Lee sings "Love Story" and joins Carol in presenting "A Doodling Song"; a drunk office employee (Tim) plans to demand a raise from his boss despite warnings that he is not in the right shape to do it from a colleague (Harvey); George faces a life-threatening operation when Zelda visits him in the hospital; a loud lady (Carol) and an exterminator (Tim) find love and more on a cruise ship; the cast and guests perform "Applause" with some comic bits included.

Comments: This show finished at Number Two for the week, the highest placement ever for the series during the regular season, thanks to most everything else on nighttime TV being in reruns, combined with Peggy Lee being a hot property thanks to her recent hit "Is That All There Is?" It is too bad the episode is not as strong creatively as it is in getting an audience, although there are certain pleasures to be enjoyed.

The Q&A starts with Carol saying it is unlikely she will do a dramatic role soon ("I would miss the laughs"), followed by an exchange with Joyce, an operator at CBS, in the "op" language—for more on this, see the Feb. 24, 1969 Q&A. A beautician offers to give Carol a free hairdo if she will bring Lyle with him, while Carol tells another audience member that she selected Lyle for his "good, big voice" (ahem). One man thanked her for a picture she sent to him and told Carol she looks even better in person. A girl brings three handmade Charwoman dolls to Carol as a gift. Finally, Carol says she would love to have the Smothers Brothers back as guests (which happens more than four years later—see Oct. 12, 1974) and reveals she has no plans for doing a USO tour.

Harvey is a hoot as Tiny Tim and Carol gets some good lines herself in "V.I.P." She tells Lyle she has been a little nauseous—not from morning sickness, but as a result of her marriage to Tiny Tim. She claimed her pregnancy occurred after they bumped into each other in the hall. This amusing bit has a duet by them that is a waste of time.

In a black gown with white curtains behind her, Peggy sings her featured number well before Carol joins her and reminds everyone Peggy just won a Grammy for her vocals on "Is That All There Is?" Carol sings a few bars of Peggy's other hits to applause, and they do a superb job with their duet too.

For the Tim-Harvey sketch, laughs come from an insistent Tim practicing how he will ask his employer for more money with Harvey. Tim accidentally stabs himself with a letter opener (and is saved from harm by his flask), then destroys the portrait of the boss on the wall. He tries to repair it with glue, but it gets stuck on his hands, as does paper and a wastebasket. Going outside, he even attracts a (fake) pigeon. When his boss (an unidentified actor) does arrive, he agrees to give Tim a raise, but Tim is so drunk and shaken he says he quits. This is pretty amusing despite little for Harvey to do in it.

After a doctor (Lyle) warns him he might die from his risky surgery, George finds no sympathy from Zelda, who gives him grief about her hardships including a problem with their cat's ear. Telling her of his possible fatal circumstances, Zelda complains she lacks a black dress to wear at the funeral. This moderately amusing but overextended sketch concludes with a frustrated George escaping from his hospital room by tying his bed sheet and lowering himself from a window, only to have Zelda accidentally cause him to fall to his presumed death.

An improvement follows as the special effects crew has a high time rocking a cruise ship set back and forth as Carol and Tim play a romantic duo. They struggle to be intimate, eat food provided by Don Crichton, and avoid getting seasick amid slanting up and down several times. A breeze blows off Tim's toupee, and he falls overboard, prompting Carol to seek help. Lyle shows up, and Carol forgets about Tim's plight and leaves with the hunk. This is a very satisfying nugget of nautical nonsense.

For the finale, Carol and Peggy sing "Applause" before being joined by the dancers and the men offering some humorous support. It is a lively presentation by all, particularly when Vicki, Carol and Peggy struggle to ring the right bells in tune with the music.

Carol plugs the repeat airing in next week's slot as she signs off. Peggy will reappear on the Jan. 5, 1972 show.

April 6, 1970: Rerun of Nov. 10, 1969 show

April 13, 1970: Nanette Fabray, Michele Lee

Q&A; Nanette and Carol are censors watching a sexy film who become aroused by what they see on the screen; Michele sings "What About Today?"; a blackout mocks the "worst commercial of the year"; Nanette sings "One Little Brick at a Time" with the male dancers and cracks a few jokes as well; Carol and Chrissy buck up Roger's confidence when he loses an expected promotion; "As the Stomach Turns" features Nanette as Marian's pill-popping addict friend being treated by Dr. Gorgeous (Lyle) and his nurse (Michele); a tribute to comic strip characters by the cast, guests and dancers.

Comments: This entry is ho-hum for the most part, nothing really terrible or spectacular in anything presented including the Q&A. Carol repeats her embarrassing summer stock experience (see the Oct. 9, 1967 episode for more) and reveals Robert Goulet will be a guest next season and Paul Newman will not. There is some excitement regarding her past though—she says she had the nickname of "Hot Lips" in junior high, and she is ecstatic and runs into the audience to embrace Buddy, her old schoolmate who was president of Hollywood High when they both attended the institution. He shows some pictures of himself with Carol during that time before the show commences.

As Carol and Nanette discuss what they want to cut out from an adult movie, it becomes obvious that they are entranced by it (nothing is heard or seen from it, mind you). Carol fans herself looking at one segment, while Nanette splashes water on herself. It is obvious and lacks wit, as evidenced by one joke about having seen a picture called *Hansel and Gretel* where a man goes to

Denmark to get a sex change and dates the doctor after the operation. Michelle's song following it is similarly passable.

The commercial blackout does have some amusement. Lyle confuses Carol for her daughter and paws after her thanks to some unspecified health and beauty product she uses. He realizes his mistake and apologies, but a horny Carol tells him to go on.

Next, Carol calls Nanette a "complete performer" who is able to do anything, and the show attempts to test that belief by giving her the thankless duty of appearing on a construction site in worker's garb to sing, dance and crack wise with the male dancers. All it does it confirm this show is going to be so-so at best.

A better—or at least tighter—offering comes with "Carol & Sis," as Carol and Chrissy prepare to celebrate Roger getting an expected raise at work. Carol's enthusiasm is dimmed some when Cindy (Elaine Joyce), the divorcee from next door, comes over to show her provocative new dress. Cindy leaves before Roger arrives, distraught that he failed to earn more money despite wearing a toupee to work for the previous two months. Thinking he has lost his youth, he is reinvigorated by Cindy returning and showing off her form to him, but his joy does not last once she leaves, as an envious Carol impersonates Cindy's high voice and pretends that she has a headache going to bed.

The show rallies a little more with "As the Stomach Turns," which is its usual strong self but does have some slow moments. Taking tranquilizers every ten minutes, Nanette is laughing, singing and otherwise acting odd toward Marian due to the drugs. Marian attempts to take action but first must deal with her daughter (Vicki), who reveals she received an "A" in sex education in college and is considered the teacher's pet. She leaves and Dr. Gorgeous (Lyle) and his nurse (Michelle) arrive, as does Nanette's husband (Harvey), a flaming queen who begs Lyle to check his heartbeat. Marian tells Harvey she blames his neglecting Nanette for her condition, and he objects vociferously, saying that he has decorated their house, cooked, cleaned and so on. He finally announces that he is going home to his mother while other plots remain unresolved.

The finale is colorful to watch and fun, if a little contrived. Carol, Nanette and Michelle are artists singing about a party before they become cartoon characters. Carol is transformed into Olive Oyl and joins a dancer playing Popeye with his familiar theme song in the background. Nanette sings the Little Orphan Annie song, while Michelle sports an animal skin dress with three male dancers in similar prehistoric costumes to perform "Alley Oop." We also get to see Harvey and Lyle as Superman and Captain Marvel respectively before the number ends.

Recalling this iffy entry, Michelle Lee noted that "Nanette Fabray was on one show with me, and everybody loved her. She was wonderful with Carol."

April 20, 1970: Pre-empted by *CBS News Special* on "Health in America"

April 27, 1970: Family Show

Q&A; slovenly Harry and Stella compile their taxes; a flamenco number by the dancers; Lyle plays a photographer from *Home Beautiful* magazine whose plans to take pictures of Carol and Harvey's apartment vanish when the couple destroys each other's furnishings deemed imperfect for the shots; Vicki and Lyle impersonate Fred Astaire and Ginger Rogers doing "Cheek to Cheek," followed by Carol and Harvey showing how the number would go if it happened in real life; Carol is a busty blonde replacing Harvey's co-star on stage; the Charwoman says goodbye to the cast and recalls highlights of the season.

Comments: The third season ends with serviceable but not outstanding offerings. The Q&A does have some fun in watching an older gentleman in the audience lie down and struggle to do pull-ups along with Carol, as part of a demonstration of the exercises she does every day. The bit is cute and tight, unlike some of this show's other pieces.

Harry and Stella, a couple in a rundown apartment previously seen on the Feb. 2, 1970 show, star in the first skit. He has a closet that opens with an avalanche of beer cans while is trying to fill out their 1040 forms. They ask Lyle, their biker son, how much he earned last year, as well as Vicki, their trashy daughter. Stella's new perfume is a disinfectant spray, which gives a good idea of the low level of comedy here. The couple will reappear in a surprisingly good installment on the Sept. 21, 1970 episode.

The flamenco number is nicely atmospheric, but any hopes that it means the rest of the show will be improving as well are dashed by the next sketch, wherein Harvey's suggestion that they move Carol's ashtray from Denmark in order to make their apartment look perfectly blended escalates into an all-out fight between the two prior to their photo shoot. Harvey throws the ashtray out the window, Carol does the same with his favorite vase. He destroys her Venetian stemware, and she responds in kind with the same move on his lattice work. Soon there are torn drapes, cotton removed from a silk sofa and other mayhem until Lyle returns, and they calmly try to portray like nothing has changed since he first pronounced their apartment perfect. While somewhat funny, there have been many better motivated and enacted destruction scenes during the show's run. The sketch is a remake from *The Garry Moore Show* episode of May 23, 1961.

The "Cheek to Cheek" spoof has some moments of enjoyment, particularly with Carol saying Harvey is making a jerk of himself and trying to get money from him during their dance. What is missing again is a certain spark to make this more than average.

Next, wearing a tight gold, spangly, low-cut gown, Carol infuriates Harvey by talking to the audience, getting her jewelry caught in her dress and eating potato chips loudly. After going on longer than needed to make its point, this skit winds up with Carol pulling off Harvey's toupee during his death scene and knocking him out the window as the curtain goes down. Nothing special here either.

After watching the end of the show, the Charwoman says goodbye to the regulars as they head off the soundstage. She then reenacts "Carol & Sis," "The Old Folks," Zelda bothering George in prison, "As the Stomach Turns" and even the Q&A. The Charwoman looks through the guest book before heading out and ending a rather disappointing closing show. Better luck next year.

Final Notes for the Season

Thanks to its general excellence as well as its lackluster competition, *The Carol Burnett Show* finished an impressive Number Thirteen for the season, its highest overall placement ever. Its average rating of 21.8 was a full point higher than what it received in 1968-1969. This would mark the only time the series finished in the top twenty for a season, but according to writer Gene Perret, that fact was fine with the star and producer.

"It would hover pretty much in the high twenties in the ratings. Carol and Joe insisted they preferred that," Perret claims. "The logic was that once the show gets into the top five or ten, the executives start forcing themselves into the creative team. In the twenties, the execs were content to leave us alone."

For the third consecutive year, *The Carol Burnett Show* earned an Emmy nomination but came up a cropper for a win as Outstanding Musical or Variety Program, losing this time to *The David Frost Show.* Unbelievably, there were no nominations for writing and directing for the series this go-round, and the supporting variety category was gone, so there was nothing for Harvey Korman to receive. The series' only other nomination went to Paul Barnes, Bob Sansom and Bill Harp for art direction and scenic design (for the Oct. 6, 1969 show). They lost to E. Jay Krause for *Mitzi's 2nd Special*. Krause would beat the trio in the same category again in 1972.

Incidentally, Carol presented the Outstanding New Series award with Gig Young during the ceremony, and *The Carol Burnett Show* was the only CBS program nominated for outstanding comedy, dramatic, new and musical or variety series categories. The latter was a sign of how the industry regarded much of the rest of the regular entertainment on CBS apart from the series as tired and trite.

At the Golden Globes earlier in the year, Carol tied with Julie Sommars as Best Television Actress, Musical or Comedy. Sommars was a regular on *The Governor and J.J.*, which beat out *The Carol Burnett Show* for Best Television Show, Musical or Comedy. The Hollywood Foreign Press, which doles out the Golden Globes, clearly had an inexplicable fondness for *The Governor and J.J.* despite the series being canceled by CBS by the end of 1970 after less than a year and a half on the air, as its male lead, Dan Dailey, won for Best Television Actress, Musical or Comedy as well.

With all this adulation came attention for writers for the series to pursue other lucrative offers. One came to Bill Angelos and Buz Kohan, who created the special musical material. "We had a chance—we thought it was a step up, but it was a step into the abyss—to write *The Pearl Bailey Show*," recalls Kohan ruefully. He and Angelos took the job for the series, which aired on ABC as a midseason replacement in January 1971 and died opposite *My Three Sons* on CBS and *NBC Saturday Night at the Movies*. "We did thirteen weeks and we were gone," Kohan says. He and Angelos will return to *The Carol Burnett Show* in 1972-1973, unfortunately with ultimately disastrous results for themselves.

During the production break, Vicki, Harvey and Lyle performed *Send Me No Flowers* in summer stock. Harvey encouraged his fellow supporting thespians to use their time away from taping their TV series to hone their talent on stage, and this was one of several examples of what they did away from *The Carol Burnett Show* in the 1970s.

One member of the staff received a promotion at the end of this season which will make him a busy contributor to *The Carol Burnett Show* in the early 1970s. "In 1970, Joe [Hamilton] asked me to be on the writing staff," says assistant director Roger Beatty, who previously contributed several "Carol & Sis" sketches as a freelancer for the series. "When I reminded him I'm the AD on the show, he told me I could do both. Great. So, for the next two and a half seasons, I did both jobs."

As a regular writer, Beatty now could contribute to a wider variety of sketches. He recalls he did several of the Zelda and George bits, and he will later become chief writer of the Tudball and Wiggins sketches from 1975-1978 (for more on that, see the 1975-1976 season introduction), among other achievements.

Beatty has nothing but praise for his immediate boss in 1970, head writer Arnie Rosen. "He was a wonderful man and a very accomplished writer," says Beatty. "He kind of took me under his wing and taught me a lot. Since I was still doing my AD job, I was only in my office performing my writing duties two days a week. Mondays I was editing the show, and Thursdays and Fridays I was in the studio doing my AD gig.

"I think some of the other writers probably didn't feel I was pulling my weight, only putting in two days a week while they were there for all five days. I expressed this feeling to Arnie, and he told me that as long as I was producing material not to worry about it. He said that I was a 'prolific' writer. I have to admit that I did quite a bit of writing at home on weekends. Also, I knew Joe well enough that if I wasn't pulling my weight, he certainly would have let me go."

By 1973 Beatty chose to be only a writer on the program, and Bob Priest became the assistant director. However, "With my five years of experience editing the show, Joe asked me to continue to edit the show in addition to writing. So, until the show's ending, Bob and myself did all of the editing and sweetening."

The Carol Burnett Show airs in reruns through July 29. On June 6, CBS begins repeats of *The Wild Wild West*, a combination sci-fi/spy/western that ran on the network from 1965 until it was cancelled in 1969 due to violence concerns. Those fears apparently subsided enough that CBS was fine with showing it again. Starring Bob Conrad and previous *Carol Burnett Show* guest Ross Martin, this includes an episode that airs June 13 featuring Harvey Korman in a rare dramatic role as an evil baron. It ends on Sept. 7 and goes into repeats on many local stations successfully as a cult series for decades.

Carol and crew returned the following week to start their fourth season. Prior to that time, there was a major shakeup in leadership at CBS. Mike Dann, who had been the top programmer for the network, quit because he was at odds with the new company president, Bob Wood, over the direction of the network's schedule.

Dann's replacement was Fred Silverman, who would play a considerable part in the fortunes of *The Carol Burnett Show* in the 1970s. His rise occurred after Wood instructed Dann to cancel *The Red Skelton Hour* and *The Jackie Gleason Show* over the latter's objections. Wood believed both series, though still popular, were attracting older audiences and would end up costing CBS money if renewed because advertisers preferred reaching younger viewers. Their dismissal meant Carol was now the top variety series performer on CBS—and on television, for that matter—just behind Jim Nabors, whose first year of helming *The Jim Nabors Hour* finished at Number Twelve after five years starring on *Gomer Pyle—USMC*. The times, they were a-changin', as the song goes.

And while NBC was keeping its movie series opposite the series, ABC was trying out regular coverage of National Football League games Monday nights starting in the fall of 1970. CBS had aired special contests in place of *The Carol Burnett Show* one time each fall since the series began in 1970, and the ratings were impressive. Suddenly Carol was facing her strongest challenge since she started, and she and her production staff knew that they needed their best effort in 1970-1971 if they were going to stay competitive.

Rita Hayworth puts aside her glamorous image to join Carol in playing a fellow Charwoman on Feb. 1, 1971 episode. Carol lost her wig during the Brown Derby sketch with Rita as herself earlier on the show, reportedly to loosen the latter's nerves about doing the comedy. They have a great rapport here, one of the few times another woman dressed in the iconic character Carol played at the end of every season. Courtesy of Getty Images.

Chapter 5

1970–1971: Standing Out from the Competition

Audience member:	"How many hours does it take you to put your face on?"
Carol (smiling):	"Sit down!"—From the Dec. 28, 1970 show

Crew Additions This Season

Recurring Bit Players: Bob Duggan, Inga Nielsen

Writers: Hal Goodman, Larry Klein, Jack Mendelsohn, Gene Moss and Jim Thurman (1970), Arthur Julian (supervisor 1970), Paul Wayne (1970), Stan Hart and Larry Siegel (1971), Woody Kling (1971)

Stage Managers: Bob Borgen, Jay Merrick

Special Music: Dick DeBenedictis, David Rogers

Additional Vocal Arrangements: Jack Elton

Wigs: Roselle Friedland

The biggest challenge for *The Carol Burnett Show* faced in the fall of 1970 turned out not to be pro football on ABC—which usually finished behind the series in the ratings—but standing out amid variety overkill. In response to complaints about excessive violence on television, coupled with the success of Carol, *Rowan and Martin's Laugh-In* and a few other similar series, the networks went whole hog on the format and installed sixteen variety series in the fall of 1970, the most since the live TV heyday of the early 1950s.

Anyone familiar with the genre realizes there is a limited amount of talent equipped to write, produce, direct and act in this challenging field, so it was not a surprise to observers that only one newcomer, *The Flip Wilson Show* on NBC, became a hit. Most were losers, including several with a connection to *The Carol Burnett Show*.

The Tim Conway Comedy Hour premiered on CBS Sunday nights from 10 p.m. to 11 p.m. Eastern and Pacific on Sept. 27, 1970. Taped at Television City with Ernie Anderson announcing, the series had a good touch of Carol's influence, and she guest starred on one program with Steve Lawrence. Their comic interplay was as magic as ever, and to his credit Tim stated that "It's because of this lady that I'm on this stage." However, *The Tim Conway Comedy Hour* flopped, so Tim returned as a guest on *The Carol Burnett Show* nearly three months after the last episode on Dec. 13, 1970.

Another variety series with a less obvious Carol connection was *The Don Knotts Show*. As Elaine Joyce became a regular on that series in the fall of 1970, her character, Cindy the next-door neighbor, vanished from "Carol & Sis." Alas, *The Don Knotts Show* lasted only one year, and Joyce never returned to *The Carol Burnett Show*.

Also affecting Carol was *The Pearl Bailey Show*, a midseason replacement on ABC produced by Bill Angelos and Buz Kohan. Their departure meant that new writers for musical numbers were needed. Carol wanted the husband-and-wife team of Ken and Mitzie Welch, who had written for her on *The Garry Moore Show* and some specials. A contract to work on *The Kraft Music Hall* on NBC prevented them from joining, but they recommended an old classmate and working partner of theirs as a replacement.

"I started off as a piano player in different jobs as shows opened in theaters," notes Dick DeBenedictis. "I finally ended up in a class with David Craig, who was the Lee Strasberg of musical theater writers. In that class were Mitzie Welch and Ken Welch." The Welches took DeBenedictis under their wing, and he helped them on productions involving Carol including *Fade In-Fade Out* while trying to make it as a composer and not just a pianist.

DeBenedictis credits Ken Welch for getting him onto *The Carol Burnett Show* to do the special material. "I was to be the musical portion, while David Rogers did the lyrics and comedy parts for it," DeBenedictis says. He was disappointed by his partner, however.

"I know there were a couple of things that worked out well, but David, working under pressure was not his thing," DeBenedictis says. "Overall, we couldn't compete with someone like Kenny."

Nevertheless, the duo endured the circumstances of getting scripts and having only a few days to write songs that sounded original and clever to use, typically in the finales. It was a fast process— "We were at production meetings, and ideas would come out for stuff next week," notes DeBenedictis— but despite the chaotic atmosphere of creating material, it was a cordial experience with Carol for his part at least.

"She was always very civil, very polite, no show business carryings-on, very professional at all times," says DeBenedictis . That impression has lingered with him longer than what he created for the series, which is a blur due to the hurried nature of what he wrote.

Other new writers joined the series for various stints this season. The most significant were Stan Hart and Larry Siegel. The two previously collaborated on several projects, including the book for *The Mad Show*, an off-Broadway musical revue hit in 1966 based on the comedy magazine for which they were contributors. That production had peppy transitions and fast delivery of gags that made some people think it influenced the pace and style of *Rowan and Martin's Laugh-In* when the latter came to television in 1968. Whatever the case, Siegel secured a job writing for the series in 1970 without Hart.

"Writing for *Laugh-In*, I did about seven or eight weeks when I got a call from Carol Burnett, or rather my agent did," says Siegel. "She said, 'I saw what this guy wrote for *Playboy*.' It was a piece about World War II movies." That topic was a favorite of Carol's, and she loved Siegel's work. (Proudly and humorously, Siegel adds that "In the 1950s and 1960s, there were two publications that helped shape and warp the minds of young men, *Playboy* and *Mad*. And I wrote for both of them.")

An impressed Burnett asked George Schlatter, executive producer of *Laugh-In*, if Siegel could come to work on her series. "I had a contract with Schlatter, but strangely enough, he gave me away," notes Siegel. "And I went over at the beginning of the 1970 season. I was delighted, because it was one of the biggest comedy shows on television."

As for connecting with Hart, says Siegel, "My agent was asked to put me there with a partner [to save costs per rules of the Writers Guild of America], so I brought in Stan Hart." Although Hart had virtually no experience writing for a variety show, he and Siegel became a potent pair working together on *The Carol Burnett Show*.

"Larry is really a very funny guy," Hart says. "He was a very strong contributor. We used to get stuck on the main ending, so we would go out to the Farmers Market [at CBS Television City] and come back to work on it. We worked very well. We worked together to make sure things were funny. He was very smart and quite productive."

Hart and Siegel specialized in movie parodies. "We both were very strong with that satire in *Mad Magazine* for years," Siegel says. "At the beginning of the week, we'd choose a movie, and you'd have to play them on a reel at the time, and see what's there to make fun of." Their greatest triumph this season will be "Lovely Story" (see Feb. 1, 1971).

Another new writer was Jack Mendelsohn, who stayed just this season because, as he frankly says, "I got more money to do another series." A cartoonist turned script writer, Mendelsohn like Siegel was a regular contributor to *Rowan and Martin's Laugh-In*, albeit in its second season (1968-1969), when it was the Number One series on TV. However, the working conditions were no laughing matter for Mendelsohn.

"We were lodged in sort of a motel that was across from Warner Brothers," he says of his workspace. There, writers had to churn out comic gold amid sporadic work hours, as George Schlatter, the series' executive producer, and the rest of the production team would take the material and force the writers to review each script in a conference room.

"We'd go page by page over every joke," Mendelsohn recalls. "*Laugh-In* scripts would be about 300 pages. Well, one night at 2 a.m., we weren't one third through a script, and I said, 'George, does it really matter where this page and this joke goes? At this rate, we'll be here till dawn!'" Schlatter stared at and purposefully ignored Mendelsohn, according to the writer. "It was like I was a non-person. At that point, I knew I was off the show."

However, he did secure an Emmy nomination for his work and was able to parlay his experience into having a regular job with Arnie Kogen as his partner writing for *The Jim Nabors Hour* during that variety series' inaugural season (1969-1970). As a guest on that series, Carol Burnett was impressed by a sketch they wrote where Jim was the Lone Ranger and his fellow regular, Ronnie Schell, was Tonto. "The next year, she wanted me, while Arnie stayed with *The Jim Nabors Hour*," says Mendelsohn. (Kogen will join *The Carol Burnett Show* in the 1972-1973 season.)

On *The Carol Burnett Show*, Mendelsohn partnered with Paul Wayne, but as noted in the first chapter, Wayne had to leave during the season due to migraines and other difficulties at work, leaving Mendelsohn as a solo contributor thereafter. Apart from his work in the season opener (see Sept. 14, 1970), Mendelsohn best remembers an incident that he credits to Carol's taste for not appearing on air. He planted his son in the audience for one Q&A and told him to ask Carol, "What do you want to be when you grow up?" Carol took the bait, looked at her breasts and quipped, "Bigger!" It got huge laughs, but Carol cut it from making the air show because Mendelsohn's son was ten years old at the time, and Carol was worried viewers would be offended by her saying that to a child of that age. "She's truly a person who cared about other people," he notes.

Mendelsohn contributed to *Mad Magazine* along with Hart and Siegel. By the fall of 1972 Arnie Kogen also had multiple credits in both *Mad* and *The Carol Burnett Show*. According to Nick Meglin, the former editor of the magazine, there were no worries about writers repeating themselves in the publication or trying to foist material cut from the series into being a piece in *Mad*.

"What works in a *Mad* page drawing wouldn't work in a sketch," Meglin flatly states. "I don't think any of our writers tapped into their own work for Carol Burnett and vice versa. *Mad*'s writing was meant to be read."

A fan of *The Carol Burnett Show*, Meglin appreciated the cast along with the writing. "I was always interested in seeing their work as performers, always so much fun," he says.

He views comparisons of the humor *Mad* writers presented on the show with what they did in the magazine as similar to that of movies based on novels, meaning that they are different forms with their own standards of success. Of the skits he remembers seeing on *The Carol Burnett Show*, "Not one of them would have made it to print in *Mad*."

Meglin is impressed that several of his writers could handle assignments for both the magazine and the series. "It's hard to believe a *Mad* takeoff could be written by the same guy, but it was!" he laughs. He notes that several other TV sketch writers submitted material to *Mad* that he rejected as unsuitable for the publications' needs, which shows there is a fine art to every style of writing.

There was also a new frequent face in the audience in the lower right corner during shots from the stage in 1970. Kathy Clements had been studying in medical school when *The Carol Burnett Show* began, so much so that when she graduated in 1968, she did not even know who Carol was, thanks in part to her family having only one TV in their house. But she liked to send for tickets to see TV shows and get autographs, and she found herself drawn to returning to see the series in person, especially to get a break from the rigors of working from 9 a.m. to 6 p.m. weekdays in a doctor's office.

"I wanted to laugh," she says of becoming a regular audience member for the series' 7:15 p.m. tapings Fridays. "It was an escape for me." She always sat in the first row, middle section, left end, which was a blessing for when she ran late. "By the end of the eleven years, the ushers knew me and said, 'Don't worry, we won't give your seat away!'"

At first she mainly came to the shows and kept to herself while getting autographs where she could. "I never met Carol until August of 1970," Clements says. "I met here when she came out of the show. I would come to talk to Joe (Hamilton), and take a snapshot and get something special." Intrigued as to who this woman was, Carol greeted Kathy, and a strong bond resulted between the two. While Kathy notes that "I don't go to her house for tea or anything," Carol did make sure during the 1970s that Kathy was treated well during the tapings, as she found her a comforting presence then and now.

"I'm one of the few people with her from the days at CBS," Clements says. "I'm safe, I'm a familiar face to her. When she sees me in the crowd, she makes a fuss."

Kathy attributes this access for the fact that Carol can be her true self with her. "There's the Carol Burnett, the one you see on TV, and the one who's very private, who does the *Los Angeles Times* crossword puzzle," Kathy says.

Interestingly, when it came to the Q&A, Kathy declined to participate. "I never raised my hand," she says.

The most cosmetic change on air this season comes in the opening. Carol emerges in front of a curtain that has tassels hanging from it to do Q&A. Next, the animated title sequence has the Charwoman appears before doors with the letters C, B and S, and Vicki, Harvey and Lyle emerge behind each respectively, with Harvey introduced first and taking a bow.

In terms of new content, there are no radical new changes, only dropping a couple of older elements. One thankfully ending is the tired "V.I.P." mock interview segments. Also going away are takeoffs of the First Family, with an odd rationale.

As Carol explained to Dick Cavett about the latter, "We had done the Johnsons, and we did the Nixons, and there was some flack. I don't really get into that much myself—and uh, the only reason really we stopped doing the Nixons was that there wasn't that much to latch onto." (At this point, the audience laughed heartily, as the interview occurred on Feb. 21, 1974, with President Nixon's approval low due to the Watergate scandal.) Carol added that "It was more fun for me to do Lady Bird, because I'm from Texas."

Perhaps the biggest surprise of the season is an unexpected pan in *The New York Times* for a rerun on March 15, 1971, following good notices from the same publication for the debut show of the season. John J. O'Connor prefaced his admiration of Burnett before saying that "it is a bit off-putting to find her spilling over into a trough of sly snickers and labored innuendo" and citing the suggestive remarks in her sketches (for specific examples of what bothered him, see the Oct. 19, 1970 entry). The TV critic was so appalled by this comedy that he made a ridiculous, inapt comparison between the series and a current hit Broadway musical featuring explicit language and nudity.

"In its very nonsnickering (sic) directness, *Hair* was and still is a beautiful show," O'Connor wrote. "The same can hardly be said for the regular portion of *The Carol Burnett Show*." The rant was so embarrassing that O'Connor apologized for it in the paper seven years later when reviewing the series' finale, blaming his negative notice on being "obviously in an uncharacteristically sour mood."

Right under O'Connor's review, an article by Jack Gould informed readers that *The Carol Burnett Show* would be moving to Wednesdays from 8 p.m. to 9 p.m. in the fall of 1971. That rescheduling turned out to be much more problematic for the series than what O'Connor had to say at the time. For now, let's see what 1970-1971 provided to viewers.

Sept. 14, 1970: Jim Nabors

** Carol, Harvey, Vicki and Lyle sing "But Alive"; an accident victim (Jim) is too modest to disrobe in front of a nurse (Carol) during treatment; George's efforts to kill himself are met only with complaints from Zelda; Jim presents "Mama, a Rainbow" and joins Carol on "They'll Never Believe Me," "My Funny Valentine" and "You Were Meant for Me"; an 87-year-old actress (Carol) who is hard of hearing and short of sight tries to make a comeback performing opposite a hammy actor (Harvey); a finale with the cast, Jim and dancers features a medley of songs from the musical *Company*.

Comments: Carol clearly had been sampling the new offerings on Broadway after last season, as this episode opens with her and the regulars doing a tune from *Applause* (a musical based on the 1950 film classic *All About Eve*) and ends with numbers from Stephen Sondheim's most recent show. Combine that with Jim soloing on a song from a short-lived 1970 Broadway production, *Minnie's Boys*, and crooning a duet with Carol that included a song from 1937's *Babes in Arms* ("My Funny Valentine"), and this episode basically could be a primer for appreciating show music.

Jack Mendelsohn and Paul Wayne wrote the Zelda sketch. As Jack remembers, George (Harvey) was on a ledge, ready to jump off for losing his money in the stock market. A policeman (Lyle) pleads for him not to kill himself, and he sends Zelda out to change his mind. True to form, all Zelda does is complain about her needs and what he has put in his will, all of which leads to George deciding to go through with his mission.

The overall theatricality of this effort did not limit the thespian talents of its star. "Carol Burnett is displaying an ever-growing feeling for the character impersonation," an impressed Jack Gould wrote about this show for *The New York Times*. "As a drone bored with her husband's suicide attempt and as an octogenarian actress bent on one more farewell, there were the seeds of a future career going beyond musical comedy." That career did happen in the future, but for now Carol's focus was on launching the series on a high note, and by all accounts this succeeded.

Sept. 21, 1970: Cass Elliot, Pat Paulsen

Opening production number with Harvey and the dancers; Q&A; a "Fireside Chat" in San Clemente by the sea with President Nixon (Harvey), first lady Pat (Carol) and their daughter Julie (Vicki); Cass sings "The Story of Love"; Lyle introduces how TV commercials inject sex appeal in their products; Pat discusses *How to Be a Sensuous Female*; Carol and Cass duet on numbers set at a beauty spa; Harry and Stella (Carol and Harvey) receive visits from Cass and Pat in their rundown tenement; Roger and Carol meet a new next-door neighbor in "Carol & Sis"; a gypsy musical finale.

Comments: The deadpan delivery of Pat Paulsen brightens what already would be an above-average episode even if he was not on board. The show commences with the unexpected sight of Harvey singing "We Can't Find an Opening for the Show" until Carol interrupts him and takes over as a red drape curtain comes down before her co-star and regular dancers. Her Q&A includes mentions of going to New York City between TV show tapings to check out the musicals, being double jointed and thinking that she would have been a teacher instead of an actress. Asked her thought on midis, the latest fashion length trend, she says, "I really don't like them," but adds she thinks there are acceptable if worn with boots. Carol also relays an anecdote about how one fan stopped her in a dress shop and said, "We watch every Monday and never like you!"

Another visit with the Nixons at home in California finds many jests about the vice president's golf game (he is so bad he beans others on the course), and his series of gaffes when speaking. "Is that Spiro's ball?" Harvey says. "It must be, it has blood on it," responds Carol. Julie (Vicki) boasts of wearing an Agnew watch: "His big foot is in his mouth." The Nixons do their usual pandering to minorities, in this case two Mexicans, and a handyman played by Lyle before the generally satisfactory sketch ends.

Wearing a black outfit a la Mae West, Cass acquits herself singing with six dancers in tuxes. Next comes a series of sexy commercial blackouts that include Bob Duggan. Vicki gets away with wearing a bikini and saying "I only had one cavity," while Lyle stands next to a beautiful blonde and boasts, "Look what I got with my Raleigh coupons!" referring to the cigarette brand. While the content spoofed is dated, this is pretty good.

Pat's sturdy monologue begins with him saying he was going to discuss *The Godfather* but got roughed up, so he would review the latest hot book on sex instead. He cracks up the audience by wearing a dress and saying "This outfit looks as good without a bra as with one." He expands on his feminizing to display painted toenails while telling the audience that "You must never bite your feet." For those who think Pat only excelled in political commentary, this is a sterling example that there was more to his talent than that.

Sporting towels on their heads in a steam room with curtains, Carol and Cass sing "Smiles" from *For Me and My Gal* before changing into robes to duet on "When I Just Wear My Smile," a track that appeared on two albums released by Cass in 1969. The ladies appear together subsequently in the Stella-Harry skit on a shabby set with tacky clothes and cranky humor. Stella worries about her daughter (Vicki, who chews gum) while Harry spits beer on her. Carol's reaction that the foam is more than she expected to receive from Harvey in this bit. Pat appears as a politician who says he has borrowed President's Nixon "sparkling personality" and is learning graft and bribery to fulfill his mission. When Cass visits Carol for food, Pat loves her despite (or maybe because of) her earthy charms and leaves with Cass. When Vicki announces she is dating a car thief, a relieved Carol says, "The kid's gonna be all right!" This quirky, distinctive sketch comes across rather well. Harry and Stella will return on the Jan. 18, 1971 show.

For "Carol & Sis," as Carol repairs the house without Roger's help, they learn the news that Cindy next door has left to live in England for a year from her equally bubbly, bounce blonde sister, Wendy (Timothy Blake). Roger assumes Wendy will take Cindy's place, but the new occupant is actually Chuck Morton (Lyle), a handsome pilot who invites the Bradfords to a party he is throwing. That fascinates Carol—until she sees the beautiful girl appearing with the pilot as they plan to throw the affair. This is a solid bit.

In the finale, Carol and Cass are garbed in red, white and blue gypsy outfits playing tambourines to "Hi De Ho" with the dancers, then joined by Vicki for another number. Clad with a scarf on his head, Pat gamely tries to fit in with singing and playing the tambourine with the rest of the troupe. Even if intentionally awkward, his contribution works here, as did everything else he did on this show. It is a shame he was used just this one time, but happily at least Cass will return again on Nov. 2, 1970.

Sept. 28, 1970: Nanette Fabray, Steve Lawrence

Steve sings "What Are You Doing the Rest of Your Life?" and "On a Clear Day You Can See Forever"; in "As the Stomach Turns" Marian is besieged by a friend who think she is undergoing a sex change (Nanette), a golf-playing priest (Steve) and several other types; Nanette performs a number in sign language with two girls and the dancers; a tribute to Columbia Pictures includes a takeoff on *Middle of the Night*, a medley from Carol and Steve of songs popularized by the studio's movies, and extended spoofs of *From Here to Eternity* and *Gilda*.

Comments: Some enjoyable movie mockery highlights this installment, which has a brief introduction of Steve's wife, Eydie Gorme, and their two sons before the scripted portion begins. Steve does fine with two contemporary numbers (neither of which were hits) as well as his Bing Crosby imitation in "As the Stomach Turns." But the sketch's real stars are Nanette and Harvey as gender-bending married characters. Nanette speaks in a deep voice and lights a cigar, while her husband Harvey is headmaster of a local ballet company who flounces about in orange tights and a floral print scarf. In case the densest of viewers cannot get the joke, Harvey's character is named Gaylord, and Nanette at one point says, "Hi, gay Gay!" Overlooking the dated stereotypes, this is an enjoyable skit.

Nanette's number came from doing "Somewhere Over the Rainbow" in sign language on the Feb. 19, 1968 episode. Following it, the Columbia tribute commences oddly by spoofing a somewhat obscure feature, 1959's *Middle of the Night* starring Kim Novak and Fredric March. Nevertheless, Nanette expertly imitates Novak's breathy vocals and tendency for weak line delivery for some good laughs. Carol and Steve then perform songs from Columbia films from the 1930s ("Pennies from Heaven") to the 1960s ("I Am Woman" from *Funny Girl*). Both shine brighter when they mock Deborah Kerr and Burt Lancaster in the beach love scene in *From Here to Eternity*. Steve grits his teeth and nails Burt's clipped speech pattern, while Carol's tight blonde hairdo is a stitch in itself. Their hugging is interrupted by a boy with a bucket and Steve yells, "Get out of here, you rotten kid!" as he resumes their passion session with Carol. They lie down on a blanket on the sand, and in an overhead shot, they are drenched by a huge wave of water, prompting guffaws from the audience.

The show concludes with "Golda," a send-up of Rita Hayworth's 1946 star-making role with Carol naturally in the lead. She nails it perfectly with her long flowing locks and a comic slinky rendition poking fun of the movie's signature tune called "Blame the Crash on Golda." Steve is amusing too with his take on Glenn Ford—here, his character keeps dropping coins every time he flips them to seem cool. Harvey plays a baron spy and Lyle a bartender at the club, where Steve decides to leave Carol for a cigarette girl at the end.

With this episode, Steve solidifies his status as an excellent foil for Carol in sketches. It also has some interesting viewer reaction—for more on that, see the Oct. 12, 1970 entry.

Oct. 5, 1970: Eydie Gorme, Joan Rivers

Q&A; Carol portrays Mrs. King Kong being interviewed by Harvey on "V.I.P."; Eydie sings "You Can Have Him"; Joan performs a comic monologue; Carol enjoys a visit by her sexy next-door neighbor (Lyle) as her love life with Roger stumbles in "Carol & Sis"; an animated cartoon interpretation of Tom Lehrer's song "Pollution"; a talk show host (Harvey) and his sidekick (Lyle) welcome the singing trio of Donna Rose and the Magnificents (Carol, Eydie and Joan); Harry Zimmerman and the orchestra appear on stage behind Eydie and Carol as they sing a medley of 31 tunes about love.

Comments: In the first of thirteen appearances she will make on the series through 1978, Eydie Gorme showcases little of her comic talent here as she will in later shows, even though she appears more than Joan Rivers. The Q&A is mostly minor queries except for one a woman asking Carol if she was the understudy for Mae West in the recent movie *Myra Breckenridge*. Carol responds that she actually held the position for Rex Reed (heh heh!). The exchange is funnier than anything in the "V.I.P." sketch, where the level of humor can be indicated by Carol saying her traditional anniversary gift from the oversized ape she married will be fur this year. At least the special effects of her being clutched in his oversized hand are impressive.

Eydie's inconsequential song features her in a black gown before Joan appears with long blonde hair. Her so-so set includes riffs about her dress, her love life, her mother, women's lib and the effects of aging. Her best line is saying she wrapped herself naked in plastic to surprise her husband, and his reaction was "Leftovers again?!" Joan will repeat one joke—about how she slowed down saying "catch me, catch me" in the bedroom with her husband as their marriage matured—when she returns to the show on Jan. 4, 1975.

"Carol & Sis" starts slowly, with Carol complaining to Roger about how dull their sex life is and making small talk with Chris, before its comic momentum escalates when new neighbor Chuck Morton is accidentally locked out of his house and asks to spend the night. Carol willingly obliges and dresses in a pink gown to impress Chuck, causing her and Roger to fight. When Chuck peels off his shirt, Roger fails to avert Carol's eyes, and when she watches Chuck do pushups, she ogles him with lust. Roger tries to compensate and gain her attention by carrying her to bed, but he is so weak he repeatedly fails to even pull her off the couch. Hearing the commotion, Chris eagerly joins Lyle to watch late night TV, as does Carol and Roger, the latter with an eye to prevent any hanky panky going on by the women. This installment zings with great comic sexual tension.

In an odd shift, Carol, a UCLA graduate, thanks Dr. Bernard Kantor, chairman of the University of Southern California Cinema Department, for the use of an animated cartoon depicting animals being affected by mankind's garbage accompanied with a satirical tune. This piece is more suited to *The Smothers Brothers Comedy Hour* than this series. Carol will amplify her anti-pollution stance in the future (see Oct. 26, 1970 for more).

A spoof of Diana Ross and the Supremes comes next, even though the group had broken up a year earlier. The glitzy wigs and outfits for the ladies look great, and Carol's glances at Joan and Eydie as she dictates what they are to say and how they are to react to Harvey is amusing. However, there is not much to the sketch beyond that, other than the trio doing a song called "Sparkling Teardrops," which is fine.

Wearing aqua blue gowns, Eydie and Carol finish the show with a long segment of numbers that allows time for a solo from Eydie. This is serviceable—the two will do better duets in the future. Carol thanks Artie Malvin for writing and arranging what she and Eydie sang, and she has members of Harry Zimmerman's orchestra take a bow before making a pitch to fight pollution and say goodbye. All in all, it is an average show.

Oct. 12, 1970: Donald O'Connor, Bernadette Peters

Q&A; Donald leads a number with himself and the other male dancers dressed as scarecrows in a rock group and the female dancers as black crows; another installment of "The Old Folks"; Bernadette sings "Come Saturday Morning"; Carol and Bernadette are at the Bridal Salon complaining about their fiancés; Roger brings home a doctor (Donald) to examine Carol surreptitiously by posing as a golf pro in "Carol & Sis"; "The Early Early Show" presents "Hooray for Hollywood Canteen," with Carol, Vicki and Bernadette as riveters and Harvey, Lyle and Donald as their suitors in a 1940s war musical spoof.

Comments: Donald O'Connor's ebullient presence saves this episode from rather wan comedy and music. The Q&A starts promisingly, with Carol revealing she was shy as a child, had received a wire from Rita Hayworth appreciating the *Golda* parody that aired two weeks earlier (a story she would repeat on the Dec. 14, 1970 show) and likes to relax by watching the late show movies. "I get ideas sometime from watching them," she said. The biggest laugh she gets from the crew is when someone asks about Harvey and she assesses her sometimes moody co-star as "He's just a happy-go-lucky guy."

"The Old Folks" appears between numbers by Donald and Bernadette that show both performers in better form than the material they have to present, even if "Come Saturday Morning" was an Oscar-nominated Best Song for 1969 (Bernadette sings it amid eye-catching draped strings of pearls surrounding her). Bert is full of vigor, wanting to see a sexy movie and tour overseas, to which Molly scoffs, "Last week you fainted watching an old Tarzan movie!" He makes the traditional move on Molly, which she tells him reminds her of the Alamo: "They didn't know when to give that up either!"

Carol and Bernadette's bit is just some banter before a duet about the challenges they face as potential newlyweds, with nothing special to offer (a typical joke has Carol saying of her husband-to-be that "Bruce likes Liberace!"). The same unexceptional quality seeps into "Carol & Sis," where Roger's efforts to find why Carol is sleeping so much involves his pal Donald trying to show proper golfing technique to her when in fact he is listening to her heartbeat and the like. Unsurprisingly, Carol thinks Donald is coming onto her until the truth is revealed. She ends up getting hit by the kitchen door this time and tells Roger she really could use a physician now.

The finale is an extended, rather generic World War II film spoof set on the home front, with Bob Duggan among the soldiers preparing to ship off. Carol's affection wavers between Lyle and Harvey until going to the latter when learning Lyle is wed, while Bernadette latches onto Donald, the canteen's one millionth serviceman. The latter two do a wonderful tap routine with the dancers and Carol sings the Andrews Sisters' hit "Boogie Woogie Bugle Boy," both by far the show's most sparkling moments. The episode ends with Carol introducing Maxine Andrews of the Andrews Sisters in the audience, who takes a bow.

Oct. 19, 1970: Nanette Fabray, Ken Berry

Q&A; "The Old Folks" celebrate their second honeymoon in Florida; Ken performs "Mr. Bojangles" and follows it with a routine along with dancers on a set resembling a 1930s movie soundstage; Carol is Harvey's lovesick boss who is appalled to find that he is enamored by her temporary replacement (Nanette) and plans revenge on the latter; Carol shows a scrapbook containing first-graders' ideas about "Who is Carol Burnett?" and follows it with a song; "The Early Early Show" mocks airplane melodramas with "Flight Thirteen to Nowhere"; Carol and Nanette fight over Ken in a post-bellum musical finale.

Comments: One of the best-remembered and most hilarious bits of interplay ever in the Q&A kicks off this installment in fine fashion. Responding to an inquiry, Carol says, "The most embarrassing question I was ever asked was whether or not I had a sex change." After the laughter dies down, the next questioner asks, "Did you?" This prompts hysteria from Carol and the audience. She plunders onward and tells another questioner she has had her driver's license for five years. "Why do you ask?" Carol concludes. "I've seen you drive," the wiseacre responds, leading Carol to blurt, "I don't believe this group tonight!" She has a calmer time introducing in the audience Jim Bailey, who she calls a new star in Las Vegas that she will have on as a guest later that season (she does—see Feb. 1, 1971), and Jackie Joseph, Ken Berry's wife at the time.

Sporting casual summer outfits, "The Old Folks" has Bert (Harvey) again trying to arouse Molly (Carol) by grabbing her leg and asking, "That remind you of anything?" Molly replies, "General Custer. He didn't stand a chance either." After remembering how Bert resembled the lifeguard, Molly joins her husband in singing about how they dated when they were teens.

For Ken's intro, Carol says she has known him for twelve years, plugs his new album and declares that "His talent is absolutely limitless." After a tap dance routine to "Mr. Bojangles" with three spotlights, Ken keeps on tapping with three other dancers and then a young girl dressed as Shirley Temple, in keeping with the Depression era theme.

Next up, dowdy but efficient secretary Carol is worried about competition for the affections of her boss while she is away from the office, so she dismisses a talented, breathy blonde (Georgene Barnes) and a tall, statuesque blonde (Inga Nielsen).When nearsighted, dumpily clothed Nanette arrives, Carol instantly hires her, only to see Nanette take off her coat and emerge as a miniskirted blonde when she trains her. Harvey is entranced, as shown when Nanette fetches coffee and asks Harvey, "Two lumps?" and he responds, "Love them!" To add innuendo, Nanette stirs coffee while her butt rotates, much in the same way Mrs. Wiggins would do when sharpening pencils on this series a few years later. Carol's attempts to sabotage Nanette ultimately backfire when she tries to push Nanette out the window but flies out herself instead. Although it has its moments, this skit is rather long in relation to the number of real laughs.

Adding to the padded feeling, Carol reads entries in a scrapbook collected by a teacher at Meadows Avenue Elementary School in Manhattan Beach, Calif., of her students' writings and pictures of who Carol is. The cuteness of seeing these wrong answers wears off fast, and Carol singing a nondescript tune while sitting on a stairwell does not help.

Funnier but spotty is "Flight Thirteen to Nowhere," with Lyle as the pilot, Bob Duggan as the copilot, and Carol as a stewardess serving such passengers as a missionary priest (Ken), a prostitute (Nanette), a drunk doctor (Harvey) and two newlyweds (Vicki and Don Crichton). Some amusement occurs when, after Carol announces she is pregnant, Lyle grumbles, "There goes our perfect safety record!" and Ken attempts to make her a moral woman by having her marry the entire crew. Also enjoyable is when love struck Vicki learns she is on the wrong plane and has been making out with someone other than her husband. Still, a better spoof of this genre will occur three years later (see Dec. 14, 1974).

For the finale, Carol and Nanette play Southern belles dueling for the attention of Col. Lee (Ken) after the Civil War. The competition becomes so intense as the ladies toss him around that he ends up destroying the set clad only in his long johns. Like much of the rest of the show, this bit has more sizzle than steak. Even so, it along with Ken's "Mr. Bojangles" number helps Ernie Flatt win his only Emmy for choreography.

Before saying goodnight and having her guests sign her book, Carol tells the audience, "Pollution affects us all, so let's fight back." This ecological message will be expanded in next week's show.

Oct. 26, 1970: Lucille Ball, Mel Torme

Opening number with regulars, guests and dancers; Q&A; Mel sings "Where Have All the Flowers Gone?"; Carol and Lucy are stage mothers angling for their own daughters to win a Broadway audition; Mel and Carol duet on songs popularized in Fred Astaire and Ginger Rogers musicals; Harvey plays a stage actor coping with a drunk leading lady (Carol); "The Early Early Show" presents "Some Like It Hotsy Totsy," with Carol and Lucy as musicians who witness a murder by gangsters Harvey, Lyle and Mel and hightail it to Florida, where they encounter dance routines and Vicki as a moll.

Comments: Carol takes a full stand for environmentalism, as Mel's themed solo number (which he sings on a swing set with an uncharacteristic mustache) follows her opener. The dancers move to "Blue Skies" and then are joined by everyone else on "Put on a Happy Face," only for white smoke to appear on stage so thick that the participants are forced to wear gas masks. "That was our salute to the lovely smog we have here in Los Angeles," Carol says after she takes off her mask and the set clears from a rather jarring but timely introduction. Going into Q&A, she discusses how she met John Steinbeck while living in the same apartment as the author in New York City, and how she had her leg in a cast for seven weeks after having broken it playing baseball with her daughters. Asked her favorite song, she joked, "Flight of the Bumblebee" and noted how one gentleman once told her, "Why don't you sing more ballads? Your singing is so sad!" She continues to kid when talking about preparations for the show ("I bind my chest"), but is sincere when she quips that "My favorite male comedian is Harvey Korman."

The first sketch has some good jokes between Carol and Lucy as competitive women instructing their daughters (played by unidentified youngsters) on how to impress the judge for a part. Both are disheartened that the part has been cast already for statuesque Inga Nielsen—even though her daughter has not yet appeared to perform. Hmmm.

The passable Carol-Mel teaming on a medley featuring "The Continental" and the like precedes a bit with a British thespian (Harvey) finding his plans to celebrate his 1,000th performance overshadowed a boozy costar (Carol) who insists on trodding the boards despite her condition. Naturally, she stumbles on the couch, fiddles with her costume and removes alcohol hidden in the scenery, such as inside the phone base. This familiar routine is nonetheless given its all by the performers.

Taking up at least the last third of the show is a spoof on *Some Like It Hot,* with Lucy and Carol in drag as the distaff equivalents to Tony Curtis and Jack Lemmon in the original. A producer (Bob Duggan) watches the duo sing and dance before they disguise themselves as men to avoid capture by three hoods they saw commit murder. Discussing having to hide their gender successfully, Carol moans, "I wish I had your voice," while Lucy shoots back with "I wish I had your body!" Hiding in a train car, Lucy meets Lyle the hood, who tells her, "You'd feel better if you got undressed" and Lucy responds, "Probably!"

Wearing mustaches and tuxes when they arrive in Florida at a nightclub, Lucy and Carol introduce molls to an audience of gangsters, and Vicki emerges wearing an oversized slot machine to do a routine. She wins the honor of being named Miss Underworld of 1927 when the joint is raided and the women's identities are exposed. Lyle pledges to save Lucy, who says he found out who she was "just south of Atlanta" on the train. Making fun of a comedy is difficult, but this sketch has satisfactory results. A 1978 tome called *TV Book* includes pictures of Lucy and Carol in tuxes and Vicki in her outfit from this episode as representative shots of the series.

This is Lucy's last appearance on the program, as she and Carol end swapping guest shots on each other's series. They stayed friends until Lucy died on April 26, 1989—the same day she had flowers delivered to Carol's house to celebrate the latter's 56th birthday.

Nov. 2, 1970: Ricardo Montalban, Cass Elliot

Q&A; George recounts to a doctor (Lyle) the extenuating circumstances of how he found himself stuck with Zelda as his wife; Cass sings "The Good Times Are Coming"; two dowdy lasses (Carol and Cass) commiserate over their bad luck in attracting men at the Over 28 Club; Ricardo sings and joins the dancers on a Mexican set; Vicki, Cass and Carol perform "Tell Us Where the Good Times Are" and "Big Yellow Taxi"; "The Early Early Show" sends up *Dangerous When Wet* with Carol as Esther Williams and Ricardo as her love interest; the Charwoman meets Emmett Kelly.

Comments: This above average entry for the season is so good that two of its elements will reappear in later installments. At the start, Carol picks a woman who has a scroll of questions for the hostess, but we only hear her ask what was the funniest thing that happened to Carol and Harvey during a sketch. Carol says there are too many to choose one instance. She also tells another audience member she would be willing to do a spoof of her job as a movie usherette when she was a child.

The story of how George met Zelda forms a great plot to kick off the show. George was drunk at an office party when he went after Zelda and woke up next to her the following morning. She informs him they got married after complaining about his snoring during the night. To his dismay, Zelda announces plans to redo "their" furniture in the apartment and quit her job to whip him into shape. Making it worse, she is having her mother live with them as well. Vicki plays the latter and mimics Carol's pitch and speaking pattern perfectly, making it even more humorous to see Harvey suffer as the sketch ends.

Cass provides excellent vocals in the next few segments, first in a solo number from her upcoming album followed by a duet with Carol on the oldie "Nobody's Heart" after a sweet seriocomic dialogue about their character's efforts to pick up men at a dance hall. Cass reveals she has lost a pound and a half over the last few months, while Carol says she is wearing a padded bra—after Cass suggests she wear one! Ricardo does fine vocalizing and dancing to "A Man and a Woman" after that, but he is outshone by what follows. The Vicki-Cass-Carol medley starts with a 1953 hit for Guy Mitchell and Mindy Carson and segues into Joni Mitchell's classic pro-ecological number from 1970, with shots of pollution interspersed with them. The women are outstanding in both tunes.

The featured movie spoof, "Slippery When Wet," is similarly strong. A playboy (Ricardo) loves Carol, who strokes her arms like a swimmer on land and delivers dialogue flatly. If that was not enough of a mockery of Esther Williams, there is film footage of Carol singing "Easy to Love" while treading amid a pool filled with lily pads. This comic sequence works so well it will be repeated in the Oct. 16, 1976 show. The skit ends with Ricardo reprising his "Baby It's Cold Outside" duet he did with Esther in the 1949 film *Neptune's Daughter*, only here with Carol her wet swimsuit dampens his own clothes when they clench romantically. There are plenty of inspired comic moments here.

For the end, the Charwoman assumes center stage at a circus and gets imagined applause for opening a can of exploding worms. After pretending to walk a tightrope with an umbrella, she gets applause from Emmett, who joins her to balance a feather on his nose—and it gets stuck there! He then sweeps the spotlight into a dot he gives to her before she sings her two tunes, with Carol singing "It's Only a Paper Moon" in the process. This sweet meeting of comic archetypes is so good that it will be seen again more than five years later, on Jan. 24, 1976.

Carol thanks Kelly, "the world's greatest clown," at the end of the show. Ricardo and Cass will reappear in cameos in the Dec. 7, 1970 show.

Nov. 9, 1970: Juliet Prowse

** Q&A; Carol performs "Gee, It's Good to Be Here" with Juliet and solos on "Meantime"; Juliet dances and sings to "Pick Yourself Up" and "Put On a Happy Face"; the Old Folks engage in repartee during their honeymoon trip to England before doing "Let Me Call You Sweetheart"; a sick Carol bedevils her theatrical costar (Harvey) during a stage performance; the Charwoman pantomimes a striptease in the finale.

Comments: Carol and her crew taped this show in London on April 12, 1970, to celebrate the series being carried on the British Broadcasting Corporation. According to Roger Beatty, Carol was so new to viewers in the United Kingdom that one of the first questions she received from the audience was a woman asking, "Who are you?"

Incidentally, Beatty was the only writer able to go to London with the show due to his status as assistant director. The other scribes had to stay in Los Angeles, as they will do again when the series goes to New York City for the March 22, 1971 show and Australia for the Dec. 8, 1973 installment.

Apart the songs and dances, most of the material presented appears to have been tweaked from earlier shows and slanted to appeal to the host country, with an assist from a guest star with international appeal (although she speaks with a British accent, Prowse actually was born in India and raised in South Africa). At least one American reviewer felt it did what it had to achieve. "The show impressed even afar as a good premiere for her British entry," assessed *Variety*. In fact, *The Carol Burnett Show* became a staple on the BBC for much of the 1970s, so this episode must have served its purpose well.

Nov. 16, 1970: Martha Raye, Ross Martin

Q&A; Carol's new hobby of painting vexes Roger when their next-door neighbor (Lyle) poses shirtless for her; Martha enacts her Benita Bizarre character from *The Bugaloos* before singing "Funny Girl"; Ross portrays Carl Sandburg as he recites the author's unpublished poem "Love"; Carol and Martha are polar opposite jurors sequestered during a trial; "Flop Theatre" presents "Storefront Hospital" with Carol as a doctor, Vicki and Lyle as interns, Ross as the hospital head, Harvey as an old physician and Martha as a patient; the ensemble performs contemporary hits as if they were done in the style of 1940s music.

Comments: Back-to-back serious solos by Martha and Ross drain away this show's energy from what is otherwise a very lively installment. The Q&A is rather blah—Carol says is not as wild at home as she is on the show, laughs off why she did not audition for *Myra Breckenridge* and does the Tarzan yell—but it leads into one of the best "Carol & Sis" entries ever. After Roger and Chrissy implore Carol to try painting to occupy her time, an unexpected subject appears when Chuck Morton (Lyle) offers to pose for her. Taking off his top and flexing his muscles, he asks, "Is this all right?" and Carol moans back "Yeah." Roger is peeved by this setup and tells Carol she could have asked him to model for her instead. "If I wanted anything pear-shaped, I could've used the bowl of fruit!" she shoots back. Roger is supposed to leave for an engagement but remains suspicious of the arrangement and keeps monitoring them. Carol notices the situation and pretends to be kissed by Chuck, prompting Roger to scurry back inside. Her amusement over his overreaction does not impress Roger, who declares that he is going to get rid of Chuck, only to have the latter hit him with the kitchen door accidentally.

From there, the show detours for the worse, starting Martha playing her witch character from *The Bugaloos*, a children's sitcom she taped at the time for NBC Saturday mornings. Martha wants to do more, but the director (Brad Trumbull) says it is a wrap, so she removes her long putty nose and wild wig to sing her contemplative version of the title tune of the movie version of *Funny Girl*. This is odd to endure, particularly for younger viewers who were fans of both shows and probably confused as to why she was out of character and seemingly unhappy about doing *The Bugaloos*. Compounding that, "one of television's finest and most versatile actors," as Carol introduces Ross, comes on next to do a lengthy monologue, first as himself and then fading into resembling Carl Sandburg with the white hair and other looks. He does it well, but no one watches *The Carol Burnett Show* for poetry recitals.

The show recovers somewhat with Martha playing her typical rowdy character, the type that is surprised to learn that a bathroom is in the same room that she shares with snooty Carol, a fellow juror. The latter is appalled by Martha drinking a beer and wielding a salami, but it turns out that despite her earthiness, Martha has the brains to figure out the guilt of the trial's suspect, leading to Carol and Martha being freed. However, seeing the hunky bailiff (Lyle), Martha grabs him and tells him to join her, since the room is already paid.

More laughs come from a combined spoof of two much-hyped and ultimately disappointing "relevant" new dramas on CBS in 1970-1971, *The Interns* and *Storefront Lawyers*. It starts by mocking the latter's theme song and its irritating opening titles where the principals happily hopped along together with their arms interlocked. Here, Lyle, Vicki, Don Crichton and two other dancers idiotically skip through the hospital's hallways as Carol arrives to meet Ross, leader of the hospital. Both emphasize they believe in professionalism before kissing passionately. Carol is diagnosed as being sick by a crusty old doctor (Harvey), but she ignores it to treat a belligerent rich patient (Martha) who ultimately rejects her. At the hospital cafeteria, where the interns have choreographed their eating habits, Carol passes out. Ross insists on operating on her without going to the ER—"I have to, I have dessert coming!" She awakes in fine condition, but it is learned that her condition is contagious to all she has kissed, so Ross and all the interns including Vicki collapse. Carol vows she will save them and all others until Harvey, fed up with her sanctimonious preaching, tapes up her mouth. Incidentally, next year *The Carol Burnett Show* will assume the time slot held by *Storefront Lawyers*.

The offbeat and surprisingly effective finale places Ross as the bandleader of an orchestra singing "My Way" in a bouncy style popular nearly 30 years earlier. That leads into him introducing Carol, Vicki and Martha doing "Spinning Wheel" like the Andrews Sisters, Harvey offering "By the Time I Get to Phoenix" in an Irish jig, and Lyle and Carol interpreting "Everybody's Talking" as a bossa nova number. There is some intentional comedy with Martha presenting "The Look of Love" as a desperate tango with Don Crichton and the other male dancers before going to Vicki singing and tap dancing to "Let It Be" with the dancers, joined by everyone at the end. Unlike other times when hit tunes of the time often faced condescension from this series, these reinterpretations appear thoughtfully with conviction by all and succeed strongly.

This episode marks the second and last guest appearance by Ross. Martha will appear once more in two months—see Jan. 25, 1971.

Nov. 23, 1970: Paul Lynde, Dyan Cannon

The ensemble performs "Happy Thanksgiving Day"; a charming insurance adjuster (Paul) loses his demeanor when Carol and Harvey file a claim; Dyan sings "Until It's Time for You to Go"; Funt and Mundane encounter difficulties as they present their farewell stage performance of "Elegant Rapture" with a grumpy stage crew; Marian tries to get money from a rich friend in "As the Stomach Turns"; Don Crichton and Shirley Kirkes are featured dancers in a routine to "More"; the dancers portray life-sized toys and dolls that become animated to the surprise of the Charwoman, who then performs "Try to Remember."

Comments: Carol reunites with Paul Lynde following their work together on *Stanley* in 1956-1957, and the outcome is so favorable that Lynde will make four other appearances on the series over the next year and a half. This episode also marks the sole appearance of Dyan Cannon, and a coup for the series, as the actress rarely appeared on variety shows.

"They approached my agent, and I was so excited to do it, I was so thankful to do it," says Cannon. She loved watching *The Carol Burnett Show* at home, as did her husband at the time, actor Cary Grant.

The series eschews the Q&A for a lively opening number that includes Paul and Dyan dressed up as Pilgrims along with the rest of the cast. The dancers set up a dining room and table during the proceedings, and Dyan and Paul appear to be having the time of their lives during the festivities, which ends with Carol dropping the turkey on the ground. That leads into Paul wooing Carol and Harvey into paying for a $700 insurance policy. "It covers fire, theft, flood and all acts of God—even if you're atheists!" he chuckles. But when Carol and Harvey's home burns a month later, Paul's family friendly attitude vanishes as they attempt to collect on the policy. "What's this about a fire?" he snarls. He calls Harvey shrill and says he'll offer $63 for the damages from the "alleged" inferno. They object, but when Lyle arrives to do a commercial, Carol tells Harvey to get in line and smile, since they'll be on TV. This is good stuff.

"She's sexy and pretty and very talented," Carol says in introducing Dyan, noting that the latter earned a New York Film Critics Circle award for supporting actress in the movie *Bob & Ted & Carol & Alice*. For her solo number, Dyan recalls, "They asked me my choice, and I was allowed to do what I wanted, and I loved it." She lends her voice to a tune written by Buffy Sainte-Marie that was a minor chart entry for Neil Diamond in 1970 (and later a top 40 entry for Elvis Presley in 1972) and provides very pleasing results on it while looking smashing in a white gown.

When Funt and Mundane tell off their sound effects, lighting and prop men (all played by male dancers, with Stan Mazin as the last one), they naturally face negative consequences for their actions on stage. Items drop down on them, a firecracker replaces a candle being lit, chairs collapse and food is tainted. Funt endures a piano's top crushing her hand, while Mundane has to return to the bench when music continues to play after he finishes tickling the ivories. By the time another actor (Lyle) enters, Funt is stuck in a window sill, then has to threaten to kill him with a banana. At the end, Stan moves the exit door so Funt crashes into a wall and passes out, and a curtain drops on top of her, Mundane and Lyle. This is very good comedy.

"More" is a pleasant fantasy sequence with a great orchestration of the Oscar-nominated tune. It leads into "As the Stomach Turns" and Dyan coping with the fact that her 94-year-old husband died just 25 hours after they wed. She inherited $700 million from him and now has a compulsion to give away money, but only to strangers, so Marian leaves and pretends to be a beggar at her door. Dyan sees through it and thanks her for trying to cheer her up. A dejected Marian greets her daughter (Vicki), a trapeze artist who leaves her baby with Marian. Vicki leaves and Harvey and Paul arrive as the identically dressed Canoga Twins, who both sneer like Paul as they enter (Paul gives Harvey a look of disgust when the latter ad libs in his voice at his expense). The twins want Marian to put away Dyan in an insane asylum while Dyan protests, prompting a bidding war between the parties to buy off Marian's affections. Unfortunately for the latter, they compromise and agree to split the take. The sketch pretty ends there with the questions about what will happen next, but it ran out of gas prior to that point.

The dancers do a superb job of freezing into position as dolls before the Charwoman puts on a pair of spectacles that magically animate the items. When she accidentally breaks the glasses, the toys stop as well, leading the Charwoman to sit on a bucket and sing the familiar hit from *The Fantasticks* on a bucket in a sentimental but nice finale. Carol then sings "It's Time to Say So Long" and then cracks up at what both Dyan and Paul write in her guest book before this generally satisfying entry comes to a close.

Regarding her fellow guest star, Dyan says, "The thing with Paul—he was just what he was, on stage and off. A wonderful, uplifting, enchanting man. He was more adjusted to doing variety shows than I was, and he made me feel so at home."

The bulk of Dyan's praise goes to Carol, however. In her opinion, Burnett was "Warm and loving and made you feel like you were stepping into her home, and not on a soundstage. When you go and do a show as a guest star, you usually don't feel like part of the company. Not with Carol. She made me feel at home. She'd invite me to her dressing room for lunch. What you saw on screen with her is what you got."

Incidentally, Cannon was the series' first female guest nominated for a Best Supporting Actress Oscar (in her case, for 1969's *Bob & Carol & Ted & Alice*) since Carol Channing and Shirley Jones in 1968-1969. Another one will pop up in the next episode.

Nov. 30, 1970: Debbie Reynolds, John Davidson

Q&A; a director (Harvey) drafts two women with no acting experience (Carol and Debbie) for a coffee commercial; John croons "Blessed is the Rain" and plays a medley of "Everything is Beautiful," "Snowbird," "Raindrops Keep Fallin' on My Head" and "Look What They've Done to My Song, Ma" on the banjo; Roger and Carol relive the events of their disastrous honeymoon; Debbie joins the dancers to do "Look at Mine"; Carol and Debbie star in a takeoff on the 1943 feature film *So Proudly We Hail*; the ensemble presents "Thank You Very Much" from the movie musical *Scrooge*.

Comments: "We've been trying for about four years to get Debbie Reynolds on our show," Carol says as she introduces the guest star for her featured number. Unfortunately, this installment fails to make full use of her talent as a comic actress and mimic, making it a disappointment overall despite her worthy contributions. Her name impresses the audience during the Q&A, wherein Carol discusses the origin of this segment of the show first. "You ought to hear some of the things we get that we cut out!" she cracks. A twelve-year-old boy from Chicago gives her a gift, then she talks about plans to do *Plaza Suite* with George Kennedy on stage next summer. After introducing longtime Los Angeles

Dodgers announcer Vin Scully in the audience, Carol speaks a little "op" language with an audience member, talks about wearing a retainer when younger and says that senior citizens have written to say they like the Old Folks skits with Molly and Bert.

A remake of the coffee commercial sketch from the Oct. 6, 1967 show is up first. Despite being shorter than the original and peppered with a few updated references such as *Sesame Street*, it is not an improvement. John's vocals on contemporary tunes are similarly competent but unexciting.

Better comedy occurs when Carol recalls her honeymoon to Chris in "Carol & Sis." Carol had worries about being intimate in her hotel room with Roger, and both inadvertently injured themselves while trying to get romantic. An unsympathetic bellhop (Bob Duggan) comments on their mishaps in this bit, which has a good share of laughs.

Debbie is in good voice for her number, which goes smoothly. So does "So Proudly We Heal," with Carol as a captain of nurses at a hospital in World War II who spouts every patriotic platitude and cliché while leading her subordinates. The latter include Vicki, who has a quick nervous breakdown and recovery, and Debbie, who is shallow and vain. Carol calls out every stock character type as she treats the men before making moves on a too-wholesome soldier (John). Meanwhile, Debbie treats and romances a wounded sergeant (Harvey). Dedicated to the war effort, Carol tells Vicki she will fight the enemy and places two grenades in the breast pockets of her jacket, prompting her to wonder why she did not think of doing so early to enhance her small bustline. This portion alone is clever enough that it will be repeated on the tenth anniversary show on April 2, 1977.

The finale comes from *Scrooge*, a movie musical version of *A Christmas Carol*. "Thank You Very Much" will be nominated for a Best Song Oscar, and another number from it will appear on the Dec. 14, 1970 show. Debbie, John and the rest do fine singing it in a Cockney dialect in a round, with "For He's a Jolly Good Fellow" thrown in for good measure. The show ends with a pitch to buy Christmas Seals by Carol before singing "It's Time to Say So Long."

Disappointingly, this is the only *Carol Burnett Show* for Reynolds. However, Davidson will return on Nov. 15, 1972.

Dec. 7, 1970: Mel Torme, Don Rickles

A production with upbeat numbers by everyone while Don is put in the stocks and gagged; Zelda and George encounter a burglar (Lyle) at their home; Mel sings "Into Something" and joins Carol in a medley; Don is a painter driven to irritation by Carol and Chrissy constantly changing their minds about redecorating their home; a send-up of *Sesame Street* for adults includes Carol as a hooker, Vicki as a bimbo, Lyle as a gambler, Harvey as the Big Bird knockoff, Don as the equivalent of Oscar the grouch and Mel as a loan shark.

Comments: This show's first half is a sequence of missed opportunities, especially contrasted with the dead-on, hysterical, cameo-laden last part. Eschewing the Q&A, everyone sings "The Way You Look Tonight," "Embraceable You" and other love songs towards Don, to his general disgust and inability to respond, since he is bound and gagged. The joke is that Don's insult humor will be held in check by everyone else, a dubious concept to use as the opener and to replace the Q&A. It leads into a plodding piece where Zelda tells Lyle where items are in her house and warns him not to steal them, prompting a desperate George to plead for the burglar to kill him and put him out of his misery. Seeing what George has to endure, Lyle gags Zelda's mouth and leaves, which thrills George, because at least his wife has shut up. The skit does come alive briefly at the end when George's happiness deflates as Zelda's mother (Vicki) arrives and is just as whiny as her daughter.

A mustachioed Mel sings a nondescript self-penned tune before he and Carol sing snippets of more than a dozen hits written by Jule Styne— "People," "It's Been a Long, Long Time," "Everything's Coming Up Roses," etc. Such familiar numbers demand a more distinctive presentation than this, which becomes just one long medley to endure.

After seeming like the show really was muzzling Don, he finally reappears as the irked painter of Carol and Roger's house. Carol cannot settle on what colors she wants, driving Don to take pills and strain to be nice, and he has a fit before he composes himself. This is amusing, and when Roger arrives, the sketch really goes into orbit. Don ad libs that he already knew Roger when Carol introduced him as her husband, prompting Carol and Vicki to leave laughing. Roger argues to Don that his wife has taste, but when Don shoots back, "You got a sty!" Harvey loses his composure. A frustrated Don paints Roger's suit and face, prompting Roger to do the same to Don (and get applause from the audience in return). Don goes for a glass of water and naturally Carol smacks him with the kitchen door for the ending. This is one of the most raucously funny "Carol & Sis" sketches ever.

This show is now cooking and continues to do so with an inspired two-part adult version of *Sesame Street* called "Poppyseed Street." On a street corner set, we meet its low-life denizens before going into the first round of surprise celebrity cameos, with Cass Elliot and Ricardo Montalban taped from the Nov. 2, 1970 show along with Lucille Ball and Dean Martin from the sets of their TV series saying words relevant for adults that begins with C (for example, Dino says "crocked"). Next up is Harvey as a big chicken telling Vicki that he is scared, mainly because Col. Sanders (an unbilled actor) is chasing him. Mel offers "It's Tough to Be Honest," an ode to the difficulties of being a crook today, and Don emerges from his trash can to tell Carol the streetwalker she needs to wear a veil to score more action. It is then back to Cass, Ricardo and Dean with "B" words— "boudoir" from Dean, for one. Lyle does a number about how one of these things is different from the rest, with a sexy young gal put next to two elderly ladies. The first section ends with "S" words from Cass, Ricardo, Dean and Jim Nabors (saying "Shazam!" just like on *Gomer Pyle—USMC*).

The laughs and surprises keep coming after the commercials, as Tim Conway shows Vicki how to count to five by taking five shots of liquor and being out like a light at the end. Dick Martin does his own number joke by fiddling with Carol's body and quipping, "I'm counting on you!" More gags follow, culminating in all the cast and dancers playing kazoos to wind up this madcap moment.

As Carol sings "It's Time to Say So Long" during the finale, Don does something off camera to crack up the audience. If such *joie de vivre* had been sustained from the start, this would have been a classic episode rather than a merely average one.

Dec. 14, 1970: Steve Lawrence, Durward Kirby, Julie Budd

Dancers dressed as Santas with ringing bells perform an interpolation of "Elegance" (from *Hello, Dolly*!) and "Winter Wonderland" followed by other Christmas carols before Carol does Q&A; Steve sings "One Day"; "Carol & Sis" has Carol and Roger forced to endure Roger's accident-prone new vice president (Durward) at their home; Julie sings "Where is Love" and "The Christmas Song"; "The Early Early Show" features "Goldman's Boy," a boxing movie takeoff; clips from the movie *Scrooge* are interspersed with the cast dressed in Victorian finery singing songs from the motion picture.

Comments: This heavily Noel-flavored show starts with a Santas number that includes one trick shot where a kick line of Kris Kringles is repeated twice on two horizontal lines, a rather ambitious video trick for the series. Carol emerges from this solid opener explaining to the audience that she has a shag cut because Gus Le Pre, her regular hairdresser, threw his back out and had no time to get her a wig. Moving on, she relates a story about meeting President Richard Nixon a year ago as part of her work for Easter Seals. The Chief Executive signaled to her to come join him in the Oval Office, which unnerved her. "I'd never been alone with a president before, and I looked at him and said, 'So, how ya been?'" Laughing it off, she adds, "He was very nice." She mentions how Rita Hayworth sent a note of appreciation to her following the *Gilda* spoof (see Sept. 28, 1970) and that the actress will be a guest later this season (see Feb. 1, 1971). The Q&A ends after a teen tells Carol about a teacher of his who was an old high school pal of hers.

In a very seasonal white outfit with green top, Carol introduces Steve, who sings a song associated with Barbra Streisand in an overcoat amid a snowy setting. Next up is "Carol & Sis," where Roger spoils plans to go away for the weekend when he has to impress a potential boss, Mr. Gordon (Durward). The latter unintentionally damages their house almost as soon as he arrives, much to Carol's chagrin. He drops golf clubs on a new lamp, spills drinks, drops cigar ashes and more, culminating by getting Carol and Roger's bedroom on fire. This time Carol winds up getting hit with the door at the end as Durward leaves the kitchen with a pail of water.

With rain falling on a window pane as she sits in an attic setting, Julie Budd belts out a song from *Oliver!* and a familiar standard written by Mel Torme and popularized by Nat "King" Cole. Julie had replaced Carol already during a two-week engagement Burnett had with Jim Nabors at Caesars Palace in Las Vegas. "Carol had to leave to go back to LA, and there was an entire weekend open," Julie recalls. "She was leaving the night I was coming in. She gave me a great hug before leaving, because she's a good soul." At the end of the final Sunday night show, Carol gave Julie a gift thanking her for filling in. "I still have that present today," Julie adds.

Under contract to CBS to do all of its variety series, Julie flew from her base in New York City to guest on *The Carol Burnett Show* and found it was run much the same way as *The Jim Nabors Hour*, on which she had previously appeared, even down to Bob Mackie designing her outfit. Regarding the choice of "Where is Love" to perform, she says, "It was part of my repertoire, and they wanted me to do it. It was perfect for my range, and it came from a Broadway show, which they liked." Carol did "Where is Love" previously (see March 16, 1970), and it will reappear again on Oct. 25, 1972.

"Goldman's Boy" has Harvey as an Italian father of Steve the violinist turned boxer, with Carol as the girl next door and Bob Duggan as a fight announcer. After winning some bouts, Steve surrounds himself with women, including a blonde, rich, bored playgirl (Vicki), and ignores Carol. Steve's manager (Durward) is unable to prevent the boxer from becoming fat. Carol warns Steve he is in no shape to fight, but when another announcer (Lyle) rings the bell, he fails miserably. Steve returns to Carol and Harvey gives his son his violin to play, but when they hear how bad it is, Carol and Harvey leave him, and the sketch ends. This is a passable parody.

The finale starts with Carol setting up a clip of *Scrooge* featuring Albert Finney as the title character singing "I Hate People." Carol and Julie sing among dancers dressed as Scrooge as another clip plays of Scrooge interacting with the Ghost of Christmas Past. Back in the TV studio, Steve and Durward appear as two Scrooge-like gentlemen joined by Carol singing "I Like Life," also from the movie, followed by male dancers dressed in pajamas and hats. The last tune is "December 25th," also from the film, with the whole cast singing as fake snow falls. This is a rather odd promotional piece for *Scrooge*, and it leaves out "Thank You Very Much," probably because the show did it on the Nov. 30, 1970 episode. But it ends the most effectively sentimental Christmas show Carol and crew ever did for the series, and on that level it succeeds.

Regarding the finale, Julie says her most priceless memory is the huge discrepancy in height between her five-foot-two frame and six-foot-five Durward as they danced together. "How they ever put me with that man in the final number, I'll never know!" she laughs.

Julie is more serious regarding how *The Carol Burnett Show* operated impacted her career positively. "Carol has a great work ethic," she says. "I was only sixteen, and it was a good thing for me to have in my life. For a kid my age, you can't believe the training it was. You had to learn quickly and under pressure—table read the script, rehearse, dress and do the show. It really makes you a different kind of artist."

Naturally, Julie has happy memories of the show's star as well. "She was always a sweet woman. She always conducted herself as a work in progress." A friend of Julie's will express similar sentiments when she does the show a few weeks later—see March 1, 1971.

Dec. 21, 1970: Rerun of April 13, 1970 show

Dec. 28, 1970: Robert Goulet, Rich Little, Pat Carroll

Q&A; Carol is monitoring a detector at airline security that uses 3,000 suspicious words to help determine who is a security risk, and Harvey is the unfortunate soul who keeps tripping it; Rich does eleven impersonations of celebrities pitching products; Robert sings solo and then duets with Carol; Zelda (Carol) aggravates not only George (Harvey) but also a waitress (Vicki) and cranky customer (Lyle) at a restaurant; Marian hears a kissing bandit (Robert) is loose in the neighborhood in "As the Stomach Turns"; the entire company toasts the new year with singing, dancing and other merriment.

Comments: One of this season's best shows missed being a disaster. Original guest star Gwen Verdon contracted an ear infection the day before the taping, and it is a measure of her talent that it took Rich Little and Pat Carroll to replace her. "They called me because I had done the show before," says Pat, referring to her prior guest effort on Feb. 23, 1970. "Once they trusted you, they knew they could rely on you in a pinch. I admire that."

Rich and Pat both do stellar work as last-minute substitutes, even though Pat does not appear until the show's second half. Before that point are some nice moments, beginning with the Q&A where the audience goads Carol into doing Shirley Temple singing "On the Good Ship Lollipop." She follows it by saying she can do an impression of a door, only to be interrupted by the sound effects man piping up a shutting sound.

Carol's first acting is as a check-in lady at the gate for TransAmerica Airlines, where Lyle tells her terms like "gun" are calibrated to set off a warning about boarding passengers. After enduring Vicki as a bimbo, Carol is forced to check out Harvey and his attaché case when he says "Adios!" and other Spanish phrases. (This was when planes being hijacked to Cuba was a big problem for flights.) After undergoing the frisking and promising to be good on the plane, Harvey ends up arrested just before he departs when he sees an old friend (Bob Duggan) and says, "Hi, Jack!"

Rich makes his series debut mocking the star spokespersons trend in commercials. He portrays Kirk Douglas, Dean Martin, Boris Karloff, Ed Sullivan, Richard Burton, Tiny Tim, and Humphrey Bogart before saving his best four for last. For John Wayne for girdles, he does the Duke's distinctive walk before venturing into political humor with Lyndon Johnson shilling for antacids, Spiro Agnew for golf balls and Richard Nixon (whom he calls "Tricky Dick") for stockings. Anyone familiar with *The Ed Sullivan Show* will find Rich's routine of the host a real stitch too, as he asks his crew, "We got time to bring on the dead bear?"

Robert sings "Without Love" in a tux before joined by Carol where both sing songs to each other. It appears to be a standard musical segment on the show as they gallop off, but then Vicki and Rich come out on the beach setting to make fun of them, with Rich getting in a few lines of "If Ever I Would Leave You" that Goulet popularized in *Camelot* on Broadway before Carol and Robert return and haul them off stage disapprovingly.

The unexpected delights continue when what appears to be a standard restaurant sketch—well, "standard" may be wrong, given the surprise of Lyle trying to feel Vicki's butt only for her to block it with a carrying tray—emerges with complications as Zelda arrives on the scene with George unwillingly tagging along. As she complains of sinus headaches, she accidentally hits Lyle with her handbag twice. Oblivious as ever, she thinks Lyle is hitting on her even while George is entranced by Vicki (staring at her breasts, he orders a pair of donuts), and she forces George to confront Lyle to defend her honor. George pretends to threaten Lyle but really offers to pay for his dinner if he ignores Zelda. Unsatisfied with George's efforts, Zelda decks Lyle and tells Vicki she did her a favor, as he would have gone after her next, "You poor, deformed creature!" The rapport and professionalism of the regulars shine through in this sprightly effort.

Pat finally appears in "As the Stomach Turns" as Sister Amy, a crusader playing "Bringing in the Sheaves" on a big drum who visits Marian to save her from giving into the temptation of a roving kissing bandit (Robert). But when Sister Amy espies the hunk, she smooches him while pounding on the drum before they part. Pat does such a great job that the audience spontaneously applauds when she leaves. But the best part comes with the arrival at the door of Harvey as an Avon lady in a blonde wig and pink outfit with matching scarf. With a high-pitched voice, Harvey convinces Marian to spray a perfume that will attract the attention of Robert. He arrives on the scene again, whereupon Harvey takes off his wig and asks Robert, "You don't remember me?!" while cracking up at how he looks now. There is not much else to this sketch, but it is hilarious enough as is.

The rousing conclusion is a classy party celebrating the end of 1970, with the male dancers in tuxes and ladies in dress suits as cast members and guests perform little bits of entertainment. Rich imitates Jack Benny, while Pat comes out in a suit covered with balloons which are popped by the men when they are not doing some impressive acrobatic maneuvers. "Although I was a tap dancer at five, I had gotten a tad heavier since then," Pat jokes about her moves here. She credits Carol for holding her hand to help her get through the routine. It ends naturally with all singing "Auld Lang Syne."

At the conclusion, Carol tells everyone about the eleventh hour switch in guests and thanks Rich and Pat before noting that the latter will be a guest on next week's show. The festive mood continues through the credits, as Robert lifts Pat up and twirls her around a little in celebration. It all makes for a dazzling way to bring in 1971.

Jan. 4, 1971: Art Carney, Pat Carroll

** Another installment of "As the Stomach Turns"; a salute to Independence Day with a medley of patriotic hits written by George M. Cohan.

Comments: Although she had much experience doing variety shows in the 1950s, including winning an Emmy for best supporting actress for *Caesar's Hour*, Pat Carroll found the tight rehearsal schedule on *The Carol Burnett Show* somewhat challenging. This was especially true during this period when she was on the show two consecutive weeks. "These were not easy to do," she says. "They were like two-act plays."

Given her opinion, it is understandable how Pat has so much appreciation for both Carol and her series. "That woman spent a lifetime in the service of laughter," she says. "Cranking out a show every week? That's World War Three! I can't do what Carol does. That woman can take dross and make it gold."

Pat recalls she first met Carol at a rather unassuming place in Manhattan during the 1950s. "At my garage at 55th Street," she laughs. "Carol at that point was married to a young Armenian man, and I had married one at the time too." Pat had heard about Carol's success as a comic actress doing club work and notes that "We got along right away." The two did not work much professionally, but her guest appearances on this series made up for that, and she enjoyed the experiences.

"They were always impeccable because of Carol," she says. "They had this anchor they could work around, and it was the best supporting cast in the world. She's just twenty-four-carat gold." Carroll will return to the series a few weeks later—see March 1, 1971.

Jan. 11, 1971: Jerry Lewis, Leslie Uggams

* Jerry and Carol are paired into dating by their high society fathers (one being Harvey); Leslie sings "This is Your Life" and "Help!" and joins Carol to do a medley of tunes written by George Gershwin; a ham actor (Harvey) finds his work sabotaged by Carol's machinations on stage; Carol and Jerry team up to sing "I've Got a Pocketful of Dreams" and "Somebody"; the Charwoman meets a janitor (Jerry) and they pantomime an elegant dining scene in a department store window.

Comments: Between disparaging females as being unfunny in comments between 1998 and 2014, Jerry Lewis recorded warm if odd praise for Carol in an interview along with their "High Society" sketch appearing as a bonus in the Time-Life DVD collection. He first met her on *The Garry Moore Show* in 1961, and she impressed him. "I was stunned at her rhythm, because it got my attention," he said. "When working with a fine artist, they usually keep all the magic to themselves. Carol was an unusual artist in that she gave pieces of herself to everyone else she ever worked with."

That's all fine, but in noting her compassionate portrayal of the Charwoman on this show and her vocal prowess, Jerry let his sexism slip some by claiming that "She never hid her femininity in the dressing room." The implication of course is that some comic actresses he knew did that, which many would argue shouldn't matter.

He added of this show that "It was an incredible night for me, because I put the experience with Carol back with the time I experienced with my dad, and my experience with great other performers I can't even name. There've been so many. But there haven't been a lot of Carols."

Lewis previously said in 1998 that "I don't like any female comedians." That quote prompted an audience member attending a Paley Center for Media tribute to the series in 2000 to ask Carol's opinion of Jerry's statement. "I think he made a big mistake. . . . He used to tell me he loved me," Carol said. "He wanted you to have his children!" interjected Vicki.

Regardless of how Jerry really felt, Carol consented to release his bit in her 2012 boxed set. It's nothing great. A rich father (Bob Duggan) wants his homely daughter (Carol) to marry a nerdish fellow scion (Jerry) of a tycoon (Harvey). They bond despite their looks after performing a comic dance. Frankly, both have done much better work solo.

Winding this up, while Jerry said in 2014 that "Seeing a woman project the kind of aggression that you have to project as a comic just rubs me wrong," he did call Carol "the greatest female entrepreneur of comedy." Make of all that what you will.

Jan. 18, 1971: Michele Lee, Mel Torme

** Carol plays Vanessa Vanilla, who goes from the excitement of being discovered as an actress at a drugstore to disillusionment about what it means to be a movie star; Michele sings "In Times Like These" and "The Green Grass Starts to Grow"; Stella and Harry (Carol and Harvey), the slovenly couple, need to get their apartment in order in preparation for a visit by a welfare worker; Mel, Michele and Carol perform a medley of "Strike Up the Band," "I Hear Music" and "The Sweetest Sounds."

Comments: Of her four guest shots on *The Carol Burnett Show*, Michele Lee has the most vivid recollections about this show. "What I really remember about guest stars was sitting with Carol and Mel Torme singing around a piano," she says. "We rehearsed a medley that Mel had written. It was brilliant. It was one of the best musical numbers they did on the show.

"It was in three parts and in harmony. It was a country medley with a sense of humor. Of course, with the brilliance of the costumes, Bob Mackie could make the three outfits look as different from each other as possible, yet cohesive to the trio."

Michele counts Mackie as invaluable to the series. "Bob Mackie was more than a genius. He had a sense of humor and knew what sketches were trying to say and just made everything funnier by the choices he made. He also knew and loved women. His designs had lines that would flatter the body. Any body—and nobody had a smaller waist than Carol."

Even so, Michele gives the ultimate credit to the series' success to Carol's personality. "She had that ability to talk to the audience and was like everybody's friend—they loved her. And of course at the end, when she would tug at her ear, we all knew she was family—that secret message that we all knew."

Mel will return to the series a final time later this year on Nov. 17, 1971. Michele will wait nearly four years before she comes back, however—see Oct. 5, 1974.

Jan. 25, 1971: Martha Raye, Edward Villella, Violette Verdy

"The Old Folks" has Bert upset that a new, handsome doctor (Lyle) will be performing checkups on him and Molly rather than a nurse; Edward and Violette dance the Don Quixote pas de deux; "Carol & Sis" has Martha appear as an Irish maid whose habits befuddle Roger and Carol; Carol and Martha duet on three songs introduced from 1928 to 1935; Zelda intrudes into George's dream about becoming a successful matador; the Charwoman appears on the set of a forest stage and encounters Edward as Robin Hood along with other ballerinas and participates in their numbers.

Comments: Carol's basic intros lead straight into "The Old Folks," where Bert boasts about his appeal to the visiting nurse. "I can't help it if she's got eyes for me," he gloats. "Too bad you got nothing for me," Molly retorts. His tune changes when Lyle arrives as the nurse's replacement, though he does get in a good word edgewise. When Lyle listens to Molly breathe, he says, "There's a little something there, but nothing to get excited about." Bert responds, "You're telling me!" while Molly glares at him. As usual, the two make up and sing a number about how they make each other feel young.

The pas de deux between Villella and prima ballerina Verdy appears next, but it is previously recorded. That does not spoil how impressive the dance is, with distinctive solo parts for both of them and spectacular footwork (and yes, Verdy dances on pointe).

"We were both at the New York City Ballet with George Balanchine and Jerry Robbins," Verdy says about her collaboration with Villella. "I was one of the three small ballerinas. He invited me to do a series of galas with him. I have a long history with Eddie."

Verdy appreciated the work of Harry Zimmerman conducting the orchestra ("He was really sensitive to our needs") as she and Edward coped with edits to their usual dance presentation to accommodate the series' time constraints. "We had to cut a little bit of the adagio, so we could do our solos and adagio. So in a way, it was sort of an excerpt."

In "Carol & Sis," Roger leaves his office at 11 a.m. to meet the new maid, a hot-looking Irish import. To his disappointment and Carol's confusion, she turns out to be Martha, who lied about her age and photo in order to get the job. Tired from her flight (Martha does a great duck walk indicating how much her feet hurt), the maid-to-be puts up her feet on the table, and her other behavior such as being scared of the vacuum cleaner eventually results in the truth—she is actually from the Bronx. The sketch ends with Martha being beaned in the head by the kitchen door when Roger opens it.

The Carol-Martha medley of "Let Me Sing and I'm Happy," "Back in Your Own Back Yard" and "I Got Plenty O' Nuttin" is rather barren except for the women's fashions. Carol's full-length black dress contrasts with Martha's black-and-white gown composed of stripes and polka dots. Incredibly, Martha has nothing else to do the rest of the show.

For the Zelda-George installment, he sleeps out on the couch to watch old movies and fantasizes he is a bullfighter in Mexico who entrances a flamenco dancer (Vicki). "I've always admired your castanets," he coos before Zelda shows up whining in a dowdy flamenco outfit with huge hoop earrings. She warns him not to pursue his profession, noting that "Animals just don't take after you," and critiques their wedding night before accidentally goring him, which probably was a relief for long-suffering George—or rather Jorge in this case, as even Zelda yells his name in Spanish.

The Charwoman dons a tutu in the finale, but keeps her hat and big boots to dance with ballerinas in *Swan Lake*. She manages to find time to slug Edward for killing a ballerina and then do a comic pas de deux with him before the fantasy ends and she sits on a pail to sing a song of lament. Prior to the credits, Carol salutes "my buddy, Maggie Raye" and learns Edward's routine is do an hour and a half class in the morning, rehearse two to three hours in the afternoon, warm up 60 to 90 minutes and then do a performance. Wow!

"Carol Burnett was really adorable," Verdy said of her experience here. "She was very endearing. She was for real. It was a wonderful atmosphere."

This passable mix of class and crass unfortunately lacked viewers, airing opposite the second part of *In Harm's Way* on ABC's movie series that night. The latter scored a huge 28.6 rating. Next week's show will do better both in terms of quality and audience size.

Feb. 1, 1971: Rita Hayworth, Jim Bailey

Carol and Vicki play star-struck crass fans of Rita who spot her at the Brown Derby and harass her for attention; Jim impersonates several female stars including Barbra Streisand and duets with Carol as the latter; Vicki dances with Don Crichton and then introduces a spoof of *Love Story*; Carol and Rita reminisce about the latter's film roles before singing together "Mutual Admiration Society."

Comments: The best episode of the season splendidly features its guest stars with one of its greatest movie parodies ever. Packed with strong material, it eschews the Q&A for a frumpy Carol and Vicki in her "dumb Dora" voice visiting the Brown Derby in Hollywood, where waiter Lyle is unimpressed by their request for a table. "There's probably one at the Taco Bell next door," he retorts. The two women nevertheless find seating when Rita, playing herself, arrives with her agent (Harvey), who wants her to play a brain surgeon in an upcoming movie. "It's not for her!" Carol says, interjecting her opinion of the role and pestering Rita for an autograph. Maneuvering to get a table next to Rita, Carol introduces Vicki as her daughter and has the latter do her cheerleading routine. Rita endures that moment along with Carol talking about how her hairdresser taught her how to do the "Put the Blame on Mame" dance from *Gilda*. The worst part for Rita comes as Carol assumes directorial duties as she tries to capture the actress on film but complains about how Rita smiles ("What is this, a tragedy?!") and how Barbara Stanwyck needed only one take to eat her Caesar salad on film.

At wit's end, Rita is relieved when Lyle tells her a fellow star wants to join her at the table (Glen Campbell, playing himself in a cameo), only to see Carol try to direct him in the scene as well. The comic pacing for the sketch is sprightly, and all participants acquit themselves nicely, including Carol in what could have been an obnoxious routine.

Next, Carol introduces impressionist Jim Bailey as someone she had seen in Las Vegas a few weeks ago and loved. "I was such a fan," recalls Jim, who eagerly accepted her offer to be on the show. "When I got back to Los Angeles, we had a meeting about what I would do on her show. Carol thought it would be a good idea to hit them with comedy first and then go into me performing as Barbra (Streisand)." And that's what happened.

Appearing in a tux in both live and pretaped segments, Jim stands next to Carol as pictures of Phyllis Diller, Judy Garland and Streisand appear on screen and he supplies his vocal impersonations of each. He then emerges in a flowing blue, purple and green in makeup as Streisand, belting out "Don't Rain on My Parade" from the latter's hit Broadway and film musical *Funny Girl*. "The Barbra gown was done by Bob Mackie," Jim says. "Bob did a sketch of it, and I liked it right away. We chose chiffon as the fabric and decided on the colors together."

Carol joins him after the song ends and says "Barbra, that was fantastic," to which Jim in character responds nonchalantly, "I know." The two play off Streisand's diva reputation even more when Carol mentions if "Barbra" remembers when they first met on *The Garry Moore Show* when Kenny Welch wrote Barbra's ballad arrangement of "Happy Days Are Here Again," and Jim quickly says "No." More laughs come as Carol stares at Jim's breasts and he says "They're real" before the scene fades made to Jim in a tux singing a duet with Carol in his normal voice.

After Vicki dances with Don in purple outfits on a jungle set bathed in blue-green light, she leads into the next big sketch as hostess of "Tearjerker Theatre," where she cries as she introduces the feature film, "Lovely Story." Carol apes Ali MacGraw's look from the film in a long dark wig and glasses as she plays a librarian hit on by Harvey, wearing a sweater with a big scarf a la Ryan O'Neal. They mock the movie's promo line as they engage in wordplay following Harvey's statement that "Love means never ever having to say I love you." They romp in slow motion in the library to show their love as four dancers enters with violins, loudly playing a knockoff of the movie's gushy theme music.

Carol and Harvey meet the latter's father (Milton Frome), who asks which of them is his son. The music gets on Carol's nerves as the scene segues to the couple's dorm room, where they are living together happily as Harvey is becoming rich and becoming the Chief Justice of the U.S. Supreme Court. "From now on, our future's going to be unlimited joy and happiness!" he tells Carol, who suddenly coughs in return. Lyle shows up as the finest doctor money can buy and examines Carol by saying, "Stick out your tongue please—uh oh!" He confidentially tells Harvey that Carol has only five minutes to live, prompting Harvey to ask what to do. "First of all, don't overact!" Lyle says. Harvey responds by jumping across the bed and telling Carol he can get anything she wants, but when she says, "I'd love a four-minute egg," he grimaces. She passes away, leading Harvey to blurt "What do you say about a girl?" when Lyle interrupts his mourning to tell him one more thing—her condition is very contagious. Harvey dies, and Lyle plays a violin with the syrupy theme in response.

"Lovely Story" is one of the series' most cutting parodies, with writers Stan Hart and Larry Siegel taking full opportunity to make fun of all the movie's irritating conventions. Both men call it one of their favorite pieces, and it shows up in several retrospectives as one of the show's best efforts. In fact, Siegel wrote a different parody of it in *Mad Magazine* and boasts that "I did a masterful job in avoiding repeating my jokes for that." However, given that it was among the most popular films in theaters at the time, Carol felt compelled to thank it at the end of this show "for bringing romance back to the motion picture industry," lest any fans of it felt offended by it.

The episode ends with Carol (in an orange outfit) telling Rita (in a red dress) about how she saw the latter's pictures when she was an usherette in the 1940s and idolized her. As clips of Rita's movies run, the two provide commentary. When *Gilda* appears with Rita in a strapless gown, Carol asks, "How'd you keep that dress up?" and Rita cracks, "Two good reasons!" Rita even dresses up as a Charwoman and meets Carol's character in a mirror, where they perform a great bump and grind routine to "Let Me Entertain You" before returning to their previous appearances to sing "Mutual Admiration Society."

Jim says Rita was suffering from early effects of Alzheimer's disease at this time. "She was an absolute gem, so sweet and vulnerable. Just before we taped the show, she asked me if I could stand offstage where she could see me. Of course I did, and I realized just how nervous she was. After the taping as we were leaving, she thanked me for helping her. She gave me a quick hug and kiss and then she was gone. What a memory to have."

The show closes with Carol thanking Columbia Pictures for the use of Rita's scenes from the studio's movies. In a rare move, Don Crichton joins the cast and guests in the featured kick line at the end due to his spotlight dance with Vicki.

There were myriad benefits emerging from this episode. The show's writers deservedly received Emmy nominations for their clever script. Rita, who rarely appeared on TV, sparkled in a guest shot worthy of showcasing her talents as an actress and star. And as Jim notes, "Doing Carol's show really boosted my popularity. I went on to do *The Tonight Show* and *Here's Lucy*." He credits Carol for giving him good advice about being careful of whom he trusted in the business and for having a friendly show.

"Carol made sure my segment was done with class and taste. Beside her immense talent, she is a warm and caring human being. She is one of the few people that has remained genuine. A true friend," Jim concludes.

Feb. 8, 1971: Rerun of Nov. 20, 1970 show

Feb. 15, 1971: Ken Berry, Totie Fields

Q&A: the handsome doctor (Lyle) returns to check up on "The Old Folks," to Molly's delight and Bert's chagrin; Ken is a mod barracks inspector in a production number with the dancers; "Dinah's Den" mocks *Dinah's Place*; Roger's old college roommate (Ken) has his engagement broken off and joins his old buddy and Roger's wife, Carol, for consolation in "Carol & Sis"; Carol reads letters from fifth graders at Thomas Jefferson Middle High School in Port Washington, Wisconsin; "As the Stomach Turns" has Totie as Marian's pal who thinks she is a werewolf; a musical farm sketch finale.

Comments: The bubbly presence of comedienne Totie Fields enlivens this edition, as well as a particularly feisty Q&A opening. A woman asks, "What kind of soap do they use to clean the floor?" Carol and most of the audience cracks up at the bizarre question, then jokes, "I think that's a little personal!" After learning it is vinyl cleaning, Carol relays the messages and queries the woman with "Do you have a vinyl floor at home?" "All over the house—just on the floor," she qualifies, prompting even more guffaws.

Other notable moments include an audience member asking if Carol's sister Chrissy nailed wallpaper at a former residence (Chrissy is in the audience and says no), Carol joshing that she got her start as a ballerina and the audience enjoying Carol's response to her idea of a utopia—a place where there is no war and you can breathe and drink the water. At least two men flirt with Carol. One asks, "How did you become so sexy?" and another says he wants to kiss the beautiful Carol Burnett. "She's not here!" cracks one cameraman in response. Carol brings out Totie, wearing a pink sparkling dress, and one lady wonders what historical character the rotund comedienne would want to be. "I'd want to be Cleopatra, but I probably will sink the boat!" she cackles.

Lyle returns as the doctor on "The Old Folks" in a sketch that is better than the previous one thanks to some sharp writing. When Bert suggestively grabs Molly's leg and goes "Ding dong!" she comes back with "I know it ain't Avon calling!" Molly flirts with Lyle by pretending to faint, which causes Lyle to tell Bert to bring her a glass of water as he puts her to bed. "Good thinking, Doc, that'll give us two hours!" Molly responds.

The Ken Berry tap routine with male dancers as soldiers follows and has some visual flair, with women coming out of the lockers to join the counterparts at one point. More effective is the next segment, where Carol sports a huge blonde wig and a gooey Southern accent to make fun of Dinah Shore and the latter's daytime talk show on TV. She introduces "a wonderful, talent starlet I've never heard of," and out pops Vicki as a bimbo with big breasts. "I won the Miss Grapefruit contest," Vicki gushes. "I came in first and second!" Totie follows as a woman instructing Dinah how to be desirable to men, and she is so persuasive that stagehands (played by the show's dancers) carry her off the set. Carol wraps it up by making fun of how Dinah used to sing her promo for her nighttime show. Considering that executive producer Bob Banner performed the same duty on that show, this might have been a little risky to do, but it is in good fun, and Dinah herself will show up later in a classic episode (see Nov. 13, 1976).

In "Carol & Sis," Carol's unintentional references to weddings and engagements upset Ken, causing Roger to get irritated with his wife. This passable entry ends with Carol hit by the kitchen door as Ken brings out a meatloaf. Carol then repeats sitting in a stairwell and reads intermittently amusing letters about herself from schoolchildren before she sings a song—the same routine appeared on the Oct. 19, 1970 show, also with Ken Berry.

As the show's momentum flags, a pretty good "As the Stomach Turns" revs up some enjoyment. Marian kisses Lyle as thanks for charging her batteries, then says goodbye to him, "Next time, baby, have a car." Totie arrives, sobbing about her condition, which also confounds a rabbi who is a golf nut (Harvey). "A Jewish werewolf?!" he exclaims. "Sammy Davis Jr. will plotz!" Also on hand are Vicki as Carol's daughter, now living with the Indians, and Ken as a golf-loving priest. The sketch ends with a good laugh about whether Lyle will visit Marian again: "Hasn't he seen enough wrecks already?"

The finale with the cast and dancers dressed as yokels dancing to "Put on Your Sunday Clothes" has as its main highlight the discovery that Totie was a pretty decent singer. After plugging the fact that February is heart month, which reaps a little audience applause, and singing "It's Time to Say So Long," Carol is amusingly upstaged by Totie, who comments on the design of her outfit's stomach that "Isn't that a funny place to put a heart?!" The laughs keep coming as Totie jumps onto Harvey to hold and kiss her as the credits ran. Totie is great—she should have done another guest shot on the show.

Feb. 22, 1971: Bob Newhart, Chita Rivera

Q&A; Roger's accountant (Bob) has an Amazon-like blonde, talented wife who makes Roger envious in "Carol & Sis"; Chita is dressed like the Catwoman to dance like a spider on a web with male dancers to Blood Sweat and Tears' hit "Lucretia Mac Evil"; Fireside Girl Alice Portnoy (Carol) blackmails a hung-over Harvey into contributing to her fundraising; the cast salutes MGM films a second time this season with parodies of *Ninotchka, The Blackboard Jungle*, *Gone With the Wind* and finally a musical operetta spoofing Nelson Eddy-Jeanette MacDonald musicals called "Naughty Rosemarie."

Comments: Making his first professional appearance with Carol since *The Entertainers* in 1964, Bob Newhart comes off well if not spectacular here, in part due to his limited use as a supporting player. He does come up in the Q&A, where Carol tells the audience he gave her a golf lesson earlier that day. Carol also reveals that during a recent earthquake, she remained calm and grabbed the youngest while Joe took care of the other two girls until the tremors passed. Regarding her summer plans, Carol says she will perform *Plaza Suite* with George Kennedy in Los Angeles (which she does). She plugs the wig shop of her stylist, Roselle Friedland, as well. There are lighter moments. A thirteen-year-old shows Carol a homemade Charwoman puppet. Carol says she has been to Chicago and "Hugh Hefner keeps begging me to come back!" An inquiry as to her favorite sport results in a quick "Paul Newman" response, but Carol was left speechless with laughter after one man asks, "What made you famous, your body or your mouth?"

In "Carol & Sis," Bob's buxom spouse (Inga Nielsen), a lawyer who loves to cook and sew, generates envy from Roger and mimicry from Carol. Roger consoles Carol, saying that her warmth and loyalty toward him count more than any attributes possessed by Bob's wife. This mild sketch has no one being hit by the kitchen door at the end.

An unexpected burst of contemporary music appears as Chita smoothly moves with Don Crichton and crew to a recent top 30 hit, with the original recording used as well, a rarity on the series. "That was a blast," Chita recalls of the routine. "That was so much fun. I would love to wear that suit again. I was all over the place in that dance."

Alice the Fireside Girl appears next, shaking down Harvey by saying she has a photo of a naked girl taken at the party held in his apartment the other night. As he tries to strangle Carol to save face, her sister (Vicki) arrives and gets a picture of the incident, forcing Harvey to donate. This is another moderately enjoyable sketch.

For the MGM salute, Carol cackles and provides a variety of other laughs cracking up as Greta Garbo to Harvey's Melvyn Douglas in *Ninotchka*, followed by Bob assuming Glenn Ford's role in *The Blackboard Jungle*. When Bob asks for the bullets from his students' guns, they respond by shooting his blackboard.

After Carol, Vicki and Chita join the dancers in a song honoring the studio, the takeoffs continue with *Gone With the Wind*. This time, Vicki is Scarlet O'Hara and Lyle is Rhett Butler, who struggles to take Vicki upstairs and not step on her hoop skirt to consummate their marriage, only to be told at the top that her room is downstairs. The segment culminates with a big production where Harvey assumes the Nelson Eddy mountie role and Carol plays the delicate Jeanette MacDonald lead. Vicki is Carol's servant taken in by Lyle, while Chita is a half-breed Indian and Bob is the Marquis de Fop. "I hate you singing," he lisps amusingly to Harvey, while Carol disguises herself as a mountie to hide from the marquis. To win the heart of Carol, Harvey and Bob host a duel as to who can hold the note the longest. Harvey wins and gets Carol, while Bob settles for Chita in time for the final song and dance number.

Before the end titles run, Carol thanks her sister Chris for her dedication in joining in the dance routine for the production number (the camera acknowledges her, smiling in the group). After wondering why a nation that can put men on the moon cannot end pollution here on Earth, she has Rivera and Newhart sign her guest book, followed by Harvey and Lyle dancing together, which is enjoyable for whatever reason they did it.

Rivera searched for more quality TV roles following this second and last guest shot on the series. They eluded her, so she returned to Broadway, earning Tony nominations for *Chicago* (1976), *Bring Back Birdie* (1981), *Merlin* (1983), and *The Visit* (2015), and winning for *The Rink* in 1984. She is philosophical about her performing career's path.

"You have to follow your lifeline, and mine was the theater, and that allowed me to get a *Carol Burnett Show*," she says. "I felt that I was presented brilliantly in those shows. The writers were familiar with me. There's not one complaint I have at all."

Incidentally, this was the only guest shot by any regular on *The Bob Newhart Show*, which preceded Carol's show for four years (1972-1976), longer than any other lead-in.

March 1, 1971: Tim Conway, Pat Carroll, Karen Wyman

** George's fantasy about being a World War I flying ace is broken up by the appearance of his nagging wife, Zelda; Karen sings "Close to You" and joins Pat, Vicki, Carol and the dancers in performing "My Feet Are Killing Me" and "There's Gotta Be Something Better Than This"; Don Crichton dances with the Charwoman on "Easy Come, Easy Go" and "MacArthur Park."

Comments: Along with her friend and fellow New York City resident, Julie Budd, Karen Wyman did many TV series in the late 1960s and early 1970s. A five-foot-two teenager with strong vocals, Karen made an immediate impression with her national TV debut on *The Dean Martin Show* in March 1969 by holding her own with the host in a five-song medley. That led to five appearances on *The Ed Sullivan Show*, visits to *The Tonight Show*, a contract with Decca Records and of course this guest shot.

"I was on a run with CBS shows," Karen recalls, noting that she did *The Jim Nabors Hour* and *The Glen Campbell Goodtime Hour* around the same time of this show. Of her big number with the other females of the show, she says, "I remember all four of us shooting out of backstage singing 'There's Gotta Be Something Than This.'" As for her solo, she believes the show suggested she cover the former Number One hit for the Carpenters. Her other main memory of this episode is of Bob Mackie designing for her what she considered a beautiful red peasant dress with puffed sleeves to wear.

Pat has plenty of recollections regarding her other guest star on this show. "I first met Tim in Columbus, Ohio, and he was directing (a local TV show). My God, that man was funny!" She loved watching him interact with Harvey Korman. "They were just two naughty boys. I wouldn't want to be a straight man around them. You saw the mischief in their eyes. They had real fun breaking each other up."

This episode represents Pat's fourth and last appearance in the series in just over a year. She did an ABC sitcom called *Getting Together* from 1971-1972 before concentrating on stage work thereafter, including an acclaimed one-woman show. "In the Seventies, I began working on Gertrude Stein, and I wanted to get my theater training going and work on my voice," she says. "I had a wonderful vocal coach. In eight years of performing, I never lost my voice. I learned more about me as an actress than any other experience."

Pat counts being on *The Carol Burnett Show* as a career highlight as well. "Everyone on the staff was top quality," she says. "Carol would do everything with such blitheness. She never lost her aplomb."

Karen adds that prior to doing this show, her manager, Kenny Greengrass, told her working with Carol would be a great experience, and she concurs with that assessment. "There couldn't have been a nicer person than Carol Burnett," Karen says. "A lady, just a real, real person."

March 8, 1971: Mike Douglas, Bernadette Peters

Q&A; Bernadette joins the dancers on "Tea for Two"; "The Brats" has Carol, Lyle, Harvey and Bernadette as kids arguing in a playground; Mike sings "Theme from *Love Story* (Where Do I Begin)"; Funt and Mundane encounter many complications on stage during a performance of "Out of the Blue" in a barn in Nebraska; Mike and Carol duet on "I Think I Love You" and "For All We Know"; "The Early Early Show" presents Carol, Lyle and Harvey in "The Most Happy Fella"; the cast, dancers and guests appear in a musical finale as senior citizens celebrating "Broadway, My Street."

Comments: While this episode serves as the last of three go-rounds for Mike Douglas as a guest, it marks the second appearance of Bernadette Peters in 1970-1971 and the only time apart from 1977-1978 where she showed up more than once in the same season. Although she had been acting since she was three-and-a-half years old (!), she recalled in a 2012 DVD commentary that doing *The Carol Burnett Show* made her nervous.

"I think I was still so young, and sort of, you know, worried, you know, making sure I was doing a great job, that I don't think I enjoyed it as much as I should have," she said. "And I'm looking back at it and going, 'This was great!'"

Bernadette credits *The Carol Burnett Show* for keeping her career afloat between stage productions. "She was hiring me more than anybody was, especially at a time when I was sort of between shows," she said. "Just kept bringing me on the show and showcasing me. She was really, really, very encouraging to my career and to me."

Having said that, this episode has negligible value overall. The wide-ranging Q&A includes Carol doing a Tarzan yell, announcing she will do *Plaza Suite* on stage with George Kennedy in the summer, giving more than $20 to two Girl Scouts and saying that her favorite character is Zelda (she will be sick of the character within two years). The rest of the show's first half is ho-hum. For the musical numbers, depicting Bernadette as going back in time to recount her courtship of Don Crichton before their wedding has good tap routines by her and the dancers but nothing scintillating. And the attempt to spice up Mike's bland sound-alike of a recent Andy Williams hit by interspersing film clips of Don Crichton (again!) and a female dancer wandering on a shoreline in love falls flat. Mike does look good in his leisure suit in the fireplace setting though.

The skit between the songs is even more inconsequential. Bernadette looks and acts like Shirley Dimple to the disgust of a tomboy (Carol). A sissy in a Little Lord Fauntleroy outfit (Harvey) is excited about Bernadette's party and tells her he has redecorated her dollhouse as a present. They leave and a Boy Scout (Lyle) offers to take Carol to the party after they learn how to kiss. This is forced and cutesy and forgettable.

The one comic sketch that works is Funt and Mundane, coping with a hick theater operator (Lyle) who allows numerous indignities on their stage—a cow and chickens appearing through the scenery, passing trains that shake the set jarringly and attacks by mosquitoes among them. By the end Lyle has to round up some loose pigs that generate bedlam on stage and laughter from the audience. But the rest is downhill from here.

The meandering movie spoof has Harvey enticing Carol to be his mail order bride by passing off Lyle as himself. When she arrives, she is so smitten with Lyle that they magnetically attach to each other as indicated by static noises, but she must marry Harvey. Eventually he finds the duo making out in a haystack and accidentally kills Carol, but that allows him to go back to dancing with Lyle as they were doing before Carol arrived. This parody never catches fire despite everyone's best efforts.

The same applies to Lyle reading an item in Walblue's Theatrical Drugstore that Ruby Keeler is now a hit on Broadway with *No No Nanette*, and that encourages him and his fellow retirees to sing their plans to audition. The set opens and shows Mike in a white tuxedo having the rest of the cast join him in dance, but there's no razzle or dazzle here.

At the end, Carol sings "It's Time to Say So Long" in her old lady voice, but this is a lost cause. Vicki does not appear in the show, indicating she might have had the right idea.

March 15, 1971: Rerun of Oct. 19, 1970 show

March 22, 1971: David Frost, Eileen Farrell, Marilyn Horne

In a show taped in New York City, Eileen sings an aria; David plays a snooty Rolls Royce salesman dealing with a crass American couple (Carol and Harvey); Marilyn's solo leads into her joining Carol and Eileen dressed as the Andrews Sisters; George fantasizes he is a gladiator impressing a fetching empress (Vicki), until Zelda arrives on the scene; David is hosting at La Scala the debut of a new operetta, "Chinderella," with Carol as the title character, Eileen and Marilyn as her evil stepsisters, Harvey as her fairy godfather and Lyle as the dashing Prince.

Comments: "You have no idea what it feels like to be back here," a clearly touched and slightly misty-eyed Carol tells the audience after a barn-burning round of applause when she appears on stage. "It's been a long time since we've been in this theatre." It's the same stage where she taped *The Garry Moore Show* nearly a decade earlier, and her first professional appearance in Manhattan since the debacles of *The Entertainers* and *Fade Out —Fade In* in 1965. This is her moment for redemption, and she sparkles in it.

With no Q&A, there are three songs by Carol and her guests, with a moderately amusing sketch in the middle. After considerable give and take, David makes Carol and Harvey swear they will refuse to degrade their automobile with gauche items such as plastic hula dolls or bobbing head dogs on the dashboard. Once the sale is complete and the couple leaves, David is revealed to be a fake British snob.

The Zelda skit puts poor George against his worst enemy, his wife, who even in ancient Rome can destroy his hope for contentment by punching through his shield. When he reluctantly kisses her before battle, she thinks he is getting fresh and smacks him. It ends with Zelda handing George his dagger for battle and accidentally stabbing him to death.

In "Chinderella," Carol sings an aria with such lyrics as "Oh woe is me-oh!" before a visit by Harvey, wearing a handlebar mustache and dressed in a tutu over long johns. This over-the-top spoofing has nice singing approximating opera by the regulars.

"Thank you all, I love being back," Carol says. The crowd clearly loved the show too. Sadly—and inexplicably—there was not another show taped in New York City after this.

March 29, 1971: Nanette Fabray, Paul Lynde

Q&A; a spoof of commercials; "The Old Folks" plan to hit the dance floor with another couple (Nanette and Paul); Carol volunteers as a temporary secretary at Roger's office with disastrous results; Don Crichton leads the Ernie Flatt Dancers in a routine backed with the theme from the movie *Tom Jones*; "As the Stomach Turns" has Marian trying to rectify her financial difficulties with the help of a friend (Nanette) and a boarder (Harvey); the Charwoman waves goodbye to the cast, sees highlights from the season's shows and sings the full verses of "It's Time to Say So Long."

Comments: For only this time, *The Carol Burnett Show* ends its season with guests instead of a Family Show, although the ones who appear on it are familiar faces who enliven it. In the Q&A, three ushers on the show line up for a kiss from Vicki, who obliges, and Carol introduces the honorary Easter Seals child in the audience.

The commercial send-ups use the tack of being the first take for each. Best of them by far is Paul as both a supposedly slick plastic sandwich bag salesman and an unwitting victim of a razor comparison test. Paul also shines along with Nanette in delivering zingers about each other while meeting Bert and Molly prior to a social gathering. As is typical in an Old Folks sketch, they all sing in unison.

With his secretary out with the flu, Roger reluctantly accepts Carol's offer to help him at work. He wants her to stay behind the desk because she is wearing hot pants and does not want anyone to hit on her. Additionally, he wants no one to know she is his wife. Roger becomes frustrated with Carol's inability to multitask in a timely manner and tries to get a replacement before a sexy co-worker (Judith McConnell) appears and tells Carol how she met Roger at the office's Christmas party. Carol's ire about this vanishes as a handsome colleague of Roger's (Lyle) visits and likes her gams on display from her hot pants. After Lyle leaves, Carol and Roger apologize to each other, ending a so-so entry.

After an elaborate dance number comes an OK "As the Stomach Turns" that could have been better if the writing was tighter. Encountering a friend with no problems (Nanette), Marian confesses she is penniless, and a visit by her daughter (Vicki) with a baby provides no solace. Marian plans to leave Canoga Falls and sell herself, prompting Nanette to say the skit's best line: "Nickels and dimes aren't going to help!" A ham actor (Harvey) arrives quickly as Marian puts out an ad for a boarder, but that does not stop the appearance of a banker (Paul) ready to foreclose on her home. He wants money so badly, he threatens to repossesses her contact lenses. Marian tries to seduce Paul, but he demurs and gives her twenty minutes to produce cash before this skit ends.

The closing follows the same template as 1969-1970's final show, only here when the Charwoman visits the sets, it cuts to clips of the Old Folks, Zelda (the Jan. 25, 1971 skit with George as a toreador), and Carol & Sis. More telling is what Carol says in the Q&A at the show's start. Noting her renewal for a fifth season by CBS programmers next year, she adds, "They've changed our time slot, and I'm very pleased." Her feelings about the switch will be quite different in later years.

Final Notes for the Season

Despite the increased competition of *ABC's Monday Night Football* for the first half of the season and a couple of strongly rated movies on the network and NBC for the rest of the season, *The Carol Burnett Show* continued to win its time slot overall. The series tied for Number Twenty-Five overall with NBC's Monday night movies and *The Partridge Family*. Its average rating of 19.8 was down a point from last season, but that still made it in line with what place it finished in the ratings in 1968-1969.

The Carol Burnett Show kept its Emmy losing streak for Outstanding Musical or Variety Program intact for a fourth consecutive year, with *The Flip Wilson Show* triumphing instead of *The David Frost Show* this time. That same program won for writing over what Carol's team offered on the Feb. 1, 1971 show. The series could take consolation with Harvey's second win for individual achievement and Ernie Flatt's first (and only) statuette for his choreography on the Oct. 19, 1970 show. Additionally, Carol did get a warm, sustained amount of applause during the ceremony when she came out at the end to present the final award for Outstanding Single Program—Drama or Comedy.

There were mixed results at the Golden Globes as well. Carol lost Best Television Actress, Musical or Comedy to Mary Tyler Moore, but *The Carol Burnett Show* triumphed as Best Television Show, Musical or Comedy, its first win in the category.

One outright win did occur from the Writers Guild of America, which named the series Best Variety and awarded Don Hinkley, Jack Mendelsohn, Stan Hart, Larry Siegel, Woody Kling, Roger Beatty, Arnie Rosen, Kenny Solms, Gail Parent and Arthur Julian for their work. The series also had better luck at the Television Champion Awards, winning for Best Variety Program (it was helped by the fact that *The Flip Wilson Show* was classified as and won the separate Best Comedy Show category), and for Best Comedienne (Carol earned the honor for a fourth consecutive year).

A major shift in leadership occurred when Bob Banner stepped down from being executive producer this year so he could form his own production company to create TV movies. His departure bumped Joe Hamilton up to the position, which most personnel on the show felt he already knew how to handle, given Banner's limited involvement in the production process. To fill his old job, Hamilton expanded Arnie Rosen's duties as head writer to encompass producer as well for the 1971-1972 season, which seemed a reasonable move at the time but would soon be a liability for the series.

A considerable loss at the end of this season is the departure of writers Kenny Solms and Gail Parent. "We did our four years of college there," Solms notes. "Gail started to write sitcoms, and I was doing variety shows."

"We had so many offers," notes Parent. She would still write occasionally for the series in 1972-1973 and Carol's specials, and Kenny did return for one guest bit. They also co-produced *The Smothers Brothers Show*—for more on that, see the intro for 1974-1975.

There was a solemn note at season's end as Harry Zimmerman departed as orchestra leader. Officially he retired, but in fact he was fired. As Cubby O'Brien recalls, "It was a very hard decision for Carol to make. It was getting to the point where he was not there all the time for the song cues as conductor. Peter Matz came out from New York, and Harry went into retirement."

"Harry was a good writer, but some felt he wrote the old school style," added saxophonist Buddy Collette. Matz fired Collette along with the majority of Zimmerman's players on *The Carol Burnett Show*, as the new conductor preferred to use musicians he already knew. Collette went on to continue a busy career with *The Flip Wilson Show* (where several other Zimmerman musicians relocated) and other opportunities through the twentieth century. As for Zimmerman, he vanished quietly from the scene after his dismissal and died six years later on Aug. 20, 1977, a week shy of his seventy-second birthday.

Also leaving this year with only twenty-six shows to their credit were Dick DeBenedictis and David Rogers, the show's special music material writers. "After that one season was over, Kenny Welch was available, and he came over to do the show, and I went to Universal," says DeBenedictis. While his temporary partner David Rogers faded from prominence, DeBenedictis flourished as a composer for dozens of dramatic TV series, including Emmy nominations for his work on *Police Story* and many others.

Summing up his short tenure on the series, DeBenedictis assesses that "It was a very good experience, and I would have liked to have stayed on, but in no way could I compete with Kenny Welch as a writer and pianist."

Reruns of *The Carol Burnett Show* will air through May 17. The next week, *Suspense Playhouse* assumes the time slot and repeats all but one show seen on *Premiere*, the 1968 summer replacement for *The Carol Burnett Show*. Three of those shows will run yet again on Mondays in the summer of 1972. Reruns of reruns of failed pilots—this is why summer programming has a bad reputation. Anyway, this series ends July 5.

Replacing it the following week is *The CBS Newcomers*, a variety show spotlighting regular upcoming talent that does little to boost their careers. That includes its host, Dave Garroway, whose stardom has drooped since he left as host of NBC's *Today* morning show in 1961. He will have no other network series after this. It runs through Sept. 6.

The Carol Burnett Show then returns to CBS—but not on Monday nights. In 1971 the Federal Communications Commission introduced the Prime Time Access Rule that took away a half hour of programming every night from the networks for use by their affiliates. CBS programming head Fred Silverman used this occasion to rid the network's schedule of hit series with popular appeal largely to older and rural audiences, including *The Jim Nabors Hour*, and replace them with ones designed to appeal to younger, upscale audiences as part of a demographics overhaul for advertisers.

To signify the massive revamp, only four series remained in their original slots. Carol's was not among them. It was not because CBS leadership had a problem with its audience makeup—far from it, in fact.

"It was one of the few shows running that (CBS President) Bob Wood and I kept after coming in charge," Silverman recounts. "It really filled the aims of what we wanted. It was a smart comedy hour, and its ratings were very, very big across the board. It was kind of a model of where we needed to take the rest of the comedy on the network."

The Carol Burnett Show had done fine dominating on Monday nights for four seasons, so Silverman felt it could blunt one of his toughest challenges for the upcoming season. NBC was moving *Adam-12*—its fourth-highest rated series in 1970-71—to be its the first show on its Wednesday evening lineup. Silverman wanted CBS to go with a proven hit to stop its momentum rather than risk competing with an untested new series.

"It was a strong show, and because of the format of the show, broad comedy, it would play well there," he says. "We needed a strong lead-in, and it was a good way to lead off Wednesday nights." Additionally, two seasons earlier, both *The Glen Campbell Goodtime Hour* and *Hee Haw* did much better as the midweek leadoff series for the network than did *Storefront Lawyers* in 1970-1971.

So, *The Carol Burnett Show* would run on Wednesdays at 8-9 p.m. Eastern and Pacific. It became the first of many changes in a season that produced the greatest turmoil backstage in the show's history. Although it was all smiles to viewers, Carol and some of her crew were frustrated creatively for the first time, and coping with the situation produced some major long-term ramifications that would shape its legacy as well as its destiny.

Buz Kohan recalls how efficiently run the series had become through contributions from everyone around Carol Burnett in its first four years, to her slight dismay. "She used to say wistfully, 'Some day, I'm going to have a show of my own,'" he says. Little did Burnett know that she had to assume a leadership role the next season in order to save her series, as it was suddenly facing the biggest challenges it had encountered since its debut.

Harvey did appear in drag a couple of times on the series, but none had the impact of Mother Marcus, which he debuted on the Nov. 7, 1971 installment of "As the Stomach Turns" opposite Carol's Marian character. Sporting an ample physique and a deliberate Yiddish-inflected speech pattern, Mother Marcus was the one character where Harvey typically cracked up the other players rather than vice versa. Courtesy of Getty Images.

Chapter 6

1971-1972: Didn't We Do This Already?

Audience member:	"What's your favorite sport?"
Carol:	"My favorite sport? Paul Newman."—From the Sept. 15, 1971 show

Crew Additions This Season

Writers: Art Baer, Ben Joelson, Ken and Mitzie Welch.

Conductor: Peter Matz.

Recalling this season, Carol revealed to *Panorama* magazine editor Lawrence Linderman in 1980 that apart from when she finally decided to end her series, "the only other time I'd embraced the idea of stopping was during our fifth season. I remember that our writers weren't coming up with sketches that Harvey Korman and I felt challenging to do, and we both felt we were starting to outgrow the show's material."

This assessment is sadly correct. Many skits seen during this season often come off as derivative, and by the Nov. 10, 1971 episode, roughly one sketch every three shows was a remake of previous efforts. It was bad enough to force Carol and Harvey to try and find an original spin on these redos, but compounding the problem was that head writer (and now producer) Arnie Rosen was making guest stars reprise their same previous roles as well, such as for Tim Conway in the Dec. 1, 1971 show, Jackie Joseph in the Dec. 15, 1971 installment and Nanette Fabray on the Jan. 19, 1972 outing. The latter had it worst of all—Nanette had to play the exact same lines she did from not just one but two earlier shows. By that point, Carol and Joe Hamilton had agreed internally that changes in the writing staff had to go, or the series was going to sink even more creatively.

Other factors may have played into Carol's low opinion of this season. In her new time slot, she competed with series starring two of her closest friends in Hollywood. *The NBC Mystery Movie* aired against Carol in her last half hour and included *McMillan and Wife* starring Rock Hudson as one of its three rotating elements (the others were *Columbo* and *McCloud*). On ABC, Elizabeth Montgomery was opposite Carol in her eighth season starring in *Bewitched*. (Ironically, *Bewitched* suffered creatively this season like Carol's series by remaking old plots for new episodes.)

As it turns out, *Bewitched* finished poorly enough that ABC moved it midseason to Saturday nights to die against *All in the Family* on CBS, while moving up *The Courtship of Eddie's Father* that followed it against the second half hour of Carol. It did no better facing off directly with the start of Carol's show, nor did the series that followed it, *The ABC Comedy Hour*. All were canned at the end of the season.

NBC was a different matter. Both *The NBC Mystery Movie* and the cop drama that preceded it, *Adam-12*, outrated *The Carol Burnett Show* in 1971-1972, the first time the series consistently lost to its competition. Additionally, *Columbo* was a critical darling that received a great amount of favorable coverage, and that attention left *The Carol Burnett Show* with the perception of being yesterday's news.

If all that drama was not enough, the arrival of Peter Matz stirred a few feathers with members of the orchestra—that is, those who remained after Peter joined. A well-regarded arranger and conductor, Peter had won two Emmys for leading orchestras, one for the *My Name is Barbra* special starring Barbra Streisand in 1965 and the other for *The Kraft Music Hall* in 1970, a series for which he was conductor from 1967-1971. Eight years prior to joining *The Carol Burnett Show*, he was a busy conductor for such series as *The Edie Adams Show* (1963-1964), *The Jimmy Dean Show* (1963-1965) and *Hullabaloo* (1965-1966). He also earned a Tony nomination as musical director for *No Strings* in 1962 and won a Grammy for his arrangement of "People" for Barbra Streisand in 1964.

With such an impressive pedigree, Peter had established clout that he could and did use when he arrived on *The Carol Burnett Show*. "When Peter Matz came out, he brought a drummer he liked, Sol Gubin, so Sol came out and joined us," says Cubby O'Brien. The show really had no room for two drummers, so Cubby and Sol uneasily alternated duties on the series for a year.

"I stayed one more year to do rehearsal drumming while Sol played on air," Cubby says of his work in 1972-1973. In early 1973, he was contacted by the Carpenters, with whom he worked twice on *The Carol Burnett Show* this season (see Sept. 22, 1971 and Jan. 19, 1972). The demands of performing meant that Karen Carpenter needed to be up front in their shows rather than behind drums as she was previously, and Cubby's talent impressed the brother and sister duo. "They asked me to go on the road with them that summer, and I stayed with them until Karen passed away in 1983," Cubby notes. Cubby's departure with Carol was amicable, and oddly enough, he became the main orchestrator for frequent Burnett guest Bernadette Peters from 1983 onward.

Despite the changes in personnel, the addition of Matz was a positive one overall for the series, giving a more contemporary edge, as did a pretty nice guest roster of old favorites and new top talent such as Burt Reynolds. There was also the invaluable contributions of Ken and Mitzie Welch, who were free to rejoin Carol after many collaborations during the early and mid-1960s thanks to the cancellation of *The Kraft Music Hall* on NBC in the spring of 1971.

The Welches had a rocky debut on the series (for more on that, see the Dec. 8, 1971 entry), but they managed to overcome that debacle and craft some memorable salutes to composers and lyricists as well as clever original music. They alternated these duties with Artie Malvin, who had been with the series from the start.

"I never worked on a show like *The Carol Burnett Show* with the spirit of the staff," Ken Welch notes. "Everybody was contributing. It was an unusually happy group. There were not cliques like on other shows.

"Joe and Carol were delightful to work with. They were very responsive to what we offered. The writers were all responsive. It was a blessed show. The whole staff was very easy to work with."

Welch makes coming up with special musical numbers with a regular writing team on the series sound like a piece of cake. "We would meet with the writers privately and find something that turned all four of us on. In a production meeting, we would announce to Carol and Joe what we wanted to do. And they were usually very favorable to what we presented."

Sometimes they crafted numbers with the dancers that included the guests. These always were done with an eye toward the known vocal limitations of several non-singers that guest starred on the show.

"We always knew in advance who the guests were going to be, several weeks in advance," Welch says. "So, we had time to think about it. We were certainly aware of people's strengths and weaknesses. That's part of the job."

Even with these precautions, Welch feels he and his wife missed the mark constantly with one guest. "What Mitzie and I did miserably were the finales for Jim Nabors," he says. He particularly dislikes the tenth season opener, a spoof of the 1930s and 1940s tropical island movie musicals that he feels really flopped (see the Sept. 25, 1976 entry).

"We thought it was a wonderful idea, and it was crap," he says. "Each time with Jim, we thought it was a wonderful idea, but when it was on its feet and on the air, it was no good. On Monday morning, we thought every show was going to be a showstopper."

In fairness to Welch, it should be noted that he and his wife deservedly won Emmys for their work on the elaborate "Cinderella Gets It On" two-part tale with the Pointer Sisters (see Nov. 29, 1975), and their Hollywood songs medley they crafted for Carol and Eydie is one of the best long-form duets ever created for television (see Feb. 12, 1977). They succeeded brilliantly overall, and all of the top episodes that air from this season onward include material by the duo that help make them a winner.

Also coming aboard was a new dancer, Bobbie Bates, who would become a top terpsichorean for the series. "That was probably the most important day of my life," she recalls of being offered to join the series. Trained as a classical ballet dancer, she first tried out for the show as a lark. "I had auditioned for the show when it started, I think I was only eighteen. We used to treat an audition as a free class." Four years later, she was one of 350 (!) women to try for a spot in 1971 and did well enough to receive a callback to compete among a group of twelve.

"I did a really good audition, because I wasn't nervous," she says. At the end, Ernie Flatt called her to be part of his troupe, and the petite talent was soon a notable mainstay on *The Carol Burnett Show*. As she puts it, "I was the one tossed from guy to guy."

Another addition was the writing duo of Art Baer and Ben Joelson, to replace the departures of Kenny Solms, Gail Parent, Arthur Julian and Jack Mendelsohn, among others, from 1970-1971. Baer and Joelson had written extensively for sitcoms in the 1960s, including multiple episodes of *Car 54, Where Are You?, The Andy Griffith Show, Gomer Pyle—USMC* and *Hogan's Heroes*, as well as created a disastrous game show, *Fractured Phrases*, which ran on NBC mornings for thirteen low-rated weeks in 1965.

A final refreshed element this season was a better recognition of all the regulars in new opening animated credits. Now at the start of each show, Harvey, Lyle and Vicki emerged from behind doors to join the Charwoman. Harvey's cartoon avatar stepped out and bowed first, followed by Vicki and Lyle's doors flanking Harvey opening simultaneously.

But none of this could compensate for Carol and Joe considering that the series' best days were behind it, and soon their belief became the stuff of industry gossip. "The word was that the Hamiltons were running scared last winter. . . . The ratings had sagged some, and critics tended to find the show uneven, not always up to the high standard of the star herself," wrote Dwight Whitney in a post-mortem of the season in *TV Guide* in 1972.

Carol and Joe eventually realized the series could be salvaged, but only if it endured its biggest creative upheaval ever. Believing part of the problem stemmed from head writer and producer Arnie Rosen allowing too much retreaded material to be included in scripts, the Hamiltons terminated working with him at season's end. Rosen told Whitney he blamed his removal on "Normal attrition. After that long, you run out of fresh ideas."

"I liked Arnie, but he got into niches, like the nudge [Zelda] and the Old Folks, and that's the way he was doing it at the time," opines Larry Siegel, who will replace him next season as head writer. "He got stuck. Arnie was sort of, like, a little old hat."

Feeling other writers were responsible for diminishing returns in tired sketches too, Joe removed Don Hinkley, Stan Burns, Mike Marmer, Art Baer and Ben Joelson and kept only Siegel, Stan Hart, Roger Beatty, and Woody Kling on staff for the 1972-1973 season. Beatty remained as assistant director as well. Hart and Siegel stayed because they contributed most of the relatively few highlights of the period with strong movie parodies, while Kling received for kudos for having created the classic new recurring Nora Desmond character in a spoof of *Sunset Boulevard* (see Dec. 29, 1971 for more).

These changes were tough on Carol, particularly as Rosen, Hinkley, Burns and Marmer had started with the series and helped it flourish, but she ultimately viewed them as necessary. "So I really thought about quitting, but then I got a second wind and changed my mind—and I'm glad I did, because I think we all would have really missed not doing the show," Carol said in her *Panorama* interview. "The following season we got several new writers, and we developed new characters and new ways of doing things."

If there was any consolation for Carol, at least the season was two shows shorter than the previous ones. CBS instituted a policy of asking for no more than twenty-four episodes per season for series rather than twenty-six. This would be the new standard for the series from here onward. Meanwhile, Carol gritted out her time change and appeared on the season opener for *The Glen Campbell Goodtime Hour* to tell his viewers she had moved to Wednesday nights. (Ironically, that series would be cancelled at the end of this season.)

With all this in mind, let's look at what is available for review for this season and assess the good as well as the bad. Remember, even a lesser grade *Carol Burnett Show* is better than most other entertainment offerings.

Sept. 15, 1971: Jim Nabors

Q&A; a bookish stenographer (Carol) mistakenly believes that an author (Harvey) is confessing to murdering eight women when he is actually dictating the plot of his new novel; Jim sings "Help Me Make It Through the Night"; Carol is a game show contestant who wins a date with Lyle but must contend with Jim as an interfering chaperone; the male dancers perform in a number about Carol having "a real bad case of the blues"; "Culture Theater" sends up the story of Anne Boleyn (Carol) and King Henry V (Harvey); a musical tribute to Jim's hometown of Sylacauga, Alabama.

Comments: The musical numbers come off as more clever and vibrant than the comedy pieces here, which dispenses with the Q&A rather quickly after Carol emerges in a beautiful green and white gown. She appears in the first sketch in an obvious and somewhat tiresome farce about mistaking Harvey's intentions while taking notes from him in a hotel room. It says something that it is of more interest to note the number of bit players needed for this scenario—Ted Ziegler as a room service waiter, Bob Duggan as a police officer and Stan Mazin as the one who takes Carol away because, of course, she is thought to be crazy for the way her mind assumed that Harvey was a killer. This is a weak way to open the fourth season.

"Help Me Make It Through the Night" was a frequently recorded hit in 1971, most popularly for Sammi Smith, and its contemporary freshness and strong overall quality mesh well with Jim's vocals. The gold accented suit and panels with bulbs behind him enhance the presentation as well.

Jim recreates his Gomer Pyle voice to supervise the activities of Carol and Lyle on a cruise to Hawaii following their win on "The Mating Game" TV show. Vicki appears as Carol's friend, and Ted pops up again as a purser. There is only so much humor you can squeeze out of Jim's yokel vocal and actions unintentionally interfering with Carol and Lyle's plans for romance, and this segment runs out of them before the finish.

The all-male dance number is better, particularly due to striking 1930s Art Deco visuals. Unfortunately, the goodwill slumps as Lyle, sporting white hair and mustache and surrounded by cobwebs, introduces a rather uninspired spoof of British historical pageant plays seen on public television in America, with Vicki as Anne's aide and an unidentified actress as Catherine of Aragon. As you might expect, there are plenty of jokes about beheading involving Anne Boleyn, and for the seemingly umpteenth time over the last year or so, Inga Nielsen shows up as a blonde bombshell who is the next queen in line. This is passable at best.

The finale is a winner, however. Tellingly, according to Carol, it is her idea. A medley of songs about different cities lead into a new one saluting Jim's native municipality in Alabama, "It's Sylacauga" (pronounced "sill-uh-CAW-guh"). Clad in red and white outfits, Jim, Carol and the dancers perform in praise of what makes the locale special, with blown-up photographs of local landmarks included. Coming off the disappointment and surprise of his variety series being canceled by CBS a few months earlier due to its audience being old and relatively poor (it ranked Number Twenty-Nine for the 1970-1971 season, usually a number good enough to guarantee renewal), this sketch seems to bolster Jim's spirits, and everyone involved make it a lively production.

Watching this show, there is little doubt that Carol and Harvey had justifiable concerns about the writers' plans for the series this season. If three derivative, slumping sketches were the best they could create after a summer break, one wonders how much lower could succeeding installments fall. Thankfully, the next show will display a marked improvement in quality.

Sept. 22, 1971: Tim Conway, the Carpenters

Q&A; the Carpenters perform "Superstar"; Tim and Carol play a do-it-yourself couple whose efforts to fix up their property backfire on them; the Carpenters sing a duet of Burt Bacharach-Hal David songs with Carol; complications ensue when an ancient doctor (Tim) joins his fellow physician (Harvey) and a buxom nurse (Vicki) in the operating room to attend to a patient; "Tearjerker Theatre" has Vicki introducing "Beyond Love Story," an imagined sequel to the movie with Harvey, Carol and Lyle; the cast, dancers and guests enact what a typical 1930s radio music show would look and sound like.

Comments: Learning who the guests are for tonight's show, the audience reacts with an impressed "Ooo!" This is because by now Tim is an established favorite guest and the Carpenters are the hottest duo on the pop charts, something not usually said about Carol's musical visitors. Tim joins Carol in a tux to pantomime impressions of animals during the Q&A, including a cat, dog, frog and finally and most memorably, a cow being milked for the first time. Tim's looks of alternating confusion, discomfort and finally pleasure about the process is most satisfying.

Karen Carpenter appears on drums while her brother, Richard, is on the piano as they obviously lip sync to "Superstar," a song that was already popular and rising on the charts when this episode was taped and later aired. This was their first TV appearance since their NBC summer series *Make Your Own Kind of Music* ended Sept. 7, 1971, and it is well-received despite the artificiality of the performance.

Tim and Carol are in top physical comedy form for the first skit as they build a room. Carol gets her hand stuck in a cement pail. Tim accidentally whacks her with a piece of wood several times and gets shocked by a drill. Unnerved by the mess they are making, they take a break to drink a bottle of Champagne, only to have the cork hit Carol. After consuming the refreshment, they throw their glasses into the fireplace and witness the latter collapsing. Tim and Carol are at their bumbling, stumbling best, which makes this miles better than most of the comedy from the previous week's show.

An eager Carol joins the Carpenters to do some songs together from the songwriters who gave the duo their first big hit, "Close to You." It is a bubbly presentation by all. Next, Tim returns on the scene this time to mainly break up Harvey in a hospital sketch by playing an elderly surgeon. The first instance occurs when Tim and Harvey look at an X-ray and Tim ad libs, "Swallowed a light bulb!" When Tim gets the X-ray stuck on his face, Harvey laughs so hard he puts the mask on his face to cover his amusement. In other shtick, Tim slowly blows up a surgical glove like a balloon and compares it to Vicki's stacked chest, and he tries to thread a needle for stitching, without much success. The segment ends rather inconsequentially, but overall it is a winner.

"Beyond Lovely Story" assumes what happens if Jenny (Carol) had lived and irked her husband (Harvey) by being too clingy. Frustrated, he tells Jenny he plans to leave her, but then she coughs and passes out again as she did in the original. Jenny's doctor (Lyle, getting applause for his first appearance on this show) gives her mouth-to-mouth resuscitation, which excites her, but when Harvey takes over doing the same thing, she dies. Surprisingly, Harvey finds himself having to console the doctor, who weeps incessantly after Jenny passes away. When asked why, Lyle says, "She was the only patient I ever had!"

The musical finale is clever and winning. "Radio Days" begins with Carol talking about recreating a live Manhattan radio show from the 1930s, leading into a production number by the dancers followed by Tim serving as host. Carol, Vicki and Karen do a brief musical bit before Lyle shows up as Wrangler Ron to croon a western tune, accompanied by Tim making the sound effects. Vicki offers "The Flat Foot Floogie" with four male dancers, and Karen follows to do a comic "Smoke Gets in Your Eyes" that includes her playing the drums. Harvey hoofs and vocalizes with four female dancers, then Carol does a solo turn with "Body and Soul" accompanied noisily by Richard on the piano, who she knocks off his stool at the end. Everyone then takes a bow at the end of this sprightly bit.

This entry sparkles much more than its predecessor. Still, creating an imaginary sequel parody to emulate the success of mocking the original the previous season (see Feb. 1, 1971) is a stretch and no doubt contributed to Carol's uneasiness about the direction of the show's comedy. Otherwise, Tim and the Carpenters were in good form. Both will return later this season, Tim several times and Karen and Richard on Jan. 19, 1972.

Oct. 6, 1971: Steve Lawrence, Carol Channing

Steve sings "In My Own Lifetime"; Roger and Carol visit a nudist colony in "Carol & Sis"; Carol C. performs "Ain't Misbehavin'," "You're the Cream in My Coffee" and "Button Up Your Overcoat"; a woman with bad luck (Carol C.) and a faith healer (Harvey) appear in "As the Stomach Turns"; an Oscar awards salute includes spoofs of *Sorry, Wrong Number, The Story of Louis Pasteur* and *The African Queen* and Carol C. as a talkative winner; Carol B. is Buster Keaton, Steve and Harvey are Laurel and Hardy, and the dancers are the Keystone Kops in a silent movie tribute.

Comments: This show earns Dave Powers his first Emmy nomination as director. It also sets a precedent of Steve Lawrence doing at least three shows every season from this point onward. He showed in previous outings he could handle more than singing, making him a big asset to the series. As writer Buz Kohan puts it, "Steve was always great as far as comedy was concerned."

"My dad would tell you, bar none, Steve Lawrence is one of the best sketch comedians," says Chris Korman.

According to Steve, he and Carol first met when they appeared on *The General Motors 50th Anniversary Show*, a special that aired on NBC on Nov. 17, 1957. He married Eydie Gorme that same year. Steve reconnected with Carol when he guest starred on *The Garry Moore Show* in 1960, and he, her and Eydie all became lifelong friends thereafter.

The confidence placed in him and Carol Channing are well earned here, as the show dispenses with the usual Q&A to open with Carol complimenting Steve on his recent guest shot acting on *Medical Center* before he solidly presents a tune from the Broadway musical *The Rothschilds*. That leads into a genuinely funny "Carol & Sis" where Carol freaks out seeing a nudist camp's host (Bob Duggan) and bellhop (Brad Trumbull) in the buff. She and Roger are there to impress Roger's client (Ted Ziegler), who has a buxom wife (Inga Nielsen), and her husband insists she disrobe to blend into the community. Carol hilariously resists stripping until finally doing so off camera, whereupon she is arrested by a cop (an unidentified actor), as the facility is busted for having a license that expired three months earlier. Covering herself with shrubbery, she yells at Roger that she won't forget this experience, and he says he won't either because the bushes she holds are poison ivy. Funny from start to the last, this has some great double entendres to boot.

Dressed up as a flapper, Carol Channing presents her medley joined by the male dancers in 1920s outfits to match when the songs were first popular. She's fun to watch here, as she is in "As the Stomach Turns" as a jinx who visits Marian wearing an all-black ensemble. There's lots of clever sexual innuendo here as Vicki arrives as Marian's daughter in the Army with the inevitable baby, followed by Harvey as an amusingly overbaked faith healer. He brings with him a boy with a sprained ankle (Steve), who suffers in pain as Harvey alleges to cure his ailment with several nice pratfalls. Harvey helps remove the bad luck Carol C. has, but it infects his hand to his dismay. This is another rollicking skit.

For the start of the Oscar salute, which Carol incorrectly says the films depicted won an Academy Award when in fact they were just nominees, Vicki plays a bedridden woman hysterical about an intruder. She calls an operator for help, but when she sees it's Lyle, she's turned on and hangs up the phone. Lyle appears next as a presenter fidgeting as Carol C. rambles on in a beautifully pretentious drawl to thank everyone for her Oscar. Her bit is broken up between the rest of the salute, during which time she becomes pregnant and gives birth to a child.

The send-up of *The Story of Louis Pasteur* has Steve as the title character whose discovery is accidentally destroyed by Harvey. That's OK, but it's overshadowed by Carol and Steve in the Katharine Hepburn and Humphrey Bogart roles in *The African Queen*, with a greasy Steve being kissed and then pushed overboard by Carol thrice as they embrace on his tramp steamer going downriver. After he climbs back aboard the last time, she finally succumbs to his charms, and he responds by throwing her off. This winning bit will pop up again as an excerpt on the 1978 series finale.

In the 2015 guest book with *The Carol Burnett Show: The Lost Episodes* DVD set, Carol is quoted as saying, "I remember sketch wasn't working during rehearsal, but Steve and I came up with the idea of tossing each other overboard again and again, and it worked!"

The silent movie tribute finale "Without a Word, Without a Sound," with the dancers dressed as the Keystone Kops, will be remade on Oct. 30, 1976 show. See that entry for more details. It caps off arguably the best show of the 1971-1972 season, with everything consistently entertaining.

Oct. 13, 1971: Ken Berry, Cass Elliot

Q&A; Ken does a tap dance routine to a ragtime jazz tune called "Razz-Ma-Tazz"; the cast and guests send up the fifth annual unforgettable commercials of the year; Cass sings "There's a Lull in My Life"; George's fantasy about being a marshal in the Old West is interrupted by the appearance of Zelda; Cass and Carol sing a medley of marriage-themed songs; a spoof of Sonja Henie musicals with Carol as a skating ingénue, Ken a brilliant but awkward songwriter in love with her, Harvey as Carol's uncle, Lyle as a movie producer and Vicki a demanding movie star.

Comments: Aside from the numbers, this show is the worst waste of Cass Elliot's comic talents on the series ever, relegating her to moments with fat jokes so notoriously bad that they were included in *Straight Shooter*, a 1988 public television documentary about the Mamas and the Papas, as an example of how TV could mistreat her skills. Otherwise, this installment sets its tone of nothing particularly special happening with a middling Q&A, where Carol signs an autograph book in several directions, meets a woman who claims she resembles the star and says she would like to do the show in Indonesia once (she never does). That is about it, followed by a standard Ken Berry song and tap number.

The show comes to life fitfully in the commercial blackouts of varying quality. They start with a crass Cass gag, where she appears in a young girl's outfit and gets attention by stomping her feet on the putting green while Harvey and Lyle are playing, causing an audible and visual shake on the course. She is excited to tell her dad (Harvey) that she has no cavities, and the reason why is "I brush my teeth sixteen times a day, after every meal!" Better is Vicki showering and telling her husband (Ken) standing in the bathroom about a better soap to use. "Man, I have a wonderful wife!" Ken exclaims. Lyle pulls back the curtain while showering with Vicki and tells Ken, "You can say that again!" Next, Carol plays Mother Nature and shows the reason why it is not nice to fool her, as she brings out a baby carriage. The segment sinks again after that with Ken supposedly washing the dishes created by Cass eating sixteen times a day, but rebounds with Harvey seeing a man in his toilet tank and flushing it in response. This is the only acting Cass does on this show, although she does fine following it with a forgettable tune she sings on a balcony set.

When Zelda turns off George's favorite western in order to show him her new nightgown, he insults her, and she forbids him to join her in bed in response. He goes to sleep and dreams that he is fighting a duel with Black Bart (Lyle) for the love of a saloon girl (Vicki). All is fine until Zelda shows up her too, blowing beer suds in George's face and getting angry when he does not pay for her purchase of the drink. She attempts to seduce Lyle to stop the duel, but when he calls her "mister," she is enraged and beats him up to take George home herself. For a George-Zelda skit, this is pretty amusing.

Joking to Carol that "I'm just as common as you," Cass joins the hostess in singing several songs such as "Ah, Sweet Mystery of Life" in honor of Cass being wed during the summer. Unfortunately, that marriage ended shortly after this episode first aired. This seven-minute medley marks the last appearance of Cass for this episode.

"Love in the Avalanche" starts with the dancers singing happily in a ski clubhouse when Lyle tells Harvey, the inn's elderly operator, that Hollywood stars are on their way to film a movie at the lodge, including a songwriter (Ken) and a diva (Vicki). Carol is a wholesome skater attracted to Ken who fakes an injury to spend the night with him and helps him write a song that they perform as a duet. They embrace and kiss just as Vicki arrives, and the incident causes her to leave and proclaim she will not be the movie's leading lady due to their activity. Undaunted, Ken suggests Carol assume the role, and in the next scene, Carol leads a Polynesian number with the dancers in Hollywood, joined by her uncle, Harvey, as well. They are all doused in snow at the end of the routine. As movie spoofs go, this is average in both the humor and music departments.

Despite her shabby treatment here, Cass will return to the series on the Nov. 10, 1971 episode, where she has a somewhat better showcase. Ken comes back on Dec. 15, 1971.

Oct. 20, 1971: Peggy Lee, Dom DeLuise

Q&A; a stenographer (Carol) warns an antique glass house operator (Dom) not to get fresh with her; Peggy sings "I Feel the Earth Move" and "Watch What Happens"; Dom hosts the game show "Do or Die" with George hampered by Zelda acting as his guest expert; Zelda appears again to nag Peggy performing "Is That All There Is?"; Alice Portnoy investigates a murder scene to help an inspector (Harvey) tell whodunit among a chef (Dom), wife (Vicki) and a chauffeur (Lyle); Carol wonders why Roger found a woman at their party particularly attractive; a musical finale with Carol and Peggy.

Comments: When bubbly Dom DeLuise is unable to spark many laughs and Carol is forced to play Zelda back to back, you definitely have a weak show. The Q&A does have a little oomph to it at least. After some in the audience respond with "whoa" upon hearing the guest lineup, Carol explains why she does not do many imitations of others. "I don't really do mimicking well at all," she claims, though she does do a good impersonation of Walter Brennan saying "Yeah!" afterward. Best of all, a woman from New Orleans who asks Carol why she does not do more movies comes on stage for an autograph and asks for a kiss from Harvey. He comes from backstage to smother her with smooches and sign her book after she praises him to the hilt.

From there, it is downhill starting with Carol arriving as a wallflower at Dom's store filled with glass antiques. One assumes she likely will destroy them when warned to be careful by Dom, and that is what she does, hitting and shrieking at a pitch that shatters them ostensibly because she thinks erroneously he is attracted to her. After Carol causes much damage, Dom loses his senses and finishes off the destruction by smashing some items off the wall. This poorly motivated humor wastes the time of everyone involved.

After Peggy sings a Carole King hit and a Tony Bennett non-hit in a yellow gown, Carol and Dom appear in another sketch with little comic momentum. Dom is given relatively little to do apart from asking relatively hard questions to Harvey as George, who answers them with ease until Zelda comes on as his guest expert. Naturally, she provides a wrong response to a question, which gets George shot in the arm as a consequence. He is then shot in the leg and put in a guillotine due to further misses by Zelda. These activities play as unfunny as they sound. Incredibly, Zelda saves George from the beheading but then accidentally shoots him thereafter for a supposedly funny ending. Vicki is in this sketch as Dom's big-breasted assistant, and she is wasted in the unfortunate proceedings along with everyone else.

As if that was not enough Zelda, she appears in the next segment to offer unnecessary commentary between lyrics for Peggy while the latter attempts to perform her hit, "Is That All There Is?" This is an overkill of the character, and one really pities that Peggy has to endure this forced sketch as well.

Stumbling onward, a cop (Bob Duggan) investigates a murder scene with Dom, Vicki and Lyle as suspect when Fireside Girl Alice Portnoy arrives to sell boxes of cookies. When the inspector (Harvey) shows up, she forces him to participate in deducing what happens after telling she knows he is zero for seventeen in solving mysteries. As with the other sketches on this show, there are lots of moments here where the performers were apparently expecting laughs that never materialized. That applies to the "surprise" ending, where it turns out the supposed victim (an unbilled actor) was faking his death— unfortunately, Harvey ends up accidentally killing him thereafter.

The final sketch is a little bit better than the preceding ones, but that hardly counts as praise. It is "Carol & Sis," just Roger and Carol cleaning up at a party before going to sleep (in separate beds, which seems anachronistic even for 1971). Carol becomes obsessed as to why Roger thought one guest was the prettiest female there. Forced on the issue, he says it was due to her looks and youth. That leads Carol to cry about him "flipping over" other women and Roger to note the attractive girl's defects to defend himself. "How dare you talk that way about my friend?!" Carol shoots back to him as she storms off, a clever, unexpected ending to an otherwise flaccid skit.

By the finale the episode has become a lost cause, but it is lively nonetheless. The male dancers appear in bowlers to move to "A Woman is a Sometime Thing," followed by Carol and Peggy singing "We're Two Little Girls With Two Little Curls" in red (Peggy) and blue (Carol) frilly outfits. The women dancers join them during the number, the one moment when the show really shines. But it is too little too late.

Given how ineffectively he was used here, it is not surprising that this was Dom's only appearance on the series, even though he and Carol had worked together well on *The Entertainers*. Peggy will return less than three months later—see Jan. 5, 1972.

Oct. 27, 1971: Diahann Carroll, Tim Conway

Q&A; two tentative customers (Tim and Carol) shop for waterbeds; Diahann sings a solo; two segments sending up how bit players try to steal scenes in movies and TV shows; Lyle, Harvey and Vicki's attempted jewelry is fouled up by the slow actions of their old henchman (Tim); Carol and the dancers perform "Saturday Morning Confusion"; "Insomnia Theatre" presents a parody of the Katharine Hepburn 1955 film *Summertime*; an extended mini-musical features Carol and Tim as the meek partners of Diahann and Harvey respectively as they hit the town for the singles scene and are joined by the dancers.

Comments: This offering is a pretty balanced presentation of the talents of all the regulars and guest stars. The Q&A has Carol discussing several outside projects. She appreciates a man with CBS Records in the audience who praises her new album that he heard on an early pressing, mentions that when she starred in the Los Angeles production of *Plaza Suite* in the summer she enjoyed the middle sketch the most and tells everyone she has taped another special with Julie Andrews (*Julie and Carol at Lincoln Center* airs Dec. 7, 1971, on CBS). The portion ends with a woman gushing, "We love you! You're a doll!"

The humor flows generously at the start as Tim and Carol fumble, stumble and become attracted to each other while rolling around testing out waterbeds. The keeper is when the bed springs a leak and Tim attempts to hide it from the salesman (Don Crichton) by sitting on it, soaking his crotch in the process. Eventually more leaks appear, which gets the duo in trouble by the end. This is a very funny piece.

Carol introduces Diahann, who is wearing a stylish cap to sing "A Song for You" amid a stark background. Diahann is quite effective in her emoting and offers one of the best solo musical numbers ever done on the show.

The actors trying to get attention in bit roles segment has two parts that combined provide an effective presentation of broad comedy. For the first, Tim plays a patron in a restaurant set who overshadow Vicki and Lyle sitting at a front table by peering and waving behind them, followed by taking sugar from their table and dousing it in his coffee cup and ultimately putting a newspaper on his head as a hat. In the second one, Lyle fires Harvey while Carol, playing a secretary, files her nails and sharpens pencils loudly, shows off her leg, removes her wig to comb it, and in a final moment to make everyone aware of her presence, put on a hat and a "beagle puss" fake nose and glasses.

The main ensemble sketch centered on Tim has him already cracking up Harvey near the start when his doddering Old Man puts a stocking over his face that distorts his features. Tim is given plenty of latitude to do his shtick here, from seeing the ample bosom on Vicki's bimbo character and exclaiming "Oh, wow!" to dancing around in time with the sound he makes while sandpapering his fingers. The ultimate gag involves Tim getting on a life-sized wheel to open a safe and being spun around as he tries to open it while the gang tries to avoid capture by police. This is a pretty good skit, if not quite prime Tim.

In "Saturday Morning Confusion," Carol soaks her feet and wears a scarf on her head while havoc appears around her in a household set by the dancers, including one dressed as a dog. She will reprise the song in a duet with Bing Crosby on the NBC special *Bing Crosby and His Friends* on Feb. 27, 1972. Both of those presentations reached more people than the original record that just cracked the top 30 in the summer of 1971 as sung by its writer, Bobby Russell (soon to be Vicki's husband).

"Arrivederci, Summertime" finds Bob Duggan as a hotel clerk and Ted Ziegler as a waiter to Carol's spinster and Harvey's Italian count. The latter two fall in love and ride a gondola steered by Stan Mazin. A good visual joke occurs as Carol literally lets her hair down and it falls in front of her face. Planning to marry, they visit Harvey's decrepit palace and encounter his mother (Vicki, who provides some entertaining facial expressions in reaction to Harvey and Carol). When a gardener (Lyle) tells Carol that Harvey wants to marry her because they need money, she decides to leave with him instead. This was a good, rather elaborate parody, although it is a shame that neither Tim nor Diahann could be shoehorned into it.

Diahann and Tim do play pivotal roles in the finale, where Diahann bucks up Carol's confidence in meeting men by singing "Chutzpah," the number the hostess first performed with Lucille Ball in the 1966 special *Carol + 2*. Afterward, the two ladies go inside a bar with the dancers, meet Harvey and Tim, and sing "Chutzpah" to the men to encourage them to dance with them. Tim pairs up with Diahann, showing how much TV had progressed since she did the show in 1967 and could not even face Richard Kiley during their love number.

Strangely, despite her evident talent on display, this will be the second and final appearance of Diahann on the series. However, she will return as Carol's summer substitute five years later (see Final Notes for the Season in 1975-1976).

Nov. 3, 1971: Bing Crosby, Paul Lynde

Q&A; in "The Old Folks" Bert's ex-commanding officer, Henry (Paul), visits to march with him in the Veterans Day parade; Bing performs a medley of love songs; "As the Stomach Turns" has Marian encountering a sadomasochistic pal (Paul), a cop-turned-priest named Father Sarge (Bing) and Mother Marcus (Harvey); Bing and Carol duet on "Sing" and "Get Happy"; Carol introduces her dancers by name before they perform a routine; "The Drunkard's Daughter" mocks vaudeville melodramas, with Bing as Carol's boozy dad, Harvey and Paul as a pair of baddies, Vicki as their showgirl accomplice and Lyle as a Canadian mountie.

Comments: The prospect of seeing how the show balances laidback Bing with manic Paul is incentive enough to watch this installment, and it is a generally satisfactory combination of pleasant music and amusing moments. The Q&A has two highlights. First, when asked, "Does the character Zelda ever come out in real life?" Carol responds with "No"—in Zelda's whiny voice, of course. And to "If you believed in reincarnation, what would you like to come back as?" Carol shoots back "Raquel Welch."

A lively installment of "The Old Folks" begins with Bert dressing up in his old soldier's uniform, which Molly says reminds her of "Yankee Doodle. It's been a long time since he went to town too." Bert feels intimidated when he sees that Henry is ready to march in the parade and appears lively. But their conversation puts those worries behind, and all three join in singing "Before the Parade Passes By" prior to the end of the sketch.

Sitting with a stool with a peace symbol behind him, Bing's solo spot is serviceable. Much more excitement is generated by a rollicking "As the Stomach Turns." After saying goodbye to Lyle as a portrait artist who painted her in the nude, Marian greets Mel Torment (Paul), who loves being in pain and scalds his hand in delight. Imagine Paul saying, "Beat me, beat me!" to Carol in his distinctive voice, plus describing his wife as "She's an angel. I hate her!" and you can surmise the laughter this generates. When Father Sarge arrives, Marian tells him he can officiate at her wedding. "I'll pray for a miracle," Bing says with a deadpan response while wearing his traditional ministerial garb. He departs, and Mel asks Marian to kick him, prompting her to say, "You need the love of a real mother!"

Harvey then enters as Mother Marcus, whose first appearance ever on the series in a bun hairdo, lipstick lips and tremendous breasts makes the audience crazy. Carol adds to the hysteria by closing the door and then opening it to find Harvey clasping Mother's bosoms and acting as they were bruised. In the 1978 series finale, Carol claims that her reaction occurred because "This was the first time I'd seen him in all that drag."

"Mother Marcus is my grandmother and my great-grandmother," Chris Korman says of his father's memorable opinionated, smothering character. His father copied their speech patterns and mannerisms, including their bear hugs, to create a character who became the third most recurring character on "As the Stomach Turns" behind Carol as Marian and Vicki as her daughter. "He could really immerse himself into his role," Chris adds.

High hilarity starts here when Mother Marcus enters and says her girdle is killing her, leading Mel to ask eagerly, "How'd you like to trade clothes?!" By the end, Mother Marcus is spanking Mel with a pan as he shouts, "More, more!" It's impressive how the series got this bit of kinky humor past the censors in 1971—and how perfectly it fits Lynde's style of humor.

Calming things down somewhat, Carol joins a tuxedoed Bing to vocalize the lyrics for "Sing" (the Carpenters' hit) while Bing interjects a little patter. They both do "Get Happy" and reprise "Sing." While the two sound great together, they are overshadowed by the next piece, where Carol introduces her dancers sitting in chairs by name. Carl Jablonski, Stan Mazin, Don Crichton, Ed Kerrigan, Eddie Heim, Ray Smith, Bobbie Bates, Patty Tribble, Shirley Kirkes, Kathie King, Gerrie Reddick and Bonnie Evans all do a number. There's nothing special here, but it is refreshing for Carol to give the names of these talented folk on air, a rarity for most dancing troupes on TV.

Harvey introduces the two-part vaudeville-style finale and does an eerily hilarious imitation of Paul Lynde as the two men threaten boozy Bing and his virtuous daughter, Carol. Lyle helps Carol in saving the day, complete with a great impersonation of Dudley Do-Right's pinched voice, and everyone repents at the end. This is a decent spoof, but it is a little unnerving the realism Bing brings to his role—his character is unshaven, and like his Oscar-nominated role in 1954's *The Country Girl*, he can vividly portray the affects of alcoholism without injecting humor.

Luckily, things do lighten up before the final credits. Carol leads the audience in booing pollution, and she amusingly does a few "bah-bah-bah-boos" next to Bing before he signs her autograph book. This was his second and last appearance on her show (for the first, see Nov. 10, 1969), but Lynde will be back twice later this season.

Nov. 10, 1971: Bernadette Peters, Cass Elliot

Q&A; a man dating Chris appears to be the same one who had an auto accident with Roger, so Carol tries to keep them apart in "Carol & Sis"; Cass sings "The Look of Love"; a drunk sound effects man (Lyle) bedevils Harvey and Carol while they act on "Heartbreak Playhouse," a live TV show; Bernadette sings the Association's hit "Cherish"; "As the Stomach Turns" has Cass as a high-fashion model,

Harvey as an underground filmmaker and Bernadette as a tap dancing nun; Carol, Bernadette and Cass do a medley of friend songs accompanied by dancers with tambourines.

Comments: As Carol hosts a show with "two of my favorite ladies in show business," a pair of missed opportunities emerge in the Q&A, one which actually was fortunate for Carol. She reveals that she plans to do a musical movie with producer Ross Hunter. Though not stated, it has to be the disastrous 1973 remake of *Lost Horizon*—Carol dodged a bullet by missing that one. The other was a request to have David Cassidy on as a guest. "I would love to have him on here," she says, but he never appears, although his father, Jack Cassidy, does next season (see Jan. 6, 1973). Other queries are "Have you ever worn braces on your teeth?" (no, but Carol did wear a retainer for a year), and "Were you popular as a child?" (she had friends but was not the star of her school).

"Carol & Sis" begin chaotically as Carol's hair dryer drowns out other noise and Chris drops groceries from a deliveryman (Don Crichton) and greets a TV deliveryman (Bob Duggan). Amid these activities, Carol meets Chrissy's date, Stanley (Tom Lowell, acknowledged vocally in the credits but like Duggan not included in the kick line at the show's end). He tells her about getting in a crash on his way to the house, and Roger arrives telling Carol the same story, so she assumes both were complaining about each other. It turns out they were involved in separate incidents, but instead of the two getting along, Stanley insults Roger's looks and shape and ultimately tweaks Roger's hurt nose, to the chagrin of Carol and Chrissy. There is too much effort to seem busy in this sketch to encourage more laughs than what really exist in the adequate but unexceptional script.

Carol introduces Cass, who is accompanied by dancers in gypsy outfits. She does well vocalizing a late 1960s hit, as does Bernadette in her turn, the latter having her in a black gown with white gloves and a blurred background. Between them is a feeble skit with wan mishaps involving sound effects (e.g., Carol blows her nose and a foghorn sounds). This unremarkable entry in the series' several depictions of offstage disasters causing havoc for onstage personnel is a remake from the May 6, 1968 episode, the first of many repeated skits this season.

Improving on the last sketch, "As the Stomach Turns" is in typically strong form as Cass appears as Marian's old pal wearing an animal print muumuu with black frills and effectively poses just like a model. She shines despite a few questionable fat jokes (e.g., she arrived there via jumbo jet) before Vicki arrives as Marian's daughter, this time working as a topless waitress at a drive-in. "Watch out for the electric windows," Marian cautions her. The other highlight is when Harvey, as an Andy Warhol-like director, has the camera around his neck drop to hit him in the crotch, causing Cass to break up. Bernadette's role is inconsequential, but it does show off her dancing skills to good form.

The finale has Carol and her guests, all in black gowns with silver star accents, being introduced by the dancers with tambourines. Their camaraderie medley thankfully has a contemporary hit, "You've Got a Friend" (a Number One record for James Taylor), and the women sing solo as well as together. Their mutual respect comes through well here.

With their appearance in only one skit, the writers seemed to have underestimated the comic talents of Cass and Bernadette, who have enough experience on their resumes to indicate they should have done more comedy on this show. Their musical numbers are on the money, however, so this episode earns a passing grade.

Nov. 17, 1971: Mel Torme, Nanette Fabray

Q&A; Carol and Nanette play two pregnant women; Nanette in a white gown sings to Freddie the Frog (Don Crichton in an animal costume); Carol and Mel perform a medley of hits written by Sammy Cahn; "Nostalgia Theatre" presents a send-up of the 1933 film *42nd Street*, with Lyle announcing the opening and then playing the choreographer along with Harvey as the demanding director, Carol as an aspiring chorus girl, Vicki as her devoted pal, Nanette as the demanding star and Mel as the male lead, joined by the dancers for a musical finale emulating Busby Berkeley's style.

Comments: With familiar guest stars who have worked together on the show previously (see Nov. 11, 1968), this show needs a special lift to rise above the ordinary but misses it. The material is uninspired, and the motion picture spoof takes up more than half of the show, much longer than it deserves. At least the Q&A is fine, with one person showing a picture of Carol when the star was a child. A twelve-year-old boy says he is "Glad they put your show on earlier!" A Cub Scout troop presents her with an Honorary Den Mother designation, and Carol says she has had four dogs as pets. Throughout it all, Carol looks splendid, sporting a beaded orange and black dress.

The bits before "Nostalgia Theatre" have little to distinguish themselves, and the absence of the regulars in them hurts too. There is a clever moment of physical comedy with Carol and Nanette as they try to pick up a quarter dropped on the ground despite their condition and Nanette finally gets it by putting gum on her shoe, but that's about all. By the time of "43rd Street," the show needs a pick-me-up that it never gets, despite great costumes (Nanette's orange outfit is a hoot in particular, as is Carol's wild geisha piece as she sings "Shanghai Sally") and shining dancing and singing. One amusing routine has Carol speed reading songs she will perform to take the place of Nanette in their Broadway show. Nanette generates a fair share of laughs too through her recurring injuries inadvertently caused by Carol (e.g., a broken neck, teeth knocked out). Bob Duggan does fine briefly as a physician.

Otherwise, it is a slog until the Berkeley-esque finale tap number involving an oversized box and overhead shots, all of which emulate the master choreographer's style perfectly. This deservedly earned Ernie Flatt an Emmy nomination for Outstanding Choreography.

This parody holds a special place for dancer Bobbie Bates. "My first speaking part was when we did the '43rd Street' one, with Harvey saying to me, 'Get it right,' and I said, 'Right!'" she recalls, saying her line in an exaggerated fashion. After the taping, Carol sent Bobbie a note with roses congratulating the latter on her first role on the show.

Bobbie is also impressed at how the dancers did the elaborate, dazzling tap number so smoothly. "I look back and can't believe it took only one week," she says.

At the closing, Carol crosses her eyes, and the studio audience laughs at something Mel does off camera. This show desperately needed much more of that frivolity from the start.

Nov. 24, 1971: Eydie Gorme, Shecky Greene

** In a send-up of TV crime dramas, Shecky and Carol play a married detective team in "Ironstreet and Wife"; spoofs of other current TV series; Eydie presents "How About Me?"; Shecky joins Funt and Mundane performing on a soap opera; a tribute to songwriters Rodgers and Hart by Eydie and Carol includes a medley of their takes on "My Funny Valentine," "Bewitched," "Falling in Love with Love" and "This Can't Be Love."

Comments: In her second teaming with Eydie on the series, Carol already has a pattern of singing multiple songs with the vocalist. The prospect intimidated the star, however. As Eydie's husband, Steve Lawrence, recalled in an interview in the 2012 *Ultimate Collection* DVD, "When Eydie did the show with her, Carol would say, 'I can't sing with Eydie Gorme, because she's the best singer in the world!' Eydie said, 'Thank you very much, and that is true, but you sing very well yourself, and don't be embarrassed to sing with anybody.'"

Regarding the parodies presented here, it should be noted that *McCloud* was the show running opposite this episode as part of *The NBC Mystery Movie* that night, and not *McMillan and Wife*.

Finally, according to Shecky's agent for a request for an interview, his client claimed he never did *The Carol Burnett Show*. Existing sources indicate otherwise.

Dec. 1, 1971: Tim Conway, Cass Elliot

** Tim joins the cast in a spoof of *A Streetcar Named Desire*; Cass and Carol browse a bookstore until a racy novel catches their attention; Cass sings "Cherries Jubilee"; a dentist (Tim) unintentionally gives a shot to himself rather than his patient (Harvey), making his body go numb and complicating treatment in the process; Cass and Carol perform a medley of children's songs; Vicki joins the dancers in an interpretation of the 1956 instrumental hit "Moonglow and Theme from Picnic."

Comments: Having Tim doing a reprise of his famous improvisation in the dental sketch from the March 3, 1969 episode is a definite sign that Arnie Rosen and the bulk of his creative team had run dry of ideas. Tim doing almost anything on the series is close to a guaranteed laugh, so the fact that nothing new could be envisioned for him—and that it revived a bit whose best parts came from Tim's improvisations in the original sketch—speaks volumes of how much the series lacked comic inspiration at this point. Incidentally, Tim credits being an athlete in high school for helping him to withstand all the pokes, prodding and pratfalls he faced when doing physical comedy on this show.

Dec. 8, 1971: Andy Griffith, Barbara McNair

** Zelda bedevils George during a flight to Hawaii; Barbara performs "It Only Takes a Moment"; a football coach is so fanatical about his love for the game that he converts his home into a playing field; Barbara and Carol duet on "Rainy Days and Mondays" and "Loneliness Remembers"; Carol recalls her dating Roger prior to their marriage in "Carol & Sis"; Andy and Barbara participate with the cast and dancers in a production number saluting Smokey the Bear.

Comments: This is the first show presenting a musical number created by Ken and Mitzie Welch, and both regretted it. As Ken recalls in his memoirs, "I don't remember what inspired us, but what we came with for a finale was 'Smokey the Bear is Alive and Well and Living in the Forest.' If it doesn't ring a bell as a memorable moment, it's no accident.

"I don't remember why we thought it was a good idea. It wasn't. I don't know what we thought it was at the time. But whatever it was, it wasn't. It wasn't funny. It wasn't charming. It wasn't powerful. And it certainly wasn't a finale for *The Carol Burnett Show*. But it aired.

"I don't know if Joe considered firing us. Maybe Carol went to bat for us. I've never asked her. But they kept us on." Ken credits the musical version of the Declaration of Independence he and Mitzie did for the next program, along with the duet they created for Carol and Peggy Lee on the Jan. 5, 1972 show, for really saving their reputation as quality contributors to the series and ensuring them to stay with the series until it ended.

Dec. 15, 1971: Dionne Warwick, Ken Berry

* Q&A; Ken performs "I Want to Be Happy" with the dancers; Roger and Carol try to remember the names of two old friends who are visiting (Ken and Jackie Joseph) in "Carol & Sis"; Dionne sings a medley of "(There's) Always Something There to Remind Me" and "One Less Bell to Answer"; Carol provides her take on "The Dolly Song"; Ken and Carol play Billy and Lily respectively, two entertainers heading to Hollywood to star in westerns in the early days of talking pictures; Dionne and Carol lead a chorus for "When in the Course of Human Events."

Comments: "Ken Berry, I think, was everybody's favorite, because we got to do numbers with him," says Bobbie Bates, who worked for him the second time here in this fairly solid predominantly musical installment that includes Berry's then-wife, Jackie Joseph, a regular at the time on *The Doris Day Show*. Before they appear, Carol addresses a few trivial queries like whether she was ever a Girl Scout. "No, I was a Boy Scout, until I flunked the physical," she cracks. Suddenly Dick Cavett emerges to surprise her and thank her for being a guest on his late night talk show on ABC while it tapes in California. "I think he is the most talented person," Carol tells her audience, who applauds in agreement. They discuss their middle names, his work as a copy boy at *Time* magazine and other items before a woman comes on stage to shake his hand and he gives an autograph where he claims to spell his name wrong the first time.

Following Ken's number, where he dances opposite Bonnie Evans, the first of only two sketches on this show is a repeat from the Sept. 25, 1967 show, which used Jackie Joseph in that original sketch in the same role as well. It's well acted by all concerned, but it does reinforce the notion that head writer and producer Arnie Rosen has become lazy in trying to offer compelling new material for Carol and her regulars and guests to perform.

Much better is "the wonderful Dionne Warwick," as Carol introduces the vocalist. Although the two numbers she performs were not hits for her, both came from her familiar writing-producing team of Burt Bacharach and Hal David, so she is quite at home and delivers both strongly.

"The Dolly Song" is a comic number Carol first performed in 1969 on the NBC special *Bing Crosby and Carol Burnett—Together Again for the First Time*, wherein she asks Santa Claus for a toy nicely at the beginning and then threatens him comically by the end. She will reprise it again on the Dec. 25, 1976 show.

The show's sole new comedy is a two-part tale of Ken trying to make it as a crooning cowboy on screen a la Gene Autry and Carol joining him in heading to Hollywood, nudged by her mother (Vicki). Though both sing off-key, their real difficulty is that Ken treats his horse better than Carol. When a grizzled next-door neighbor (Harvey) tells Carol about a job as a stunt horse rider which she wins, Ken gets drunk in response, feeling he is a failure in comparison to her because he is unemployed. A movie director (Lyle) throws them both a twist by saying he wants to make Ken's horse a star.

In the second half, Lyle's abuse of Carol as a stunt double for a star (Vicki) leads to Carol dying a long death where she spouts clichés. She call out for someone to find Ken before she expires. Ken's horse informs about Carol's situation, and Ken arrives on the set to tell her the good news that she will be a mother, as his horse is pregnant. This fairly original skit is pretty good but overlong.

"When in the Course of Human Events" is a recitation of the Declaration of Independence set to music for a chorale to sing, as done here with Dionne and Carol alternately singing lead. Ken and Mitzie Welch wrote the number for a musical years earlier that never was produced, and they offered it to be used in this show, where it went over better than their previous "Smokey the Bear is Alive and Well and Living in the Forest" effort. In fact, Carol thanks them at the end of the show by name for creating it. The series will reuse the material again on the Jan. 31, 1976 show. Obviously, there is a lot of recycling of material associated with this program.

Most times including this one when Ken was on this series from 1969-1973, sharp-eyed viewers would note two male dancers regularly appeared beside him in numbers. "Carl Jablonski and I bookended him," Stan Mazin said. "We loved when he was on the show."

Jablonski was dancing professionally on Broadway while he was a teenager when he first encountered choreographer Ernie Flatt. "I was in the original Broadway company of *My Fair Lady*, and I had been recommended to Ernie to replace a dancer on a show," he recalls. "I was eighteen at the time, and he was doing *Your Hit Parade*." While Carl wowed Ernie with his variety of dance styles including tap, he told him, "You're just too young for me" and let him go.

Following that, Carl worked four years entertaining in Paris along with Josephine Baker, then was drafted and served two years at Fort Hood, where he choreographed and directed shows. "Ernie kept in touch with me," Carl says. "He said, 'When you get out the Army, I'll give you a job.'" He was good to his word, and Carl worked with Ernie and Carol on the *Calamity Jane* special on Nov. 12, 1963 and *Fade Out—Fade In* on Broadway in 1964-1965. Between those jobs, he assisted Ernie with routines for *The Judy Garland Show* on CBS from 1963-1964.

Like fellow Burnett dancer Randy Doney, Carl then worked in Mitzi Gaynor's stage show before getting a call to join the series. "Ernie said, 'I'd love for you to come out to California and dance with her, because I need dancers," he says.

The decision gratified Jablonski, for as he notes, "It was such a phenomenal time in my life." He distinctly recalls how excited he was when Betty Grable did the series (see Feb. 12, 1968) and during breaks in rehearsals, she would spend her downtime with the gypsies. "I nearly peed in my pants," he says.

Jablonski says most of his dances even without Ken Berry had him working with Stan Mazin. "Stan and I were about the same size, and we were both tap dancers," he says. He never soloed on any dance routine during his five years with Burnett. That was not the reason why he left in 1973, when he was officially the assistant choreographer—he just had bigger ambitions for his career.

"In 1973, I thought, 'I'm thirty-five, and I want to choreograph," Carl says. Since Ernie was not leaving the series, when Carl received an offer to do the dance routines for a new show on another network called *NBC Follies*, he jumped on it. Unfortunately, the series lasted only thirteen weeks. However, Carl did earn an Emmy nomination for his choreography in 1974, and so did Ernie for *The Carol Burnett Show.* Both lost to Tony Charmoli for a Mitzi Gaynor special. Carl went on choreograph numbers for many other series including *The Love Boat*, which beat *The Carol Burnett Show* in the ratings in 1977.

Dec. 22, 1971: Rerun of Sept. 22, 1971 show

Dec. 29, 1971: Steve Lawrence, Dick Martin

Q&A; Carol and Vicki are two rival airline representatives who keep topping each other with the promises for Dick, a potential customer; Steve sings "Losing My Mind" and then plays Secretary of State Henry Kissingame being interviewed by reporter Barbara Waters (Vicki); Marian in "As the Stomach Turns" uses the powers of Madame Latisha to predict her future; a spoof of Oscar-nominated movies including *Some Like It Hot*, *Tea & Sympathy* and *Sunset Boulevard*; and a finale with cast, guests and dancers in a tribute to the Disney studio.

Comments: This episode provides much credence to Burnett's belief that her writers were now repeating themselves. The airline sketch was an overdone rehash of what Carol, Lucille Ball and Tim Conway did four years earlier (see Oct. 2, 1967), the Oscar parodies were the second one in four months and marked the second time of mocking *Some Like It Hot* after doing it last season, again with Ball (see Oct. 26, 1970), and even the Disney salute was on its second go-round (see March 23, 1970). Combine that with a few other missteps, and this was a rather poor effort for the series to close out 1971.

The Q&A starts promisingly, with Carol joking that she had made an album for Columbia that has been out for three weeks and sold one copy. Before she does her Tarzan yell, the sound effects man plays the original shout from the movie over her vocals to her surprise and amusement. The fun atmosphere disappears as the rather long and ragged first skit has Vicki for Presidential Airlines and Carol for Trans America vying for the attention and service of Dick Martin with escalating offers and counteroffers. While getting drunk from Carol's complimentary Champagne, Dick hears Carol promise him a contract with 20th Century-Fox, Van Cliburn playing in first class and Liberace in coach if he goes with Trans America. Vicki ups the ante by promising topless entertainment on Presidential and finally ends by kissing him passionately. Carol's final stroke is the show's already tired practice of bringing out an unbilled statuesque blonde beauty to seduce Dick (or as Carol puts it to the bimbo, "Kill!").

Steve's version of "Losing My Mind" is adequate, but his take on doing a Henry Kissinger parody with Groucho Marx inflections shows how desperate and confused his sketch is, as is Vicki's efforts as his straight man. She looks and sounds nothing like Barbara Walters, and by calling her a CBS correspondent for a show called *Washington Report* rather than reflect Walters' job at the time as co-host on *Today* dissipates its impact. Combine that with rather flat punch lines, which included Steve dropping Groucho's old TV series title—"You bet your life!"—and this effort is best forgotten.

The disappointment continues with one of the weakest "As the Stomach Turns" ever. After a policeman (Lyle) helping Marian report seeing a naked man leaves, Madame Latisha (Vivian Bonnell, unbilled even though she appears in the show's closing) tells Marian her fortune from cards. She draws an ace, which produces a handsome black pilot at Marian's door, then a two of hearts, which summons Vicki as Marian's daughter with a baby produced from her time with a football team. Next Latisha draws an eight of hearts, leading to Dick playing gigolo dance teacher Cesar DeNiro, sporting a plastic helmet of hair like a Ken doll. He romances Marian until Latisha's draw of a thirteen of hearts indicates the affair was over. As he leaves, Latisha reveals a joker, which prompts Harvey to finally emerge on the show as nasal Sam Snorty, mayor of Canoga Falls. He patronizes the soothsayer, telling her "My favorite show is Flip Wilson!" as she rebuffs his attempts to win her vote. The bit sluggishly ends with Marian's traditional "Wait, before you go, there's something you all need to know," and Harvey makes goo-goo eyes to try to spice up some laughs. But with strained jokes such as Lyle saying of DeNiro, "Will Ralph Nader recall his fee?" there is not much any hamming can do to save it.

After little enjoyment with the send-ups of *Some Like It Hot* (with Dick in drag, obviously reading off cue cards the way he did in "As the Stomach Turns") and *Tea & Sympathy* (Vicki learns her efforts to seduce the possibly gay Dick are for naught because he already has a girlfriend), Carol and Steve duet on several Academy Award-nominated Best Songs. It is passable but not a showstopper.

The show finally catches fire with *Sunset Boulevard*, which introduces Carol's mad silent star Nora Desmond and Harvey as her bald assistant, Max, who speaks with a clipped German accent. With Steve as William Holden's reporter character, this spoof is top notch in every respect. Harvey's bullying delivery to Steve of orders such as how Nora does not do TV commercials is dead-on, while Carol's debut is memorable, stumbling down her mansion's staircase and throwing her necklace around. With a finger ring holding her cigarette, the audience is already laughing before Steve asks her why she did not make in talkies and screeches in response, "I dunno!" The sketch gests wilder as Harvey makes Steve tap dance on his knees while the former directs Nora in a risqué Theda Bara outfit with a whip. She accidentally shoots Harvey, and another bullet goes off, prompting Nora to search her body (including her breast for it) before Steve learns he has killed himself. Harvey returns with a bandage on his forehead, which Nora strips off to put on her head to end the sketch.

The high continues with a bubbly Disney tribute, with eight dancers in costumes such as Goofy on loan from Disneyland. The stars dressed up as classic characters—Vicki as Snow White, Steve as Pinocchio, Lyle as the White Rabbit (with buck teeth) and Carol as Peter Pan, flying over the set and being the only one singing. She promotes Disney's latest film, *Bedknobs and Broomsticks*, in appreciation of the studio's help in the bit.

But this segment and *Sunset Boulevard* are not enough to rally this show from being a lesser series entry. The overall air of sloppiness all adds up to a rather ragged show for the holiday season.

Jan. 5, 1972: Peggy Lee, Paul Lynde

** A snooty couple bickers; Peggy performs "Sing a Rainbow"; a spoof of *The Seventh Veil*; Carol and Peggy perform a medley of "Happy New Year," "Something's Coming" and "Great Day" in honor of the start of 1972; a finale set in a circus includes the cast and dancers doing "Here Come the Clowns," "Clown Alley" and "Be a Clown."

Comments: Notorious for having an opinion about anyone and anything, as well as possessing a reputation for being difficult in certain quarters, Paul Lynde seemed to like doing this series and vice versa. He and Carol had established a friendly working relationship ever since they starred on the NBC sitcom *Stanley* in 1956-1957. This was his fourth of five appearances he made over the last two seasons, and he had admirers for his work on it. As he related to Boze Hadleigh in *Hollywood Gays*, "Jack Benny sent me a note after I did Carol Burnett—she's nice too. He's so complimentary, so lovely."

Lynde also was a regular on *The Hollywood Squares* daytime game show on NBC during this period. The series taped on the weekends, allowing him time to guest star on programs like *The Carol Burnett Show*. A frequent guest with more than 40 appearances on *The Hollywood Squares* during its run from 1966 to 1980 was Harvey Korman. On one occasion, the latter failed to recognize a quote that had come from Carol Burnett.

Jan. 12, 1972: Pre-empted by *National Geographic* special on "The Lost Tribe of Rindanad"

Jan. 19, 1972: Ken Berry, Nanette Fabray, the Carpenters

Q&A; the Carpenters perform "Hurting Each Other"; Carol portrays a plain secretary who envies how her glamorous colleague (Nanette) attracts the affection of their boss (Lyle); Ken and Nanette sing "Coffee in a Cardboard Cup" in a restaurant setting; Carol and the Carpenters duet on a medley of the latter's hits; "Nostalgia Theatre" presents "The Ballad of Broadway," a tale of a song-and-dance vaudeville team (Carol and Ken) who break up when he is enticed to go solo by a multimillion patron of the arts (Nanette) and she gets her own sponsor (Harvey), with each performer having varying success.

Comments: When a show waits until two-thirds the way through to bring on Harvey Korman, it is usually a sign it will be disappointing, which is true here. The most unfortunate waste of talent is Nanette Fabray, who has to re-enact two characterizations similar to what she had done on the show previously. The only ones who impress are the Carpenters, who figure in the Q&A as well. A young girl in the audience asks to kiss Richard, who comes out and complies. That is it for that segment, but Richard reappears next with Karen as they lip sync "Hurting Each Other," their just-released record which will be their sixth million seller. Even with their band members having to mime playing their instruments in the background, this is one of the program's few enjoyable moments.

The first sketch re-enacts what Carol and Nanette did on the Nov. 6, 1967 show, with the only differences being Nanette has a more buxom figure with a blonde wig, a different set layout, and Lyle and Vicki in place of Harvey and an unidentified actress as the boss and the wife who walks in on him making out with Nanette from the original. Nanette even recreates rotating her rear as she sharpens a pencil like she did in the first go-round. It ends again with Carol falling out of the window when she cannot see where she is going—an apt metaphor for the choice of recreating this skit.

Nanette dons a waitress outfit to join Ken as a fellow server as they sing "Coffee in a Cardboard Cup" at a cafe surrounded by the dancers dressed up as protesting hippies and senior citizens. It is nothing more than acceptable. A livelier number follows when Carol, wearing a rainbow-colored skirt with a burgundy top, accompanies the Carpenters on "Just an Old Fashioned Love Song," "We've Only Just Begun," "I Kept On Loving You," "Let Me Be the One" and a reprise of "Just an Old-Fashioned Love Song." Their harmonies sound great, and it is refreshing to hear the Carpenters sing live.

The second half of the show concerns a generic send-up of rags-to-riches show business movies. Nanette's character and actions bear a striking resemblance to what she did on the Nov. 11, 1968 show, as a temptress who woos Ken away from Carol so he can become a ballet star (?!). Carol visits him when he is a success and he ignores her pleas of being broke, so she plays a song on a piano lamenting how empty her life is. When it ends, Harvey appears as a backer overhearing her and promises to make her a star if she vocalizes similar tunes of depression. Speaking with a voice crossed with Peter Lorre and his Max characterization from the Nora Desmond bits, Harvey amuses Carol and provides the only spark in Act One of this parody.

The last act finds Ken dancing drunkenly on stage during a Russian ballet number, leading to Nanette to dismiss him (Nanette gives her all in providing comic villainy here). Carol and Harvey pass by Ken performing on the street (a monkey grinds the music while Ken dances), and she fails to recognize him, a plot development that happened in the aforementioned Nov. 11, 1968 show. Ken, looking like a bum, then reunites with Carol on stage but falls to the ground ill. She offers to give him brandy to revive him but he says it will kill him. Forced to choose between love and no riches and being famous without Ken, she chooses the latter and makes him take a swig, causing his death. This intermittently amusing spoof would have fared better if it ran shorter.

Before ending the show with her usual festivities including a reminder to fight pollution, Carol animatedly says Ray Charles' name in announcing him as one of her guests next week. Too bad this show was not as exciting to watch as Carol's pronunciation here is.

Jan. 26, 1972: Ray Charles, Tim Conway

Vicki and Harvey's daughter (Carol) is a tomboy that they want to feminize, so they invite a male peer (Tim) over to bring out that side of her; Ray performs "Look What They've Done to My Song Ma"; Tim is a billboard hanger afraid of heights scaling a building's exterior with Harvey; "Tearjerker Theatre" presents a spoof of 1930s movie melodramas with Carol recounting her life to a priest (Tim) about the sacrifices she made for the sake of her husband and her son (both played by Harvey); the Charwoman dances and sings with Ray and his band.

Comments: Though this show won the Emmy for best writing, one suspects it was more the Television Academy's way of acknowledging the staff for its five years of work on the series rather than for its quality, which is better than most of this season's other entries but not quite top-of-the-line Burnett. The real excitement comes from the appearance of Ray Charles, whose name draws cheers from the audience prior to the first skit. Carol resists Harvey's entreaties to lose her masculine habits and wear a dress, telling him that "Every time some guy tackles me, he'll see my underwear!" Nonetheless, Harvey forces her to change while Tim, her supposed date, nervously fidgets waiting for her. Awkwardly approaching Tim in high heels with the dress on, Carol sits on a table with her legs open, and Tim demurely crosses them. They converse, and Carol is so impressed by Tim that she tells Harvey she is going to a sleepover at Tim's house, to Harvey's horror. This is good but not exceptional.

"The genius of Ray Charles," as Carol introduces her musical guest, puts on a killer version of a hit for the New Seekers in 1970 that what will become a minor chart entry for Ray later in 1972. Joined by four Raelettes, a bassist, a guitarist and a drummer, Charles riffs delightfully on this number, the most soulful music spot the show had presented up to this time.

From there, the obligatory Harvey-Tim moment has Tim freaking out as he and Harvey go up the side of a building and he sees how high he is. He tries to maintain his composure but winds up spilling milk on his lap. Even worse, he nearly falls off the ladder when he tries to grab an orange thrown to him by Harvey, clinging to dear life on the billboard they are handling at one point. Finally going about his business, Tim gets glue stuck on his hand along with a fake pigeon. Harvey removes the latter but loses his lucky hat and heads down to the street, leaving a terrified Tim alone. Despite no real ending, this is an enjoyable excursion, but again, not the best of their work.

Better is the two-act parody "Sinful Woman," which starts with a prisoner (Carol) confessing to a priest (Tim), whose phrases such as "fry in the electric chair" and "your grave" fail to comfort her while she sits on death row. Nonetheless, she tells how her life went wrong when she was working under Lyle in a honky tonk bar. There, she met a brokenhearted millionaire (Harvey), who is entranced by Carol and weds her. His family annuls his marriage, however, so he takes a frigid, mean debutante (Vicki) as his wife. Carol arrives with her son by Harvey, but news of her situation could derail Harvey's plan to be governor, so Vicki forces Carol to give the child up to her and Harvey. (Vicki and Carol stretch the baby ridiculously like they are in a tug of war before Carol relinquishes control.)

In Act Two, 25 years have passed, and Carol now works as a domestic who unwittingly returns to Harvey's residence to apply for the job. He is dead, but their son (also Harvey) is a flamboyant district attorney groomed for success. Carol still mothers him—and cracks up Harvey from overfeeding his mouth at one point—but plans to hide her secret until Lyle arrives and threatens to blackmail her over her past. They argue and she accidentally kills Lyle. Put on trial for the crime with her son as the prosecuting attorney (and Brad Trumbull playing her lawyer), Carol refuses to plead self-defense so that Harvey will win his case. A return to the present finds Tim has been sleeping while Carol told her tale of woe, but he wakes up as music is played. Brad arrives to tell Carol there has been no reprieve from the governor, while Tim offers her a raffle ticket for the church's drawing. Then Harvey appears and says he has learned her story and gives her flowers for Mother's Day. He is governor now, but she still gets the chair anyway. This above average old movie takeoff works very well, with great bits for everyone involved, and it will appear as a highlight in the tenth anniversary show in 1977.

The real highlight, however, is the rocking finale, as the Charwoman cleans Ray Charles' piano after a concert and conjures up the dancers, Ray Charles and the Raelettes. Ray starts the joint jumping with "St. Louis Blues," Carol enters with "Kansas City," and she joins Ray and the Raelettes on "Swanee River" and "You Are My Sunshine." The scene then fades to black with just Carol and Ray side by side on his piano singing "Crying Time" and "Georgia on My Mind." Carol launches into the second verse of the latter while Ray does "Yesterday," then both of them do "God Bless the Child" and "Hallelujah I Love

Her So." The dancers and Raelettes reappear to join the duo on "What'd I Say" until they all vanish and we are left with the Charwoman reprising "St. Louis Blues." This is a superbly entertaining number.

Ray does autograph Carol's book at the end. He will return ten months later—see Nov. 22, 1972. A fun fact worth mentioning is that Carol's daughter Jody loved watching Ray Charles on *The Ed Sullivan Show* so much that she kissed him on the TV and claimed he was her husband. He later embraced her backstage when he guest starred here.

Feb. 2, 1972: Rerun of Oct. 6, 1971 show

Feb. 9, 1972: Vincent Price, Eydie Gorme

** Vincent recites "Desiderata"; Carol and Eydie do a gypsy medley; "The House of Terror" mocks horror films; Eydie performs "The Way of Love" and joins Vicki and Carol to sing "What We Really Need is a Boy" and "Perfect Young Ladies"; a salute to the Roaring Twenties.

Comments: Following a scripted bit where Vincent attempts to hypnotize Carol into calling him a pussycat, Carol introduces him presenting what was a hit spoken word record in 1971. The only thing is that she screws up pronouncing "Desiderata" for several times, as shown in the blooper reel.

Emmy nominations for this show went to art directors Paul Barnes and Bob Sansom and set decorator Bill Harp.

Feb. 16, 1972: Steve Lawrence, Kaye Ballard

* "Operation Minestrone" sends up World War II thriller films; Steve sings a medley of "Ain't No Sunshine" and "You are My Sunshine"; Carol performs "If I Could Write a Song" sitting on a staircase after reading letters from children; Kaye sings "Cabaret" and "Don't Tell Mama" with the dancers; a salute to the music of Cole Porter.

Comments: "A musical comedy performer equally adept with humor and singing who was raised by her grandmother" describes Kaye Ballard as much as Carol. Kaye acknowledges that in her autobiography, noting that "Even with all those similarities, or perhaps because of them, at one time I was extremely envious of Carol and all that came her way."

What particularly peeved her was one guest shot she lost to Carol. "We were both on *The Garry Moore Show*, and I—being stubborn and ignorant—I said, 'This isn't funny,'" she says. For complaining about her material, Kaye not only lost her part, but also got to witness Carol became a hit on the series and snag one of its producers, Joe Hamilton, as her husband. Kaye adds that she was also under consideration to star in *Once Upon a Mattress* on Broadway before Carol won the lead in 1959.

Now, nearly a decade later, Kaye was grateful to obtain this guest spot by her perceived competitor, an occasion which dissipated her resentment toward Carol. "She couldn't have been more gracious to me," Kaye says.

Her affection carried over particularly to one of the regulars and her fellow guest star. "I love Harvey Korman more than I can tell you," she says. As for Steve Lawrence, "I adore him," and adds that he sent ten gowns from his wife, Eydie Gorme, as a gift to her.

On her website, Kaye has a clip of her solo performance from this show. Carol introduces Kaye as "a terrific lady, and I'm so glad she's on our show." The interpolation with the dancers works well, including a gag where Kaye's mother (played by Kaye in a blonde wig) criticizes her at the end. Kaye says the idea of her doing "Cabaret" came from the production staff, undoubtedly because the film version of the musical had just opened in major cities.

Combined with her sketches and other songs, Kaye says the experience of this show made her very happy. "I couldn't tell you how absolutely wonderful they were," she notes. Her enthusiasm and great work here allowed for her to make a return appearance less than a year later—see Feb. 27, 1973.

Incidentally, "If I Could Write a Song" is the featured title tune for Carol's new album. Alas, it had already peaked at Number 199 a few weeks earlier on *Billboard*'s LP chart. It consisted of mostly contemporary tunes, including two popularized by the Carpenters and "Saturday Morning Confusion," which she presented on the Oct. 27, 1971 show. The album will be Carol's only solo one to make the music charts. Ironically, a year later at this time, Vicki Lawrence will have a huge solo hit. See the Feb. 3, 1973 entry for the story behind "The Night the Lights Went Out in Georgia."

Feb. 23, 1972: Nanette Fabray, Burt Reynolds

Q&A; a series of commercial spoofs interspersed through the show; Burt deliberately awkwardly plays the piano, sings and hoofs his way through "As Time Goes By" with the female dancers; Zelda spoils George's efforts to enjoy a camping trip in the woods; Nanette performs "It's a Musical World" with the dancers; Carol sings "Al" in a library setting; "Wednesday Night Adventure Movie" presents a spoof of *The Scarlet Pimpernel*; a finale on the completion of the transcontinental railroad system connecting the coasts of America in the 1800s features Carol, Nanette and the dancers performing "She'll Be Comin' Round the Mountain."

Comments: What this installment lacks occasionally in execution often has plenty of energy to compensate for its shortcomings, chiefly because there's a lot of excitement surrounding the male guest. Nanette Fabray has acknowledged having a crush on Burt Reynolds as a fellow panelist on *The Hollywood Squares* in the early 1970s, so one can surmise that this was an especially chummy set during this week of rehearsal and taping. Another big admirer of Burt's was Carol herself—but only shortly before this show.

As Carol recounted on *The Dick Cavett Show* on Dec. 7, 1971, prior to the host bringing out Burt as a guest, her initial impression of him was negative. "The first time I met Burt was on *The David Frost Show*," Carol says, immediately apologizing to Cavett for mentioning a potential competitor, which Dick shrugs off. She thought based on his largely dramatic roles that he would not have a sense of humor, but to her surprise, he was able to joke freely. "He is just so funny," she concluded. "A funny, nice man."

For his part, following Carol's spot on *The Dick Cavett Show*, Burt said, "I have a thing for her too." Some in the audience laughed, but he was sincere in his appreciation for Carol. "I think she is one of the sexiest women in the world. I truly believe that," Burt said. With flattery like that, it's not surprising he was asked to guest star on the series not long after Cavett's show aired.

Burt's name at the top of the show elicits screams from the audience which recur a few times later during his appearance. After naming her two favorite teachers, Carol brings out Burt, "a living doll," to answer questions about how many movies he's made, during which he plugs the theatrical release of *Deliverance* in six months, and his start as a stuntman. That latter background goes to great use as he sings a standard associated with the 1943 film classic *Casablanca* in a burlesque where he accidentally removes one dancer's wig and has a piano crash after he pretends to tickle the ivories while trying to seduce another female. He lunges at her but misses her embrace and falls down a long, curling staircase to land on a table that he breaks before stumbling off and finishing the number to more squeals from the audience. This comic scene is so memorable that it will appear in the show's 1978 finale.

Between Q&A and Burt's scene is the first of several ad parodies, most not really impressive. For example, the first has Harvey in drag as a stereotypically flaming flight attendant. The best is Carol doing a testimonial for a detergent wherein she launches into a frenzied diatribe about how bad her home life is. Otherwise, the show has done better.

The George and Zelda bit finds the long-suffering husband trying to shoot his wife while she's in a tent and missing, and even a bear that plans to attack Zelda finds himself so appalled by her yelling that the creature offers sympathy to George before shuffling away. Zelda also bends George's shotgun in this acceptable but unexceptional entry.

Nanette's number has her singing while the dancers are dressed in various costumes. It's visually impressive but fails to engage attention throughout its rather long duration. The same can be said for Carol's solo as a bookworm upset by other library patrons (the dancers) who belittle her lack of social involvement. The show looks wobbly here.

Luckily, the enthusiasm comes back with "The Lavender Pimpernel," featuring Burt as Charles de Gay (another sissy stereotype on the show) who transforms into the masculine title character in disguise to save Carol from marrying an evil nobleman (Harvey). The period costumes (France in 1790) are incredible even by Bob Mackie's dazzling standards, and the wild slapstick has Burt doing everything from busting through doors and windows several times to carrying Carol on his shoulders. His broad, mugging performance in saving her fuels a lot of the humor and makes this a winner, but at least one co-writer of the parody was not impressed.

Stan Hart thinks this piece he wrote with Larry Siegel lacks the comic impact they anticipated due to Burt's interpretation. "We thought they'd all come out well," Hart says of his send-ups with Siegel. "Some didn't. *The Scarlet Pimpernel*, Burt Reynolds asked, 'Should I be Clark Gable?' We couldn't help him out." The 1935 movie actually starred Leslie Howard, and it is hard to conceive how Reynolds could have achieved a successful approximation of that actor's British lilt. He does fine on his own terms, even if it was a different character than the original screen version. Lyle, Nanette and Bob Duggan as a cardinal also take part in this skit. (Vicki does only the ad spoofs on this show.)

For the musical conclusion, Carol plays a gruff frontier woman greeting the uneasy Nanette, a genteel woman from the East, as they meet to connect the coasts via railroad. With the dancers dressed in period costumes doing a familiar number, it's lively enough.

Recalling this show on *The Carol Burnett Show: The Lost Episodes* DVD set, Burt said, "I couldn't have had a better time." He called Nanette Fabray "Always wonderful. Great fun" and praised Carol to the hilt. Burt will return to the series in the Q&A next season (see Jan. 27, 1973), while oddly this was Nanette's thirteenth and last appearance with Carol and crew. Maybe she thought working with Burt was hard to top.

March 1, 1972: Eydie Gorme, Tim Conway

Q&A; Roger's poker game aggravates his wife in "Carol & Sis"; Eydie sings "A House is Not a Home"; Harvey and Tim are cops pretending to be a couple (with Tim in drag) to catch a mugger in park; "Midnight Theatre" mocks the James Bond film *Dr. No* features Harvey as the title villain, Vicki as his assistant, Tim as a secret agent and Carol as a tempting *femme fatale*; a young girl (Carol) resents the attention spent on a new baby in the family during the turn of the century in a production number with everyone called "Angel Child."

Comments: Apart from Eydie's solo and the Harvey-Tim skit, none of the bits succeed in this misfire, which if nothing else shows remaking old material was not the series' only problem this season. Everything feels overlong except the Q&A, where there are only two queries. Carol says besides her husband, she would want to stranded on a desert island with Burt Reynolds (he had said the same thing earlier publicly) or Peter Ustinov ("He's terrific, gosh, he's got stories."). And for her favorite silent film actress, she named Mabel Normand even though she admits she hadn't seen any of her films.

From there, the show slogs starting with a "Carol & Sis" where Carol endures Tim, Lyle, Bob Duggan and Brad Trumbull coming to play poker with Roger. She yells that she wants them out by eleven and Roger agrees, but he asks her to fetch a sandwich and some beers for them. Tim accidentally spills ketchup and mustard on Carol's outfit, and she loses her patience and tries to throw the men out before Roger accidentally knocks her out with the kitchen door. With few laughs, little plot and the disappearance of Vicki at the outset to go a movie, this plays like a poor version of "Carol & Sis" from 1967.

Eydie nails a 1964 Burt Bacharach-Hal David composition after this, but this triumph is limited, as she lip syncs the tune. Similar limited pleasure comes from Tim sporting a blonde wig, purse, high heels and gaudy print dress as he and Harvey attempt to play a romantic cover. Tim plays with his hair and makeup to great comic effect at Harvey's expense (naturally), and rubbing Harvey's knees while sharing a bench with him produces more guffaws. After they have a "lovers' quarrel," the mugger (Lyle) arrives, discovers who they are and handcuffs them to the bench, where they leave in a huff. This segment is pretty good, but there have been stronger Harvey-Tim collaborations.

Spottier enjoyment comes from "Dr. Nose," where James Blond (Tim in a golden-haired wig again, albeit without curls) has some of the women dancers fight for his affection as he kills hidden foes. His equipment specialist (Lyle) gives him a gun to put over his finger that James accidentally discharges a few times, including around Passion Plenty (Carol in a long wig), who challenges James to a "kiss off" before the latter heads to confront Dr. Nose (Harvey with a huge proboscis and overdone makeup facial makeup). The doctor and his aide (Vicki) try to murder James in their laboratory by tying him to a slab and using a laser a la the 1965 film *Goldfinger*, but Passion enters to defeat their effort. She tricks Dr. Nose to adjust his proboscis to face his own ear, then sprays pepper in his direction to make Dr. Nose sneeze bullets and blow his brain out, so to speak. Passion celebrates the victory with James, who ends up accidentally killing her and himself by unintentionally activating his finger gun. The entire plot is ridiculous (not unlike the ones in many Bond films), and its execution is oddly inconsistent by the cast, making a promising parody pretty much a mess.

The finale is an operetta with Carol upset with how her grandparents (Harvey and Vicki) and aunt and uncle (Eydie and Tim) fawn over her infant sibling, featuring trilling solos by Vicki and Eydie. By the extended time Carol gets attention focused back on her and explains she is envious because today is her birthday, any hopes of this being pleasant have faded. Worse yet, there's little for the dancers to do here (or the rest of the episode). At least the costumes and sets convey a good sense of early 1900s Americana.

Carol sings "It's Time to Say So Long" in her child's voice at the end to add a little spark, but this show is a lost cause. Tim and Eydie will be better served next season.

March 8, 1972: Jack Klugman, Tony Randall

** The cast presents takeoffs of the TV show *This is Your Life* and the 1944 film *Lady in the Dark*; an elaborate tribute to Broadway musicals includes Carol singing "Adelaide's Lament" from *Guys and Dolls* and joining Jack to do "You'll Never Get Away from Me" from *Gypsy* (in which Jack starred on the New York stage in 1959), plus Jack, Tony and Harvey present "Brush Up Your Shakespeare" from *Kiss Me Kate*.

Comments: This is the only instance of Carol having two stars from the same series appearing as guest simultaneously, and this may have been an effort to encourage ABC to renew Jack and Tony's sitcom *The Odd Couple*, whose ratings were iffy this season. The network did pick the series up, and *The Odd Couple* ran until 1975.

Recalling his father's impressions of the guests, Chris Korman says, "He loved Jack Klugman. Tony Randall was sort of a priss."

Jack and Tony will guest separately on this series four years later, and ironically in back-to-back episodes. See Feb. 21, 1976 (Tony) and March 6, 1976 (Jack) for more details.

March 15, 1972: Rerun of Nov. 3, 1971 show

March 22, 1972: Paul Lynde, Karen Black

** Carol and Harvey are couple bedeviled by bad construction on their residence, and their complaints are dismissed by a smarmy project overseer (Paul); Karen performs "Gee, But I Hate to Go Home Alone" and "Flowers in the Morning"; Carol vocalizes on "I Don't Care"; Vicki presents her version of "It's Too Late"; Karen, Carol and Vicki portray three women out on the town who do "Waiting for the Girls Upstairs"; the Charwoman checks out the scene at an exclusive health spa.

Comments: Stan Mazin recalled that this show's female guest star was one of the most difficult ones to handle. "Karen Black, she was over Dave Powers' shoulder, saying, 'Why don't you shoot over there?'" he said. Not surprisingly, Mazin claims her interfering efforts in the show's direction led her to miss her own spot to be in camera range during the taping.

The home builder sketch is so awful that even the bloopers for it are not funny. As for Paul Lynde, this will be his swan song on the series, and ironically his own sitcom will air on ABC against *The Carol Burnett Show* the next season.

March 29, 1972: Family Show

Q&A; the cast does a five-part send-up of the 1945 film *The Dolly Sisters*, with Carol as a musical stage performer, Vicki as her sister and co-star, Harvey as an emcee who wants to marry Carol but cannot do so as complications arise, and Lyle as a talent booker who becomes attracted to Vicki; the Charwoman receives costumes and hugs from Harvey, Lyle and Vicki as they leave the soundstage, waves goodbye to the dancers, puts out a sign saying the show is closed for the season and sings all the lyrics to "It's Time to Say So Long."

Comments: The series' rocky season comes to a close with what Carol professes is one of her favorite episodes—a full-length musical comedy where she gets to assume a role originally played by one of her idols, Betty Grable. Stan Hart and Larry Siegel spent a couple of days hashing out the elaborate script.

"We wanted to do a whole show, and the Welches did the music," says Hart. "Ken and Mitzie Welch were wonderful. I loved working with them."

"We knew it was a challenge, but it was fun to work on," Ken Welch recalls. "We had a special relationship, a very good relationship with Stan and Larry."

"The Doily Sisters" is actually only intermittently dazzling, but Carol's love for the original material and the fact it had not been tried on the show before makes it dear to her heart, even though most viewers probably will be just mildly impressed by it today. As she tells the audience at the start, "We've had a ball doing it. . . . I really know of no other bunch who could've done it in two days." The Q&A has two highlights. Astronaut Buzz Aldrin is in the audience with his wife, and Carol asks him when we might expect to see a woman in space. "When we find some fully qualified," he replies. Also, Larry the lead usher (no last name given) is leaving his post after three years to be a management trainee. "I have to find a real job, no offense," he tells Carol, who cracks up in response.

"The Doily Sisters" commences in 1912 New York, where Harvey is the host at Budapest Cafe, which needs twin girls to replace a missing act. The proprietor (Larry Gelman) drafts Carol and Vicki as replacements, even though they have no act. They decide to sing about the cafe's name—how "Buda" and "pest" meshed—and it goes over so well that Harvey wants to work with them as an act. He sings a tune about Mr. Moon, and Carol adores both him and the song. The trio head to a vaudeville theatre run by Lyle, who tells them he will only book a duo. Carol offers to drop out, but when Harvey proposes to her and she rejects him to protect her sister, he forges out on his own.

Act Two begins with an elaborate production number, as the women dancers appear in various makeup to accompany Vicki and Carol singing about being naturally beauties. A montage show them appearing at various venues until they reach New York City, where Harvey sings his Mr. Moon song again when the ladies suddenly arrive. Carol tells Harvey she made a mistake not marrying him, but he does not want to live in her shadow and tells her to forget about him. Concerned, Carol convinces Lyle to book Harvey at the Palace, and when Harvey finds out, she pledges to wed him and end her career. But World War I has begun, and Harvey enlists as a soldier first.

In Act Three, Harvey does the moon song again, this time in a trench in France, and as luck would have it, Carol and Vicki show up to entertain, wearing Wonder Woman-style outfits and presenting patriotic tunes which inspire the troops until they sing a line about referring to whether the men will be able to come home. Harvey tells them not to give up their career as he plans to lead a charge against the enemy, but another soldier (Roy Stuart) wants Carol and Vicki to head them into battle instead, which the gals do. That leads to Act Four in Monte Carlo after the war, with a playboy (Bob Duggan) toasting Carol fruitlessly, as she still pines for Harvey. She also tells Vicki she realizes her sister loves Lyle and encourages her to wed him and break up their act. Carol finds getting solo attention is hard—she is ticked off by others singing accompaniment to her at the roulette wheel and hates that the spotlight stops following her wherever she walks. A count (Ken Greenwald) offers to wed her, but she sustains a car crash (with only a scratch on her face, naturally) that her doctor (Brad Trumbull) rules is amnesia.

Finally in Act Five, in New York five years later, a waiter (Trumbull again) drafts a still-amnesiac

Carol to become a fellow server. As Harvey sings his moon song for the umpteenth time, another waitress accidentally hits her on the head, and she remembers everything. She spots Vicki, who tells her that Lyle ran away and becomes hysterical. Spotting Harvey, Carol pleads that he wed both her and Vicki to make everyone happy. "Whatever!" says Harvey as the whole sings together at the finale.

The rest of the show is the standard season closer, with nothing special. Given all the costume changes, dialogue and new songs everyone had to learn in a crunch, that probably was a wise decision. Larry Siegel, who co-wrote the entire musical, said that James Cagney watched the show and phoned Carol afterward to tell her it was the greatest television sketch ever. Additionally, art directors Paul Barnes and Bob Sansom and set decorator Bill Harp earned Emmy nominations for their work, but due to the eligibility period, they receive their nods a year later at the 1973 ceremony. The trio lost to Brian Bartholomew and Keaton S. Walker for *The Julie Andrews Hour*.

Final Notes for the Season

For such a lowly regarded season, *The Carol Burnett Show* did surprisingly well in the ratings. The average numbers were up over the last (21.2 versus 19.8), and the series tied for Number Twenty-Three with *The Doris Day Show*, a slightly better showing than Number Twenty-Five in 1970-1971. But with *Adam-12* at Number Eight and *The NBC Mystery Movie* at Number Fourteen, the series no longer was the top destination for Wednesday night viewers the way it was on Mondays.

Still, the show was a hit, and there was optimism about the next season, because despite all its failings, *The Carol Burnett Show* finally won the Emmy for Outstanding Variety Series—Musical, along with the writing category for the Jan. 26, 1972 show. That might have been a little uneasy, since the award came after the massive firings on the show, but Larry Siegel remembers it as an unintentionally embarrassing episode for himself.

"I was kind of a pushy guy in those days," he recalls. "We had lost the year before to *The Flip Wilson Show*. Then next year, we came out and half the staff came on there. Right away, I grabbed the microphone from Arnie Rosen and said, 'This is the first Emmy Carol Burnett has won. It's about time!'" Of course, it was not the first win for Carol or for the show either, and Siegel's exclamation came back to haunt him as Harvey teased him about his unbridled passion on stage during the ceremony.

Also at the Emmys, Harvey Korman won for Outstanding Achievement by a Performer in Music or Variety after the category resumed following a hiatus from the previous year. He beat Ruth Buzzi and Lily Tomlin from *Rowan and Martin's Laugh-In*. Both actresses would appear on *The Carol Burnett Show* as guests next season.

Other nominations went to Dave Powers for direction of the Oct. 6, 1971 show (he lost to Art Fisher for *The Sonny and Cher Comedy Hour*), Ernie Flatt for choreography on the Nov. 11, 1971 show (Alan Johnson beat him for his work on the NBC special *Jack Lemmon in 'S Wonderful, 'S Marvelous, 'S*

Gershwin), and Paul Barnes, Bob Sansom and Bill Harp for art direction and scenic design for the Feb. 9, 1972 show (E. Jay Krause won for the special *Diana!* instead).

The series did not claim a Golden Globe this year, unlike last, but Carol did win in the Best Television Actress, Musical or Comedy category. Besides Best TV Show—Musical/Comedy, the series had another nomination, for Harvey Korman as Best Supporting Actor—Television. For the Television Champion Awards, Carol won Best Comedienne for a fifth straight year, while *The Carol Burnett Show* won Best Variety Program for a second consecutive year.

About the only person not nominated during this period was Lyle Waggoner. Looking to expand his activities and broaden his resume, Lyle signed up to became host in the fall of 1972 of *It's Your Bet*, a syndicated game show that had been on the air since 1969 with a new host virtually every season. Unfortunately for him, the show's popularity began to wane, and it went off the air in 1973. Vicki Lawrence will appear as a guest to support him before the unsuccessful endeavor ends.

Even with all the honors earned this season, Joe Hamilton declined to reinstate any of the dismissed scribes, including head writer Arnie Rosen. After his departure, Rosen stayed fairly busy on TV but never had another Emmy nomination or success on the level of *The Carol Burnett Show*. His first post-Burnett job, producing and co-writing with ex-*Carol Burnett Show* veterans Don Hinkley and Woody Kling an updated TV adaptation of the 1931 Broadway musical *Of Thee I Sing*, aired on CBS Oct. 24, 1972, and used Dave Powers as director. He re-teamed with Hinkley and other former Burnett personnel Stan Burns, Mike Marmer and Arthur Julian to write for *The Mac Davis Show*, which Rosen co-produced as a summer show on NBC in 1974 and a midseason replacement in the 1974-1975 season. Rosen later was a supervising producer for *C.P.O. Sharkey*, a sitcom starring Don Rickles on NBC from 1976-1978, before he died of cancer on Jan. 30, 1980.

Apart from their jobs previously mentioned, Don Hinkley, Mike Marmer, Stan Burns, Art Baer and Ben Joelson continued to write on TV. Hinkley contributed to *The Flip Wilson Show* and *The Muppet Show* before he died in 1981. Marmer went from the highs of writing for *The Flip Wilson Show* and *The Dean Martin Show* in the 1970s down to the mediocrity of *The Love Boat* and *Punky Brewster* in the 1980s before hitting rock bottom as creative consultant for the ill-fated Fox late night talk show *The Chevy Chase Show* in 1993. He died in 2002. Burns compiled even lesser credits in the 1980s as he split from being Marmer's partner before he passed away in 2002 as well. Baer and Joelson continued their collaboration and did scripts for *Happy Days*, *Alice* and many more sitcoms before becoming producers on *The Love Boat* from 1979-1986. Joelson passed away in 1996, while his partner died ten years later.

Meanwhile, their efforts for *The Carol Burnett Show* in 1971-1972 became largely hidden from view. Most of the 1972 shows are virtually impossible to find in any form in archives or bootlegs, more than any other season. Some of this scarcity may be due to the low regard Carol has regarding the shows' quality, but there are other contributing factors. Quite frankly, Carol does not like the way she came across on air in this period.

"I really cringe when I look back at some of the things I did during the first five years," Carol told *Panorama* magazine. That included putting herself down during the Q&A as well as what she felt was unnecessary mugging in sketches.

Another hurdle has been ownership of the series. Although he left as producer of *The Carol Burnett Show* in the spring of 1971, Bob Banner retained a controlling interest on the series this season until Joe Hamilton bought out all the rights for his own production company after this season. Banner died on June 15, 2011, two months shy to the day of turning 90, but his heirs have remained co-owners of rights to the content for the first five years since that time, and they expect to be compensated for public showings.

In fact, a year after the death of the company's namesake, Bob Banner Associates filed suit against Carol's production company seeking compensation and accounting in part from profits generated by DVDs of *The Carol Burnett Show* that included selected portions of shows from 1967-1972. Bob Banner Associates planned to sell a DVD of Carol's appearances on *The Garry Moore Show* in 2013 that Carol's lawyers blocked. To avoid an impasse and make everyone happy—including fans who had long wanted to see the material—Carol and the Banner heirs came to an agreement with her selling *The Lost Episodes*, a DVD set released in 2015 that featured 45 episodes from the 1967-1972 seasons, including nine from this season (but notably only three of them from 1972).

Getting back to 1972, this season's episodes air in reruns through May 31. Two variety series serve as summer replacements—*The Melba Moore-Clifton Davis Show* from June 7 through July 5, followed by a special the next week and then *The David Steinberg Show* from July 19 through Aug. 16. During this period, Vicki will wed songwriter Bobby Russell. No one from the series or her family will show up for the event. It is a bad omen for the marriage, which will end in divorce two years later.

Carol spends her time off filming *Pete 'n' Tillie* with Walter Matthau, her first movie since 1963's *Who's Been Sleeping in My Bed?* (for more on that, see the Sept. 25, 1967 entry). A moderate success, she will promote it by singing its theme next season on the Jan. 20, 1973 show and reference it occasionally in following years, most notably in the Oct. 18, 1975 and Jan. 10, 1976 shows.

When Carol's series returns in the fall, a new creative crew is in place. Arnie Rosen's departure results in open position on the series for both head writer and producer, and one writing duo to survive the cuts this season wanted the former role badly.

"Stan [Hart] and I were pushing to be head writers," Larry Siegel says. "Stan and I were pretty sure we could be producers the following season." Given their expert work on the series for two years, Hamilton did name the duo co-head writers.

For the producer position, Hamilton looked to the past and installed Buz Kohan and Bill Angelos, who had written the same sort of movie parodies for *The Carol Burnett Show* from 1967-1970 that Hart and Siegel had since excelled following the departure of Kohan and Angelos. Hamilton saw no problems with the new setup, but he sadly miscalculated the personalities involved in their new roles.

Almost immediately, envy, resentment and friction resulted between the new head writers and producers. As a result, the transition in the series' sixth season was nowhere near as smooth as Hamilton had hoped. The final outcome was that no one won except for the series, which somehow survived the tense atmosphere between the quartet to produce a markedly better season than this one.

Olympic swimming winner Mark Shpritz (Lyle Waggoner) watches Carol's Charo character Chimango shake her body vigorously while a talk show host (Steve Lawrence) attempts to maintain decorum on the hilarious Dec. 23, 1972 episode. Lyle often appeared shirtless on the series, as seen here. The real Charo proved to be such a good sport about liking this parody that she will appear as a guest on Sept. 22, 1973. Courtesy of Getty Images.

Chapter 7

1972-1973: A Midseason Shift, A Season-Long Squabble

Audience member:	"Will this be shown in Argentina?"
Carol:	"Yes. It won't be shown in America."—From the Oct. 18, 1972 show

Crew Additions This Season

Producers/Writers: Bill Angelos, Buz Kohan

Writers: Stan Hart and Larry Siegel (head writers), Gail Parent, Woody Kling, Roger Beatty, Tom Patchett and Jay Tarses, Robert Hilliard, Arnie Kogen.

Assistant Choreographer: Carl Jablonski

More than 40 years later, this season's clash between new head writers Larry Siegel and Stan Hart opposite new producers Buz Kohan and Bill Angelos on *The Carol Burnett Show* remains fresh in all their minds. Here is how each player describes the tense tone of their working relationship and what essential disagreements they had.

"Buz and Billy, I liked them, but I never spoke to them," Siegel says.

"We just didn't think they were funny, and it was a comedy show," Hart says. Both he and Siegel considered contributions by Kohan and Angelos to be limited at best.

"We had a tough season that year, because Buz and Billy didn't know what they were doing, and Joe didn't want producers," adds Siegel. "And we were really doing the whole show, the best sketches."

"They were kind of evil, and we didn't want to work with them," Kohan responds.

"During that year, there was out-and-out jealousy for no reason," maintains Angelos. "The clashes were really due to a show business phenomenon I have seen elsewhere, and that is jealousy."

"They all just didn't get along," concludes Arnie Kogen, a newcomer who observed the dueling duos when he joined *The Carol Burnett Show*. Siegel and Hart were among those who recommended him to join the series. As with those gentlemen, Kogen had established himself previously as a top contributor to *Mad Magazine*.

"Another was Steve Lawrence, who I wrote for his nightclub act," adds Kogen. He also credits his agent at the time, Mike Ovitz, for making a recommendation.

Kogen spent the first year teamed with Gail Parent, who returned without Kenny Solms. "Often I took existing characters, but if I wanted to do something new, I did it," he says of his writing assignments. His fine work this season included the invisible baby sketch (Dec. 16, 1972) and Tim as an elderly firefighter (Feb. 17, 1973).

He also specialized in one of the series' best recurring features. "They'd say, 'Do commercial blackouts,' and I'd do it," he says.

Though Kogen stayed clear of the Hart-Siegel-Kohan-Angelos stalemate, most of the other writers found themselves taking sides in the conflict. They included Robert Hilliard, previously wrote for *The Jackie Gleason Show* in the 1960s, and the team of Tom Patchett and Jay Tarses. The latter duo appeared on the 1971 NBC summer series *Make Your Own Kind of Music* before they pursued writing comedy over performing it.

Carol and Joe eventually recognized the animosity occurring, but at the same time, the series was enjoying an evident increase in quality, and they did not want to rock the boat. For her part, Carol was becoming a more active part of the show during production meetings, especially in contributing ideas, including suggestions for movie spoofs. She liked the direction it was heading, even if there was some backstage strife.

Also energizing the series was the arrival of Carlton Johnson, a sprightly black member of the Ernie Flatt Dancers with a thick mustache. With a bright smile and confident attitude, he was able to do some bit parts on the series that thankfully did not involve using his skin color as a source of humor (although some did, unfortunately). "He was very outrageous," recalled Stan Mazin fondly of Johnson, who died in 1986 at age 52.

What really boosted the series this year was a midseason change in its time slot that CBS programming head Fred Silverman calls a "checkerboard move" done more to protect *The Sonny and Cher Comedy Hour* than anything else. Having started as a summer series replacing *The Ed Sullivan Show* in 1971, *The Sonny and Cher Comedy Hour* returned to CBS in the middle of the 1971-1972 season and became a top 30 when it replace *My Three Sons* and *Arnie*, two sitcoms which faltered as the initial Monday night successors for *The Carol Burnett Show*. But the series drooped opposite NBC's top sitcom, *Sanford and Son*, in the leadoff position for Friday nights in the fall of 1972.

"It was an ill-advised move," Silverman says. "It was shredded. I considered it our pride and joy."

Seeing the success of *The Carol Burnett Show* on Wednesday nights, Silverman decided that would be the best new time for *The Sonny and Cher Comedy Hour*.

As it happened, CBS was so strong in the ratings that there were few options where to relocate *The Carol Burnett Show* without having to switch to Fridays for certain death. The only exception was *Mission: Impossible*, which despite winning its slot on Saturday nights was losing a lot of viewers from its lead-in, the new hit sitcom *The Bob Newhart Show*. "I knew it would make a terrific comedy block," says Silverman, so he moved *Mission: Impossible* to Fridays, where it flopped against *Sanford and Son*, and rescheduled *The Carol Burnett Show* for Saturdays from 10-11 p.m. Eastern and Pacific.

"I think *Mission: Impossible* was kind of in its final period, it was a sacrificial lamb," allows Silverman. "But we had two hit variety shows that were very good for CBS."

At the end of November, *The Carol Burnett Show* completed its stint on Wednesdays and moved to Saturdays on Dec. 16, 1972. Despite a lackluster opening episode on that date, the program retained most of the audience much better than *Mission: Impossible*, and it easily beat movies on NBC and a rotating crime anthology series on ABC called *The Men* to finish the season at a strong Number Twenty-Three. The switch was so perfect that Carol would stay on Saturdays from 10-11 p.m. Eastern and Pacific for the next five years.

Carol was grateful for the change, as she related nearly five years later to UPI reporter Vernon Scott. "We're not an 8 o'clock show," she contended. "We do a lot of movie spoofs and sophisticated comedy—in addition to slapstick and other humor—to which the younger audience doesn't relate. And our music isn't rock oriented. The 10 o'clock time period allows us more freedom to reach a more varied audience. So after the Wednesday night catastrophe, we moved to Saturdays."

Despite Carol's beliefs, the time spent on Wednesdays probably boosted the series' appeal in the long run. Its exposure to a younger audience led many of them to follow it on Saturday nights, where many could stay up late and watch the series because they had no school the next day. Indeed, the influx of more children in the audience during the 1970s is quite noticeable when comparing the Q&A segments to those in the 1960s. In essence, *The Carol Burnett Show* had cemented itself as a family show by this season.

Carol also appeared on CBS Dec. 12, 1972, in a remake of *Once Upon a Mattress* as a ninety-minute special. As she told Johnny Carson on *The Tonight Show* four days prior to its airing, she did it to introduce it to a new generation with a color version (the presentation on June 3, 1964 was in black and white). Jack Gilford and Jane White returned from the 1964 show (and Gilford guest starred on Carol's series twice this season to boot). With Ken Berry, Bernadette Peters and Lyle Waggoner in the cast, Dave Powers as director and Joe Hamilton as executive producer, it almost felt like an extended episode of *The Carol Burnett Show*. It earned Emmy nominations for Outstanding Single Program—Variety and Popular Music and direction for the same.

Carol discussed with Carson how certain plot points could occur on the special that were forbidden in 1964. "We owe that to Archie Bunker," she said with a twinkle in her eye. Carol clearly was happy as much to be on the same night as *All in the Family* as she was to enjoy loosening restrictions on TV comedy for her series. Best of all, her work paid off with better shows than last season—even if some of the staff was unhappy backstage.

Sept. 13, 1972: Jim Nabors

* Another installment of "Carol & Sis"; Stella Toddler (Carol) attends a theater dedication in her name and winds up being inadvertently hurt by the emcee (Harvey), the architect (Lyle) and an old friend (Vicki) in the process several times; Jim sings "The Way of Love" and joins Carol on "Maggie Blues"; Carol presents "If I Could Write a Song"; a send-up of 1940s wartime movie musicals.

Comments: The new production team wisely opened the sixth season with a fair balance of sketches and songs, including Carol's second presentation of "If I Could Write a Song" in seven months (for the first, see Feb. 16, 1972). The highlight is the debut of Stella Toddler, a ninety-four-year-old actress with short, unkempt hair, drooping stockings around her knees, "granny glasses" and a low, halting voice that Carol says she developed in a restroom stall to the shock of other patrons. The indignities she endures in her theater dedication include falling off the stage, onto the floor and into the rostrum, getting a shovel stuck in her stomach as Harvey gives it to her to lay a cornerstone and gets crushed by Vicki's embrace. In a brilliant slapstick ending, a wrecking ball hits her and she rides on top of it before falling off and the cornerstone falls on top of her.

A favorable *Variety* review noted "But the best of the night was the closing 'Hollywood Canteen,' an on-target needle of sappy World War II pictures. Complete with '40s costumes and then-hip slang, Miss Burnett and her friends deftly picked apart the girl-meets-soldier corn that constituted reel life in Hollywood in those days. A good example of what she does best." Incidentally, there was a 1944 film called *Hollywood Canteen*.

Sept. 20, 1972: Carol Channing, Marty Feldman

Q&A; Harvey and Marty are pilots and Carol Burnett is a flight attendant who play pranks on their passengers; Carol Channing sings "How I Love Them Old Songs"; Marty is a demented plastic surgeon with Vicki as his assistant, Carol Burnett as his patient and Harvey as an escaped convict who wants his face altered; the sixth annual "Unforgettable Commercials" parody segment; Carol learns that Roger's new secretary has appeared in a girly magazine centerfold in "Carol & Sis"; a mini-musical comedy-drama with the regulars and guests saluting Johnny Mercer with more than twenty tunes by the songwriter.

Comments: This show does an excellent job of showcasing the wild-eyed (literally and figuratively) approaches to humor provided by Carol Channing and Marty Feldman. In fact, Carol brings Marty out during the Q&A to tell everyone how she loved his work as a regular on the 1970 summer series *Dean Martin Presents the Golddiggers in London*. She also blows a kiss to a woman's husband at work, per that lady's request in the audience.

While their jet is on automatic pilot, Harvey and Marty have a grand time in the cockpit declaring disturbing fictional scenarios on the intercom, like telling people they needed to move their luggage as they flew. Carol provides them with running commentary about the passengers' confused reactions, which ends with them jumping out of the plane to escape the pilots' mischief. This is a pretty amusing sketch.

Carol Channing wears a spangly gold outfit while performing a song said to have been written for her by Mickey Newbury. That claim is odd, given that he primarily composed country music. When it ends, she does another country number, "Jambalaya (on the Bayou)," with Don Crichton and the dancers. It is an unusual but acceptable bit.

The friskiest segment of the show has Marty is in manic form as a doctor who irons Lyle's face to get rid of his dimple before being confronted by Harvey at gunpoint, demanding work to hide his looks. After hitting Harvey with a shoe in a flawed attempt at acupuncture, Marty throws Carol, a nose job patient, off the operating table to accommodate Harvey. Channing then appears to whisk Harvey to surgery—but not before she sings "Hello, Dolly!" (in reference to the moving table) in Harvey's voice. This raucously effective sketch is briskly performed by the cast.

The commercials medley is sprightly and hilarious. When Harvey argues with Burnett over whether a product is a candy mint or a breath mint, she solves the dispute by clobbering him with a sledgehammer. Lyle says he will shave without water—and without blades, because he is in an insane asylum. Channing appears with big bosoms and Harvey inquires, "Is it really you?" "Cross my heart!" responds Channing, but when she does the motion, her bustline deflates. Lyle is in bed shirtless announcing "I didn't use my deodorant yesterday, and I may not today," to which Vicki, lying beside him wearing a gas mask, says, "You have till tomorrow!" Mocking retired NBC reporter Chet Huntley's series of plane commercials, Harvey says, "This is Hunt Chetley reminding you to fly Universal Airlines" before Marty appears as a hijacker who demands the in-flight pianist play "La Cucaracha." Finally, as Vicki Boone, Burnett talks about how much she loved eating ice cream as a child, then stands up with a fat bottom and legs and accidentally knocks down a table of bottles as well as crashes through a door.

The merriment ebbs with a ho-hum one-joke "Carol & Sis" installment. Roger's new secretary, Trixie, was a model, but in 1950, when he learns to his dismay when Trixie visits with her daughter, Pixie (both unidentified actresses). There is not much more to this, except for Carol announcing plans to put the bed out in the garage due to Roger's perceived lascivious interest in other women.

Much better is the elaborate finale, where Burnett is a waitress shutting down a restaurant singing "On the Atchison, Topeka and Santa Fe" to kick off an operetta that uses classic Mercer songs in interesting, unconventional depictions, both in solos and duos. For example, Harvey sees Channing and woos her with "Tangerine," and Marty provides energetic renditions of "Accentuate the

Positive" and "Jubilation T. Cornpone" wearing balloons and playing a recorder. Best of all is when Marty and Channing sing "Jeepers Creepers" about each one's bulging eyes, one of the most inspired music presentations ever done on the series. Marty and Channing leave together, but Harvey decides to depart without Burnett, bidding her farewell with "Moon River." She wistfully reprises "On the Atchison, Topeka and Santa Fe" before this satisfying piece concludes.

The show ends with a promotion to watch *The Sonny and Cher Comedy Hour* on Fridays on CBS. Three months later, that show will assume this time slot.

Sept. 27, 1972: Andy Griffith, Helen Reddy

Q&A; Andy sings "Turn Your Radio On" from his new album, joined by the dancers; a husband (Harvey) encounters an unkempt house due to his wife (Carol) spending more time obsessed by reading gossip magazines that cleaning up; Helen performs "I Am Woman"; Andy is a warden who allows a prisoner (Harvey) a conjugal visit with his wife (Carol) but keeps interrupting their lovemaking activities; Carol and Helen banter and sing about how to speak Australian; "The Old Old Movie" parodies the 1940 Oscar winner *Rebecca* with Carol in the title role; a musical finale on the chains of life.

Comments: Helen makes the first of several appearances on the series, while Andy has his third and final one. This is understandable, because whereas Helen shows a good sense of timing and delivery, Andy's down-home, low-key humor meshes uneasily with the rowdier brand Carol and crew employ. Carol describes Andy as "A gentleman we all very much love around here" before his solo number, which follows the Q&A. For this go-round, she informs the audience that she will be appearing on screen soon in *Pete 'n' Tillie*, reprising *Once Upon a Mattress* as a TV special next year and continuing to take part in an exercise class at the studio. Two Quebec women representing the Bucket Sitters of Canada present Carol with an award for Outstanding Bucket Sitting of 1972 on behalf of all charwomen. The interplay ends when a boy tells here "Everybody needs milk. What does your body need?" Grinning, Carol shoots back, "Sit down!"

Andy energetically performs a gospel-tinged song that was a modest hit for Ray Stevens in 1971 to kick off the show's entertainment. Standing on a podium, he is accompanied by the dancers in black and red outfits under a tent setting whose moves add to the electricity. This is about as spiritual as *The Carol Burnett Show* ever reaches.

Next up, when Harvey arrives home from work to a messy kitchen and living room, he is greeted by Carol, overcome with grief that Warren Beatty has broken up with his girlfriend. An enraged Harvey tells her she is learning nothing from reading such trash instead of neglecting household duties. Carol responds by doing dead-on impersonations of Bette Davis and Katharine Hepburn. Fed up, Harvey throws Carol out the window along with the trash. This is moderately amusing if you avoid the inherent sexism.

Ironically juxtaposing the preceding sketch's chauvinist theme, Helen sings "I Am Woman" in a purple outfit, with multiple superimpositions shown to indicate she is lip-syncing the chorus too. When this episode first aired, "I Am Woman" had just re-entered the pop chart after a brief run in the summer. It became Reddy's first Number One record, and while this performance may not have led to its success, it certainly did not hinder it.

When Carol arrives to spend the night with Harvey, her convict husband, she is so horny that Andy frisking her before she enters Harvey's cell makes her hot. Andy reappears several times with questions and suggestions to delay passionate embraces between Carol and Harvey. They finally shake him off, only for Carol to learn that Harvey has cheated on her during their twelve years of separation with another woman—Emily, a mop he painted. Carol slaps the mop in retaliation, then realizes she is in the wrong cell. Andy offers to help, but she is so frustrated that she knocks him out and stays with Harvey anyway. A little bumpy at points, this is moderately amusing nonetheless.

Carol and Helen's routine about Australian pronunciations is passable, but it is outshined by the next sketch, "Rebecky," where Aunt Celia (Shelia Bartow) tries to help Rebecky (Carol) become mistress of Roundelay, overseen by Max (Harvey). Harvey breaks character when his leg is soaked by tea poured all over it. More laughter comes from when Carol blows into a tissue and stuffs it into her bra, then asks Harvey for another tissue to balance out her bustline. "One for show, one for blow," he dryly notes. When the two arrive at Roundelay, Mrs. Danvers (Vicki) warns Rebecky about living there and discovering Max's secret. Rebecky finds it out at the end that Max has his mother there too, as Harvey emerges in his big-breasted Mother Marcus outfit.

The finale has three teams of duets performing—Carol and Andy, Harvey and Helen and finally Vicki and Lyle—joined by the dancers. The men are in tuxedos, and the women sport halter tops and long skirts. It caps off a disjointed but overall pretty good episode.

The end credits reveal that "Turn Your Radio On" and "I Am Woman" are pre-recorded. Following that, Chad Everett's voiceover promotes that *Medical Center* is next on most CBS stations. It may have been unnecessary—that series slightly outperformed *The Carol Burnett Show* in the ratings at season's end.

Oct. 4, 1972: Steve Lawrence, Paul Sand

Zelda and George are in the audience before the show starts; Q&A; Steve sings "In the Wee Small Hours"; "The Very Friendly 11 O'clock News" has an anchor (Harvey), sports reporter (Steve), weathercaster (Carol) and man on the street (Lyle) engaging in trivial talk; Paul is aggravated by a record on "How to Win a Friend"; Carol vocalizes on "Of Thee I Sing"; Roger and Carol think Chrissy has an overnight date in "Carol & Sis"; Steve sings "The End"; a spoof of *The Petrified Forest*; an Indian dance finale with Carol and Steve performing "Singin' in the Rain."

Comments: An excellent showcase for Steve's comic talents, this opens with Carol and Harvey seated with others in the studio as Zelda and George, with Zelda caustically commenting on their situation. "I'd rather be shopping at the Farmer's Market," she grouses. "I can't want to see Harvey

Korman," he says. "Boy, do I love him! Don't you?" "Who is he?" Zelda shoots back. Her opinions include "The people who ask the questions are all actors!" "That's not her real voice!" and, regarding Carol's dance routine, "She waits until the audience leaves and does it one step at a time!" It's a good bit taking shots at some criticisms of the series. Both leave before the show starts, and Carol comes out to do a brief Q&A in a pink gown. She says she loves show business, reveals she has three daughters and most amusingly signs multiple autographs for one girl.

Carol introduces Steve as a specialist in making all kinds of music sounds good, but what starts as a standard number emerges as something quite funny. As he vocalizes in a trench coat on the steps of a late night brownstone apartment on a street set, a woman yells from a window for him to shut up, then a drunk stumbles along, as do two guys fighting. It gets worse—a person drives by and throws out a dead body onto the ground, and an old couple mugs Steve and strips him to his underwear. By the time he valiantly struggles to finish his tune, the woman shouting out her window drops a bucket of water on him.

The first sketch targets the "happy news" craze sweeping local TV stations at the time, where anchors engaging in friendly banter seemed to take precedence over delivering the top stories. Here, the crew of Channel 8 crack jokes, hug and kiss each other no matter how adverse the news. That includes Lyle talking to a victim of a fire (Paul) with questions so vacuous that the interviewee pleads, "I wish you would've left me in the ambulance!" Back in the studio, Harvey's plans to go out with Carol upsets Steve, who hugs her passionately. In retaliation, Harvey hits Steve, who then insults Carol, resulting in all three fighting on the air. This is a solid, funny piece.

Carol tells the audience she first saw Paul as a guest on *The Mary Tyler Moore Show* (in 1970, where he played an IRS auditor smitten by Mary). His featured bit has him listen to a self-help record while on a bed and perform the actions requested longer than the time given for his response, causing him to fall behind and argue with the album as it plays. The record ends up with the upper hand, of course, skipping at the conclusion to tell him that "I'll be your friend till the end . . . the end . . ."

"I did that with Second City and took it to Broadway on *Story Theatre*," Paul recalls (he modestly omits that he won the Tony for Best Supporting Actor when *Story Theatre* ran from 1970-1971). The sketch came to him after he had studied mime in Paris under Marcel Marceau and then joined the Second City improvisational troupe in Chicago but was too timid to participate in the group's antics initially. While trying to conquer this problem, he noticed a gentleman on a bus reading *How to Influence People*, and when he received a suggestion from the audience on stage one night to do something involving a phonograph, he riffed on how an aural version of that book might interact with his shy self. The result was comic gold, as shown here and thankfully preserved.

Carol and Steve's OK but bland solo numbers are separated by "Carol & Sis," where Chrissy's date, Larry (Paul), a medical student, picks her up for the weekend for a retreat. His parents are joining them, but Chrissy tells him to omit that detail to make Carol and Roger think they will be out of town without chaperones. Naturally, Carol wants to do everything to stop their possible hanky panky until she learns the truth when Larry's parents arrive. For a simple farcical idea, this sketch wrings out some pretty good laughs.

"The Old Old Movie" presents "The Putrefied Forest," with Steve in Humphrey Bogart's star role. Paul is his henchman who is known as a mad dog and thus decides to act like a pooch whenever possible. Both take over a cafe where Carol is a waitress, Vicki is a grandmother and Harvey is a poet. This swift, effective parody ends up with Carol being greedier than the robbers and killing Harvey for money from his life insurance policy.

The only part of the show that does not hold up well is the politically incorrect depiction of Aztecs by the dancers and Carol as the tribal elder woman in the finale. Even so, she and Steve do a great job with "Singin' in the Rain" as they are joined by the rest of the cast before saying goodbye. Steve keeps the American native theme going when Carol announces his wife, Eydie Gorme, will be a guest on next week's show and he responds, "My squaw!" It is a great line from a show with several nice moments overall.

Oct. 11, 1972: Eydie Gorme, Jack Gilford

* Q&A; Jack is a hypochondriac physician in the medical drama spoof "Terminal Hospital"; Eydie sings "But Not for Me"; a man (Jack) dominated by his wife (Carol) is transformed into a magnetic personality when he wears a hat at a department store; Harvey is a writer struggling to compose a novel featuring Jack, Carol and Vicki as characters; Carol and Roger think Chris has been kidnapped by a solicitor at their door (Jack); Eydie, Carol and the dancers perform a medley of songs written by Harold Arlen, including "Over the Rainbow," "Stormy Weather" and "The Man That Got Away."

Comments: Jack Gilford's honey-voiced, unassuming persona is central to most of the skits here. In the hat sketch, for example, he is so low-key that he is ignored and even treated as a mannequin by a prissy store clerk (Harvey) until he dons a hat that Lyle says looks terrific and Harvey claims makes him resemble a superstar. After Vicki praises him, a gaggle of females strip him as he sings "All the Way" contentedly. But then he loses the hat, and Carol comes back, aggravated that he has not gotten the items she wanted on her list while he is now down to his underwear. This equally funny and poignant vignette is one of writer Larry Siegel's favorite pieces he created.

For "Carol & Sis," Jack is even more hilariously modest in contrast to what Carol and Roger believe he is. He knocks on the Bradfords' door to raise money for a music center, but Chris is the only one home, preparing a fake ransom note as a prop for a stage play she is doing. Jack says he will come back when Roger is home, while Vicki is in a hurry and accidentally forgets the note as well as knocks over a lamp as she leaves. Naturally, Carol assumes the worst due to the circumstances, and when Jack returns, she and Harvey amusingly misinterpret his moves and demands as threats in case they do not pay enough to release Chris. Their hysteria leads them to holding Jack down before Chris returns to explain the misunderstanding. This is an above average episode involving the Bradfords.

"The Playwright" has Jack as a shifty, mysterious stranger aboard a life raft with Carol, Vicki, Lyle and Don Crichton. Harvey appears superimposed in the upper left corner, pecking away at his keyboard and dictating the action while the players follow his instructions in pantomime. He changes his scenarios frequently, and the characters follow suit. For example, when he decides Vicki should be pregnant, she blows up her stomach in response. Jack's character is said to play his hand, and he does so, treating his fingers like a trumpet, before he pulls out a luger to threaten everyone. Carol ends up shooting him and everyone else after helping Vicki deliver twins before Harvey decides he is creatively shot on this work. He takes an aspirin, and that results on a big pill landing on top of the characters to end the sketch. This is a novel approach for the show and probably its best rendition apart from its weak ending. It will reappear in the Nov. 29, 1972 show in a variation before being revived and worn out in the last season.

As for the rest of the show, the Q&A is pretty negligible. Carol does the Tarzan yell and meets a woman who knows a friend's uncle who is an old pal of Carol's, but the woman does not know much more of him beyond that. One man's inquiry of "How do you keep your fantastic shape?" prompts Carol to quip, "I'm the only one who wants it!"

Eydie confines herself solely to music segments. That will change when she appears again on Feb. 24, 1973. Jack will return as well, on Jan. 20, 1973.

Oct. 18, 1972: Joel Grey, Cass Elliot

Q&A; Joel performs "Me and Julio Down by the Schoolyard" with the dancers; a candidate (Harvey) loses his voice during a paid political broadcast and his wife (Carol) supplies bad answers in his place; Cass plays an usher and Mae West in her solo spot; Carol mistakes Vicki for an old pal named Mary McCluskey; Lyle, Harvey and Joel are dogs waiting to be bought at Elsie's Pet Shop; Cass and Carol duet on several tunes sung in rounds; Carol and Cass are foreign film fanatics who watch several spoofs of the genre followed by a multilingual spy production number.

Comments: While Joel Grey is a top draw thanks to his role as the emcee in the movie version of *Cabaret*, and does fine, Cass shines more in this richly elaborate outing. For the start, a tan Carol selects a twelve-year-old girl in the audience, who upon learning Lyle is married follows up with "Will his wife mind if he kissed me?" Also, learning that a man is from Scotland, Carol queries him about what the natives wear under their kilts. "You'll see me after the show?!" she says in mock horror when repeating his answer.

Calling him "sensational in *Cabaret*," Carol introduces Joel in a yellow outfit vocalizing Paul Simon's recent hit, joined by the women dancers in Carmen Miranda getups and the men in Bob Fosse-ish stripes. It is a bizarre presentation, but at least it is contemporary.

"Meet the Candidate" features Carol making politically incorrect patter with guest bit players, as Harvey's character has laryngitis and she covers for him badly while working with Lyle as the host and a slew of unidentified actors as reporters. She boasts about how they live beside their Chicano and Puerto Rican friends, ruefully adding, "Can't really avoid them, they're all over the place." To Harvey's chagrin, she relates that their youngest child is in Phoenix fighting extradition. Her interviews with the press are similar disastrous—she seems not to care that she misidentifies a Chinese reporter as Japanese and fails to convince a black newswoman that some of her and Harvey's best friends are of that race. By the time she breaks into "Aquarius," the conference is in shambles as Harvey attempts to shut her up. This is a good sketch overall.

First dressed as an usher, Cass passionately sings "If I Could Only Be a Movie Star" before the scene fades to her dressed as a glamorous Mae West, vocalizing the 1930s chestnut "Life is Just a Bowl of Cherries" surrounded by male dancers in white tuxes. This sparkling segment confirms Cass as one of the show's greatest musical talents.

In "Mary McCluskey," Carol claims Vicki is her old pal, Mary, despite constant denials from the latter. Compounding insult to injury, Carol criticizes "Mary" for alleged bad habits, leading Vicki to hit Carol with spaghetti and give her $2 to get away from her. She does—only to spot another woman and claim she remembers her. This sketch is brief enough that it makes its points effectively and scores some good laughs.

When Lyle is sold at Elsie's Pet Shop, his dog buddies (Harvey and Joel) try their best to be purchased too, with Joel even singing bits of "Yankee Doodle Dandy" (which he did in the 1968 Broadway musical *George M!*) and "Wilkommen" (from *Cabaret*). But it is Harvey who looks ready to go, until he bites the lady who picked him to take home. The duo then sing a song of friendship. The whole exercise is somewhat corny but passable.

Carol and Cass alternate in taking the lead to tunes like "Row Row Row Your Boat," "Frere Jacques," "The Old Grey Goose," "The Man in the Flying Trapeze" and more. Although a medley of rounds using mostly folk numbers is somewhat dubious as entertainment on a variety show, the women's vocals and professionalism make it work.

The ladies return in the final spot as two foreign film fanatics seated in a theatre eating foods themed to the countries whose pictures are display. They eat pizza while watching a spoof of *The Bicycle Thief*, where Joel and Lyle see that Cass has brought back Joe's missing bike but broken it, apparently an unfunny reference to Cass's weight. The parody of *And God Created Woman* has an unidentified actress who reveals what she is wearing covers up her flat-chested physique. In *The Seven Samurai* takeoff, Joel and Harvey are stereotyped Oriental combatants whose duel ends when their swords collapse because the latter were made in Japan. For *Never on Sunday*, the humor comes from Harvey pinching Vicki's butt and fighting Lyle, who leaves with Carol the prostitute, all while the overdubbed translation claims only innocent events are occurring.

One bit from a parody of *The Blue Angel* unfortunately did not make it to air. As the character originally played by Emil Jannings, Harvey lacked enough to make a quick change from a tuxedo to a chicken suit, so entered the scene in a chicken suit on top and just jockey shorts on the bottom. Carol laughed so hard, they had to stop taping.

Overshadowing all this is "Heist," an imaginative seven-language espionage caper. A diamond switches hands from Lyle to Cass to Joel to Vicki to Harvey in Germany, Italy, Japan, France and Casablanca, interrupted at each stop by Carol intercepting the gem temporarily as the others are arrested. Carol ultimately gains control of the jewel, only to see it crack. Elaborately choreographed with the dancers and finely shot and edited, this is one of the series' most ambitious offerings ever.

At the closing, Cass, still clad in a trench coat like her character was in "Heist," offers Carol the diamond. She should have kept it—her contributions here were that invaluable.

Oct. 25, 1972: Tim Conway, Pearl Bailey

Q&A; Nora Desmond (Carol) considers doing a TV commercial pitched by a meek adman (Tim) with the help of Max (Harvey); Pearl sings "Where is Love?"; the Old Man (Tim) tries to help a fellow slave (Harvey) row a ship; a psychiatrist (Pearl) overly sympathizes with her client (Carol); an accused murderess (Carol) needs help from a life-sized rabbit lawyer (Tim) to clear her name; the cast engage in a series of spoofs of 20th Century Fox films, including *The Sound of Music, Love Me Tender* and *Anastasia*; Carol, Vicki, Pearl and the dancers present "Alexander's Ragtime Band."

Comments: Producers Buz Kohan and Bill Angelos reunite with the distaff guest star after having produced the failed *Pearl Bailey Show* (1971). Unfortunately, Pearlie Mae is not too well served in her only guest appearance in this up-and-down outing. It kicks off with a Q&A where it seems everyone in the audience wants to kiss at least one member of the cast, so Carol promises they will do during breaks between taping. She also says she has three pet dogs—Phoebe, Phoebe's daughter, Fern, and a poodle named Jingles.

The Nora Desmond sketch is fine, with the usual delusions by Nora (she mistakes Tim for Rudolf Valentino and then her hairdresser and smacks him both times). Rehearsing for the Knock 'Em Dead bug spray ad, she kills her co-star, Billy Bedbug, an insect she squashes when she does a monologue about how she fantasizes they will become rich and famous and then he cheats on her. Tim replaces Billy only to be accidentally impaled by a sword Nora uses, followed by Harvey accidentally (actually, it looks to have been planned) jumping on the sword with his crotch, causing to him cross his eyes in pain. Max accidentally strikes Nora with the sword as well, resulting in all falling down dead.

Pearl's number had appeared previously on March 16, 1970 and Dec. 14, 1970, and given that plus her lack of association with it or the play from whence it came, *Oliver!*, it comes off as a waste. Better is the slave ship sketch, where Tim does a stellar job of destroying Harvey throughout, starting with singing "By the Beautiful Sea" before he sits next to Harvey and including picking up a piece of bread with his toes and pulling it up to his face by his shackled ankle. Having said that, give credit to the writers for coming up with great physical comedy involving Tim and Harvey rowing the oars, as well as situations like Tim shaking Harvey's hand as an introduction and saying "I'm a leper" to the latter's dismay. Tim also amuses Lyle, playing the slave driver, when the latter finds on the floor Tim's effort to escape and says, "The key, huh?" and Tim responds, "He speaks Spanish." The sketch ends strong too—when Lyle throws Tim overboard for attempting to escape, Harvey is still shackled with him and follows him off the ship.

Unfortunately, a flat routine follows where Pearl is a psychiatrist constantly interrupting Carol before singing the lament about their situations that "A Good Man is Hard to Find." Pearl ends up being the one lying on the couch revealing her troubles to Carol. Eh.

Next is a skit that fans either find stupid or endearingly silly. Carol approaches Lyle to represent her in court, but he is too busy and pawns her off to his law partner, F. (for "Fluffy) Lee Bunny. Wearing floppy ears, whiskers and white paws in a business suit, Tim earnestly acts as a hare, twitching his nose and chewing greens and carrots while discussing the case with Carol, even shaking his leg in appreciation when Carol pets him. When she accepts him for the job, Tim hops for joy at getting his first murder case and says "That's all, folks!" before closing the door leaving his office.

For the 20th Century Fox salute, the first three efforts miss the mark in varying degrees. *The Sound of Music* has Maria (Carol) being introduced to the family of Capt. Von Trapp (Harvey), which include Lyle as one of his sons. When Carol sees him, she stops singing "Do Re Mi" and leaps into his arms—that's the big joke. *Love Me Tender* is similarly ho hum, with Tim as Elvis Presley mumbling to his dying brother before accidentally knocking him out with his guitar. Carol is Carmen Miranda in a number with the dancers, and while the costumes, choreography and orchestrations are bright, Carmen is such a camp icon that this comes off more of an impression than a send-up.

Better is a longer roasting of *Anastasia*, wherein the empress (Carol) follows the imploring of her aide (Harvey) to review candidates claiming to be her granddaughter. Vicki is proven to be a fake from Brooklyn, but Pearl (wearing a wig of long black straight hair) convinces the empress she is the real deal by doing the Kiev High School cheerleading song. After crowning Pearl, Carol gives her a list of tasks she is to do now, and an appalled Pearl proclaims, "I don't do windows! Who is this broad?" and leaves. This is the one moment in the show Pearl truly is able to showcase comic chops, and Carol is great in putting on a nasal tone every time her pince-nez clips onto her nose.

In tribute to the 20th Century Fox 1938 film of the same name, the leading women perform "Alexander's Ragtime Band" and give the classic Irving Berlin composition their all in beautiful black outfits. Pearl looks comfortable, and obviously enjoys dancing solo as well as singing. The fact that the show rarely stopped for retakes is clear in this piece, as Don Crichton's top hat falls off his head for a time in the dance routine.

At the end, Harvey kisses Tim on the head, but Lyle demurs doing the same. Pearl seems happy on the kick line, so apparently she enjoyed the show despite its occasional faults.

Nov. 1, 1972: Peggy Lee, Anne Meara, Jerry Stiller

Q&A; a takeoff of the "Mary Worth" comic strip with Carol bothering a happy couple (Harvey and Vicki); Peggy sings "A Song for You"; a comedy routine by Anne and Jerry; Carol and Peggy duet on "Girl Talk"; Marian helps a bearded lady (Anne) determine who is trying to sabotage the circus in "As the Stomach Turns"; a contrast in how the sexes handle an auto accident; a rich couple (Carol and Harvey) are aghast by their crass fellow in-laws (Anne and Jerry), and all four hate the street wedding of their children (Vicki and Lyle) in the musical finale.

Comments: Even though it leads with a sketch Carol loathes, this one of the series' top shows, with all guests seamlessly integrated into top musical and comic moments. The Q&A encompasses Carol's plans to make another record (she does, but her label does not, she jokes) to visits to Australia (a gentleman from the land down under says it is his second time to come to her taping, and she assures him she will get there soon, a promise she will hold—see Dec. 8, 1973 for more) to Mark Spitz. Getting a little flustered talking about the six-time Olympic gold medal winner, she says, "I think he's very cute, he's adorable, he's, yeah, I'd like to have him give me a few swimming lessons!"

"Mary Worthless" was planned to be a recurring item until this bombed with Carol even more than the audience. Seen first in a Sunday comic panel on screen, Carol plays the title character with a white wig and apron who expresses her philosophy of being a do-gooder before we cut to Harvey and Vicki as a rapturously romantic couple. They do everything together and skip effortlessly across their apartment before Carol arrives to meddle as their new maid and insinuates each is lying to the other, including implying Vicki is sleeping with Harvey's boss (Lyle). The obviousness of what is happening produces limited chuckles, so in the second taping Harvey takes advantage when things go awry, first hearing a doorbell before it rings, then mugging his way to the door and opening it to see Lyle accidentally drop a watch he was twirling on his fingers. Sensing the disarray, Harvey knocks out Lyle, then Carol comes up with a cake and Vicki promptly smashes it into Harvey's face before leaving. With his life in tatters, Harvey jumps out a window and nearly hurts himself in the pratfall. Following this chaos, Carol says with some chuckles, "Because bringing happiness is the only thing important to me, don't be surprised if I show up on your unhappy doorstep some day. Better yet, be surprised, because I'm not doing this again!" The sketch is not as bad as Carol thinks it is, and it actually has some amusing moments before Harvey takes charge.

Next, Peggy strongly delivers a tune that was a minor chart entry for Andy Williams in 1971. The set makes it appear as if stars are behind her in the dimly lit presentation.

Lightening the mood, Stiller and Meara portray Mr. and Mrs. Chou En-Lai after President Richard M. Nixon and his wife had left from visiting China. Anne complains how the chief executive wrote "Dickie loves Pat" on the Great Wall, while Jerry confesses he thought Barbara Walters was the First Lady. Both are glad to have given pandas to the Nixons, with Anne adding, "I didn't have the heart to tell them they were gay!" This is a tight and enjoyable set.

In "Girl Talk," Carol and Peggy gossip between singing at a beauty shop where Carol is a manicurist and Peggy is a customer. This satisfactory entry is quickly overshadowed by a top "As the Stomach Turns" set in a circus tent. Marian meets several amusing suspected saboteurs, including the strongman (Lyle), whom Marian feels up for concealed weapons, and Evil McQueevil (Jerry), a daredevil who has made one jump too many. Also on tap is Harry Harriet, a person who has one side male and the other female (Vicki gets applause for a bit where she literally argues with both sides of herself) and a lion tamer who is a coward (Harvey). This brisk piece gives everyone involved great business to perform.

The depiction of how two men handle car crashes versus women may be somewhat dated and sexist today, but still funny overall. To be honest, Harvey and Jerry yelling at each other and threatening to fight is just as much a cartoon as Carol and Anne belittling the damages to their vehicles in favor of empathizing with each other.

The wonderful finale starts with snobbish Carol and Harvey mortified that their son (Lyle) is marrying into a family led by shabby Anne and Jerry. Carol's affected phony laugh is a gem in itself, but the interaction between all four is golden. When Lyle arrives with Vicki and announces they are going to marry on the street in the village, Carol and Anne faint in their husbands' arms. In the half-hour reruns the sketch ends here, but the original show cuts to the dancers who appear as flower children decorating the in-laws with headbands while Peggy officiates the ceremony by singing "The Rhythm of Life" accompanied by tambourines. Even with Peggy obviously reading lyrics from cue cards, this is a vibrant, spirited number that includes the bonus of seeing Jerry surprisingly spry on his feet. Interestingly, Stiller and Meara were appearing as in-laws at the same time in frequent guest shots on *The Paul Lynde Show*, which aired on ABC opposite this series.

"I have the flower headband for that sketch," notes Carol's super fan Kathy Clements. "Carol took it off and didn't want it."

Given how well they came off here, it is a shame Stiller and Meara do not appear on the series again. At least Peggy Lee will return—see March 17, 1973.

Nov. 8, 1972: Lily Tomlin, Steve Lawrence

An interpolation of "We're All Playing in the Same Band" and "I Believe in Music" starring the whole cast; Lily performs a comic monologue; Roger becomes enamored with Carol's divorced friend (Lily) in "Carol & Sis"; Steve sings a medley of "I Get Along Without You Very Well" and "Without You"; Carol is the innocent bride of the Godfather (Steve), who does his crime business while they are on honeymoon; a parody of the 1950 film *Caged* with Carol, Vicki, Lily, Steve and Harvey; the Charwoman fantasizes herself in a glamorous outfit singing "If My Friends Could See Me Now."

Comments: It is easy to see why this episode won the Emmy for Outstanding Writing. Every aspect is top-notch, including the dazzling opener where Carol is joined by Steve, Lily and then the rest of the cast in singing an upbeat tune that fell short of the top 40 in 1970 by Bert Sommer. They segue into a 1972 hit by Gallery as Carol, Steve and Lily have heart designs attached to their shoulders to make them resemble the splendid minstrel look in black jumpsuits with silver accents that everyone else is wearing.

From that rousing bit, Carol introduces Lily as "truly one of the finest performers I've ever seen in my life." Playing a woman at a restaurant waiting for her boyfriend to return and looking into the camera, Lily warns us that there is weirdness out there as she unwraps a cigar. The audience applauds at the spiffy way she throws up her lighter and catches it in her coat after starting to puff her stogie. After musing on how love works, she vows that she will find her soul mate one day. "And then I'll hurt him!" It is a great monologue with a killer ending from an always magnetic comedienne.

Lily appears next as a recent divorcee who is not taking her situation nearly as gravely as Carol feared. Her appearance and attitude entrance Roger, who offers to show her golf moves instead of going to practice the game as he vowed earlier. An envious Carol tries to goad Roger to go, but he stays and dances the funky chicken with Lily—even after the music stops. Any hopes he had of going further vanish when Lily says she has to leave for dinner with her first ex-husband, to Carol's shock, and any anger Carol has about Roger's behavior vanishes when he gets his back caught doing the funky chicken again and cannot play golf. By "Carol & Sis" standards, this is a better-than-average entry.

Steve does something to crack up Carol and the audience before she introduces him singing on a bench. His medley is helped by the second number being a contemporary hit, as is the theme of the next sketch. With huge wads of cotton in his cheeks, Steve does a broad but winning approximation of Marlon Brando as the Godfather as a newlywed along with Carol. She seems oblivious when he kisses his henchman (Lyle) for 30 seconds, which it turns out to be the kiss of death as Lyle is shot. (In a great comic death scene, Lyle lands on his stomach, then pushes himself up with his hands to twirl over and fall on his back.) Carol remains clueless when Harvey arrives to beg for a favor and even gets into bed with Carol and Steve to make his case. Steve grants Harvey his wish to be a U.S. senator and then has his cronies appear from under the bed to escort Harvey out. Steve and Carol appear ready to consummate when Carol reveals she is really Kevin, his arch rival's son, and shoots him. As he dies, Steve ends this smooth sketch with a great final line: "Sorry you did that, Kevin, I still think our marriage could've worked!"

In the last and best sketch, "Caged Dames," Lily is a warden who slaps her inmates down the line as part of her mean streak, one of them being her mom! Carol is a new arrival ready to break out, but her efforts are hampered by her cellmate (Vicki), a clod who plays the harmonica just with her hands and botches Carol's plan to escape. In response to the latter, Lily scrapes her fingernails down a chalkboard to torture Carol. But Carol gets a cake with a file in it to pick a lock, grab Lily and get her gun. As she plans to escape, a priest (Steve) arrives and sings "My Yiddishe Mama" to Carol to remind her he is her brother and tries to save her. Lily grabs for her gun to kill Carol but accidentally shoots herself instead. She does not die immediately and beckons Carol to come closer—at which point she scratches on the blackboard one last time. Carol prepares to face the electric chair when suddenly Mother Marcus (Harvey) arrives with the governor (an unidentified actor) to free her daughter. Clutching her children to her ample bosoms (and making Steve giggle), Mother Marcus is so overbearing with her love that Carol announces "I'd rather go to the chair!" and leaves. Both Carol and Larry Siegel (who co-wrote this sketch with Stan Hart) believe this is some of Vicki's best work.

Anything following all this could have been anticlimactic. However, the Charwoman fantasy bit with her singing along with a mirror vision of herself in a white robe on both "If They Could See Me Now" from *Sweet Charity* and "Baby Dream Your Dream" is quite effective in an understated manner.

Carol coerces Steve and Lily to sing "It's Time to Say So Long" with her at the end. The camaraderie reflects the great job and chemistry displayed by all on this winning entry.

Nov. 15, 1972: John Davidson, Ruth Buzzi

Zelda and Gladys Ormphby (Ruth) visit the studio audience for *The Carol Burnett Show*; Q&A; actor Alfred Mundane (Harvey) insists on doing his play with the original actress, which he regrets when he sees how much bigger physically she has become; John sings a song while pictures of his newborn son flash in the background; Harvey is a beauty show host awkwardly interacting with a contestant (Vicki) and last year's winner (Ruth); Zelda and Gladys replace Carol and Ruth in a dance number with John; a comic and musical tribute to MGM studios by the cast, guests and dancers.

Comments: This lively episode continues the series' hot streak, with an inspired start as two of TV's frumpiest comic creations meet for the first time. Ruth had popularized her dowdy character in a hair net on *Rowan and Martin's Laugh-In*, so the audience immediately reacts to her and vice versa—she actually hits a man with her purse! Gladys joins Zelda because George gave up his ticket (probably because he saw it earlier—see Oct. 4, 1972), and Zelda provides her pal with the lowdown on what to expect. Zelda says a special camera lens disguises Lyle, who is short and fat in real life. Asked by Gladys why they cannot do that for Carol, Zelda grouses, "Nothing works for Carol Burnett!" Zelda calls the show's star the "Wicked Witch of the North" before we cut to the stage and Carol does the Q&A, where she confirms that Zelda is her favorite character (at least for now). She also says she watches what she eats, loves the Rehearsal Club in New York and receives compliments from twenty New Zealanders visiting her in the studio.

Carol dons a fat suit and blonde wig to play Harvey's former co-star in "The Madcap Lover" for the first skit. The brilliantly plotted script hilariously maximizes Harvey's dilemma of accommodating her weight gain, from being bounced onto the floor as he rushes into her arms to hug her to trying to hide her bulging breasts when he puts her into a closet. This one gets lots of laughs throughout.

As proud new father John Davidson appears with Carol, she shows a clip from *The Entertainers,* the 1964-1965 series where both of them were regulars (as was Ruth Buzzi), where he sang to Carol's newborn daughter, Carrie, who cried as he vocalized. Looking even younger than he did seven years earlier with a shag haircut, John then sings a passable tune with pictures of his son behind him.

Great humor returns as Harvey introduces Vicki breaking balloons to "The Blue Danube Waltz" and then answering a question while blowing bubble gum in a spoof of pageants. Asked what she would like to be if reincarnated, Vicki in her "bimbo" voice says she would like to be Mom's apple pie. If that were not enough, the previous queen (Ruth) stumbles out drunk and weighed down by her robe. She embarrasses Harvey by revealing she has been locked in a hotel room with him and remarks, "Have I got a surprise for you on Father's Day!" As with the previous skit, this is an obvious target for parody, and the writers and actors make the most of it.

Ruth appears next as the namesake owner of Greta's Greenery who talks to her plants and loves them so much that she tries to prevent a customer (Carol) from taking any of them. The struggle becomes so intense that Carol grabs a sprayer to claim one, but Ruth overcomes her. A defeated Carol vows to get back at the operator and leaves. After that, Ruth tells her plants not to worry—she will protect them from Carol, who is obviously bananas. Although forced at time, this is pretty good overall.

"It started out with me being the flower shop customer and Carol as the owner," Buzzi recalls. "In rehearsal, the customer got all the laughs. Before I knew it, Carol had my part, and I had hers. I had to take the shop owner part and make it funny. I did, and it really worked great. In fact, that sketch turned out to have been one of my favorite moments on television."

The festive atmosphere deepens as a typical production bit with Carol, Ruth, John and the dancers is interrupted by previously taped shots of Zelda and Gladys providing biting commentary about what they are seeing. Suddenly the scene transforms to Zelda and Gladys assuming the lead female roles on stage, assaulting the dancers, weighing down John and even having dogs joined them. This unexpected change of pace is a delight.

The show wraps up wonderfully with a peppy salute to Metro-Goldwyn-Meyer pictures. For *Lust for Life*, Vincent Van Gogh (Lyle) presents his ear to his girlfriend (Vicki) as a gift, and she says "I love you"—only he can't hear her now. In *National Velvet*, Carol puts on a hat to disguise herself as a jockey, but when she turns around and shows her buxom figure, John tells her she will need two more hats to pass as a man. John sings a tune from *Broadway Melody of 1940* before we have a splendid roasting of *Camille*. Here, Carol excels in trying to hide her coughing spells from her lover in a pillow and other hilarious methods. When the truth is revealed to Harvey, he wonders how Carol got sick. Enter Lyle the butler, who begins huffing a lot. Everyone including the dancers and guests join in singing a medley of hits from the studio for a fine finish.

During the closing, John amuses Carol by showing her a bottle with the Charwoman's head as a stopper. It is a cute moment for a show brimming with similar pleasures.

This was Ruth's first extended appearance since March 18, 1968, but this time she received billing up front. As with her previous guest shot, she was still a regular on *Rowan and Martin's Laugh-In*. "We had different nights of the week for taping, so it was very easy to accommodate our needs when I guested on her show," Ruth says.

Regarding the differences between the variety series, she notes that "*Laugh-In* was much more casual. Everything was rushed, but there was a tremendous amount of trust between the producers and the directors and all of us regulars. We were allowed to take our characters and go with them. On Carol's show, everything was extremely scripted except Carol's interaction with Harvey and Tim." She loved reuniting with John Davidson and adds, "I never worked with a more professional performer, or anyone more gracious."

Nov. 22, 1972: Ray Charles, Vincent Price

* Carol overhears a phone conversation by Chris and misconstrues it to mean her sister is pregnant in "Carol & Sis"; Ray performs "Every Saturday Night"; George fantasizes about being a card shark in the Old West playing opposite Lyle and romancing saloon girl Vicki until Zelda arrives and breaks his spirit; Vincent presents a soliloquy titled "Reviewing the Situation"; a tribute to horror films includes takeoffs on *The Mummy* and *The Bride of Frankenstein*; Ray plays a cocktail lounge pianist and duets with Carol on "Tess's Torch Song" and "I Guess I'll Hang My Tears Out to Dry."

Comments: With a reliance on familiar characters, this show feels like a so-so installment from the previous season. The best thing about "Carol & Sis" is that it is short. Chris is trying to be accepted to nursing school, but all Carol hears makes her tell Roger her sister is with child, probably by her new boyfriend. Carol and Roger drop hints to try to get Chris to confess, such as Roger saying it has not rained in nine months. Chris is oblivious to it, and she lets a priest (an unidentified actor) enter when Roger and Carol are in another room. When the duo returns, Chris says, "Carol, Roger, say hello to the new father," and Carol faints. At least there is a payoff at the end.

Moving on, after Zelda interrupts George watching a riverboat gambler movie on TV, he dreams that he is a nineteenth century poker player who is the envy of Lyle and the object of desire of Vicki. "Oh, Beauregard, you got the best pair at the table," coos Vicki, as George stares at her chest. His reverie ends abruptly with the arrival of Zelda in a huge, ratty hoop skirt, and she is such a distraction that he loses all his money to Lyle. Zelda tells her husband to stop worrying and whining. "I'm going to boggle his libido," she proclaims, but Lyle refuses her attempted wooing as well as her desire to play him in cards. Frustrated, she challenges Lyle to a duel and makes George participate after accidentally shooting him in the foot. The joke turns out to be on Zelda—Lyle hates to see a guy suffer, so he shoots her instead. As Zelda skits go, this is above average.

There is variable comedy as Lyle plays Count Dracula and introduces two scary movie spoofs. The first has Vincent opening King Tut's tomb and finds a couple making out instead of a mummy. After that supposed humorous bit comes a more elaborate parody with Vincent as Dr. Frankenstein, Vicki as his assistant, Harvey as a horny monster and Carol as his bride who fails to impress him. She walks to a mirror and finds herself ugly too, so she paints lipstick on her cheek and powders her forehead in an attempt to beautify. It works, and the monster gives her a rose and Vincent weds them. However, any hope the monster has for the honeymoon dissolves when Carol growls, "Not tonight—headache!" This is all right, but one feels the series could have done better for Vincent.

On a happier note, the clip of Ray with Carol singing with him on this show will appear on the series finale.

Nov. 29, 1972: Melba Moore, Carl Reiner

Q&A; Carol and Harvey are contestants waiting to get on a *Let's Make a Deal*-styled game show; Melba sings "You've Got a Friend"; "Terminal Hospital" features Carol and Melba as nurses, Lyle and Carl as doctors, Harvey as a sissy male attendant and Vicki as a society lady suspected of murder; Harvey is an author constantly rewriting the plot of a story involving Carol and Carl; Carol and Melba duet on "Have a Little Talk with Myself"; "Non-Violent Theatre" presents "The Plot to Hurt Hitler"; "The Rip-Off" has Carol and Melba as suspected juvenile delinquents in an elaborate musical mini-drama.

Comments: This spottily pleasing installment opens with Carol in the Q&A giving a little girl an autograph and telling a gentleman that she keeps her figure by watching what she eats on weekdays and splurging on "bad foods" during weekends. From there, we have Harvey standing in front of an audience line as an ice cream cone and Carol dressed as a kangaroo. "You haven't changed a bit," Harvey says to her admiringly. Both compare the ways they plan to attract the attention of the game show's host to be selected to play—he with a horn, she with a bell—before the emcee (Lyle) appears with the payoff line: He tells them they need to get into costume before appearing on his show.

From that iffy start, Carol introduces "one of the best singers around today." Wearing large earrings, Melba effectively vamps through a 1971 hit written by Carole King.

Next up is a rather silly, forced bit wherein head nurse Carol bosses around her protégé (Melba), Harvey speaks in a Paul Lynde imitation and Carl arrives in a top hat and tails as part of the insanity, and inanity, as they prepare for an operation. Carl claims he cannot handle surgery because his hands are trembling, prompting Carol to sit on them in ecstasy (amazing that the censors let that pass in 1972). As they prepare to operate on a patient (Roy Stuart), Harvey reveals he used to be a doctor until he performed surgery on Carl that left the latter's hands shaking. Carl informs Harvey that his work was a success, as Carl used to shake all over. It ends with Vicki scaring her husband to death with a yell—in other words, it is a sketch that assumes being frantic equals being genuinely funny.

Much better is the next offering, which Buz Kohan claims he wrote on a Wednesday night when a sketch was a disaster during rehearsal (and if it was worse than what preceded it here, it must have stunk). With Harvey on a typewriter in the lower left corner of the screen, Carol is under a lamppost smoking, until Harvey changes course and has her put on a lipstick instead, nearly forcing Carol to choke on her smoke until she is finished. Harvey's next plot development has Carl appear, look at Carol's butt and say "At last we meet, Monique!" The author's directions forces the characters into difficult tasks, like Carol batting her eyes to say 1,000 things with them and having to smoke two cigarettes at one time. He writes a fight scene with a flurry of guns and knives between Carl and Carol, then feels it is horrible and rips the paper out of the typewriter and crumples it, prompting Carl and Carol to fall down to the ground uselessly. The sketch ends poignantly as the discarded characters reach out to hold their hands.

Carol and Melba's duet on an obscure number is highlighted by their smashing black gowns, with Carol's complemented by blue feathers and Melba's by purple ones. Next comes a takeoff of *The Plot to Murder Hitler*, a CBS special nominated for an Emmy for Outstanding Docu-Drama in 1972. Here Carl is a turncoat Nazi who collaborates with a waitress (Vicki) and French barkeep (Carol) to overthrow the Fuhrer with the help of fellow officer Harvey. Bombs are out as too violent, as are Carol's hickeys, in favor of Carl putting a "Kick me" sign around his back while Harvey takes a picture of them. Hitler (an unnamed actor) discovers their plot and plans to kill them, but since it's non-violent, he has his officers tickle Carol, Carl and Vicki to death. This has lots of crackups and goofs by the players that are actually enjoyable rather than contrived. In a part that does not make it to broadcast, Harvey's chair collapses to the ground when he returns from talking to Carol, plus he accidentally pulls out the wick from the bomb.

The finale, written by Buz Kohan and Bill Angelos, has Carol and Melba in pigtails who on a dare from friends including Harvey and Lyle steal jelly beans from Carl, a candy store owner. Put on trial, they face Harvey as the judge with eight jurors in a stylized courtroom where they are able to avoid prison time. The girls end up returning the stolen jelly beans, only to see Carl put up a sign saying "Free jelly beans today."

This was the last *Carol Burnett Show* seen on Wednesdays. CBS gave the star and her gang a two-week break before moving to Saturdays.

Dec. 16, 1972: Anthony Newley, Bernadette Peters

Bernadette stars in a production number called "Frankie" with the dancers; Carol voices her frustrations to a new neighbor (Bernadette) about having an invisible son; Anthony performs a song he wrote with support from the dancers, does a routine with Vicki, Harvey, Lyle and Carol about the effects of his English dialect and duets with Carol on "Where is the Love"; a two-act spoof of Shirley Temple's 1938 film *Little Miss Broadway* features Carol as Shirley, Vicki as the operator of an orphanage, Harvey as Shirley's uncle, Anthony as Harvey's brother, a broken-down tap dancer, and Bernadette as Anthony's girlfriend.

Comments: This episode is a treat if you like Anthony Newley's distinctive singing and mugging. If not, well, at least it begins strongly with Carol saying, "I wish she was on every week, Miss Bernadette Peters!" and the guest star dazzles as always. Peters slinks along with four male dancers in white coats and black ties and pants before the scene fades to her riding in a cab driven by Carlton Johnson to go to a club where the female dancers are floozies. As the featured male dancer, Don Crichton has his shirt removed before Bernadette kills him and goes to jail unrepentant. Peters gets well-deserved applause for her vocals and moves in a somewhat risqué number that fades back to the opening.

Bernadette has good comic chops as well in a rather obvious but still funny sketch where she learns that Carol has a son no one can see (voice by Harvey). Carol is embarrassed by her situation ("I kept diapering the wrong end!" she wails in recalling his childhood), and great special effects coupled with her exaggerated reactions make her plight convincing. The boy leaves and Harvey appears as his father, who wonders how he and Carol ever created an invisible child. The answer appears when Carol opens the door and we hear Lyle's voice for that of the invisible milkman, whom Carol tries to hide from Harvey.

From here onward, the show is mostly dominated by a man Carol introduces as a lyricist, composer, performer, actor and singer, "Mr. Tony Newley." At a piano with enlarged sheet music, Newley launches into his stylistic tones, wearing a shirt that exposes his hairy chest as dancers and handclaps are superimposed while he sings. When it ends, Carol banters with him about his accent. That leads into a belabored routine of Anthony wowing Vicki (in a Brooklynese dialect), Harvey (a hardhat) and Lyle (a cop) in different instances with his British voice. Carol witnesses it all and tries it out on Lyle and Harvey, with the latter hitting her on the nose and saying, "A Julie Andrews she ain't!" Hopes for this being a winning episode dissolve at this point, and Carol and Anthony's wan version of a recent hit by Roberta Flack and Donny Hathaway afterward does not help either.

The last half of the show is "Little Miss Showbiz," with Carol's Shirley Temple character Honey Bunny cheering up fellow residents at Happytime Orphanage in a production number featuring the female dancers as young girls. Her efforts impress the elderly operator (Vicki) and Carol's newly arrived uncles (Harvey and Anthony), who come to take her away. The orphan girls say goodbye to Honey Bunny, who sings a thank you in response. As Carol leaves with Harvey, Anthony sings to the orphan girls to get happy.

After three forgettable production numbers, Act II is an improvement when Bernadette appears to tap dance and sing with Anthony (and surpasses him in both departments). Carol arrives at the couple's apartment while Anthony works on music for a Broadway show, and she is clearly envious of Bernadette dating her uncle. Nevertheless, she takes a keen interest in Anthony's work and writes a song for the show, "Yummy Yummy Yummy," a nice send-up of "On the Good Ship Lollipop." A producer (Lyle) who looks through a window to see the trio perform the tune offers to back Anthony's show, causing everyone to celebrate, with Carol forcing her way between Bernadette and Anthony.

But to Carol's chagrin, Harvey returns to fight for custody of his niece before an elderly judge (Don Crichton). All appears lost until Carol sings in her defense, then Anthony, Bernadette and the jurors, who are the dancers, join in. A spectacular scenery change occurs with the judge's bench turning around to reveal Vicki as Lady Justice in an Art Deco arch in white, gold and black. The dancers do one more number in spangly outfits, and all ends well, even though Carol still wants Bernadette to stop romancing Anthony.

At the end, Carol sings the last line of "It's Time to Say So Long" like Shirley Temple. The moment stresses cuteness over cleverness, as most of the show unfortunately does. "Little Miss Showbiz" will reappear twice despite its so-so quality, in a remake on the Dec. 18, 1976 episode and as a clip in the 1997 documentary *Moon Over Broadway*. The latter presumably occurred because Bernadette Peters appears later in the film. Peter Matz wins his sole Emmy for this series for his musical direction on this episode.

Dec. 23, 1972: Steve Lawrence, Tim Conway

Q&A; *The Tonight Show* has a substitute host (Steve) who loses control of the show through the antics of a sexy-Mexi singer (Carol), Mark Spritz (Lyle) clad only in a swimsuit and Mark's agent (Harvey); Steve sings "The Good Life"; Harvey is a World War II parachutist with Tim as his idiot partner; stage actors Funt and Mundane (Harvey and Carol) must appear on TV during a technicians' strike; a parody of *Columbo* with Steve as the title detective, Carol and Harvey as crime suspects and Tim as the butler; a musical salute to bells and songs about them.

Comments: Arguably the season's best show and definitely one of the series' strongest, this has top sketches and a finale tangentially and cleverly connected to the time of the year that makes a holiday treat. The Q&A includes a woman complimenting Carol effusively, causing the hostess to remark, "You all know my Aunt Louise," and a Carol saying it was the fourth time she was wearing her dress on stage in some form this season. To a query about whether Carol would do a commercial for milk with Mark Spitz, she says, "I'll ask him." That byplay probably stoked suspicions from conspiracy theorists that this segment had plants because a parody of Spitz follows immediately.

Lyle appears in a red, white and blue bikini with gold medallions after Steve introduces guests to his talk show. A blonde bimbo (Vicki) promotes her new movie, "The Beast With Two Backs" (which somehow got past the censor). Next is Chimango (Carol), a Charo takeoff with malapropisms intact (e.g., "For three years, I was in a commissary" instead of missionary). She laughs at Steve's jokes only to calm down and say with a straight face, "I no get it." When Lyle enters with three milk bottles, Carol goes gaga, bumping, grinding and molesting him over the protest of Harvey, who is trying to protect his client. Amid the chaos, Steve cuts to a commercial, and there appears a slide of rabbits with the phrase "No More to Come," mocking the "More to Come" stills used as bumpers in and out of ads on *The Tonight Show* during the Johnny Carson years.

Steve's song is overshadowed by the next hysterical sketch. Lyle (as a pilot) and Harvey both crack up early as Tim goes to the bathroom on the plane to the sound of a jiggling toilet handle. As Lyle goes to the cockpit, Harvey endures Tim showing a map of the target area on his body and pulling up his shirt to reveal a dark eyelash drawn above his left nipple. Harvey tries to compose himself, as well as when each man puts what looks like chocolate pudding on each others' faces to camouflage themselves—Tim thinks he resembles Al Jolson in blackface, so he breaks into singing "Mammy." Later Tim takes a grenade, winds it up like a pitch, and tells Harvey that he is keeping it to hold off the player on second base. Tim accidentally pulls off Harvey's parachute when the latter jumps, but Harvey does blow up the target when he lands, so all ends well relatively.

When Lyle tells assured theatrical stars Funt and Mundane that their performance on TV will have to occur with substitute cameramen and technicians, they valiantly decide to carry on, but mishaps overwhelm them. The camera misses its mark, a boom mike drops too low and comes between them during a love scene, and the opening of a curtain on the set reveals Stan Mazin as a striking employee. By the time a scab cameraman comes too close and knocks out Carol's teeth and makes her slur her speech, Harvey has had enough and throws a vase back at the camera to indicate their frustrations.

The fourth superbly written and acted sketch makes this a classic. "Cobumble" has Harvey and Carol discussing how to hide their murder of Carol's mean twin sister when the detective arrives. Tim answers the door, but first retreats to adjust the angle of a dish on the mantel, then retraces his steps back to reposition Harvey's leg, causing the actor to crack up. When Tim gets to the door, Harvey warns that the oversized gold knob has been polished. Tim's hands slip trying to grasp it, and efforts using rope fail as well. Desperate, he grabs the top of the door and swings down to straddle the knob, which provides his crotch with a huge golden cover due to its appearance. After composing himself, Harvey pushes Tim's body to open the door, only for it to swing back and Tim to indicate the motion irritated his privates. Steve enters as Cobumble, and having watched Tim's antics, he shifts the picture on the mantel back for additional laughs. Cobumble quickly deduces that Carol is not her twin because of ill-fitting shoes and her ignorance of state capitals. She kills Harvey and plants the gun on Tim, who learns Cobumble believes he is guilty because "the butler always did it." As music plays to end the sketch, an impish Harvey pulls on Tim's legs as the latter tries to exit.

After plenty of comedy, Carol appears on stage with an array of bells, joined by dancers and the cast plus Steve to sing snippets of tunes such as "Carol of the Bells" and "Winter Wonderland." The latter are the only ones that indicate this show originally airs two days before Christmas. Tim keeps the laughs going in the end credits by giving Carol the golden knob from "Cobumble" as a souvenir as she hugs him.

This episode is a total triumph and could have won the series the Emmy for best writing alone if the Nov. 8 edition with Steve and Lily Tomlin had not been chosen. Having the last skit mocking the series that had given the show its biggest competition for viewers until the recent switch to Saturday nights makes it even sweeter to watch and enjoy.

Dec. 30, 1972: Repeat of Oct. 4, 1972 show

Jan. 6, 1973: Tim Conway, Jack Cassidy

An orphanage operator (Vicki) offers a prospective mother and father (Carol and Harvey) the chance to adopt one of three adorable boys—or one 35-year-old man (Tim); Jack performs "Gesticulations"; an angel (Harvey) dislikes it when he is forced to live on his cloud with a cherub (Tim) who clumsily tries to ingratiate himself; a three-part send-up of *A Star is Born* features Jack as a fading, drunk actor, Carol as his devoted wife who becomes a rising star, Harvey as an agent for both, Vicki as a gossip columnist and Tim as a geriatric, horny movie studio head.

Comments: With no Lyle and a goodly amount of Tim's shenanigans, this episode feels like an average entry from the ninth and tenth seasons. First, Tim tries to impress a skeptical Harvey and Carol to add him to their household by doing a somersault and crashing a table in the process. His plea about how he has suffered without parents is obviously ad libbed, as he breaks up Carol and Harvey by telling them how he had to go throw and fetch a ball by himself. Carol then tells Harvey Tim's lifetime of rejection by other families means that he needs them, and Tim punching Harvey in the gut seals the deal by blackmailing him. They take him in, only to see Tim introduce them to his wife and two children who will be coming too. This is a very funny and winning sketch.

Introducing her other guest, Carol says, "I've known him for quite a while. I had the honor of appearing in a Broadway show with him." (She neglects to name it was the ill-fated *Fade Out—Fade In*.) Jack acceptably presents his tune in a tux before Tim makes a shambles of Harvey's happy heavenly abode. As Tim plays a Jew's harp with his mouth and a harmonica with his nose to provide twangy music and bungles his attempts to get into the top bunk, Harvey loses it a lot in this sketch—he covers his face twice within the first few minutes to hide his laughter, for example. He is so rattled that he tells Tim to polish harps instead of halos, and when Tim does the latter, miraculously one of the hoops lands around one of Harvey's wings, prompting more laughter. This solid skit ends with Harvey shooting off Tim's wings so the latter will fall out of heaven.

The show's final element varies in quality. For "The Old Old Movie," Vicki introduces "The Story of a Star," with Jack as a debonair, egotistical motion picture idol unwittingly on his way down when he meets Carol, a cute, freckle-faced chanteuse. After literally wiping off the freckles from Carol's face, Jack invites her to join him on set, where he vows to make her a success. That leads to the skit's best part, where droning reporter Rhonda Babbitt (Vicki) tells of Carol and Jack's wedding followed immediately by troubles in their relationship. Carol approaches white-haired Mr. Mogul (Tim) to plead for another job for Jack following his dismissal from a movie. Mogul lusts after Carol but cannot keep up in trying to follow her (Tim is great as usual being exaggeratedly slow). Finally, after Carol says she will do anything to get Jack employed, Tim dies after being turned on so much. A third musical number is being filmed before an intoxicated Jack interrupts it, leading to his firing.

The last portion has Rhonda both saying Carol is now an Oscar nominee and encouraging Jack to kill himself as the rest of Hollywood is demanding. Carol's agent (Harvey) warns her not to do a dangerous trapeze stunt prior to the Academy Awards, but she does and breaks many bones. This causes Harvey to have to carry her crumpled body on stage when she wins her Oscar while screaming in pain. She composes herself to pay tribute to Jack in her speech, and he emerges from inside a piano to reunite with her—and unintentionally crush her more by hugging her. As part of this so-so parody, Brad Trumbull appears as the maitre d' (he also was in the start of the orphanage sketch), Bob Duggan is a director and Jan Arvan is the Oscar emcee.

As the credits roll quickly, there are no dancers, and Carol does not sing "It's Time to Say So Long." Jack just signs the guest book and joins Tim and the regulars to wave goodbye. The rushed ending gives the episode an overall unfinished feeling despite several strong attributes. As Tim's sketches are so short and the *A Star is Born* spoof is so long, this show is one of the few that could not be edited successfully into a half-hour version for *Carol Burnett and Friends* in syndication and thus disappeared for more than 40 years before being included in the *Carol's Crack Ups* DVD in 2014.

Jan. 13, 1973: Pre-empted by special *Marlene Dietrich—I Wish You Love*

Jan. 20, 1973: Jack Gilford, Ruth Buzzi

Q&A; Vicki and Carol illustrate how the show tries to censor its material prior to going on the air; Ruth stars in a fantasy musical number where she envisions herself as Tina Turner; Carol mistakenly believes Roger's description of his auto accident actually describes an affair with another woman; Jack sings two songs as the father of a bride (Carol); Zelda disturbs George's nautical fantasy; Carol lends her vocals to "Love's the Only Game in Town"; a send-up of Snow White; a medley of songs popularized by Al Jolson ("Swanee," "Mammy," "You Made Me Love You," etc.).

Comments: Sagging after the first skit, this rebounds nicely during the second half. In the Q&A, Carol reveals that on Christmas Eve, Xavier Cugat sent over a painting to her house with a nice note on the back from his wife to say how much they loved her impersonation of Charo, also known as Mrs. Cugat. After that, Carol launches into an opening bit where she and Vicki supposedly are rehearsing next week's show but are constantly interrupted by others claiming what they are saying is offensive. Director Dave Powers (actually the voice of Harvey) tells them to drop the use of a Jewish surname, while fake prop man Carmine Dellasandro (Stan Mazin) objects to the use of an Italian one too. Cameraman Hans Kaufman (an unidentified black actor) requests his own changes, and when Carol suggests references to a sister or brother, a priest and a nun (both unidentified actors) wave their fingers silently to indicate disapproval. By the time the boom operator (Don Crichton) protest the use of a dog, all Carol and Vicki are left to do are say hello to each other and then goodnight. This is an amusing poke at the foibles of free speech on TV in 1973.

"She's one of our favorite guests," says Carol in introducing Ruth, emoting in a casino how she will be a swinging lady before the scene transforms into her as a long-haired star knockoff of the Ike and Tina Turner Revue. There is a lot of different flashy angles seen here—including one shot where the marks of where everyone was to stand on the floor appear clearly—before we return to Ruth singing solo and breaking the bank on a one-armed bandit at the conclusion. The number is odd and somewhat forced but tolerable.

"Carol & Sis" relies on tired mistaken assumptions for humor, as Carol goes to the bedroom thinking Roger is cheating on her while he comes home to tell Chris he just had an accident. Naturally, Chris leaves before Carol returns and tells Roger she realizes what is happening, prompting an unknowing Roger to make comments that imply he wants a divorce. The tired concept at least does not run too long (about five minutes) and has a great ending when an unidentified actress greets Carol at the door and says, "Is your husband here? I'd like to talk to him about our little accident" before taking off her coat and unveiling her pregnant stomach, leading Carol to faint. This should have been better.

On Carol's wedding day, her nervous father (Jack) sings "I'm Calm," and they duet on "More Than I Can Wish You." At six minutes, this is overlong and too cloying. The time spent with Zelda the nudge is largely wasted as well, although Harvey tries to spark laughs by fiddling with his eye patch as the captain. When Zelda arrives as a pirate who throws away Harvey's pistol, sword and knife, it allows Lyle and his band of rogues to take over the ship and tell Harvey he will be chained to Zelda for a year. This prompts Harvey to jump overboard, as do Lyle and the men when they realize they will be stuck with Zelda. Zelda's shtick is wearing thin now.

Just as the show looks to be a dud, Carol vibrantly sings the theme to her recent movie, *Pete 'n' Tillie*, noting that John Williams composed the music and Alan and Marilyn Bergman supplied lyrics. Surpassing that pleasant moment is a vaudeville-style turn with Carol as Snow White fifteen years after her marriage to Prince Charming (Harvey). Her breasts are sagging, making her less attractive according to her wisecracking mirror on the wall (Lyle), while her husband is rotund and effeminate. Hearing Snow White plead for help, her fairy godmother (Ruth Buzzi) returns to grant her one more wish to free her from her loveless marriage. This leads to the arrival of horny Bashful (Jack), and the wicked witch (Vicki), who gives a poisoned apple that the prince eats and dies, allowing Snow White to leave with Bashful. This is silly but swift and raucous fun.

The finale has Jack and Ruth wearing bowlers and spangly outfits along with the dancers in a tribute to Jolson's most famous movie character, the lead in *The Jazz Singer*. This show marks Ruth Buzzi's third of four official guest shots (for the last, see Dec. 15, 1973) and Jack Gilford's second and final appearance.

Jan. 27, 1973: Tim Conway, Kaye Ballard

Q&A; a service station attendant (Tim) mucks up the getaway plans of a crook (Harvey); Carol introduces Kaye singing "Go In the Best of Health," a number from the latter's upcoming Broadway musical version of *The Goldbergs*; Vicki, Carol and Kaye are buddies dining out who are so intoxicated that they cannot figure out how to split their bill properly; a spoof of *The Dating Game* has Lyle as the host and Harvey as the contestant having to chose between Kaye, Carol—or Tim; the cast, guests and dancers appear in a tribute to vaudeville's Palace Theatre.

Comments: This outstanding show starts in the stratosphere with a superb Q&A. After a lady asks about Carol saying in a recent magazine article that she read 128 scripts before picking *Pete 'n'*

Tillie to do as a movie (Carol's first feature film since 1963), the hostess says she rejected other offers because they were just extensions of what she does on her series. Then Burt Reynolds emerges to screams to ask Carol if she fools around. "Yes!" she responds as he joins her on stage and kisses her, causing Carol to collapse in mock ecstasy. "That what I like—hard to get!" he cracks. Burt takes questions and sign lots of autographs, including about his recent nude centerfold in *Cosmopolitan*. "When is Burt going to pose for another magazine?" asks one lady. "Listen, darling, I don't take my clothes off to take a bath anymore," he quips. Another lady compliments Carol when Burt thinks she meant him, causing him to mock collapse in this very charming segment.

The solid opener has Harvey trying to outrun the police and relying on Tim for help at a convenience store. Tim insists on singing the brand's theme song and telling Harvey he will get a complimentary glass for filling up his tank. An angry Harvey tells Tim to get to work, but to his irritation Tim insists on washing every window inside and outside of Harvey's car, including on Harvey's glasses. When Tim opens the hood to check on the engine, Harvey slams it down on him and gets shot multiple times by cops. As Harvey lies dying, Tim escapes to tell Harvey he has won a trip to Hawaii. Tim's guileless earnest nature opposite Harvey's desperate pleas produces some hearty chuckles here.

Calling Kaye her good friend, Carol sits with her guest star on a set filled with radios as they impersonate old-time shows, with Kaye doing the Shadow and Carol the creaking door from *Inner Sanctum*. Carol recalls *The Goldbergs* and notes that Kaye will soon play the lead character from that series created by Gertrude Berg in a Broadway musical called *Molly's World* (it will be titled simply *Molly* when it opens on Nov. 1, 1973). This scene transitions to a taped piece where Kaye appears as Molly, singing the touching "Go in the Best of Health" from her apartment window to the street below following the news that her children want to leave home. The number was meant to attract financial backers to support the musical as well as provide the show with national exposure during tryouts.

"That was a wonderful show," Kaye remembers of *Molly*. She credits Carol for putting the number on the series because "She thought I'd be a big success with *Molly*." But weak reviews and sales forced the musical to close by the start of 1974. At least this show preserves part of the history of *Molly* for posterity's sake.

Kaye appears with Carol and Vicki as a trio smashed at lunch to the disgust of their snippy waiter (Lyle). As they finalize payment, each insults the others, and all look like they will part as enemies before they agree to do it again soon. The effervescence and camaraderie between the women make this piece of fluff an enjoyable excursion.

The last sketch is even more on target. As a crew member on "The Dater's Game," Tim prepares bachelorettes Carol, Kaye and Vicki when he unintentionally tears off the latter's dress, prompting her to leave in a huff and forcing Tim to assume her place. The taping begins with Lyle encouraging Harvey, a swinging bachelor in a Nehru jacket, to make suggestive questions to the three contestants he cannot see. During the proceedings, Carol and Kaye snipe at each other, with Carol implying Kaye is a slut and Kaye impugning Carol's looks. Tim just answers honestly, telling Harvey he would be willing to go fishing or see a ballgame with him, and that attitude makes Harvey select Tim as his date. Kaye slaps Harvey (a little harder than he expects, based on his reaction) and Carol punches him in the stomach before Tim emerges. Shocked by his choice, Harvey nonetheless puts his arm around Tim's shoulder and caresses his face before the skit ends. From start to finish, this one flows smoothly and gets great laughs.

The extended ending recreates a night of vaudeville entertainment with acrobats, dancers (Don Crichton and Stan Mazin hoofing as Niles & Edgar, the Tippy Tap Brothers), music and comedy. Harvey plays the xylophone and mistakenly believes the hoots and applause are for him rather than Vicki shimmying and disrobing behind him. Tim is Pops Lindo, the world's oldest magician, who looks up in an instruction book how to pull a rabbit out of a hat. He cracks up Lyle, his assistant, often as he attempts to disappear on stage too.

Next up is Kaye as "Sophie Talker," a character familiar to her from her experience in show business. "Oh yes, I knew Sophie Tucker," Kaye says. Between belting songs, Kaye as Sophie recounts a tale about her injury on stage and thinks she can be heard fine without a microphone near her. It all ends with Harvey driving a piano on a bicycle with Carol perched atop to sign "Tea for Two" as the dancers join in, interrupted briefly by Tim and Kaye coming out on a bench where she makes moves on his uncomfortable self. Elaborate, flashy and fun, this is a smashing finale for the show.

This marked Kaye's second and last appearance on the series (for the first, see Feb. 16, 1972). She believes that of the dozens of variety series from the 1950s through 1980s on which she was a guest or regular, *The Carol Burnett Show* outdid them all. "Carol's was the best," Kaye says. "It really was. It was so perfect. That show was so well produced that it was not a challenge for anyone to do."

Feb. 3, 1973: Family Show

** Carol reconnects with an old high school flame and Roger resents the rekindling in "Carol & Sis"; the dancers do a routine to a song called "Hoedown"; Carol offers her interpretation of the standard "I've Got You Under My Skin"; Vicki sings "The Night the Lights Went Out in Georgia"; "Waterloo Bilge," a send-up of the 1940 film *Waterloo Bridge*, has Carol and Harvey assuming the lead roles originated by Vivien Leigh and Robert Taylor, with Lyle as an elderly English nobleman and Vicki as a street girl.

Comments: This show's key distinction is the debut of the only hit produced by the series, "The Night the Lights Went Out in Georgia." Vicki Lawrence had released flop records on Elf in 1969 and United Artists in 1971 when her husband, Bobby Russell, presented her in October 1972 with the tune. Based on an actual event with details changed to avoid a lawsuit, the number took Russell several months to complete. Originally the song expressed a male point of view, and Russell planned to record it until he had Vicki record a demo in one take.

Russell presented the demo to Sonny Bono to have Bono's then-wife, Cher, record the song.

Bono felt its depiction of backwoods justice, where a judge convicts a man framed for murder by the narrator who did the actual killing, would offend listeners of the title state and negatively affect Cher's career, so he nixed it.

But Cher's producer, Snuff Garrett, felt it was a hit. He offered to have his client, Liza Minnelli, cut the tune. Russell argued that Liza would be wrong and that Vicki would do fine, since she loved the song and her demo had impressed Garrett. So, with an ominous arrangement by Artie Butler, Garrett had twenty-one musicians cut the instrumental backing for "The Night the Lights Went Out in Georgia" in one session, followed by Vicki cutting her lead vocals and harmonies. Snuff mixed, mastered, dubbed and had the song shipped to New York City in only three hours, reportedly his quickest production of a record ever.

The single entered *Billboard*'s pop chart one week after its debut on this show, at the very bottom position at Number 100. The eerie story song moved up gradually each week due in part to dedicated pushing by Bell Records' national promotion director, Steve Wachs, to have more markets play it after it broke out in the South. "It turned out that the job we had to do with this record was to convince radio in the rest of the country that we didn't just have a regional hit," Wachs told Nat Freedland in *Billboard* in 1973. Ironically, given Sonny Bono's concerns, the first radio stations to play it were ones in Georgia.

"The Night the Lights Went Out in Georgia" reached Number One for two weeks. But Vicki could not match its success. Her follow-up, "He Did With Me," stopped at Number Seventy-Five in 1973. She returned to the chart in 1975 with "The Other Woman," which peaked at Number Eighty-One. Vicki had her final album release four years later.

Russell became jealous about his wife's success with "The Night the Lights Went Out in Georgia," and the couple divorced in 1974. The song had a longer life than the marriage. It became the title tune of a lousy 1981 movie featuring Mark Hamill and Kristy McNichol, popped as one of the clues on the *Win Lose or Draw* game show hosted by Lawrence from 1987-1989, and went to Number Twelve country when Reba McIntire redid it in 1992 (Vicki's original made Number Thirty-Six on that chart in 1973). The song will receive special recognition by Carol later this season—see the March 24, 1973 show for more.

Feb. 10, 1973: Petula Clark, John Byner

Q&A; Petula sings "Without You"; John does a monologue with multiple impersonations; Molly and Bert host a garage sale; a salute to TV commercials features five takeoffs; a criminal in a zoot suit (John) and his doltish assistant (Harvey) end up regretting that they kidnapped Fireside Girl Alice Portnoy by mistake; Vicki hosts a public service program on modern art that recounts a starving illustrator (Harvey) and his weak wife (Carol) trying to survive in Paris on their meager income; Harvey is a studio head who has to fire Donald Duck (John); Carol and Petula duet on a medley.

Comments: This above average outing's only deficits are mundane musical moments and an unexceptional "The Old Folks" skit. The Q&A starts with one man wondering about Carol's age when she co-starred with Buddy Hackett on *Stanley* in 1956-1957 ("Twelve and a half," Carol quips), and how she felt about actor Christopher George telling *Los Angeles Times* columnist Joyce Haber that Carol is a very sexy lady ("He's very nice"). She reveals her daughters' ages and said they may go into acting as adults. When a woman suggests Lyle should be the next centerfold for *Cosmopolitan*, Carol references its editor and said, "Helen Gurley Brown, if you are watching." (Lyle later will appear modestly nude in *Playgirl* magazine this year.) The age-obsessed audience asks Carol how old she was when she began her series. "I started when I was twenty, so it's been seven years," she jokes.

Carol says this is the first time she has met Petula Clark and "She's a delight." Petula's number, different from Nilsson's recent Number One hit of the same title, is well performed, but hardly rousing. More exciting is John's monologue, which Carol prefaces by hugging him and noting that if Harvey had been tied up with John on one side and Tim Conway on the other, "Harvey would laugh himself to death." "Harvey was a fan," John recalls of Korman, who previously directed Byner when he was a regular on *The Steve Allen Comedy Hour* in 1967. "I couldn't impersonate Johnny Mathis enough in his company."

In fact, John does his Johnny Mathis impression on air for Carol to her delight, then he pretends to be seagulls choking on smog and a lizard. His interpretations include David Brinkley working at a casual dining restaurant, John Wayne as a physician, Ed Sullivan as a maitre d', Jimmy Stewart as a slow drawling Air Force colonel and Tonto studying interior decorating at night school. The latter bit would draw frowns today, as John portrays the character with a lisp and high voice. Otherwise, this is fine stuff.

"The Old Folks" has a good bit where Bert grabs Molly's leg and she says it reminds her of Joe Namath, "Because you'll need ten other men to help you score." Otherwise, this effort that ends with both singing a song of devotion to each other is best forgotten.

The show rebounds strongly with excellent spoofs. The Marlboro Man (Lyle in a gaucho outfit) lights cigarettes for himself and for a woman (Carol in a swimsuit), then begins coughing uncontrollable after puffing a little. His fit is so intense, he knocks over a palm tree. Next, Vicki asks John if he wants a second cup of coffee, and he destroys their kitchen in response. "He's not fooling me with those little excuses, he really doesn't like my coffee!" says Vicki afterward. Petula shows up starving at a McDougal's restaurant, and her server (Lyle) leads the male dancers in a number telling her that "You deserve a rest today" while Petula passes out from hunger. Vicki is a flight attendant going down a plane's aisle who sings "Come on and fly me" off-key, resulting in a pie in the face. Best of all, Harvey offers a grocery shopper (Carol) two detergents in exchange for her Tidy brand. She spurns him as well as his repeated efforts to bribe her up to $100, so Harvey shoots her and steals her detergent. Don Crichton emerges and says to Carol, "Lady, you've been shot!" "Never mind me, get my Tidy!" she pleads to him.

Following this is what John claims is one of his favorite skits to do on the series, as he and witless Harvey are terrorized by Fireside Girl Alice Portnoy. John cracks up Harvey by repeatedly banging his head into Harvey's chest over frustration that they kidnapped the wrong girl, and more aggravations soon follow. Alice is able to con Harvey into giving her his club, which she uses to hit him on the leg, and steals a gun to hit John on his head before Harvey gets control of her. The men learn that Alice's dad actually wants $10,000 from the crooks to take the busybody back. John releases her, but she returns to get $10,000 herself and blackmails them with her products. Her activities so unnerve John and Harvey that they end up jumping out of a window to escape her.

A more ragged but generally likeable routine has Carol as the dedicated but weary wife of Harvey the starving artist. He props her up with a broom to paint her before Lyle arrives as an art dealer who offers him money for his work. Harvey rejects Lyle's offer as insufficient, leading Carol to want to kill herself except she is too weak to stab her stomach. Harvey accidentally knocks her out the window, and she comes back with a mangled face that inspires him to draw it like Picasso and presumably success thereafter.

In a golden comic segment, John is dressed up as Donald Duck as Harvey reluctantly tries to fire him. John says the writers were inspired by his killer duck impersonation to do this skit. One ingenious bit has John doing Donald Duck imitating John Wayne. Later, Harvey's wife calls him up for food for dinner and he tries to kill John in response, as the latter catches on and tries to avoid capture. This is a howling good time.

As Petula just had a baby, she and Carol sit on stools to sing tunes related to children, such as "Turn Around." It is a nice but rather subdued ending for a generally lively show. John and Petula will return to the show next season, both with even better efforts than they had here. See Oct. 27, 1973 for John and Nov. 10, 1973 for Petula.

Feb. 17, 1973: Valerie Harper, Tim Conway

Q&A; Funt (Harvey) learns that a producer (Lyle) has Charo (Carol) ready to serve as a replacement for the actor's ailing wife onstage; Valerie sings and dances with Don Crichton in a number; Valerie and Carol are teens on a double blind date with Harvey and Tim; Tim is an elderly firefighter sent to rescue Harvey at the latter's burning residence; Carol sings "The Ladies Who Lunch" in a fantasy sequence with Valerie and Vicki; Marian comforts a man afraid of women (Lyle) in "As the Stomach Turns"; "The Good Old Bad Old Days" is a finale set around newspapers.

Comments: Valerie's appearance marks the first time another regular from CBS's powerhouse Saturday comedy lineup guests on *The Carol Burnett Show* simultaneously, in this case *The Mary Tyler Moore Show*, where Valerie played Mary's pal, Rhoda. She does a serviceable if not stellar turn here, which begins after a brief Q&A where when asked what her favorite character is, Carol responds with "I'm working on her—Elizabeth Taylor." (She and Taylor will actually collaborate on an HBO movie ten years later, *Best Friends*.) Carol also invites three Girl Scouts on stage and gives them $20 for their cookies—an impressive amount for 1973—before getting the show underway.

The usual Funt-Mundane stage show with complications is given a juicy twist with Carol's Charo bumping and grinding her way during a performance with Harvey's upright British thespian. She gets angry when Harvey dictates what she is to do in their play while portraying a dying woman and tells the audience he is using a fake gun that will not kill her. Harvey is livid by her work, which includes her shaking her body during her death scene and constantly getting up thereafter, even when he covers her with a blanket. Finally, Harvey shoots himself, but his death scene is upstaged by Carol's dancing as the curtain drops. The humor is fairly obvious, but this sketch is a winner.

Still wearing her Charo getup, Carol introduces Valerie, wearing a red gown as she is joined by Don Crichton in a red bowler hat and black outfit. Her number with him, "The Last Blues Song," is a little flat vocally but otherwise acceptable.

Tim comes next, as he enlists Harvey's advice on what to do during his first date with Carol, as does Carol with Valerie. Trying to bond, Carol and Tim spray citronella on themselves (it is a hot summer night) and make small talk as they keep checking back with their friends. During one meeting, Harvey says Tim is as dumb as Carol, prompting Valerie to defend her pal and leave Harvey. She plans to go home with Carol, but the latter is smooching Tim so well that her leg is shaking, prompting Valerie and Harvey to leave disgustedly on their own. This sketch sails smoothly thanks to great work by all.

Even better is one of the top Tim-Harvey combos, with Tim starting the laughs early as he constantly smashes out all of Harvey's window and then some with an axe before climbing into the house. "Tim took about ten minutes to get through that window," laughs Arnie Kogen, who co-wrote the skit. A member of the Sun City Hook and Ladder Fire Department, Tim quips to Harvey that "I love my work. That's why they call me the Happy Hooker." Harvey saying he is short of breath and needs mouth-to-mouth resuscitation. Tim first grabs Harvey by the butt and says, "Look like you're going to be all right. You're starting to get some color in your cheeks." This is all part of the script, but the rest comes from Tim, according to Kogen. Tim turns around to face Harvey, sprays Harvey's mouth as well as his, grooms himself and brings Harvey into hysteria by wrapping his arms around him and asking, "Where are you from?" By the time Tim says, "I hope you'll be gentle when you talk about this," the entire audience is consumed in laughter. Harvey supposedly dies at the end, but this sketch shines brightly throughout.

Unfortunately, next Valerie and Vicki make small talk with Carol before the latter sings a plaintive tune from the 1970 Broadway musical *Company*. This obvious piece dampens the festive mood. Carol's love of the composer will be put to better use when she does *Side by Side by Sondheim* on Broadway some 25 years later. Here, it is just dreary.

The laughs do resume, albeit not quite as strongly, with "As the Stomach Turns" providing Lyle and Vicki their only real roles for the show. Carol kisses Lyle repeatedly to help him overcome his fear of the fairer sex before the arrival of Vicki as a gossip columnist in the style of Rona Barrett who attempts to talk to Lyle about his condition. He goes upstairs at Marian's house to change while Vicki leaves, and Valerie arrives as the town's naughty lady. She claims to have reformed, but when Lyle arrives downstairs wearing just a towel around his waist, Valerie makes out with him immediately. To retaliate, an envious Marian pours hot coffee on Lyle's rear (!), prompting him to go upstairs again and change. Valerie then repents and becomes a nun, even though she is Jewish. Speaking of Jewish, Mother Marcus (Harvey) arrives, and she is hysterical as ever in claiming Lyle is her son before we learn we have to wait for the next episode for more details. Apart from the weak ending—and inexplicably no part for Tim—this is a very good entry.

In a set designed like the front page of a newspaper, Carol and Valerie appear in one photo box, Harvey, Vicki and Lyle in another one, and Tim in his own one. Dancers dressed up as delivery boys complement their number, which is fair enough.

Although Valerie appeared on this series just once, she remained thankful for Carol later testifying on her behalf for her successful lawsuit against the producers of her series *Valerie*, who fired her. The full story can be found in Harper's memoirs, *I, Rhoda* (2013).

Feb. 24, 1973: Eydie Gorme, Ken Berry

* Q&A; Roger insists on having quiet while doing his taxes but Carol and Chris inadvertently bother him with their behaviors in "Carol & Sis"; the Three Stooges (Carol as Larry, Ken as Curly and Harvey as Moe) attempt to run a bank; Eydie offers her interpretation of "I Am Woman"; a salute to Fred Astaire includes Eydie and Carol singing his hits followed by Ken and Ernie Flatt's crew imitating his dancing style; a salute to the RKO Radio movie studio includes parodies of *The Pride of the Yankees*, *Notorious*, *The Outlaw* and *The Hunchback of Notre Dame*.

Comments: The writers lack compelling material for the two frequently seen guests here, making this just average. The Q&A includes a cute moment with two boys. Cub Scouts Bruce and Jay make Carol an honorary den mother, and Jay pleads for Carol to tell parents watching *The Carol Burnett Show* to let their kids stay up to watch the series in its new later time slot as well. "I'll tell 'em, Jay!" Carol responds.

Carol and Chris unintentionally irritating Roger is a pretty obvious setup. Carol ends up being loud holding back a sneeze, and she talks on the phone saying figures that Roger incorporates while doing his taxes. Chris snaps her gum and Carol crunches potato chips, aggravating Roger more. Exasperated by his demands for quiet, Carol tells Roger can sleep in the den and drapes the cover of his body. Roger does not care—he finally has peace to do his taxes. This is a waste.

The salute to RKO references two films the series never spoofed—*The Best Years of Our Lives* and *Citizen Kane*—before offering flat bits on others. For example, the supposed humor for *Pride of the Yankees* is that Lou Gehrig (Ken) speaks in echoes even when not addressing the stadium. *The*

Outlaw has Eydie sporting breasts so big a la Jane Russell that she knocks down Ken. The longest is a loud, labored version of *The Hunchback of Notre Dame* with Harvey as Quasimodo, Carol as a gypsy girl and Ken as a poor gypsy poet. Lyle, the duke, accuses Carol of thievery before she is saved by Quasimodo, whose ringing of the bell tower where he stays drives her nuts. Ken warns her Lyle is about to arrive and pays off her debt to have her stay with him, but she gets stuck in the bell and develops a hunchback like Quasimodo. It plays as forced as it sounds.

What does redeem the episode somewhat is a clever salute to Fred Astaire contained in the Ernie Flatt collection at the Paley Center for Media. Carol and Eydie sing "Cheek to Cheek," "They Can't Take That Away from Me" and many more superimposed on stills of Fred. Ken then leads the dancers in tails, tuxes and gowns to recreate the artist's terpsichorean style from the 1930s in a dazzling piece of showmanship. The other skit with Ken is unseen by this author but is praised by writers of *The Three Stooges Scrapbook*, so it may have made the show somewhat better than the half-hour version implies.

Incidentally, Lyle made a rare guest acting appearance away from *The Carol Burnett Show* three days after this show aired, as a politician on *Marcus Welby, M.D.* on ABC.

March 3, 1973: Pre-empted by *The Grammy Awards* special

March 10, 1973: Paula Kelly, David Hartman

* Q&A; Nora Desmond asks Max to protect her from autograph hounds when they go out to eat at a restaurant; Paula sings "Killing Me Softly With His Song" and accompanies Carol on "I Ain't Down Yet"; a doctor (David) providing a house call for George learns Zelda thinks she deserves more attention and treatment; Carol and David duet on "We Could Be Close"; a takeoff on *This is Your Life* has a tribute go awry when the honoree (Carol) has gained considerable weight since her glory years; the cast, guests and dancers do a musical salute to politics.

Comments: This is a surprisingly good installment considering that actress Paula Kelly and actor David Hartman are not associated with this sort of raucous comedy on display. The Q&A includes a girl saying she came to the series instead of going out with a guy. One wagers she made the right decision in terms of entertainment at least.

The delusional Nora is brought down to earth when a restaurant run by Lyle fails to produce the obsessive fans she tells Max she fears will attack her. She slaps Max often before Don Crichton's comment that there are no stars in the room makes her realize no one recognizes her. To prompt memories, she re-enacts a scene from a 1929 film in front of an unimpressed Stan Mazin, who tells her to take a walk. Max throws Stan out in response. Desperate, she takes off her coat to reveal her sagging breasts and emotes for the crowd, giving out the same look for every command shouted by Max. It is for naught, as a Swedish actress (Vicki) mistakes Nora for a waitress. Nora hits her with a salad and gooey dessert before being thrown out. Subtle it ain't, but this is a solid piece of comedy.

Wearing a pink shirt and green pants that are shocking in every sense of the word, Zelda sprays down George to prevent his germs from coming near her. She adjusts her large rear before letting David enter. Thinking he is a quack, Zelda interferes with David's examination by asking him to check on her irritated throat. Trying to accommodate her, David tells Zelda to take off her blouse. She hits him for the request and growls, "You animal!" David discovers Harvey has the flu while Zelda takes his stethoscope to perform a self examination. (In this season's blooper reel, Carol in one unaired taping put the stethoscope under her fake breast, cracking up the audience and the other actors.) David prepares a shot to help George, then injects Zelda so she will shut up and he will have peace of mind. It usually is smart for any Zelda sketch to have karma come back to bite her in the end, and this one is expertly done by all involved at every part.

The brief acting Paula does on this show comes when she brings a plump actress planning a comeback (Carol) into Jack La Lard's reducing salon. She leaves as Harvey surprises Carol with a camera and crew saying, "This is your lifetime!" Carol smacks him before sinking down into a coach and grimacing as he recounts her story. Her old singing partner (Lyle) is so dumb that he goes off stage when he cannot recognize her bloated figure. Carol's identical sister (Vicki) looks so spiffy and svelte in a black gown that Carol bumps her away. Worst of all, the arrival of her estranged husband (David) leads to a fight between the two of them, as she is livid that he has the gall to return after going out one night to get bread and never to return. Trying to keep the proceeds in check, Harvey has all the participants gather together for a group picture, and Carol wreaks revenge by knocking back everyone on the couch. The laughs are fast and furious here.

Hartman says this was his first time meeting Carol, and he was delighted. "They called and asked if I wanted to be on the show," Hartman says. His appearance was a rarity—an actor concurrently a regular on a dramatic TV series from another network, as his series *The New Doctors* (1969-1973) ended its run on NBC this season. The only other person fitting this qualification was Rock Hudson when *McMillan and Wife* ran on NBC from 1971-1977, who will make his full-fledged guest debut on Feb. 15, 1975.

Regarding his work here, he notes that "I didn't do sketch comedy, but when you're working with them, you just have to play straight to go along. They're just brilliant."

Hartman also recalls that regarding Paula Kelly's solo, "They used some interesting slo-mo stuff. She was a beautiful dancer." He says he did a number from the musical *Fiorello*, "Politics and Poker," as part of the show's finale as well.

"It was a wonderful experience doing the program," Hartman says in summarizing his appearance. "I don't know how they did that every week." Curiously, his future co-host on *Good Morning America*, Nancy Dussault, will do the series too—see Oct. 15, 1977.

March 17, 1973: Peggy Lee, William Conrad

* Q&A; a police sergeant (William) seems focused on everything but Roger's testimony about being mugged in "Carol & Sis"; William sings "A Quiet Girl" and "A Married Man"; Peggy performs "When I Found You" and joins Carol on "It's a Good Day"; Carol and Vicki present a duet on "I Don't Know Enough About You"; a series of skits mock TV series popular during this season, including *The Sonny and Cher Comedy Hour*, *Password*, *The Golddiggers* and *Maude*; a salute to songs written by Peggy Lee include the cast and guests harmonizing on "Manana."

Comments: The comedy here is some of the best the series ever offers, although William Conrad croaking tunes prevents this from being a classic. It includes a better than average "Carol & Sis" where William gently tweaks his current role as a detective on *Cannon* by being a wistful investigator more interested in relaxing and talking to Carol and Chris than hearing Roger recount being a victim of a crime. Chris leaves but Carol stays and learns that Roger's supposedly intimidating assailant was really a short, 60-year-old man who outran Roger after a neighborhood block, prompting her to laugh hysterically. She leaves and soon returns to inform Roger that in fact he had mugged the 60-year-old and not the other way around, as his wallet was left in their bedroom. Thinking quick, Roger claims to have found his wallet, but William said that does not end the case, since the alleged "mugger" is a municipal judge who probably will want to see Roger in court. The unexpected twists in this skit plus William's endearing portrayal make this a winner.

Even more enjoyable are the TV spoofs starting with "Stunny and Glare," with Carol and Harvey as the title couple (Harvey kneels on his knees to indicate the height difference) and Vicki as their daughter. As in the original series, the adults swap insults while the daughter smiles uncomprehendingly until she makes fun of the father as well. Adding to the verisimilitude, this uses the set for *The Sonny and Cher Comedy Hour*.

For "The Golgigglers," Carol, Vicki and five of the female dancers jiggle and squeal like morons as William, a famous author, reads to them about the Civil War. "I think we had no business being there," interrupts Carol to William's confusion. They cling all over him while he recites the Gettysburg Address before bursting out into frantic moves with the music. In *Backstage at the Dean Martin Show*, author Lee Hale claims he and other personnel laughed heartily at this send-up of a syndicated variety series spun off from *The Dean Martin Show*, where the women had been had been regulars since 1966 before getting their own program in 1971. Everyone executive producer Greg Garrison, that is, possibly because he was upset at making fun of a group he created for the show.

The richest roasting is the last. "Broad" has Harvey in a dress shirt and underwear getting booze from his home bar when his stepdaughter (Vicki) says there is a chorus of WASPs singing on the front porch that might bother her mother and his wife. Before they can intervene, Broad (Carol) enters and yells offstage, "Why don't you get some Mexican Americans in your group?" Wearing a dead-on outfit and hairdo to resemble Bea Arthur, and nicely approximating her voice, Carol mentions that

Vicki has a son that no one sees before greeting an applicant for a housekeeper. New Jersey, played by old series semi regular Isabel Sanford, now a regular on *All in the Family* (which coincidentally was where *Maude* was spun off into a series), is a militant woman who demands that Harvey do so much of her cleaning work if she is to join the household that he feels their gender roles have been reversed. He expresses his fear to Broad, who listens to him by having him sit on her lap and cuddle. This skit nails the conventions of the original series so well that it really helps seeing an episode of *Maude* in advance to get the full humor here.

Peggy Lee makes her fifth and last appearance on this show. William Conrad will return nearly two years later—see Jan. 25, 1975.

March 24, 1973: Family Show

The cast and dancers sing "Keep it in the Family"; Q&A; Carol, Harvey, Lyle and Vicki are dolls who come to life when put in bed; the dancers play feuding Hatfields and McCoys in a medley of "Dueling Banjos" and "Arkansas Traveler"; Vicki and Lyle are thieves hiding out in an X-rated movie theater; Carol and Lyle are orthopedic specialists celebrating the opening of their own offices; "The Old Old Movie" presents a spoof of *Random Harvest*, with Carol and Harvey as the leads; the Charwoman visits Carol's dressing room and characters emerge as she puts up the wardrobe.

Comments: Nearly everyone sings clad in pantsuits (Carol's is orange, Vicki's red, the female dancers yellow and male dancers off brown) before Harvey and Lyle join them on a set with leaves in the background, each sporting the first name of a dancer. Vicki leads the title tune, which mentions the half-dozen years the show has been on the air. After the number, Carol comes out in a black gown to do Q&A and praises *The Effect of Gamma Rays on Man-on-the-Moon Marigolds* ("It is one of the best movies I have seen") before she cracks up when a young lady asks if Carol was discovered when she was a cleaning lady at CBS. Next, Carol brings out a startled Vicki (still in her pantsuit) and announces, "Vicki, you got a gold record!" as she presents it to the singer of "The Night the Lights Went Out in Georgia." Another bit of serendipity follows when Carol tells Lyle a woman in the audience wants a kiss from him, and he brings out and sets up a table with checkered cloth, two chairs, a bottle and a candle that unfortunately goes out. Undaunted, Lyle pours out a little bubbly for his guest and they toast, with him adding, "I'm glad that we're up here, 'cause I'm a little light on the show!" That amuses the girl before she receives Lyle's kiss and he escorts her back to her seat.

In the first sketch a little girl (Cari Ann Wander) puts her dolls in bed and leaves, allowing Barbary (Carol) and Ben (Harvey) to come alive in her absence and complain about their treatment. They assume their former positions when the girl adds another doll, G.I. Jack (Lyle), who turns on Barbary considerably before the girl comes back with one more doll. This one is Betsy Wetsy (Vicki), whose mere name makes the rest of the dolls run off the bed. This is a silly but swift and short segment.

A good, offbeat presentation has the dancers dressed as feuding hillbillies, with Don Crichton wearing a crooked nose to boot. Following that is an acceptable if unexceptional skit where cops (the lead portrayed by Brad Trumbull) try to locate Vicki and Lyle, criminals on the run who accidentally duck into an erotic feature. Vicki cringes at what is shown on screen and hides behind beagle puss glasses while Lyle tells her to stay calm. When Brad and the other cops arrived, they are so mesmerized by what they see on screen that Vicki and Lyle are able to escape with their loot.

Also passable but longer in execution is Carol and Harvey as doctors signing "Dem Bones" to a skeleton in a stately fashion before they loosen up with some Champagne. Carol realizes they missed the elbow during their duet, so they perform an ode to it before they end up falling in love, naturally.

Better executed and more humorous is "Rancid Harvest," with Harvey (in a dead-on Ronald Colman impersonation) as an amnesiac in England in 1918 being treated by a hospital doctor (Lyle). Carol arrives with a squeeze box, which she gets stuck briefly on her chest when contracting the instrument and accidentally hurts the injured soldiers while playing. After being befuddled by Harvey's short-term memory problems (which produce several laughs), Carol persuades Harvey to live in her cottage, but he still has difficulties such as forgetting where the bathroom is located. Carol is happy nonetheless until she reads a newspaper report that Harvey's fiancée is searching for him and that he is really a lord. There is a great routine where Carol keeps beating a radio to bits as the voice of the announcer (Lyle) keeps attempting to deliver the news. She then takes advantage of Harvey's condition and tells him he asked her to marry him. Before that happens, however, Harvey goes outside and is hit by a taxi that drags him back to his ancestral home and reminds him who he really is.

In Act II, Harvey is now a mean groom to his butler (Lyle) and his fiancée (Vicki), and he needs a secretary to help him. Carol pops up as an applicant and tries to remind Harvey of their time together while he belittles her. It takes Vicki hitting Harvey on the head to jog his memory, and seeing what has happened, Vicki hits him again so that he reverts to his crusty self. Then Lyle opens a door and knocks both Harvey and Carol, giving her amnesia and causing Harvey to have a taxi hit her and bring her back to Harvey in her original form. It may sound contrived and confusing, but it is expertly done on stage and easily the best part of this show.

For the finale, as the Charwoman goes through Carol's discarded costumes, each comes to life, first Zelda, then Charo, Nora Desmond, Alice Portnoy and Stella Toddler, and all sing along to the tune "Without Me She is Nothing." It is a great display of overdubbing as well as onscreen trickery before it ends with the Charwoman sitting on a bucket on the empty soundstage to sing "It's Time to Say So Long" in full verse before leaving.

Although not the best show of the season, this episode did earn an Emmy nomination for writing in 1974 (the Emmy eligibility calendar at the time ran from March to March each year). It lost to the Feb. 16, 1974 episode of *The Carol Burnett Show*, with mostly different writers. There will be more on that situation shortly.

Final Notes for the Season

In the spring of 1973, CBS announced its Saturday night lineup for the next season would be *All in the Family*, *M*A*S*H*, *The Mary Tyler Moore Show*, *The Bob Newhart Show* and *The Carol Burnett Show*. Putting these powerhouse comedies back to back was so intimidating that an official at another network moaned to *Variety* that it wasn't fair.

"I think it was probably the best night of television in the history of the medium," CBS programming head Fred Silverman says in recalling arguably his greatest legacy forty years later. "Every one of them hit the bull's eye in terms of getting audiences. I think the lowest show of the night was a forty share." That meant that four out of all ten TV sets in use that night were watching the CBS lineup, an incredible feat then and even more so today. "It was a terrific night, and I can't think there's ever been a night to equal it."

Even so, there were guarded reasons to celebrate this boost for those on Carol's show. One involved the mixed Emmy results presented on May 23, 1973. The series won for writing (see Nov. 8, 1972), music direction (see Dec. 16, 1972) and Tim's work as a supporting performer, but choreography and art direction lost, and there was no nomination for Dave Powers (he did receive his only Directors Guild of America nomination for the series this year, however). Worst of all, it lost the statuette for Outstanding Variety Musical Series to *The Julie Andrews Hour*. The win was an upset, as that series stayed near the bottom of the ratings and had mixed critical reaction at best.

The Julie Andrews Hour also ends the two-year streak *The Carol Burnett Show* had for Best Variety Program from the Television Champion Awards, but Carol wins a record sixth straight time as Best Comedienne. That ceremony will end in 1974. The series also ends its three-year streak of at least one Golden Globe, getting only nominations for Carol, Harvey and Vicki (and for the first time no nomination for the series itself).

More problematic for the series was dissention among the writing staff. The friction between head writers Larry Siegel and Stan Hart and producers Buz Kohan and Bill Angelos became so great that the latter duo resigned, frustrated by the atmosphere.

"It did not end happily then," Angelos says. However, he notes that he did run into Larry Siegel at CBS a few years later and "He spent at least an hour I'd say apologizing, and it was heartfelt."

"I think good stuff was being done this year, I just don't think we were doing it," Kohan assesses of the standoff. "It was an untenable position by that last year. We split up that year as well."

Kohan remained active in the business, while Angelos curtailed his show business activities by the early 1980s to pursue spiritual and environmental activities. "When I left show business, I left," Angelos says. "I chose to work with the masses."

Hart and Siegel appeared poised to assume Angelos and Kohen's role in the aftermath, but Joe Hamilton decided he did not need the position and that they could remain head writers. That did not set well with the duo, and they decided to leave as well.

"Stan wasn't that comfortable to come back to the show, and we sort of had a falling out with Joe [Hamilton]," says Larry Siegel. "We all knew that the producers title to Joe was just a name, but we wanted that on our resumes." Ironically, like Kohan and Angelos, Siegel and Hart then parted professionally. Hart moved to New York, married a woman who had part of the Topps bubblegum fortune and stopped writing for TV.

Siegel had a new agent who pitched him to return to the series as a writer in 1977. "He contacted Joe, and Joe was happy to take me alone. But everybody then had partners, and it wasn't as exciting as before. I didn't do as many great or memorable things," he recalls of his second go-round, which lasted just one year as Carol decided to end the series.

If these departures were not enough, Gail Parent, Woody Kling, Robert Hilliard and Tom Patchett and Jay Tarses left the series as well. "Everyone didn't get along with everyone else," says Arnie Kogen of the writers' situation. "They cleaned house, and myself and Roger Beatty were the only ones to survive."

"I have to say that I can't remember ever having any conversations with Stan and Larry," Beatty says of this period. That probably helped his status in being a returning writer.

Parent went back to freelancing and eventually producing, scoring a success with *The Golden Girls* sitcom from 1985-1992. Kling did scripts for Saturday morning cartoons until his death in 1988. Hilliard faded from view with few and minor credits thereafter. Patchett and Tarses had more success writing and producing *The Bob Newhart Show* before separating for other writing and producing assignments in the 1980s and 1990s.

For the summer replacement, CBS opted to move *Mission: Impossible* back to the time slot it started in the fall of 1972 for its last shows in reruns, while running *60 Minutes* in the Friday time slot *Mission: Impossible* previously occupied. *Mission: Impossible* stayed there until Sept. 8. *The Carol Burnett Show* returned a week later with a virtually new slate of writers with their own mission of making sure their work met if not surpassed the same high public and critical reception of their predecessors.

Carol and Vicki sing as Elizabethan vendors in the musical finale with Ken Berry for the Oct. 20, 1973 episode. By this point Berry was a regular guest at least once every season and Vicki's recording of "The Night The Lights Went Out in Georgia" had sold more than 3 million copies. It would be the last big hit written by Bobby Russell, who divorced Vicki in 1974 as he became jealous of her success. Courtesy of Getty Images.

Chapter 8

1973-1974: New Writers, and a New Family

Young girl: "You think you're a good actor?"
Carol (looking down at her own chest):
"I'm a better actor than an actress!"—From the Oct. 20, 1973 show

Crew Additions This Season:
Supervising Writer: Ed Simmons
Writers: Gary Belkin, Bill Richmond and Gene Perret, Rudy DeLuca and Barry Levinson, Dick Clair and Jenna McMahon, Barry Harman
Music Director: Irwin Kostal (temporary replacement for Peter Matz Feb. 23, 1974, March 16, 1974 and March 23, 1974 at least)

Ed Simmons joined *The Carol Burnett Show* as its new head writer with an impressive pedigree. In the 1950s he and his writing partner, Norman Lear, won kudos for their scripts for *The Colgate Comedy Hour* and other variety series. Writing solo in the 1960s, he did a smooth job transitioning *The Red Skelton Show* from a half hour show in 1961 to an hour-long entry in 1964, when he left to pursue other projects, including helming scripts for *The Jerry Lewis Show* from 1967-1969 and *This is Tom Jones* in 1969, before *The Carol Burnett Show* came calling for his services at the end of the 1972-1973 season.

"I think that after the turmoil of that season, Carol wanted a solid guy on the show," says Arnie Kogen of the decision to recruit Simmons. "He was a pacifying force."

One writer to work with Simmons later on the series, Bob Illes, described him as "a beatnik kind of guy, old school." Illes thinks Simmons may have envied how Norman Lear, his ex-partner, was the top situation comedy producer in the 1970s, earning fame and fortune helming *All in the Family*, *Sanford and Son*, *Maude* and more. Even so, all indications otherwise are that he was very happy in his new position.

Simmons managed his writers fairly loosely, relying on their input rather than dictating orders to them. Sometimes a writing team would be asked to create sketches for certain guests. Otherwise, there would be brainstorming sessions for any premises that were funny. There appears to be more rewriting under Simmons than previous head writers to fix problems on the show being produced that week—even edits made between the dress and air tapings—but in general it was business as usual for the writers as in past years.

The new writers on the show came from many different backgrounds. Gene Perret and Bill Richmond both had written for *Rowan and Martin's Laugh-In*, but they were hired individually before being reunited on *The Carol Burnett Show*.

"I had been writing on *The New Bill Cosby Show* (1972-1973) that year, and either the powers that be on the Burnett show saw some sketches they liked and asked who wrote them, or they asked some people on the Cosby show about writers," recalls Perret. He interviewed with both Joe Hamilton and Ed Simmons and made the cut.

"Joe Hamilton was the real power on that show. . . . Probably most of the decisions to accept a sketch or reject came from Carol and Joe," Perret says. He says Simmons served as a liaison between the writers to the star and the producer in this regard.

"All of the bosses, Joe, Ed and Carol—after all, it was her show—were all understanding of writers and their problems," adds Perret. "None of them would rant and rave if a sketch didn't work or some of the lines weren't funny. We all sensed that they realized that writers have good days and off days. Knowing that allows a writer much more freedom to create."

Perret and Richmond specialized in outlandish, absurd situations taken to extremes. They most like the one on the ninth season opener (Sept. 13, 1975), where Tim Conway played a brooding soldier left with no internal organs after swallowing a grenade to save his company. A queen (Carol) attempts to honor him, but the "hollow hero" rebuffs her medals—he wants a pony instead.

"The reason this is our favorite is because it was so much fun to write," says Perret. "It derived from a joke. We put it into sketch form, and each line seemed to be a punch line. We laughed uproariously as we were writing it. Others would come into our office to find out what was so funny. As we described the sketch, they laughed just as loudly."

Among those writers laughing was Gary Belkin, a newcomer who cut his comic teeth on *Caesar's Hour* and earned his first two Emmy nominations there in the 1950s. Another nomination followed for *The Danny Kaye Show* in 1964 and a win in 1970 as one of the scribes for the special *Annie, the Women in the Life of a Man*. He also wrote for *Mad Magazine* in the early 1960s, joining the ranks of Stan Hart, Larry Siegel and Jack Mendelsohn of those who wrote for that publication and *The Carol Burnett Show*.

Simmons had to accept at least two new writers on his staff without consent. Barry Levinson and Rudy DeLuca had worked together as improvisational actors on late night television in Los Angeles in the 1960s before they became sketch contributors and occasional bit players on *The Tim Conway Comedy Hour* in 1970. After that bombed, they scrambled to find work and had to go over to the United Kingdom for their next regular variety series, *The Marty Feldman Comedy Machine*, which aired in the United States on ABC in the summer of 1972. Job offers stagnated after that for a year.

"We were considered outsiders of comedy, a little too crazy at that point in time," recalls Levinson of the duo's reputation. But they had a powerful agent then working at the William Morris Agency and a connection with a favorite on the series that helped them secure a spot with *The Carol Burnett Show*.

"I'm guessing that Michael Ovitz was our agent, and we had worked with Tim Conway, so it was probably a combination of both," Levinson says.

"He'd been trying to get us on the show for years," DeLuca says of Ovitz.

The duo's next obstacle was the skeptical new head writer. "Ed Simmons didn't quite understand us," asserts DeLuca. "At the beginning, we had a rough time. We went weeks without a sketch." Simmons excluded their material until the season's sixth show.

However, "Dr. Jekyll and Ms. Hyde" was a hit when it aired on Oct. 20, 1973, and the two were busy thereafter for the next three years. Levinson cites Tim as the Old Man conductor in the Australia show (Dec. 8, 1973) and the Tim-Harvey submarine sketch (Feb. 16, 1974) as prime examples of the physical humor he and DeLuca created.

Levinson allows that their improvisational background did help occasionally in writing sketches. "Sometimes we would just be playing out something and write it down. You'd play the character and do that." He adds, "We did such crazy sketches that they never came from daily life."

The other new major writing team played a pivotal role in freshening the series with a setup that supplanted the increasingly tired "Carol & Sis" skits. Carol, Roger and Chrissy relocated to an apartment, but the change of scenery did not increase the humor level. Worse, the addition of Jim Connell as an elevator operator added only irritation and confusion as to why he was part of the mix. He lasted just three episodes in 1973. Like much of her audience, Carol found "Carol & Sis" bland and wanted something better.

Enter Dick Clair and Jenna McMahon. The duo previously acted on TV as a couple on *The Funny Side*, a NBC comedy variety series in 1971. Eager to prove their writing chops for the series, they worked for weeks to create a bit for Carol, Harvey, Vicki and Roddy McDowall on the March 16, 1974 show. The called the skit "The Family."

"'The Family' was purely based on Dick or Jenna's family," notes Arnie Kogen. Both were shocked at what happened during the table reading. Carol was to play the mother and Vicki the flighty daughter married to Harvey, but Carol felt drawn to the latter character, Eunice, who reminded her of her own mother with unfulfilled dreams. She not only switched parts with Vicki, now playing cranky Mama

Harper, but also added a Texas accent that all the others adopted too except Roddy McDowall, who decided to keep his incongruous British lilt even though he played a member of this Southern clan.

The changes upset Dick and Jenna, but Carol remained steadfast in her approach. Bob Mackie had Vicki play a senior citizen wearing just a soft round baby bunting "body" into a slip covered with a polyester frock, gray wig, glasses, knee socks, old shoes and no lipstick or eye makeup. By doing this, narrowing her eyes, jutting her chin and using her Southern mother-in-law's twang, Vicki created an indelible character. Her interactions with Carol and Harvey as her daughter and son-in-law respectively are an immediate hit. By next season "The Family" will be a regular feature and "Carol & Sis" will die out.

This segment airs a day before Carol stars on CBS in *6 RMS RIV VU*, a TV adaptation of a recent Broadway comedy. She taped the special in New York City during a break in taping her series in February 1974, and it earns Carol her first Emmy nomination apart from her show. Clearly, all transitions this season were working well for Carol.

Sept. 15, 1973: Jim Nabors

* Carol performs "Come Back to Me" with special lyrics in the introduction and later offers "True Blue Love"; an elevator operator (Jim Connell) is in love with Carol amid Roger's confusion on "Carol & Sis"; Jim sings "And I Love You So"; a two-part parody of *Kung Fu* features Jim in the lead role played by David Carradine, Harvey as his master teacher, Carol as a squaw, Vicki as a saloon gal and Lyle as a prejudiced cowboy out to kill Jim and Carol; the cast and dancers perform in a medley of band numbers.

Comments: Hewing closely to the mix of what the previous new creative team used to open last season, this opener is a pretty fair balance of comedy and music. The latter is more effective than the former, as only one of the two skits hits the mark. The flop is "Carol & Sis," wherein a new character resembling a young Marvin Kaplan in a shag cut provides an unpleasant addition. Talented Jim Connell has to play a thankless role—a geek in his twenties with stalker tendencies in his devotion toward fortysomething Carol. The concept does not lend itself to hilarity except for Roger's stunned reaction that someone younger than him finds his wife sexy. Even so, the show inexplicably will have him come back to do the same routine on Sept. 29, 1973 and Dec. 1, 1973.

Better is the elaborate TV series spoof "Yung Fool." Jim Nabors dons a skullcap to appear bald and assumes his Gomer Pyle twang to imply idiocy. He visits a saloon menaced by Black Archie (Lyle) and run by Vicki, who interviews a new Native American applicant named after her parents, Red Fox (Carol). Wearing a white martial combat outfit with black belt, Jim shows his moves but detests violence, to Carol and Vicki's chagrin, as bigoted Black Archie plans to kill them all. Jim explains his beliefs in flashbacks to his old mentor (Harvey), a bald philosopher who is unimpressed by Jim doing everything he tells him, such as burning his hands by holding onto a steaming pot.

For the second part, Harvey hilariously defends making a pass at a young Asian woman (an unidentified actress) as fulfilling the needs of an old man living alone in a garden before returning to the present. Vicki gives an impassioned patriotic speech about ecumenicalism to impress Black Archie, but it fails. As Carol puts it, "In the name of my people, I call you Talking Bull." She plans to marry Jim but must endure another flashback, this time with her involved in a purity test by Harvey prior to her wedding. Told she has to walk across a footbridge to show she is chaste, she falls off and gets water up to her knee and quips, "Because I don't go all the way!" Back to the present, Jim reluctantly fights in slow motion, aping the convention of *Kung Fu*, and defeats Black Archie, prompting Harvey to "flash forward" to marry Jim and Carol. But Carol beats up Harvey to get a ring and informs Jim that things are going to be different when they get married as she starts bossing him around. Although somewhat politically incorrect, this is a generally hilarious parody throughout.

Incidentally, this season marks the first time since Nov. 9, 1970 where *The Carol Burnett Show* had another show besides Jim's to feature only one guest—in fact, there will be several of them. Others will include Gloria Swanson (Sept. 29, 1973), John Byner (Oct. 27, 1973), Carl Reiner (Jan. 19, 1974) and Steve Lawrence (March 9, 1974).

Sept. 22, 1973: Tim Conway, Charo

A meek man (Tim) attempts to get a haircut in a unisex salon run by a mouthy, impersonal stylist (Carol); Charo strums and sings "Midnight Guitar"; Tim tries to stay awake during a boring speech by Vicki; a mild-mannered reporter (Tim) has an interview with a Hispanic bombshell (Charo) interrupted by her overprotective mother (Carol); Carol learns from a radio reporter (Lyle) about everything that is putting her life in jeopardy; the Campbellock Dancers groove to "Scorpio"; Lyle leaves an oblivious Carol for Vicki at a party; Carol, Vicki and Charo do "Luck Be a Lady" with the dancers.

Comments: For a rare *Carol Burnett Show* of this era without Harvey in it (with no reason given for his disappearance), the results still work, although this episode varies wildly in tone from raucous to run-of-the-mill. The first skit has Tim bedeviled by inconsiderate behavior by Carol, sporting a huge wavy platinum silver coif. His barber chair bobs up and down and spins around while Carol preps him (Tim earns deserved applause for this), he nearly drowns being shampooed and gets a hot towel dropped on his lap by Carol, who keeps forgetting Tim's name. After having a mudpack and a hair dryer cap being on his face, Tim stumbles around, hits a wall and falls into a laundry bag that Don Crichton removes without realizing there is a person in it. This is a good sketch but it could have been funnier and shorter.

Charo does an excellent job of displaying her real talents as a guitarist and vocalist in her number, a mellow offering that belies her reputation as the hyperactive "coochie coochie" girl. "I was playing one night on *The Tonight Show* a classical number, and Carol saw it," Charo recalls. "She insisted that after the first comedy act that we see a side of reality from me on her show. I was extremely grateful. I was a very well-trained musician at the age of sixteen, seventeen, eighteen. She told me, 'I want you to play the guitar. I want the audience to see both sides of you.'" The segment succeeds in that mission.

Following it is another amusing effort with Tim that should have been edited and tightened some to be really great. As Vicki drones on at a podium, Tim sits next to Lyle in a dais in front of her and gets drowsy. His hairpiece falls off and his cigar lands in his lap, and he even uses Lyle's shoulder as a pillow at one point. Exhausted, Tim finally pulls the tablecloth over himself to go to bed to wind up this decently done pantomime.

The show really sparks next when Tim meets Lyle, who represents Chiquita (Charo), a lively Latina. She alternately makes moves on Tim and pushes him away, haughtily announcing, "You think I was born tomorrow!?" The festivities end when Carol appears as Chiquita's mother, wearing the same shiny red halter top and tights as her daughter, only with sagging breasts and huge buttocks, an outfit that convulses the audience. Carol's mimicry of Charo's accent and hip shaking amuse viewers as well, as she tells her daughter she does not trust her and puts soap in her mouth for talking about her body. As Charo shimmies into a corner, Carol complains about what her daughter as done to Tim, but his dropping of words like "bedtime" and "behind" makes her think he is impure, and she slaps him across the couch several times before banishing him. This is wonderful, one of the best and funniest uses of a guest star's persona ever on this series.

"The funniest thing that everybody says they saw was Carol playing my mother," notes Charo, pointing out the skit's high number of hits on YouTube. She vividly recalls seeing Carol's outfit the first time. "She knocked on my dressing room door, and I was hysterical when I saw it." Carol told her she was showing her the getup so that Charo would not crack up on stage when they did the sketch. "But it is so difficult, because you're so funny!" Charo responded, adding that Carol's accent and shaking of the fake breasts—or "those maracas down to the floor," as Charo termed them—amused her endlessly as well. Nonetheless, she composed herself and did the bit perfectly straitlaced, immensely adding to its appeal and effectiveness.

The excitement ebbs in the next segment that starts slowly but does improve. Arriving home, Carol engages in trivial dialogue and actions until reports from a radio announcer (Lyle) inadvertently creep her out about the hazards she has in her house. For example, when he talks about an oil spill, she gets petroleum out of her faucet. Lyle mentions that a brand of tranquilizers has problems, and Carol's knees buckle after taking the medication. It culminates with Lyle (playing Carol's husband) coming home to her relief, but he tells her he is so depressed about being fired that he is experiencing a personal "power failure" and is thus impotent. Carol's mugging and increased pacing as the complication ensure make this ultimately a winning effort—but just barely.

Real excitement comes when Carol introduces a sextet of dancers she saw profiled recently on a Los Angeles news station. Formed by Don Campbell and choreographed here by Toni Basil (she had the Number One hit "Mickey" in 1982), the Campbellock Dancers provide the funkiest entertainment ever seen on *The Carol Burnett Show*, accompanied by a recent slinky top ten pop hit. A member of this troupe showing an impressive early example of the "locking" dance style is Fred Berry, who will become Rerun on the ABC sitcom *What's Happening!* in 1977.

The last skit has Vicki's surprise party for her friend (Carol) and the latter's new husband (Lyle) resulting in him going after Vicki instead. As Carol belts out "As Long as He Needs Me" from *Oliver*, Lyle strips her of her flower and dress to give to Vicki and finally knocks her down before leaving with Vicki. This is a fresh take on the typical "Carol loses a man to Vicki due to looks" scenario, and it is short and effective.

Dressed as jockeys along with several of the male dancers (the remaining ones are men placing bets on the horse races), Carol, Vicki and Charo present a pleasant rendition of a tune from *Guys and Dolls* that nonetheless runs longer than needed. Following that, Carol pretends to be in pain as she mimics Charo's maneuvers during the closing.

Although Charo appeared just once on the series, Carol has indicated she liked working with her. "She's really a terrific girl," she told Dick Cavett in 1974. Charo is similarly effusive about Carol and the series. "She became friends with whoever she was working with," she says. "She was very nice to me with the guitar, the costumes and everything."

Sept. 29, 1973: Gloria Swanson

Q&A; Carol and Roger try to persuade a lovesick elevator operator to drop his obsession of her in "Carol & Sis"; Gloria sings and dances the tango with Stan Mazin; Bert plans to play golf despite Molly's skepticism in "The Old Folks"; Carol and Vicki perform "Mama's Got a Date"; Harvey is overcome with guilt as he tries to tell his wife (Carol) he has cheated on her; the Charwoman plays a film in an abandoned silent movie projection room and imagines Charlie Chaplin (Swanson) invites her to join him in his Little Tramp guise on screen.

Comments: In her 1980 autobiography *Swanson on Swanson*, this show's guest star called this show her favorite TV appearance ever, and it does display her to excellent effect, with her work compensating for a few deficiencies in other parts of the episode. In the Q&A, an actor in the audience asks her to confirm while they shot *Pete 'n' Tillie* that he accidentally broke two ribs of the wardrobe lady, and a woman compliments Carol's appearance before Gloria comes out. Carol shows the first Nora Desmond sketch (see Dec. 29, 1971) and notes how Gloria wrote a letter telling her how much she loved the parody. The final scene of the real *Sunset Boulevard* airs before Gloria emerges in a black-and-white gown accompanied with Lyle. Gloria thanks Carol for giving Lyle to her and is intrigued to learn he recently posed for *Playgirl* magazine. "Do you fool around?" she asks him before learning that he is not a "weirdo" and goes for Harvey instead. Gloria does a fine job of delivering the somewhat stilted scripted repartee here.

The "Carol & Sis" installment kicks off the show sluggishly, as Carol has invited her apartment building's young, bespectacled elevator man (Jim Connell) to dinner in order to convince him how much Roger loves her and give up his pursuit of her. When the man arrives with flowers, Roger and Carol's passionate kiss fail to make an impression on him, nor does Roger's attempts to explain unconvincingly his love of Carol and even Roger's attempt to match up Chrissy with the guy. Finally, the elevator man gets the message and says he thought it was no problem to say how much he loves Carol while knowing and respecting her marriage. Carol apologizes for the situation and invites him to dinner—and he responds saying they can go to the movies while Roger and Chrissy do the dishes. Jim Connell gets to appear in the kick line at the show's end and will return on Dec. 1, 1973, but his character remains an unappealing one to watch.

Next, Gloria looks smooth along with Stan Mazin and his pomade-covered hair and says "groovy" to boot. (Mazin says he got to dance with Gloria because Don Crichton was too tall to match well with the petite actress.) Following it was "The Old Folks," where Bert brings out his clubs to play the links over Molly's doubts. "Your old bag is cracked and dry!" she gripes. "Nobody said you had to come!" he rejoinders. Trying to be affectionate with Molly, he grabs her leg. She says it reminds her of their mailman during the postal strike—"He couldn't deliver either!" As the jokes indicate, for the most part this bit and the song accompanying it at the end do little more than kill time.

The big revelation in Carol and Vicki's number is that after they appear as teenage girls in pajamas singing their number about their mother's big romance, the person in question does arrive in the form of Harvey as Mother Marcus, showing "her" ring to her two daughters. It's a funny enough payoff, as is the next sketch, where Harvey brings roses and acts nervous to an oblivious Carol before admitting his adulterous ways and vowing never to repeat the acts. Carol says she understands, then she poisons him with cinnamon.

The Charwoman fantasy is a big step up from the so-so bits preceding it, as Gloria's dead-on Little Tramp transports Carol into "his" black-and-white film and romances her while chased by a cop (Harvey). Gloria mimics the way Lyle woos Vicki in a fancy restaurant by filling the Charwoman's boot with Champagne before the Charwoman insists she must return to the present. Gloria bids her adieu with a flower. When the movie ends, Carol is back in the projection room with a flower in her pocket, and she sees Chaplin on screen blowing her a kiss before she sings a tune.

At the end, Carol thanks Paramount for the use of the *Sunset Boulevard* clip and promotes the studio's new movie, *Scalawag*, as good for the whole family. *Scalawag* turned out to disappoint the studio, which is the same that can be said of several parts of this show without Gloria. Oh, well.

Oct. 6, 1973: Helen Reddy, John Byner

Q&A; a comic monologue by John; thinking that she is dying, Nora Desmond enlists George Jessel (John) to provide an appropriate eulogy for her upcoming funeral and runs through the possibilities with him; Helen sings "Don't Mess With a Woman"; a best legs contest; a happily married Hollywood couple (Carol and Harvey) go at each other's throats due to insinuations made by interfering gossip columnist Rona Rumor (Vicki) while interviewing them; Helen, Carol and the dancers present "A Little Bit of Sunday" and "Dixie Firehouse," with a spoof of several commercials between the numbers.

Comments: Helen Reddy and John Byner previously worked together professionally. "Helen opened for me at Mr. Kelly's nightclub in Chicago before working together on any TV show," John notes. "I love Helen and think that she is a terrific talent." Together, they are dynamite on this show, one of the season's best.

The Q&A begins with trivial queries about Carol's fluency in French, her age and her summer plans before sparking when someone asks if it is true that redheads have hot tempers. "I wouldn't know," she says, showing her dark roots to applause and laughter. She jokes about posing for Hugh Hefner in *Playboy* and says her favorite game shows are *Password*, *Split Second* and *Jeopardy!* Finally, when a woman says she gave Harvey a wild pair of glasses for Carol to wear, Carol interjects that "He wears them himself!"

Introducing John by saying "We just love him around here," the impressionist does a routine about singers that is rather inconsequential until he launches into dead-on impersonations of Johnny Mathis, Frank Sinatra and Elvis Presley. He thrusts his hips so much like the latter that he is shot from behind, presumably to placate the censor.

Max slaps a doctor (Lyle) repeatedly for saying Nora Desmond is suffering from an ordinary virus, as Madame has nothing common about herself. Nora enters down the stairs bellowing Max's name and reveals a pair of sagging breasts while proclaiming she is dying. George Jessel (John) arrives and reels off sample eulogies he did for others, but none meet with her favor, nor does a new one he offers as Nora stages her death. Max chokes George, who is so desperate that he delivers another effort like a musical. A still unimpressed Nora decides she will give her own eulogy and makes George pretend to be a corpse. After several failed attempts, George gets up and leaves the freaky scene, only to be shot by Max. Nora tells him to put him in the pool along with the other bodies. Carol's devoted fan, Kathy Clements, says this was her favorite sketch on the series.

After Helen's song, Carol holds a best legs contest, with the joke being that Harvey, Lyle, John and three men dancers are the one displaying their gams behind a curtain covering their top halves. This is an amusing variation on what happened earlier on the Feb. 12, 1968 show. (For the record, the winner was bearded dancer Eddie Heim.)

Next, a monotone Vicki twisting the statements made by Carol and Harvey into something sinister for her reporter commentary is the central conceit of the Hollywood couple skit. Done swiftly and nimbly by the participants, it leads to Carol and Harvey having a loud fight that Vicki then captures by a cameraman (Don Crichton) she signals to come and film the brouhaha. It's a bit that really clicks on all counts.

Helen and Carol's two beautifully sung duets with the dancer bookend the series' best collection of commercial send-ups ever, with everything scoring. Harvey is a sergeant in drag telling Lyle about the great shave he has and then hitting him with the purse, complaining "You never call!" and cracking Lyle up. Vicki points at the neck of an embarrassed priest (John) and yells "Dirt around the collar!" (People shouted "Ring around the collar!" to those with messy shirts in the original.) Lyle shows lousy furniture he built by hand that collapses when he sprays cleaner on the items.

The most elaborate and hilarious parody follows. Helen gives her husband (Harvey) margarine, and he suddenly gets a crown on his head. "Your majesty," Lyle says as he enters, bows and warns a stunned Harvey about discontent in his kingdom. A ragged peasant (John) stabs Harvey, and a courtier (Vicki) runs by, crying out "The king is dead! Long live the king!" A shocked Helen returns to the kitchen and asks what happened. "I don't want any more of that margarine!" moans Harvey before dying. This is a perfect example of taking a message to its logical extreme and wringing laughs out of it.

But wait, there's more! Lyle has black tape over his underarms to indicate where perspiration stains are located, which a grossed-out Carol rips off, to his pain. Euell Gibbons (John) eats everything outdoors until he is shown to have escaped from an insane asylum. Bing Crosby (John) swings in a hammock while his wife (Helen) makes breakfast. "No women's lib for my old lady," crows John before she pours orange juice on his head and he attempts to croon afterward. John's imitation is humorously dead on here. Finally, Carol greets a locker room of football players (the male dancers), and compliments them all until one of them pulls them into the shower, to her enjoyment.

The combination of John and Helen is a potent one. The series will team them together again for an equally fulfilling installment next season—see Nov. 9, 1974.

Oct. 13, 1973: Eydie Gorme, Paul Sand

Carol plays a dirty blonde celebrating the release of her husband (Harvey) from jail at a diner where she insults several people to his chagrin; Eydie sings "Take One Step"; Paul is a nervous newlywed trying to find a hotel to celebrate his honeymoon with his wife (Carol); Harvey appears with the male dancers in a medieval kingdom production number; a tribute to film series roasts Dr. Kildare, the Cisco Kid, Tarzan and the Wolfman; a finale inspired by the Bowery Boys has Carol, Harvey, Paul, Eydie and two male dancers play a gang who sing "Gee Officer Krupke."

Comments: The first third of this episode is tedious before it picks up the pace and becomes a winner, sparked by Harvey's featured number. Before that, there is an acknowledgment of thanks to Peter Matz and two overlong flat skits broken up by Eydie singing her latest single, which had some minor action on the adult contemporary music chart. The initial diner sketch includes Vicki as a floozy waitress (Carol's character even calls herself that), a cop (Bob Duggan) and a leather biker (Lyle). Carol insults the latter two, and Lyle prepares to fight her when Harvey accidentally stabs him. He plants the weapon on Carol and celebrates her being taken away with Vicki.

That's much ado about nothing, as is the routine with Paul confessing to Carol that he is driving by hotels because he misses how much they were in love when they were single and is afraid the honeymoon will be a disappointment. If that makes little sense, imagine how it plays out with Paul zooming past hotels and Carol screaming at him over and over repeatedly. Paul differs in recalling it years later, however. "It was such great fun," he said between laughs. "I was just sort of shy about sex. What a great show that was."

Harvey's performance of "Royalty," a song from his upcoming movie *Huckleberry Finn*, sloughs off the show's creeping lethargy. Dressed regally by Bob Mackie as a king with Ernie Flatt's male crew joining him as members of his court, it is a rousing bit.

The blackouts concerning movie series are similarly bright. Young Dr. Kildare (Paul) finds himself facing a doddering senior surgeon (Harvey in a great Lionel Barrymore impersonation) who insists the junior physician needs to give a nose job to a patient who is dead. The Cisco Kid (Paul) and Pancho (Lyle) meet at their favorite cantina to reunite with sweet Carmelita (Carol in her Charo routine), who claims to still be pure even though Zorro's "Z" is slashed on the seat of her pants. Tarzan (Lyle in a coat without a shirt) joins Jane (Carol in a superb Maureen O'Sullivan characterization) in a fancy New York restaurant and tries to follow etiquette but no waiters will serve them. Seeing she is ignored too, Jane gets attention by doing a Tarzan yell.

The longest and best parody has Carol and Paul entering an old castle and meeting a white-haired hag (Eydie). She hears a howling wolf and says "My master is calling." Eydie screams off (to applause) while Vicki emerges as an ancient fortune teller who shames Paul and Carol for seeing what they did last night. The flustered couple learns that a werewolf will bite Carol tonight unless she stops him with a stick with a silver tip, a wooden stake through the heart or a Bavarian cream pie in the face, or as Carol puts it, "A stick, a stake and a shtick." Harvey arrives as the owner who grimaces when he hears talk about a full moon and plans to transform into a wolf until hit by the pie in the puss. There is applause for that as well as Harvey's exaggerated death scene, where he says, "Cheerio!" before passing away. Carol and Paul leave hurriedly thereafter when Vicki says a physician down the street can help them—he is Dr. Frankenstein.

For the closing number, Lyle plays a cop who hears the gang whistle "Pop Goes the Weasel" and threatens to arrest them before they break into a tune from *West Side Story*. After this lively presentation ends, Carol follows her usual anti-pollution message by doing "It's Time to Say So Long" in the same doofus voice she employed in the sketch.

Interestingly, Sand will be back on the show three weeks with Eydie's husband, Steve Lawrence—see Nov. 3, 1973 for more info.

Oct. 20, 1973: Jack Weston, Ken Berry

Q&A; Jack and Carol share a common interest in trivial facts on a date; Ken performs "It's Not Where You Start" with the dancers; Ken is a patient whose operation is in jeopardy due to bickering between three doctors (Harvey, Jack and Carol) and a nurse (Vicki); Carol is a tackily dressed vocalist doing "The Lady is a Tramp"; Jack learns that a singer (Carol) is just as loud and brassy off stage as on; "Dr. Jekyll and Ms. Hyde" involves gender switching between Carol, Harvey, Vicki and Lyle; Ken, Carol and Vicki join the dancers in "New Elizabethan Rhythm."

Comments: In the DVD introduction to this episode, Harvey says, "This is a hummer," then corrects himself to say he meant "humdinger." Actually, it is more of the former, humming along well but just shy of being among the all-time best, with top contributions by Jack Weston and Ken Berry ("our old buddy" and "so great with his body," Carol says of them respectively in the commentary). The Q&A sets a nice tone, with four Campfire Girls making Carol an honorary member and supplying three dolls for each of her daughters. Carol reveals she has no plans to make a milk commercial like Mark Spitz and that Vicki's "The Night the Lights Went Out in Georgia" has sold more than 3 million copies, and jokingly agrees with a woman that she cannot stand having the gorgeous Lyle and Harvey around her. Finally, to the query of "Do you get nervous before you go on?" Carol says "No," then fakes fainting on stage.

Carol and Jack are dates matched by a computer who think they have nothing in common until they realize they can spout obscure records that make them amorous, like the longest distance a Champagne cork was popped. They connect nicely until Jack suggests they wed and try to surpass the number of having the most children, leading Carol to throw him out. Afterward, she notes how she thinks she will beat the record for oldest living virgin. This fun bit is especially impressive regarding how much obscure information Jack and Carol have to deliver authoritatively.

Ken's number starts with the male dancers at his 1937 high school graduation, then repeats the song with the female ones at a 1944 USO and finally with all the dancers in Las Vegas in 1973. This routine sports incredible costumes and sets, and Ken is even more energetic than usual—and he takes a pie to the face at the end.

Next up, Ken is on the operating table when Carol demands a divorce from Harvey before starting the procedure. She talks about suffering from Harvey ignoring her while Ken gives great reactions as he endures pain as the anesthetic wears off. Ken's efforts to have them resolve their problems and get his operation going are undermined when the nurse (Vicki) reveals she has been seeing Harvey, prompting harsh words from Carol (she calls Vicki "Silicone Sally" at one point). Harvey leaves and Jack plans to take over, but he is upset because Vicki is his wife. Disgusted, he and Carol both leave, and a worried Ken calls for someone to help him. The answer comes from an elderly doctor (Tim Conway in a cameo) who stumbles all over the operating room in response. After the sketch ends, Carol asks for a round of applause for both Ken and Tim, telling the audience after Tim takes a bow that the staff called him up the morning of this taping to put the final touch on this. It was a smart move, and it showed that the sketch needed a little more tightening to be great rather than just acceptable.

After a funny bit with Carol wearing "granny glasses" and mugging as a homely torch singer, she channels Ethel Merman and even does "There's No Business Like Show Business" at a nightclub at the start. A patron (Jack) bribes the maitre d' (Lyle) to meet her, but to his shock, she belts out statements in talking just as much as she does when singing. As he tries to run away, she challenges him with "Anything You Can Do" and grabs onto him and sings "Together." Even for those without a rudimentary knowledge of Merman and her hits, this will produce some chuckles.

In "Dr. Jekyll and Ms. Hyde," the doctor (Harvey) involuntarily changes into a woman (Carol), and his fellow physician (Lyle) becomes a woman (Vicki) uncontrollably too. The transformations between the participants behind a sofa and curtains are cleverly handled, with the audience most enjoying when Lyle goes from dancing with Carol into doing the same with Harvey, who pleads, "Just one more time around, OK?" Lyle reveals his situation and wants to marry Carol, but she refuses, so he proposes they drink a potion to split all the personalities. It succeeds, except the two women now have the voices of two men and vice versa. This take on gender identity is splendidly handled by all here.

At an old European street festival, Carol and Vicki are selling their wares while Ken, a performing minstrel, sings "New Elizabethan Rhythm" and joins the dancers. This leads into Vicki and Carol singing "Fascinating Rhythm" before returning to their sales duties. It is a nice albeit rather standard finale.

This would be the only appearance of Jack and Ken this season. Some of this show was preempted this evening due to live coverage of what became known as the "Saturday night massacre," where two attorneys general resigned on the same evening to protest President Richard Nixon's firing of Archibald Cox, the special Watergate prosecutor.

Oct. 27, 1973: John Byner

* Q&A; Chris hosts a group therapy session wherein Carol and Roger proceed to get on each other's nerves while sharing their emotions; John appears as a cowboy ready for a showdown in a saloon with Harvey; Carol sings "I've Gotta Be Me"; John's testimony during a trial meets with scoffing from a courtroom stenographer (Carol) who takes over grilling him from the attorney (Harvey); the cast parodies the daytime tribute show *The Girl in My Life*; a finale of tunes that have kept Americans' spirit soaring since the start of World War I to the present.

Comments: The fact that John Byner guests solo on the show just three weeks after his debut indicates just how much Carol and her staff appreciated his wacky sense of humor and great vocal and physical dexterity. This episode is slightly less wild and effective than his premiere shot, though none of it is his fault. It is a shame he is kept out of the first skit, since his reactions probably could have made a pretty good "Carol & Sis" into a great one. As it stands, Roger thinks the group therapy class held by Chris consists of kooks and refuses to join Carol in it until he sees a buxom woman (Inga Nielsen) is participating. Inga accompanies Lyle, who is seen along with Stan Mazin and Brad Trumbull, and she so mesmerizes Roger that he sits next to her as well as Carol. Carol stabs him with her fingernails for his new obsession and admits to everyone that she feels threatened by Inga's body. Inga shocks Carol and Roger by saying he is ignoring her the way her husband does at home. To comfort Inga—and get back at Roger—Carol tells everyone he does not act like an adult, prompting him to announce that she undresses in the closet. This leads to a verbal brouhaha that spreads across the group and causes it to degenerate in chaos, ending an amiable segment.

John shines in the next two bits. He first swaggers into a saloon to demand whiskey from a bartender (Lyle) when he stumbles across an effeminate cowboy (Harvey) who has an implied relationship with Carlton Johnson. John tells Harvey he is going to make him dance and Harvey complies, leading the other cowboys (played by the male dancers) in a kick line and a production number shot from overhead like the June Taylor Dancers on *The Ed Sullivan Show*. Impressed by what he sees, John leaves and reveals that his name is indeed June Taylor. This is wonderfully silly, offbeat and swift in presentation.

For the trial sketch, Carol openly scoffs at John's answers to the prosecutor (Harvey) while transcribing the discussion. Disgusted by Harvey's approach, she interrupts by declaring, "It's an open-and-shut case!" and openly labels John the killer of his wife and business associate. John's voice quavers as she approaches him, but slowly the two connect and she sympathizes with his story, even grabbing his hand and kissing it. However, John's claim that the butler murdered his wife makes her smack him off the stand and rant that "I was sucked in! I believed him!" She confronts Harvey during his summation and asks, "Where did you learn to practice law—in the White House?!" (There is much applause for this line.) To ensure John is put behind bars, she has him accidentally shoot Harvey. This is nutty and delightful all the way through.

John will make one more appearance on the series this season (see March 23, 1974) and two more in the next, making him the most frequently seen male guest in the period over the next two years apart from Tim Conway and Steve Lawrence.

Nov. 3, 1973: Steve Lawrence, Paul Sand

Q&A; Carol is an obese woman doing her morning exercises under the guidance of a TV fitness instructor (Lyle) who ends damaging herself and her surroundings in the process; Steve performs "I've Got You Under My Skin"; a pregnant woman (Carol) thinks her husband (Paul) is jealous of her condition; an extended spoof of *Double Indemnity* features Carol and Steve as adulterous lovers, Harvey as Carol's husband, Vicki as Carol's stepdaughter and Lyle as Steve's boss; the cast, guests and dancers celebrate Irving Berlin turning 85 by performing a medley of the composer's hits.

Comments: In the second joint guest appearance by Paul Sand and Steve Lawrence (for the first, see Oct. 4, 1972), Paul unfortunately has a weak showcase here, doing only one rather poor skit and participating only in a minor way in the finale. Before all that happens, of course, there is a lively Q&A, where after Carol reveals her height (five feet, six and a half inches), a gentleman follows up with "What are the rest of the measurements?" Carol mistakes a woman from Rhode Island for being British but learns that woman makes the tubes in the show's cameras. After saying she hopes to do a special with Julie Andrews soon, our hostess becomes involved in a discussion of astrological signs when talking to a man who aunt shares the same birthday as Carol. After surveying her audience, she is actually able to get away with saying, "We got the bulls and the goats—any jackasses?" without being bleeped. TV is getting more mature in 1973 indeed.

In "Exercise with Jack Lay Lonnie," Carol is a huge woman in black shorts valiantly replicating the moves she sees Lyle do on her TV screen. She swings her hips and shakes her big breasts, then tries to touch her toes but cannot get her hands past her waist. She crushes a chair and hits a curtain for another exercise. Her efforts to do sit-ups fail when she barely can raise her neck, and her push-ups are so meager that she appears to be swimming on land. While jumping the rope, the camera shakes to indicate her impact when landing, and she ends up breaking a table and falling over a couch from exhaustion. Calling out for help, Lyle comes out from the back room, who complains to her that he slept too late and missed his own show. Overlooking the politically incorrect portrayal of being overweight, this is a superb example of Carol's knack for physical comedy.

Wearing a tux, Steve sings a 1936 Oscar Best Song nominee in fine style, although it is odd to do a Cole Porter number in a show later saluting one of his rivals, Irving Berlin. Next comes a monotonous outing where Paul tells his expecting wife (Carol) that he would rather sleep than hear her talk about her pregnancy. When Carol goes into labor, however, he is shown to be unnerved and envious of his wife's condition, culminating in Paul claiming to have labor pains of his own and Carol having to call the ambulance for them. As with the Oct. 13, 1973 show, this Carol-Paul segment is unfocused and weak, and the performers seem to sense that by yelling half their lines to generate some yocks.

Luckily, more laughs appear in the strong "Double Calamity" sketch, where Steve assumes Fred MacMurray's role in dictating to a tape recorder how his love for a blonde with big earrings and a loud anklet (Carol) went sour. The two plot to kill Carol's husband (Harvey), who is so oblivious he fails to note their smooching. When Harvey's daughter (Vicki) witnesses him sign an insurance renewal policy, she knows what is occurring and has a hilarious scene of hysteria before leaving. In the second act, Carol and Steve meet at a grocery store and discuss their plans for Steve to choke Harvey at home and throw him out of a blimp to make it look like an accident. Steve does that, but his boss (Lyle) visits him in his office to say how weird it was that Harvey's body landed in a tuba in the Rose Bowl. Vicki visits Steve again and makes another overemotional scene while inadvertently revealing that Carol is double crossing Steve. Infuriated, he confronts her at her home, and Carol and Steve exchange rounds of gunfire between apologies and words of love saying how great they could have been as a couple. There is a great moment where Carol bends over and shoots Steve between her legs, and he responds by taking a shot at her butt. After the gunplay, we return to Steve in present time at the office, where he discovers he forgot to turn on the recorder. He starts to talk again but Lyle enters and says he has heard it all, plus introduces a visitor—Carol, who comes to shoot Steve to death. This is a solid spoof all around.

The finale features snippets of roughly twenty Berlin tunes, beginning with Carol and the dancers doing "Say It With Music." Highlights include Steve, Vicki and Lyle doing "Alexander's Ragtime Band," Paul and Harvey singing "I Love a Piano" (sitting at a piano, naturally), Carol and Steve doing "I Got the Sun in the Morning," plus bits with the dancers in "Oh, How I Hate to Get Up the Morning," "God Bless America," "Easter Parade," "A Couple of Swells" and everyone singing "There's No Business Like Show Business." It's a nice tribute, ending with an original song about Berlin being 85 in 1973.

Both Lawrence and Sand will return later this season, with Sand making his final appearance on the series with Steve's wife—see Jan. 12, 1974.

Nov. 10, 1973: Tim Conway, Petula Clark

Q&A; havoc results at the latest Funt and Mundane dramatic performance when the stage manager (Lyle) accidentally knocks out the contact lenses of the main actress; Petula sings "Silver Spoon"; Tim aggravates Harvey checking in for a flight; Carol fantasizes how she might reap revenge on an old flame (Harvey); Marian encounters a mincing lawyer (Harvey), an old obscene phone caller (Tim), and an alleged twin sister (Petula) and the latter's bellhop (Lyle) in "As the Stomach Turns"; a recreation of an early 1960s TV dance show with Harvey as host and Carol and Petula performing with the dancers.

Comments: This was the show where Harvey was so grouchy that Carol threatened to fire him after the taping. Though Carol later claimed his demeanor that week so unnerved him that she was horrible throughout the episode, the truth is she only bobbles a couple of lines in "As the Stomach Turns" and otherwise contributes a smooth performance. But the look and kiss she gives him at the end, ooo! Let's cover the highlights first.

The Q&A has Carol saying she hopes to do a movie next year and confirming Jimmy Stewart is her favorite actor. When a boy asks her age, Carol says "Take a guess." Someone else yells out "Twenty-five" and she thanks that person immediately. A man mentions seeing her during the summer doing *I Do, I Do* with Rock Hudson ("I'm no fool!" she interjects) and wants her to do the bump-and-grind routine from the play, which Carol said she would do after this show ends. A brother and sister present her with a little koala bear bank for her upcoming trip to Australia, and a man says he understood the queen would be there at the same time. "He means the Queen of England!" she says to some snickering that he meant a gay man. As to whether Carol would be portraying the queen, she surprised everyone by saying she is scheduled to interview Her Royal Majesty for *Good Housekeeping* magazine. (Carol will spoof a member of royalty highly reminiscent of Queen Elizabeth a year later on this series.)

The Funt and Mundane bit is pure Burnett slapstick. A backstage accident that impairs her eyesight prompts Carol to squint and run the wrong direction, walking over a table and stumbling behind a couch along the way. While Harvey admires the outside view, Carol does the same staring at the butt of a nude painting. There is a good routine where Carol valiantly struggles to place a record album on a turntable, and more laughs when she "shoots" him with a brush, then caresses his dying body at his legs, thinking they are his face. The brilliant skit ends with Carol planning to leap out a window to her death but knocking down the back walls instead.

After Petula lip syncs her non-hit "Silver Spoon" in a red gown, there are solid laughs with Tim as a check-in man for Speedo Airlines, delivering the company's message to an agitated Harvey in a hurry. Tim cracks Harvey up immediately by stamping everything in his boarding pass, including the key to Harvey's carry-on suitcase. The latter breaks off in the lock as Tim attempts to open it, so Tim saws and drills into it to find out what it contains to Harvey's distress, as it holds valuable film he has taken. Tim accidentally sets off a can of shaving cream into the suitcase, and his efforts to remedy the situation by wrapping the suitcase with tape ends with him adhering to it as well as Harvey drags him to the gate.

The show's momentum screeches to a halt in the next installment, where Carol eats with Vicki at a restaurant, spies Harvey at another table and imagines a scenario where she could confront him and he would grovel in response. Switching back to reality, Carol addresses Harvey, who ignores her and then grudgingly and indifferently listens to her express her feelings. She ends up making a scene and realizing that the person she really is destroying is herself. This obvious, unfunny skit is poorly written and slackly paced, and it is overextended several minutes beyond making its unimpressive point.

Thankfully, the show rebounds with a great "As the Stomach Turns." A swishy attorney (Harvey) informs Marian she has inherited $50,000 from her dead uncle, which is actually good news, as her daughter (Vicki) has become a Girl Scout. Fearing no tragedy in her life, she is thrilled to see Petula show up claiming to be her long-lost twin with muscular Lyle carrying Petula's bags. As they settle in upstairs, Tim arrives as a heavily breathing Old Man who had been on the phone with Marian and pulls up the carpet with his feet as he shambles along. This is hysterical, as is Tim calling his dad, laughing so repeatedly that Carol briefly leaves the stage and then returns to crack up when Tim ad libs, "Don't you get it?!" His excellent comic abilities continue as he tumbles backward on a chair across the living room set, earning applause when he lands. Vicki comes downstairs claiming she has Lyle's baby, but Lyle says he is already married, and Petula whispers a secret to Carol before this nice skit ends with these unanswered questions.

After Carol and Petula sing "Yesterday Once More," Harvey appears as a Dick Clark-ish emcee introducing several hip acts in an energetic setting from a decade earlier. Vicki presents "Born to Hand Jive" with the dancers in surprisingly provocative outfits, then Harvey himself vocalizes "The Peppermint Twist" with Carol and Petula joining in the gang, wearing wild outfits sporting multiple tassels. This is a pleasant change of pace from the usual medley of standards in the show's finale.

However, during the taping of the number Friday morning so that it would be played back on the monitors for the studio audience later that day, Harvey scowled at Carol. Taken aback by his grouchiness, she asked what was wrong, only to be curtly dismissed by Harvey, who said he would rather go home and never come back.

With that in mind, at the end, Carol provides Harvey with only the most perfunctory kiss she has ever given him on the show. Backstage afterward, she tells Harvey in his dressing room that his behavior unnerved her so much that he is fired. Shocked, he asks Carol for a reprieve, which she grants only if he is cheerful at work thereafter.

The following Monday morning, the elevator door opened before Carol, and out came Harvey whistling, dancing and skipping down the hall. The following week, Harvey had a plaque placed on his dressing room door: "Mr. Happy-Go-Lucky." All was fine again.

Nov. 17, 1973: Repeat of March 17, 1973 show

Nov. 24, 1973: Pre-empted by *Miss Teenage America Pageant*

Dec. 1, 1973: Family Show

A spoof of commercials; models Harvey, Lyle and Carol pose exaggeratedly at their homes; Carol presents a comic needlepoint number; a sick Carol asks Chrissy for help because she knows Roger is afraid of catching her disease, only to find unwanted assistance from the elevator guy (Jim Connell); Vicki sings "Ships in the Night"; a send-up of the movie *Back Street* where a groom (Harvey) tells a bridesmaid (Carol) obsessed with him to wait for his return, and she does repeatedly—while he stays married; Harvey and Carol are ex-bar owners who sing "Those Were the Days."

Comments: A minor family show, this closed the door on any chance of Jim Connell becoming a series regular despite his dedicated efforts. With no Q&A, it starts with the best segment. The topper is a bra ad parody. Carol wears the Cross My Body brand over her sweater to show its features, only to have Harvey come out wearing underwear over his pants to tell her she looks ridiculous, to audience hysteria.

From there, Harvey, Lyle and Carol's artificial model stances and fake bright smiles contrast strongly with their dialogue. All three score well, but the point could have been made more effectively if the skit was not dragged out longer than needed. Better is the segment that follows, which pays off when it is revealed Carol has been seated doing needlepoint while singing "The Shape of Things" for a reason—she's very pregnant.

The rest of the show is a waste. "Carol & Sis" is a trying affair where Roger wants to stay away from a flu-ridden Carol, forcing Chrissy to call out her secret weapon to help her sister—Jim the love-struck elevator guy. His obsession with Carol is still creepy and unfunny, but it does prompt Roger to intervene and save his wife. She thanks Roger by kissing him, to his horror. This is old hat for 1973, and the participants can do nothing to make it spark. Not surprisingly, this marks the swan song for Jim in these skits.

After an unremarkable tune from Vicki comes "Back Alley," a lifeless, overextended mockery which takes the original film's premise to absurd lengths only to drain the humor. Carol waits for months after Harvey goes on his honeymoon but proclaims he will return to her, and she keeps putting up with his prolonged disappearances as he promises to divorce his wife and marry her. By the third time Harvey is with Carol, who is seen graying and surrounded by more rabbits every time he returns, the amusement is largely gone, and the arrival of the rest of the cast in other roles fail to help either. The final number with Carol and Harvey does not improve the mood much.

This disappointing effort is a rare entry without the dancers. Apparently the series was saving up here for costs of its next show, which thankfully was much better than this.

Dec. 8, 1973: Australia Show (Tim Conway, Edward Villella, Lucette Aldous)

Harvey, Lyle, Tim, Vicki and Carol banter on their flight to Australia; Carol enters the Sydney Opera House to sing "It's Today"; Q&A; the oldest conductor (Tim) takes the baton from Harvey as he leads his 358th farewell concert; Edward and Lucette dance to "Le Corsaire"; Funt (Harvey) performs "Triangle of Love" with an understudy (Vicki) at the Down Under Theatre in the Round before his drunk wife, Mundane (Carol) arrives and forces her way onstage; the Charwoman sees the Sydney Ballet Swan Lake trunk and is shocked as ballerinas materialize and make her part of their performance.

Comments: The last show Carol and the crew will tape outside CBS Television City in Hollywood is a winner. After a scripted bit where she and her regulars and Tim debate whether they gain or lose a day going to Australia, Carol receives massive applause at the Sydney Opera House as she sings a new song that includes lyrics about being on a seventeen-hour flight. She falls to the ground at the end, then gets up and says, "I'm so thrilled to be here." Carol announces that the guests include Lucette Aldous, an Australian Ballet Company prima ballerina who will dance with Edward Villella, then does a very brief Q&A. Regarding one of the continent's best-known tunes, Carol tells the assembled that "I think 'Waltzing Matilda' is one of the most beautiful melodies I've ever heard in my life" and earns claps for that, naturally.

The first sketch is a hoot. Tim's old conductor cannot get up the stairs, so he pulls the step up on its side, sits on it and rotates to land on the podium. He announces that the musicians will present "The Surprise Concert" in C sharp. "Tonight, we will play it in B flat. Surprise!" When he hits his baton on the music stand, he cannot stop it from vibrating for a time. He looks at the music sheet quizzically and hums the tune before approving where it is going. The music goes back on the stand, which now pops up and down, and then he temporarily loses his baton in his shirt sleeve. He appears to be ready for the concert when Tim hears Harvey's squeaky violin and stops the proceedings to tune it, then propels himself back onto the podium. The concert begins with the musicians playing "The William Tell Overture" at a steady pace as a fly bothers Tim. He takes out a swatter in place of the baton and follows it in time with the music, culminating in Tim somersaulting into the orchestra pit. This is ingenious pantomime at its best.

Sporting a headband and no shirt, Villella dances with Aldous, wearing a golden beaded tutu. He then offers a solo turn and leaps majestically across the wide opera house stage, which deserves kudos to the cameramen and director for following him so well. Despite appearing to have applause dubbed at parts, the dance is a fine showcase deserving of respect nonetheless.

After outside shots of the opera house before and after the midway commercial break, a great Funt and Mundane sketch has Harvey and Vicki playing things on stage straight until Carol runs through the audience and stumbles through the orchestra, clutching a bottle of booze while demanding she do her original role. After failing to get rid of her, Harvey encourages Vicki to pretend Carol is not there. That fails, as Carol perseveres to play her role and even finds more alcohol she has hidden on stage that she drinks while causing more mayhem. Lyle arrives playing a spurned lover with a gun, prompting Carol to scream and think it is a real firearm. Exasperated, Harvey knocks Carol out and puts her behind a sofa, but she emerges with a hammer hitting the floor like a construction worker and saying "The opera house is finished!" Lyle "shoots" Vicki, who screams and falls down to Carol's confusion. Harvey mourns Vicki, but Carol informs him she is not dead and props her up before tearing off Vicki's wig and Harvey's toupee as this raucous, enjoyable segment ends.

The Charwoman wears a tutu and brown boots to join the dancers in "Swan Lake." She gets next to Edward and Lucette and loves their moves until Edward's bow shoots Lucette, prompting Carol to smack him in his face. Carol and Edward do a comic pas de deux where he cannot lift her but she can hoist him. The other dancers come on stage and Edward disappears before the Charwoman can thank him. Alone, she comes down stage to sing "For All We Know" (not the 1970 Oscar-winning song) before we fade to black.

"You were just sensational, thank you so much!" Carol says at the end, and the audience heartily indicates it was just as fond of her too. Although some personnel flew over from the United States, the bulk came from the Australian Broadcasting Commission, the National Nine Network and Pat Condon Services Pty. Ltd. as credited.

Incidentally, several romantic liaisons occurred during this trip. Harvey's then-wife Donna had an affair with Villella, while Vicki fell in love with the show's makeup man, Al Schultz. Ironically, Harvey recognized the latter union immediately but missed his wife's cheating. Al and Vicki subsequently grew closer while they both were in miserable marriages and divorced their partners. They would wed in 1974.

Dec. 15, 1973: Ruth Buzzi, Richard Crenna

Q&A; a cop (Richard) learns that his wife and partner at work (Carol) wants a divorce; Ruth is a life-sized children's toy who leads a production number featuring "Oh, You Beautiful Doll" with the dancers; Lyle hosts "Celebrities and Peasants," a game show teaming a shallow actress (Ruth) with a beaten-down librarian contestant (Carol); a salute to naughty ladies in films has quick send-ups of *The Graduate* and *All About Eve* and an extended takeoff of *Born to be Bad*; Ruth, Carol and Vicki join the female dancers in a tribute to the U.S. Constitution's Article Nineteen allowing women to vote.

Comments: Following an ambitious show taped overseas can be a tough order, but this episode is a real letdown despite Ruth Buzzi's fourth guest shot. Even the Q&A is minor. A woman in Toronto says hi, and Carol reveals she has never been to Canada. A man from Acapulco says Carol speaks great Spanish in his country, which leads Carol to say how she met a statuesque woman and a meek man who dubbed her and Harvey for Mexican broadcasts respectively. Finally, asked how she got her series by a young girl, she quips, "I just asked to be on the air and CBS was so nice, they said OK."

The first flat sketch has Richard and Carol fighting while trying to catch a burglar (voice of Don Crichton). She had an affair because she wants more affection from Richard, even though he secured her a job as a cop working alongside him. Their arguments become so heated that the burglar leaves and the duo learn that they have been reported to their fellow officers as being in a domestic dispute. It plays as unfunny as it reads.

Another missed opportunity follows with Ruth singing a song more than fifty years old while tempting her fellow boy dolls and irritating the girl ones with her adorable looks (at least according to the doll maker). This is cute at best. Much worse is the next sketch, apparently a parody of *Password*, but every character and situation is so generic, it is hard to tell or care. Lyle, Ruth and Carol try to enliven their worn-out types, with Carol indicating how desperate her character is to win that she parted with everything she had in Akron, Ohio, and lived in a park for a month. Ruth has no idea that the answer to Carol's clues "president," "American" and "first" is George Washington, and Ruth's own hints for "the Vatican" are ridiculous, so Carol yells at Ruth for being the worst celebrity to play with and tears off her wig and clothes. This is tough to endure.

There is a glimmer of hope with the film parodies, but they turn out to be flat. The joke of *The Graduate* is that Mrs. Robinson (Ruth) is trying to seduce a Boy Scout (Richard, doing his high-pitched Walter Denton voice he used in *Our Miss Brooks* twenty years earlier). In *All About Eve*, Margo (Carol, in a good exaggeration of Bette Davis) dismisses Eve (Vicki) after the latter eyes one of her costumes and cries for help from her boyfriend, Bill (Harvey), who turns out to wanting to wear that same outfit himself. This leads into "Raised to be Rotten," a mockery of a somewhat obscure 1950 film with Carol as Ruth's bad cousin, seducing Ruth's rich fiancé (Harvey) while at the same time romancing a nice guy (Richard). Carol fools Harvey into thinking Ruth wants him only for his money and weds him, but it is an unhappy marriage and she still has the hots for Richard. Harvey breaks up with Carol because of that and runs to Ruth, but the implication is that she has learned to be just as manipulative as her cousin in the interim. The costumes are impressive, and that is about the high point of this mess.

The musical finale has all the women regulars and Ruth in a production number centered around working on a mimeograph machine in the 1910s, another waste of time for all concerned. It leads into Carol making a pitch for Christmas seals at the end, followed by only the female dancers joining the regulars and the guests to wave goodbye—apparently the male dancers knew what a stinker this one was.

Ruth and Richard never returned to the series after this episode, which is understandable given its quality. For her part, Buzzi claims that she was not let down here. "Carol had the best writers in the industry. They would never deliberately present me with what one would consider 'weak' material. . . . I was happy to work with her, and loved the challenge of taking a lesser part and trying to make it even better."

Dec. 22, 1973: Dick Martin, Anthony Newley

* Harvey's nomination of Dick to the Wine Tasters Hall of Fame ruffles the feathers of another aspirant to the position (Anthony); Carol and Tony duet on "I'd Like to Teach the World to Sing" and have the dancers join them as they present "The People Tree"; Vicki is a newcomer to a singles bar who is

shown the ropes by a veteran (Carol); Anthony sings "What Did You Do in the War Daddy?"; a salute to movie detectives sends up Sherlock Holmes, Sam Spade and Miss Marple; everyone but Dick participates in a tribute to songs written by Anthony.

Comments: Dick and Anthony appeared separately in flawed installments in previous Decembers (Dick on Dec. 29, 1971 and Anthony on Dec. 16, 1972), and this episode is similarly lackluster, with overlong skits and music that is hard to endure if you are not a Newley fan. The opening sketch putters along as Harvey picks a skid row bum (Dick) to be the latest member of a wine tasting club, infuriating Anthony, who is envious that his old romantic rival is being selected. Anthony dares to have Dick identify a wine, which he does so incorrectly because Anthony switched the cards. Harvey appoints himself as judge of a "taste-off" between the men, as each alternates sipping and identifying wines from 100 bottles. Down to the last two glasses, Anthony loses when he incorrectly identifies the wrong year of a vintage. He pulls out a gun to prevent Dick from assuming his nomination when Harvey informs him Dick has been dead for two minutes—Harvey just wanted to continue the contest to see if Anthony truly was well versed. Impressed, Anthony toasts the body of Dick, who in a voiceover slurs out, "I'll drink to that. Hic!" Apart from Dick's amusing drunk routine, this is a flat concoction.

After two songs with Anthony, Carol acts as an advisor and protector to Vicki, rebuffing one man (Bob Duggan) as he makes a move on her younger pal. Next, Carol hits on a disinterested patron (Brad Trumbull) and mocks him as he departs. After everyone is gone, Vicki strikes up a conversation with the bartender (Lyle) and leaves with him, telling Carol she will call her in the morning. "Sure you will" says Carol in a weary voice. Meant to be poignant, this ending comes off as pathos instead, and it has little humor preceding either. Anthony's solo number does not help improve matters.

Two weak entries occur before there are finally some solid laughs with the last of the cinematic sleuth spoofs. Sherlock Holmes (Anthony) admits he has one mystery he has never solved—the first name of Dr. Watson (Harvey). "If you'd like, you can call me Priscilla," the latter reveals. *The Maltese Falcon* takeoff has Dick as a slurring Sam Spade (a bad mockery of Humphrey Bogart's lisp) who doesn't realize that the dame needing his help (Carol) has died. All looks lost before "Miss Marble Screams Bloody Murder!" gets chuckles flowing with Carol as the elderly, plump title investigator arriving as Anthony and Vicki get ready to read the will of their late father, joined by Dick as a butler and Harvey as an inspector. As expected, Carol's obesity is the target of a few gags, chiefly about her getting stuck in a sofa, and there are several clear plot twists that make this a tolerable takeoff. But it can't save the show's now-deadly atmosphere.

Wrapping up this blah episode are excerpts of a few familiar tunes by Anthony, including "What Kind of Fool Am I" and "The Candy Man." The mini-revue ends with Anthony, Carol, Harvey, Lyle and Vicki getting on trapezes that lift up in the final shot. Too bad this show itself never really gets airborne.

Dec. 29, 1973: Repeat of Oct. 6, 1973 show

Jan. 5, 1974: Steve Lawrence, Tim Conway

Carol and Tim are lovers meeting Carol's father (Harvey) when Tim's reaction to a shot for a chimp bite makes him go ape; Steve sings "Maybe This Time"; Stella Toddler (Carol) prepares to put her feet in concrete in front of Grauman's Chinese Theatre along with an unctuous emcee (Harvey); Carol and Steve are shy, homely types who blossom into beauties upon meeting and sing together; Tim is a client who finds himself fought over by Harvey and Steve like he is their lover; the cast, guests and dancers perform "With a Pow! Pow! With a Bang! Bang! Bang!"

Comments: A ponderous, mawkish middle part drags down some great moments here. Before getting there, the show starts with Tim acting like a monkey while visiting Harvey, his prospective in-law, including checking Harvey for ticks and putting the latter's hairpiece in his mouth, which cracks up Harvey, of course. By the time Tim climbs a bookcase in a bit of comic athleticism and throws fruit at Carol and Harvey, the latter is calling 911 for help. Carol and Harvey climb the bookcase too, and Harvey's squawks somehow connect with Tim and calm him down to leave with Carol. But his antics continue as two policemen (Don Crichton and Stan Mazin) arrive, and they carry Harvey away in believing he is the chimp imitator. Carol and Tim return, but their bliss is shattered when Tim accidentally bites and she acts like a gorilla herself. As Tim's sketches go, this is average in execution and could have been tighter, but it does get funnier as it progresses.

After Steve's acceptable number in a tux, a nice segment features Stella Toddler as an unintended victim of others while receiving a tribute for her work as an acting teacher, first by being tangled in the red carpet when she arrives at the theatre. Harvey knocks her over on her back with her slip showing, and Lyle is a white-haired singer whose vocals into a megaphone drop her down as well. Another accidental hit by Harvey pushes her onto the spotlight on both sides, and when he tries to plant her feet in cement, she makes a plea that would define her character: "I've been hurt a lot. I don't want to be hurt again." Unfortunately for Stella, her feet get stuck, and when reporters ask Harvey for a few more photos, he trips her into the cement, where she sinks. Ever the unflappable host, Harvey tells those assembled that they have just witnessed Hollywood's latest shrine to one of its own. This is a good showcase for Stella.

The show's momentum then crashes with an awkward romantic interlude, as Carol is a dowdy lass singing a sticky number called "In Buddy's Eyes" before the appearance of her bespectacled, meek date (Steve). They are immediately smitten with each other and fantasize themselves as glamorous types as Steve sings his part of "In Buddy's Eyes" and then they duet on it. By the time they finally revert to their normal selves at the end, viewers are left wondering if the show will maintain this gooey tone.

Happily, the show goes into overdrive with two very humorous, lively pieces. In the first, Tim and Harvey are being served at a restaurant by Lyle the waiter while Harvey attempts to woo Tim's business much like a love scene, lighting up two cigarettes and giving one to Tim (who cracks up) and then pleading, "I want your account!" Steve suddenly joins them in the booth to Tim's discomfort, since Steve already has Tim's account. Staring intently at a nervous Tim, Steve witheringly summarizes how Harvey treated a competitor with such zing that the audience applauds after his delivery. Even so, Tim announces to Steve that he is ending his relationship with the latter, prompting Steve to bring out a gun (from another client, naturally) and shoots Harvey, in a good death scene. Steve calls it a crime of passion, and an unnerved Tim pushes Harvey's body to the floor (cracking up Harvey slightly) as Steve orders for both himself and Tim. This "clients as lovers" gambit is very effective and will be reused twice in the following season, but this is the best of the bunch.

Death plays a major role in the finale, as the cast and guests tell Carol they want to dramatize great scenes of people expiring. Vicki particularly insists on recreating the passing of the ballerina from the 1948 film classic *The Red Shoes*, and Tim deadpans, "There's something you can sink your teeth into, see? Like twirling yourself to death!" Between a number talking about the ways to die comes last moments portrayed by Steve as James Cagney being shot, Lyle as a cowboy in a shootout (Birl Johns nails him between his legs), Harvey as Peter Lorre and even the dancers in another shootout. Carol plays a concerto one last time at the request of Harvey, who then tells her, "That wasn't it!" before she dies. After trying to insert himself earlier, Tim does a great pantomime of a pilot having engine trouble, assisted nicely with sound effects. And Vicki has her ballerina death scene, topped by Steve saying afterward in an affected voice that "The ballet of the Red Shoes will not be danced tonight!" Mock bombs then appear to fall and blow up and kill everyone on stage—until Tim gets up to say he has one more idea and Carol mock shoots him, causing him to shut up.

The finale is a surprisingly enjoyable twist from the usual. So is the ending, when Carol invites Steve and Tim to sing "It's Time to Say So Long" with her, but with Tim off-key, she tells him to just listen, and he reacts with fake disgust. It is a rousing finish for what could have been a classic if they had just dropped Carol and Steve's bit in the middle.

Jan. 12, 1974: Paul Sand, Eydie Gorme

** Astronauts bicker on their way to land on Mars; Paul and Carol are newlyweds who argue even before they leave from church; Eydie sings "I'll Take Romance"; blackouts on the energy crisis; the dancers perform to "End of Summer"; a musical finale celebrates the leading ladies of Broadway with the songs they made famous.

Comments: This was the last of four guest shots by Paul Sand in little more than a year. His appearances here helped make him a hot property and land his own starring series, *Paul Sand in Friends and Lovers*, on CBS Saturdays in the fall of 1974. Unfortunately, too many viewers tuned out when the show aired between *All in the Family* and *The Mary Tyler Moore Show*, so it went off after thirteen weeks. Paul was free to return to the show after that, but his representative had other plans for his career, to his regret.

"It was an agent—greed," Paul says nearly four decades later. "I would've done a lot more shows if I could've."

While Paul has no memories about working with Eydie, even though this is his second show with her, he does remember thinking that Steve Lawrence was funny off stage. His most vivid recollections involve Carol ("She's so spontaneous. A co-player") and the pleasant atmosphere on the set.

"It was all so easy," he said. "There wasn't a problem with anybody. You'd get up, and she'd make the actors comfortable. I would just pack a lunch and go to work."

Eydie Gorme will return to the series in five weeks—see Feb. 23, 1974 for more.

Jan. 19, 1974: Carl Reiner

Q&A; Carl plays a man who tries to get insurance for his wife (Carol) from Harvey while trying to hide her accident-prone tendencies; a dramatic vignette between Carol and Harvey leads into a song; a marriage counselor (Carl) helps a man (Harvey) coping with the never-ending spate of jokes from his comedienne wife (Carol); Harvey's attempts to go on a date with a blonde bimbo falter when he meets a loud, rowdy checkout clerk (Carol); the entire cast portrays Los Muchachitos y Los Muchachitas de Mexico, a troupe from Mexico enacting a Spanish-language musical version of "Little Red Riding Hood."

Comments: This episode gets better as it goes along, although the Q&A starts well. A lady from Philadelphia said she received a letter signed by Carol and is happy to be in the audience. "Will Tim Conway ever been a regular?" one girl asks. "If I have anything to say about it, yes," Carol answers. "If he can fit into my dresses, he can come on and be (laughter). I love him very much. He's matter of fact doing a pilot of his own, so let's all say a prayer for him that it goes real well. I'd love to see him have his own show." *The Boys* fails to make CBS's fall 1974 lineup (nor does an adaptation of *Pete 'n' Tillie* which would have had Cloris Leachman assume Carol's movie role). Luckily, this meant more of Tim on the show in 1974-1975 and a regular spot the following season.

Also, Carol reveals her makeup man is Al Schultz. "He's a little old guy, but you know, I feel like people like that should be given a chance," she cracks about Vicki's future husband to audience laughter. He comes out and Carol kisses him. The segment ends with a girl asking Carol to do Shirley Temple, and coaxed by the audience, she does a short and sweet "On the Good Ship Lollipop." To top it off, one gentleman inquires, "Is this a repeat show?" and Carol responds, "No, we're live here" to audience hysteria.

Less laughter emerges in a somewhat tiresome opening sketch, where the gag is Carol always hurts herself with whatever she does at a restaurant despite Carl's entreaties to act normal so they can earn coverage from Harvey. So, when Harvey accidentally knocks hot shrimp from a waiter (Lyle) into Carol's lap, she grimaces before pouring water on it to cool down. She plays it cool when a violinist (Stan Mazin) accidentally removes her wig with his bow as well. When it appears she is covered for insurance, Carl celebrates, but Harvey tells him Carol must sign the document, and her hands have endured having so much glass broken on them and having Carl accidentally stomp on them that she cannot write. Harvey closes his briefcase to leave, only to get Carol's hand stuck in it, which forces her to leave with him. This is a messy, pretty one-note affair, and while the participants act well in it, one thinks it could have been tighter and better.

Another questionable maneuver follows as Carol plays Harvey's boss whose unrequited love for him is shattered by him getting married. In response, she goes to a typewriter when he leaves and sings "Send in the Clowns" straight. This deadly dull moment thankfully vanishes when Carol next appears as a brassy redhead in a loud outfit who keeps joking with her husband (Harvey) and their marriage counselor (Carl) despite their pleas for her to be serious—she even does a Jimmy Durante impression. Carl decides to employ "shock treatment" on Carol where he presents the setups to jokes and forbids her to say their punch lines. She passes out, and Harvey tells Carl he is an exorcist. But the cure fails, as Carol blurts out one more punch line, and a disgusted Harvey throws her out the window, where she lands with a drum's "ba dum pum" sound like at a nightclub. This is swift and focused, two attributes missing from the scripted parts that preceded them.

Even better is the next bit where Harvey has lined up a floozy (Jennifer Blake) to take home, but he needs to buy some items first to set their lovemaking scene. Carol is an unimpressed woman at the register who irks him by asking for a price check on incense (Don Crichton's voice gives her the answer) and haggling with him, while a Boy Scout (Don again!) offers to pay for Harvey's date until he learns her price is too high. Harvey writes Carol a check and she needs his driver's license to validate it, and his photo cracks her up along with her fellow checkout gal (Vicki), as well as everyone else in the store. That includes Lyle, who shows up to whisk away Harvey's date while the latter drops his groceries. The ribald fun flows naturally, and all involved sparkle here.

The show ends with "La Capecita Rogo" ("Little Red Riding Hood" in Spanglish), where with a nice dialect Vicki narrates the actions of Carol as the title character if played by Charo. Lyle plays a bullfighter who wants her cookies, but the bull (Carl) has bigger plans in store for Carol, who is on her way to see her grandmother, played by Harvey as the Castilian Mother Marcus, right down to singing about her castanets with a lisp. Carl hides Harvey away and pretends to be her in bed. Carol arrives and notes how "horny" Carl looks (possibly the first time a CBS censor let the word be used in a possible context of the word meaning sex-crazed). Lyle arrives to kill Carl but ends up running away, forcing Carol to try to subdue the creature. Her efforts end when her grandmother arrives and professes her love for the bull, leading to Carl and Harvey looking like they were about to kiss, to the audience's shock and/or amusement. The skit ends with Carol throwing the treats in her basket to the audience. Keeping the theme when saying goodnight, Carol sings the first two lines of "It's Time to Say So Long" in Spanish, and everyone says "Adios" instead of "so long" at the end as well.

"That was very funny, and the production on that show was as good as any show," says Reiner of the sketch, the only one he did on the series that he remembers clearly among his three guest shots (the first was on Nov. 29, 1972). Incredibly, Ken and Mitzie Welch originally wrote it for ventriloquist Shari Lewis! Reiner will return on Dec. 14, 1974.

Jan. 26, 1974: Pre-empted by *Entertainer of the Year Awards* (Carol performs on the special)

Feb. 2, 1974: Steve Lawrence, Tim Conway

Carol is a housewife whose bathroom and kitchen are bombarded by appearances from characters from TV commercials; a British stage actor (Harvey) needs a quick costume change from his doddering backstage dresser (Tim); Carol introduces a clip of Tim cracking up repeatedly during the dress rehearsal of a skit he, Steve and Harvey did on the Jan. 5, 1974 show; Lyle bets Steve, the guest of honor at a bachelor party, that the latter cannot seduce Carol; a pantomime sketch between a couple (Carol and Tim) working different job shifts; a musical salute to George Gershwin.

Comments: The opening sketch (no Q&A here) is excellent, with Carol beautifully bewildered by quick bits featuring all the regulars plus the dancers, some with dialogue. The elements are so broad and funny that a viewer does not have to be familiar with the advertising to enjoy them all, such as Carol smacking Stan Mazin out of her house when he carries a huge stick of gum. The best part arguably is Harvey as Peter Pan, sending up the character as an effeminate pusher of peanut butter. There is a slight storyline in that Steve shows up and Carol pleas for him to save her, only see him leaving with Vicki as a bimbo stewardess. Dejected, Carol goes to the refrigerator, takes out a beer and ends up prompting a bull to attack her. This brilliantly written, directed and acted sketch is helped immeasurably by the talents of the stage crew and sound effects.

The high level of comedy continues in the next skit, where Harvey has his most uncontrolled fit of laughter ever. It comes after he already is amused by Tim drawling "koala" and other business, such as Tim messing with Harvey's mustache and slippery spirit gum. After Tim dawdles with accidentally gripping Harvey's toupee and thinking it is a fungus, Harvey begins to lose it more when he asks the unseen stage manager how many more minutes until he has to go on and receives no answer. Tim has a great set of physical comedy involving a hand towel dispenser (he pulls on it until he is flat on his back on stage, then sneezes and goes up so quick as the towels retract that he hits the machine). He tops that by getting into an automatic clothing rack that Harvey operates that goes both directions, and each time Tim's face and position is changed. Harvey is laughing so hard that you can hear the trembling in his voice pleading Tim to stop. The sketch ends with Harvey putting on a coat that accidentally wraps Tim behind him.

Apparently in an effort for fair time to show Tim could "pull a Harvey," Carol shows her guest star laughing uncontrollably during the first taping of the "clients in love" sketch that aired just three weeks earlier. Tim said the audience had been so quiet during the opening minutes setting up the sketch that all he heard was the air conditioning, and the thought the sketch people thought would be a hit was apparently bombing amused him no end. It is cute enough that Steve apparently was fine with it running it place of what normally would have been his solo singing spot on any other *Carol Burnett Show*.

The next effort suffers in comparison to the great comedy that preceded it due to lumpy pacing and a somewhat uneasy storyline. Steve's efforts to seduce Carol and win a bet with Lyle are thrown awry when Steve learns she is the sister of his fiancée. When Carol tells him she forgets everything when she is drunk, he attempts to get her plastered so he can still win the bet, but Lyle unintentionally lets their plan slip to Carol. Her reaction is "If you mention this to my husband, I'll kill you!" The use of cheating combined with drinking gives this an unpleasant air to watch, especially with what had appeared earlier.

Lyle introduces Carol as a wife working days and Tim as a husband working nights when they meet between shifts in their apartment. This is a great wordless piece of physical comedy through the end, when Carol suddenly announces, "We're going to have a baby" and an exasperated Tim responds "No way!"

On an art deco set, Carol, Steve, Vicki, Harvey and the dancers appear in various combinations in tribute of one of America's greatest songwriters. Many of the numbers date back to the 1920s and 1930s naturally, including "Someone to Watch Over Me," "SWonderful," and seventeen others, as Carol and Steve play lovers who meet, marry and part. The segment ends with a freeze frame of all participants doing "I Got Rhythm," with "Summertime" dubbed on at the end. Carol ends the show with a pledge for the Heart Fund, as February is heart month, and Steve joins her in singing the last verse of "It's Time to Say So Long." All in all, this is a pretty strong episode.

Feb. 9, 1974: Joel Grey, Vincent Price

Q&A; Carol and Roger learn that Chrissy's new boyfriend (Joel) is nowhere near as hip and swinging as he claims; child star Shirley Dimple (Carol) terrorizes director Maximilian Von Terhoff (Harvey) and others on a movie set; Vincent delivers a monologue recalling the wit and wisdom of Abraham Lincoln; a hotel operator (Carol) listens into the interesting conversations between two conventioneers (Joel and Vincent) and their two friends (Vicki and Lyle); Harvey exchanges secrets with a fellow spy (Vincent) but comes up short with the payout; Vincent is a puppeteer presenting Punch (Joel) and Judy (Carol) to amused townsfolk.

Comments: Afterthe briefest of Q&As comes the first scripted material, which is a shame because most of the pieces are serviceable but needed some trimming that would have allowed more of this segment. The only question of note involves Dustin Hoffman, Robert Redford and Paul Newman. Carol says she will be asking to work with them next week, but she has no plans to do movies with any of the trio.

From there, Joel has a decent showcase as Chrissy's new beau. Looking like a stud for 1974 with a mustache and bedazzled jean jacket, Joel even hits on Carol to show what a make out artist he is. However, his efforts are constantly thwarted by several phone calls from his mother, who reminds him to take his allergy pill, brush his teeth and even talk to Roger to hear what his voice sounds like. An embarrassed Joel leaves with Chrissy, but when his mom calls one more time, an impish Roger cannot resist telling her that Joel has taken off all his clothes in the living room and has burned his toothbrush.

Some OK chuckles also come from Carol's Shirley Dimple taking on Harvey's tyrannical director with her own obnoxious behavior, such as pushing away in a wheelchair an older actor (Lyle) playing her grandfather and blackmailing Harvey for a close-up (he wears women's underwear, as she shows by cutting his pants). It is revealed that her hairdresser (Vicki) is her mother and that she smokes as well. But the director gets the last laugh—he brings in the camera so tight for Shirley's close-up that she falls off the set.

In an interlude that is odd both for its pretext (the celebration of the 165th anniversary of the birth of President Lincoln) and purpose, Vincent presents some stories meant to show why America's sixteenth president is considered to be the first humorist to occupy the White House. Apart from giving Vincent the chance to say "jackass," this is a mild piece of patriotism, and while this recitation would be fine on *The Ed Sullivan Show*, its inclusion here seems flimsy and desperate.

The next sketch is far and above everything else in this show, a cleverly plotted and wonderfully executed piece. In the center of the screen, Carol is a hotel operator who eavesdrops on escalating conversations, starting with Vincent (in the upper left) talking to ditzy Vicki (lower right) about a rendezvous. She turns him down, so Vincent calls and sets up a dinner date with fellow conventioneer Joel (in the upper right) for dinner. However, Vicki calls Vincent to say she has changed her mind, so to accommodate her, he calls Joel to cancel, saying he has a headache. At the same time, Lyle (lower left) calls up Vicki for a date tonight, and she says yes and tells Vincent their date is off. Joel rings up Lyle for dinner, but he turns him down without saying Vicki is the reason, so Joel checks with Vicki, who decides to go with him and calls things off with Lyle. Vincent hits Vicki back and pleads to meet with him, so she acquiesces and tells Joel he is now history. On the rebound, Joel asks Lyle to dinner, who says yes—and they plan to go to the same restaurant as Vincent and Vicki. Carol, who has listened intently to the interactions, asks "What about reservations?" while all are on the line saying the same thing. Informed by the parties of what they need, a gleeful Carol calls the restaurant and requests their spots, along with a table for one for a magnificent view of those other guests. This bit really dazzles by all involved.

Disappointingly, the following skit just makes the grade. When Harvey, speaking like Peter Lorre, learns he is $20 short in a $750,000 transaction to Vincent, his fellow trench coat-wearing spy, he tries to make up the difference with $8 in cash from his wallet, before selling parts of his clothing to Vincent, until all he has is 10 cents for bus fare while clad in only an undershirt and boxers. He leaves Vincent to go to the bus stop, where four of the male dancers are waiting in undershirts too. The sharp ending fails to compensate for the tedium of watching Harvey disrobe by offering his pants, shoes, etc.

The finale fails to rouse the show's torpor, as it slogs rather than sparkles. Vincent says the lines of "Comedy Tonight" as the emcee presenting Punch and Judy, whose horseplay on a stage in an unidentified village leads the audience (the dancers, of course) to mimic their behavior with broomsticks and boards before the residents run off Vincent out of town. This leaves Carol and Joel to finish singing "Comedy Tonight."

At the end, Joel's hand is still in the glove he wore as Punch, so to sign Carol's book, he awkwardly grabs the whole pen. The move is a good symbol of how most things on this show just seem "off" and missing the mark.

Feb. 16, 1974: Bernadette Peters, Tim Conway

Q&A; Marian discovers her visiting niece (Bernadette) is possessed by the devil and needs an exorcist (Tim) in "As the Stomach Turns"; Bernadette sings "Blame It on My Youth"; Vicki reconnects with Carol, her old chum, and the latter dismisses much of what she is doing; Tim is a Japanese submarine captain and Harvey his subordinate as they plan to attack Cleveland; a gangster (Tim) fumbles a hit on an enemy at a barbershop; a mini-musical set in the 1930s features Harry Warren's songs as Carol has the hots for fellow college student Harvey even though he only wants Bernadette.

Comments: This could be subtitled "Who Needs Lyle?" because the performer barely appears—a brief shot at the end of a sketch, an introduction of another and that is it. It makes a persuasive case that the show will be fine without him next season (for more on this, see Final Notes of the Season). The quick Q&A consists of a teenage girl coming on stage to show Carol her imitation of Zelda that she did at school (rather ironic, as the series stopped doing the character after this show). Following that, Carol mentions Cicely Tyson's recent performance on the TV-movie *The Autobiography of Miss Jane Pittman* and comments, "I think that's one of the most terrific things I've ever seen. Boy, she's got my vote for the Emmy." (Tyson did win the statuette for her work later in 1974—and one person she beat was Carol for *6 RMS RIV VU*.)

A strong "As the Stomach Turns" kicks off the festivities. There are great amusing bits from the start with Marian pretending to talk to Maude from the TV series of the same name, followed by her endlessly turning the pages of her photo album of the funerals of her ex-husband. She is expecting her niece (Bernadette) even though she has no brothers and sisters, and the child is a blonde goody two shoes in pigtails. She comes from Washington, D.C., and her gifts for Marian include two tapes, presumably from what President Nixon tried to keep secret from the Watergate hearings. Her too-cheerful demeanor suddenly vanishes as she destroys flowers and candy in the house, and a chair levitates in the house.

When the niece slugs Marian in her belly, the latter decides she needs an exorcist (Tim), a low-key gentleman dressed in all black. After some repartee, he tells Marian that the niece's possession can be broken by symbols of goodness that they show her. These include a picture of Doris Day drinking milk, a white shoe worn by Pat Boone and ultimately a set of Shirley Temple glasses used by the Johnny Mann Singers doing a tribute to "America the Beautiful" with special guest star Kate Smith. Tim says this has cured Bernadette. "She has nothing but goodness and purity in her heart and her soul and a little bit in her knee," he tells the women, causing Carol to lose it as she spits out her lines between chuckles. Tim sits on a chair that rises followed by final questions. Will Marian never again have relations in the house? Will the niece return to D.C., where strange behavior is taken for granted? And why was Lyle exorcised from this script? (He comes out a side door but is cut off before he speaks, although he does serve as narrator.) This shines from start to finish.

Bernadette's solo is slow and passable, although she looks great in a white gown and lighting that highlights her facial beauty. Better is the next skit that Lyle introduces (and then disappears until the end credits). Carol is an opinionated woman sitting at a restaurant table whose bluntness unnerves Vicki, her long-lost pal. She belittles Vicki's marriage, recording contract, acting career (she is in a Neil Simon play that is going to be a movie with Mike Nichols directing it), and even Robert Redford for being selected as Vicki's co-star. "You call that a movie star?" she sniffs. Carol's dismissal of these accomplishments leads Vicki to tears about her life as she exits. After that, Carol sits up and gets a table for two, proving that she is not as successful as she implied. This is a good, cutting sketch, well done on all parts.

The comic momentum stays tight with a solid Tim-Harvey bit, although their imitation of Japanese military men during the 1940s unfortunately has tinges of insensitivity today (thankfully they do not use demeaning makeup in their guises). Getting beyond that, there are laughs aplenty as hits from other subs springs leaks they have to plug, and it is especially amusing watching Tim grapple with a periscope Harvey raises and lowers at will. Sometimes it crushes his head, others it lifts him high and then drops him with a thud. During the latter bit, Tim really grimaces and cracks up some about the pain of the landing (supposedly he had undergone a vasectomy shortly before this taping, adding to his real aggravation). They shoot a torpedo at a target, only for it to go the wrong direction toward them. Tim pushes it back, but Harvey sees an opportunity and launches the torpedo with Tim attached to it as it blows up. This is smart, fast and funny overall.

Tim appears once again with Harvey as the latter is a barber preparing to shave Stan Mazin, who is Tim's target for a mob hit. While Harvey is preoccupied, Tim tries many failed efforts to kill Stan, culminating in Tim accidentally blowing himself up. Any hope that Stan is safe is dashed when Harvey sneezes and unintentionally slashes his customer's neck. Despite a somewhat unsettling end, this is pretty good.

The musical finale has Carol playing the songs of Harry Warren when Harvey, her classmate, visits and is so impressed, he asks her to help him serenade Bernadette before pinning her. Carol loves Harvey so much that she swallows her pride, and in a nice scene change, the background behind her is lit up to show the dancers in outfits with Art Deco black-and-white designs in a number. That leads to a superb tap routine with Bernadette joining the dancers, and all the male dancers end up pinning her while Harvey inadvertently loses his pin for her. He sings his sorrows to the female dancers, then has a few romantic numbers with Carol before Bernadette reappears. Though Harvey leaves with her, he sees the error of his ways and rejoins Carol. The production is a winning one.

This top-of-the-line entry deservedly won the Emmy for best writing.

Feb. 23, 1974: Eydie Gorme, Tim Conway

Q&A; a housewife (Carol) hears a radio interview show and realizes her neighbor is sleeping with the housewife's husband; Eydie sings "The Way We Were"; a series of blackouts based around musical numbers with the cast and guests; Nazi officer Wolfgang Schveinholt (Tim) sees his attempts along with his subordinate (Harvey) to interrogate an American prisoner (Lyle) go haywire; a gypsy teller (Vicki) predicts the future of a woman (Carol); a dinner party is interrupted by investigators (Lyle and Vicki); Tim and Harvey take on *Lost Horizon*; Carol and Eydie do a medley with the dancers.

Comments: Conway sings! Or at least he tries, among the highlights of this spotty but generally above average effort. In the Q&A, Carol tells a set of girl twins how she once pretended to a guy that she had her own double for four days, and says her favorite characters to play are Nora Desmond and Charo (this would later change to be Eunice). The first sketch is golden: Carol's mostly mimed reactions to when she learns her neighbor (voice of Vicki) is telling a radio host (voice of Harvey) that she's having sex with Carol's husband is beautiful. To add to the fun, Vicki's commentary lets Carol know that her husband (Lyle) will be dropping by to get items to add to their romantic rendezvous. Thus alerted, Carol passes off sticks of dynamite to Lyle as candles, which he eagerly grabs and lights, causing an explosion at the cheating lovers' house. A satisfied Carol then sings the last line of "My Way" to celebrate.

Eydie does a fine job of the Oscar-winning Best Song, and the effect of starting and ending it with an overhead shot of a window pane with rain was pleasing as well. Singing will continue in the next bit, but this time with comedy emphasized. The recurring element has Tim vocalizing the first line of "Ebb Tide" before getting hit with buckets of water every direction repeatedly, even while protecting himself with umbrellas from directions he had been doused previously. Between each take, the following happens:

1) Lyle sings "Goodnight Irene" to Vicki, whose character name is Helen, so she punches him (and he hits her back, not exactly a funny move);

2) Dressed as a construction worker, Harvey does the first two lines of "Blowing in the Wind" about being a man before mincing off the stage;

3) Eydie's rendition of "The Boy Next Door" ends when Harvey enters walking on his knees, looking like Toulouse Lautrec (and he hits her, again not funny);

4) A mugger (Harvey) tries to get cash from a broke woman (Carol), who responds with "I Can't Give You Anything But Love (Baby)"—he gives her $20 to leave him alone and she smacks him in response;

5) Vicki croons "Getting to Know You" to Tim who inadvertently bumbles and crashes all over her apartment (she hits him followed by him hitting her); and

6) Harvey intones "I Talk to the Trees" until two male dancers including Don Crichton take him away to a mental hospital.

The sketch ends with Tim getting a pie in the face. Overall, this is funny apart from the implied female abuse, but it feels like these bits had already been done on *Laugh-In*.

More inspired is Tim's World War II bit, where his Aryan officer generates guffaws as he jumps onto a desk on his knees and puts on a hand puppet of Adolf Hitler to squeak "I've Been Working on the Railroad" in a high-pitched voice. Lyle cracks up at this while being interrogated, plus Tim has the puppet grab a pencil and say "He's gonna hit you with that club!" Lyle escapes with his secrets intact, but Tim was the real winner here.

Unfortunately, the next sketch goes awry, as potentially funny complications never quite pan out. As a fortune teller (Vicki) looks into a crystal ball, she predicts a great future for her guest (Carol), starting with the arrival of a tall, dark stranger (Lyle). From there, however, while Vicki sees good times, Carol loses Lyle to a jilted woman (Eydie) who kills him and gives her the gun for protection. Don Crichton appears to arrest Carol for Lyle's murder, but then Stan Mazin and his henchman knock Don out and demand Carol give them some microfilm. Tim interrupts the proceedings as a Central American leader and thanks Carol for denying the microfilm. She is rewarded with a toy and teddy bear by the president of Tim's country (Harvey), but he puts her on the firing squad when he learns she is from Akron, Ohio (apparently this season's big in-joke—see Dec. 15, 1973 for another reference). Harvey's men shoot her, then she crawls back to Vicki to pay her money, and Vicki asks her if she really believed what she had been saying. There is too much going on here for too long, and it should have been changed at the end—seeing anybody blindfolded and mock shot is not funny to witness.

Two quick skits follow. The first is a trivial one where the joke is that Lyle and Vicki have arrived at a dinner party to arrest Harvey as a suspect in a crime, but the duo arrived at the wrong event to make the charge. Better is a mini-spoof of 1937's *Lost Horizon*, with Harvey doing a precise Ronald Colman impersonation to ask for the philosophy of life from Tim's old High Lama. He provides such dubious wisdom as beer being the source of his longevity. This is silly but more amusing than the two previous efforts, and it is always fun watching Harvey and Tim try to stifle laughter with each other.

The medley finale with Carol and Eydie is chiefly of note because of their dazzling black spangly pantsuits and that the most current song Eydie sings is "The Beat Goes On." That tune was popularized by Sonny and Cher in 1966, and contemporary viewers must have wondered why that couple's series excelled in presenting the current music scene as compared to what was offered here. Anyhow, Carol cracks up over Tim's off-key and off-the-beat vocals at the end and imitates them as she does "It's Time to Say So Long." Likewise, this episode is just slightly off on being the best of what this series can offer.

March 2, 1974: Pre-empted by the Grammy Awards

March 9, 1974: Steve Lawrence

* A TV reporter (Harvey) interviews Houdini's daughter (Carol), who plans to escape from a trunk; an Italian woman (Carol) tries to comprehend the moves being made on her by an American barfly (Harvey); Steve performs "You Will Be My Music"; auditions for a PTA show directed by a Russian (Steve) pits a veteran star (Carol) against an upstart (Vicki); Carol puts a hit out on her husband (Harvey) without knowing details about it; Vicki and Harvey are a couple dressed as their opposite gender who start acting the way they look; a finale based on a "Lonesome Road" medley.

Comments: Only two of the five sketches presented here catches fire, making this installment a lost effort. Though all three misses were tough to endure, Carol's top fan Kathy Clements said one sketch was one the star loathed doing the most along with "Mary Worthless" (see Nov. 1, 1972), as much because some key props went awry during the first taping as because it simply was awful.

As Carol explains in a preface on the air show before the tape runs, "I didn't want to do it again because it was a shambles. And we decided we're going to show it anyway, just to let you know, because it was so silly and dumb. . . . At one point you'll see a second time I sit down on a crate and it's supposed to break, and it didn't, and, ah, so I kept trying to break it, and finally it did. And then at the end, I was supposed to get all wrapped around in a microphone cord, and it's supposed to pull me off the end of the pier, but it broke. . . . And I was cracking up the whole time and poor Harvey was there with me. So at the end, I just jumped off the pier, and I didn't want to do the sketch again. So we're going to show you what we did. Please forgive us."

Carol's summary is much funnier that watching her as Flo Ziegfeld Houdini tell a reporter (Harvey) that she plans to follow in her father's steps by being handcuffed hand and foot, and bound and gagged, before being put in a trunk that will have cement poured on it and be locked, then dumped in the ocean. The supposed humor is that the zipper on her jacket becomes stuck and she cannot remove it properly, along with her butt becoming stuck on a crate when she sits on it. The problem during the taping was not just the crate failed to collapse, as Carol noted, but also a tiresome setup as she supposedly makes other entanglements in which she could not escape. It is sloppy slapstick that would have failed even if everything else went right during this bit, which includes most of the male dancers acting as Harvey's TV crew members.

More tedium occurs as Harvey eyes Carol, a curly-haired brunette, and spends nearly five long minutes at a lounge trying to seduce her despite a language barrier that brings many misunderstandings. For example, when he indicates to a bartender (Don Crichton) that he wants to buy a double, Carol interprets it as him implying that she is a hooker. Frustrated, Harvey leaves, and to little surprise, Carol reveals she knew what he was saying and only pretending to be Italian. Steve then covers a song that was a minor entry for Frank Sinatra on the easy listening charts in 1974, which does not help brighten the pace.

Stumbling onward, Sheila Rogers introduces Steve to a group of suburban moms. He is a professional director from the Soviet Union who will lead this year's PTA production of *My Fair Lady*. As first lady of the local theatre scene, Carol assumes she naturally will have the lead, but Vicki arrives to audition with a rousing rendition of "I Could've Danced All Night." Carol interrupts Vicki's singing to offer her mangled take on the tune, but she realizes she is no match, so she threatens to withdraw her husband's sizable financial donations to the school unless she become Eliza Doolittle. Improbably, she has a change of heart and reluctantly lets Vicki take the part. For a third consecutive time, a sketch starts nowhere and goes little beyond that.

Thankfully, classic Carol emerges when she tells her friend (Vicki) that she has paid a man to kill her husband (Harvey), but she does not know who, when, where or how. When Harvey arrives at the restaurant, a nervous Vicki crawls away on her hands and knees to avoid any possible collateral damage. The waiter who takes their order (Lyle) seems to be winking at Carol and pointing at Harvey's temple, making her assume he is the assailant. But when Carol learns Harvey has become a millionaire due to an inheritance from his late uncle, she takes drastic actions to preserve her husband from being shot. She learns that Steve is the real killer as he complains that her check bounced on him. A seemingly unwitting Harvey pays the check, which leads to Carol, Steve and Harvey all fighting over Steve's gun. Carol ends up getting shot, followed by Harvey asking Steve, "How much do I owe you?" "Nothing," Steve responds. "I said *her* check bounced. Yours was fine. Mind if I join you?" A great setup, snappy dialogue, clever mugging all make this a humorous offering the previous skits should have emulated.

Slightly less enjoyable but still good is Harvey dressed as a woman and Vicki as a man returning from a masquerade party who have failed to realized a hypnotist has put a spell on them to act like the opposite sex once they hear the sound of a clap. The series once again puts a light but insightful spin on traditional human behavior, and Vicki and Harvey's acting carry this across winningly. The finale was fine as well.

This episode marks Steve's fourth appearance on the series this season. It will be the most he made on the series in one season until 1977-1978, as well as the highest number by a male guest star apart from Tim Conway in any season.

March 16, 1974: Roddy McDowall, the Jackson 5

Q&A; Roddy and Carol do a love medley duet, followed by Roddy showing how he becomes made into an ape; Lyle introduces the debut of "The Family," with Roddy visiting his self-absorbed sister, brother-in-law and mother; two male carpenters (Harvey and Lyle) dismissive the new female (Carol) on their project; the Jackson 5 lip sync to "Dancing Machine"; a phone call interrupts Carol,

Harvey, Lyle and Vicki as they wait at a bus stop; Carol and Roddy have a modern "Brief Encounter"; a substitute teacher (Carol) gets hip with her class of the Jackson 5 and the dancers.

Comments: This key episode is the first appearance for not only Eunice and her clan but also its guests, two of the most durable and enjoyable acts to appear on the series. Overall this is a solid output. The Q&A is mostly trivial—another redhead asks Carol if she likes her hair color, Carol reveals her favorite color (yellow) and her favorite actor again (Jimmy Stewart). "Have I gone streaking?" she laughs at one query. "No, I think there's enough violence on television!" Before saying she will perform *I Do I Do* in summer stock with Rock Hudson in a few months, Carol's most enlightening moment here is saying the new character she is doing tonight in the Family sketch is one she really enjoys, and that it is based upon her grandmother as well.

"One of Hollywood's nicest gentlemen," Carol introduces Roddy, who comes out in a tux with his face made up as an ape. Without acknowledging his looks, he says *Cleopatra* was the one film he did that had the greatest influence on himself and quotes from it. They perform parts of six romantic songs including "Tea for Two" before Carol dispenses with their contrived banter and reveals it took Roddy three and a half hours to do his makeup for the show as a reminder of his role in the *Planet of the Apes* movies (he will star in the disastrous TV series spinoff of them on CBS later in 1974). Roddy then narrates a film clip showing how he transformed from man into an ape character, ending with a shot of him smoking, and gives Carol his fake ears before heading offstage to get back to normal. This bit is more interesting than funny but still effective.

The first encounter with "The Family" occurs next, and it already has many elements that will be discussed in the future, including a mention of Ed's assistant Mickey Hart, whom Eunice calls a lamebrain. The plot has Philip (Roddy), a successful writer, visiting his mother's house and meeting an ecstatic Eunice, while Ed chews on an apple and brags about his hardware store. When Philip mentions he has won the Nobel and Pulitzer prizes, an unimpressed Ed and Eunice argue instead about where they put the *TV Guide*. Mama finally emerges and complains about how her hair looks bad thanks to Eunice causing her to miss her hair appointment. The interplay alone between Carol and Vicki during this dialogue is crackling, unlike anything else the two had done previously, and shows this is a new element worthy of keeping on the series.

Getting back to the segment, Mama is just as disinterested in Philip's activities when Eunice tells everyone to look at how cute Mama's dog, Topaz, looks sleeping. Philip makes a noise to accidentally wake the canine, to everyone's distress, then says he cannot stay long as he has to go to London to interview Princess Anne. This prompts the others to discuss gossip about the Royal Family before Mama interjects that Philip is the only one in the family with talent. Eunice becomes defensive and argues before Topaz acts cute again (offstage), and the Family turns their attention to him. A puzzled Philip leaves as the remaining trio dismisses him unceremoniously. It is a strong start for the series' best-remember continuing characters, although its writers thought it was just a one-shot.

"I'll never forget the first reading of 'The Family' that they did," says Barry Levinson. "I said to Dick Clair [who co-wrote it with Jenna McMahon], 'You could just do a series of these sketches for the show.' Dick said, 'I don't know how we'll be doing another one.'" But the demand was there, and the will found a way. From this point onward, Clair and McMahon will write only "The Family" sketches for *The Carol Burnett Show*.

Less impressive is a tolerable piece where Harvey and Lyle dilly dally and fight while Carol, their new fellow carpenter, finishes installing panels for a building. They decline Carol's offer to buy them a beer but change their minds to escort her as she takes off her overalls to reveal a sexy skirt underneath it. This is a muddled, dated take on women's rights that at least does not run too long.

Saying "They've been a delight at all week," Carol says she hopes the series will see more of the Jackson 5. Despite not playing live, the gents are smoothly professional with their moves, with the highlight being Michael performing the Robot dance. They are now really the Jackson 6, as the youngest member, Randy, has joined them, along with an unidentified organist and drummer backing them. "Dancing Machine" is just entering the charts when this show first runs, and this shot gives the series the distinction of its first time of featuring a Number One soul hit by the original artists.

Next up are two relative quick skits, both good. In the first, a public phone rings as Carol, Harvey, Vicki and Lyle sit at a bus stop, and they learn that it is from the Dial-a-Buck radio show where they can win money. The answer is the day's newspaper, and as they go to the trash to retrieve it, a drunk (Stan Mazin) hangs up the phone ("That was fun," Stan recalls of that role.) The quartet cry about their lost anticipated winnings before going back to their routines. A clever, well-paced piece follows as Carol and Roddy exchange one-word answers as they discuss a possible affair at a restaurant table. The kicker is that Carol decides to leave him when he answers with a full sentence.

Even better is the finale, as students of the Glendale Musical School show their prim substitute teacher (Carol) how to become funky. After some dialogue that includes Michael Jackson cracking that he thinks Frankie Laine is one of the old singers like David Cassidy, Carol leads them in singing "This Old Man." A minor earthquake occurs and freaks out some on stage as Carol ad libs that it is nothing but the ground shaking. Continuing onward, the Jackson 5 break out into their 1970 hit "ABC" accompanied by the dancers in bright green outfits, and Carol shimmies along with the gang. This is a bright, lively way to close out the show.

There are so many Jacksons that at the end of the show, they were unable to finish signing their names until after the credits finished. It is a cute moment in a show abundant with them.

March 23, 1974: John Byner, Francine Beers

Q&A; two criminals (Carol and Harvey) have to pretend to be a waitress and cook when cops (Lyle and Don Crichton) arrive at the restaurant they intend to rob; John performs a comic monologue; Roger and Carol's efforts to celebrate their anniversary romantically are impaired by a woman (Francine) who is locked out of her apartment; Vicki lip syncs to "Mama's Gonna Make It All Better"; Harvey and John are scientists competing to see which one of their female robots (Carol and Vicki) is the best one; a send-up of country music awards by John, the regulars and the dancers.

Comments: What appears to be a substandard episode is redeemed by one of the most hilarious finales the series ever presented. The brief Q&A has Carol giving some Girl Scouts $20 for their cookies and saying the show will return next season. After that, Carol and Harvey must serve policemen and other patrons after they botch a theft at a diner. Carol becomes proficient in delivering orders in restaurant lingo, and Harvey whips up food instantly. After a montage indicating the passage of time during the night, the place becomes so crowded and crazy that Carol quits, but Harvey is proud of his new talent and refuses to leave, planning to go straight instead. The cops then confront them and plan to arrest the duo when they and other customers become sick from their meals. Harvey frets that he just was not cut out for cooking as they take money from everyone before leaving. This promising concept loses its comic potential by running too long.

John begins his monologue by saying, "I love working with Carol Burnett. Such a nice lady. Really sweet." He then launches a rambling monologue touching on being backstage with animals during *The Ed Sullivan Show* and having to act like you are not crying during a movie if you are a man. Despite using few impersonations, this is an acceptable if not outstanding piece.

After having acted opposite Carol in *6 RMS RIV VU* on CBS six days earlier, Francine Beers appears as a woman down the hall from Roger and Carol who is locked out of her apartment. The couple is excited that Chrissy is out and plans a romantic dinner, but when Francine cannot reach the building manager and says she will wait in the drafty dark hallway for him to arrive, Carol pressures Roger to let Francine stay with them. After promising to sit in the living room quietly, Francine butts in and joins the couple at their table while they exchange gifts. Francine's running commentary about the activities irks them so much that Roger leaves his apartment key with Francine as he and Carol leave to get their own place for solitude. This is unfocused and somewhat boring.

Vicki looks and sounds OK in her number, but she fares better in the next bit as a glamorous platinum blonde robot created by Harvey. John has one too, but Carol is a raggedy-haired metallic schlub that makes chugging noises. An unimpressed Harvey shows John how Vicki can make him a drink. Hearing the music that accompanies Vicki in this task, John ad libs, "She sounds like the beginning of *Wagon Train*," which amuses the cast. John gets the upper hand when it is revealed Carol can speak and Vicki cannot. Carol mocks Vicki with jokes until the latter collapses, but John cannot revel in his triumph, as Carol now nags him as they leave. This is the show's first good sketch.

The show soars into the comic stratosphere with "The Annual Rural Music Awards Show" from the Molly Bee Auditorium. This hysterical spoof of the 1970s country music scene has Carol and Vicki mock Loretta Lynn and Donna Fargo respectively and Harvey as Johnny Money (a Johnny Cash send-up) along with John as the host with a huge blond pompadour. Harvey has uproarious lines about songs that appeared that year, including a take-off name on Vicki's hit—"The Night My Tights Wore Out in Georgia"—"Tie a Yellow Ribbon Round the Old Redneck" and many more. After a number by Big John Black (Lyle), Vicki presents a great mockery of Tammy Wynette's hit "D-I-V-O-R-C-E" called "Split," and Harvey shines in a Cash-like original, "Fifteen Minutes to Go." Even with that, Carol's shining turn and an excellent, boisterous hoedown by the dancers, this is John's star turn. His hooting, hollering and whistling for the acts is amusing, and his own number, "Me and Little Suzy," about a man in love with his sow, lets him imitate playing a harmonica and snorting like a pig, both of which he delivers beautifully.

Continuing the theme, Carol sings "It's Time to Say So Long" in a country twang except for the last two words. Francine appears in the end credits to sign Carol's book as well.

March 30, 1974: Pre-empted by special *Grammy Salutes Oscar*

April 6, 1974: Family Show

Q&A; spoof of commercials; a manic depressive barfly (Carol) accuses another patron (Harvey) of trying to pick her up before she pours out her feelings to him; Carol sings "Al"; "Lucky Lady" has Lyle hosting a game show wherein a stylish Palm Springs beauty (Vicki) competes against a suffering women in a neck brace and leg casts (Carol); the dancers perform to "Apache Talk," a bolo ball samba number; "The Old Folks" wait early in the morning for a gas station to open; a tribute to songwriter Jule Styne; the Charwoman bids the cast farewell for the season.

Comments: Apart for a weak sketch, this season closer is satisfying. Carol includes mentioning the Ernie Flatt Dancers at the top as part of the family, which is nice, then cracks up when someone asks if she had silicone shots to improve her bust. On another topical matter, Carol quips, "I think streaking is all right. It keeps the kids on the streets." She thanks a woman praising her work in *6 RMS RIV VU* and reminds everyone of doing *I Do I Do* in stock with Rock Hudson this summer. Finally, asked what makes her so sensual, Carol replies with a deadpan face that "You're born with it!"

The commercials are a strong lot. Among the highlights, as Harvey robs a bank, he turns to the camera to brag, "You know what I'm doing right now? I'm cleaning my bathroom bowl!" Nasal congestion is like having a stopped-up drain, and Harvey has a drain on his nose to show that as a fact. The final two are classics. Vicki is considering what brand to use to treat irregularity when she is told to talk to her doctor. She waves at Harvey, her physician, but he blurts out, "Can't talk now!" as he urgently goes to the bathroom himself. Carol matches that by appearing as actress Ann Blyth, boasting how having a screen career makes her an expert on selling Hosties dessert products. "They have none of those pesky vitamins and minerals," she extols to home viewers before she gets up, revealing an obese lower body as she loses her balance and slams through a wall.

Too bad what follows is tough to endure, as a somewhat inebriated Carol vacillates between yelling at Harvey ("I hate all men!" she exclaims in one outburst) to thanking him for understanding her. Carol's yo-yoing between despair and ecstasy is as trying for viewers as Harvey, who finally tells her he must leave to go back to her wife. When another man (Brad Trumbull) enters the bar, it's obvious that she is going to start the whole hoary routine on him again. This mess should not have made the cut for air.

After a passable straight solo number, Carol fares better playing a game show contestant from the lower east side of Appalachia who lives in a box and supports fourteen children as she waits for her husband to return from World War II and has a brother on fire. She wants to win against Vicki, a posh socialite, in a spoof of *Queen for a Day*-type shows featuring needy women. This works because of the utter comic disdain Vicki and Lyle (as the smarmy host) display to Carol—for example, Lyle wraps his microphone cord around Carol and constrains her as he interviews Vicki intently. When the audience votes to award Carol as most deserving but Lyle picks Vicki instead, an enraged Carol removes her cast and crutches, decks Lyle and Vicki, and walks through the aisle in the studio audience to leave the show amid much applause and laughter.

Dressed in Mexican outfits, the dancers do a solid job in their feature number, which leads into Bert and Molly sitting in a jalopy in the early morning to beat the crowds for gas. Since this is 1974, there are jokes about the energy crisis and other topical matters. Bert's leg grab reminds Molly of *The Exorcist*—"It would take a supernatural miracle," she says, in reference to his move leading to sex. Molly adds, "Our love life is like the Watergate tapes. Eighteen minutes of nothing!" It ends with Bert learning the station is out of gas and telling Molly she will need to siphon some from another car instead. If one can bear with the dated references, this is a very good entry for "The Old Folks."

The finale has a storyline where a stagehand (Carol) loves a clown (Harvey), but he has eyes only for a trapeze artist (Vicki). She in turn has the hots for the ringmaster (Lyle) and leaves with him, while Carol and Harvey connect as well. With more than ten Jule Styne tunes used, many of them familiar, and a colorful circus setting, this is a better-than-average salute to a songwriter by the show.

The final goodbye is rather quick—the usual Charwoman watching on TV to hear the show will be in reruns, followed by her saying so long to the dancers, Harvey, Vicki and Lyle, then singing all of "It's Time to Say So Long" while sitting on a bucket after hearing a recorded version of the first verse and leaving the studio through the audience. There's no special acknowledgment about Lyle leaving, but at least he had some good work in this episode to end seven years with the show.

Despite the irritating barfly sketch, this show managed to earn a writing Emmy nomination, which it lost to another episode of *The Carol Burnett Show* (see Feb. 16, 1974). The fact that two episodes of the series made the cut over entries from other variety series speaks volumes about the quality of the writing in the genre this season.

Final Notes for the Season

The Carol Burnett Show finished at Number Twenty-Seven and easily beat its competition, movies on NBC (which will remain its competition through the end of 1977) and *Griff* and its midseason replacement *Owen Marshall, Counselor at Law* on ABC. Its Emmy success was even better. It won for variety series, directing (the first for Dave Powers, deservedly for the Dec. 8, 1973 show from Australia), writing (the Feb. 16, 1974 show thankfully beat out 1973's so-so "Family Show" closer, which somehow fell into this nomination period) and supporting actor (Harvey Korman, beating out Tim Conway listed in the same category for his work on *The Carol Burnett Show*).

Other Emmy nominations included Vicki Lawrence for supporting actress, Paul Barnes and Bob Sansom for art direction and Bill Harp for set decoration for the Feb. 16, 1974 show, and Ernie Flatt for his choreography and Peter Matz for his music direction, both of the latter two for the Australia show. The show had ten nominations, its highest to date.

For its second and last time, the Writers Guild of America awarded the Best Variety accolade to the series this year (the first was in 1971). Golden Globe nominations occurred for the series, Carol and Harvey. Dave Powers lost his sole nomination ever from the Directors Guild of America for Best Direction in Musical-Variety Shows to Dwight Hemion for the special *Barbra Streisand & Other Musical Instruments*.

About the only person not nominated this year was Lyle Waggoner, as had been the case previously. Seeing little room for professional growth or higher pay, he left the series to pursue better acting opportunities. He remained friends with Al Schultz, Vicki's husband, but otherwise saw little of the show's regulars.

"Lyle in his own way was as good as what he was given," opines Arnie Kogen. The problem was that there was not much to give him. He did not find another regular TV series role until *Wonder Woman* on ABC starting Dec. 18, 1976, which ran three seasons (the last two on CBS). Ironically, he was playing support again to another woman, only this time in a comic book adventure series.

Vicki divorced Bobby Russell by the end of this season, less than a year after they were wed. An alcoholic addicted to uppers, he abused Vicki and her dog and cheated on her openly. Bobby collected Nazi uniforms and once told her because she was part Jewish, if Hitler was alive, she would have been dead. His professional career went downward shortly after their split. Bobby died on Nov. 19, 1992 of a heart attack at age fifty-one.

In the wake of all this off-screen drama, as with the previous summer, CBS moves reruns of an action adventure series, this time *Barnaby Jones*, to fill in for *The Carol Burnett Show* in 1974, while having *60 Minutes* assume the Sunday night slot held by *Barnaby Jones* during the 1973-1974 season. When *The Carol Burnett Show* returns in September, it and *Mannix* will hold the record as the oldest nighttime series on CBS. *Mannix* will not last beyond 1975, but *The Carol Burnett Show* will—even though the series for some reason will produce shows that have the most up-and-down quality ever in one season.

Flanked by Jean Stapleton and Phil Silvers, the latter a big fan of the series, Carol tugs her left ear as she traditionally did after "It's Time to Say So Long" as a nod to how she greeted her grandmother at home. This penultimate episode of the 1974-1975 season was one of several shows done without a pregnant Vicki Lawrence in what was a rather rocky period for the series. Courtesy of Getty Images.

Chapter 9

1974–1975: Who's on the Show Tonight?

Audience member:	"I'm getting married, and I want to know if you can give me some advice. Maybe sing?"
Carol:	"The first advice I give you is not to have me sing at your wedding! . . . He's an Arab and you're Polish? I wouldn't touch that!"—From the Jan. 25, 1975 show

Crew Additions This Season

Conductor: Irwin Kostal (temporary replacement for Peter Matz Jan. 4 and 11, 1975)

All outward signs showed *The Carol Burnett Show* looking unbeatable as the series embarked on its eighth season. Its lead-in, *The Bob Newhart Show*, remained popular, and its fall competition on ABC, *Nakia*, bombed so badly that the network began offering movies midseason just as NBC was doing, virtually guaranteeing Carol an audience for anyone who missed the first hour of each. And for once in the 1970s, the writing team remained the same, with the exception of the loss of Barry Harman from 1973-1974.

There were some troublesome signs in the air, however. One was an alarming dip in the variety genre. In the fall of 1974, *The Carol Burnett Show* was now just one of two network variety series. The other was *The Sonny Bono Comedy Revue* on ABC, which resulted from his divorce of Cher earlier in 1974 that also canned their series. It was a flop, and his wife's effort, *Cher* on CBS, started out strong in the start of 1975 but faded in its second season as well. Also gone now were former NBC hits *The Dean Martin Show* and *The Flip Wilson Show*. Yet this proved to be a temporary slump, and in fact more variety series emerged in the 1975-1976 season, including NBC's late night *Saturday Night Live*, which would outlast them all and still be on the air 40 years later.

The lack of competition in its genre turned out not to harm *The Carol Burnett Show* as much as it seemed the show floundered without Lyle Waggoner, of all things. The decision not to replace him somewhat surprisingly left the series with what sometimes felt like a hole in its ensemble in skits and musical numbers.

Indeed, fluctuations among appearances by the regulars added to viewer frustration. Harvey missed the Nov. 9, 1974 show. Vicki became pregnant with her first daughter, Courtney, and when she began showing her condition by early 1975, Joe Hamilton wanted to keep her off for the rest of the season, citing that she had violated a "deformity clause" in her contract. After missing a few shows, she returned when Carol intervened, primarily because Carol missed doing Eunice and "The Family." The cast call at the end of the 1975 shows indicated she was pregnant, but the show did not acknowledge that fact until the season finale. (To top it off, Vicki had a frizzy hairdo in the first few shows that viewers loathed, so she dropped it by 1975.)

Another complication was that Joe Hamilton also assumed executive producer responsibility on *The Smothers Brothers Show* that began airing in midseason on NBC. More on that can be found in the Oct. 12, 1974 entry, but suffice it to say that running two variety shows at the same time is a time consuming chore that can affect one's judgment, and that possibly had an effect on this season's shows as well.

Seemingly to compensate for all these shortcomings, more regulars from popular CBS series will appear than *The Carol Burnett Show* ever had or would use in other seasons to attract viewers. Three of the network's top detectives will appear—Telly Savalas (*Kojak*), William Conrad (*Cannon*) and Buddy Ebsen (*Barnaby Jones*). So will Nancy Walker, the mother on *Rhoda*. Also dropping by are two stars from *M*A*S*H*, Alan Alda and Wayne Rogers, as well as a pair from *All in the Family*, Jean Stapleton and Sally Struthers. (The star of *All in the Family*, Carroll O'Connor, will team up with Carol to play her husband on guest shots on the NBC sitcom *Mad About You* in the 1990s. As to why the series' other star, Rob Reiner, never did *The Carol Burnett Show*, his father, Carl Reiner, quips, "I don't know, maybe they didn't ask him?").

The series tried another tactic usually employed in desperation to goose up the ratings by adding child performers, in this case Lena Zavaroni and Steven Warner, something that had not been employed since Julie Budd and Karen Wyman appeared in the 1970-1971 season. Neither was as popular as the Jackson 5, a holdover from the prior season.

Several guest stars also will spend an inordinate amount of time on air this season in part due to Vicki's condition, such as Alan Alda in every sketch and musical number on his show (plus the Q&A!), and Jean Stapleton and Rock Hudson in all but one skit in theirs. It all left the impression that the series was now concentrating on Carol and her guests over the regular ensemble, which is fine but not what *The Carol Burnett Show* is about.

While these developments seemed chaotic to watch unfold on screen, all the writers interviewed indicated the comings and goings of the regulars were not problematic for them. As Barry Levinson says, "We were just back in our rooms writing."

That may be one reason why the series' overall quality became more variable within most episodes than in 1973-1974 despite having the same essential personnel. Few shows this season managed to be consistently funny or entertaining overall (for one exception, see Nov. 9, 1974). There seemed to be a disjointed air, as if the production was trying to find its way for new sources of humor but often relying on old ones to the point of exhaustion. Indeed, this would be the last season to employ the increasingly overdone characters of Norma Desmond, Fireside Girl Alice Portnoy, "The Old Folks" and "Carol & Sis."

Variety bears out this opinion, as for the first time, a reviewer panned the series' season opener, hating everything except its opening and closing numbers. This brickbat indicated there was some stagnation with the production that needed to be addressed.

To be fair, there were several excellent skits scattered throughout the season, just not enough to result in consistently outstanding shows. If nothing else, 1974-1975 solidified the appeal of "The Family," as previously indicated by the demand for a pregnant Vicki to rejoin the series just to do Mama again. However, those sketches produced their own headache for head writer Ed Simmons due to the way Dick Clair and Jenna McMahon wrote them, according to fellow scribe Gene Perret.

"They spent an inordinate amount of time on them and wrote them so that they were almost full sitcom scripts rather than sketches for a variety show," Perret says. "Ed Simmons had the task of cutting these down to usable size."

Apart from that, other elements were fine this season more often than not. The show just needed a kick—and it will get one next season with Tim Conway becoming a regular.

This season's introduction has an animated Charwoman opening doors to find Harvey and then Vicki in her poorly received curly hairstyle. An uncharacteristic wah-wah guitar plays music as Carol shows up briefly in three wild getups such as a mermaid, then goes back to the Charwoman who comes on stage, smiles at the camera and sees the latter stick its tongue out at her in derision before it explodes and the curtain descends to display "The Carol Burnett Show" title, with the Charwoman peeking out from the bottom at the end. Like most of the 1974-1975 episodes, it seems somewhat off the mark.

The 1974 CBS fall preview airing before the season opener, "See the Best," featured Ernie Anderson as narrator, a sign of the impact Carol's show had on this year's festivities. Ted Knight played Ted Baxter of *The Mary Tyler Moore Show* announcing returning shows as a news story with a generous helping of Burnett clips from the previous season interspersed within his routine, including the March 16, 1974 skit with Harvey and Lyle as handymen, even though Lyle is now gone. When the preview showed what was on each night at the end, it naturally ended on Saturday with a shot of Carol doing Q&A. That's how it begins this season too, but with a little twist added before it.

Sept. 14, 1974: Jim Nabors

The dancers perform "With an A, B, C" to introduce Carol; Q&A; Eunice, Ed and Mama meditate on a sermon on brotherly love; Carol is a housewife who learns about people leaving her in a peculiar fashion; Jim sings "One Life"; Harvey has to comfort Carol as they go to bed and she lists her dislikes about her features; Carol sings "Just a Gigolo" as a hint to Vicki about the true intentions of Harvey; Jim faces the consequences at an arcade when he outdraws the game character Black Bart; the finale "Rimshot" salutes jokes and drummers who punctuate them.

Comments: While the negative *Variety* review for this show seems overly harsh and misses some good elements, the critic was correct in noting how surprisingly poorly several skits miss their mark. There is no indication of that happening from the start, as the dancers sprightly carry placards, each with a large letter on it, that rapidly spell out words derived from "Carol Burnett" before displaying the star's name. The incredible choreography is performed with split-second precision and sets an energetic tone for Carol to come out and start the Q&A, which has a hysterical and classic exchange. "Did you ever go to acting school?" asks one girl. "Yes, I did. I took acting at UCLA, and then I went to Jeff Corey's class out here for a short while," Carol responds. The woman shoots back "Done any good, do you think?" and the audience shrieks in laughter, as does Carol, who composes herself to say, "I don't think it did!"

"The Family" has its weakest episode ever on this series. Mama, Ed and Eunice come home impressed by a sermon on brotherly love from their preacher, although the effects vary—Mama tears up remembering her late husband, while Ed just wants to eat at the Waffle Palace. Mama demands that they all eat at her home, to Ed's chagrin. Eunice calls up her sister, Ellen, to let her know she forgives the latter for her behavior, but she argues with Mama about being petty first. When Eunice does reach Ellen by phone, her sister rejects the offer, and Eunice slams the receiver down. Mama does Eunice no favors by rhapsodizing how her late husband loved Ellen, prompting more yelling between the two. The trip down memory lane makes Mama want to visit her husband's gravesite, but Eunice says that will not happen in order to avoid Mama making a "jackass" of herself, leading to more arguments. Finally, Eunice acquiesces to Mama's demand, Ed reads the Bible and they all leave together. This is overextended (fifteen minutes) and has the actors shout repeatedly in a vain effort to generate laughs.

Things improve when Carol enters a kitchen and opens her refrigerator door to see a note written on a roll of toilet paper hanging from it from her son complaining that her current tissue is not soft enough. The writers take this parody of a commercial to very funny extremes, with Carol's son writing that he has run away and her daughter leaving a roll on the shelves saying she has split too, this time with a motorcycle gang. A deliveryman (Randy Doney) gives her a roll from her husband, another hater of the not-soft-enough tissue who has departed with a lady chiropractor. A toilet paper roll crashes through her window, and Carol learns it is from her neighbors who want her to move. Carol's cleaning lady is wrapped in the closet by a robber who hated her toilet paper, and finally the

Jolly Green Giant drops a huge roll that busts through her kitchen door. This is good, with Carol's wails between reading each roll adding to the laughs.

Jim's lip-syncing of his operatic vocals for his solo number in a leisure suit afterward generates little excitement. Neither does Carol and Harvey's routine, which like the Family one runs too long and emphasizes raised voices. Harvey dismisses Carol's unhappiness with her body until he notes lines on her body she points out to him. She complains about a blotch on his head to get back at him, they bicker and then make up and go to bed—then Harvey starts worrying about the blotch again. This plot and theme will be revised for the March 13, 1976 show, where it is funnier and better.

Also variably funny is Carol in a nightclub saluting Vicki and Harvey as a couple that will be married in two weeks with "Just a Gigolo," with the lyrics and Carol's movements serving as hints to Vicki about what a cad Harvey really is. After some mildly amusing reactions, it ends with Vicki planting a pie in Harvey's face.

The real downer is the arcade sketch, where Jim (using his Gomer Pyle voice) learns from an aged coin lady (Carol) that his success in outdrawing Black Bart at a game means that more gunslingers will be after him now in person. The first is Harvey, who is killed by Jim and falls onto a pinball machine. Vicki emerges as a showgirl mourning Harvey as he dies and vows to get vengeance even though he pleads for her not to do it. Carol implores Jim to stay and protect the arcade's customers as a new marshal before Ernie Anderson shows up as an officer to arrest Jim for Harvey's murder. There is nothing clever in extending this fake dueling scenario to extremes, and it is tedious.

At least the finale is an improvement, with a silhouette of a drummer on screen being featured center stage while Carol, Jim, Vicki and Harvey appear in red and white outfits to sing and tell jokes before the dancers appear, accompanied with a strong drumbeat naturally. As in the opener, the dancers are exceptional in their performances.

Carol ends the show cracking up the audience by saying, "And remember, the next time you see someone causing pollution, hit them in the mouth!" Too bad the bulk of this show lacked the energetic delivery she displays here.

Sept. 21, 1974: Steve Lawrence

* Roger and Carol both confess to Chris individually that they have spent the afternoon drinking but do not want her to let their spouse know this, a secret which she slyly agrees to keep with each of them; a roast of Nora Desmond which includes Steve as the host and Vicki as Phyllis Diller cracking jokes shocks the honoree and her assistant Max; a mini-musical set in Las Vegas acts as a tribute to composer Frank Loesser and includes "Luck Be a Lady Tonight."

Comments: As a half hour repeat, this show comes off as a lesser entry, and given that Joe Hamilton usually edited each program down to its comic highlights, this one looks like a miss overall. The last outing for "Carol & Sis" includes one jarring note that is unfunny now, as Carol's tipsy bridge group winds down and an unidentified actress brags how she can drive drunk no problem. "Don't worry about a thing. There's not a cop in the world who can catch me!" she cackles. After that disturbing comment, Carol confesses to Chris what had happened while making her sister pledge not to tell her husband as she goes to cook dinner. When Roger enters, he admits having martinis at a business lunch, but like Carol, he does not want Chris to spill the beans to his spouse. Naturally, both stumble and fumble until they learn something is amiss with each other—in Carol's case, she thinks Roger does not love her anymore—before they collapse in each other's arms, giggling and making up. The freshness of the plots for these characters has long passed the expiration date since last season, and this is a merciful albeit messy way to end what had been a regular feature on the series since the premiere.

Somewhat better is Steve and Phyllis Diller (Vicki) throwing verbal jabs at Nora Desmond on a dais. When an enraged Max grabs Steve and tells him that "Madame does not do shtick!" the shaken host turns over the floor to Phyllis, who lets loose with lines like "She's the only other woman on Earth besides me who wears prescription underwear!" That leads Max to choke her until she crawls away under the table. Seeing how the proceedings are going, Steve then asks Max to take the podium to praise his boss. He does so, until he slips when saying, "She is committed—at least she should be!" Hearing laughter, he mocks Nora's figure and face as well before she pulls him down and he apologizes to her. She comes up to speak next and goes on a roll making fun of Max. With its relatively brief length and some funny lines, this is pretty good overall.

This marks the second time in as many seasons where Steve appears solo as a guest.

Sept. 28, 1974: The Pointer Sisters, James Coco

Q&A; a housewife (Carol) has a verbal tussle with her margarine container that says it is butter; The Pointer Sisters perform "Steam Heat"; a hooker (Carol) is interrogated about a "floozy murder" by a bald cop (Harvey) in a *Kojak* spoof; James is an anxious man set up on a blind date by Harvey, who tries to bolster his confidence; Carol and the Pointers sing "Salt Peanuts"; a takeoff of the 1932 film *One Way Passage* features James romancing Carol on a ship while she has a fatal illness; everyone participates in a production number centered around "The Entertainer."

Comments: Lively if a little lumpy, this offering features the first of six sparkling appearances by the Pointer Sisters. "We were watching the show before we did it," says Anita Pointer. "My mom, dad, everybody would watch it. We were so happy to do it." She and her sisters had done some variety series prior to this, including *The Helen Reddy Show*, and Anita credits their agent for securing this appearance.

The group was hot thanks to its first hit in 1973, "Yes We Can Can," but unfortunately they do not get a chance to do their next smash, "Fairytale," on this show, even though it will make the charts in a few weeks. Carol and the production team preferred them usually to do period tunes despite their contemporary success. Regarding the selection of what numbers they performed, Anita says, "I would imagine our producers probably worked with the producers on the show. We didn't have any say on the show."

For this show, Carol tells an audience member that Peter Matz conducts the orchestra before going into a silly but swift bit based on a popular albeit irritating commercial of the period. Carol gets so angry with her margarine tub talking back to her that she slaps it, then wails her apology about how she has tried to make her relationship work. She and the tub (voice of Harvey) reconcile before Harvey arrives home. "How's the margarine?" he asks. "Not bad," Carol says with a smile on her face. This is cute, tight and enjoyable.

In bright outfits, the Pointer Sisters trio smoothly performs a song from *The Pajama Game* in front of a backdrop with tea kettles floating aid white clouds. They lead into Harvey playing Krojak, a laidback detective assisting some cops (Ernie Anderson, Brad Trumbull, Stan Mazin and Randy Doney) in a bar where he announces, "There's a fruitcake in this town who likes going around killing bimbos!" He zeros in on Carol, a cranky prostitute who finally confesses she did the killings and reveals she is Krojak's daughter by pulling off her wig and revealing her bald head. Other bar patrons (played by the dancers) do the same to indicate they are Krojak's spawn as well. This is good but should have been shortened for better impact.

James Coco finally appears as a nervous pantyhose salesman who drinks a lot to calm his nerves while Harvey offers support. By the time Vicki arrives as James' date, he unloads all the pretend scenarios of their marriage he considered earlier onto her and finished with a flourish as he tells her his attorney will contact her the next day for their divorce. James' expert overplaying makes this sketch sing.

Likewise, Carol's energetic riffs on a 1945 Dizzy Gillespie hit with the Pointers enliven the following segment. "That was a great song," says Anita Pointer. The Pointers actually consulted the original artist to get advice on presenting it, and Anita adds that "Dizzy Gillespie said, 'I played it a little different every note.'" Carol includes a clip of this number as part of her one-woman stage show.

In "One Way Ticket," a dying Carol finds love from James in a white tux and toupee. Harvey (with an Irish brogue) is a cop who pursues James to go to the electric chair for the murder of 48 people, while Vicki is Dr. Ouspenskaya (a nod to Slavic character actress Maria Ouspenskaya, who Vicki imitates), who confirms Carol is deathly ill and needs to avoid doing "whatnot." James eventually stabs Harvey to spend more time with Carol, but she does not want Vicki to tell James she is dying, even while Carol has just two minutes to live. ("Right on the nose," Vicki notes when Carol passes.) We go to a New Year's Eve party where the ghosts of Carol and James reunite romantically. "And They Died Happily Ever After," notes a graphic on screen. This is an above-average old movie spoof with clever lines and snappy delivery by all.

The show wraps up delightfully with a presentation involving a 1903 Scott Joplin tune popularized again by Marvin Hamlisch as an instrumental in the movie *The Sting*. Here the Pointers and Carol, decked out in white finery and feathers, supply the lyrics while James plays the piano. He is as engaging in this minor role as he is in the rest of the show, and one wishes this was not his sole appearance on the series.

The *Variety* reviewer who roasted the season opener checked in again and liked this much better, although he noted that "The comedy writing still needs some sharpening, and new approaches would be helpful." Good thing he did not review the next show.

Oct. 5, 1974: Jack Weston, Michele Lee

A series of misunderstandings has a nurse (Carol) fear that her patient (Jack) is dying when in fact his wife (Vicki) wants a divorce to wed his doctor (Harvey); Carol hears an elaborate story from her husband (Harvey) about why he was late coming home; Michele performs "Well, Did You Evah?" with the dancers; Michele and Harvey's dinner to celebrate their engagement is hampered by an argument between her sister (Carol) and brother-in-law (Jack); a sot (Carol) berates a woman waiting for her date on a street corner (Vicki); a salute to songwriter Stephen Sondheim.

Comments: Apart from the second sketch, this is one of the series' weakest episodes ever, with many interminable unfunny moments that waste two talented guest stars. Any Q&A would have been better than the leadoff, an aggravating piece where Carol's confusion about what Harvey is saying causes her to going from laughing at Jack's jokes to crying about his supposed fatal diagnosis. After running far too long, it finally ends with Harvey and Vicki leaving and Carol and Jack having some chuckles over his bad jokes. Any farce where all the characters are having to mug and giggle over each other's comments to generate humor is a sign that it is not clicking, and that is the case here.

A glimmer of hope comes next with a truly clever skit. Harvey tells an irate Carol that his car battery died, which leads a complicated tale of how he encountered a driver and his sister who helped him, a motorcycle cop who stopped them, a juggler who hitchhiked a ride, an elderly woman at a hospital and a waitress. Realizing that Carol would disbelieve him, Harvey has all the participants sit in the living room and confirm the details. Stunned, Carol apologizes and all leave—but not before Harvey pays each and thanks them for participating in the cover-up, including a woman who kisses Harvey and gets ready for their next affair. The dancers, Ernie Anderson and Brad Trumbull play these roles rather than the guests, which is a shame given what Jack and Michele have to do the rest of the show.

Wearing a stunning blue grown, Michele sleekly moves and belts out a Cole Porter classic in a contemporary evening party scenario. This is well presented, but unfortunately it is downhill from there. Michele makes cutesy baby talk with Harvey sluggishly at a restaurant before Carol and Jack join them and snipe at each other. The two leave separately after Carol dumps a salad on Jack's head, and the incident chastens Michelle into giving the ring back to Harvey and departing, causing him to sigh in relief. This diatribe about marriage is both pointless and largely unfunny.

Even worse is a melodramatic mess where Carol sits on a stoop and harasses Vicki (and later Harvey, Vicki's date) while recounting her failed life. She forces Harvey to promise to treat Vicki well before he leaves. The pathos is so calculated that Carol picks up a wandering cat and bonds with it as her only friend at the end. This interminable piece is so enervating that the musical finale cannot rescue the show from failure.

This episode marks Weston and Lee's swan song on the series. It is a shame that it is such a poor sendoff for them, as they deserved better, as did viewers.

Oct. 12, 1974: Telly Savalas, the Smothers Brothers

Q&A; a comic monologue by Tom and Dick Smothers; Eunice's brother, Jack Harper (Tom Smothers), find himself less than comforted by a visit from his family while in the hospital for an operation; Telly sings "Rubber Bands and Bits of String"; Harvey is a businessman who finds that his merger with Telly's company is off; the regulars and the Smothers salute the eighth annual to the most unforgettable commercials of the year; Algiers' Casbah is the site where Telly meets a fez-wearing inspector (Harvey) and becomes transfixed by a beautiful exotic visitor (Carol).

Comments: TV's favorite bald cop and musical/comedy duo are an odd combination for any show, and more surprisingly Telly Savalas comes off better here, with relatively little for Dick Smothers to do as well. "The ladies here at CBS have been coming out of the woodwork to see Telly this week," Carol tells her audience at the end of a quick Q&A which includes Carol saying, "Are my measurements the same as Cher's? No, mine are the same as Sonny's." This leads into a somewhat meandering Smothers Brothers routine in tuxes where Tom claims not to know the words to their duet but Dick informs him it is a madrigal in which he should improvise lyrics. It is OK, meaning Smothers Brothers fans will like it while others will fidget waiting for the next segment.

The Family sketch is a better laugh-getter, as a doctor (Ernie Anderson) informs Jack (Tom) that his older sister Eunice has come to visit, to Jack's dismay, as he knows how his family is. While Ed feels nauseous in the hospital, he is able to warn Jack about possible bad times following an operation. Eunice puts down Ed's mention of his partner, Mickey Hart, as "the original twit," and argues with Ed about the latter's worth in his business. Mama arrives with a puzzle she found for Jack in the gift shop and fights with Eunice over claims that Jack's doctor is a quack. After threatening to leave and saying Jack is "practically at death's door," Mama accidentally pushes Jack's toupee off to the side before asking him if he has made a will. When Jack says he is leaving everything to his wife and kids, Eunice and Mama have a spat over what items they deserve to inherit from his home instead. During this discussion, Eunice blabs that if Jack dies, his wife will run off with the plumber she is seeing on the side. The regulars leave, and an enraged Jack calls his wife to get more information about their plumber. This is wonderful fun. Incidentally, Jack never will be mentioned in later Family sketches.

Telly's "talk-singing" of his featured number is not too bad as these things go, but he really shines in the next skit. This variation from the Jan. 5, 1974 show features Telly informing Harvey that their business deal has fallen through because "We're not right for each other." "There's another company, isn't there?" Harvey says. "You're making it sound so cheap!" Telly snaps back. If there was any doubt this is a mock lovers' quarrel, a piano plays "The Way We Were" and Harvey notes that it is "The song they were playing the night you proposed our merger." He recounts the meeting in loving detail, as Telly tries to console him by saying they can do future business with each other. "What kind of company do you think I am?! . . . I gave you something I never gave anybody else—my debentures!" At this point, Telly cracks up but composes himself to tell Harvey they should end this quietly and remember the good times. Harvey looks as if he will kiss Telly before leaving, leading Telly to laugh some more and the audience to applaud and whistle. Telly then lets Ernie Anderson know they can now merge, only to have Ernie turn him down, to Telly's sorrow. This is a brilliant, top-notch comic bit.

The commercial parodies are a chunky mix of great and so-so, mainly the latter. The first is the best, with Harvey as an interviewer who has a shopper (Carol) tell him which one of the three cups of coffee looks the richest. After carefully eyeing them, she picks the right one, and Harvey has her drink it to see if she thinks it tastes as rich as it looks. After failing to say the phrase initially, Harvey shakes her into a confession and she runs away screaming. Harvey then smiles and says this was an unsolicited testimonial.

Another pleasing takeoff has the dancers flashing their index fingers to indicate a diet drink has just one calorie before it cuts to Carol in a fat suit doing the same while surrounded by hundreds of bottles. Less enjoyable are a bandage spoof with Harvey and Dick, a moment with Tom on "Pepto-Dismal" (he asks if people mind if he speaks about diarrhea, and they let him know they do), and Dick not having used soap for three years. The next shot is of the camera crew all wearing gas masks. Har de har har.

Replacing the usual musical finale is a swell segment where Harvey impersonates Peter Lorre as he attempts to intimidate Telly in a cafe. Telly shrugs him off in favor of Carol, who so entrances him he wants to leave with her even though Harvey threatens to kill him if he escapes. As it turns out, Carol is an undercover cop who shoots Telly instead. As the latter dies, he vows that he will be reincarnated and call himself Barnaby Jones. The snappy delivery of lines and great atmosphere make this a winner.

Though ill-used here, the Smothers Brothers did agree to have Joe Hamilton as executive producer for their new series on NBC at the star of 1975. *The Smothers Brothers Show* was a disaster for all involved, including Kenny Solms and Gail Parent, former writers on *The Carol Burnett Show* who were very unhappy working with Hamilton here. He left after just three weeks, forcing Solms and Parent to guide a misbegotten revival that lacked the bite and verve of what the Smothers Brothers did with their variety series from 1967-1969. Ironically, the Smothers Brothers had rejected Gail as a writer for their series in 1967 prior to her joining *The Carol Burnett Show* because they did not want a female.

Oct. 19, 1974: Pre-empted by *CBS Reports* news documentary on "The Case of the Plastic Peril"

Oct. 26, 1974: Rich Little, Eydie Gorme

* Harvey and Carol are a couple so argumentative that they refuse to speak as they make pointed actions involving each other's gifts to get on their spouse's nerves; Eydie sings "You'll Remember Me"; Rich portrays a portly Alfred Hitchcock as part of a salute to the director's films, including takeoffs of *North by Northwest*, *Psycho* and *Rebecca* where Rich plays the butler, Vicki the maid, Harvey the master of the house and Carol as the title character; the regulars and guests appear in a musical finale saluting songwriter Jerome Kern.

Comments: The two principal skits here available for viewing on syndicated reruns are so good that one is tempted to conclude the rest of the show dazzles as well. Carol and Harvey have one of their best one-on-one vignettes ever, a near-pantomime that starts with the two entering their house and Carol deliberately closing the door on Harvey, followed by Harvey emphatically slamming it in response as the two glare at each other. He makes a drink, and she responds by smoking a cigarette and blowing puffs in his face. Carol takes flowers Harvey has given her out of a vase and stomps on them. He in turn takes his cigars from a humidor she gave him and grinds them in a blender, puts the pulpy residue in the flower vase, shakes it like mixing a cocktail and throws it at Carol's feet. Livid, she takes apart his tennis trophy, pulling off the ball on top and knocking it away with his racquet. Unfazed, Harvey takes the base of the trophy to smash Carol's china set on the wall. She breaks his racquet's strings on the trophy to retaliate. After Harvey demolishes her cups and flips her tea set, Carol throws his clothes outside, but Harvey locks her out. At that point, he finally speaks through the peephole: "Happy anniversary!" She then pokes him in the eye. This is masterfully done in all respects.

The Hitchcock tribute is dandy. Rich does his sparkling take on Cary Grant as he accidentally drops Vicki off Mount Rushmore. Vicki is a cleaning woman who screams in horror at a shower scene, only for Eydie to come out in a towel yelling, "Hey, well, you're no raving beauty yourself, you know!" Then Little's dead-on Hitchcock imitation introduces "Rebekky," written by Barry Levinson and Rudy DeLuca, the latter of which considers it one of his favorite sketches. Even though the series had parodied the movie two years earlier (see Sept. 27, 1972), this is better, with the regulars and Little having a delightful time as Harvey attempts to drive Carol crazy but she ends up doing it to him instead. It also has several ad libs when a tabletop malfunction and Harvey covers for it and Carol forgets the lyrics to "The Windmills of Your Mind." Best of all is when Little impersonates James Mason and Harvey responds "That's very good, Claude, I wish we had time for your Cagney, but we must press on." This sort of interplay shows there is still life left in *The Carol Burnett Show* this season.

Nov. 2, 1974: Alan King, Lena Zavaroni

* Alan is a baseball fan pestered by Carol, who is more interested in him than in the game; Lena belts out "If They Could See Me Now"; Carol becomes fascinated by a package at a bus stop; Harvey and Carol are two fading silent screen celebrities who talk while polishing stars in their honor located on Hollywood Boulevard; the finale honors songwriters B.G. "Buddy" DeSylva, Lew Brown and Ray Henderson.

Comments: While there are thankfully few sad stories to tell about Carol and her guests, Lena Zavaroni is an exception. A ten-year-old Scottish singer with a booming voice, she appeared poised for greatness as an adult, but she never made as much a splash with American audiences as she did with British ones. She endured battles with anorexia nervosa and depression beginning in her teen years and suffered other setbacks before dying of pneumonia a month before her thirty-sixth birthday. At least Lena appears bright in her appearance here in a skit on the half hour syndicated rerun of this show.

In it, Carol is a dowdy, bespectacled type who sees a package with a purple bow as she sits on a bus bench. Harvey joins her and asks what's in the present that she clutches in her hands. She deflects him as he recognizes the wrapping paper is from an upscale store. Vicki arrives and knows it is an expensive gift too. Carol awkwardly insists to both she paid good money for it. As Harvey and Vicki get a cab, Lena joins Carol at the bus stop, and she is Carol's student who Carol gave an F for her composition on honesty. As you expect, Carol opens up the package and sees it's a tape recorder. Lena claims it is hers and announces she will play it back to her fellow students in Carol's class tomorrow morning before running away with the recorder. Carol yells negotiating tactics to Lena as this slight but fairly amusing outing ends.

The other skit with Alan is acceptable but nothing special. He will reappear on the show as a solo guest on Dec. 4, 1976.

Nov. 9, 1974: John Byner, Helen Reddy

Q&A; Helen performs "Angie Baby"; "The Family" plays a board game that brings up nothing but aggravation for Eunice as Ed and Mama make moves that beat her while playing; John offers a comic monologue centered around mocking the conventions of *The Adventures of Ozzie and Harriet*; "The Pickup" has Harvey and John as would-be Lotharios trying to impress two wallflowers (Carol and Helen) at a bar to end the night with them; Helen, Carol, Vicki and the women singer and dancers appear in an all-female finale paying tribute to songwriters of the distaff persuasion.

Comments: John and Helen are just as endearing as their last joint appearance on Oct. 6, 1973, even slightly better in some respects in this, the season's top show. After saying "I love Elvis Presley" and laughing off a man wanting her to run for governor of California in the Q&A, Carol introduces Kenny Solms playing a tuxedo-wearing alleged winner of a scholarship in her name. He tells her he blew all of his prize money on a first-class plane ticket to Los Angeles, then announces his plans to join her show to Carol's astonishment. "I'm going to change my name first," he says. "To what?" Carol asks. "Lyle," he says to much laughter, in reference to the former regular. After saying he is getting his dressing room ready and telling Carol she can take him out to dinner whenever, the show's former writer leaves the stage in one of the best scripted parts of Q&A ever.

Helen is "a wonderful person and the holder of nine gold records," Carol says in introducing her musical guest. Reddy will earn her tenth gold with the prerecorded song presented here. Imaginatively and adroitly dramatizing the oblique lyrics are shots of a female dancer entrancing men in a bedroom set superimposed on Helen singing. It is distinctive and one of the series' best presentations of a guest vocal performance ever.

Up next is a classic Family sketch with Mama complaining about Eunice's cleaning skills when Eunice suggests they play Sorry! (a registered trademark). Eunice's insistence on following the rules backfires as Mama and Ed take the lead at her expense. In one outtake from this part, Vicki meant to say "got durn dice" as scripted, but slipped and said a profanity instead. Carol lost it, then composed herself and asked Dave Powers, "Can we go back?" "How about Questions and Answers?" he shot back, making Carol laugh more.

Proceeding onward, Eunice vents her anger toward Ed's failures in business and Mama's put-downs by ranting and tearing apart their couch pillows. This leads to a priceless exchange by Mama telling off Eunice with, "I think somebody blew your pilot light out!" Caught off guard by the ad lib, Carol tries to hide her laughter and then says, "That's a new one, Mama!" to audience appreciation. "You wait, there's more, Eunice!" Vicki responds. "You know what? You got splinters in the windmills of your mind! You're playing hockey with a warped puck!" The audience whoops it up. For the second taping, also unaired like the outtake, Vicki came equipped with new cracks ("Everybody [on the staff] was loading her up," recalled Harvey in the 2001 special *Show Stoppers*), and she hit Carol with "I think you done sprung a leak in your dinghy! What's the problem, Eunice? Is it your time of month or something? Are you riding the cotton pony?!" Carol turned her head away before Vicki made the first comment, and by the last part she was in hysterics as Vicki tried to pull her face forward and say, "Look at me, Eunice!"

The skit ends with Eunice throwing the game dice down in frustration, resulting in double sixes. That results in her turning around and playing Sorry again while saying, "Isn't this a good game!?" It is a perfect final line for a golden sketch.

John has the unenviable job of following this moment but does well given the challenge. After kidding about some conventions of the 1950s, he zeroes in on a sitcom that ran on ABC from 1952 to 1966 as his primary target of scorn. He cracks on Ozzie's name and voice as well as the show's fashions and conventions, and especially he notes how out of date the series would be if it was still on the air now, riffing on Ozzie and Harriet's son Ricky coming over to mope about his wife being pregnant (interestingly, there actually was a semi-revival of the series called *Ozzie's Girls* in syndication in 1973-1974). Even without having a working knowledge of the series, Byner does a fine job in conveying its basics to generate several solid laughs for any observer.

Byner is in even better form with Harvey as a pair of desperate losers trying to seduce Helen and Carol, dressed as plain Janes. After hearing "25 or 6 to 4" played in a club (which gives a nice contemporary feel even though it is not the hit version by Chicago), Helen freaks out when another customer (Dick Patterson) asks for the time. "He was using me to get to you!" she tells Carol. John and Harvey cautiously approach the ladies but turn away when the women try to look at their faces. The men retreat, so Carol tries to entice them by "flaunting" herself, which in her case means taking off her jacket and running to the ladies room. John makes a move on Helen but runs away scared after he touches her.

The bartender (Stan Mazin) announces last call, so each side gives their best shot. Helen warns that if the men do seduce them, "We stick together." Carol concurs and humorously paraphrases the lyrics of Helen's hit "I Am Woman" by saying "We are strong, we are invincible." As the woman slowly trudge out, Carol drops a hankie and Harvey picks it up. He presents it to her and she screams and scurries out with Helen, while John grabs onto a cracking up Harvey for dear life. "I think maybe we were too pushy," Harvey concludes. John calls this sketch his favorite of the series along with the Alice Portnoy one on Feb. 10, 1973. He especially likes the part where it is last call and the slow-moving guys bemoan, "If we only had more time!"

The finale is themed toward women's liberation in design as well as presentation, as the panels behind the women list their names as well as the female composers and lyricists they celebrate. It is a nice salute only a chauvinist would dislike. During the closing, Kenny Solms returns hilariously with his own book for the guests to sign like Carol normally does, a clever move that nicely caps off this wonderful installment.

Nov. 16, 1974: John Byner, Kenneth Mars

Q&A; John offers a monologue set at a record store with him hawking "100 Top Hits from Puberty to Senility"; Kenneth instructs John on how to break up with Carol, but his suggestions backfire; a secretary (Vicki) encounters a torrent of alliteration as she answers the phone; a soap opera viewer (Carol) is so enraptured by the storyline that she ignores others who visit her; Vicki performs with the male dancers; a husband and wife (Carol and Kenneth) have dream sequences about each cheating on the other; Carol hosts the twenty-ninth annual Mr. Globe Award for Most Beautiful Man.

Comments: Despite a lack of Harvey and the female dancers, this is a solid show due to generally strong writing and clever comic timing by John and Kenneth, the latter subbing for Harvey (and who worked with John in the 1971 movie comedy *What's Up, Doc?*). The brief Q&A includes a young man saying he rented Carol's 1972 movie *Pete 'n' Tillie* for showings in his basement for seven nights straight. "I lost $50. Nobody came," he adds, to laughter from Carol. Next, John's monologue mocks special music offers on TV by having him hawk the ultimate album containing songs for all ages. While his impersonations of Glen Campbell doing "Galveston" and Frank Sinatra interpreting "Waltzing Matilda" are middling, John does score with dead-on takes of Perry Como, Mel Tormé, Johnny Mathis and Frankie Laine. It ends with his inevitable impression of John Wayne for a pretty good monologue overall.

After giving a waiter (Stan Mazin) his order, Kenneth suavely provides pointers to a clearly nervous John about how to end the latter's relationship with Carol at a fancy restaurant. Carol's response is to make a scene and loudly tell patrons how she has been seeing John behind his wife's back. John's abject embarrassment and horror over Carol's revelations are a delight, especially when she tightens his tie to choke him and his voice sounds like a duck in response. She blackmails him for $70,000 not to reveal the dirtiest of his escapades, then gives the check over to Kenneth, her co-conspirator. Their celebration is short-lived, however, as Kenneth is breaking up with Carol, prompting her to make another scene in response. This is nimbly handled by all. John Byner adds that "Kenneth Mars and I spoke a short time before he left this planet, and he didn't remember doing 'It's Over' with me on Carol's show. I've always admired his work."

Vicki's solo segment is similarly pleasurable. She has to talk with people and discuss items that all begin with "B"—for example, the broken ball bearings at Burt, Burns, Broughton and Ballback. After reeling off a series of similar sounds, she is asked by Ernie Anderson to substitute for his secretary, and she does so, only to use lots of words starting with "C" instead. This is cleverly written and crisply delivered by Vicki.

The comic pace continues strong with Carol watching "Search for Love," narrated by Ernie Anderson, with the melodrama between Don Crichton and an unidentified female on screen so enthralling Carol that she closes the door on a senior citizen collecting money for an orphanage. A physician (Kenneth) arrives to check on Carol's dying husband to similar indifference, and Carol's neglect even extends to Vicki, who becomes hysterical in relating that her husband is seeing another woman and plans to kill herself in response (she leaves with applause for her impassioned take). Kenneth tells Carol her husband is very sick, and she still cares little, but when her husband (Ernie) emerges and passes out on her TV, she is upset—she tells the phone operator she needs help because she cannot watch her soap opera anymore. This one scores just like all the previous skits.

After Vicki lip syncs to an acceptable number comes the weakest sketch, where Carol dreams that Kenneth tells her he is leaving her for Vicki, a trashy bimbo, and will kill Carol rather than divorce her. She wakes up and apologizes for her outburst to Kenneth, who goes back to sleep and has his own vision of Carol having affairs with the milkman (Stan Mazin), the window washer (Birl Johns), a cop (Don Crichton) and eventually the rest of the male dancers, all of whom he is unable to kill with his gun. He awakens, apologizes and then leaves with a hidden Vicki after thinking Carol was back asleep. Seeing the coast is clear, Carol has her male suitors join her as well. Besides being uninspired and trite, this sketch suffers because it has Kenneth assuming a role normally done by Harvey, and since viewers lack a history and rapport with the actor playing opposite Carol, his efforts to mistreat and kill her come off as menacing and discomforting instead of funny.

The show rebounds with the finale, where Kenneth plays an awkward announcer presiding over a male beauty pageant hosted by Carol. She introduces Mr. Australia (Don Crichton), Mr. Token from Kenya (Carlton Johnson), Mr. USA (Birl Johns), Mr. Siberia (Stan Mazin) and Mr. Hong Kong (John, in an unfortunately dated Asian caricature that allows him only to mug in stereotypical fashion). Bob Mackie's outfits for each are outstanding, and Carol's breathless delivery and Kenneth's stilted interview with an ancient pageant director (Vicki) are joys to behold as well in this obvious but generally on-target spoof.

Surprisingly, this is Byner's sixth and last appearance on the show. He probably would have made a wonderful series regular, but regarding that prospect, he says, "I never thought of the 'regular' possibilities on any show. It was a family of people who wanted to do a family show. I loved working with all of them." Mars will work with Carol again on *Carol Burnett and Company* five years later. For more on that, see the final chapter.

The biggest disappointment for this show is its scheduling during its first airing. The first part of the TV premiere of *The Godfather* swamped it with a 37 rating for NBC, one of the highest ever. Maybe that competition is why Harvey did not show up here.

Nov. 23, 1974: Maggie Smith, Tim Conway

Q&A; Simba the lion (Tim) learns he must go into the jungle from the parents who raised him (Carol and Harvey); Maggie and Carol complement each other musically in "You're So London"; two military privates (Harvey and Tim) stranded on an island whose relationship alters drastically when Harvey learns he has been promoted to second lieutenant; a movie star (Maggie) endures aggravating behavior from her old college chum (Carol) and the latter's husband (Harvey); two cops (Harvey and Dick Patterson) have doubts about the story told by a suspect (Vicki); the Charwoman imagines she is Betty Grable in the finale.

Comments: This episode runs hot and cold. Tim is excellent but absent from the last half of the show, while Maggie Smith is used not to full advantage here. The Q&A starts well with a joke from Carol about her favorite rock star—"Rock Hudson"—an introduction of Alice Ghostley in the audience, a Tarzan yell and an announcement that Alan Alda will be a guest next month. Carol cracks up the most when an unknowing woman asks, "Does your husband ever come to your show?" She responds, "No, he can't stand me!"

The show starts strong with a send-up of *Born Free*, which was running as a failed series on NBC at the time. This spoof is based more on the 1966 movie, as Harvey demands that Carol dismiss Simba (Tim, dressed in a lion outfit), from their home near the jungle. Tim wonderfully acts like a human in his pantomime, offering Carol coffee and reading the newspaper as she tries to coax him to go outside. Harvey returns after Carol's efforts fail, and he demands that Simba exit. Here is where the comedy really shines. Tim ad libs as he gets his suitcase and slowly moves around after Harvey repeatedly asks him to go. After hearing a toilet flush that catches Harvey off guard, hysterics ensue as Tim emerges with a bowler on his head and a business suit around his mane as he heads out. Once Carol closes the door, she and Harvey clearly lose it before the sketch fades to black.

Unfortunately, the next bit is not as short and sweet. Stating that "I have made a brand new friend," Carol introduces Maggie, who is wearing the same red-brown spangly outfit as Carol. After Maggie talks about how she is touring the United States on stage in *Private Lives*, Carol musically pleads how she wants to be classy like Maggie in "You're So London," while Maggie extols Carol's virtues in return. It is a passable moment but overloaded with lyrics that make an obvious point over and over again.

The show gets back into the funny groove when a military mail drop informs Harvey he now holds a higher rank than Tim on an island, and he starts lording over his buddy with his new position. Harvey has the "company" fall in as Tim pretends to be several men hilariously, then demands the troop pass in review before him, where Tim's comic gifts go into overdrive. Offstage, he yells as if he several people, cracking Harvey up as the latter pleads for him to begin. Tim first walks by waving a baton and losing it as he throws it into the air, followed by holding a long banner in the front—and in the back! He emerges with a shipwrecked woman, and since she is a corporal, she can only mess with enlisted men like Tim, so he goes with her and leaves Harvey alone. This is a delight.

Just as the humorous momentum builds, it disintegrates with an overlong, sluggish skit where Carol and Harvey's behavior irritates viewers almost as much as it does Maggie when she visits them. They hound her about Hollywood life and even argue about whether to get marijuana for Maggie to smoke—a rare excursion into drug humor for the series that nonetheless fails to stop the torpor. Finally fed up with their activities, Maggie uses her acting talents to tell Carol and Harvey that she has indeed changed from the days she and Carol were in charge and must go. The actors make a go of it, but this sketch needed much more tightening or should have been dropped instead of what emerged.

An interlude of silly humor follows as Vicki's confession to Harvey and Dick turns out to the story of Goldilocks and the three Bears. An irked Harvey is convinced Vicki is holding back and finally gets her to crack. It turns out that she was wearing a red riding hood while going to see her grandmother. It is childish but works, unlike the previous sketch.

The evening winds down with the Charwoman doing silhouettes on the curtain of an empty stage (Carol's studio in a bit taped without the audience). Seeing a sign that the recent program was a tribute to pinup girl films, the Charwoman sings "Oh to Be a Movie Star" before fantasizing about being Betty Grable singing "Cuddle Up a Little Closer, Lovey Mine" in a production number with the dancers in tuxes, tails and gowns. She gets to show off her gams before it goes back to the Charwoman reprising "Oh to Be a Movie Star." It is fine but not spectacular.

At the end, Tim wears the bowler he sported in the *Born Free* sketch. It is a reminder that this show could have used more of his antics. He and Maggie will fare much better in their next outing together—see Oct. 18, 1975.

Nov. 30, 1974: Pre-empted by special *Miss Teenage America*

Dec. 7, 1974: Steve Lawrence, Tim Conway, Steven Warner

The godfather of Canoga Falls (Steve) blackmails Marian, who must raise $5,000 from her son (Vicki), her doddering uncle (Tim) and Mother Marcus (Harvey) in "As the Stomach Turns"; Steve sings "On a Clear Day You Can See Forever"; a cop on a stakeout (Carol) is mistaken for being a prostitute by a meek but horny man (Tim); Carol sings the title tune from the movie *The Little Prince* and talks to Steven, its star, with clips shown; Tim is a highly suggestible patient in a waiting room; a salute to the music of Alan Jay Lerner and Frederick Loewe.

Comments: This show could have been a classic had it not been forced to include obvious promotion for the flop movie musical adaptation of Lerner and Loewe's *The Little Prince*. There is no Q&A apart from Carol doing the Tarzan yell. Luckily, that means we can get into one of the best "As the Stomach Turns" installments ever.

Wearing a dress black on one side and white on the other because she has attended a funeral and a wedding today, Marian meets Steve the godfather, who has a scandalous picture of her with the town acrobat on a chandelier. He wants $10,000 in order not to show the image to anyone else, but Marian only has half that amount. The godfather gives her five minutes to collect the rest before having to leave—"I've got to see a man about a horse," he says before wheezing a few chuckles out. Marian waits for help at her door from "Someone really ca-RING!" she shouts as a hint to the sound effects man, who finally activates the door buzzer. It is her son (Vicki), who is a female impersonator ("I've looked at love from both sides now"). Faking compassion, Marian offers Vicki use of her room if she puts up $5,000 in advance, but with no deal, she throws Vicki out.

Next, Marian's rich uncle (Tim) rolls down the stairs and keeps his momentum going to wrap himself up in her rug. She pulls him out and puts him into a chair, but he starts drooping forward, and twice the crumpled rug hampers Marian's efforts to put a table underneath him, prompting Tim to take advantage and slump face forward to the floor each failed effort. Finally upright, Tim tells here he cannot give her $5,000 because he has a fiancée, Mother Marcus (Harvey), and he buries his head into her sizable chest when she appears. Tim bumbles upstairs to open a safe, but he has only fake money. When the godfather returns to collect from Marian, Mother Marcus recognizes him as her son, and he breaks out into singing "My Yiddishe Mama." This is wonderfully golden nonsense, beautifully written, directed and acted by all.

After Steve finely sings a Lerner and Loewe tune (talk about promotion overkill!), Vicki is a hooker thrown out of her room by Carol the cop and her aide (Dick Patterson). Carol uses the location as a stakeout and is told that she will get a new partner from the Eleventh District to help her. At the same time, Harvey sets up Tim to go to where Vicki had worked. Arriving at the room, Tim assumes Carol is a prostitute and she does the same about him being a cop, leading to numerous smart double entendres. "We could be here a couple of days," Carol tells him. "Wow," a nervous Tim responds. Tim preps himself in the bathroom and comes out clad in yellow children's pajamas with fuzzy bunny slippers, while Carol tells him the first time she did something like this was in a phone booth across the street from Disneyland. This scares him even more, so he goes back into the bathroom while the case breaks and Carol leaves to get the perpetrators. In a brilliant ending, Steve shows up as the new cop and says to Tim, "I'm the Eleventh [District] man. Who are you?" "I guess I was the tenth guy," Tim shoots back.

The show's momentum slows when Carol sings the Oscar-nominated but now virtually forgotten theme song for *The Little Prince* over scenes from the film. She brings out its 8-year-old star, the adorable Steven Warner, who says he is a first-time singer and performs "Why is the Desert" from the picture, with more scenes from the movie shown during this number. This is the most blatant and uncomfortable huckstering the series ever did, and it really drags down the otherwise pleasant vibes this show possesses.

Tim rescues the mood with a typically wild performance that generates laughs from the start, as Carol provides Harvey with amateur diagnoses of others in the doctor's waiting room and Tim assumes he has them because he takes the medication Carol mentions. Watching Tim pantomime side effects such as dizziness, arm and leg spasms, and depression alternating with laughter, is a joy to behold. Tim faints at the end per Carol's instructions, but when the doctor (Dick Patterson) comes out, Carol recommends that he look at Harvey because he is a very sick man.

This Lerner-Loewe love fest ends with a dazzling finale where everyone except Tim has a number to perform, but that does not stop him from unsuccessfully trying to vocalize wherever possible. Steve does "Brigadoon" and "Gigi," Harvey "They Call the Wind Maria," Vicki "I Could Have Danced All Night" with the male dancers, Carol and Harvey "I Remember It Well," and Vicki and Steven "Thank Heaven for Little Boys" with the female dancers. All are presented with great vigor, as is the last one, "Camelot," where Tim is even allowed to sing along with everyone else in Elizabethan outfits. This production is funny, swift and entertaining to watch.

At the end, Carol makes a plea for viewers to buy Christmas seals. She will be more in the spirit of the season two weeks later—see Dec. 21, 1974.

Dec. 14, 1974: Carl Reiner, Ken Berry

Q&A; Ken performs "Razzle Dazzle" with the dancers; "The Biggest Movie of the Week" presents "Disaster '75," with Carol as a flight attendant, Ken, Harvey and Vicki as passengers and Carl as the man who saves them; four musical blackouts feature Carol, Ken, Harvey and Vicki; Harvey and Carol are a bickering couple who alternately sulk at each other; Alistair Cookie (Harvey) introduces public television's musical version of *Hamlet*, with Ken as the lead, Carl as his father's ghost, Carol as Ophelia, Harvey as Ken's stepfather, Vicki as Ken's mother, and the dancers as members of the royal court.

Comments: This is hit-or-miss throughout, even during the Q&A, where trivial, familiar items like Carol's favorite perfume, her introduction to acting and the Tarzan yell are broken up by a couple of memorable moments. She says she would have been a sex symbol if not an actress and interjects, "You've never seen Raquel Welch and me together, have you? We're the same person." A girl remarks that "My friend, Theresa Renteria, couldn't come tonight," and Carol picks up the unique sound and rhythm of that moniker while saying hi to Theresa. "That's my favorite new name!" she says. The series remembers it and will invoke the name more than a year later—see Feb. 14, 1976.

Best of all, a group of girls ask if Carol used to date a gentleman and, when Carol confirms, they tell her his daughter is in their troupe. "You could've been mine!" Carol exclaims as she hugs the girl and tells how she dated her father in Hollywood High. It is an adorable moment, one of the best ever in the Q&A.

Ken's take on "Razzle Dazzle" is more of interest now because when it was first performed, it had just appeared in the Broadway musical *Chicago*, which was moderately successful but not as big as in its revivals in the 1990s and the 2002 movie version. Unfortunately, the presentation fails to live up to the title, as Ken merely joins the male dancers in a turn-of-the-century barbershop set to dance with a mop designed to resemble a woman. The women dancers do appear in petticoats, and everyone contributes their best here, but this is adequate rather than exceptional.

A two-part send-up of *Airport 1975* is the show's highlight. Escaping from a cockpit full of horny pilots, Carol greets those flying Titanic Airlines Flight 1313, including a man needing a nose transplant (Ken), the singing Smothers Sisters (Vicki and a female dancer), and the great Nora Desmond dictating her memoirs to Max. (Gloria Swanson played herself in *Airport 1975*.) Another plane hits the cockpit, but before Carol can move, Harvey brandishes a gun and announces he has dynamite in his briefcase. "You know how hard it is for a guy to find work who used to be in charge of Friday nights on ABC?!" he tells the passengers before Carol lets him know that his plot happened four years earlier in the original movie, which leads him to sit down and apologize. Vicki plays "99 Bottles of Beer" to calm everyone as Carol radios for help from air traffic control, where Carl and his assistant (Dick Patterson) provide little help at first. Carl and Carol had a spat before the flight, and he mocks every claim she makes to her distress.

In the second half, Dick informs Carl that Carol is correct, and her plane does need help. As chaos breaks out in the cabin—Vicki knocks out Ken after he complained about her singing, Harvey tries to hijack the plane until told that was another movie too—Carol grudgingly apologizes to Carol to get his assistance, but she learns she cannot pilot the plane. She tells Carl he must help while she occupies the passengers by turning up the lights and taking questions. Just like a certain variety star, she says Jimmy Stewart is her favorite pilot, gives her height and reveals other details before asked about her age, when she returns to the cockpit.

From there, Carl jumps up via trampoline to join her and successfully land the plane. Carol returns to the cabin to tell everyone some basic information, including a 60 percent chance of an earthquake, which then shakes up everyone as the graphics over them says, "But That's Another

Movie." This spoof runs the gamut from stupid to clever, but it keeps moving, everyone gives it their all, and it is nice to see a contemporary motion picture mocked for a change.

Laughter continues in four enjoyable blackouts based on hits. Vicki sings "I've Gotta Be Me" while removing her wig, dentures and falsies. Ken learns his blind date is Charo (Carol), and sings the Beatles' "Something" to her until she bumps him to the ground. Harvey is a bum who sings "Tramp Tramp Tramp" before mincingly walking down a highway (not unlike what he did previously with "Blowing in the Wind"—see Feb. 23, 1974). Finally, Harvey sings "A Baby is Coming" to Carol, his equally slovenly wife in a slum apartment who is pregnant and disinterested. She knocks him out at the end.

From here out, it is like watching the air go slowly out of a balloon. The Harvey-Carol skit has each comforting the other over unexplained slights which look to be resolved before they go to bed, until Harvey asks Carol once again what provoked their arguments and she mopes. This irritating bit starts and goes nowhere for five long minutes.

Winding up things wobbly is "Hold Me, Hamlet," a near-operetta whose highlights are the costumes (especially the sexy outfits worn by the female dancers as the castle guards), sets and makeup. The comic numbers lack zing, and the scenario is stale. In fact *Gilligan's Island* did a similarly themed production eight years earlier, and it was funnier, tighter and brighter than this, plus it had the talents of Phil Silvers, an upcoming guest here (see March 29, 1975). Rather incredibly, the outlandishness of this concept failed to resonate with some show business types, and *Rockabye Hamlet* actually appeared on Broadway less than two years after this for seven painful performances.

This show marked the last appearance on the series of Carl. Ken will not return until nearly two years later—see Nov. 20, 1976.

Dec. 21, 1974: Alan Alda

Q&A; Eunice surprises Mama with a visit by Larry (Alan), Eunice's brother, who is a commercial illustrator spending his first Christmas with the family since he was a child; Carol is a harried gift wrapper and Alan an exhausted Santa at a department store who console each other by singing "Nobody Does It Like Me"; a woman (Carol) finds that her date (Alan) has been stealing lines from old movies to impress her; the cast and dancers perform a medley of songs related to New York City starting with "Take Me Back to Manhattan" in a street setting.

Comments: Although Carol has had a few shows with just one guest previously, none used that person as prominently in every part as this one with Alan Alda. He even shows up in the Q&A, where a girl in the audience gives him a rose and a kiss amid a swarm of others presenting Carol with gifts (it is the Christmas show). After collecting a pillow with the UCLA emblem on it, a pin cushion, flowers, a plant and a letter, Carol exclaims "What a haul!" She takes a few inconsequential queries before the show begins.

The Family is in usual form, with Eunice in a garish Christmas apron to celebrate the holiday by the appearance of her brother, Larry, who Ed admits he thought was a "nance" (and makes a limp wrist to underline the notion) because Larry is an artist. Eunice and Ed talk over Larry after asking him what he's doing before Mama arrives and adds her own little digs at her estranged son, like how he always had bad timing. Larry's gift to the family of a coffee table reference book goes over like a lead balloon, and he is similarly unimpressed by their present of a paint-by-numbers set illustrating a hog. "We got it for the boys, but thought it would be too sissified for them," Ed explains, while Mama implores Larry to thank Ed and Eunice for the item. Reaching his limit, Larry rants about how he is a successful artist whose talent they fail to recognize, throws his gift on the floor and leaves in a huff (with applause). An unfazed Ed, Eunice and Mama go back to arguing about how to celebrate Christmas. This is a strong, energetic start for the show.

The next segment is a fine seriocomic musical romance with Carol and Alan musing over the challenges of their jobs before connecting as lovers. Following it is a nice but unfortunately prolonged bit where Carol finds out after ending her date with Alan that he cribbed what Harvey said to Vicki (in a blonde wig) in a black-and-white old movie shown on TV. She confronts him about doing this, and he confesses that he did it because he was an only child, and the movies were his only outlet growing up in learning how to deal with the opposite sex. They reconcile, but when he leaves, Carol turns on the TV and sees Harvey saying the same words in a film. Enraged, Carol demands that Alan be himself, and even though he proclaims to be dull—and he is—she is fine with that. The cute moments here would have been more effective if this had tighter pacing. Harvey cracked up during a taping of his segment when he blew out candles on a dinner table with Vicki and the crew turned out all the lights to make the entire set dark in response.

Alan telling Carol that he lives back East and commutes to Los Angeles to film *M*A*S*H* serves as the setup for the musical finale. The dancers do "New York, New York,""Lullaby of Broadway" in a mock subway, "42nd Street" and many more. As Carol and Alan stroll through various scenes, it is most impressive how the regulars make quick costume changes. Harvey first is a taxi driver, then a pickpocket and a drunk, while Vicki goes from a posh socialite to a hooker singing "Rose of Washington Square" to a cop. It's nimbly performed by all involved, who get showered by fake snow at the end.

Throughout it all, Carol's former co-start in *6 RMS RIV VU* is excellent and has a real rapport with her. It's a shame this was his only visit to the series.

Dec. 28, 1974: Repeat of Sept. 28, 1974 show

Jan. 4, 1975: Joan Rivers, Vincent Price

Q&A; Alice Portnoy (Carol) blackmails a famous author (Vincent) in order to appear with him on a TV interview; Carol, Vicki and the dancers do "Born in Brooklyn," a musical tribute to introduce Joan, who does a comic monologue; Funt and Mundane (Carol and Harvey) have their play's closing night wrecked by their envious understudies (Vicki and Vincent); spoofs of new TV series of the fall season include *Police Woman*, *Chico and the Man*, *Rhoda*, *Tony Orlando and Dawn* and *The Waltons*; Vicki hosts a mock young people's concert, "Sara and the Moose," with the ensemble.

Comments: This generally enjoyable outing has its weakest elements up front, including a rather ho-hum Q&A, with such things as a lady delivering Carol a letter on stage that she had planned to mail to her and a query about whether Carol wears contact lenses (she does not). The only item of note is Carol saying she wants to continue doing the show when she is seventy and does her greeting in her Stella Toddler voice. Even less exciting is the last and arguably least appearance of Fireside Girl Alice Portnoy, this time interrupting the mystery writer of the year (Vincent) by pointing out errors in his works and noting that she saw him with a blonde in the back seat of a car as well. When his interviewer (Dick Patterson) decides to include the imp in their live segment, Alice makes Vincent fork over money to keep her from blabbing these details. This drawn-out affair has nothing new to add, which could explain why this is Alice's deserved swan song.

A spirited number about celebrities born in Joan's hometown is so great the comedienne applauds the dancers before she launches into her routine. Sitting up front on a stool, Joan takes swipes at her body, her mother-in-law, her marriage, and the differences between first and second wives, illustrating the latter by talking to people in the front row. Joan being Joan, she characterizes one woman as "adorable with no bra." This material is breezily and sprightly delivered, if a little more prickly than the usual Burnett humor.

As Funt and Mundane prepare for their final performance, they belittle their understudies for never having the chance to replace them onstage. But the latter two undermine them, starting with Vincent breaking Harvey's foot during a change offstage and assuming his place. Vicki gives Carol lemon juice to make the latter pucker and drops a window down on Carol's fingers. The comic whirlwind escalates to where Vicki flips back a couch with Carol on it and stomps on the actress repeatedly. Funt and Mundane keep returning despite every physical ailment thrown their way, but at the end Vicki and Vincent appear before the curtain to applause. This is top-level farce done wonderfully by all.

Next up is a strong set of send-ups of new TV shows. In "Police Lady," Vicki pleads with Vincent not to think of her just as a cop, only to ticket his vehicle. In "Chiquita and the Man," Carol's Charo bumps and grinds are so raucous, they lead to a heart attack by her prospective boss (Harvey), and Carol says it's not her job to get him his medication. "Rhonda" mocks the first season opening titles for the spin-off from *The Mary Tyler Moore Show*, with Joan primping her hair and making jokes until she is mugged on the streets of New York City and yells in response, "I recognize you, Mary!" For "Tony Tallahassee and Dusk," Harvey, Carol and Vicki sing "Wrap Those Jammies Round the Old White Pine" before the real Tony Orlando and Dawn show up to replace them.

These modestly amusing bits are capped off by "The Walnuts," where John Girl (Carol), Grandma and Grandpa (Vicki and Harvey), and Mama Woman and Daddy Man (Joan and Vincent) refuse a $1 million offer for their property from a rich man (Dick Patterson) after John Girl tells them how the money would corrupt them. She talks of her memories of skipping rocks and how they could not enjoy that activity with swimming pools in place, for example. After throwing the rich man out, John Girl says good night while in bed with her family, with Grandpa thrown out of bed after he tries to make a move on Grandma. John Girl's voiceover at the end tells us she realizes as an adult what idiots her family members were. Even ardent fans of *The Waltons* have to recognize there is enough truth about the series' conventions behind the comedy to make this very effective.

The unconventional finale has everyone dressed in black gowns and tuxes and divided by singing voices representing the themes of the story's participants. Basses support the moose, altos do the same for Sara (Joan), tenors for the forest ranger (Don Crichton) and sopranos for Aunt Fanny (Carol). With each section's sounds, we learn that Sara has a moose call for a birthday present that she shows the forest ranger before giving it to Aunt Fanny, who accidentally swallows it and prompts the moose to be amorous towards her. Despite a somewhat flat ending, this is an enjoyable and distinctive piece.

This was the last appearance for Vincent and Joan on the series, both of whom are excellent here. The two would remain friends in real life until Price's death in 1993.

Jan. 11, 1975: Tim Conway

Q&A; a cleanup crew member at a Japanese steakhouse (Tim) volunteers to cook dinner with disastrous results as the maitre d' (Harvey) helplessly observes; Bert wants to go to an X-rated movie but Molly protests the notion; Carol does a novelty number; Harvey referees a match wherein Tim is flustered by the flirting of Carol, his opponent; the dancers perform to "Wild Party"; a witness to a car accident (Carol) argues with another one (Harvey) about what really happened; Carol confronts Vicki at the latter's apartment about Vicki taking dictation from Carol's boss; everyone participates in a pirate-themed musical number.

Comments: Everything here runs from passable to great in another wildly variable outing. It starts with Carol getting two kisses from men, one having a strong Southern accent and the other taking up her dare regarding how she reacted to the recent minor earthquake. "If you want to feel the earth move, honey, come up here and kiss me!" she jokes, and he follows through to her shock. Trivial queries follow about her clothes, children and hair color until a man from Holland tells Carol his reaction about watching her show for the first time the last three weeks. "I was amazed!" he exclaims, cracking Carol up because he sounded surprised the series even got on the air.

The first sketch has an employee (Dick Patterson) at the Beniha-ha restaurant tell Harvey that the chef has broken his leg and they have no replacement. A desperate Harvey allows Tim to take over, only to regret his decision once Tim accidentally sticks the carving knife in his crotch and checks to see if there was any damage from the maneuver. More snafus follow as customers at the table watch in dismay as Tim accidentally cooks Harvey's toupee along with their food and places the hot rug back on Harvey's head. Tim figures out how to divvy what he is making by writing numbers on Harvey's blue tuxedo, then finds a contact lens lost by Harvey on the hot surface and puts it into Harvey's eye, all of which irk Harvey. The food catches fire and Tim has to extinguish it, prompting customers to leave. Harvey fires Tim, who dejectedly sings "It's Time to Say So Long" and pulls on his ear before leaving. Dampening this skit's enjoyment is the dated Asian stereotypes Harvey and Tim employ in their characters' dialects to change L's into R's (Harvey calls Tim "Chef Ruby Keerer," for example) and the sporadic humor it contains.

"The Old Folks" putters along with two memorable moments. When Bert tells Molly, "You're about as exciting as a WIN button," referencing President Gerald Ford's program to "Whip Inflation Now," and gets only a few titters from the audience, Harvey ad libs "About as effective" to everyone's amusement. Also, when Bert once again grabs Molly's leg, she quips, "Reminds me of many years ago . . . and you had that stupid hunting dog." Bert asks what that means, and she shoots back, "He was always barking up the wrong tree too!"

The next offering is one joke that becomes pretty stale by its conclusion. Carol sings "All of Me" superimposed on a blue screen background that makes her appear as if she is becoming invisible as she removes every object of clothing, leaving only her right hand in view by the end. At least the number intends to be funny rather than earnestly serious.

In "The Boxerette," fight announcer Ernie Anderson introduces Tim versus Carol in the ring, and the game is anything but competitive. Carol plays with Tim's emotions by crying and making advances to throw him off so she can actually beat him. However, her swing at him misses and hits her in the face, knocking her out. As Harvey does the count, an indignant Tim comes to Carol's defense and punches Harvey down. For the modest comic purpose of this segment, it is pretty effective.

Outside a courtroom, Carol and Harvey agree to get their stories straight about what happened in an auto crash they saw to save time during their depositions. Carol slants the story to favor the woman driver who hit a man over Harvey's reluctant objections. They head into the courtroom with their stories matching as Vicki arrives and thanks Carol, her sister who flew into town to help Vicki with the story she fabricated. This short and sweet attraction has a good payoff at the end.

Even better is the concluding skit, where Carol and Vicki's dramatic dialogue over Vicki's work for Carol's boss makes it sound like they are women fighting for the affection of the same man rather than an office dispute. "He needed me," Carol intones, recalling her secretarial devotion to her boss. "I typed my fingers to the bone for him!" Vicki confronts Carol with her typing mistakes that led to the boss asking Vicki to help out instead and boasts how she enjoys working with him. When Vicki snubs Carol's offer to buy her off, Carol threatens to kill her until Vicki says she was really having an affair with him and did not want to work for him. A grateful Carol thanks Vicki for the confession, but Vicki says she will use her status with the boss to have Carol fired for confronting her. This is well-written and well-acted.

The "Mack the Black" finale has a beautifully costumed cast on the deck of a Caribbean ship as Carol, Vicki and the lady dancers pleading musically with Captain Bligh (Harvey) to protect them from the clutches of the title character, played by Tim. Naturally, Tim is not as threatening as his name suggests, as he gets caught up in the rope flying onto the deck and does some other bits that obviously were edited out, as the final take shows Harvey cracking up at something Tim did as he turns away from the camera for more music to play. Somehow Tim accidentally impales all the male crew, and an impressed Carol wants to leave with him, but Tim remains confounded by the rope on his leg. Although not entirely successful, this is a good change of pace from the usual movie send-ups and tributes to songwriters that normally end each show.

The episode wraps up with Harvey whispering into Tim's ear and the latter pretending to be in pain after listening to it. This prompts Harvey to mockingly cut off Tim's ear. The show could have used a little more wildness like this to be a truly outstanding effort instead of the merely acceptable one it is.

Jan. 18, 1975: Pre-empted by special *Entertainer of the Year Awards* (Carol is an honoree)

Jan. 25, 1975: William Conrad, the Jackson 5

Q&A; the Jackson 5 perform "Life of the Party"; Carol is a woman who becomes unglued when her husband (Harvey) says his former flame will be attending a party with them; William sings "Movies Were Movies" from the Broadway musical *Mack and Mabel;* Harvey and William are two doctors who have an argument after Harvey learns his patient has been treated by William as well; Mama has a new beau (William) that Eunice fears wants her only for her money; the Jackson 5 sings tributes to other vocal groups, with sister Janet Jackson joining them to play Cher.

Comments: This show misses the mark often in the first half, yet clicks strongly enough for the remainder to make it finish as a winner. The Q&A is fine. A gentleman inquires, "Do you remember me, Carol?" "Alvin, yeah!" she yells back. "Wonderful lady!" he tells the audience in response. Asked why she is so uninhibited, Carol quips, "I guess I've got a lot to show!" A gentleman approves that she has three daughters, and she reveals they like Eunice because they can imitate that character. She says she may read children's fan letters on the show again sometime, signs an autograph on both sides for a fan, introduces the Los Angeles County March of Dimes poster child in the audience and cannily names the Jackson 5 as her favorite rock group.

"Life of the Party" was not a hit for the Jackson 5, and likewise this lip-synced performance is not one of the group's best, despite some nice split screen shots of the piano, guitar and band at the same time. Nevertheless, Michael is absolutely dynamic with his large, fluffy Afro and infectious stage presence, and there are some fun close-ups of Randy pounding on the bongos (it's actually the Jackson 6 at this point). The group will compensate for this minor disappointment later in the show.

A party host (Dick Patterson) informs Harvey that the latter's ex-girlfriend will appear soon. That worries Harvey, who knows that his wife (Carol) reacts strongly to such news. She denies it, but as he recounts his affair, Carol destroys her chair and a pillow, stammers and has head spasms before she calms down. When Vicki arrives in a low-cut gown, Carol freaks out again, and Harvey escorts her out. As they leave, a handsome man (Tony Young) grabs Carol and kisses her. She introduces him to Harvey as their milkman, and his presence causes Harvey to start having spastic reactions on his own. This sketch owes a lot to Carol and Harvey's mugging to make it work well.

A cornball moment follows as William Conrad sings—or rather bellows—about his love of silent movies when he was a kid. The dancers show up in various guises to illustrate his point, such as Don Crichton as a Keystone Kop, ending with Birl Johns launching a relay of pies to the faces of all the dancers. The wall behind them opens to a street set with Oliver Hardy (William) wanting a banana from Stan Laurel (Bill Richmond). Stan gives him a peel without a banana which he throws on the ground in disgust, and a policeman trips on it and blames Oliver for his fall. This leads back to William reprising his song at full blast. The overall bombastic effect hardly inspires nostalgia.

The show sluggishly tries to gain momentum with William and Harvey playing physicians after a round of golf who have a scene when Harvey is envious that William has been treating one of his patients. He feels inadequate because it was his first patient, and William tries to console him by telling the man has seen every doctor in town. When William reveals the patient is a hypochondriac, Harvey is so upset he splashes his glass in William's face. Finally, William reveals that he has been sleeping with Harvey's wife as well, prompting Harvey to say, "When you have bad news and good news, give the good news first!" This is a so-so variant on Harvey's jealousy bit with Telly Savalas from the Oct. 12, 1974 show, and thankfully the last time the show tries using it.

Excitement finally arrives with a nice Family sketch, as Mama has a new beau (William, in white hair) who Eunice thinks is a money grabber even though he is rich. Ed hopes he will take Mama off his hands, but Eunice remains unnerved by his frisky demeanor, such as smacking Mama's behind. When Eunice goes into the kitchen and learns Mama and her boyfriend plans to go to New York City—and that Mama knew William and had the hots for him before meeting Eunice's father—she becomes livid and hits her head repeatedly against the refrigerator door. Eunice returns to the living room and begins a tirade with Mama about how the latter used to hate traveling with her father but is fine in doing so with William. Both of them call Ed a failure, which prompts him to say he should have walked out on Eunice a long time ago. They end their bickering and leave with Eunice scrunching her expression and saying, "I want you to take a good look at this face, Mama, because it's the last time you'll ever see it!" Having uneasily watched these proceedings, William gives Mama some money and leaves, obviously worried that Mama will continue to react like her daughter in the future. This is splendid in all departments.

The show is now on a roll as the Jacksons do solid vocal and dancing impressions of the Mills Brothers and the Coasters—as well as three of the men doing the Andrews Sisters and the other three doing the Supremes. For the latter, Michael strongly approximates Diana Ross performing "Stop in the Name of Love" down to the arm movements. Finally, they perform "Dancing Machine," with Michael dancing the Robot, while Randy sits out the song to join Janet in a feather boa (!) to act as Sonny and Cher rocking out "The Beat Goes On." Carol and the rest of the Jackson 5 join them for a rousing ending.

Bill Richmond joins in the closing of the show. This is William Conrad's second and last appearance on the show, but the Jackson 5 will return next season—see Jan. 24, 1976.

Feb. 1, 1975: Rerun of Oct. 5, 1974 show

Feb. 8, 1975: Tim Conway, the Pointer Sisters

* Q&A; Tim is a hobby program TV host dealing with a surly crew, including a hung-over assistant whose antics nearly hurt him badly; Stella Toddler attends a game show and suffers many indignities under the supposed help of the unctuous host (Harvey) and her celebrity guest partners (the Pointer Sisters); Tim plays a man auditioning to replace Max as Nora Desmond's assistant and soon regretting his decision to do so; the Pointers perform "Love in Them There Hills" with Carol along with a Duke Ellington medley and "It Ain't Gonna Run No Mo."

Comments: It is a shame this full episode is not available anywhere as of this writing, for what does exist indicates it may well be the most consistently funny edition of this season. The Q&A has Carol doing her usual response regarding her film career ("I've got a lot of plans to do more movies. The producers don't") before saying that La Jolla, California is OK and naming Robert Redford, Alan Alda and Burt Reynolds as the sexiest actors. Four teenagers give her a homemade pillow and a shirt that says "Raquel Welch, eat your heart out" with two fried eggs over the chest area, which amuses Carol. Finally, one man says his ten-year-old son wants know if Carol will be a *Playboy* centerfold. "*Field and Stream* beat 'em to it!" she cracks.

Tim's contributions are solid. He is hilariously deadpan as always trying to teach home repair techniques while dealing with offstage personnel doing thing like throwing missing tools at his body. Tim is just as unflappable as he responds to an ad Max has made because the latter is going to direct a toilet commercial and needs someone to act as Nora's consort in his absence. Entering as an applicant with a Hitler mustache and a bowler covering his bald head, he endures Nora smacking him up her staircase (and gets applause from the audience for his great work doing so) and Max ripping off his mustache because Nora dislikes it. Max threatens to kill a reluctant Tim if he does not try to pretend to be him, so in a proto-Tudball voice, Tim does his best impersonation. But when Max unexpectedly returns, Nora is confused as to which of them is real and ends up accidentally shooting Tim through the keyhole, causing Max to dump Tim's body in the pool. Apart from a weak ending, this is a good bit.

Stella Toddler makes an appearance in the game show parody "Up Your Income," where the unflappable host (Harvey) introduced the Sha Na Na Na Noony sisters (the Pointers) to help the contestant. When Harvey calls out Stella's name, she is asleep in the audience, so Don Crichton and Randy Doney bring her up unconscious on stage, where she asks Harvey not to make much noise, and of course he ignores her. Stella endures being hit a boom mike and falling over as she cannot punch her way out of an oversized bag.

The final humiliation comes when she has to face an oversized fan to collect dollar bills blown across the stage by it—Stella is pushed back by the wind pressure, and the wigs fall off the sisters as well. "That was our idea, to put the ribbons under our wigs, so when they blew off, the ribbons would blow as well," notes Anita Pointer. This funny bit runs a little longer than needed, as shown by how much overacting Harvey has to put into it.

By the way, Carol says in the Q&A that Vicki Lawrence is on this show, even though she is missing in the half-hour version. The Pointer Sisters will appear again thrice next season, the most of any guest in 1975-1976, beginning with the Oct. 25, 1975 show.

Feb. 15, 1975: Rock Hudson, Nancy Walker

Q&A; Rock and Nancy sing and dance in "Mine"; a series of blackouts make fun of commercials; Harvey does a monologue with a ventriloquist trying to separate from the dummy in his act; "The Late Late Show" mocks the 1948 film *When My Baby Smiles at Me* in two acts, with Carol a stage performer in love with boozing and carousing Rock, Vicki as Carol's cynical pal, Harvey as a producer who wants to sign Carol for his own show and have her as his wife, and Nancy as a wealthy millionaire who wants to have Rock all to herself.

Comments: This uneven offering is brightened by the first guest shot by Rock Hudson, supplying the show with the handsome hunk type not seen since Lyle's departure. The announcement of his name draws screams from the audience, while Carol says she is happy because this show allows her to play a role by one of her idols, Betty Grable, with all original music. She tells those assembled that the show has received great reaction for Eunice and the Family sketches, that her favorite game show is *Password* (where she has appeared several times) and that Ernie Anderson will appear in tonight's show. Carol also smartly quips that "The cameramen like the dancers. They even like the girls!"

The show begins with Carol claiming Marge Champion has choreographed the hot new dance team of Rock and Nancy. Officially Rock is sixteen inches taller than Nancy, and they make the most of the mismatch by having Nancy sing to his chest at one point and letting Rock pick her up and swing her around stage as well. Despite a little stiffness by Rock (dressed in tie and tails), he and Nancy (in a white outfit with a frilly wrap) come off fairly enchanting, and Carol emerges at the end to have them take a bow.

The generally strong commercial takeoffs show how much heavy lifting the guest stars must do this season, as either Rock or Nancy is in nearly every one of them. The first boggles the mind in retrospect. Harvey is Joe Namath wearing pantyhose and promoting the product when Rock appears along with the dancers with towels wrapped around their waists in the locker room and sneers to

Harvey, "OK, the guys are all done. You can use the shower now." Knowing Rock's homosexuality nowadays, the apparent joke that Harvey is gay and thus needs to be kept away from the "normal" athletes makes one cringe at its implications. The other spots are funnier and less troublesome. Nancy cleans an oven with her feet, which is too involved to explain why here. Rock argues with a tub of margarine that claims it is butter, and Vicki is sick of Rock's quarrel so she shoots him—only for the wound to claim she stabbed him instead. Laying his head on a roll of toilet paper, Rock extols its virtues until Carol yells from the bathroom, "Bring that back here!" Two of the dancers are nicked shaving and an offstage voice says, "Gotcha!" before Harvey appears and gets goosed from behind with a "Gotcha!" as well. Finally, Rock boasts about his wife's ridiculous accomplishments before Nancy arrives, haggard from all the activities she supposedly has handled.

Harvey's dramatic monologue that follows is a change of pace. Given the challenge of having to tell a dummy he is breaking up the act because the latter gets all the laughs, yet coming around to conceding that they need to stay together, Harvey does a masterful job of delivery and showing his range, although it does seem somewhat lengthy.

"When My Baby Laughs at Me" consumes the show's second half and has a few high points. Vicki's real-life pregnancy is obvious, but most of the parody has Nancy manipulating Rock to forget Carol and come work with her instead. In a great visual, Nancy stands on a table to talk to Rock face to face before she implores Carol to leave Rock, which the latter does. In Act II, a newly divorced Carol dances with the men dressing her as she plans to wed Harvey reluctantly. When he says he might burst with excitement, Carol warns him "You're a straight part!" Vicki and then Rock arrive to congratulate Carol, and Carol and Rock do their old number which emotionally exhausts her before he leaves. A stage manager (Ernie Anderson) tells Rock that he is a washed-up drunk. Carol helps Rock do his routine on stage with her, during which she confesses that she did not marry Harvey and is ready to go back to him. However, Nancy arrives on stage with a box to stand on again to tell Rock that she is ready to have him star in another production, so he says goodbye to Carol. Dejected, Carol sees Harvey arrive on stage, but any love they have may vanish because he wants to be a solo star too. Brightly performed and sung, this nonetheless should have been tighter and funnier.

Despite this show's faults, it is nice to see two stars of a concurrent dramatic TV series (in this case, *McMillan and Wife* on NBC) showing their musical comedy talents. Though this is Walker's only guest shot on the series, Hudson will return—see Jan. 29, 1977.

Feb. 22, 1975: Tim Conway

Q&A; Mama is in a wheelchair living with Ed and Eunice following an accident and getting on their nerves; a police lieutenant (Harvey) gently interrogates an old man (Tim) hospitalized with a blow to his head about what the latter witnessed in a restaurant murder; a "Mama's Got a Date" number with Carol, Vicki and Harvey; Carol and Harvey play a couple debating about their supposed wishes;

a robbery involving Tim and Harvey goes awry; Cleopatra (Carol) performs "Row Row Row My Boat" and "Up a Lazy River" with a centurion (Harvey) and the dancers as Egyptians.

Comments: This show is a winner considering how disastrous it could have been. Originally singer/songwriter Paul Williams let the staff know a day before taping that he was uncomfortable with his material and dropped out of the show. This was surprising, given how he appeared frequently on almost all other 1970s variety series. The series does not hold a grudge against him as a songwriter at least, as Hal Linden will perform his composition "I Won't Last A Day Without You" two years later (see March 5, 1977).

In any event, the situation left a hole for his featured spot, which the show fills by rerunning the "Mama's Got a Date" musical number from the Sept. 29, 1973 show where Carol and Vicki played teenagers singing about the engagement of their mother (Harvey as Mother Marcus). For his speaking parts, the reliable supporting actor Dick Patterson takes Williams' place, and he deservedly appears in a tuxedo for bows at the end of the show for doing a superb job at the last minute.

This situation is hidden from the studio audience, which learns that Tim was the guest before Carol does the Tarzan yell, says she likes the Family sketches and mentions that Bob Mackie designs her gowns. More intriguing is when a man asks to feel her double-jointed hip that she can dislocate as she revealed recently on *The Dick Cavett Show* and requests her to "Take it slow!" to everyone's amusement. She does, and then a girl asks, "What else is double-jointed?" Carol responds by making her knuckle disappear. She notes Harvey's recent Golden Globe win that was not shown on the telecast and tries out a little Spanish in the audience when learning she has three male visitors from Columbia, Chile and Holland in the audience. Then it's off to the main show.

As Ed collects material from Mama's house, Eunice tells her sister, Ellen, on the phone that Mama passed out from fumes when cleaning the upstairs bathroom and then fell down the stairs and injured her right ankle. Coming out from the back room in a wheelchair (and sheets covering Vicki's pregnant stomach), Mama insists that everyone keep their usual routine—until she complains about Ed watching *Bowling for Dollars*, reading the newspaper, buying so many Japanese rabbit traps in believing they would be a hot item and bringing the wrong jar of hand cream from her home. Eunice receives grief from Mama too, for having sticky drinking glasses and a dirty floor and drinking alcohol. "That's your fourth beer today," she tells her daughter. "And I'm going to tell you something, I needed every one of them!" Eunice shoots back to Mama. Ellen calls again and Mama sings praises to her other daughter before noting all the things wrong with her room at Eunice's home. That prompts Ed to finally have it with Mama, and she says she will go stay at a nursing home instead. However, she falls out of her wheelchair in her room, prompting Eunice to plead to God to save her mother. When it is clear Mama is OK, Eunice vows to Mama that she and Ed will be more understanding of her condition—and then the fighting starts again. This is a top entry in the Family sketches.

Even funnier is the next offering, where a doctor (Dick) warns Harvey of Tim's precarious nature as a patient as Harvey works a murder investigation. Tim lays in his hospital bed with his feet rather than head on the pillow, then rearranges his position and giving Harvey three bedpans during the transition, prompting the first of several crackups by the latter in this bit. The next comes when Tim looks up Harvey's nose and ad libs in mock horror, "Is that loaded?!" Tim then alternately passes out and awakens in relating trivial details about the murder, and he causes Harvey to break character again when he pulls his eyelids down one time. Tim becomes lucid enough to describe the suspect's face, and Harvey ends up drawing Mickey Mouse. "That's him! He's gonna kill me!" Tim exclaims. Harvey figures Tim needs to get a sedative, while a scared Tim thinks the suspect is loose and tries to leave by putting his slippers on. He thinks they were on the wrong feet the first time when actually there were correct.

Harvey re-enters and knocks Tim on the head, who lies down on the bed with his body bent. To correct the situation, Harvey adjusts the bed too fast and propels Tim forward into swinging off the front of the curtain rod. The doctor arrives and gets Tim down with Harvey, then they leave to get Tim a wheelchair. Still scared of the killer, Tim attempts to wrap the curtain around his bed, but it gets stuck midway. As he stands to adjust it, Harvey pushes back the curtain several times to find him, and Tim hits the wall each time. Amid this nuttiness, Ernie Anderson arrives to say they have cornered the suspect, causing Harvey and Dick to leave. But Tim plays with his motorized wheelchair that backs him up into a window and knocks him out of the chair, causing him to fall out.

This is a brilliantly presented piece of physical comedy, and the audience in the first taping got even more enjoyment because the original plan was for the chair to bust through the hospital wall, but it failed after repeated attempts by Tim to navigate it and knock it down. Finally and amusingly frustrated, Tim gave up and finally walked through the wall himself. An edited version of this appeared in the *Show Stoppers* special in 2001.

After "Mama's Got a Date," Carol wonders if Harvey's hopes at a wishing well involve their upcoming wedding. Her fears lead her to make her own wish, which she confesses him was to find out Harvey's secret request. He reveals to her that it was to see her in the well and pushes her over—a disquieting ending to an otherwise acceptable sketch.

Tim returns as a bartender being robbed by Dick, who is upset to find only $3 in Tim's cash register. Harvey appears to steal too, and Tim says where more money is at before a cop (Don Crichton) appears and arrests Harvey and Dick. Left alone, it is revealed that Tim actually was the bar's first robber. It is a nice twist to end a pretty good skit.

The finale is enjoyably flashy and fast moving. If Paul Williams was to be part of it, Carol, Harvey and the dancers cover his absence flawlessly. During the credits, Vicki is big as a barn in her pregnancy, which goes unacknowledged. Regardless, were it not for the repeated number—and the wishing well one—this show would rank in the top 25 shows of the series. Dick Patterson will continue doing bit parts on the series next season.

March 1, 1975: Pre-empted by the Grammy Awards

March 8, 1975: Buddy Ebsen, Wayne Rogers

** Buddy and Wayne appear in a spoof of military movies called "War is Heck"; the Old Folks make an appearance; Buddy dances to "Rendezvous," a song for which he wrote the lyrics; Carol is an accident prone wife; a musical finale called "County Fair."

Comments: Nearly forty years after making his sole guest appearance on the series, Wayne Rogers chuckles a lot when recalling his work on this program. "I remember a skit Harvey and I did with her, and she was a chanteuse at a nightclub," he says, recounting "War Is Heck." "Harvey and I played Gestapo officers raiding the nightclub. We had these Aryan accents, and they amused her."

As Buddy, Wayne and Harvey serenade Carol, she starts laughing wildly at their vocals. "She laughed so hard, she fell down on the floor," Rogers says. "We were in hysterics too." Trying to regain control, Harvey asks Wayne, "Are things this funny on *M*A*S*H*?" before Carol speaks in her Eunice voice and shoots Wayne. Rogers also recalls a spoof of *The Bridge on the River Kwai* where he played Alec Guinness's character and cracked up over Harvey's Japanese accent there as well.

Rogers adds that when he guest starred on *Cher* this same season with Tatum O'Neal and Raquel Welch (an episode that lost the writing Emmy this season to *The Carol Burnett Show*), the latter was upset with the size of her dressing room at CBS Television City. George Schlatter, executive producer of *Cher*, pleaded with Rogers to appease her.

"I took her around and showed her all the dressing rooms, and the biggest was Carol's," he says. "Otherwise, she'd have to another studio and be shuttled. So she finally settled on Carol's dressing room. I told Carol later, and she said, 'I would've helped you if I'd known!'" Welch's diva behavior here may be the reason why Carol nixed the idea of her as a guest star when an audience member suggests it on the Nov. 15, 1975 Q&A.

As for his overall impression of the series, Rogers says, "Carol was wonderful. She was a great improviser, and she didn't take herself too seriously. And Harvey and Tim were superb actors for what they did. I think that the ensemble part made that show. Everybody on that show contributed to its success. Good people."

March 15, 1975: Roddy McDowall, Bernadette Peters

Q&A; Eunice, Ed and Mama visit Eunice's brother Philip (Roddy) at his home in Hollywood for the first time; Bernadette performs "All That Jazz" with the dancers; Carol and Bernadette are two synchronized electronic typists; "The Late, Late Movie" roasts *The Heiress* with Carol as a wallflower, Harvey her domineering father, Vicki her sister and Roddy her suitor, all perfectly spoofing the acting styles of Olivia deHavilland, Ralph Richardson, Miriam Hopkins and Montgomery Clift, respectively; a mini-musical tribute to Broadway songwriters Sheldon Harnick and Jerry Bock with the cast and dancers set in a Gay Nineties Parisian nightclub.

Comments: This episode is a very good showcase for two of Carol's favorite guest stars, giving them meaty roles both comically and musically. The Q&A has a Canadian theme. One woman from the country wants to know if Carol has visited America's neighbor to the north, and Carol says no. Then a gentleman asks her, "What do you think of bald men, and I will take you over the border." "In that case, I love them!" Carol responds.

Philip Harper (Roddy) tells his houseboy (Dick Patterson) how excited he is that his family is coming to visit. That feeling dissipates once they arrive, with Mama the first to be cranky about the trip. "I've had gas for three days for eating at truck stops!" she wails before wanting to watch her soap opera which airs at a different time back home. Ed wants to see Disneyland, while Mama chimes in that the "Only one I want to meet is Lawrence Welk." Then Eunice hints to her screenwriting brother that Francis Ford Coppola wrote a part in *The Godfather Part II* that his sister, Talia Shire, was able to play. If her star making efforts were not aggravating enough to Philip, Ed says his script needs to add Three Stooges routines to spice it up.

Eunice takes over the conversation to moan how she envies the awards and respect Philip has earned in the family and posits that if she had not married Ed, Philip would willing put her in his movie. Ed shoots back that if he did not wed Eunice, he could have traveled more and had more fun and own a chain of hardware stores. Mama interjects by eating caviar and crying out, "What the hell is this goo?!" Amid this racket, Philip announces he is going to a motel room to work on revision by himself and leaves incognito. His disappearance fails to faze Ed, who decides to get into Philip's pool and pulls off his pants to reveal swimsuits underneath. Mama and Eunice go with him to the pool as a very satisfying installment of "The Family" ends.

Bernadette ("a lady we like a lot around here," says Carol in her intro) resembles Betty Boop in a black gown with spangles as she listens to a Victrola before she segues into a leisurely paced version of a song from the recent Broadway hit *Chicago*. Working alongside the male dancers clad in purple shirts and open collars, later joined by the female ones in purple outfits, Bernadette smoothly delivers her featured spot.

Sitting beside each other at desks, Carol and Bernadette mimic each other's activities, though not always with the same results—for example, Bernadette gets a date on her phone while Carol's efforts fall flat. After they gossip, each woman realizes they are going on separate vacations and Carol wishing that they were not. Bernadette agrees, saying, "Yeah, it'd be fun doing things together for a change." What sounds like a trifle in description is a nice little comic gem due to tight writing, directing and acting.

In "The Lady Heir," we see mousy Carol doing needlepoint when she meets Roddy, a ne'er-do-well nouveau riche opportunist who is after Carol's money, to the disdain of her stuffy father (Harvey). Carol hides in the piano until Roddy professes his love for her by calling her clever, even though she cannot remember the punch lines of jokes. Harvey reluctantly gives his blessing for the two to marry, but he tells Roddy if they elope, he will disinherit Carol, so Roddy calls off his plans and leaves.

Carol holds her breath for a year before Harvey reveals what had occurred, which prompts her to verbally attack Harvey and the latter to have a heart attack.

Two years later, Roddy returns and learns from Carol's sister (Vicki) that his one-time paramour has become a hot, confident senorita. Carol tells Roddy she still wants to marry him and gives him her fortune in a bag to take outside in advance of that wedding. As he leaves, Carol tells Vicki to hit the deck, because she really gave Roddy a bomb that will activate if he opens up the purse, and of course he does that. Carol then opens up the window, says goodbye to Roddy and tells him to say hi to her father on the other side. This takeoff falls a little short of a laugh fest, but considering its dour 1949 movie as source material, the cast and crew wrung out about as much humor as possible in the situation. Roddy added to the verisimilitude of the project by having his hair curled in the same style Montgomery Clift sported in the original.

In the musical finale, Carol acts as proprietor of a nightspot where Roddy and Bernadette are singles seeking love. Naturally, Carol puts them together, as well as herself with Harvey. Roddy offers decent vocals as he and the rest of the cast and dancers tell the stories by Harnick-Bock tunes, including Harvey singing "If I Were a Rich Man" from *Fiddler on the Roof* partly in French. Incidentally, dancer Randy Doney worked with Roddy in the Broadway musical *Camelot* in 1960.

The credits follow, with Carol and her regulars and guests somehow unable to choreograph the kick line in the right direction in the end. It was the only obvious moment out of sync in a nice episode.

March 22, 1975: Steve Lawrence, Sally Struthers

Q&A; Steve sings "Make It Easy on Yourself" and "Ain't No Sunshine"; Carol lip syncs to her version of "The Trolley Song," then pantomimes having noisy body functions while in a movie theater; Sally and the dancers present "Next to Lovin'" from the musical *Shenandoah*; Steve impersonates James Cagney in a two-part spoof of the 1939 movie *The Roaring Twenties,* along with Sally as a chanteuse, Carol as the operator of a speakeasy and Harvey as the law graduate who plans to prosecute Steve as a criminal; a finale centered around compositions with the word "time" in their titles.

Comments: This music-heavy lesser entry is of note more for what supposedly precedes it. According to some sources including a question on the game show *Jeopardy*, McLean Stevenson made a cameo at the start of this show as his Lt. Henry Blake character from *M*A*S*H*. The latter series had killed off his character just four days earlier as Stevenson made an unsuccessful bid to star in his own program. As the rumor goes, public outcry about Henry's demise was so strong that he appeared to be afloat saying "I'm alive!" rather than being shot down overseas in a plane as stated on *M*A*S*H*. It's questionable if such a taped segment did in fact air. It certainly does not appear in the audiotape for the series, although that may have left out this piece as a separate element. Incidentally, McLean and Vicki briefly dated in 1972, and she claims was the one who convinced him to audition for the TV version of *M*A*S*H*. If McLean did in fact appear here, it would have been his only on the series. Vicki is not on this episode either.

The show is mostly flat, from Steve's blah contemporary medley to Sally's overdone singing and dancing. Even the Q&A bores, with talk about Cher wearing Carol's hand-me-downs, Carol's first TV job with Paul Winchell, her last *Garry Moore Show* and her stage work in Kansas City in 1973. The only amusing parts are Carol's lip-sync job and pantomime. The former copies what Carol did in the Nov. 18, 1968 show, only this time Dave Powers bets $1 that she cannot follow the recording as it slows down and speeds up. (When the 1968 segment reappears on the tenth anniversary show in 1977, Carol mistakenly remembers this bet here as occurring then.) Carol also shines as she coughs, blows her nose and has her stomach growl as she tries to stay quiet while catching a film.

As for the featured parody on "The Late Late Movie," "The Boring Twenties" starts with Carol in 1933 recounting to an unwilling drunk (Dick Patterson) how she met Steve thirteen years earlier along with Harvey, an aspiring lawyer bought off by Steve as part of his empire during Prohibition. Claiming they are on easy street, he tells Carol he will wed her until a platinum blonde (Sally) who wants to be in his show attracts his fancy. Despite missing notes while singing "Melancholy Baby," Steve hires her and dumps Carol.

In the second half, Sally loves Harvey and Steve threatens to kill him before accepting the inevitable. Carol tells Steve that they can marry instead, but he starts drinking wine from a straw and becomes a sot. He disappears until he walks into Carol's bar and proposes to her while Sally asks Eddie to support Harvey's bid for governor. But Steve is unable to shake his underworld connections and is shot more than 30 times on the street, hit with bullets so strongly that he even does pushups with his body. Carol then asks if he's been hit, he says "Rosebud" before dying, and she recounts to an unwitting cop who has arrived the story of their relationship. Like Steve's Cagney impression, this skit wears out its welcome long past its conclusion.

The finale bunches more than ten mostly forgettable songs (with the exception of "As Time Goes By") delivered rapidly by the cast and guests, who mug shamelessly to inject some life in the bit. It does end cleverly segueing into Carol frenetically singing "It's Time to Say So Long" at the end, but it's too little too late to save this effort.

For people who did not have enough of the *All in the Family* guest star experience with Sally here, another cast member appears on a better episode the following week.

March 29, 1975: Jean Stapleton, Phil Silvers

Carol sings "Alice Blue Gown" as Cher; Q&A; Phil is a grump unhappily married to a devoted wife (Carol), while next door Harvey endures his cranky spouse (Jean); Jean sings "Losing My Mind"; a series of commercial blackouts; Carol and Jean are residents on an apartment stoop who do a duet on "Flings"; "The Old Folks" celebrate their anniversary; a feminist (Jean) complains of sexist treatment from a man (Harvey) at an office building; Phil is a sergeant leading his men with Harvey as his lieutenant when Carol's all-female troop arrives with Jean as her aide in a musical finale.

Comments: This is a critical episode in many respects, even though the installment itself falls a little short of being one of the greatest entries. It commences hilariously with a spotlight shot of Carol in a metallic blue wrap covering her body as she sings the first stanza, then the lights come alive as Carol struts down the runway. As she removes the wrap, Carol reveals a pair of sagging breasts in a halter top, complemented with a large (foam prosthetic) belly and hips and long, flowing hair. The result is a perfect send-up of how Cher was opening her variety series that had begun just a few weeks earlier, down to Carol dropping supposedly hip slang and telling the audience, "Hey, let's hear it for the dress!" before reprising the song. Since he dressed Cher at the same time, credit is due to Bob Mackie for making fun of his own style here.

Carol then emerges to do Q&A, though she can't resist saying "How's it going?" in the same manner she did in the previous sketch. She says a special hello to Becky Morton two different times in this segment, although it may be the result of combining both tapings. Becky was a twelve-year-old longtime fan dying of cancer who bonded with Carol during the production of this week's show, with Carol visiting her in the hospital and even giving her a preview of a musical number Carol would do with Vicki the following week. By the time this show aired, Becky had passed away, with Carol at her bedside.

Perhaps realizing the emotional investment Carol had made that week, Harvey lightens up the mood during the Q&A by appearing in the audience and yelling out, "Who's the nicest person you ever worked with?" (Luckily, she said he was.) Other hilarity pops up a lot here, with Carol cracking up as someone asks of the opening sketch, "Was that your real belly button?" One lady asks, "Have you ever thought about having your mouth insured?" and Carol shoots back with "There's not enough money!" As she recognizes some in the audience as children of her best school friend, she recounts how she and her old chum pretended to be sick so they could play jacks in the bathroom. She says her own daughters have not pulled that trick on her because "I'm onto them!" After the Tarzan yell and a joke about her husband, Carol is asked about her everyday personality. She allows that she runs hot and cold. When the stagehands laugh uproariously to that, Carol asks why, and announcer Ernie Anderson tells her that her husband said from the booth he agrees with that assessment. "Oh, how would he know?!" Carol guffaws.

Phil and Jean play individuals grumpy for different reasons. He cannot stand his sweetly devoted wife (Carol), while on the adjacent balcony, Jean is a frizzy-haired nag treating her husband (Harvey) poorly. As they go inside their apartments, Harvey discovers Carol's happy demeanor, and both become entranced with each other and run inside to have a rendezvous. Returning outside, Phil and Jean cannot find their mates but do locate their shared love of being gruff to each other. The new couples emerge in different balconies singing "Cheek to Cheek." This nice piece leaves out a blooper by Carol during one taping where she offers Harvey a piece of bass but pronounces it as "base" instead, leaving him to say he will have some "claims" (instead of clams) to go with it.

In a blue gown and a hazy background, Jean's musical number offers little to enjoy. Thankfully, the show quickly recovers with a quick series of ad takeoffs. Because they are offered tightly, these ten skits have a high success average for all involved, but the best involve Harvey. As former baseball player "Moe DiMaggio," he drinks from a coffeemaker and hates the taste so much he uses a bat both on his cup and the glass pot containing the liquid. Ending the blackouts, he arrives home for a trip complaining to Carol about the flight's irregularity and she forces him to take a laxative. Harvey tells her he meant his plane was late, then says "Uh oh" and heads straight to the bathroom.

The show's momentum fades again with Carol and Jean's seriocomic duet, the only item of interest being the nighttime urban set where they sing. Better is the series' final Old Folks sketch, which is funny and thankfully dispenses the usual song at the end.

Following this, Jean stars in a sketch that Carol found uncomfortable to perform. When Harvey offers to open the door for Jean, she calls him a male chauvinist pig and demands he go through the door first. He declines, saying that he was taught to hold the door for women. This leads Jean onto statements about how she is worthy of equal pay and "I am not a sex object!" Finally, she goes through the door first before she realizes Harvey is the man she is meeting for an interview regarding a job in the complaints department. Carol's instinct on this one was right—although fitfully amusing, there is an anti-women's rights tone overall that diminishes its enjoyment.

After the evening's up-and-down offerings comes a strong closing where Phil reminds everyone of his success in playing Sgt. Bilko on TV in the 1950s as he appears in military garb and tells Harvey he worries about the efficiency of his men. At that point, Carol and her female troop appear to do a song-and-dance face-off against their male counterparts. As Carol, Jean, Phil and Harvey sing "Anything You Can Do," the dancers sound off, march in time and tap in unison. Carol and Jean sing "I'm a Woman" to seduce Phil and Harvey respectively, and the female dancers follow suit on the males. By the end, Harvey and Phil sing "Alright, OK, You Win" to the delight of Jean and Carol.

The shows ends with Carol saying good night to Becky Morton once more. Phil mimics Carol and tugs his own ear after signing her book, then hugs and dances with Harvey and even grabs him on the butt. Clearly, Phil enjoyed the show no matter its deficiencies.

April 5, 1975: Family Show

Q&A; Eunice and Mama visit Ed's hardware store to go to lunch, but to their dismay he wants to wait for Mickey Hart to come back from getting flathead screws; Carol and Vicki do a medley of lullabies; a blackout with Carol singing "When Your Love is Gone" in the shower; the Old Man (Tim) irks a customer (Harvey) who wants to have his grandfather clock repaired quickly; the dancers perform to "Ain't That Nothing"; the Charwoman says goodbyes to the cast, remembers highlights of the season and sings "The Two of Us" with a marionette form of herself.

Comments: The inclusion of Tim Conway (because we consider him family, Carol says) foreshadows his involvement as a regular next season, though no one in the audience knows that during the taping. There is a lot of good stuff on display here, so all the Q&A consists of is a montage of Carol doing the Tarzan yell eleven times during the past eight seasons. She then performs it one more time before getting a mock gunshot for doing so. Carol will reprise this bit on her March 29, 1978 finale.

The Eunice sketch is the best example of Carol's contention that the segment contained no jokes, just inflections by the cast that kept it from being a tense drama otherwise. Ed tells a joke to a customer (Dick Patterson) before the latter leaves and Eunice and Mama enter his store and get on Ed's nerves. Mama is obsessed with finding the right rubber stopper for her tub, while Eunice is incensed by the attention Ed lavishes on a pretty brunette shopper (Sandra De Bruin) as well as having to wait for Mickey to return. When Mickey does arrive, Tim's ad lib complimenting Mama on her blue hair has the other regulars trying to stifle giggles in response. Mickey delivers an involved story explaining why he could not find the screws Ed wants but can get some similar ones, and Ed encourages him to do that immediately while Ed will handle the store during lunchtime. This infuriates Eunice even more, as she accuses Ed of deliberately trying to avoid spending time with her and Mama. As she leaves with her mother arguing about what movie to go see, Eunice spits out sarcastically, "Ed, thanks for the swell lunch. Because that's what you're gonna get for dinner!" Dick Patterson returns and asks Ed to join him at the Weenie King for lunch, which Ed does, saying it's the best offer he has had all day.

This sketch has a little more honesty than humor, but still is enjoyable. Vicki has a great line addressing what some viewers had been thinking when she yells to Mickey, "Why the hell you keep calling me Mother Harper?! Ain't you got a mother of your own?!" Meanwhile, Harvey already was tiring of his character in this segment, according to his son. "He hated to do Ed because Mama and Eunice butchered him every show," says Chris Korman. "He also didn't like the shrillness of it."

Carol had played her and Vicki's lullaby medley for Becky Morton before she died two days before this taping. Dressed in checkerboard gowns—Carol's in red and Vicki's in green—both ladies discuss potential names for Vicki's baby, with Vicki doing her Mama voice to insist it will not be Eunice if it is a girl. They sing parts of more than twenty familiar standards for children such as "Frere Jacques" and "Twinkle Twinkle Little Star" while seated on a wire bench with nice floral settings and eye-catching lighting changes to emphasize different tunes. Though a little long, it is hard to fault this segment, given with the women's emotional harmonies and the happiness surrounding Vicki's pregnancy.

The shortest and least enjoyable bit has Carol sing a portion of a song and come out of the shower as the camera closes in and reveal the male dancers playing instruments in it. This remake from the Nov. 24, 1969 show is just as unfunny here as it was then.

The show recovers adroitly with Tim slowly shuffling along to date a claim check for Harvey at the start of a skit where the latter breaks up several times. The first is when Tim tells him he can give him a loaner clock shaped like an owl with the hour and minute hands in place of its left and right eyes respectively. "Wanna see quarter to three?" Tim says as he crosses his eyes. Harvey barely recovers from that when Tim says he has a clock from Australia in the shape of a koala, an in-joke between the men. Tim does wonderful shtick trying to open and close the top door his desk before going to the grandfather clock, whipping out a stethoscope and saying "Wanna turn your face and cough?" Harvey loses it again after that, as he does when Tim busts through the top of the clock and exclaims, "I can see the marina!"

When Harvey tests the clock by setting its hands at twelve o'clock, it rings so loud that Tim, still inside it, breaks through the sides to undo the change. Tim's damage to the clock prompts Harvey to destroy all the other clocks in retaliation, only to learn that Tim's place is owned by his hulking son (played by an unidentified actor), who tells Harvey to put everything back together. As Harvey-Tim sketches go, this ranks among the top ten.

The dancers' routine is a Bob Fosse-esque number with everyone in denim-covered top hats and overall, with bright shirts underneath. There are several male-female duos and trios spotlighted in this energetic piece.

The Charwoman watches the end of the show, turns off the TV and says goodbye to the dancers—and Roddy McDowall, who appears unannounced but happy—then kisses Tim, Harvey and Vicki before turning the "Closed for the Season" sign. Finding costumes on a rack, the Charwoman puts them against her body and imagines herself recreating scenes from the season involving Nora Desmond, Eunice and the Old Folks, with clips from each. She then opens a locker with props and finds a marionette doppelganger. The two sing together before the puppet vanishes and Carol goes to sing the full version of "It's Time to Say So Long" before leaving the studio.

Final Notes for the Season

In what was a rocky year for variety series, *The Carol Burnett Show* survived relatively unscathed. Although its overall finish at Number Twenty-Nine was two places lower than the last season, average ratings actually went up slightly, and once again the series vanquished all comers against it. Its most impressive feat actually occurred during its reruns. The May 10, 1975 repeat with Telly Savalas and the Smothers Brothers finished as the Number One show in that week's ratings, indicating that the series remained a potent performer for CBS.

Part of it had to do with weak competition. While NBC stuck with movies as always, ABC bombed with *Nakia* and then its own unimpressive movie series. Incredibly, the latter network will follow pretty much the same formula in 1975-1976, bombing this time twice with action adventure shows (*Matt Helm* and *Bert D'Angelo—Superstar*) before resorting to movies again at season's end against *The Carol Burnett Show*.

This marked one of at least two of Rudy DeLuca's three seasons with the series where during the wrap party for cast and crew, he impersonated Carol taking questions from the audience, decked out in a wig, red dress and boots. It left everyone in good spirits for the conclusion of the season.

As far as members of the Television Academy were concerned, they thought the series remained golden and awarded it with Emmys for comedy-variety or musical series (its only competition was the undeserving *Cher*), writing and directing (both for the Dec. 21, 1974 Alan Alda show). Tim Conway and Vicki Lawrence lost as supporting performers in their genders to Jack Albertson and Cloris Leachman respectively, both for *Cher*.

In other award news, Harvey Korman earned a Best Supporting Actor Golden Globe for his work on the series, the series' first win there in three years. Other Golden Globe nominations occurred for the series itself, Carol and Vicki. The Writers Guild of America also gave this year's scribes its top honor for a second time, the first being in 1971.

Amid these awards came an ominous note for the series in terms of executive leadership. Fed up with the bureaucracy at CBS, Fred Silverman left as the network's head programmer to go to ABC for the fall of 1975. Silverman's acumen had kept CBS just as strong as the overall ratings leader since Mike Dann's tenure in the 1960s, and his skills as a counterprogramming genius positioned him as someone able to give *The Carol Burnett Show* its biggest challenge from ABC since it debuted. It loomed as a potential large threat for Carol and company, but luckily it did not materialize immediately.

Instead, things were mostly business as usual, including the series having its traditional summer hiatus. After CBS ended repeats of *The Carol Burnett Show* on June 14, the network installed *Moses—The Lawgiver* as its first fill-in a week later. A miniseries based on the life of the Biblical character starring Burt Lancaster, it ran until Aug. 2. On Aug. 16, *The Dick Cavett Show* featured ABC's former late night talk show host doing interviews and some comedy bits for four weeks through Sept. 6.

The following week, *The Carol Burnett Show* returned with Tim Conway installed as a regular. Would he have the same effect he did with *Rango*, *The Tim Conway Show* and *The Tim Conway Comedy Hour* and cause it to lose ratings quickly? Or would he enliven a series that sometimes seemed moribund this season? Those were the questions that would have to be answered as *The Carol Burnett Show* entered its ninth season.

Carol is the Queen, putting up with the idiotic comments and demands of a military hero (Tim) at the behest of her stuffy husband (Harvey) because the soldier saved his troop by swallowing a grenade and is now hollow. This is one of several characters introduced in 1975-1976 that reinvigorated the series and made it into the best season overall. Courtesy of Getty Images.

Chapter 10

1975-1976: Conway Comes Aboard

Audience member:	"If you could be any age you wanted to be, what age would you be?"
Carol:	"I think 33. Maybe I'll change my mind when I get there."—From the March 13, 1976 show

Crew Additions This Season

Regular: Tim Conway

Writers: Tim Conway, Ray Jessel, Bo Kaprall (Feb. 14 and 21, March 6 and 13, 1976), Pat Proft (Feb. 14 and 21, March 6 and 13, 1976).

Rejuvenation" is the best way to describe what happened to *The Carol Burnett Show* this season—maybe "transformational" too. Much of it stemmed from Tim being a regular performer and writer, much to the delight of everyone, including the show's scribes.

"He was Tim all the time, on and off," says Bob Illes, who worked with Conway in 1977-1978. "Always hysterical."

"Carol, Harvey, Vicki and Tim worked so well together that they helped make the writing easier," says Gene Perret. "They respected the writing yet were also willing to add bits and pieces during the rehearsal that made the writing appear stronger than it actually was."

"He worked extremely well with Carol, in Mrs. Wiggins and Tudball, and he and Harvey Korman always hit it off in so many sketches that he became part of the show," notes Barry Levinson of Conway. "He was very influential, and at the same time, he never deflected from Carol. He was such a playmaker."

The Wiggins and Tudball Levinson mentions was the big new recurring addition this season. Carol played the dumb blonde to end all dumb blondes who worked as a secretary to Tim's Mr. Wiggins, a boss with a protruding stomach and a short temper dealing with her. Introduced in the Jan. 10, 1976 show, the bit always generates strong guffaws.

Tim told how the Tudball voice came about in the 2012 DVD commentary. "My mother was Romanian, and we used to go visit the Romanian folks on Sunday, and-uh, they would-uh sit around and-uh talk-uh like that."

As for the inspiration of the rest of the sketch, there was a secretary down the hall who could not use the intercom properly. That woman, Charlene Beatty, became Tim's wife in 1984. She previously had been married to Roger Beatty, the series' assistant director, and she had been working with Carol and Joe since *The Garry Moore Show*. Tim and Charlene remained friendly with their ex-spouses.

Wiggins was to be an old woman, but Bob Mackie thought that was overdone. He gave Carol a platinum blonde wig and a skirt that bagged, forcing her to stick her knees into it and jut out her butt in back. That produced the "Wiggins walk," a great source for laughs.

Also becoming a mainstay of the series was at least one Tim-Harvey pairing in a skit. Being the devil that he was, Tim would examine the scripts and the sets to study where he could improvise to crack up Harvey in each of these, and invariably he achieved his goal.

"Harvey and Tim were incredible together," recalls Stan Mazin. "Tim never let on what he was going to do. All Tim had to do was catch his eye, and Harvey was gone." Mazin himself managed to stay composed during such moments even though he was in many of the sketches with the duo. "I was afraid to break up, because I was a dancer," he says.

One holdover sketch, "The Family," became more popular than ever. Joe suggested that Vicki do Mama as a spinoff in 1975 shortly after Courtney was born, but she nixed it. Without Carol and Harvey, she saw no purpose to it, and she doubted whether she could return to the show. Instead, she stayed and won an Emmy this season to boot.

Carol loved these developments on her show. "Tim brought us new life and new characters, and boosted us a whole lot," Carol said in *Panorama* magazine. "That's why I think our ninth season was our best. We'd really developed into a well-oiled machine by then, and we had the show's best combination of cast and writers."

Indeed, the new characters were more enjoyable to watch than their predecessors. "The Family" outshone "Carol & Sis." Tudball and Wiggins produced more laughs in one skit than several of "The Old Folks" combined. Any appearance by Stella Toddler surpassed the tired con shenanigans of Alice Portnoy or the whining of Zelda.

The new guests were fantastic as well. They included winners of Oscars (Cher and Shirley MacLaine), Emmys (Betty White, Jessica Walter and Dick Van Dyke), and even an EGOT (Emmy-Grammy-Oscar-Tony winner), Rita Moreno. Additionally, most were Carol's age or younger, making the show seem fresher and hipper than before.

Another writer helped add to the fun this season, but only halfway. "I brought in Roy Jessel," notes

Arnie Kogen. "We wrote for Joey Bishop, and we later did *The Jacksons* and *Donny and Marie* shows." Finding acclaim for their work, the two men left *The Carol Burnett Show* in midseason to write for *The Rich Little Show* from February to June of 1976 followed by the latter two series Kogen mentions.

Kogen and Jessel's departure resulted in a curious and rare case of discontentment among the writing staff this season. Joe Hamilton hired Bo Kaprall and Pat Proft, who had worked separately as writers and actors on TV. They first worked together professionally with the Kentucky Fried Theatre, a Los Angeles-based comedy stage performance group that served as the springboard for its creators, David Zucker, Jim Abrahams and Jerry Zucker, to produce hit movies beginning with *Airplane!* in 1980.

By the mid-1970s the two men were getting a fair amount of work, with Bo being offered a regular job on a new NBC series, *Saturday Night Live*. "But my agent said, 'No, you're getting hot here,' so I stayed in Hollywood," Bo says. John Belushi went to New York City in Bo's place. Bo kept content by writing for shows such as *When Things Were Rotten,* a short-lived 1975 sitcom on ABC he did with Pat, before their agent told them they had secured employment writing as a team on *The Carol Burnett Show*.

According to Pat, the reason the two received an offer to write for *The Carol Burnett Show* was a recommendation by a previous duo there. "It was Kenny Solms and Gail Parent," Pat says. "They had produced the show I had written for, *The Smothers Brothers Show*." Kenny and Gail hated doing that NBC series with Joe Hamilton in 1975, and similar negative feelings emerged between the newcomers to the executive producer.

"There's nobody better than her," Bo says of Carol. "Her husband was a prick. Total polar opposites."

Joe was not the only source of their discomfort—so was the head writer. "Ed Simmons and I had a fight," Pat says. "During a table read through, I thought, 'This stuff should've been shorter.'" Ed did not appreciate Pat's opinion (even though it was a valid one that should have been considered more often during pre-production), and he let him know that clearly in a way that unsettled the new writer.

"I went to Catholic school, and he seemed like a big, mean man to me," Pat adds.

Others on the writing staff provided no solace for the duo either. "For us, this wasn't fun, because we were not welcome," Bo says. "The older guys were always bitter." He singles out Rudy De Luca as particularly dismissive. "He was pissed we were on the show, because he didn't think that we had paid our dues."

"I knew Rudy De Luca and Barry Levinson, but it didn't seem like they knew me," adds Pat.

Rudy denies that assertion. "I think they felt as uncomfortable as we did when we first joined because of Ed Simmons," he says. "He was a little tough."

Even more discouraging, Bo and Pat found received an office space with pipes overhead and no windows, hardly the best circumstances to create hilarity on page. To Bo, this was the production staff indicating to them that "We were the low guys on the totem pole," and Pat felt disconnected enough to detach his commitment to the series by leaving before the end of each workweek. "I don't think I was there for tape days," Pat says.

Given the circumstances, it's not surprising that at most just two skits of at least eleven they wrote made it to air. Pat recalls writing the over-efficient office sketch that leads off the March 6, 1976 show, while Bo believes they contributed to a Tudball and Wiggins entry the following week. After that, they were dismissed after just four weeks of work.

"I just felt like we never fit in," Pat concludes. "It just didn't feel right."

Both men broke up professionally afterward, but each flourished professionally as writers and occasional actors on TV shows and movies the next 40 years. Pat joined forces with David Zucker, Jim Abrahams and Jerry Zucker to co-wrote several hit comedies, including *The Naked Gun* series with Leslie Nielsen. Meanwhile, by the twenty-first century, Bo ironically was writing several skits for *Saturday Night Live*, the same variety show for which he had been considered as a regular several decades earlier.

Despite their experiences, Pat and Bo are able to look past their disappointing tenure with the series to add praise to it overall. "It was a smart show. It was a good show," Pat says. "It was the cream of the crop," says Bo.

It certainly was, and it was a superior one often this season, beginning with its first show.

Sept. 13, 1975: Jim Nabors

Q&A; the Queen (Carol) finds that a military private (Tim) does not want a medal she is attempting to pin on him; Jim performs a medley of saloon songs and duets with Carol; Harvey shows Tim how to woo a woman by using his charms on Vicki, with disastrous results as Tim attempts to do the same with Carol; Eunice vents to Mama her anger over an incident involving Ed, who enters Mama's house to apologize along with Mickey; a tribute to towns made famous in the founding of America in advance of the country's upcoming Bicentennial.

Comments: The series' best season opener ever has lots of joy and good humor flowing throughout. After having Jim come out for a kiss, Carol takes a few queries, including one that cracks her up. "Did they ask me to audition for Jaws?" she repeats with amusement, in reference to the toothy title shark of 1975's most popular summer movie. She brings out Harvey, Vicki and new regular Tim before the festivities commence.

The next sketch is one that Gene Perret claims was the most fun he ever had writing for the series. A sullen soldier (Tim) rejects an honor from his queen. "I don't want your medal. Stick it in your ear!" he tells the Queen. She repeats his comments to her husband (Harvey), who warns her not to do it. Wondering how the idiot got such an importance post, Carol recalls that Tim is the hollow hero. She yells into his mouth and gets an echo as proof, to audience applause. Harvey and Carol determine that they need to give Tim a pony like he requested so that he will take the medal, only he tells them he wants a blue pony. This infuriates the Queen, who gripes that "I'm out here, busting my royal bustle, trying to please you!" After that, Tim decides he wants the medal, but Harvey makes Tim fall to the ground to pay for his behavior. This rollicking skit went so well during the first taping that Joe Hamilton suggested they just repeat it for viewing on the monitors for the second one, but Carol told him the cast so enjoyed doing it that they would re-enact it. The Queen will become a new recurring character for Carol in the next two seasons.

After Jim sings his medley, Carol joins him for laughs as they review clips of her intros of him at the start of every season. They look at old pictures of themselves with some laughs while singing "I Feel at Home with You." This is a breeze to watch.

Another strong sketch has a shy Tim make a move on a bar patron with long bangs (Carol), urged on by a friend (Harvey) who has just shown him how to score with a different woman (Vicki). Tim engages in wildly inappropriate behavior toward Carol, such as telling her, "Well, I see it's 9 o'clock, better take out my eyes and wash them," and pretends to put his peepers in a glass of water before putting them back and coming out cross-eyed when he opens his lids. Carol is mute and clearly unimpressed until after he damages some items at the bar, when she says a quiet "Wow." Tim takes that as an opportunity to smooch on her, leading to a fracas where Carol tries to get away from him. This great piece confirms that Conway was overdue to be a regular on the series.

Eunice witnesses Ed visiting a massage parlor and wails about it to Mama, who is more interested on her movie on TV. To combat that, Eunice tells her the ending to force a conversation, only to be interrupted by the taxi driver (Jim) who transported Eunice and needs change from her. She does not have it, so Mama searches for cash while wondering how Eunice will survive if she divorces Ed as she threatens. Eunice says she will get a job and live with Mama, which irritates the latter almost as much as Jim waiting for his money. Ed arrives with Mickey, who unsuccessfully lies about what Ed was doing before the latter confesses to the massage. "It is a sin!" yells Eunice. Ed suggests that they separate and Eunice can have the house—a notion Mama endorses while calling the persistent Jim a jackass. But she has a change of heart and talks common sense to them, and Ed, Eunice and Mickey all leave before Mama throws Jim out. The latest installment of "The Family" is as strong as the show's earlier winners, and it's good to see them use Jim effectively in it, since he is a native Southerner.

The finale incorporates everything from traditional tunes such as "This Land is Your Land" to comic contrivances by Tim to salute America's upcoming 200th birthday. It's a rousing end. To top off the happy vibe, during the closing, Carol has Vicki bring out her baby daughter, who was born on May 3. It all makes a promising start to a great season.

Sept. 20, 1975: Sammy Davis, Jr.

Q&A; an entertainer (Sammy) returns to his hometown twenty years later and discovers an old classmate (Carol) still unknowingly harbors some prejudices; Sammy performs a medley of songs associated with him; Tim is a passenger on a no-frills section of an airplane who finds that Harvey is receiving much better treatment than he is, particularly from their flight attendant (Carol); a marshal (Harvey) receives a visit from an old gunslinger (Sammy) he planned to deputize; a mini-musical salute to Harold Arlen has the cast dancing and singing in a tropical lounge featuring Tim as a beleaguered tourist.

Comments: "I'm so thrilled that we've got this gentleman on our show," Carol says in introducing Sammy during his medley, adding that they had wanted him as a guest since the start but scheduling problems had prevented that until now. It is worth the wait, as Sammy is as winning as ever, even if the material could have been a little better. The Q&A is just Carol telling the disappointed audience she is not doing Eunice tonight, yet she copies much of that character's vocal inflections and timing in portraying Sammy's old classmate at a theater clearly set somewhere in the South. After Don Crichton congratulates Sammy on a great show and reporters including Randy Doney and Stan Mazin ask him questions, Sammy uneasily greets Carol, whose family had Sammy's mother as their maid before he became a success. Carol cluelessly makes condescending comments about Sammy—how much her dad liked the way he cleaned his boots, what great diction he has and so on. As Sammy smokes while choking back words, Carol tells him that her husband was at the bar and awkwardly avoids using the N-word that her husband gave in categorizing him. When Sammy tells Carol the mayor and his wife are joining him for dinner, Carol points out that her husband has his own restaurant and all the waiters are black there too. "Naturally, the cashier is white," she adds. A few more insults follow, including Carol using the term "colored," before Sammy ushers Carol out—but not before telling her with a grimace, "Please forgive me for acting uppity." She plans to shake his hand but retracts it before leaving. This funny but prickly take on race relations in 1975 unfortunately remains the same among certain people 40 years later, which makes it possibly even more difficult to watch today.

Thankfully, Carol is happy to kiss Sammy before his strong medley, which includes accompaniment by George Rhodes, Sammy's longtime accompanist. Wearing rings on all his fingers and smoking again, he smoothly performs parts of "Something's Gotta Give, "Hey There," "The Candy Man" and "What Kind of Fool Am I?" (but strangely not "I've Gotta Be Me"), and even gets the audience to clap along some.

Next is a classic sketch introduced by Vicki on what the "no-frills" trend in airlines is providing customers. The idea on this came from Carol, and writers Gene Perret and Bill Richmond take it and milk every possible laugh. Tim, in his typical hangdog expression, endures endless obstacles as he sits behind Harvey. A spare tire and jack falls out from his overhead bin. The rug ends before his seat. Carol takes his jacket, rolls it up and puts it behind Harvey's back to give the latter more comfort. Carol whispers the emergency procedures to everyone but Tim, who has a rope tied around him to serve as a seat belt. Tim learns his window is a hole, finds out the music he gets to hear is Carol singing to him, and has his cigarette (smoking for the third segment in a row, probably a record for the show) extinguished by Carol. When turbulence hits, Harvey is unaffected, but Tim's seat bounces up and down wildly, spilling his drink on himself and causing other damage. He hears Carol asking Harvey if he was going to Chicago, and Tim says that is his stop, to which Carol responds by pushing him out the exit door while the plane keeps flying. This segment sparkles on every level. A fellow writer on the series, Arnie Kogen, terms it as "Hysterical. Just a brilliant sketch, perfect for Tim."

A funny but less successful skit follows where a barkeeper (Ernie Anderson) tells a saloon girl (Vicki) that Harvey is getting drunk because he misses his deputy. Sammy arrives, and after some fancy gun twirling that draws applause, he wonders why Harvey never made him his deputy and left him along with a posse. Their discussion clearly mimics a lovers' quarrel, as Harvey offers Sammy to become his new deputy, but Sammy demurs, saying there is somebody else he works for now—Wyatt Earp. "Earp?!" Harvey responds, in a delivery that squeezes out the maximum laughter for such a simple line. When a gang arrives, Sammy tells Harvey that he will join him in the fight, only don't tell Earp he was cheating on him. In a clever nod, this sketch undermines what Carol's earlier character said about black entertainers not being able to appear in a western.

We conclude with the dancers doing "Happiness is a Thing Called Joe" to begin the finale, as Sammy attempts to entice Tim with the pleasures of Vicki by singing "Get Happy." Carol, Tim's partner, arrives and is upset with the situation, and commiserates with Sammy by singing "Come Rain or Come Shine," among other solos and duets with him. Harvey arrives wearing a pith helmet singing "Gotta Right to Sing the Blues" and "Stormy Weather" and wins Carol's affection, while Sammy wraps it all up by doing "Ac-cent-tchu-ate the Positive" with dancers in counterpoint to Carol and Harvey reprising "Get Happy." With some humorous mugging by Tim and Harvey, who does a wacky dance, this sixteen-song set moves nicely.

It is obvious at the end that Carol adored working with Sammy, as she looks on him affectionately while starting "It's Time to Say So Long." The appreciation was mutual. Harvey reveals in the 2004 DVD commentary that Sammy surprised everyone with a private concert during rehearsals. Sammy will return to the show on Oct. 2, 1976.

Sept. 27, 1975: Cher

Q&A; Tim and Harvey are dueling classical pianists who vent their frustrations on each other's instruments; Cher sings "Just This One Time" and then joins Carol for banter and a joint duet called "Variety"; Carol is a homely mistress to Harvey, who proudly reveals his adultery with her to his glamorous wife (Cher); the cast and Cher observe the ninth annual salute to TV commercials; "As the Stomach Turns" has Marian encounter a native American (Cher) and a snooty friend (Vicki) enjoying their hairdos from a new stylist (Tim); everyone appears in the rock finale "Solid Silver Platform Shoes."

Comments: Appearing as part of a swap deal where Carol guest starred on her variety series last season, Cher is much more confident and charismatic than when she appeared on *The Carol Burnett Show* with then-husband Sonny on Nov. 6, 1967. Carol introduces Cher as a "brilliantly talented, nice lady" in the Q&A before making a memorable quip for a query about whether she liked her first kiss: "Well, it was from a dog." That leads into the first of several excellent skits, starting with Tim (in a frizzy wig making him resemble Van Cliburn) as the protégé who irks Harvey by fidgeting with his music (he wants to play Ponchielli's "Dance of the Hours," the tune behind Allan Sherman's 1964 hit "Hello Muddah, Hello Fadduh!"). They volley in destruction. Harvey smashes Tim's piano, Tim removes the legs of Harvey's piano and Harvey closes the piano cover on Tim's fingers. Before the latter, the offstage pianist starts playing while Harvey's fingers are in the air, prompting Harvey to praise a higher power for doing it for him. It finally comes down to Tim stomping on Harvey's piano top down to its springs, prompting Harvey to retaliate by jumping on his piano's keys to propel Tim up and through the latter's piano. It is a brilliant piece of physical comedy by two performers in peak form.

"Just This One Time" was not a hit, but Cher does it well, along with her banter with Carol, who wears a black dress with silver spangle accents to contrast with Cher's white gown with black and silver accents. The two sing "Variety" in honor of what fun it is to have your own TV show, but their efforts to go out in the audience and corral people to sing along with the audience are mixed at best and slightly uncomfortable to watch.

Better is the next offering, where Carol, looking truly dowdy in an off-kilter brown wig, shabby clothes and uneven teeth, is paraded by Harvey to Cher as the type of women he wishes she would be. Naturally, Cher is unfazed by Carol at first, but Harvey grabs Carol by the neck and pushes her around to emphasize her natural charms to Cher's indifference. He breaks through, and Cher calls Carol a "brazen hussy," while claiming "I'm just an ordinary housewife" (even Cher cracks up trying to say that straight). Seeing his wife in distress and needing him, Harvey goes back to Cher and leaves Carol to get her head hit twice on the door as the duo ignores her to reunite.

The five TV commercial spoofs are mildly amusing, with the best being the last. Cher wears a slinky outfit and asks Harvey if he wants more coffee. "I have one in the bedroom," she purrs. "Oh yeah," moans Harvey as he follows her. Carol, as Harvey's oblivious wife, looks into the camera and says, "Gee, that's funny. Jim never wants a second cup of coffee."

For "As the Stomach Turns," the milkman (Dick Patterson) turns down Marian's request for "other" service, and she is bored as a result. "It seems any gypsy, tramp or thief has more fun than I have," she exclaims in reference to Cher's 1971 hit, and sure enough, Cher shows up in her white native American outfit she wore on TV to promote "Half Breed" in 1973. As Pocahontas Pirelli, she tells Marian that her new coiffure came courtesy of hairdresser Warren Pretty (Tim, wearing a dark mullet a la Warren Beatty's character in the film *Shampoo*), whose motorcycle busts through Marian's door after Pocahontas leaves. He is not wild about doing Carol's hair, but he is for that of Marian's nouveau riche gal pal (Vicki), who ends up with a wildly poufy and curly look. As she departs, Mother Marcus soon enters, and Harvey wrings out laughs with every line and move, even amusing Tim at one point. Warren plans to do her hair before the "But wait" section appears at the end. Sexual allusions abound in this generally on-point entry.

Dressed as the Who, What, When, Where, How and Why rock group in flashy refinery, the dancers join Carol and Cher in big frizzy wigs and Tina Turner-esque dresses shredded at the thighs. Accompanying them is Harvey as a long-haired guitarist and Tim as Elton John in the latter's Captain Fantastic outfit (a great visual dead-on). Add a set lit up like *Don Kirshner's Rock Concert*, and the result is a lively production number.

Although not totally successful, Cher's vibrant stage presence and earnest performances by all make this a winning entry. Alas, it was not enough to draw viewers to watch Cher's rapidly sinking variety series, which went off CBS four months later.

Oct. 4, 1975: Shirley MacLaine

Q&A; Eunice remembers how she and Ed became husband and wife; Shirley and Carol read amusing letters sent to them before performing "Fan Mail"; a palace guard (Tim) is resolute in keeping the Queen (Carol) and King (Harvey) from entering their residence; a Little League mother (Carol) and a baseball coach (Harvey) are upset with the child of another mother (Shirley) who lost a game; Harvey's commentary in "200 Years Ago Today" puzzles an eighteenth century patriot (Tim); Shirley sings "Gorgeous" with Carol followed by "I Love to Dance Like They Used to Dance" with the dancers.

Comments: Although featured in roughly half of this show, Shirley MacLaine is seen less than Don Crichton, who appears in all of her segments plus the royalty sketch. Apart from that anomaly, this is another top-notch episode, with its only deficiencies being relatively little for Vicki and Tim to do and a weak sketch featuring Shirley. The Q&A is pretty short and unremarkable. A woman from Missouri learns she missed Carol when the latter performed *I Do, I Do* with Rock Hudson outdoors last summer. "It was 105 degrees on stage every night," Carol noted, as well as mentioning her fears about the cottonweed trees attacking her with their seeds. Asked if she had ever worked the Catskill Mountains, Carol affirms that—"As a performer," she adds, prompting much laughter.

The Family kicks off the festivities as Eunice and Ed come to pick Mama up for a movie while leaving their boys with a sitter. "Is she reliable?" Mama inquires. "No, Mama, she's on probation from the penitentiary!" Eunice snaps back. As Ed takes his time to get together, Mama remarks that "I will never figure out why you married that man anyway." That leads to a flashback with Ed sporting a head full of dark hair as he and Eunice come home from a date to her house while her parents are out. After letting Ed know Betty Grable is her favorite musical performer (as it is with Carol herself), Eunice realizes they both have parents who disrespect themselves. That fact becomes evident when Mama unexpectedly surprises them by being home along her husband, Carl (voice of Dick Clair). Wearing dark hair in curlers, Mama lets Eunice know that even though the latter has dated Ed for two months, he is not right for her. Mama tries to enlist Carl to help out, but he prefers to stay in the bathroom, even after she opens the door to complain to him while he presumably is sitting on the toilet (a risqué move for TV in 1975). Undaunted, Mama tells Ed she never wants to see him again and he leaves, leading Eunice to become infuriated and say that she is going to marry Ed before running out the door. Returning to the present, Eunice says she knows why she and Ed are together, and she tells him to explain what happened later that night, which leaves Ed nervous. "I get your drift, Eunice," Mama said, implying that Ed impregnated Eunice that evening. She gets a good one in by adding, "Welcome to the club." A mortified Eunice leaves with them. This is incisive, funny and touching comedy handled well all around.

Coming out to whistles, Shirley joins Carol in reading two letters apiece before launching into their tune about the correspondence they receive, broken up by a few more pieces of mail. The funniest one for Shirley is from a woman who said like the actress, her brother got all the good looks in the family! (Shirley's brother is Warren Beatty.) Randy Doney and Don Crichton bring out separate mail carts for the women to sit on for part of the number, then push them offstage before they reunite at the end under a flurry of envelopes dropped on their heads—good symbolism for an enjoyable bit.

The hollow hero reappears, this time obstinate in denying the Queen and Prince passage into the palace at the gate, even when Harvey hints that the Queen needs to go to the bathroom. He refuses to allow admittance until they can produce a buffalo popsicle for him. An ice cream man (Don) informs the couple there is no such thing, so Tim makes an even more ridiculous request, prompting the Queen to go into a tirade which causes her tiara to move from the side and then back of her head. Harvey interjects that he thinks he sees a buffalo popsicle in the back of Don's cart, and when Tim goes to check it out, Harvey kicks him into it, Don drives away and the couple enter safely. This is great.

A letdown follows as Shirley is put on the defensive at a bar by an angry Carol and Harvey for her child losing a baseball game. Carol grouses directly at Shirley while Harvey bemoans the incident to a barkeep (Don once again) before confronting Shirley as well. After proclaiming that winning isn't everything, Shirley becomes weepy talking about how her family has had to move several times because their child lost games for teams in other cities. Her pleas for one more chance move Harvey and Carol after learning her plight. They leave, and the final joke enters—Shirley's child "Billy" is a girl. It is a long way (five minutes) to go for a supposed kicker that has now dated, and it is a shame that this is the only segment to feature Shirley, a great comic actress.

Better is a takeoff of the *Bicentennial Minutes* CBS aired between programs from 1974-1976 to celebrate the nation's 200th birthday. Here Harvey narrates the tale of a drummer (Tim in a portrait frame next to Harvey), saying the latter withstood obstacles such as cannons firing at him at all directions during the Revolutionary War. Increasingly harried by portraying the hazards Harvey describes, Tim is delighted when Harvey says a band of roving divorcees set upon the drummer, then is vexed when Harvey says the drummer resisted their charms to lead America to victory. Tim announces he is not doing that, drops his drum on Harvey's head and leaves with the divorcees (played by the female dancers). This runs half the time as the previous skit yet has twice the laughs.

Closing the show is Carol and Shirley, wearing identical white gowns with blue beads and seeing each other as mirror images as they sing and dance together. This leads to Don dancing with Shirley in tails before having the others join him, with the women in blue gowns and the men in tails as well. All the men get to dance with Shirley, but she ends with Don before returning to see Carol in the mirror as they reprise "Gorgeous." Taped before the studio audience arrived, this number had several retakes, one with Shirley flubbing a line with Carol and another with the male dancers not coming in time to hold a twirling Shirley. Still, the end product is a shining one, and it is a shame the dancers do not take a bow at the end of the show along with Shirley and the regulars.

"She was a fun guest," Carol recalled of Shirley on her 2004 DVD release. MacLaine never did the series again but did have a special pre-empt this series on March 12, 1977.

Oct. 11, 1975: Bernadette Peters

Q&A; Harvey is a therapist and Carol is his patient who learns they have a key childhood connection with each other that involves a pail; Tim plays Perry Como in a series of blackouts; Bernadette performs "He's the Wizard" from the musical *The Wiz* with the dancers; Stella Toddler tells two police investigators (Harvey and Dick Patterson) that Tim has mugged her; a man being treated for a snakebite (Tim) is at the mercy of a conflict between the doctor (Harvey) and the nurses (Vicki and Bernadette) treating him in the emergency room; a tribute to Irving Berlin.

Comments: Two classic sketches highlight this appearance by Bernadette, who is absent from both. Otherwise, this is average, as is the Q&A, where Carol mentions having three daughters, discusses how her portrayal of the Queen is not meant to be Queen Elizabeth II specifically and notes how she would love to do a film with Lucille Ball (she never does).

From there comes "The Pail," which Arnie Kogen claims is one of the favorite sketches he wrote. He loves how when Carol discovers Harvey was the fat boy who stole her pail, the jokes keep topping each other, particularly when Carol and Harvey recount their own versions of what happened during the incident. Harvey mocks Carol's lisp, while she makes fun of his waddle. After she threatens to expose his past to his patients, he capitulates and gives her a pail, but not the one she had stolen. Reluctantly, Harvey lets Carol check his closet, and a cascade of plastic buckets falls out. That is not all, however.

"It had like five different endings," Kogen notes. Indeed, this sketch could have finished with Carol getting her pail back, but then she asks for the shovel—and Harvey has it hidden in his pocket! This brilliant piece builds beautifully and ends strong.

Less impressive are three blackouts by Tim that bookend Bernadette's feature number. Dressed in a sweater to resemble "Mr. C" back when he did his TV series with a boom microphone and music stand clearly on stage—a setup that ended twenty years earlier than when this first ran—Tim drops the lyric sheet to "White Christmas," has his mike replaced with a noose when the crew hears his tone-deaf rendition of "Once in Love with Amy" and witnesses the studio audience walk out (in a previously recorded clip) as he tries "Fools Rush In." All the gags are as decades old and tired as the songs Tim sings.

"He's the Wiz" is an odd routine where the dancers wear captains hats and faces with crossed eyes over their over their top halves and have fake arms dangle beside them while boogieing with Bernadette. The Wiz (Stan Mazin) joins them in a matching yellow fright wig and jumpsuit, and the emphasis is on frivolity, as indicated by the scoring. This attempt to be cute falls considerably short of how much better the number works in the original production, which was a hit when this was first presented.

The show comes back to life when Stella reaps unintentional abuse at a police station from a sergeant (Harvey) who has more sympathy toward her accused mugger (Tim). Stella re-enacts how she had her purse stolen in a great physical bit that has Harvey fighting not to laugh, but Tim looks like he will get away with the crime until he accidentally confesses. However, Harvey needs to confiscate Stella's purse for evidence, thus continuing her pattern of abuse. This is a joy thanks largely to Carol's clowning.

For the next skit, Tim freaks out after Harvey criticizes Bernadette for being slow in administering the lifesaving serum for Tim and Vicki tells her not to inject Tim in order to protest Harvey's brusque behavior. As Tim pleads for the medicine and starts showing symptoms of his condition (loss of vision, itchiness), Bernadette waits for an apology from Harvey, which finally occurs. Tim is not out of the woods, however—Vicki plans to give the shot when Bernadette complains that will make Vicki look like a hero and not her. They fight and accidentally put the needle in Tim's buttocks, and he scampers away to avoid more problems. This bit has some laughs but should have generated more.

Ken and Mitzie Welch and Artie Malvin will earn Emmy nominations for the mini-musical that closes this show. They will lose to themselves. For more, see Nov. 29, 1975.

Oct. 18, 1975: Maggie Smith

Q&A; Carol is an actress who extracts much physical revenge on her fellow thespians, namely her husband (Harvey) and his mistress (Maggie), when they all appear together on stage; Vicki sings "The Other Woman"; the Queen (Carol) is ready to christen a ship when she faces again a hollowed-out, irritating soldier (Tim), accompanied by his girlfriend (Maggie); a parody of *Jaws* with Harvey, Tim, Vicki and Dick Patterson; a finale with Carol as the mother of two girls (Vicki and Maggie) who sing and dance for the affections of suitors at an antebellum cotillion.

Comments: Maggie has some great moments in another top entry for this season. The audience already appears lively when Carol comes out in a multicolored jacket for Q&A. She reveals she has a twin sister—Raquel Welch—and introduces Miss California in the audience. When one gentleman asks her age, she turns the tables and instructs him to guess. "Old enough," he says. "You're right there!" Carol responds.

Another actors-in-distress-onstage sketch has the novelty of one of the performers causing mayhem this time. Wearing a blonde wig, Carol sees Harvey woo Maggie before their play, with a great in-joke of "They're thinking of us for *Pete 'n' Tillie Part Two*!" Curtain's up, and Carol is on the move, stabbing Harvey with a pen and smacking him on the side while kissing him. Alert to what is happening, Maggie pounds on Carol's foot with her cane and tries to choke her with a necklace, only to have Carol evade her and stomp Maggie's foot instead. The women stumble along until Carol is able push Maggie outside a window and put on "beagle puss" glasses to shock Harvey during a scene of intimacy. The scene degenerates to where the women are pulling off each other's wigs and fighting with pillows. It is a superb exercise in physical humor by all involved.

"Hey gang, Vicki's got a new record out!" Carol announces in introducing her cast member's number. Unfortunately, "The Other Woman" was her last entry on the pop chart, and a minor one at that. At least the presentation is nice, with blurred and kaleidoscope visuals of Vicki singing in a red gown.

The rest of the cast appears in a skit where Carol's regal Queen is ruffled again by Tim's inconsiderate, disobedient soldier as she prepares to launch a ship. This one had several bloopers removed from the final broadcast, such as Carol stepping one of Harvey's lines and the prop bottle for the christening breaking prior to the event. What remains is still very hilarious, and Maggie looks smashing as Tim's tart girlfriend in a short skirt who blasts him into getting in line and following Carol's requests.

"Jowls" is a fine parody of the shark horror film. The best part has Tim ad libbing as the shark hunter fishing in a bathroom while Harvey and Vicki attempt to stay poker faced. However, Tim himself cracks up (in a blooper left out of the show) when he recounts a story of how a woman in Hawaii tried to get away from a shark in the water and loses his composure when he says, "She would've made it too, if she hadn't worn her lucky ham!"

The closing piece features a little humor (Tim as a Southern colonel) amid such bits as the male dancers performing to "I'll Go Home with Bonnie Jean" from *Brigadoon* and Harvey singing "Almost Like Being in Love" to Maggie (and she returning the favor with "Show Me"). With costume resembling what the show would offer a year later in its spoof of *Gone With the Wind*, the production ends on a sentimental note with the party having ended and Carol saying good night to her late husband.

Before the credits roll, Carol sings "It's Time to Say So Long" in a Southern accent, to some amusement. All in all, this is a fine outing.

Oct. 25, 1975: The Pointer Sisters

Q&A; Ed, Eunice, Mama and Mickey play charades; the Pointer Sisters sing "How Long (Betcha' Got a Chick on the Side)"; Harvey is a bartender who drives Carol, his customer, crazy with responding to her tales of woe with jokes; Tim portrays Perry Como in a pair of blackouts; dick jockey Sheepman Jack (Harvey) is appalled by his squeaky clean radio show guests (the Pointer Sisters); Tim is a bum who can win $1 for himself and Carol, a fellow hobo, if he boxes Harvey; a finale with the women alone doing "Get Me to the Church on Time."

Comments: This show is a subtle tribute to women power, although the men get a chance to shine too. Carol could use some energy in the Q&A, as her voice cracks twice before she nails the Tarzan yell on her third try. She reveals that the set designer is "Paul Barnes, a delightful man" and what is going on in the booth behind the audience with the director and his staff. "They're all drunk, and it's bulletproof glass," she quips. After thanking someone noting an award she received, Carol is asked if she would make another movie with Walter Matthau. "I'd love to. He's a crazy, lovely man," she responds. She also notes that she never got to play Juliet to someone else's Romeo. "I don't know why, I'm so perfect for it!" she exclaims.

When Ed's helper, Mickey Hart, unexpectedly arrives, Eunice suggests they play charades, which she is excited about as much as her partner, Mama, could care less. Eunice irks Mama with her display of signals she has a hard time remembering, while Mama's suggestion of one title for Ed and Mickey to do, "Under the Bamboo Tree," meets with disdain from Eunice, but she writes it down. She has more faith that *The Scarlet Pimpernel*, which she saw on TV the other night, will stump the men, who are first up. Ed fails to convey to Mickey "bamboo" by pretending to shove some shoots under a person's fingernails, and he loses his cool when Mickey cannot figure out "under" is the opposite of "over." Mickey gets upset when Ed calls him dumb, but they make up even though they ran out of time. Now it is Mama's turn, and after seeing her title is "Supplemental Hardware Guide," she announces, "We're sunk, Eunice." She cannot get Eunice to identify even one word, and Eunice is livid about having to guess it. Next, Ed needs only five seconds to identify *The Scarlet Pimpernel*, since it is Mickey's favorite movie and the men had been discussing it. Eunice is the last player, and she is aggravated when doing the second word in "Wait Till the Sun Shines Nellie" that Mama sees it sounds like pill and guesses daffodil. This causes Eunice to break her silence and tell Mama to concentrate. Mama finally gets the answer two minutes past the time limit, which infuriates Eunice. She makes a scene about the injustice, only to change her tune to sweetness when Ed suggests they have another game. This is a classic bit.

The Pointer Sisters lip sync their future top twenty pop and Number One soul song in silver purple dresses in front of jukeboxes. It's the only time they perform one of their current hits on the series. That sizzling bit is followed by a cool but good comedy-drama of Carol recounting being dumped by her boyfriend of three years to Harvey while he serves her a drink. He tells her several jokes in response, leading her to get angry before he tells her it is the only way he has learned to cope with everyone telling him their troubles. Carol says she is willing to hear his problems, so he describes how his wife left his best friend, and Carol responds with a comeback. They two of them bond before the scene ends.

Bigger laughs come with back-to-back quick bits with Tim, sporting a white sweater, walking onto a podium with a stand to ape how Perry Como did his early TV series. For the first entry, he sings "Just in Time" before his stool breaks, and in the second, he stands up and intones "Make Someone Happy" before falling through the floor.

The laughs keep coming as Harvey sends up Wolfman Jack as a raucous radio host. "The Sheepman's baa-aack, baa-acck, baa-ack!" he yells into his microphone, getting applause for his lamb vocal impersonation. The electric atmosphere disappears when the Pointer Sisters play a proper vocal group in pink prom dresses and tell the Sheepman in their on-air interview that "We don't sing rock and roll." Their inspiration is the Andrews Sisters, and they do the first chorus of "The Sound of Music" to the Sheepman's horror. He gets them off the air, only to confess that he detests what he has to play, and the women break out in an up-tempo tune. While this sketch does feed into the show's anti-rock perception, Korman's delivery alone is hilarious enough to negate such concerns.

Less effective but tolerable is an old-timey skit taped in black and white with Tim fighting in the ring against Harvey, wearing a bedazzled boxing outfit. With Ernie Anderson as the referee, there is the expected physical comedy of everyone stepping on each other toes before Tim improbably wins thanks to Carol putting a horseshoe in his glove. Carol and Tim go outside with the $1 they have won to buy hot dogs, but when they see two other struggling people, they give the money to them to use instead.

In the finale, Carol is a nervous bride who boozes it up at the bachelorette party before singing "Get Me to the Church on Time" with Vicki as her mother and the Pointer Sisters as her bridesmaids. The Pointers move very well with the female dancers who make up the wedding party, and it ends with Carol passing out.

At the end, Carol urges her viewers to conserve energy—the electrical kind, not the enthusiasm shown by all tonight despite some material not being quite as good as last week's installment. The male dancers do not take a bow at the end, even though they appeared in the boxing sketch. They do appear when the Pointer Sisters return again just five weeks later (see Nov. 29, 1975).

Nov. 1, 1975: Roddy McDowall

Q&A; Carol interrupts Harvey's wedding proposal at a restaurant by cackling over another patron's misfortune; Roddy performs a medley of musical tongue twisters with Carol; Tim tries to buck up Harvey, his fellow trucker, when he breaks down at a restaurant about how lonely he is; the work Carol, Roddy and Tim are doing on an assembly line is greatly impeded when Carol tells Roddy she wants a divorce; a window washer (Tim) transforms an office worker (Vicki); a takeoff of the 1941 film *The Little Foxes*; the entire cast participates in a mini-musical using Cole Porter's compositions.

Comments: After a shaky first third, this show finally clicks as it progresses. The Q&A is not a letdown, with several amusing moments revolving around Carol's looks. She lets loose a monologue about how she prepares herself for the tapings. "Being in comedy, you can't be too beautiful, or people wouldn't laugh at you," she starts. "So what I do in the morning, I get up, I cut my eyelashes, because overnight, they grow so long, they make Elizabeth Taylor's eyes look bald. The next thing I do is bind my chest. And then I darken my hair, and put my teeth in. . . ." To someone wanting to know how she keeps so slim, Carol seriously responds, "Just no junk food." Finally, she blends jokes and sincerity when asked about her nationality. "I'm Oriental," she quips first, then adds truthfully that "I'm Irish and English and I think Dutch and some German, and part American Indian, Cherokee."

The first sketch is so forced, one wonders how it made the cut in rehearsal. In a restaurant, Carol laughs uproariously at an unseen man who has whipped cream on his nose while Harvey asks for her hand in marriage. Another patron (Stan Mazin) complains about Carol, only to join in with her when he witnesses the scene too. A waiter (Tim) and another man (Roddy) intervene to calm down everyone, but they bust a gut as well. When Carol gets dip on her nose, that finally amuses Harvey, to Carol's anger, so she coats his nose along with Tim's and Roddy's with the dip, and that's it. This sketch with no point has the cast laughing harder than the audience for little reason. It's a waste.

Carol banters with Roddy about how she loves his enunciation, and he tells her that tongue twisters can help. They do several rounds of this together, then Carol has one man in the audience try "Toy Boat," and he slips up on it wonderfully. The routine ends with Carol and Roddy singing "Moses Supposes," and though not classic, this is much better than what preceded it.

The show unexpectedly slumps again with a forgettable Harvey-Tim bit. All sporting Southern accents, Tim and Harvey give their meal orders to wisecracking waitress Vicki before Harvey sobs about being a lonesome divorcee. Tim tries to build up Harvey's confidence, but he loses his bearings too when the jukebox plays an old tune he shared with his wife. They compose themselves before leaving, after which Vicki complains to her co-worker that the two do not take love seriously. This has no ad libbing by Tim, probably because there is nothing to add to this limp seriocomic item.

From there, things pick up as Roddy drills, Carols nails and Tim adjusts a board with a wrench on an assembly line. Amid great sound effects for these duties, Carol tells Roddy she wants to leave him "Because your work comes before me." There is also someone else she likes, and Tim grimaces as she delivers that news. When they take a break, Carol babies a nervous Tim, while Roddy vows revenge on who has been seeing Carol, and shows it by drilling multiple times. Harvey arrives as their boss and tells the arguing Carol and Roddy to report to his office, leaving Tim to have to do all three jobs on the assembly line, which leads to a great time where he accidentally activates the drill in his pants. Carol and Roddy return, and there are so oblivious in their reconciliation that they end up drilling and adjusting Tim to the conveyer belt. It is nicely played by all.

A quickie follows with Vicki happy to leave her work desk to interact with a window washer (Tim). His words of care lead her to break out in singing "For Once in My Life" at the same time his rig collapses on one side, and he dangles and pleads for help unnoticed while Vicki continues, even as Tim is getting electrocuted by a wire. When she finishes, he applauds for her and accidentally falls down. This is tight, light and just right.

"The Little Foxies" has Roddy as the brother-in-law of Harvey, Vicki as Harvey's drunk wife, Tim as their cross-eyed son and Carol as Roddy's scheming spouse in a mansion so Southern the doorbell plays "Camptown Races." The latter four want an ill Roddy dead so they can inherit his fortune, but Tim's efforts are so irritating that everyone slaps him—even himself—and Roddy hits him so hard Tim rolls up the staircase. Carol's attempts to poison Roddy's heart medicine when Harvey asks her the status of her work. "Not yet, now get out!" she barks. "Chitlins!" Harvey exclaims as he closes the door. His ad lib forces Carol to compose herself before blurting, "Oh, he makes me laugh sometimes!"

Carol keeps Roddy's medication away from him, leading to a prolonged death scene where he goes up and down the stairs and rises repeatedly from the ground before collapsing. All enter as Carol reads the will, which says that Vicki will inherit Roddy's money first, leading Harvey to kill her. Harvey is next in line, so Tim takes his gun and shoots him (the show kept out one taping where Tim shot Harvey in his crotch, followed by Carol quipping, "I'm sure there wasn't much there in the first place!"). Carol says she is next in line after Tim, so to save her time, Tim shoots on each side of his face and then the middle, saying "I can see! I can see!" before dying. Opening the safe, Carol encounters a cannonball to the face, after which Roddy gets up and happily celebrates everyone's passing. This is one of the series' best old movie spoofs ever.

The finale has a 1700s style party with the dancers dressed for a royal party and performing to "Anything Goes." Carol and Roddy are servants who join the dancers in "It's DeLovely," followed by Tim noisily trumpeting the arrival of Harvey and Vicki, who sing "Love for Sale" and "Let's Fall in Love." Carol, Roddy, Harvey and Vicki all become amorous before there is a reprise of "Anything Goes." The rich atmosphere and familiar tunes sprinkled with humor works well here.

Now an annual guest, Roddy will return to the series again on Oct. 30, 1976.

Nov. 8, 1975: Helen Reddy

Q&A; a housewife (Carol) struggles to open products with labels that tell her what to do; Helen performs "Ain't No Way to Treat a Lady"; Tim reluctantly helps Harvey search for the deadly great white phantom squid; a TV phone conversation between Helen and Carol has the latter trying to hide Tim, Helen's husband who has been cheating with Carol, from being seen during the call; Vicki and Carol devolve into rancor with the revelations from their fortune cookies at a restaurant; Carol, Helen and the dancers participate in the "You Don't Need a Reason to Sing" finale.

Comments: With this episode, the series launches a consecutive quartet of superior installments, superb on every level. Following a trivial Q&A (some girls want to give gifts to Tim, and Carol reveals she is a Taurus and Bob Mackie does the clothes), Carol reads the instructions (voiced by Dick Patterson—the other instructions will have voiceovers by the dancers) on how to open a bag of macaroons but cannot crack it. More difficulties with products follow after she hears voiceovers of their instructions, such as Carol gashing her thumb trying to get into bag of crackers and then being confounded on how to release a bandage from its protective wrapper. The finger ring to her can of soda comes off, so she slugs it with a rolling pin, but the can remains intact. When she needs aspirin and hears the difficulty of the directions, she throws it into a can while it is still talking (the audience applauds). As she breaks down, her husband (Harvey) enters and consoles her. He suggests she get romantic with him. She eagerly agrees—but then Harvey cannot undo the zipper on Carol's blouse, making her burst into hysterics. This is a classic bit of comedy.

Wearing flippers on a ship's deck, Tim appears as Harvey's assistant, speaking French gibberish about his fears of confronting a thirty-foot squid in the water. He is so worried that he asks Harvey for a lullaby, which obviously is an ad lib based on Harvey's reaction. Tim acquiesces and fights the squid, then asks for Harvey's help. The latter gets taken away by the squid, and Tim apologizes to the viewing audience. Although a little short of their classic routines in laughs, this is still very enjoyable.

Helen gets into the comedy act by talking to her friend Carol on their new video phone (a piece of technology planned in the 1970s that did not occur until four decades later). Carol is having a tryst with Tim, Helen's husband, at her house and has to conceal him in various ways, including him having to pretend his exposed arms are Carol's as she sits in a chair while conversing with Helen. Helen makes Carol uncomfortable by saying she suspects Tim is cheating on her, but when Helen cites as evidence finding long blonde strands of hair and a big bra, Carol realizes he is going behind her back too and retaliates on Tim. The setup is ingenious, everyone's delivery is tight, and this is a winner.

Vicki's contribution to the humor is opening fortune cookies from a waiter (Dick Patterson) along with Carol at lunch, and each woman finds the epigrams prompt them to question their friendship. Vicki's fortune of "Do not lose the one you love to the one you trust" particularly makes her think Carol is seeing her husband, Harold (Harvey). "I can take Harold away from you in front of your fat face!" Carol retorts, as she and Vicki demand two more cookies. After Carol does a great vocal routine of showing Vicki how bellowing really sounds, the two women fight over a bowl of fortune cookies when Harold arrives and tells them to stop. They reconcile and Vicki goes to pay her share, during which we learn Carol really does have something with Harvey. This is beautifully played throughout, and if the payoff really is not a surprise, it still is a satisfying one.

The smashing finale cleverly interpolates the new title tune with "I'd Like to Teach the World to Sing" and Carol and Helen doing "Sing" and "I Believe in Music" while Ernie Flatt's crew performs a square dance. The contemporary numbers are performed with gusto and make this a great ending. Given the verve she shows here, it is not surprising that Helen becomes a recurring solo guest on the series for the next two seasons.

Nov. 15, 1975: Maggie Smith

Q&A; a housewife (Carol) tries to keep her upset husband (Harvey) from noticing that their kitchen is falling apart; Maggie teaches Carol how to speak with a Cockney accent through a song; a sick patient (Harvey) suffers as he endures the efforts of an elderly house doctor (Tim) treating him; a teacher (Maggie) meets Eunice, Ed and Mama as the parents of an underperforming student and realizes they are the cause of his behavior; Carol and Maggie sing "That's Show Biz" as carpenters in overalls as the intro to a fantasy sequence involving the talents of the ensemble.

Comments: Maggie Smith is the season's first repeat guest, and as pleasant as her entry was just four weeks earlier, this one surpasses it and ranks one of the series' best. Everything scores mightily here, including the Q&A, where Carol looks iffy about a suggestion to do a burlesque number with Raquel Welch—who Carol referenced in the last Q&A with Maggie! She gets a pair of goofy glasses, recounts how she performed *Once Upon a Mattress* in five theaters in New York City in one year and introduces Alice Ghostley in the audience. When asked to share a story about her relationship with Lucille Ball, one crew member cracks "Desi Arnaz!" in reference to Lucy's ex-husband.

The first sketch is prime *Carol Burnett Show* physical comedy. Harvey comes home after a day as head of the Consumer Protection Bureau and says he does not want to hear any more complaints or see anything else go wrong. As luck would have it, Carol's redecorated kitchen was a botch job, resulting in calamities such as the freezer door handle breaking off, the shelf doors opening easily, and finally everything collapsing, to audience applause. Harvey becomes hysterical and goes outside to his car, which ends up exploding and sends his pants through the window. A worn out Carol tries to console herself with a bottle of booze, only to drop it. This is well-done, well-motivated humor presented in top form at all levels.

Maggie's number "Ain't She the Limey Now" is a cute duet with Carol that comes off fine. Even better is the Harvey-Tim segment, wherein Tim's ancient physician gets his feet caught under Harvey's rug, washes his hands in a goldfish bowl, momentarily thinks the fish is a shark that has bit off his fingers, and pulls down the curtain to shine his glasses and shoes. A barely composed Harvey loses it when Tim comes to treat him on the sofa and says the word "koala," an in-joke from their visit to Australia (see Dec. 8, 1973). Tim takes Harvey's pulse by wrapping the patient's arms around him in the couch and getting into a comfortable romantic clutch before Harvey dismisses it. Poor Harvey is giggling again when Tim puts on a monkey mask to force him to take a pill. The sketch ends with the arrival of another doctor (an unidentified actor)—Tim's even older father. In one taping not seen on air, Harvey can barely say his lines before opening the door for the father due to his laughter over Tim's antics. The end product is just as enjoyable for viewers as it was amusing for Harvey.

When the cast first rehearsed the sketch where Maggie serves as teacher to Bubba, Eunice and Ed's son, they did it straight without comic inflections, and the dramatic effect is one Carol remembered long afterward. Here of course it has humor, once Maggie says goodbye to some other parents during conferences about their students. One is played by Stan Mazin, who ad libs, "Thank you, ma'am" in a Southern drawl as he left. "I just wanted to talk to Maggie Smith," Mazin recalls, amused at his audacity, which was kept in the show.

In her classroom, Maggie tells Ed, Eunice and Mama that Bubba has been going downhill since the first grade, being smart-mouthed and mean to others. That point is lost among the trio. Mama complains about the lunch meat Eunice serves Bubba, for one. When Maggie shows a drawing where Bubba depicted himself as a dot lorded over by a crabby Ed and Eunice, Eunice complains about the way her hair is depicted, while Ed quips he thinks drawing is for sissies. More discussion by the trio occurs, all irrelevant of what Maggie is telling them, and Eunice leaves in a huff, thinking that everyone is against her. She returns and blames Ed's capital punishment as the reason for Bubba's attitude. Ed defends his actions by saying his father's spankings made a man out of him, prompting Mama to interject, "I think maybe he was a couple of wallopings short." "You're really on thin ice, old woman," Ed shoots back (with some claps from the audience).

Eunice turns the conversation back to herself and blames the way Mama raised her as a contributing factor when Maggie slaps a desk for order. She says that she thought Bubba was a bully until she met his uncaring family and demands that they show more love to the child. Maggie tells them she will check up on him and forcefully tells the group they are dismissed, where they mutter about their treatment and eventually turn on each other. "Why the hell did you drag me here?!" Mama tells Ed and Eunice. "Who the hell needs you?!" both respond. Maggie frets that there is a lot of work they will have to do for Bubba. That's not the case of this bit, however. This is one of the finest Family skits in every respect.

The finale uses the pretense of being a backstage fantasy to allow everyone to do some clever solo takes. This includes Harvey's dead-on Anthony Newley vocals in presenting "Be a Clown" on bended knee, Vicki offering "Let Me Entertain You" with three male dancers, and Tim doing some mock acrobatic and magic tricks. It culminates in Carol doing a sultry "There's No Business Like Show Business" with Vicki and Maggie shimmying like a stripper (!) before fading into an empty soundstage with Maggie and Carol. This is a haunting end to a fun production number.

At the end, there are sweeping leg kicks done by the regulars and Maggie. It is an apt metaphor—this is one high-stepping installment, as is the next one.

Nov. 22, 1975: Betty White

Q&A; an executive (Harvey) with the German auto company Luftvagon brings in a district manager (Tim) to give a pep talk to the sales team to combat sluggish activity; Carol sings "By the Time I Get to Phoenix"; Tim and Carol are a couple disturbed by an ugly bug; the dancers present the Roach, the Bump, the Snake and their version of the New York Hustle; Mama's birthday prompts friction between Eunice and her sister, Ellen (Betty); Betty helps Carol overcome her fear of parades by a performance from the Locke High School Marching Band in Los Angeles.

Comments: This is the first of three guest shots by one of TV's all-time favorite personalities, and each time Betty White delivers some of the series' best work. Apparently because it is her first time and the writers are unsure how to use her, she acts only in the last half of the show, but Carol rectifies that by bringing Betty, "a wonderful lady," for a bow in the Q&A. In a scripted bit with Carol, Betty talks about her role as Sue Ann on *The Mary Tyler Moore Show* and refers to its spin-offs, *Rhoda* and *Phyllis*, by saying, "It's easy to be mean knowing that I'm the only woman in the cast who isn't getting a show on her own!" Before that, Betty's husband, Allen Ludden, is seen in front of a man who has a copy of Carol's book he wants her to sign. When he arrives on stage wearing a University of Southern California shirt, Carol notes that "I'm from UCLA," the cross-town rival to USC. "I'm sorry," the man quips in response to laughter as she grimaces.

Harvey is already giggling before Tim enters in the first sketch—perhaps he remembers how Tim played his German character from the Feb. 23, 1974 show. Tim jumps on a table and lands on his knees to make a point to his sales team (four of the male dancers), then gets one leg down and wonders where the other went, while Harvey struggles to stay composed. After hopscotching to the

Luftvagon sales chart, he follows the line of sales decline and hits his head. Harvey wants his salesmen to be hurt in retaliation, but instead Tim leads them in wild cheers that break up Harvey again. To check out the competition, Tim puts on a hat and crosses his eyes behind glasses as he calls an American car dealer, and makes Harvey wear a blonde wig and pretend to be his wife even though they are only on the phone. The offer from the dealer is so good that they both leave to buy the vehicle. The ending is weak, but the comedy on display otherwise is great.

Carol's take on the Glen Campbell standard is unexpectedly and wonderfully humorous. As a woman planning to leave her husband, she gets in a station wagon singing the tune straight, but the car will not start. She checks out the engine as she vocalizes, and a stuck horn drowns out part of her vocals in the process. Exasperated, she gets on a tricycle, only to have her suitcase open and spill out her clothes. Harvey then comes out to complain about the noise and tells Carol to come make breakfast, which she does. This bit is very effective and amusing in its delivery.

The same can be said of the Tim-Carol excursion where Carol freaks out over a bug crawling over her. A somewhat dubious Tim helps her look for it, finds it and puts it under a glass. They go to bed, but Carol worries the bug will get out, so Tim checks it out and ends up getting the bug on his back. He walks hilariously in paralyzed fear out the door and gets rid of the bug, to Carol's relief, but she passes out when she sees he now has an iguana on his back. This is a wonderful skit.

The Ernie Flatt Dancers present a very lively overview of top current dance styles, replete with glitter outfits and silver platform shoes. With the women in really high heels, sequins and bikini tops, it was a provocative routine for the time. As Bobbie Bates notes, "My grandma said, 'Don't let anybody see that number!'"

It is a prelude to the first on-camera appearance of Eunice's snooty sister Ellen. Betty sinks her teeth into the role, flashing fake Southern sincerity at all turns to Eunice's disgust. For example, she regards Ed's job as a lowly one by the way she tells him that she always says, "Be a bush if you can't be a tree!" After discussing memories about how Ellen and Eunice argued as kids, Mama opens her birthday gifts—a mink stole from Ellen and a fly swatter from Ed and Eunice. Ellen offers to give the latter to her trash man, leading Eunice to snarl about Ellen's inconsiderate nature. This prompts Ellen to call Eunice a jackass. Undeterred, Eunice spouts out how Ellen stole the only man she ever loved (to Ed's dismay). Ellen denies the man ever loved Eunice and calls her a jackass once more before leaving to applause. This is a great sketch showing the dynamics in the Harper clan and cemented Ellen becoming part of the Family fixture.

The finale basically consists of a pretext for having a marching band present its spirited version of "Pick Up the Pieces," a Number One instrumental hit earlier in 1975. The bright presentation of contemporary songs by the band and the dancers earlier, combined with top contributions by all other parties, make this a keeper.

Incidentally, Betty borrowed the black and white gown she wore in the Q&A when she attended the 1976 Emmys. She got to show it off well to the TV audience, as Betty won a statuette for best supporting actress on *The Mary Tyler Moore Show*.

Nov. 29, 1975: The Pointer Sisters

Q&A; the cast except for the guests present the 9th annual TV commercial awards; the Pointers sing "Save the Bones for Henry Jones"; Tim is a political candidate who makes noise and distractions at the dais while his running mate (Harvey) speaks at the podium; Carol is a woman constantly overlooked at a restaurant by her dining partner (Vicki), waiter (Harvey) and busboy (Tim); "Cinderella Gets It On" has Vicki as the evil stepmother and the Pointers as her daughters going to a rock concert featuring Elfin John (Tim) without Cinderella (Carol) until her Fairy Godmother (Harvey) intervenes.

Q&A: This is a very 1975 episode, as indicated from the start when a preppy-looking gentleman asks Carol, "You know how to hustle?" in reference to the recent Number One Van McCoy dance hit. Carol milks the laughter before nodding her head. She sets a rowdy tone by coming out with a butterscotch in her mouth that she did not want to remove, and from there on this Q&A is really animated. Mrs. Miller, a senior citizen who was an audience regular for many tapings, tells Carol she could not get a front seat, so Carol said the cast will speak louder to help her. Then a lady up front offers to change seats with Mrs. Miller, so Carol goes out into the audience to orchestrate the transfer, to the amusement of spectators. Once that ends, one lady perplexes our hostess who wonders if she is serious about her query as to whether Carol is making more money on TV than she would have if she pursued the newspaper career she portrayed in the movie *The Front Page*. Dazed, Carol smiles and carries onward.

In a memorable moment, Ruth Pointer's son, Malik, asks if Carol's right hip can go out of joint like he has heard. She invites him onstage to feel it while swearing to the audience she had no idea who he was. Malik feels Carol's hip as she displaces her body and cracks up. As to whether that question was planned, Malik's aunt, Anita, laughs and says, "No, not all, that was just Malik! He was just a bright, bold little boy, and he's still like that as an adult!" That ends the Q&A and leads into a sparkling installment.

The first in a strong edition of commercial blackouts has housewife Carol telling interviewer Harvey that she keeps her hand so soft while washing dishes thanks to Jay. Harvey shows a bottle named Jay, but Carol interrupts him and brings out the Jay she meant—Tim, who saunters out in an apron to clean. Vicki says her headache has gone thanks to the pain reliever she took last night, but when Harvey makes moves on her, she tells him the headache has returned. Carol shows a torso-sized pill she needs to take for healthy living, Tim gets shocked for trying to start six cars with one battery, and Vicki looks for a plumber in the phone directory and finds one when a hand with a wrench emerges from the book. A questionable bit of humor has Tim as Hitler using an American Depress credit card, which prompts Harvey the waiter to ask for another form of ID.

The best bits are near the end. Carol plays an old lady upset by wearing braces until she meets Harvey with one tooth (in the original toothpaste commercial, it was self-conscious teenagers). Harvey and Carol argue whether a piece of seafood is too salty or fishy before he eats it and loves it, to which Carol responds, "It's a veal cutlet, you dumb cluck." In the outtakes for this, Carol originally called Harvey a, um, type of hole on the first take, followed by him using the word on her in the second, director Dave Powers saying it as he cued them for the third, the clapper using it for the fourth, the entire crew yelling the obscenity and finally Carol replacing it with another off-color word. It's amazing that they somehow got this taped.

After the Pointers energetically perform a non-hit, Tim offers a great performance introducing his fellow politician on the ticket (Harvey) and unintentionally taking attention away from him by crunching on potato chips, chewing a mint he hates and spitting it out into a handkerchief, and nearly choking on a peanut. For the latter, he wipes his mouth with his handkerchief, and the mint's remnants there blacken his face and amuse the audience. Harvey thinks they are laughing about his comments until he sees Tim and cleans him up. More havoc is on the way as Tim munches on celery and spits out the tip of a cigar that ricochets and hits him. By the time Tim is coughing on his cigar, a disgusted Harvey hits him with the microphone, causing Tim to fall out a window and Harvey to carry on without him. This is a nice piece.

The next sketch goes to comic extremes to show Carol ignored by everyone while eating in public, struggling to get served and even being forgotten temporarily by her dining companion (Vicki). Desperate to have an impact, she trips Tim, who hits Harvey as they both knock down people at other tables and flowers drop from the wall. Tim tells everyone he thinks he tripped on his own, prompting them to go back avoiding Carol. This is silly but effective and well done.

The big musical finale features wildly imaginative flashy outfits even by Bob Mackie's standards, with Harvey as a Mother Marcus-styled fairy in a dazzling blue gown and gossamer wings on her back. She provides Cinderella (Carol) with a hip motorcycle and a silver fringe outfit to take her to the disco, where naturally she impresses Elfin John, as does Mother Marcus leading everyone in a dance called "The Schlump," which paraphrases "Rock Around the Clock." The twist here is that at the end the fairy changes Elfin into a nebbish, with Tim assuming his Mr. Tudball voice in a business outfit.

"It was a long scene, and it was so much fun," Anita Pointer recalls about "Cinderella Gets It On." "I could just see myself doing that crazy dancing!" Ken and Mitzie Welch and Artie Malvin deservingly won Emmys for their great music here.

The Pointer Sisters did well in their acting bits, even though there were only three of them here. They will show up on the show two months later—see Jan. 31, 1976.

Dec. 6, 1975: Eydie Gorme

Q&A; a doctor at a hospital (Harvey) neglects a sick Stella Toddler in favor of her roommate, a pampered, demanding actress (Eydie); Eydie performs "As Time Goes By" with Peter Matz and the orchestra on stage behind her; Tim fights with a life-sized plant he is trying to return to a flower shop operator (Carol); a housewife (Carol) finds herself overrun with people from TV commercials; a suitor from centuries past (Harvey) unwisely employs the feeble efforts of the old man (Tim) to torture an unwilling lass (Vicki) into joining him in matrimony; a musical salute to composer Richard Rodgers.

Comments: Slightly less successful than its four predecessors, this installment still is a pleasure overall. The Q&A is not much. Carol says if she had the power to change the world in three ways, she would have universal peace, no disease and time on a desert island with Paul Newman. Asked "How's your love life?" she shoots back, "G-rated."

The Stella bit is swell, as she gets dropped and pressed in her adjustable hospital bed while Harvey tries fruitlessly to impress Eydie with his impersonations. Eydie is similarly insensitive to Stella, which boomerangs on her when she accidentally takes Stella's sedative and two orderlies (Don Crichton and Stan Mazin) wheel her out on a dolly to get an unneeded appendectomy. Carol's mugging as Stella is as charming as always.

Eydie's sultry take on a number best remembered from *Casablanca* is overshadowed by Tim's hilarious work following it. While Carol tells him to be nice to the plant because it can hear him, the plant pummels him every time she goes to the back of her store, forcing Tim to punch back. "I was the plant," Randy Doney says. "Working with Tim, that was incredible. As we just were doing it, when he's feeding me, I respond." After seeing the fighting continue, Carol dismisses Tim without the plant, then smacks the plant for being an idiot again that she could not sell. This is a very good, laugh-inducing skit.

The commercials segment is dated but still funny as Carol is pushed around by the regulars, Eydie and even a few dancers. It is somewhat better than an Old Man skit where Tim fights cobwebs, gets a hot poker caught under his armpit, has a mouse overpower him, and loses control of a mace that wraps around his neck and hits him. When Harvey learns that Vicki is just playing hard to get to marry him, he accidentally crushes Tim on a bed of nails that collapse on the latter. This has some amusement, but it is a lesser Old Man entry in terms of tightness and overall humor.

As with Bernadette's appearance on Oct. 11, this show's musical finale has been deleted from the DVD release at the time of this writing. What remains is enjoyable enough.

Dec. 13, 1975: Jessica Walter

Q&A; Mama is grief stricken about the passing of an aunt to the chagrin of Eunice and Ed as they prepare to go to the funeral; Jessica performs "Could It Be Magic"; Carol, Tim, Harvey and Jessica portray two married couples living next door to each other whose individual versions of the truth produce curious conversational complications; Tim and Harvey play respective leaders of the 1905 peace treaty signing by Japan and Russia; a life insurance agent (Harvey) tries to get Carol and Jessica to sign policies naming each as the other's beneficiary; a salute to lyricist Dorothy Fields.

Comments: This episode has some strong elements but falls short of being an above average entry. Before an animated audience, Carol mentions tonight's guest is an Emmy winner (omitting that NBC canceled *Amy Prentiss*, the series for which Jessica Walter won for outstanding lead actress, the previous season) and talks at length about her upcoming special with Beverly Sills. A dental hygienist from the University of South California asks to clean Carol's teeth for her coursework, to the amusement of the hostess. Not as entranced is a man in the audience who asks, "Is the acting part of the show going to start?!" Taking that as a cue, Carol closes the Q&A.

Eunice and Ed grin and bear it as Mama moans about how her aunt died watching *The Mike Douglas Show* while Mama was too busy cleaning her oven. As the trio wait to go the aunt's funeral with Eunice's sister and brother-in-law, Eunice realizes Mama is not impressed by being in public with just her and Ed. Mama eventually reveals she still has an animus against Eunice for her behavior at the funeral of Carl, Mama's husband and Eunice's father. "I bust my butt for you, old lady!" Eunice retorts as she recounts how Mama called her aunt mean and selfish before all plan to head to the funeral. Although good overall, this Family sketch relies on yelling that weaken its comic impact.

Jessica provides surprisingly good vocals to a recent Barry Manilow hit before joining Carol and the male regulars in a spotty skit. After complaining to Harvey about his bad parking in the apartment lot, Carol lies to her husband (Tim) about how nice she was in informing him of the oversight, yet claims he was mean back to her. She encourages Tim to confront Harvey, and he does, but he says he told Carol to shut up about the things she was saying about Harvey because he wanted to keep their friendship intact. Then, Harvey tells his spouse (Jessica) that he was ready to hit Tim for his accusations about his behavior, prompting Jessica to say she will confront Carol. Naturally, Jessica is sorry about Harvey's "actions," and Carol does the same about Tim's supposed statements to Harvey. Carol then tells Tim that he has their neighbors quaking in their boots, and he notes it just proves what he thinks—"You tell them the truth, and they'll crumble every time!" Despite the great ending line, this roundelay meanders too much and fails to become as strong a laugh generator as its intriguing premise would suggest.

The next segment is hampered by stereotyping (Tim in glasses playing an Asian broadly) and is just not a well-motivated comedy as is expected by a teaming with Harvey. Tim plays musical chairs when there are only two seats but three members in his entourage counting himself, Randy Doney and Don Crichton, then gets his fingers stuck while trying to open a folding chair. Meanwhile, Harvey is upset by Japan's proposed borders that would leave Russia a small country, so he destroys the map and forces Tim to sign Harvey's own treaty. When Tim's pen leaks onto Harvey's suit, it is a battle royale between the men and their aides, culminating in a sword fight where Tim lacks a blade and finally both men charging at each other with flags and missing, going into their opposite walls instead. This generates some chuckles, but not the usual amount.

The final sketch is obvious from his setup as a mincing lawyer (Harvey) tells two business partners (Carol and Jessica) their insurance plans are such that if one of them dies, the other will get $25,000. So of course, both try to kill each other and then reconcile, which is good, because Harvey returns to tell them he forgot to get their signatures to make the documents legal. This goes on too long to be successful.

The tribute to a woman who supplied words to many hits from the 1920s through the 1970s is fine but not spectacular. Walter still sings and dances surprisingly well, making her an unexpectedly delightful guest. Still, this was her only appearance on the series.

Dec. 20, 1975: Steve Lawrence

* The Old Man (Tim) finds an sudden opportunity for romance when Stella Toddler comes into his store to try on new shoes; Steve sings "Now That We're in Love" and joins Carol in an alternating duet, "The Way a Man Can Aggravate a Woman/The Way a Woman Can Aggravate a Man"; customers wreak revenge on an overbearing cafe patron; Steve plays the lead detective and Carol the supposed victim in a spoof of the film noir classic *Laura*, with Harvey as a newspaper columnist and Vicki as a screaming housekeeper; a mini-musical tribute to composer Sammy Cahn.

Comments: Although only the half hour version of this series is available as of this writing, its combination of a great teaming of recurring characters and one of the best classic film parodies ever strongly suggests the full version is a top entry. The Old Man-Stella meeting is golden. The store owner (Dick Patterson) leaves the Old Man in charge during lunch hour, and his encounter with Stella is golden at every turn. Both alternate in accidentally hurting each other while she shops for shoes. A typical bit has the Old Man hitting Stella in the head and stomach with boxes he pushes out from the back. At the end the two connect, but Stella asks him if he can promise he won't get fresh with her. When he says no, she immediately says OK and leaves with him. This is a joy at every moment.

"The Late Late Movie" presents "Flora," where Steve and a cop (Dick Patterson) encounter a chalk outline of a woman's body before Harvey identifies himself as a columnist and "closet animal lover." Vicki is hysterical upon her entrance before leaving, while Harvey notes that Steve seems obsessed by the painting of the dead woman over the mantle before departing as well. Suddenly Carol arrives as Flora, and she and Steve wordlessly (and humorously) stare at the chalk outline and rock back and forth as they kiss. He then realizes someone else has been murdered, as proven when Carol lies within the outline and her chest is smaller than that of the busty deceased woman. Carol loves Steve because they have the same theme song, but their romance ends when Harvey arrives and throws a hissy fit. When Steve leaves, a hidden Harvey leaps out, grabs a shotgun from a grandfather clock and cocks it when Steve opens the door and triggers Harvey to shoot Carol. Steve shoots Harvey in response, but Carol moans "Why couldn't you knock?" as she dies. She and Harvey review the problems they have faced in life and commiserate over their experiences before they both expire. Steve pledges his undying love for Flora, but when he sees Vicki in a hot maid's outfit, that vow goes away. However, Vicki starts griping about her difficulties as well, so he shoots her and leaves. Unlike some film takeoffs on the series, not a moment is wasted, and humorous incidents abound at everyone point, making this among the best ever presented by Carol and crew.

The mini-musical included familiar standards from the 1960s such as "Call Me Irresponsible,"

"Thoroughly Modern Millie" and "My Kind of Town," which gives it a contemporary sheen. Incidentally, Steve's solo, "Now That We're In Love," was written by Sammy Cahn, this week's feted lyricist. Although not a hit for him, it was a 1975 Oscar nominee from the forgettable movie *Whiffs*, and Steve got a lot of mileage out of it, singing the tune at the 1976 Academy Awards and including it as a track on *Hallelujah*, an album he recorded with Eydie Gorme (naturally).

Dec. 27, 1975: Repeat of Sept. 20, 1975 show

Jan. 3, 1976: Rita Moreno

Q&A; the Queen and Prince (Carol and Harvey) are dismayed that their daughter (Vicki) plans to marry the hollow man (Tim); Rita does "Some Cats Know" accompanied by four male dancers; Tim is a military officer flummoxed trying to demote a soldier (Harvey); a bank robber (Harvey) and a teller (Carol) instruct their trainees (Tim and Vicki, respectively) on how to conduct their activities properly; an accident prone woman (Carol) is bedeviled by a nurse (Rita) supposedly keeping her safe; Rita, Carol and Vicki sing "Much More" and "There's Gotta Be Something Better Than This" with the dancers.

Comments: The multitalented Rita Moreno is unfortunately limited to just one sketch here, and it is the weakest one. Otherwise, this is another strong outing, beginning with Carol introducing Beverly Sills and her husband in the audience to let everyone know they will be taping the special *Sills and Burnett at the Met* in March. The only query shown in the Q&A has Carol stunned. A woman asks, "Have you ever had any hair removed by electrolysis?" because she is studying to be an aesthetician. "If I had, I wouldn't tell!" Carol responds, then adds, "Well, maybe on my chest."

The hollow hero sketch has little new to add except for Vicki's squeaky British dialect and Tim nearly succeeding in cracking Harvey and Carol up by repeatedly laughing at his own joke. Harvey tries to dissuade Tim from hitching up with Vicki by saying she will someday resemble the Queen, while Tim upsets Vicki by rejecting her choice of the wedding location. ("Take the palace and stick it in your ear," he says.) It ends with Vicki smashing a vase over Tim's head to get rid of him. Although not as well executed as previous outings, the characters are so endearing that it is hard to discount this effort.

Rita's routine is a sultry routine she lip syncs in a white beaded gown while the men sport mustaches and hairy chests, some of which were fake (it was in style for the time). We do not see her again until after two more skits. The first has Tim in virtual pantomime mode after addressing Harvey unexpectedly in his Mr. Tudball voice about the charges, cracking Harvey up. He struts like a peacock walking on both sides of Harvey as he ends up tearing up more of his outfits than Harvey's, which has one rope part that Tim pulls out endlessly and buttons that stay stuck. After Tim accidentally unbuckles his pants to reveal red, white and blue-striped boxers, he announces that he has given up and Harvey will remain in the military, whereupon the four dancers dressed as officers in the background have their equipment malfunction. This is a nice Tim-Harvey bit as always.

The best skit is next. A novice blonde teller (Vicki in her dumb Dora voice) encounters Tim as a nervous criminal newcomer. "This is a mess up, so don't stick around!" he screws up in announcing his intentions. As Vicki's mentor, Carol laughs at Tim's goofs like failing to leave the car running for the getaway and forgetting to bring a bag to carry the money, but Harvey, as Tim's trainer, encourages Tim despite his errors. Sensing an opportunity to show how it is done, Carol dons a visor and shows Vicki how to count out $300,000 by shuffling money, which she gives to Tim and Harvey along with a calendar and a piggy bank. Impressed by her efficiency, Harvey gets romantic with Carol even though he knows it is wrong. "One of the first rules about the bank robbery business is never get involved with the bank tellers," he coos. A similarly smitten Carol tells him, "It'll never work. . . . I'm nine-to-five. You're ten-to-twenty [as in years in prison]." She confesses that she hit the silent alarm, which leads to Don Crichton to arrive as a cop—with his own bumbling trainee for the arrest. Luckily for Don, when Harvey tells Tim to use the gun, Tim gives it to the officers rather than shoot it.

Gene Perret recalls this bit came from a brainstorming meeting among the writers where one scribe mentioned eating out the previous night and being served by a waitress with a trainee tagging along. This excellently written sketch was the result of that experience.

Unfortunately, the next is substandard, with Harvey going out of town and leaving Carol, his supposedly uncoordinated wife, in the hands of Rita, who torments Carol by "accidentally" hurting her. Rita had already done a similar act in her role on public television's *The Electric Company*, playing a rich woman who knocked down items and placed the blame on the clerk by saying, "Clumsy, clumsy!" It was shorter and funnier than this sketch, where Carol naturally gets the upper hand and retaliates amid obvious plotting. Both ladies give their all in this forced sketch.

Rita fares much better in the finale, washing dishes in a restaurant kitchen and musing about her dream career with Carol and Vicki amid dancing waiters and waitresses. Rita speaks in her Hispanic accent for part of the spirited number.

At the end, Carol encourages viewers to write to the Environmental Protection Agency to learn how they can address pollution. "I'm going to stop reminding you about the pollution problem, because I know by now all of us are very much aware of it," she says, ending her campaign on the show. She did want viewers to be proactive, however, and this is a nice move to wrap up nearly six years of her speaking out on the topic.

Jan. 10, 1976: Steve Lawrence

Q&A; a husband and wife (Carol and Harvey) cannot seem to plan when they can meet amid their hectic work schedules; Steve performs "In the Still of the Night"; Carol is perplexed by riddles offered by Vicki and Steve, who refuse to share the answers with her; Mr. Tudball (Tim) loses his patience trying to teach his dense secretary, Mrs. Wiggins (Carol), how to use their intercom; Carol and Steve do a medley of songs written in 1915; a salute to Universal Studios features five parodies that lead into a tribute to the Glenn Miller Orchestra with the dancers.

Comments: The first installment of Tudball and Wiggins highlight this above-average entry, which is hampered only by the second sketch and the medley being just fair in comparison to everything else. Peter Matz appears on camera at the opening, probably because he will be conducting the Glenn Miller number later on stage, followed by two guests in the audience. Don Sutton, pitcher for the Los Angeles Dodgers, does a little banter with Carol, who jokingly wonders about how the loss of Jerry West (a basketball player) will affect the baseball team. The other visitor is Nick Benedict, then starring on *All My Children*, Carol's favorite soap opera, who gets on stage and takes questions while hugging and kissing Carol a lot.

From there, a great sketch kicks off the show. Sitting at opposite ends of a long dining table at breakfast, Carol and Harvey try to make time to see other during work, but they go two weeks without finding a suitable opening. Suddenly, Carol makes a face, says, "I think it's time, I better get to the hospital," and stands up to reveal she is pregnant. "Do you need me?" Harvey asks. "No, I won't be long," she says. To top it off after she leaves, Harvey adds, "I wonder how that happened." Short and sweet, this is a delight.

Steve presents an upbeat version of a 1930s hit with the orchestra on stage behind him, foreshadowing its presence later in the show. That leads to a bit where Vicki asks Carol what is the color of a bear that walks by a room with an all southern exposure, and Carol is frustrated in not knowing the answer. Steve joins them at the table with another puzzle that is even more complex, but Vicki knows the answer and whispers it to Steve, who confirms she is right. They refuse to share the solution to Carol, prompting her to go on a tirade that makes them leave. Harvey then joins Carol to ask her the same riddle Vicki did, prompting her to punch him in the face. The audience is almost as aggravated by Carol by this trying setup, but it moves well and is acceptable for what it is.

Better than that is what would become a staple for the rest of the show's run, as a repairman (Randy Doney) tells Mr. Tudball his new intercom system is ready. What follows is precise comic timing by Tim and Carol, with Wiggins repeatedly unable to understand she is not supposed to press the button until Tudball has finished talking. He gets her into his office by talking to her in person, but twice he does it without saying she needs to have a pad for his dictation. Tudball's slow burn has some excellent lines ("Thanks for taking time of your busy schedule" as Wiggins wiggles to get paper the second time) and funny gestures, like him being unable to break a pencil in half in frustration. Finally, he gives up and puts the intercom boxes into a file cabinet, which Wiggins opens and says into one box, "I'm going to lunch now." This great launching point for both characters leaves you wanting more, as any top sketch does.

The momentum slows some when Steve and Carol offer a ho-hum discussion involving quizzes on matchbooks followed by songs made popular fifty years earlier in honor of the creation of the gramophone. This weak excuse to sing mostly obscure tunes at least does not run too long. The pace picks up afterward with blackouts of mostly recent films except for *Hamlet*, which Carol incorrectly claims was the first Universal film to win the Oscar for Best Picture (*All Quiet on the Western Front* from 1930 preceded it). Harvey impersonates Laurence Olivier to reveal that Yorick's skull amuses him because it sports a big fake nose and glasses. Next is *Pete 'n' Tillie* ("It starred Walter Matthau and others," Vicki says, slyly omitting Carol's starring role), where Carol throws out Harvey as Walter in his underwear playing piano, only to be replaced by Steve doing the same thing. For *Rooster Cogburn*, Carol's dead-on quavering impersonation of Katharine Hepburn leads Harvey's John Wayne to put his eye patch over her mouth to shut her up. *Freud* has Steve in a weak bathroom joke involving the doctor, but *Earthquake* redeems that slip by having him and Carol kiss right when a tremor hits Los Angeles, leading Steve to offer her a cigarette afterward and mumble, "I never knew it could be like this."

A mention of *The Glenn Miller Story* prompts Carol to sing "Moonlight Serenade," followed by a shot of the Peter Matz Orchestra dressed up in blue outfits to resemble Miller's orchestra on stage. Among the highlights, Vicki sings "Perfidia" with some original members of the band, the dancers jitterbug to "Pennsylvania 6-5000," Harvey offers "I Got a Gal in Kalamazoo," Carol does "Jukebox Saturday Night" and Steve leads "Many Moons Ago" before all join in a reprise of "Moonlight Serenade." This is winningly and respectfully performed, with the only drawback being that along with the earlier numbers, one had the unfortunate feeling that the show lacked interest in any music written after 1950. This show marked Steve's second and final appearance this season, the lowest number of times he did *The Carol Burnett Show* since 1970-1971.

At the end, Carol is able to get away with twitching the top of her low-cut dress over her breasts while singing goodbye. She nicely pulls Peter Matz out to take a bow with everyone else, which he does before conducting the end of the show.

Jan. 17, 1976: Pre-empted by *Super Night at the Super Bowl* special

Jan. 24, 1976: The Jackson 5, Emmett Kelly

Q&A; Carol sings "Anybody Named Jackson" to introduce her musical guests, who perform "Forever Came Today"; a politician (Harvey) has a deranged wife (Carol) who assaults his aide (Tim) as the latter prepares his boss for a White House visit; Vicki learns how to groove with the dancers and the Jackson 5 in "Body Language"; "The Late Late Movie" sends up the Bette Davis film *A Stolen Life*; the Charwoman cleans a three-ring circus where she encounters affection from a clown dressed as a hobo (Emmett) and sings "It's Only a Paper Moon" and "Look for the Silver Lining."

Comments: "The world's greatest clown" (as Carol introduces Emmett at the outset) and the last public appearance of the Jackson 5 under that name (they left Motown shortly after this show was taped and the record company assumed ownership, forcing them to become the Jacksons thereafter) are at peak form as are everyone else in this winning entry. Everything is so good that there is only a short Q&A, during which a woman asks about Carol's recent book on children. "Can you just pick it up anywhere?" she asks. "Well, I'd rather you buy it!" Carol shoots back.

Carol lists Andrew, Stonewall, Glenda, Mahalia and Shoeless Joe as other famous Jacksons before bringing out Michael and his brothers on an aqua-green set with silver tinge and the J5 logo in the background. Each Jackson is named by Carol and describes himself, with Jackie being the oldest one, Tito the swingingest (sic), Marlon the dancingest (sic), Michael the skinniest and Randy the cutest. The quintet then lay down "Forever Came Today" beautifully, with on-point choreography and a solo dance by Michael that amaze even despite the group lip-syncing the disco record. To its credit, the show allows them to perform the extended version, and the Jacksons do so expertly.

This sets the stage for a great skit wherein Carol, recuperating from a head injury that has left her crazy, goes on a rampage and terrorizes helpless Tim as he tries to get his boss (Harvey) ready for an interview with the president on a cabinet appointment. While Harvey is preoccupied, Carol swings from a chandelier, puts her leg in Tim's hands repeatedly, hits his nose, chokes him on his tie, and most incredibly does a running leap onto Tim and wraps her legs around him, with Tim impressively walking around carrying Carol while trying to pry her off him. Following each incident, Harvey sees Tim disheveled and scared to explain his predicament. When Carol pours water all over Tim's suit, paints a mustache on his face, stamps his forehead and then rips his pants down, he is so pathetically shabby that Harvey fires him (and the audience applauds him for his superb comic reactions). But one more twist awaits—as Harvey and Carol prepare to leave for his White House meeting, Harvey shows he is just as messed up his wife as he talks to a coat rack and congratulates it on being named Tim's replacement. This is wonderfully written, directed and acted in all departments.

The Jackson 5 return to build confidence up for Vicki, who sits on the steps of the exterior of a brownstone apartment telling the guys she cannot dance. With their prodding, however, the "foxy lady" (as the Jacksons call her) joins them and the dancers dressed as passerby to make some fancy moves to the group's tune "Body Language." Everybody nails their steps strongly in this vibrant routine.

The hits keep coming with "A Swiped Life," a great takeoff where Carol plays twins, a wallflower named Patsy who loves sketching lighthouses ("It says to me, 'Hi, Paaaaatsy!'" Carol says, imitating the building's sounds) and her tart sister, Vera. Harvey appears as the lighthouse keeper who has burnt out his bulb and encounters Patsy, who swoons when she kisses him. While Patsy retrieves a light for Harvey (which in a great sight gag is an inflated balloon shaped like a bulb), Vera appears on the scene and goes gaga for Harvey until her Aunt Leona (Vicki) informs Harvey Vera is really Patsy's twin. He is nevertheless undeterred and marries Vera, to Patsy's chagrin. Later, Patsy goes sailing with Harvey and Vera, and the latter dies during a storm at sea, prompting Patsy to assume her identity.

In Act Two, Patsy learns the drawbacks of her impersonation when Harvey says he wants a divorce because Vera has been cheating on him. This is apparent to Patsy, as she has to fight off the advances of a prowling Italian lover (Tim), a butler (Don Crichton) and even a policeman (Stan Mazin). She reveals the truth to Harvey, who is upset she lied to him and leaves with the maid (Leslie Dalton). Figuring she has nothing to lose, Patsy whistles for the men to come back and accost her. Carol's mock Bette Davis accent is just one of many highlights in this fun romp.

The sentimental ending is either a remake or rerun of Carol's meeting with Emmett Kelly from the Nov. 2, 1970 episode. Regardless, it is a pleasant and deserved reprise.

At the end, Carol is excited to have Kelly sign her book, while viewers will be happy they watched. This is one of the best *Carol Burnett Show* episodes on all counts.

Jan. 31, 1976: The Pointer Sisters

Q&A; a pigeon lady (Carol) imparts wisdom to a park cleaner (Harvey); the Pointer Sisters sing "That's A Plenty"; a robber (Harvey) demands treatment from a nurse (Vicki) who is so irritated by her boyfriend (Tim) that she forces him to pretend to be a doctor; Carol, Vicki and the Pointer Sisters perform songs written by Fats Waller; Harvey goes to get a prescription filled by an odd pharmacist (Tim); Carol tries to seduce a playboy (Harvey) on a cruise; the Pointer Sisters join Carol, the dancers and the George Becker Singers in a musical salute to the Declaration of Independence.

Comments: "Does the type of audience you have affect the way you perform?" asks someone in the Q&A. "Yes. Wow, that's an intelligent question," Carol answers. Saying that "You get vibes from an audience," she tells them that the more "hot" they are in responding to the actors, the livelier the performances will be. Unfortunately, there is little to make the audience warm in this subpar outing apart from great vocals from the Pointer Sisters (Ruth, Anita and Bonnie in this installment) and a hilarious second sketch. The Q&A has some pleasures too, such as a lady complimenting Harvey and a man from the Los Angeles College of Chiropractic Medicine doing the same for Carol's spine. "Oh, you like my back. Well, that's half of it!" she quips. Suddenly a clown on roller skates comes on stage and tells Carol, "We have voted you . . . a Doctor of Clown Humanities." She is Peggy Williams, the first lady clown with Ringling Brothers Barnum and Bailey Circus, and Carol graciously accepts the honor. After answering that she painted her toenails red with a "What other color would I use?" look, Carol concludes Q&A by kissing a nervous fourteen-year-old. "Have you really ever thought in terms of an older woman?" "I'm gonna faint!" he says before she smooches him.

Chanting "Coo coo, pigeons!" Carol tells Harvey that the world needs to be nice to the birds and spread love and peace throughout the world. She hammers variations that notion for several minutes with only a couple of witty lines. By the end of this middling sketch, one wonders why Harvey does not tell her to shut up or leave.

The atmosphere brightens with the Pointers energetically presenting "That's A Plenty" in 1920s gowns with fringe. Lip syncing to a track previously released as the title tune for a 1974 album for the group, the sisters perform with verve that makes this a winner.

The good mood sets the stage for a hilarious modification of what Tim did previously in the dentist sketch on March 3, 1969. Harvey arrives as Tim is breaking up with Vicki in a doctor's office. Shot in the leg during a robbery, Harvey waves a gun to make Vicki help him. She tells Harvey Tim is a physician, forcing the latter to fake his way. Tim puts alcohol on Harvey's leg, which stings so much that Harvey beats him up. He then asks Vicki for a drug to numb Harvey's pain, but it gets accidentally injected in Tim's hand, and from there the fun really begins. He tries to cut the pants leg with scissors before he injects his leg as well (by this point Harvey is cracking up seeing Tim go limp again). To top it off, Tim confuses the syringe with a pencil and stabs his tongue as he plans to write something down, forcing him to mumble threats. Vicki grabs Harvey's gun and Tim threatens to poke him in the eyes unsuccessfully, then tries to turn pages in the phonebook to get help and gets his thumb stuck in his mouth while doing so. Eventually he calls for help incoherently in the phone before yelling unintelligibly out the window. As Harvey is about to be captured, he confesses to Vicki that he loves her and hoped to leave the country with $1 million with her. Sensing the opportunity, when two cops (Birl Johns and Carlton Johnson) arrive, Vicki tells them to arrest Tim instead. This is a hoot.

Harvey introduces the salute to Thomas "Fats" Waller, with the male dancers wearing bowlers and pretending to play pianos while each Pointer Sister walks down a mazelike runway separating the men to sing a different tune, followed by Vicki and Carol. The latter leads them all in doing "Honeysuckle Rose" together. It's not near the quality of the later hit Broadway revue *Ain't Misbehavin'* (whose title tune is performed here as well), but it is an enjoyable presentation nonetheless.

Next comes a rarity—a Tim and Harvey matchup that fails to catch fire. It suffers from a weak premise, that Harvey is a heart patient receiving elaborate concoctions that Tim claims are the drug that Harvey's doctor ordered for him. The first effort explodes, the second one requires Tim to chase something down with a net in the back of the pharmacy and the third needs Tim to solder part of it. None of this is particularly funny. By the last effort, Harvey says he will take what Tim has made only if Tim consumes it himself. He does, and he becomes a werewolf ready to attack Harvey. The fact that Harvey never even cracks a smile during this skit indicates how much of a dud it is.

Similarly weak is Carol as a stuffy nosed office worker whose friend (Vicki) tells her to cut loose before wishing her bon voyage. Carol notices Harvey (in a black toupee) on deck and fantasizes being so sophisticated with him that he offers her to leave with him and live on his private island. Back to reality, she approaches Harvey, hitting her head on a pipe while trying to get his attention. When she does, he is indifferent until he says he can use her to help him seduce a hot number (Bonnie Evans). She responds by telling the woman to watch out, he has a bad condition before she leaves. Like Carol's other skit in this show, this seriocomic piece falls flat as both humor and drama.

The show has at least a rousing finish with Carol and the Pointers in white gloves standing in the middle of two rows with fourteen men in tuxes and ten women in black and white gowns to recite the Declaration of Independence with musical accompaniment. Some of those on stage are just the dancers mouthing the words, but like everyone else, they are committed in presenting a moving ode to patriotism in preparation for the country's upcoming bicentennial. For the story behind this number, see Dec. 15, 1971.

The Pointer Sisters will return for a final time next season—see Nov. 27, 1976.

Feb. 7, 1976: Family Show

* Eunice, Ed and Mama visit an upscale restaurant, but their typical behavior and loud voices limits their enjoyment of the occasion; the dancers perform to "Down Home Rag"; the Old Man (Tim) is a sheriff in the wild west who slowly stands off against a bandit (Harvey) in a saloon with a waitress (Vicki) and others seeking help from the law; Vicki is a processor at the department of motor vehicles whose demands for paperwork tax the patience of a frustrated customer (Harvey); the finale features Carol, Harvey and Vicki singing "There Once Was a Man."

Comments: This show was explicitly designed to win Vicki an Emmy, and it succeeded. She is seen in every skit to great effect, starting with Mama's complaints about walking and dislike of the lady's room attendant that prompts her to steal toilet paper at a fancy dining establishment. The maitre d' (Jan Arvan) and other customers become impatient with the uncouth behavior of the trio, such as Ed's boorish interactions and Mama's problems with the tongs at the salad bar. Eunice loves the elegant atmosphere but cannot contain her frustrations with Ed being upset about the menu's prices and Mama's skepticism of her drink, a pink lady. When Mama has problems seasoning her salad, a flustered Eunice exclaims, "It is a mill, Mama! It's a pepper mill! You grind it!" As she shows how to do it, a patron at the adjacent booth (Stan Mazin) interjects, "I wonder if you mind lowering your voices. We came here for a peaceful dinner!"

Mortified by the comments, Eunice tries to contain herself but loses composure again when a violinist comes by playing "Smoke Gets in Your Eyes" and she sings along with the tune. Mama and Ed are unimpressed, however, causing Eunice to get into a spat with them that is so loud that the maitre d' asks them to leave per the request of other customers. While Ed and Mama say goodbye and good riddance, Eunice looks longingly at the lounge before having to depart. Funny and poignant, this is a beautiful skit.

Vicki's main purpose in the cowboy sketch is set up the conflict between a not-so-tough bank robber (Harvey), who says "Give me a mai tai" before playing cards, and the town's ancient sheriff (Tim), who gets stuck on the saloon's swinging doors before walking underneath him. When he does the latter, another customer enters and knocks Tim to Harvey's table to play seven-card stud. Before he deals, Tim tries to roll a cigarette and gets cards stuck on his moistened thumb, amusing Harvey, who takes over dealing instead. Tim leans back in his chair more each time he sees his cards before having a duel with Harvey. Vicki intervenes and shoots Harvey to save Tim's life, but the latter accidentally discharges his gun. A bullet ricochets and damages many parts of the saloon before hitting Tim in the butt. It's silly but sleek.

For the other main sketch, Vicki really shines as a demanding bureaucrat offering little help to an annoyed, suffering Harvey. Her rote, emotionless tone contrasts with his desperation as he tries to comply with her demands and produces a lot of laughs for anyone who has had to deal with an unsympathetic worker at an agency. Combine that with her usual enthusiastic musical delivery, and it is not surprising that Vicki won her first Emmy here, and on her first nomination. With this win,

The Carol Burnett Show becomes the first variety series where all of its on-air regulars earn at least one Emmy.

Feb. 14, 1976: Joanne Woodward

An old pal of Eunice's (Joanne) accompanies her for an afternoon of drinking, much to the dismay of Mama and Ed; a bickering couple (Harvey and Vicki) have their servants (Tim and Carol) act as surrogates for much of their activities and arguments; Carol and Joanne are wallflowers at a dance party; Mr. Tudball becomes frustrated as he briefs Mrs. Wiggins on what she should do during an upcoming meeting, yet she constantly fails to perform it properly during their rehearsals; Carol, Vicki and Joanne perform "Everything Old is New Again" in floral print dresses with the dancers.

Comments: Everything except an overdone premise in the middle glitters in this show, which begins with Carol heaping praise on her guest in place of the Q&A. "She's an even nicer lady than she is a great actress. . . . It's kind of sad to see this week come to an end," Carol says. Joanne shows why in the Family sketch, as a floozy who stays for dinner with Eunice following an afternoon of drinking and merriment. An old high school buddy with a past, Joanne returns to town from Chicago and impresses an envious Eunice with her liberated single life. But her presence enrages Mama ("I thought this town got rid of that alley cat!"), who spouts plenty of unsubtle digs. Eunice defends Mama's implication that Joanne has shown little achievement in life, which Mama denies. She adds, "Besides, being a failure is nothing to be ashamed of. Hell, look at Ed there!" Ed had been subdued but also verbally attacks Joanne, prompting her to threaten to punch Mama for calling her indecent and to reveal that Ed had gotten fresh with her in high school. Joanne leaves in a huff and tells Eunice she is sorry the latter has to stay with these two people. Sensing Eunice's disgust and anger, Ed and Mama quietly decide to prepare dinner. The first Family show with a guest star playing a character who is a friend of Eunice's is cracking good.

The regulars are at peak form next as Carol and Tim sport deadpan expressions as they virtually pantomime their services requested by Vicki and Harvey, respectively. The latter upscale duo is being fed by their maid and butler, and then some—Tim burps Harvey, while Carol puts on lipstick for Vicki. When Harvey and Vicki have a verbal dispute, they make Tim and Carol perform the actions they describe, and the servants hit each other back and forth. Finally, Vicki has Carol get a gun and says she is going to kill herself, to Carol's horror. Dutifully, however, she shoots herself, and Harvey follows it by claiming he cannot go on living without Vicki, to Tim's chagrin. He shoots himself and elaborately cleans up where his body will fall. Harvey and Vicki reunite, and Carol and Tim raise their heads to ask, "Will that be all?" and being told "Yes" by their masters. It is nonsensical slapstick that works wonderfully.

This episode is looking great before stumbling with the overdone Carol-and-female-guest-star seriocomic setup of being homely women ignored at a social function. This tired notion had been done all the way back to Oct. 9, 1967 with Imogene Coca. Nothing new occurs here except Carol and Joanne try to sing and make themselves happy after each fails to win over Harvey. As an in-joke, Carol calls her character Theresa Renteria, a name that first appeared in the Q&A a year earlier (see Dec. 14, 1974).

Luckily, the program rebounds from this misstep with a Tudball and Wiggins segment that may have been written by Pat Proft and Bo Kaprall. Tudball is trying to page Wiggins, who has just painted her fingernails, so he has to tell her in person to come into his office. Watching her move, he notes that "You're the only person I know who can actually tailgate herself!" Tudball wants Wiggins to buzz him when he stands up during his noon meeting so that he can stall and find the answer his visitor wants, and he has her practice doing it with disastrous results. He calls her in his office again, and after she takes her time getting there ("You're a real Jesse Owens!" he snarls), he informs her that they should switch positions and pretend to be each other to understand what he is saying. Carol does a great job of Wiggins impersonating Tudball as she asks Tudball who is calling for "him," and the scenario so inflames Tudball that he announces he is quitting working for himself. Tim's ad libs are icing on a delightful comedy cake here.

The finale is relatively restrained by the show's standards, but it works fine in presenting Joanne as a dancing and singing equal to Carol and Vicki. Joanne hoofs it up well with Don Crichton, and it is a hoot to see Vicki do the Charleston with Randy Doney.

Chris Korman says this is one of his father's favorite episodes because Woodward's husband, Paul Newman, attended the taping and apparently felt intimidated watching his wife in action. As Chris notes, "He sweated more than she did after doing it live!"

Feb. 21, 1976: Dick Van Dyke, Tony Randall

Q&A; a encyclopedia salesman (Dick) is caught in the crossfire between a bickering couple (Carol and Harvey); Tony sings "Madeira, M'Dear?"; Dick and Tony are two men on vacation whose efforts to deal with a monetary discrepancy lead to a verbal sparring; Dick performs "Ballin' the Jack" as a scuba diving professor showing the dancers how to move in flippers; Tony is livid that his wife (Carol) forgot their secret signals during their party; an Ira Gershwin mini-musical set on a movie stage features Harvey as a director, Tony and Vicki as lead actors, and Carol and Dick as lovers.

Comments: Tim wants time off this week to vacation with his wife, or so Carol explains to a disappointed audience. Two top comic actors replace him, but despite their efforts, this installment is spotty. The respectful audience applauds Peter Matz, and the Q&A has a few fun moments. Carol recounts the plot on *All My Children* and reveals she will guest on it (she wants to do Stella Toddler, but that does not happen). Asked what she wanted to be as a child, she says, "I wanted to be an artist and have my own comic strip." She also relates signing an autograph for a woman who could not read her handwriting.

A nice skit that could have been better kicks off the show, as meek Dick bears the brunt of Carol's anger toward her husband (Harvey). She threatens to jump off a ledge, but Dick talks her not to do it, and Harvey comes back to reconcile with Carol. Harvey plans to buy Dick's encyclopedia as a sign of appreciation, but the cost of the down payment leads him into an argument with Carol, and Dick slinks out from them during the melee. With a little tightening, this would have sparked, but as it is, it is a lukewarm offering.

Tony dresses up to present a song about a lover's efforts to poison another person. It is somewhat too precious to endure but acceptable, and Tony performs it enthusiastically.

The next segment feels like a Tim-Harvey routine, and its writer, Gene Perret, confirms it was envisioned as such. At a bar, Tony is upset he has lost $10. To bolster his pal, Dick nonchalantly burns a $10 bill. But when Tony finds the missing $10, Dick demands Tony give it to him to make up for his loss. Tony refuses but proposes a compromise and have them split it. He gives his $10 bill to the bartender (Don Crichton), who accidentally hands out four $5 bills for a $20 instead of a $10. Following this, Tony gives Dick $5 as promised, but Dick wants another $5 to even out the overpayment. Tony returns it to him, but Don returns to his register and realizes his mistake, so he takes the two $5 bills in front of Dick, who is enraged. Vicki comes by selling flowers, and Tony proposes buying them to settle their problem. Unfortunately, Dick realizes that Vicki has stolen his money and watch and leaves to get it. Meanwhile, Tony orders two drinks from Don and gets a double star on his receipt, meaning both drinks are free. "Cheers!" Tony says in response.

This clever bit moves sprightly. Perret is proud how he and his partner, Bill Richmond, overcame the initial premise problem once Tony found the money. "Bill and I stayed with it, and we came up with several plot points that kept the comedy alive," he says.

Carol tells everyone that Dick will have his own variety series on NBC next fall, "and deserves it," before he leads an enjoyable hokey pokey style routine with the dancers which is especially impressive given that all are wearing flippers. This is followed by a strong playlet where Tony and Carol play a couple who have developed body maneuvers to serve as code at parties, but Carol forgot to follow the protocol. As Tony recounts what she missed with his hands and body and she apologizes and retaliates in the same manner, the physical humor between him and Carol is pitch perfect. It concludes with Carol trying to console Tony, only for him to signal "Not tonight, I have a headache."

The show unfortunately concludes with a so-so, too prolonged segment stuffed uncomfortably with ten songs and a choppy scenario. Carol and Dick are part of the crew on a movie musical who are forced to stand in for the stars (Tony and Vicki) and fall in love as Harvey directs them. This seriocomic exercise ends with Tony picking Carol to be his next lead, but of course she leaves him for her newfound romance with Dick. Apart from Dick missing his cue from Harvey so the latter said "Lights, camera, action" to himself, this is none too amusing.

This is Tony's last guest shot, but Dick will return after the failure of his variety show. See Dec. 18, 1976 for more information.

Feb. 28, 1976: Pre-empted by *The Grammy Awards* special

March 6, 1976: Jack Klugman

Q&A; Tim tries to find a place and way to work with Carol and Harvey in a very cramped accounting office; Jack and Carol talk-sing "Where Were You?" about missing each other for appointments; an author (Jack) is dissatisfied with the predictions made by a clairvoyant (Harvey) who is dating the sister (Vicki) of his wife (Carol); Carol complains to a silent Tim about his indifferent treatment of her; Tim is a robber trying to purloin the Pink Pussycat diamond; a Southern congressman (Jack) and his wife (Carol) sing "The Country's in the Best of Hands" to their constituents.

Comments: Two weeks after Tony Randall guest starred, his former co-star on *The Odd Couple* appears as the guest in this week's generally good but not great installment. Carol describes him at the outset as "the adorable Jack Klugman" before a Q&A with time for just one question. "Has Vicki had her baby yet?" asks one person. "Oh, I hope so. She's nine months old!" Carol says of the infant.

Vicki appears in the first skit in a minor role. Harvey has to walk over his desk behind Carol to begin work, where they precisely time sending items back and forth to each other down to Carol yelling "File!" and Harvey ducking down as an enormous drawer zooms over his head nearly out the window. The latter visual joke is so strong that the audience applauds. Tim arrives as a new member of the accounting team and stumbles to find a place to sit, to Carol and Harvey's disgust, and an umbrella opening up on him does not help his efforts. He straddles a folding chair and then angles it between Harvey's desk and the window sill to sit down, and more complications arise as he tries to answer the phone Carol throws to him. Vicki comes in with a bottle of bubbly to surprise Carol and Harvey in celebrating their twentieth anniversary with the firm today and gives them both the day off, leaving Tim alone. Any chance he has to celebrate finding comfort is short-lived, as he accidentally activates opening the long file drawer that hits him in the face. This is a rollicking good start to the show.

Carol and Jack have a pleasant bit of banter broken up with occasional singing about who is right about missing events they have planned. Eventually it is determined that he was right and wanted to propose to Carol, a sweet ending for a battle of the sexes depiction.

Less successful is Jack in his trademark growling role, upset by the arrival of Harvey, a soothsayer in a purple and print dress suit, in his residence as the date of his sister-in-law (Vicki). When Harvey predicts the children's books written by Jack's wife (Carol) will be a success, Jack scoffs, particularly because Harvey says he does not see Jack with Carol to enjoy her fame and fortune. Harvey's comments that he sees Jack as a failure prompts an incensed Jack to go on a harangue over Harvey and his life in general. The rant has more anger than humor, and what little energy there is in the skit drains particularly when Jack leaves in anger—there is no real ending for this, a wasted opportunity overall.

Much better is Carol griping to an oblivious Tim, reading a newspaper in a comfortable chair. She runs the gamut of emotions as she goes from complaining about her tough life to professing her love for him while wanting their relationship to change, but he says nothing and seems to be ignoring her in response. Then in a killer twist, a car pulls up, Carol yells, "It's my husband!" and Tim comes to life and leaps out the window.

Tim gets a shining solo turn next in a segment based on a scene from the 1975 movie *The Return of the Pink Panther*, accompanied by a smart variation on "The Pink Panther" theme played by the orchestra in the background. A guard (Dick Patterson) tells a group played by the dancers about the elaborate security system surrounding the Pink Pussycat diamond before closing the exhibit room. Tim is a burglar who lowers himself on a rope and encounters many difficulties. The rope is too low to reach the ground, so he swings it and gets his crotch hit by a statue. When he finally hits the floor, he finds the diamond is guarded by an electrified field that lights up a bulb he holds (great special effects here). He survives nearly electrocuting himself to reach the glass case, only to find he cannot cut into it and learn that he has a drill too short to reach a plug. When he discovers the case has no top, he climbs above it but gets stuck. At that point, another crook (Stan Mazin) runs into the room, steals the diamond and activates the alarm, leaving Tim helpless—and the audience appreciative of some good laughs here with his alternately desperate and nonplussed reactions.

For the finale, a mayor (Harvey) introduces an elected official and his wife (Jack and Carol) assuring a group at a community assembly that everything is fine with America. The patriotic ode with a sense of humor includes good tap work with Vicki along with the dancers and provides a fresh, fun closing for the show.

TV Guide used a still from the kick line at the end in an article honoring the series in 1982. Anything to make up for Cleveland Amory's pan of the series in 1967, one supposes.

March 13, 1976: Family Show

Q&A; Eunice is upset to learn that Ed plans to take Mickey Hart to a convention in Chicago rather than her; Mr. Tudball holds a surprise birthday party for Mrs. Wiggins, who is indifferent to the occasion; the dancers perform a routine to "Baby Face"; a couple (Carol and Harvey) are inspired to be honest in discussing what they dislike about each other after watching a movie stressing that theme; the Charwoman says goodbye to the cast as they leave and recalls top moments from the season while visiting sets in the empty studio.

Comments: Carol and crew wrap up the ninth season with nary a misstep in this tight entry, beginning with a lively Q&A session where Carol first says she would be OK with her daughters going into acting. A woman tells Carol that "On account of your show, my grandchildren and I always get in trouble, because when I babysit the children, I let them stay up to watch your show." Learning that the audience member's daughter is named Carol (!), the hostess looks into the camera and says, "Carol, leave her alone." A man who knows Murray in charge of sound effects mentions him and Carol interjects "He's marvelous" as she displays his technique by hitting her head with a fist to a large thump. For her hiatus this year, Carol notes that "I'm going to be in Las Vegas May 27 for two weeks at the MGM Grand Hotel. I'll be there with Tim Conway and the Pointer Sisters." A boy says his grandfather in Canada thinks Carol is sexy and "Can I make him jealous by kissing you?" As he comes up on stage, the fourteen-year-old ("You're not supposed to be in here, but that's all right," jokes Carol) redhead nervously rolls his eyes to laughter from the audience, and his stunned reaction after the smooch even amuses Carol.

Mickey Hart prepares to take Ed to the airport when his entreaties to come along win Ed over, who tells Mickey he has a special emergency fund that can pay for his ticket. He warns Mickey not to tell Eunice, who has returned after taking Mama to the foot doctor. Mama wants to soak her feet and gets on Eunice's nerves, but not enough to distract Eunice when she overhears Mickey telling Ed they need to stop at his house to get pajamas. Ed reveals the truth to Eunice, who is livid and badgers Ed to take her to Chicago (Carol is especially winning here in pleading her case). Facing the onslaught, Ed gives up. A zombie-like Ed pours Epsom salts over Mama's legs while Eunice excitedly packs and tells Ed all the stuff she plans to do. Eunice's demands on the trip finally drive Ed nuts and he explodes, telling Eunice she is no fun and would hurt his efforts on the trip. He says Mickey will go with him to Chicago and they will see go-go girls before he leaves. Left at home, Eunice tells Mama she hopes Ed does have his laughs in Chicago, "Because that's the last ones he'll ever get!" This is good stuff.

For Tudball and Wiggins, the secretary is ready to leave, but her boss has her enter to take a dictation: "Happy birthday to yew, happy birthday to yew, happy birthday, Missus-Uh-Hwiggins, happy birthday to yew." She writes it and asks where he wants it sent, since has it addressed to a Mrs. Higgins. Trying to explain himself, Tudball solders on and gives her a cup with her name on it as a gift, but she is unimpressed because it is past 5 o'clock and she wants to leave. Tudball raises his voice about her time watching, prompting her to scribble a note, stuff it in the complaint box and sulk. An aggravated Tudball opens the box and tells her he was not yelling at her, then proceeds with the party to her indifference, culminating with bringing out a birthday cake and hearing Wiggins say she cannot eat it because she will break out with acne. As she leaves, she forgets her purse and Tudball picks it up. Unfortunately, it is under the cake, causing the latter to hit him in the crotch. Despite a weak ending, this is great fun, especially Tim's multiple ad libs sarcastically calling Wiggins a fast walker (he says during one strut by her that the eyes dry out so they cannot go "blinky winky," for one example).

"Baby Face" uses the old standard's 1976 dance hit version by one-hit wonder studio group The Wing and a Prayer Fife and Drum Corps in a cutely satisfying piece with the female dancers garbed in pink frills and the men in blue pajamas. Next is one of the best Carol-Harvey skits ever, as a loving couple disrupted when Carol wants them to follow the lead of the film they saw and implores Harvey to say what one of her flaws are. Pressed, he says she has a high forehead. Taken aback, Carol says she did not think he would be addressing her looks. To make peace, Harvey tells her to criticize him, and she says, "Your ears are irregular" and notes one wiggles lower than the other. Harvey is unfazed by that comment, so she pleads for another shot, and he acquiesces. Carol notes he has an "outsy" belly button that sexy men lack, which ticks off Harvey to respond that Carol's toes curl up. Realizing how petty their attacks are, both make up and say how they like their alleged flaws, but when Harvey accidentally quips, "I love your turkey neck," Carol goes into hysterics and looks it at in the mirror for any possible blemishes. Written, performed and directed expertly, this bit flows with wonderful humor.

The wrap-up is similar to last season's finale, only less elaborate. The Charwoman waves and kisses everyone as they leave, goes on the sets and remembers clips from Eunice, Tudball and Wiggins, and the Queen, and then sings "It's Time to Say So Long" on a bucket before leaving. Given how well this season turned out, it is a satisfactory finale.

Final Notes for the Season

The Carol Burnett Show finished in the ratings virtually the same as in 1974-1975 at Number Twenty-Nine. Its Emmy tally was lower, thanks largely to *Saturday Night Live* in its first season. The latter beat *The Carol Burnett Show* in variety series, writing (over the Sept. 13, 1975 Jim Nabors show), director (over one of the Maggie Smith shows) and supporting actor (Chevy Chase triumphed over both Harvey Korman and Tim Conway). The series did win for Ken and Mitzie Welch and Artie Malvin for special musical material in the Nov. 29, 1975 show, and Vicki Lawrence as supporting actress in variety or music, winning over Cloris Leachman in the special *Telly... Who Loves Ya, Baby?*

Other Emmy losses were in special classification (Ken and Mitzie Welch and Artie Malvin for their Irving Berlin finale on Oct. 11, 1975), art design (art directors Paul Barnes and Bob Sansom and set director Bill Harp for the Jan. 31, 1976 show) and choreography (Ernie Flatt for the March 15, 1975 show finale—the nomination period extended to the previous season). The ten Emmy nominations tied the series' previous best in 1973-1974.

At the Golden Globes, Tim Conway earned a statuette as Best Supporting Actor, tied with Edward Asner for *The Mary Tyler Moore Show*. Carol received a nomination as well, but oddly there was none for the series, the same as it was in 1973.

Despite this season's success—or perhaps because of it—there were more changes on the writing staff beyond the premature departure of Bo Kaprall and Pat Proft. Barry Levinson and Rudy DeLuca had managed to write *Silent Movie* for Mel Brooks while doing the show and decided to leave to pursue successful careers in motion pictures that lasted into the twenty-first century. DeLuca stayed as a writer, while Levinson branched into directing as well and won an Oscar in 1988 for *Rain Man*.

CBS replaced repeats of *The Carol Burnett Show* with two variety series, *Dinah and Her New Best Friends* starring Dinah Shore from June 5 through July 31 and *The Diahann Carroll Show* from Aug. 14 through Sept. 4. Three weeks later, the series began in earnest its tenth season—a length of time less than 1 percent of all TV series ever reach.

"I saw it in the window and couldn't resist it": Here it is, the Bob Mackie dress so famous that it's now in the Smithsonian. Two NBC pages, Rich Hawkins and Liz Sage, wrote "Went With the Wind" with Carol as Starlet O'Hara, and the enthusiastic audience reaction when it aired on Nov. 13, 1976 led them to become regular writers. Incidentally, Harvey didn't crack up on stage because Carol showed it to him in advance. Courtesy of Getty Images.

Chapter 11

1976–1977: Celebration, Challenges and Complacency

Girl in the audience:	"I have a 'nothing book' and I want you to sign it."
Carol:	"I would be the biggest nothing in the book, right?"—From the Oct. 16, 1976 show

Crew Additions This Season

Writers: Elias Davis, David Pollock, Rick Hawkins, Liz Sage, Adele Styler, Burt Styler.

The tenth season of *The Carol Burnett Show* had remarkably little change in tone and feel from the ninth one, a welcome respite for the cast and crew given the notable on- and off-air upheavals that had happened previously for most of the 1970s. Oddly, however, the consistency may have been a slight drawback to the series for these shows.

For example, by now, even though the guest list remained strong, there was some staleness setting into what the series offered. Besides Jim Nabors opening each season and a family show closing it, also guaranteed to show up at least once would be Steve Lawrence, Eydie Gorme, Ken Berry, Helen Reddy, Roddy McDowall and Bernadette Peters (who missed this season while she starred in the failed CBS sitcom *All's Fair* most of the year). That makes at least eight shows out of twenty-four each season, or one out of every three, where viewers knew what the guest lineup would be. That is not a smart way to encourage people to tune into a program that supposedly promote spontaneity.

Also, virtually no new recurring characters will be launched this season, unless one counts Vicki playing Mr. Tudball's amply endowed wife with an accent similar to her husband. "I remember thinking that Mrs. Tudball was a little over the top, like, really, we've gone too far," Lawrence said in the

2012 DVD commentary. Nonetheless, she performed her with gusto, making a winning if improbable character to enjoy.

This does not mean that the returning writers and new ones were losing their touch, however. Indeed, this was the season with the classic *Gone with the Wind* sketch written by Rich Hawkins and Liz Sage, newcomers to the writing staff who were in their early twenties at the time. Many other great one-off skits would occur from them and the other newcomers and returnees as well. The musical numbers remained strong as well, with new input coming in that area too.

A newcomer to the terpsichorean talents on the show this season was Sande Johnson. "Ernie Flatt, the choreographer, decided to get two new dancers," she recalled. "Toni Kaye and I had worked a few years before at the Disneyland Horseshoe Review, so she put in a good word about me being multitalented." The comment could not hurt, as Johnson was one of more than 300 women trying out for the pair of available slots. She credited her classical training as giving her an edge during her audition.

Johnson had grown up in Texas watching *The Carol Burnett Show* and was thrilled to be part of the series. Her petite size determined who would be her regular partner for most dances. "We were matched size-wise. I was working with Stan Mazin or Eddie Heim."

Meanwhile, Randy Doney assumed the role of assistant choreographer this season, a title he would hold the rest of the series' run as he helped Ernie Flatt teach the elaborate numbers to the dancers, regulars and guests. He continued to dance, and as he told Flatt, "I still want to be in the sketches." He was allowed to do that as well.

The only real change in content astute viewers might have noticed was the complete absence of Stella Toddler and Nora Desmond, coupled with only four appearances of Tim's Old Man character. Their almost total disappearance occurred in response to Lydia Bragger, chair of the New York-based Gray Panthers Media Watch Task Force, writing a letter to CBS complaining that such characters portrayed senior citizens as "cranky, stubborn, crumbling human beings." Sensitive to the criticism (about the only serious complaint about the series' content), Carol and crew made changes in response, although Vicki's ornery Mama was too established to be dropped.

Amid all this relative stability within the show, an unexpected challenge emerged in the series' lead-in this season. To the surprise of CBS, ABC's move of *Starsky & Hutch* to Saturday nights opposite *The Mary Tyler Moore Show* and *The Bob Newhart Show* in the fall of 1976 really took a bite out of the audiences for the latter two series. Carol's show still handily defeated ABC's crime drama *Most Wanted* that followed *Starsky & Hutch*, but CBS wanted to retain the strong edge it had on Saturdays for most of the 1970s and made changes in order to preserve its strong night.

In November 1976, the network moved *The Mary Tyler Moore Show* and *The Bob Newhart Show* back an hour and installed *All in the Family* and *Alice* in their place. Those sitcoms flourished, while Carol had no problems with ABC's replacements for *Most Wanted*, *Dog and Cat* and then *The Feather and Father Gang*—all tiresome cop dramas. This admittedly was not the best work of ABC's head programmer, Fred Silverman, who otherwise was taking his network to Number One this season. But he had other plans in store that would have a more drastic effect on *The Carol Burnett Show*.

In October, Peter Andrews with *The New York Times* announced that Harvey would be leaving *The Carol Burnett Show* at the end of the season to star in his own situation comedy. Silverman had mentioned the idea to Harvey in 1975 as part of his strategy to make ABC stronger by making weakening hits on competing programs. (For example, he convinced Redd Foxx to leave *Sanford and Son* on NBC in 1977 to do his own variety series on ABC, which flopped but did lead to cancellation for *Sanford and Son*.)

The article claimed that there had been talk when Silverman was head of programming at CBS from 1970-1975 of spinning off Harvey to have his own series, but the network was worried about tampering the show's winning format. Silverman clarifies this contention.

"I was very happy with *The Carol Burnett Show* as constituted and didn't want to fool around with it," he says. "Why break it up? He was an integral part of *The Carol Burnett Show*. It would be taking the life out of the show. I got the idea of having Harvey do his own show when I went to ABC. When I went to ABC, it was fair game to go after him."

Korman seemed conflicted about the change when talking to Andrews. "I was very happy with Carol, but I was getting a little restless after ten years and wanted to deepen my life and my career. I was a contracted slave, and a lot of people should try not to be anything more, but I guess there was a little more Spartacus in me than I realized. This could turn out to be a colossal mistake, but at this time in my life, it is something I have to try."

This desire by Korman was understandable. After all, before doing Carol's show, he had spent four years previously as a regular on *The Danny Kaye Show*. That makes fourteen years as a top supporting comic actor, and as he was turning fifty in 1977 while being in strong demand in movies during the hiatus of *The Carol Burnett Show*, it was the optimum time for him to pursue being the lead of his own comedy series.

Beyond wanting to avoid being typecast as a sketch comic, Korman told Michael J. Hoy of the Copley News Service in November 1976 another reason he wanted to leave. "This is the first time in five years that I felt I wanted to get out and do a summer stock tour—and returning to the show was a prospect I didn't face with much enthusiasm," he said.

In retrospect, Korman appears more perceptive about the quality of *The Carol Burnett Show* than other principals at the time. While this season will offer some of the all-time funniest moments on the series, there are several moments when the series appears to be desperate to find anything to fill time. The most egregious example is the "Little Miss Showbiz" remake on Dec. 18, 1976, but other ones will be noted as well.

Additionally, there are three family shows, more than any other season previously. Why a series that has been showered with honors and is celebrating a decade run is unable (or possibly too cheap) to get guests for two shows more than usual is a confusing development that suggests greed and negligence to viewers.

The most questionable decision was to continue to feature Korman so prominently in the series. By placing him as an integral part in the majority of skits and musical numbers throughout this year, *The Carol Burnett Show* proved he was indispensable to its success. This seeded doubts into the audience about who if anyone could (or should) take his place in the series, a source of skepticism the series could ill afford at this point.

As for Korman, the downside of his decision was that future success was not guaranteed, despite his experience and many awards, because he was relying on other producers to fashion a successful vehicle around him. Korman realized that obstacle acutely.

"We have such a great staff on Carol's show," he said to Andrews. "How am I going to get people that good for my show? And where am I going to find another Carol Burnett?"

Those questions would have to be answered later. For now, *The Carol Burnett Show* proceeded onward, still making some of the best moments in TV history.

Sept. 25, 1976: Jim Nabors

Introduction of Jim; Harvey introduces a takeoff of *Mary Hartman, Mary Hartman* with Carol as the title character, Vicki as her pal, Jim as Vicki's husband and Tim as Carol's grandfather; Jim presents "Let Me Be There" with the dancers; Tim plays a tired businessman eager to get some sleep but too many distractions in his hotel prevents that; Eunice, Ed and Mama play a game with predictably rowdy results; "Shipwrecked in Tahiti" salutes the music of composer Nacio Herb Brown featuring Tim as a witch doctor, Carol and Harvey as natives, and Jim and Vicki as a couple washed ashore.

Comments: To start the tenth season, Carol's "special buddy" Jim Nabors comes out and laughs with the audience at a clip of the "I Believe in You" duet from the debut show, along with Carol trying to teach Jim how to say "The rain in Spain stays mainly on the plain" without a Southern twang. They reprise that phrase in a scripted bit where Carol ends up sounding like Jim's Gomer Pyle character. Although a little forced, it works.

That leads into Harvey appearing as "Norman Blear, Sultan of Sitcoms." Head writer Ed Simmons gets a few jabs at his former collaborator as Harvey boasts of his successes and announces his latest spinoff, a soap opera for children called "Mary Mary Quite Contrary, Mary Mary Quite Contrary." Carol does a dead-on send-up of Louise Lasser's nervous tics and nasal voice, starting with her emerging from underneath a kitchen sink to answer "Good morning" on the phone and then apologizes profusely for not checking to see if it indeed was good. The caller is the police, telling her that her grandfather, Wee Willie (Tim), has been arrested for "peek-a-booing." While trying to adjust to this news and learn what it means, her next-door friend (Vicki), a country singer, comes to tell her about a spider that sat down beside her while she was eating curds and whey. More weirdness comes as her horny husband (Jim) says that Wee Willie is going to the house with an old woman living in a shoe with many children and no husband.

These circumstances lead Carol into a rant before calming down with some coffee, which draws applause from the audience. Wee Willie shows up, flashing his nightgown with a teddy bear design on the stomach to everyone, including the police outside. Mary freaks out—even wonders about her little lamb—and goes back under the sink, while her neighbors go home to have sex and Wee Willie flashes the phone while calling the Humpty Dumpty hotline. This alternately silly and ribald piece moves so well that an audience member asks Carol on the Oct. 30, 1976 show if she will reprise the character. (She does not, in part because *Mary Hartman, Mary Hartman* was losing popularity.)

With the dancers dressed like they are going on a hoedown, Jim lip syncs his take on Olivia Newton-John's 1974 country-rock hit to good effect. This leads to a superb near-solo pantomime by Tim as a man so exhausted in getting into his hotel room that he cannot even tip his bellhop (Don Crichton). He fights with clothes hangers to put up his coat, and the blinds on the window drop down on him. A couple next door (voices of Harvey and Vicki) have a shouting match, and a lamp is thrown through the wall and hits Tim. As he finally gets settled, a fly buzzes whenever he turns out the light. He walks out the door to have the fly follow him, then stumbles through the transom on top to get back inside. When he hears a knock at the door, he answers and the fly re-enters. He manages to trap the pest under the glass, but it taps loudly against it, so he grabs it, only for the fly to take control and pull Tim to fall outside the window. This is brilliant physical comedy.

We visit the Family next, and when Eunice lands on Boardwalk, she is ecstatic, because she owns Park Place too, and for the first time ever, she has the two most expensive properties in the board game. Carol plays her enthusiasm so well the audience applauds. But Eunice's joy dissipates as Ed and Mama lose interest in the game, and she forces them back to play with her. Her pleasure in buying houses on her properties vanishes when she lands on properties owned by Mama and then Ed that bankrupt her. Eunice goes out in the rain to bemoan to the world that she has lost again, getting more applause, but as she returns soaking wet, Mama cares nothing about her plight. She is more interested in getting back in the game and beating Ed, or as she puts it, "I'm going to bury this bozo!" Eunice's disappointment ends this fine if standard installment.

The show culminates with an island setting that allows viewers to see all the principals (except Vicki and Jim) and the dancers in sarongs, with the men wearing leis to cover their chests. Viewers still get to view a good amount of skin nonetheless amid a thin storyline with Tim administering his love spell to the natives where requested. Carol and Harvey do not need such assistance until the dancers bring Jim and Vicki's unconscious bodies before them, and a love struck Carol asks Tim to mesmerize Jim. The successful request prompts an envious Harvey to ask Tim to create a volcano, which he does and more. Vicki wakes up doing "Singing in the Rain" amid the tumult and Jim goes back to her, while Harvey takes advantage of the situation and has Tim put a spell on Carol. All ends well for the couples, and even Tim wins over a woman dancer to call his own.

Everything here is in fine form, but it lacks a little something extra that would make it an unabashed classic. It may be that it is slightly overstuffed and rushed, a contention borne out by the fact Carol does not sing "It's Time to Say So Long" at the end. Regardless, it is a serviceable, sturdy start for the season.

Oct. 2, 1976: Sammy Davis Jr.

Q&A; Sammy sings "What Became of Me" at a club setting with the dancers; a snob (Carol) tries to intimidate her nurse (Vicki), but her efforts backfire; while facing the wrath of Harvey, Tim is a slave rowing on a galleon thrown off by the behavior of his new foppish seatmate (Sammy); the Queen and Prince (Carol and Harvey) find that they owe money to an American loan shark (Sammy) and try to avoid his efforts to reclaim the alleged principal and interest; Carol and Sammy sing a medley of Broadway hits, including ones they popularized themselves.

Comments: Just as with 1975-1976, Sammy is this season's second guest. His return is slightly less successful due to the somewhat lower quality of skits, but Sammy gives 100-plus percent as always. Coming out to applause for the Q&A, Carol thanks the audience with her mock Bette Davis voice saying "Not bad at all!" This segment runs the gamut—a woman wants Carol to sign her picture book, a person remembers her from doing *Stanley* in 1956-1957, a woman compliments her hair style, Carol says why she pulls on her earlobe and does the Tarzan yell. Asked for advice on show business, she jokes, "Stay out!" then says stay in school first. For a boy wanting a kiss, she inquires about his age and he quips in reference to the minimum age listed on the tickets that "I'm supposed to be fourteen!" "The show is so long tonight, you may be fourteen by the end!" Carol responds. Also, Carol is offered to be an honored orientation member for her alma mater, UCLA. "You counsel freshman," she is told of her potential role. "So far I love it," Carol shoots back.

If all this were not enough, Carol takes time to note a very special guest in the audience (at the first taping only, according to Kathy Clements) by saying, "If possible, he's even nicer than he is talented—Laurence Olivier!" The crowd gives the legendary actor in a blue leisure suit (well, it was 1976) a standing ovation, which Carol notes is the first time it has happened on her series. "You want one?" asks an audience member in return. Carol laughs it off, then mockingly warns them next time she will. Incidentally, Carol first met Olivier a year earlier when he rented her Malibu beach house.

Sammy's number is sparkling, but unfortunately following it is a sketch with a point that fails to pay off. As Carol's rich witch insinuates to Vicki that the latter's husband may leave her, Carol receives her comeuppance when the nurse finds out Carol has ordered all the flowers in her hospital room for herself. This dramatic twist is meant as food for thought, but comes across as shallow in execution.

An improvement occurs when Tim's doddering slave character is intimidated by the arrival of Sammy, a prissy type with long, curly looks, frills and a handbag. In case anyone is too dense to realize the implications, the name of Sammy's character is Bruce. Sammy cleans his sitting place for rowing on the ship with a hanky ("It is a bit tacky, tacky, tacky," he frets), and his efforts to help

Tim just produce suffering instead under Harvey, their slave driver with an eye patch. For example, when Sammy informs Harvey that Tim is thirsty, Harvey breaks a water jug on Tim's head. Somehow, Sammy has smuggled a handgun on board and uses it to shoot off the chain constraining them, but the bullet make a hole into the bottom of the ship, forcing Tim to sit on the newly created water spout to conceal it as it soaks his crotch. In an effort to fish with a line supplied by Sammy, Tim loses the oar, and Sammy loses composure as he tries to tell Harvey what happened. Amid the chaos, Sammy steals Harvey's whip and plans to take over the ship when Tim grabs the handgun and shoots Sammy, because he hates troublemakers on the ship. This variant of a sketch Tim did with Harvey originally on the Oct. 25, 1972 show is just as clever and enjoyable as the original.

Less amusing is another revamp of Carol and Harvey as royalty, this time besieged by Sammy as a representative from Vito the loan shark coming to collect money owed. Sammy uses phrases like "jive turkey" and "Can you dig that, sister?" to bring home his threat. In response, Harvey says "Sticks and stones" as he squats down to Sammy's height, prompting laughter from the latter, and his promised retaliation is meaningless since the black guard (Carlton Johnson) prefers to strut and bond with Sammy. When Sammy gets out a gun, Carol says she will give a speech to the public on her balcony confessing their wrongs and invites Sammy to join her and Harvey. Carol announces that she will raise taxes 128 percent to the angry mob below, then she and Harvey duck. Sammy returns with arrows across his body and dies. Back-to-back skits ending with Sammy's passing seem in poor taste even though they are comical, and the Queen and Prince are much funnier being tormented by Tim's hollow soldier than by a blackmailer.

The show improves markedly with the finale, wherein Sammy sports a leisure suit and Carol a black dress with silver spangles as they sit on trunks with the names of Broadway musicals plastered on them. They do snippets of approximately twenty show tunes, including Sammy's hit "Mr. Wonderful" and "Shy" from Carol's *Once Upon a Mattress*, which Sammy sings as well.

"Sammy was so fantastic to work with," recalls Ken Welch, who crafted this finale with his wife, Mitzie. "He loved this so much that he bought us a tape recorder." This smooth, professional collaboration ends the show on a rousing note. Hopefully the soon-to-be Sir Laurence Olivier enjoyed the episode overall from his audience seat as well.

Oct. 9, 1976: Family Show

* A two-part spoof of the 1944 film *National Velvet* features Carol in the Elizabeth Taylor ingénue role, Vicki as her mother, Tim as a jockey and Harvey as the race supervisor; Carol and Harvey are a couple struggling to remain calm as they host their weekly grievance session; Vicki and Carol perform a medley of "I'm Not at All in Love," "A Wonderful Guy" and "I'm Not Getting Married Today"; the cast and dancers participate in a musical salute to Las Vegas.

Comments: The earliest family show to date in a season stands out mainly with its superb movie send-up. In "Natural Velvet," Carol is so devoted to horses that she acts like one in her house. Tim assumes a mock Cockney accent to and does a hilarious bit showing how an upcoming race will be run by stumbling on furniture in Carol and Vicki's house. Determined to compete in the derby, Carol pretends to be a male jockey, but her ruse appears in jeopardy when a judge (Harvey) tells all the men in the locker room to strip to the waist to prove they are not women. It is amusing watching Harvey inspect the chests of the male dancers here, but what sends it over the top is Tim dressed up with huge breasts and blonde hair in a form-fitting jockey outfit to deflect attention from Carol. His gambit works (and breaks up Harvey, of course), and Carol competes and wins, ending the race astride Tim. This is one of the series' best spoofs ever.

There will be one more family show this season before the usual one at the end. For that, see Dec. 25, 1976.

Oct. 16, 1976: Madeline Kahn

Q&A; Eunice rehearses a local production of *Mary of Scotland* with a visiting, pretentious movie actress (Madeline); Carol and Madeline duet on "Friends"; Mr. Tudball attempts to buy coffee from a malfunctioning vending machine, and he attacks it in response, prompting the ire of an office security guard (Harvey) speaking in an Irish brogue; the movie spoof "That's Entertainment Part 86" has Tim and Harvey as ancient hosts recalling moments that ape Ann Miller's tap dancing (Vicki), Nelson Eddy and Jeanette MacDonald operettas (Harvey and Madeline), Fred Astaire (Tim) and Carol as Esther Williams in a swimming routine.

Comments: "I have been dying to have her on our show ever since I saw her in the movies," Carol says at the outset about tonight's guest. The anticipation pays off excellently, with comic and vocal material tailored to display Madeline Kahn's talents at peak form. First, Carol has some nice audience interactions during the Q&A. She reveals she raised nearly $16,000 for Dr. Jonas Salk's cancer research from her recent garage sale before being asked to autograph a special publication from a fan. After telling a fourteen-year-old girl she will be glad once she gets her braces off, Carol receives her own compliment when a boy asks from whom she inherited her gorgeous legs. "How old are you?" she says a little stunned. "You little devil! Have you ever thought in terms of an older woman?" She then answers that she got them from O.J. Simpson. The adorability factor goes off the scales as a tiny girl comes onto the stage with a paper in her hand, claims Carol is her aunt and hugs her tightly. Carol recognizes who she is but fails to tell the audience. A woman wants Carol to come to Colorado and Carol responds "OK!" Finally, a twenty-year-old gentleman from Tulsa complimented her on nine great seasons on TV and says it keeps getting better, then asks Carol how old she was when she started. "I was eleven," she says, implying she was the same age as him.

Eunice is in a tizzy as Ed and Mama play a board game noisily while she rehearses her theatre role with the star (Madeline), whose previous credit was appearing in the movie *Cat Women on Mars*.

An emotive type, Madeline has Eunice lightly meditate and adopt the mantra "In our circles" before launching into their scene, but Eunice's delivery is overstated. Madeline suggests Eunice pretend to be a butterfly, but that fails as well, so the actress proposes Ed and Mama read parts to help out. The results are disastrous, with Mama and Eunice arguing about how the latter acts, and when Madeline says the line, "A bastard profanes the English throne," a shocked Mama asks, "What kind of smut is this?!" Ed, who has been overenthusiastic in his readings, agrees with Mama that the play stinks, while Madeline attempts to move onward and critiques Eunice thoroughly about her mistakes. During her tirade, Madeline reveals she wanted to can Eunice until she pleaded to stay in the production. Eunice shoots back by belittling Madeline's movie role, which chastens the actress somewhat before she fires Eunice, even though the latter has bought 100 tickets to the play at a cost of $200. As Madeline leaves and Eunice mopes, Mama consoles her with "Poor baby, she's failed again. . . . Failure's not so hard. You still got us." The look on Carol's face at the end is priceless, as is this top sketch.

"Friends" is specially written for Carol and Madeline to sing on stools. Carol says she wrote a fan letter to Madeline after seeing her in *Young Frankenstein* and complimented her on her previous work, after which Madeline did the same. Their vocals balance each other delightfully, and they even dance a little to serve as icing on the cake here.

The good times continue with the twist of using Harvey as the foil for Mr. Tudball. Tim cracks him up several times as he defends hitting the haywire machine. The first time he puts in a dime and gets nothing, the second the coffee is dispensed but no cup appears to catch it, and the third he gets a cup along with the coffee, but the cup has no bottom. Tim's reactions to Harvey's warnings after each incident are priceless. The difficulties appear to end when Harvey puts in a dime and everything goes well, so he leaves, but too much coffee comes out, and Tim bangs on the machine again. An agitated Harvey returns only to find a similarly irked Tudball grab his gun and shoot at the machine. Finally, that results in a perfect cup of coffee coming out, and Harvey leaves. Mrs. Wiggins enters, sees the scene, murmurs "Free coffee" and leaves with the cup to Mr. Tudball's dismay. It is a killer closer to a great segment, and it is hard to believe any other star the magnitude of Carol would be willing to get dressed up in costume just to deliver two words in a bit that lasts less than ten seconds, even if that action produces huge laughs.

An excellent set of parodies occurs in "That's Entertainment Part 86," chief among them Madeline's wonderful trilling and Carol's gurgling vocals in doing water choreography in an impersonation filmed outdoors in a pool (that bit is a repeat from the Nov. 2, 1970 show). The capper is having all the artists come out with the dancers at the end having aged considerably—Vicki has white hair with fat thighs and drooping bosoms, Madeline is doddering in glasses while still trying to hit the high notes, and best of all Carol drops down from the rafters on a swing in a flowered swimsuit with water sprinkling out everywhere from her on stage and on the cast.

At the end, Madeline spends a considerable amount of time writing in Carol's book. One hopefully assumes it was a lengthy note in appreciation of everyone presenting her delightfully in one of her best TV guest shots ever, and of the series' best entries.

Oct. 23, 1976: Steve Lawrence

Q&A; a housewife (Carol) copes with intrusions by characters and situations from TV commercials; Steve sings "I Write the Songs"; Carol is a recovering soap opera addict whose husband (Harvey) worries she may be slipping as her friend (Vicki) reveals the latest plot developments; a military leader (Harvey) entrusts an inadequate subordinate (Tim) to operate a cannon during a charge against the enemy; a nightclub comedian (Steve) tries his failing routine on his wife (Carol) to help him improve; "Old and New Fashioned Love Song" has Carol doing the former and Vicki the latter along with Steve and the dancers.

Comments: This is a top episode, ranging from pretty good to great sketches and a strong ending. The Q&A is quick—Carol jokes that her favorite baseball player is basketball star Jerry West and says there is no more time for questions when someone inquires about her age—to get into a great commercials bit featuring Carol. She grinds up an irritating miniature character in the garbage disposal, tells a fast-running O.J. Simpson (Carlton Johnson) that she does not know where he can find his rental car, and endures Tim peddling dog and cat chow even though she has no pets. The wildest bit has Harvey wearing underwear over his pants and telling Carol how great he feels. Amid this insanity, Carol calls for a cop (Don Crichton), but he is too busy enjoying some sweets. It culminates with Tim stripping Carol of her blouse and skirt after she refuses to give them to him and Carol having to fight a bear over a beer she has to calm her nerves. Though some references are obscure now, this well-written sketch still clicks along nicely.

With the Peter Matz Orchestra onstage behind him, Steve offers an acceptable if not quite impassioned version of Barry Manilow's recent Number One hit. After that, Carol tells Vicki that she and Harvey threw out their TV set and are doing fine without it. This impresses Vicki, who, after wondering how Carol could lose her curiosity for *All My Children*, *As the World Turns* and *General Hospital*, recounts each show's latest plots. A musical "sting" hilariously indicates Carol's shock and interest in what is happening, which alarms Harvey. He does not want her to slip back into her old habits, but he allows Vicki to share one revelation, the knowledge of which leads Carol in a golden comic breakdown in hysterics recounting fake developments on the soap operas. Vicki is sorry about what has happened and says she should have just stayed home to watch the football game, which sparks Harvey on a rant about how bad Dallas was last season. He vows that he and Carol will get a big new color TV to watch what they are missing, a perfect ending to a gently pointed commentary on our culture's obsession with video.

Next is one of the best Tim-Harvey concoctions ever. As Harvey leads an attack, Tim cannot load a cannonball properly to be fired, forcing Harvey to retreat and try again. On the second go-round, Tim accidentally knocks out a cannonball already put in the mouth of the firearm and attempts to replace it with a ball too big to fit. That ball ends up falling into Tim's pants and weighs him down until he attempts to shove it into the cannon in a way that looks like he is trying to impregnate the device. (Somehow this hilarious sequence passed muster with the censors in 1976.) More hysterical failed attempts include another ball falling out and hitting Tim in the crotch, losing the plunger inside the cannon and being unable to light the fuse. By the last attempt, Harvey returns in his long johns and forces Tim to lead the attack while he works the cannon. Tim agrees, only to accidentally shoot Harvey before going onto the battlefield. This sparkles.

The last skit is generally effective if not as laugh-inducing as what preceded it. In a loud pink and red tuxedo, a dejected Steve presents his jokes to Carol while she acts as a heckler to improve his performance as a comedian. After witnessing his poor Edward G. Robinson and James Cagney impersonations, Carol tells Steve he stinks and belittles him, prompting him to insult her in response. She presses him to do more and tells him he is good while doing that, building up his confidence. He thanks her for the psychological strategy employed, but the last shot indicates Carol really has doubts about his potential.

The entertaining finale has Carol singing standards (plus "An Old Fashioned Love Song" from 1971) while Vicki belts hits from the 1960s and 1970s in a competition to woo favor from Steve between them. Carol gets Steve to do "Our Love is Here to Stay" with her, even though he did it as the title tune for a TV special with Eydie in 1975 (hmm). Vicki responds by enticing him with "Love Will Keep Us Together." This interplay occurs through roughly twenty numbers, but fast pacing and fine selections make this relatively easy to enjoy. Seeing Vicki bump her hips against Steve while doing Joe Tex's 1972 funk hit "I Gotcha" is amusing if a little cheesy, along with her doing some other upbeat recent tunes like "Lady Marmalade" and "Get Down Tonight." Carol's reactions of dismay and determination are as great as her singing. The most notable part comes when all three do "Feelings," and Carol moans out the "whoa" part of the chorus, a send-up she will refine later this season (see Feb. 12, 1977 for more).

This marks Steve's nineteenth guest shot on the show. His twentieth will come on Jan. 29, 1977.

Oct. 30, 1976: Roddy McDowall

Q&A; Mr. Tudball (Tim) installs an automatic door lock that confounds Mrs. Wiggins (Carol); a cinematographer (Roddy) directs a ditzy nurse (Vicki) and a surgeon (Harvey) on how to manipulate their work on a patient (Tim) in the operating room for maximum drama; Vicki sings "Hollywood Seven"; two old chums (Carol and Roddy) meet in an elevator in London and exchange memories and hopes via one-word answers; a married couple (Carol and Harvey), hung over after a party, check with their pal (Vicki) to learn what happened amid each other's fears of having slept around; a salute to silent movies.

Comments: Had there been a little trimming of the sketches and a better feature song, this episode might have been a classic, but it has to settle for being very good, which is still impressive. In the busy but sparkling Q&A, Carol does the old joke of having plans to do movies while producers of them do not, recommends vitamins for energy, plugs her special with Beverly Sills on Thanksgiving night, and says Glenda Jackson and Shirley MacLaine are her two favorite actresses. After doing the Tarzan yell, she accepts praise for the "Mary Mary Quite Contrary" skit (see Sept. 25, 1976); talks about a recent garage sale she had; thanks a woman from Newark, New Jersey, who says this is her third consecutive year visiting Los Angeles where seeing a taping of Carol's show is the highlight of her trip; recounts the current plots on *All My Children*; and reviews the fact that Eunice has three brothers. There's even more in the Q&A, but that will suffice.

Tudball and Wiggins are right on the mark, as his efforts to explain to her how the new automatic door works wring out plenty of laughs in multiple scenarios where she takes advantage of his unintentional missteps. It all culminates with him getting stuck on a ledge as he tries to get into his locked office via a window due to Wiggins refusing him admittance. Before that happens, Tim releases a great ad lib by eyeing Wiggins' puffy posterior and quipping, "If you get to a gas station, you ought to check that left rear!"

The skit with Roddy does not quite ignite despite the determined efforts of Vicki in her "dumb Dora" voice and Harvey in his Germanic accent. Roddy complaints about various aspects of the surgery as he films, and Vicki and Harvey accommodate him over Tim's objections. One amusing bit involves an exploding balloon, but like much of the sketch, that emphasizes noise and chaos over true humor. At the end, Tim runs out of the ER when Harvey suggests he have a sex change operation instead of removal of gallstones.

"Hollywood Seven" is an ersatz emulation of the ominous mood and sound of "The Nights the Lights Went Out in Georgia," and its tale of a would-be starlet who arrives in Los Angeles only to become a hooker to support herself and then dies is the hoariest of clichés. On the opposite end, Carol and Roddy's vignette is fresh and clever, as their short comments to each reveal they are old lovers who unsuccessfully try to connect for one last fling. Although not a gut buster, it is cute.

There are some chuckles as Harvey apologizes to Carol for an affair he thinks he carried out over the previous evening, only for Carol to learn from Vicki that Harvey actually slept with Carol. However, this is overextended for the amount of laughs generated.

Roddy harmonizes nicely with Carol and Harvey on "Without a Word, Without a Sound," a tune that serves as an introduction to the recreation of classic early movie comedy scenes. When they leave through three doors upstage, the show goes to black and white as the dancers emerge as the Keystone Kops, followed by Carol as Buster Keaton and Roddy and Harvey as Laurel and Hardy, respectively. They do a bit that includes Tim and Vicki as a wealthy couple trying to decide whether to use Buster's ice cream cart or Laurel and Hardy's. The conflict between the two camps lead to attacks on each that result in an unintentional pie in the face to Vicki, causing Tim to run after the trio amid the bungling of the Keystone Kops before the show returns to color and the present day. As with the previous sketch, this is overlong in terms of the amount of enjoyment reaped.

At the end, Carol cracks up as she announces Dinah Shore will be next week's guest. In an apparent last-minute switch, Dinah actually will appear two weeks later, at least on air.

Nov. 6, 1976: Kay Cole

Q&A; a man faking a lawsuit from an injury (Harvey) receives a visit from his apologetic alleged perpetrator (Carol) who soon deduces his scheme; Carol introduces Kay and Harvey, Tim and Vicki provide the guest with unsolicited advice on how to perform on the show before she sings and dances to "Boys and Girls Like You and Me" with Don Crichton and another number with the dancers; Eunice, Ed and Mama visit Mickey Hart's apartment for supper and surprise revelations; Carol, Vicki and Kay sing a medley of songs with rain themes at an outdoor cafe with the dancers.

Comments: Billed as the TV debut for singer/dancer (and later director/choreographer) Kay Cole, this show technically was incorrect. "I had done a lot of TV as a kid—*Climax*, *Playhouse 90*," Cole says. "I was a working child personality. This was my first musical foray." In the 1960s through the mid-1970s, she concentrated on stage work over TV.

Carol introduces Cole as someone who impressed her when she saw *A Chorus Line* twice on Broadway. Cole does not recall Carol coming backstage during either visit. "But I do remember when she got to the set," she says. "Everybody there made me feel really comfortable. Carol set the tone."

Cole learned through her agent that Carol wanted her on the series, which was a pleasant shock. "I had just left *A Chorus Line*," she says. "It came out of nowhere." A fan of the show ("Carol was someone I admired. Like everyone else in the United States, I watched every week"), her adventure with it was a memorable one from the start.

"I did have a costume fitting prior to the week rehearsal and show with Bob Mackie," she says. "The dress I wore, he redesigned for Marie Osmond." Next came rehearsals with the dancers. "It was a very quick learn, very organized, very comfortable," Cole recalls.

This show is a winning showcase for her talents except as a thespian—she does no skits, which was a shame. It is rather ironic considering her later career, as Cole notes that "The odd thing is, as I teach acting, I do not teach singing. I haven't sung in many years."

Getting into the show itself, the Q&A includes one bit where a young man wants to see if Carol's finger fits his class ring. He thanks Carol for the opportunity and tells her she is his favorite star—except for Lucille Ball. Carol introduces four cast members in the Los Angeles production of *A Chorus Line* in the audience. A man with a frizzy coiffure asks her if she ever has stage fright and she responds, "Once in a while, and when I do, my hair goes out like yours!" to hysteria. She mentions that *Once Upon a Mattress* and *6 RMS RIV VU* may be rerun soon, then tells a child requesting that she do Nora Desmond that she needs drag to get into the character. Carol asks the youth if he knows what she means, and he says yes—a drag is a cigarette. After clearing that up, Carol gets Tim out to give a handshake to a long-haired gentleman and a kiss to a young girl.

From there, this entry divides into roughly four equal chunks. First, Harvey wears a neck brace and props up a leg with a cast in a wheelchair as he pretends to be the victim of an accident. Carol begs forgiveness for supposedly harming him, but she notes when looking for an item in his apartment that it is placed too high for someone claiming to be paralyzed from the waist down. She tests him by tickling his feet, but he is able to avoid revealing the truth. (He does break up at one face she makes, however.) Desperate, Carol pretends to die, and Harvey arises to help her. She raises her finger accusingly at him, and he backs away, only to fall down and really hurt his leg and back, making Carol grimace. The bit overall is solid, though it falls a little short of the show's best comedy.

Next, the regulars bicker about how to address the audience (and Harvey bobbles saying "dignity" in the process) before they leave for Kay to perform, first with Don Crichton and then the rest of the dancers amid a nightline backdrop. Kay's belting and terpsichorean talents are well represented despite the height difference with Crichton. "One of the biggest challenges was that he was so tall and I was so tiny," she said.

In "The Family," to celebrate his fifth anniversary of working with Ed, Mickey invites the Higgins and Mother Harper to his tiny apartment. "I thought your place was a disaster area," Thelma says to Eunice in comparing Mickey's threadbare living quarters. Mama falls into a low-slung chair and has to get Ed and Mickey to angle it and her to hold her arms out as they push her out. Vicki obviously is holding back a laugh here, but all the cast members provide great looks and line deliveries. Carol gets applause when Mama starts to complain and shoots back, "Do not start with me, don't start! I'm poised with every fiber of my body!" Another top laugh generator is when Mickey goes to pick up Chinese food and Carol mutters, "God only know where that man's hands have been." When Mickey returns and they eat, Mama has a memorable monologue showing her prejudice about Chinese restaurants. "You couldn't pay me to go into one. My Aunt Frances had a friend go in there and never come out!"

But the key part revolves around Eunice being livid when she learns Ed has given Mickey a raise while she has to struggle on their meager income. She and Mama plan to leave in protest, but Ed is determined to celebrate with his friend and gives her the car keys, saying he will take a taxi home. A defensive Eunice tells him, "It's either Mickey Hart or me." After a pause, Ed intones, "Drive carefully." Eunice leaves in a snit, only to come back and grab boxes of food. "At least my sons are gonna have a good meal!" she lets out. But Ed remains with Mickey. This is one of the best "Family" sketches ever.

For the musical finale, amid gray skies and imaginary precipitation, Carol plays a café operator with Kay and Vicki as customers, and all three alternate singing portions of appropriate tunes, joined by dancers for the last three-fourths. There are "Here's That Rainy Day" (Carol), "Cloudy" (Vicki), "Soon It's Gonna Rain" (Kay), "Rain on the Roof" (female dancers), "I Get the Blues When It Rains" (Carol), "Singin' in the Rain" (an instrumental version, with the male dancers waving umbrellas), "Rainy Days and Mondays" (Carol, Kay and Vicki, with great harmony) and "When the Sun Comes Out" (Carol and Kay). Inexplicably omitted are some recent hits such as "Raindrops Keep Falling on My Head" and "Here Comes That Rainy Day Feeling Again." Even so, this is a distinctive number in theme and approach, and Cole nails her vocals beautifully.

"I'd never heard such a big voice come out of such a little person, and she's been a joy to work with all week," Carol says in praising Cole before the end credits roll. More than thirty years later, Cole returned the compliment by saying of this episode, "I had a great time. It's a lovely memory, and something I treasure having the opportunity to do it."

Nov. 13, 1976: Dinah Shore

A businessman (Harvey) has something other than just sales figures in mind as he presents materials for review to a colleague (Carol) during a business lunch; Dinah sings "50 Ways to Leave Your Lover"; Harvey is aggravated by the slow service offered by the Old Man (Tim) working at a butcher store; a two-part parody of *Gone With the Wind* features Carol as Starlet O'Hara, Harvey as Rat Butler, Dinah as Melody, Tim as Brashly and Vicki as Cissy; Dinah, Carol, Harvey, Vicki and the dancers present eight blues songs in a French Quarter setting.

Comments: Yes, yes, "Went with the Wind" is brilliantly written, arguably the series' finest movie takeoff, but let's not overlook other great work here. Although there is no Q&A, it is a delight for Carol to present at the outset Anthony Hopkins, "my favorite actor today," in the audience. That leads into a sketch showing the superb rapport Carol and Harvey have developed. Harvey proposes marriage to Carol as a business presentation, showing papers indicating such things as their optimal number of children based on research (one point three) and signs of an increase for affection since fiscal year 1974. However, Carol reminds him of one dip. He rallies back by saying that both of them love each other, prompting her to take notes. The innuendo-laden script is tight and hilarious and caps off nicely when Harvey steps out and Carol gets on the phone and changes her stern personality into a giggly lass telling her mother excitedly that he proposed to her.

The best thing about Dinah's slow version of Paul Simon's Number One hit is that she looks beautiful in the blue gown. The show's momentum recovers from that misstep with Tim's usual bumbling shtick with Harvey, such as accidentally grinding the latter's tie along with some beef and making musical sounds with a block of Swiss cheese and hanging meats. At one point he tears off Harvey's pants, and a woman (an unbilled actress) comes into the butcher's shop, yells "Pervert!" at Harvey and has a cop (Stan Mazin) arrest him. Although somewhat short of a top-grade sketch, this bit nonetheless is a winner overall.

What really sends the show into the stratosphere is "Went With the Wind," where Rick Hawkins and Liz Sage created a send-up of the epic 1939 film classic where nary a moment is wasted. Starlet hates nice Melody to the point where she tells her to stick her head in a bowl of punch because she's so sweet—and Melody does! Melody also has wed Starlet's obsession, Brashley, prompting Starlet to throw a vase which Rat catches. He has the hots for her, but the Civil War breaks out, and he and Brashley leave to fight. As Starlet's plantation is attacked, Melody starts having a baby, and Sissy, the hysterical servant tries to help deliver the child. Starlet makes her famous "As God is my witness" speech, only to be drowned out by Melody's labor pains and Sissy's warbling.

Act Two has a Union soldier (Don Crichton) come to get back taxes, only to get knocked out by the women. Brashley returns and Starlet hugs him at the same time Melody does. Brashley notes that Rat is now rich, and when he returns to the plantation, Starlet is determined to impress him by using material from her curtains. After Sissy stalls him with casual conversation, Starlet arrives with a curtain rod sticking out of her outfit. Velvet drapery is attached to the rod, as golden curtain tassels are tied at the waist and Starlet wears a hat with more tassels. When Carol appears at the top of the stairs in the getup, the laughter generated is so intense that the show has to edit it out of the final broadcast. As Starlet arrives at the bottom of the stairs, Rat raves about her gown. "Thank you, I saw it in the window and couldn't resist it," which prompts almost as much laughter and applause as the first appearance of the outfit. It became so recognized as one of the series' best moments that the dress now resides in the Smithsonian.

From there, things quickly progress as Melody appears atop the stairs and asks to see Starlet before she dies. Starlet complies, and Melody pushes her down the staircase, getting more applause for Carol, as does Dinah mocking herself by saying, "Bye, y'all!" and blowing a kiss the way she ended her variety series in the 1950s and 1960s. Brashley leaves and so does Rat, but Starlet closes the door on the latter before he completes his famous line. As Starlet cries about what she will do know, Sissy slaps her on the face the way Starlet had been doing to her earlier and says, "Frankly, Miss Starlet, I don't give a damn!" Everything from the acting (including Harvey's precise imitation of Clark Gable's looks and inflections, which he nailed just prior to the performance) to the sets, costuming, direction, even music which has fun with the familiar "Tara's Theme," are just right here. This sketch is one of the series' greatest triumphs.

The show wraps up with the dancers in wildly designed orange outfits moving below Vicki, Dinah and Carol in black beaded dresses and colorful feathered boas, who sing in various combinations in a balcony overlooking the scene. Harvey joins the scene as a trumpeter and not only sings solo but gets to kiss and even lick (!) Dinah. Considering the unbridled hilarity that preceded it, this is a pleasant way to wind down the evening.

At the end, Harvey tries to play the trumpet off screen and flops so badly it causes some laughter. Also, Tim comes out with one of the boas the ladies used in the finale wrapped around his neck. It's a loose, amusing ending to an overall well-done entry.

Nov. 20, 1976: Ken Berry

Q&A; the old man (Tim) is a cook who aggravates Harvey while trying to make a hot dog and a chocolate shake; Ken performs "Stolen Love" with the dancers, all dressed in their finest tennis whites; a two-part spoof of *Mildred Pierce* has Carol as the title character, Vicki as her bratty daughter, Harvey as Carol's lover and Tim as a law enforcement officer hearing Carol's confession for killing Harvey; a mini-musical salute to lyricist Johnny Mercer has Harvey as a saloon pianist, Carol as a woman in love with Ken, the bar operator, and Vicki as Ken's love interest.

Comments: This is Ken Berry's most satisfying time on the series, even though he is confined to the musical segments. Nevertheless, everything presented is warm and funny, including the brief Q&A. Carol talks about liking pockets in her gowns so she has a place to put her hands and jokes that the character that best portrays is Raquel Welch. Also, if she was not an actress, she might have been a teacher—"College boys!" she quips.

After Don Crichton asks for directions and says goodbye to an absent cook at an outdoor stand, the old man emerges as Harvey arrives to tell him where to go. Harvey ignores Tim's delayed response and places an order that so perplexes Tim that he has Harvey write it down and cannot read it. Tim milks the slowness of his character beautifully here, cracking up Harvey as he struggles scooping up hard ice cream and hitting him with some choice ad libs that also make Harvey lose composure. When Harvey tells him, "What's a hot dog without a bun?" Tim quips, "A lonely weenie." Complaining about the service, Harvey gripes, "I never saw a place like this in my life!" "Well, it's the only one on the block," Tim shoots back. After having confused his hot dog with his cigar, Harvey finally blows a fuse when he recognizes that his shake tastes awful because Tim used mashed potatoes instead of ice cream. "I'll have to charge you for the blue plate special then," Tim responds as Harvey fumes. It's a solid ending to a great comic piece.

Ken's number is brightened by a nice presentation of having him and the dancers appear to be taking a break from a tennis tournament. Visually appealing, it has an unexpected ending with him being pelted with tennis balls, making it a cut above the usual.

The show really shines with "Mildred Fierce," a takeoff that follows the 1945 movie more faithfully than the effort the series did on the Jan. 26, 1970 show. Beautifully made up as Joan Crawford with exaggerated eyebrows, Carol enters a police station and tells a cop (Stan Mazin) that "I'd like to confess to a murder." An interested lieutenant at the express desk (Tim) offers to listen to her story. After ripping out a page in a magazine ("Good recipe"), she describes how her daughter (Vicki) was snippy and demanding about her mother working at a diner. When Mildred owns the chain, Vicki remains disgusted and complains about a billboard featuring her mom promoting at Mildred's Fatburgers in a waitress outfit. "I belong in a mansion or beach house!" Vicki snaps before slapping her mom (Carol has a great reaction shot here). The disharmony dissolves when Harvey arrives to buy Mildred's restaurants and takes an interest in her—and Vicki. Sensing opportunity, Vicki implores Carol to wed the rich entrepreneur. Shimmying her shoulders, Carol tells Harvey she expects marriage as part of their deal, and he agrees. When he embraces Carol, he kisses Vicki standing behind her as well.

In the second section, Carol says she shot Harvey for being unfaithful, but Tim tells her they found the real killer. They bring in Vicki, who is upset that her mother could not lie for her. Carol then reveals the truth—she came home early one night and found Vicki and Harvey kissing. She resignedly accepts Harvey's demands to get a divorce so he can wed Vicki, saying, "I don't need a brick to fall on my head" (and several fake ones do just that—silly but funny). When Vicki learns Harvey's statement of marriage was false and just meant to get rid of Carol, she shoots him. Carol returns and stumbles over the body as Vicki tells her she has to take the blame because she spoiled Vicki rotten, to which Carol agrees and gives her $50,000 to hide for a few days. Back at the station with her story finished, Carol implores Tim to be easy on Vicki—"This was her first murder!" Hearing how Harvey was lecherous, Tim agrees to let Vicki go in Carol's custody. Just as soon as that happens, Vicki gripes again incessantly about Carol's failures. We hear several shots and Carol coming to the door to blow wind to knock down Vicki's body before she returns to Tim's desk and says, "I'd like to confess to a murder" as he eagerly scribbles. This is a classic on every level, one of the best parodies ever on TV.

The evening keeps going on a sprightly note with a finale that cleverly uses the titles of two Johnny Mercer hits of the name of the characters Carol and Vicki play, "Laura" and "Tangerine" respectively. At least six other Mercer tunes including "Accentuate the Positive" appear during this love quadrangle set at a bar during the gold rush era. With great music, delightful costumes and unexpected plot twists, this is a minor gem.

Despite all the great trappings of this show, during its first run, the 1971 movie *Billy Jack* made its network TV debut opposite it on NBC and overwhelmed it with a 27.5 rating. Thankfully, the main sketches have been repeated frequently, making them probably more familiar to contemporary audiences than *Billy Jack* in fact.

Nov. 27, 1976: The Pointer Sisters

* Mr. Tudball asks Mrs. Wiggins to lie for him to cover for a situation he is trying to hide; the Pointer Sisters sing the old Sam Cooke hit "Havin' a Party"; Carol is a mother offering heartfelt advice to her daughter (Vicki) prior to the latter's wedding; an English lady (Carol) and her butler (Tim) listen to her husband's stories as they attempt to murder him; a cranky construction shop worker (Tim) attempts to fix a priceless Stradivarius violin owned by Harvey, with a disastrous outcome; the cast and the Pointer Sisters do a musical salute to Ray Charles.

Comments: "I loved working with the Pointer Sisters," says dancer Bobbie Bates. So apparently did the rest of the cast and crew, as this marks the group's sixth appearance on the series, the most of any musical act on the show.

"Carol Burnett was so great," Anita Pointer says. "All the clothes we wore were made by Bob Mackie, and she gave us all the clothing after the shows. It was so beautiful." The show also made personalized directors chairs with the name of each Pointer to sit in during rehearsals, and Anita says has kept that too.

The sisters' connection to Carol extended beyond the series. "We went on the road with here, Las Vegas with her and Tim Conway," Anita says. June was not able to make it for one show, so Tim just wore her costume and came out with the other sisters. "It was just so hilarious," laughs Anita.

Apart from the musical selections, this show has a worn feel with the setups, especially Tim's characters. The segments have flashes of humor but in general they are not as fresh as in previous outings. Carol's seriocomic scene with Vicki does not help, and the revelation that she and Tim end up killing themselves accidentally after listening to Harvey's descriptions about other murders he knows is a trite one. The series clearly is starting to show its age. No more musical groups guest starred on the series after this entry, unless you consider the Captain and Tennille one (see Jan. 29, 1978).

Dec. 4, 1976: Alan King

Q&A; a husband (Tim) who comes home to make breakfast inadvertently makes loud noises that keep waking up his wife (Carol) and their child; Alan performs a monologue on the airline industry and joins Carol in a song; a patient (Carol) has her explanation of a recurring nightmare interrupted by calls to her doctor (Alan); a salute to Warner Brothers films includes send-ups of *The Fountainhead* (Alan and Vicki), *They Died With Their Boots On* (Tim and Harvey), *Ceiling Zero* (Harvey, Vicki and Alan), *Night and Day* (Carol and Harvey) and Busby Berkeley musicals (everyone except Tim).

Comments: After a promising first third, the potential for this to be a memorable show flame out rather quickly, with precious little time for Tim and a pretty good waste of Carol and Vicki's talents as well. The audience seems to be more interested in previous guests in the Q&A. Asked about Rock Hudson, Carol describes him as "One of the nicest people I ever worked with in my life. He is a doll. I love him very much." A woman wonders when Carol and Lily Tomlin will team up. "Lily was on our show once before, and I loved working with her," Carol says (see Nov. 8, 1972). "She does a lot of specials, you know? And it's very difficult to get her. We asked for her this year to be a guest. I like working with her." The one non-star query comes from a boy who said he waved to Carol at LAX airport three years ago and she waved back. "Do you remember me?" he asks. "I sure do," she responds. "Stand up. (He does.) You've grown!"

The first sketch is as much a triumph for the props department as it is for Tim. Hungry and trying to be respectful of Carol, who has finally gotten their baby to sleep and wants to do the same, he winds up destroying their kitchen by accidentally pulling out all the shelves and other unintentional mischief. The best bit may be when he cracks an egg and nothing comes out, leading him to say, "Must be on the pill" and getting applause. The sounds become enough for Carol to come out a final time, get her hands burned by Tim's heated frying pan he hands to her, and everything in the kitchen falls apart, waking up the baby again with loud cries. Assessing the situation, Tim tells Carol he will get something at the office for breakfast instead but will be home for lunch—a solid end to a sturdy comic piece. Too bad Tim will appear only once more this show.

"Alan and I are very old and dear friends," Carol says in introducing her guest, who tears into an ad promising to get fliers to Cincinnati every 30 minutes ("Why?!") and grouses about airline food and damage to his suitcases. This is fairly funny if a little rough to endure, as Alan has a tendency to shout his jokes. He then asks to sing with Carol, as they reference "all those years with Garry (Moore)" where they first met. They do "You Say the Nicest Things," where they alternate singing each other's praises as the recipient merely responds with a short "yeah" or the like. There is a good line here where Carol notes that "If I married you, I'd be Carol King!"

Sadly, the show sags with an infuriating skit wherein a nervous patient (Carol) has to retell the setup of a horrible dream she is having to a doctor (Alan). Each time she is about to reveal what she saw, his phone rings. This happens five times, and each one is just as aggravating to viewers as it is for Carol to endure. The supposed humor of interruptions by Alan's ex-wife trying to blackmail him and his mother's irritating conversations never materializes. By the time Carol realizes Alan's frustrations and they switch places so that she can interview him—after informing the secretary to hold all calls—this bit is a lost cause.

The show tries to rally sluggishly with parodies thereafter, but they are mostly weak. For *The Fountainhead*, Alan confesses to Vicki his one mistake in making his office building was that he forgot to install bathrooms. In *They Died With Their Boots On*, Col. Custer (Harvey) has his aide (Tim) dress like himself so he can escape as an Indian during battle. Inexplicably, *Casablanca* just has Carol singing as "As Time Goes By." The return to alleged humor has Harvey and Alan faking a fight so that Vicki will fly a doomed plane instead of either one of them in *Ceiling Zero*. The last comic routine is a funny but long parody of *Night and Day*, where a recovering Cole Porter (Harvey, doing a dead-on Cary Grant) is told by a nurse (Carol) to write a hit song, and the activities performed by her and other soldiers (played by the male dancers) give him the ideas for lyrics of his tunes.

In the finale, a nurse (Carol) and doctor (Harvey) each have a vision of a double for the other one (Vicki and Alan, respectively). In a great set piece, sixteen dancers join them for a spectacular Busby Berkeley number. Even Alan moves well. But it is too little too late.

At the end, Carol just says good night without singing "It's Time to Say So Long" (although the orchestra plays it), and the kick line is awkward as well, both serving as good indications of how this often missed the mark. Thankfully, it will recover strongly the next week with one of its greatest installments ever.

Dec. 11, 1976: Betty White

Q&A; Eunice's sister, Ellen (Betty), joins her and Ed in helping to clean out Mama's attic, where treasured items are discovered; Carol and Betty are two surviving members of the Class of '32 Waxahatchie University who reminisce about old times; Tim is a bar patron who learns Carol has a phony $20 bill and tries to help her out; a tribute to the Ziegfeld Follies has Harvey as the emcee, Betty as a showgirl, Tim as the star of a solo comic pantomime, Vicki as a Fanny Brice-like star of a mock ballet and Carol as the featured final act.

Comments: In the Columbia House introduction to this episode, Carol praises Betty White to the hilt. "She does the bitchy roles so great. . . . I always loved working with her." That adoration is obvious in the Q&A, where Carol in a nice white suit describes her guest as "my very dear friend, the wonderful Betty White." Carol also notes Betty's husband, Allen Ludden, is in the audience and has him take a bow while noting that "I love him very much." She additionally reveals Anthony Hopkins is her favorite actor currently and tells an aspiring singer to study and keep auditioning—Carol even does her audition of doing "The Whiffenpoof Song" solo when her partner was missing, which generates applause (she previously did it on the Sept. 23, 1968 show). After Carol notes that you can never find celebrities on Hollywood Boulevard, a woman in the audience interjects that "You can see them at the unemployment agency!" A mature gentleman asks, "What do you do with your old clothes?" and Carol responds with, "Are you asking for yourself, sir?" before they kid around a little more. Other revelations are that Carol's maiden name is Creighton, taken from her mother's maiden name, and that her crew wears jackets that read "Burnett's Bums" before this segment ends.

Before Ed goes bowling, he has to help his wife and Mama open boxes in the latter's attic when Ellen arrives. Wearing a blonde bouffant wig, Ellen apologizes to Ed for calling him a plumber when they first meet and explains that it is because every time she sees him, she thinks of septic tanks. Eunice is unhappy with the appearance of her snooty sibling but puts that aside when she sees a picture of her beloved bunny, Fluffy, who disappeared from its cage one day when she came home from school. Moving on, she and Ellen see an old Andrews Sisters record and sing it, and their imitation brings applause to the audience. But their truce ends when Ellen finds a lampshade and claims it as her own even though Eunice wants it. Ed locates other items he can sell in the store but argues with Mama, who asks for any profits made from them to be split evenly.

Eunice becomes more agitated when Ellen grabs some fine china to claim for her own because her house is better than Eunice's, at which point Ed loses it. He goes on a tirade about how the arguments exasperate him and concludes it with "I can't take three of you damn dragons!" which gets applause. Ellen then reveals to Eunice that Mama cooked Fluffy for dinner, making Eunice exclaim that they were cannibals. Ed tries to comfort his wife by threatening to hit Ellen, but she brushes him off as Eunice confronts Mama about the Fluffy tragedy. Mama discounts it, saying "It would be dead now of old age!" A dejected Eunice breaks the Tiffany lamp and china to spite Ellen, who vows people will lock up Eunice in an insane asylum before she leaves in a huff (and to applause). Eunice tells Ed to start opening more boxes, as she is going to find some treasures to use herself. Betty nails down Ellen's fake sincerity and manners perfectly in this top vignette, whose plotline will be recycled for inclusion in the 1982 special *Eunice*.

Betty turns up next as a hard-of-hearing college alumnus of Carol's, who herself is shortsighted. Both are spirited despite being the only ones at their large table in a banquet hall, and dressed in their old cheerleader outfits, they provide great harmony in singing "Ready to Begin Again," an optimistic ode to old age. This is both funny and touching.

The shows keeps rolling as Tim is hit up at a bar by Carol, who says she discovered that someone gave her a counterfeit $20 bill and wondered what to do. Tim says if she gives it to the police, they will invalidate it and not compensate her for the loss, so he suggests she pass it along to someone else. He orders drinks from Harvey the bartender and ad libs "You got any chips?" Harvey smiles tightly and answers, "No, just popcorn." A cop (Brad Trumbull) arrives as Tim plans to pay, so he takes back the $20 while the policeman notices something is odd between Tim and Carol. She tells the cop that she gave Tim the $20 bill for four $5 ones, and he gives her those dollars as the officer leaves. Tim then asks for his $5 bills back and Carol says no, and the hubbub attracts the attention of Harvey, who learns about the fake $20 and also tells Carol that the four bills Tim gave her are phony too. Tim then pays $37, all he has to compensate for the counterfeit money, before Harvey throws him out. Carol and Harvey then dump out a container of bills they had been collecting from their con game as the operative who played the cop joins them in celebrating their take. The wonderfully written sketch works like a charm, and one even bets Betty could have been just fine as the cop in it too.

The Ziegfeld tribute is an entertaining finale, with Harvey in white tails first introducing Betty, speaking with a French accent as she struts along with the male dancers. Her outfit revealed plenty of her legs, and she later said people later complimented her on her gorgeous gams on display. After her number, Tim amusingly played a drunk trying to mail a letter, followed by Vicki's bright pseudo ballet with the female dancers dressed as a bird with a Germanic accent. It ends with Carol doing a number seated on a platform with a moon crescent design that is swung wildly by the male dancers, forcing Carol to cling onto it to prevent falling. Her reactions and the presentation are much better than a similar number that appeared in the 1974 film *Mame* starring Carol's idol, Lucille Ball. She gets to come down to the stage to do the final goodbyes for the show.

When it comes to bringing something extra to *The Carol Burnett Show* as a performer, few are as all-around talented and spirited as White is in her guest shots. Her delivery, singing and dancing contribute to make this one of the greatest episodes of the series.

Dec. 18, 1976: Dick Van Dyke

Q&A; a policeman (Tim) clumsily interrogates two criminal suspects (Harvey and Vicki) and winds up hurting himself more than getting to the truth; Carol and Dick are in all-white outfits and he paints parts of her as sings about how he "colors" her world; a wallflower at a party (Carol) meets a nerd (Dick) and both discuss their daydreams to try to impress the other one; a two-act spoof of Shirley Temple's 1938 film *Little Miss Broadway* features Carol as Shirley, Harvey as Shirley's uncle, Dick as Harvey's brother, a broken-down tap dancer, and Vicki as Dick's girlfriend.

Comments: What seems to be a classic episode for the first third of this show dissolves with the inexplicable decision to remake the "Little Miss Showbiz" sketch from the Dec. 16, 1972 show. Before then, it is pretty smooth sailing starting with the Q&A, as Carol tells one man that the guests that she has had the most fun with include Dick Van Dyke, Maggie Smith, Joanne Woodward, and from her specials Beverly Sills, Alan Alda and Julie Andrews (she does not say the latter's surname). The audience is disappointed that there will be no Eunice tonight, but Carol impersonates her briefly in saying she does not want people to be tired of her. She bolsters their spirits by telling them she will be doing Shirley Temple instead, although one wonders if they would be happy if they realized it was a re-enactment of a four-year-old bit. Finally, Carol guarantees a woman asking on behalf of her husband that Farrah Fawcett will not be a guest on her show.

Tim's cross-examination of Vicki and Harvey is a setup whose physical humor is so obvious that it should not make you chuckle, but thanks to Tim's expert movements and reactions, it sparkles. Sporting an interesting Southern accent with a tough guy attitude, Tim electrocutes himself, hits himself in the face with a low-hanging lamp, and in a routine that challenges Harvey's composure, gets tape caught on pieces of paper. He finishes up by accidentally detonating shotguns held in storage, which knock him out and allow Harvey and Vicki to escape. Sadly, this is Tim's only appearance for this show.

More giggles emerge as Dick paints Carol's mouth, eyebrows and hair as she sings about how to color them based on the emotions she is feeling, based on the John Kander-Fred Ebb standard "My Coloring Book." What could have been the usual sentimental number is rendered instead as a great messy comic essay, and Carol handles the dripping paint admirably.

Dick and Carol are back in a more subdued setting next as awkward types looking for love and describing their fantasies about their own ideal mate so intently that they turn each other off. The two really click here and generate laughs sometimes just by their body language toward each other. It is on the long side but still enjoyable.

Hopes for a strong finish vanish with a nearly rote redo of "Little Miss Showbiz," with Carol and Harvey playing the same roles as in the original and the sets and outfits being similar. The headmistress role is gone so that Vicki can assume what was Bernadette's part, and Dick's portrayal of what Anthony previously did meant more tap dancing for his character. Additionally, in place of Lyle Waggoner as the producer who wants Carol, Vicki and Dick to put on a show is an unbilled Brad Trumbull. Otherwise, it is nearly a recreation of what happened previously right down to Don Crichton as an elderly judge. Tim's absence from this parody does not help.

Even at the finale, Carol impersonates Shirley as she sings "It's Time to Say So Long" like she did in 1972. At least Ernie Anderson acknowledges verbally during the credits that the sketch was by Larry Siegel and Stan Hart. The best one can hope from this is that Dick had a great time doing the show, as shown by his enthusiasm at the end, and that "Little Miss Showbiz" did well enough to encourage the show to rehire Larry as a writer next season. Otherwise, this is a missed opportunity at greatness.

Dec. 25, 1976: Family Show

* Tudball takes Wiggins to lunch to celebrate National Secretaries Week, but she has little interest in the affair and a snippy waiter (Harvey) does not help matters for Tudball either; Carol performs "The Dolly Song"; a bar serves as an unlikely setting for two married sophisticates to become interested in each other; Carol stars in a gender-altered spoof of the recent miniseries *Rich Man, Poor Man*

that covers 30 years of life events in less than a quarter hour; everyone participates in a medley of "Money, Money" from *Cabaret* and joins in singing some Christmas carols.

Comments: This Yuletide has two very amusing highlights. The restaurant skit with Tudball includes great ad libs by Tim calling Harvey "stork legs" and threatening to give him a five-cent tip while enduring an unimpressed Wiggins as he treats her to lunch. "Rich Lady, Broke Lady" has Carol as a protagonist weary as she ages amid enduring much travail in her life. For the rest, "The Dolly Song" might have triggered memories among longtime viewers, as Carol sang it on the Dec. 15, 1971 show. This is one of the rare programs of this season not available in full form on the trading circuit, in archives or on DVD as of this writing.

Jan. 1, 1977: Repeat of Oct. 16, 1976 show

Jan. 8, 1977: Pre-empted by special *Super Night at the Super Bowl*

Jan. 15, 1977: Glen Campbell

Q&A; Tim suffers the after effects a swine flu vaccine by acting like a pig, to Carol and Harvey's consternation; Glen performs "Southern Nights"; Carol attempts to keep Vicki from seeing that the latter's husband (Harvey) is at another table with a blonde; an office supplies boss (Harvey) dictates a letter to his secretary (Carol), who is injured often by the company's products; Glen and Carol mock the promotional pose for *A Star is Born*; Vicki and Harvey have an interesting elevator encounter; Tim and Carol are slobs living together; Glen sings a medley with Carol, joined by the dancers.

Comments: Nearly six years after his cameo on Feb. 1, 1971, Glen Campbell finally makes his full-fledged guest debut on the series, and every bit of this show is wonderful from start to finish. Even the Q&A has one of its greatest moments. After Glen's name elicits screams of approval from the audience, Carol reveals she and Dick Van Dyke will be performing *Same Time Next Year* in summer stock and shows her roots to prove she is not a natural redhead. And then a woman asks her if Bea Arthur is in the audience, or rather Bea Arthur as Maude. The latter tells Carol she has been mistaken for Bea and loving it, and then says she wants to sing a song. Her name is Carrie McCann, and she requests the orchestra play "You Made Me Love You" in the key of G. Carol cracks up at her audacious request. Even better, Carrie nails it. Carol joins her midway to sing along in harmony, and the audience loves it, especially when Carol hits the wrong note and Carrie says, "You screwed it up!" It's a top launch for a great show.

The strong start has Carol, Harvey and Tim celebrating the latter's successful test of a swine flu—and Carol and Tim's upcoming marriage—at a restaurant when Tim suddenly sports a snout and tells the waitress (Vicki) he wants a bushel of corn. "You want that on a plate or in a trough?" she shoots back at him. Carol and Harvey try to play it cool, but when Tim starts snorting, Carol finds she has to speak pig Latin for him to understand. It sounds worthy of groans, but everyone plays it earnestly, and seeing Tim act like an animal is always good for a laugh, particularly when he gets a banana and eats only the peel (that ad lib cracks up Harvey). Tim eventually learns his condition and leaves, even though Harvey tells him it is just a temporary side effect of the drug. It is also contagious, so when Carol drinks out of the same glass as Tim's, she gets a snout as well. Silliness in the spirit of fun is a hallmark of this series, and this sketch bears (or maybe pigs) it out beautifully.

Next, Glen performs his last major crossover hit, "Southern Nights," just as it is being released. He plays it live, with nice close-ups of him fingering his guitar, and better yet, it has more verses than the single release and includes his falsetto to boot.

What follows is more top broad comedy, as Carol keeps tripping Tim the waiter to divert Vicki from seeing the latter's husband (Harvey) at a nearby table with a blonde. "You aren't going to do this till you get it right, are you?" a disgusted Tim tells Carol after her second effort. After some more machinations by Carol, Vicki finally spots Harvey, and Carol learns that the blonde is Harvey's younger sister. A mortified Carol apologizes to them and she attempts to pay for the damage she did to Tim, who backs away from her in fear—and gets tripped up again. Once again, the cast plays this smoothly all around.

The laughs remain strong as an elderly Carol endures a string of calamities while taking a letter from her boss (Harvey). Her pencil breaks, her coffee cup has no bottom, and when she hits the return on her typewriter, the carriage flies out the window. When she checks figures for Harvey on a calculator, it explodes and knocks her back into a chair that collapses. She encounters a file cabinet that is stuck and breaks her foot through a wall in trying to pry it open before its contents pop out on her. Carol finds the right file Harvey needs and places it on a table, which falls down. Finally, she pulls down a light to illuminate the office, only to have it pull her up and have her hanging as Harvey leaves. Throughout it all, Harvey is wonderfully oblivious to the proceedings, while Carol masterfully handles every piece of slapstick.

Glen finally acts in the show, and it is a stitch. Resembling a shirtless Kris Kristofferson and Barbra Streisand, Glen and Carol are stuck in the duo's iconic pose from *A Star is Born* because a 2-year-old super glued them together. The dog gets pasted on Glen's leg too, and Carol tells him to be careful not to wake the pet up. When Carol's husband (voice of Harvey) arrives home, she tells Glen, "Act natural," but their attempt to hide fails as Harvey calls for the dog and drags them along. This is appropriately short and sweet, as is the next bit, where a formal and reserved Vicki and Harvey get on an elevator and instantly dance wildly when a song plays before the doors open and they part ways.

The last sketch has a shaggy Carol wearing rainbow socks ironing clothes when her slovenly husband (Tim) arrives in their apartment and compares her to a reptile. The insults fly fast between the two, and Carol ad libs a basketball score that makes Tim break character. He finally declares he is fed up and leaving her—only to return and ask if she wants to go to a movie with him. This is more solid fun.

The finale matches the excitement previously generated, with Glen showing his talents playing many instruments on familiar songs. First Glen plays "Walk Right In" on a ukulele and references Carol, who joins in to sing her own lyrics. He follows that with a six-string guitar to do his old hit

"Wichita Lineman" exquisitely, and Carol tries to sing and strum the guitar to keep up. Glen has Carol try to play "Classical Gas" with him as the dancers emerge, the men in all black and the women in yellow skirts. Carol sings a bluesy "I Got Rhythm" with Glen accompanying her, and then we unexpectedly get a polka from Glen while Carol dances with all the men. Finally, Glen offers "Baby Face" on the banjo and "Sugarfoot Rag" on the guitar, with Carol adding some vocals and the dancers participating as well. This very satisfyingly concludes the show.

This episode had enough entertainment to fill two shows. It is a shame this was Glen's only star appearance on the series, but as it is, it definitely was worth the wait.

Jan. 22, 1977: Family Show

Q&A; Tim and Carol are a married couple at odds when he receives a phone call late at night and claims it was nothing; Carol portrays a woman desperately eager to go to a party at the apartment next door; the dancers perform to "Nadia's Theme"; "The Recital" features the regulars in an unconventional concert; Vicki tries to build up Tim's confidence as a vacuum cleaner salesman; "The Late Late Show" sends up the 1953 Joan Crawford vehicle *Torch Song* with Carol in the lead as a demanding Broadway star and Harvey as her nearsighted pianist who loves her.

Comments: This episode displays the mature comic excellence of Carol and her regulars possess, yet also provides disquieting hints that the series had run its course. None of the latter is evident in the animated Q&A, where a girl asking Carol how to overcome stage fright and the hostess saying that when she was auditioning in New York City, a friend told her to imagine everyone in the audience sitting on the toilet. Carol obliges a child's request for a shout out to Carol's fans at Rosemont High School in San Diego. A woman with a Southern voice cracks up Carol by exclaiming, "I'd like to know where the hell you got the idea for the Ed-Eunice skit!" Finally, she deflects a comment from one gentleman who asked, "Weren't you a lot heavier when you worked with Garry Moore?" "No!" she quickly responds. "You had a fat television set!" After saying she was thin and gained some weight, she concludes, "I know, you got me mixed up with Raquel Welch!"

The first scripted bit of business has Tim and Carol in single beds for blocking the scene and not censorship, as a phone in the nightstand between them provides the source of conflict. Tim answers the late night call and then hangs up. Carol asks who it was, he tells her no one said anything and it was probably a wrong number. A suspicious Carol thinks it could be a signal to Tim to confuse her, maybe from a girlfriend waiting outside to make a rendezvous. Tim assures her she is overreacting and tells her to go to sleep. Once she does that, he gets out of bed and prepares to leave when Carol cocks a shotgun and threatens him with "You open that door and I'll blow you to (laughter drowns out the rest)." Quick and funny, the skit does what it needs to do in the right amount of time.

Next, Carol is in curlers and pajamas when she hears a party next door. She calls the building operator to connect her with the adjoining apartment, and she tells the host next door she needs ice and asks to borrow some from him. When he says yes, she hangs up and changes quickly in a formal outfit, but the man next door (Joel Lawrence) thwarts her plans by bringing ice over himself. Trying another strategy, Carol calls the host and pretends to be the hotel operator to say that Carol's mother has tried calling her daughter but could not get through, so can she use your phone instead? This prompts the return of the host, who invites Carol to come over, but her phone rings as she plans to leave, and yes, it really is her mother calling her. Then Harvey rings her doorbell, thinking that her apartment was hosting the party. She takes advantage of the situation by claiming her date canceled on taking her to the event and asking Harvey if she could go with him instead. Unfortunately, Harvey is a lecher who promises he could show her a better time than the party. He attacks her and she decks him, and as luck would have it, when he recuperates leaning on the next door apartment's door, someone opens it and lets him in. Suddenly Tim comes out from the back room in an undershirt and tells Carol, "Hey honey, the ball game's over. You wanna come to bed?"

This near-perfect sketch has a jarring note occurs at the end when a dejected Carol turns on the TV, hears herself singing "It's Time to Say So Long" and in response mockingly tugs her ear, yells "Shut up!" and throws a glass that destroys the TV set. It probably seemed funny to the show's creative personnel to make a joke at its expense, but in doing so, it implied the viewers that while there are parties going on Saturday nights, you are content to stay home and watch Carol. This slight probably was unintentional, but it hurt this show's credibility and simply was unneeded for another otherwise fine piece.

Next is one of the show's best dance routines ever, with the men in red jumpsuits and the women in pink gowns moving on a pink set to "Nadia's Theme," a song most Americans know better as the theme to *The Young and the Restless*, then in its fourth year on the air. Peter Matz and the orchestra provide an intensity matched by the dancers, with some nice slow-motion effects added to create a vivid, memorably atmospheric number.

Harvey and Tim walk out in tuxes and Carol and Vicki in black gowns before they assume their positions on stage to make a quite discordant noise. Vicki trills off key, Carol plunks on wrong notes of a piano, Harvey squeaks on a recorder and Tim randomly plucks on a harp in solos before they all join together to make a racket at the end, then bow and leave. While amusing enough, it recalls what Howard Morris said in *The Box*, an oral history of early TV, about how he, Sid Caesar, Imogene Coca and Carl Reiner had done so much on *Your Show of Shows* that they thought they had reached the point where all they could do was just come out and sit on a stage. One surmises something similar hit Mitzie Welch, who wrote this as a spoof. It got some laughs, but this group should be doing something more creative at this stage of working together so long. (The bit also had one man leave a taping in a huff, not getting it was a joke, according to Ken Welch.)

The final comedy-only skit has Tim so flustered and lacking confidence in selling a vacuum cleaner to a housewife (Vicki) that he cries thinking that she will not buy it. He is so discouraged that Vicki winds up trying to sell him the unit and even apologizing to him for taking up his time. This switch play is nicely written and presented.

The ending has Carol scarily perfect as Joan Crawford starring in "Torchy Song" as a demanding Broadway actress, intimidating her stage manager (Don Crichton) and even her dance partner (Randy Doney), who she has removed from her upcoming production. She gives the same dismissive treatment to Harvey when he arrives, not realizing he is a former critic who loved her even before she developed her trademark pose of extending her legs. When Carol's maid (Vicki) convinces the star she needs a man in her life, she romances Harvey. At one point while romancing Harvey, Carol bobbles a line, causing him to ad lib, "I can't see, and you can't talk!" They get back on track and sing a duet, but the lyrics about her becoming a mother creep her out, and she has Harvey put away in the piano by the end. This is a lively spoof.

At the conclusion, Carol places her wig on Tim's head and peels off her fake long eyebrows to make them resemble a mustache above her mouth. This nice, light moment reflects the camaraderie and talent on the show despite its few flaws. A still of the quartet doing the kick line is one of the most circulated pictures taken during the show's run.

Jan. 29, 1977: Rock Hudson, Steve Lawrence

Q&A; Mrs. Wiggins has a date for lunch (Rock) while separated for her husband, and both the circumstances and the boyfriend astound Mr. Tudball; Steve performs "You Take My Heart Away"; married news anchors (Carol and Rock) read reports that act as double entendres about his affair and her discovery of it; Tim, Vicki, Harvey and Carol present "In the Mood" by imitating chickens; Carol and Steve exhibit dubious behavior as Harvey and Vicki consider them to serve as their children's godparents; a salute to Jule Styne uses his music in a 1940s movies setting with everyone except Tim.

Comments: Though she always projected as best possible an air of excitement regarding her guests, Carol's body language and general demeanor could indicate when she was really enjoying herself, and that is the case here, in one of the best showcases for two of her favorites. We see them in action quickly, for the Q&A only has a few questions, such as if Carol knew if any of her daughters wanted to act (she did not, but said she would encourage them). As for another query, "Is my hair naturally red? Hey, OK, don't go away, we've got a big show for you!"

The strong start has Tudball complaining about his Japanese hairpiece until he hears Wiggins wondering where to go to lunch now they she has split up with her husband. That startles him, but he has her go back to work, and she sharpens pencils by wiggling her butt, drawing applause even though the bit had been done several times before (for the first, see Nov. 6, 1967). "It's like the aerial view of the Black Sea," quips Tudball. Wiggins' boyfriend (Rock) arrives early so she has him stand in the corner and sharpen pencils too. Tudball is stunned by Rock's looks—"I'd like to borrow that and go to the beach for a couple of hours!"—and asks him what he sees in Wiggins, who Rock calls "Bun Buns." Rock says he realizes he is unworthy of Wiggins, which confounds Tudball, especially when he learns Rock is a successful franchise owner. Meanwhile, Wiggins gets a call from her husband to reunite and she agrees, so she has Tudball break the bad news to Rock. Learning that they are history, Rock walks on his knees to plead with Wiggins, but she is adamant. Then a blonde woman (an unbilled actress) shows up to ask a question, and Rock goes immediately after her. Tudball offers to take Wiggins to lunch instead, and she agrees—only to accidentally lock him in the office. This sketch shines from start to finish.

Wearing a leisure suit, Steve lip syncs to a song that was a minor disco entry for Laura Green. It is an upbeat contemporary number, and as such, it is one of his more magnetic presentations, even if he is only mouthing what he sang earlier.

Rock appears next with Carol in another great skit, this time as married co-anchors whose first lines of their stories indicate how they are really feeling, as Carol learns Rock has been cheating on her with his secretary. He eventually apologizes, but Carol uses her platform to squeeze out a public promise of a new mink coat and diamond ring to atone for his misdeed. Every word has great comic impact and meaning here, and Carol and Rock wring out all the laughs possible from it.

Following this is a silly but amusing lip sync by the regulars dressed in formal outfits to a re-make of Glenn Miller's 1940 hit. Here they mimic chicken clucking noises made on record by Ray Stevens (in a single that made the top 40 briefly in early 1977 under the fake group name of Hen-house Five Plus Too). The chuckles continue with Steve's only sketch of the night, as he and Carol fake arguments about each other's families and personal habits in an effort to make their unwitting fellow couple (Vicki and Harvey) think they are the wrong persons to take care of the latter's children as godparents. The plan backfires because Harvey and Vicki tell them that listening to their bickering reminded them of the way they act home with their children. This is relatively short and sweet and hits the mark nicely.

For the finale, the male dancers are dressed as sailors singing "Everything's Coming Up Roses," followed by fellow sailors Rock, Harvey and Steve doing "Together." Harvey reunites with Vicki, his long-lost flame, and they present "It's Been a Long, Long Time," while new romantic couple Steve and Carol exclaim about their situation that "It's Magic." Rock is a bookworm who offers a decent version of "People" to indicate his solitude, and an interested Carol, seeing Steve attracted to one of the girl dancers, offers to him that "I'm Just a Little Girl from Little Rock." "You Are Woman, I Am Man" Rock sings in response, but before they become too passionate, Vicki singing "The Party's Over" to Harvey indicates that the shore leave has ended for the sailors and they all must return. Familiar music and a compelling storyline make this one pop.

At the end, Carol seems giddy with her time with both men, as does the audience, as there are whistles in appreciation of a stellar outing. Unfortunately, relatively few watched this show originally, as Part 7 of the miniseries *Roots* dominated the night with a 42.3 rating, placing it among the 100 highest-rated TV shows ever. Ironically, one of that production's stars will be a guest on Carol's show four weeks later—see Feb. 26, 1977.

Feb. 5, 1977: Helen Reddy

Q&A; Wiggins is caught in the middle of an argument between Mr. Tudball and his wife (Vicki) on his gambling habits; Helen accompanies the dancers to present "Feeling Too Good Today Blues"; a woman who has recovered from a nervous breakdown (Carol) faces a challenge when confronted with her husband's habits; the regulars audition to be Helen's backup group; Harvey and Tim are con men looking to score action from two innocent women from Little Rock, Arkansas (Carol and Vicki) arriving at a Los Angeles bus station; Helen and Carol perform a medley of nearly 50 hits from the 1960s.

Comments: With Helen not singing her hits and sketches having variable quality, this show is somewhat of a letdown, although still pretty enjoyable overall. The Q&A has a man ask about a recent incident on the ABC daytime soap opera *All My Children* where one character, Nigel Fargate, a charlatan physician, claimed he would be on Carol's show. Carol says she loved that bit and then gossips about more plot developments, which leads the crew to turn off the studio lights temporarily in an unsuccessful effort to stop her. As a bonus, she notes that Francesca James and Peter White, who play star-crossed lovers on the soap, are in the audience and has them stand up and chat some.

The show starts strong with the hilarious introduction of Mrs. Tudball, who refused to let her husband sleep at home because he lost track of time playing cards. He tells Wiggins that is why he had to sleep in the office all night. Wiggins could care less about his dilemma and sharpens pencils. As her posterior wiggles, Mr. Tudball quips, "That reminds me, I got to get my tires rotated." When Mrs. Tudball arrives, he barks, "It's good to hear the clippity clop of your orthopedic shoes again!" She threatens to divorce him after fourteen years of marriage while dropping choice jokes at the expense of him and Wiggins. Mr. Tudball swears he will not play cards again, but a call comes through, and Wiggins relays that it was a man calling to confirm plans for tonight's game. Mrs. Tudball hits her husband with her purse as this raucous installment comes to a close.

Helen's number after this is lively as well, as she does a smooth tap number with the dancers in a pool hall setting. Unfortunately, what follows is a skit in dubious taste today, as Carol goes batty while Harvey repeatedly engages in baby talk, slurping, loud laughing and tapping his fingers during lunch. His behavior leads her to pull off a tablecloth and remove the wig of another patron, forcing a waiter (Don Crichton) to throw her out. Vicki then joins Harvey to celebrate driving Carol back to a sanitarium for at least six months so they can continue their affair. As contemporary sensitivities toward mental problems are more acute now than in 1976, it lessens the enjoyment of this in that light.

Next, Carol, Harvey, Vicki and Tim offer to be backup singers for Helen as she performs "Leave Me Alone (Ruby Red Dress)." Their "ooo, ooo, ooo" and singing of the title phrase are off key and mistimed, as is their dancing, and Helen stops the song midway to tell them they are awful. That thrills the quartet, as they tell here it is the nicest thing anyone ever said about them. This is mildly amusing but rather meaningless overall.

The last skit has Tim and Harvey pretending to be film producers spotting the visiting Carol and Vicki as new talent that they want to audition (actually sleep with) at a hotel room. The men's plans go awry when Stan Mazin tells the girls that all the luggage has been picked up from the bus that dropped them off. Without their bags, the women have to money to pay for a hotel room, so Tim and Harvey scrounge up $72 to help them pay for their rooms, and the women tell the men they will meet them there. All leave, but the women return and pretend to be coming off another bus so that they can actually con men out of money and not the other way. This is decently executed but does not really spark.

The end medley is the most jam-packed collection of tunes in one sitting shown on the series. For nearly fifteen minutes, Helen and Carol singly and together offer dozens of hits popularized in the preceding decade, along with a few ringers from 1971 that somehow made the cut ("If," "Put Your Hand in the Hand" and "(Where Do I Begin) Love Story"). After playfully switching their roles to do the introduction, the two ladies in black pantsuits with sparkling studs on one corner launch into "Sgt. Pepper's Lonely Hearts Club Band" and do mostly lighter numbers, including three hits by Glen Campbell and several other Beatles songs. They even throw in the theme from *Sesame Street* and "A Spoonful of Sugar" before reprising "Sgt. Pepper's Lonely Hearts Club Band" at the end. Due to the familiarity of these numbers and their speedy presentation, this is a mostly breezy spot to watch and appreciate despite the length. Even so, it will be surpassed by what Carol does with Eydie Gorme for the finale in next week's show.

Feb. 12, 1977: Eydie Gorme

Tudball teaches Wiggins how to play blackjack before she goes to Las Vegas—and regrets doing so; Eydie sings "Kiss Today Goodbye" from *A Chorus Line*; Carol is a woman whose husband is kidnapped and becomes more theatrical as she recounts her situation to a reporter for the nightly news (Harvey); Eunice is excited about being invited to sing "Feelings" on *The Gong Show* despite the trepidations Mama has about her daughter's appearance; Eydie and Carol do a medley of more than twenty songs popularized in the movies over the last fifty years, joined by the dancers.

Comments: Despite having no mention at the top of the show and being in no sketches, this is Eydie's finest hour on the series. Her booming vocals are perfect for her material, and the skits surrounding her work are just as strong, beginning with Wiggins beating Tudball in cards much the same way Judy Holliday unexpectedly won gin rummy in *Born Yesterday*. So naive that she is unsure if she could look at her cards, Wiggins nonetheless wins three hands and costs Tudball money. Worried about his losses, Tudball pleads for Wiggins not to tell his wife he lost at gambling with her. Wiggins agrees—but only if she gets two weeks of vacation in Vegas. This is smart, solid comedy.

Eydie's first number is one of the series' best solo turns ever. She nails the song's emotion perfectly on every note and gets deserved whistles from the audience for her work. Carol follows it with a bit where she supposedly misreads headlines from a gossip magazine indicating Steve and Eydie are breaking up. It's trivial but short and acceptable.

Carol shines next as a cop (Brad Trumbull) and then a TV interviewer (Harvey) ask her questions about her husband's recent abduction. Everyone plays it somber as Carol recounts her situation and cries. But when the sound engineer (Stan Mazin) says the level was wrong, forcing the interview to be redone, Carol comes off as less emotional, so Harvey interrupts and asks her to try once more. She puts more of herself into it, then tells Harvey she wants one more time because she can really nail her performance, and she puts on makeup and reacts more broadly than before. Carol's transformation from timid wife to determined media starlet within minutes is complete as she takes control of Harvey's microphone, looks straight into the camera and so dramatically pleads with her kidnappers to release her husband that the audience applauds her work. It ends with the crew leaving and a star struck Carol telling a friend to look for her on the news that night. This ranks as one of her best acting jobs ever.

She manages to top even that in her next bit, as Eunice ignore her family and spends $500 on a new green gown and tiara to appear on *The Gong Show*. Enthused at the potential the show offers her "class A act," Eunice performs her routine before Mama and Ed, complete with a dramatic monologue inserted in the middle of "Feelings," the notorious sappy hit ballad of 1976. She heads to Hollywood when Mama calls her backstage and implores her to at least change part of the monologue, but Eunice is determined to pursue her dream, and she tells Ed on the phone that she is never coming home. A cut to *The Gong Show* set has host Chuck Barris introducing Raytown's Eunice to an unimpressed panel of Jamie Farr, Jaye P. Morgan and Allen Ludden, making this the only appearance on *The Carol Burnett Show* for all except Ludden. All three gong her, and in a breathtaking shot, the lights around Eunice go dark and her disappointed face is frozen as it zooms out of vision, providing a poignant and affecting ending to Eunice's continuing woes. "Feelings" will appear on the show for laughs again on Jan. 1, 1978.

A spirited medley starts with "The Way We Were" by Eydie and "Raindrops Keep Falling On My Head" by Carol and goes back in time to mostly familiar tunes. They sing solos and duets as the dancers join them as background assistance for several occasions—for example, one is dressed as Mary Poppins as the two do "Chim Chim Cheree," and the ensemble dresses up in greasepaint as both ladies offer "Be a Clown." All the vocals are great, but particularly outstanding are Eydie's Spanish lyrics to "The Continental" and Carol's reprise of her Shirley Temple impression for "On the Good Ship Lollipop" and "Animal Crackers in My Soup." The energy and enthusiasm runs a good ten minutes and climaxes with "Hooray for Hollywood," which at the end cuts from the studio to a filmed bit where Eydie and Carol sing the ending from the Hollywood hills sign as the shot zooms out and away on a helicopter. This jaw-dropping visual capper is so distinctive that it is used as the last segment on musical guests for the show's 1978 finale.

Carol's Number One fan Kathy Clements has called this medley her favorite number ever from the show and remembers the extra efforts required of Carol and Eydie for the final shot. "The day when they taped the show and that was the finale, they put them in painters getups, lowered them down the hill and then they had what Carol said were combat boots to walk there. You can see the two ropes they used on TV."

This show is so jam-packed with goodies that Carol has no time to sing "It's Time to Say So Long" at the end. Regardless, as one of the series' greatest and most elaborate shows, this earned an Emmy nomination for the writers and a win for director Dave Powers.

Feb. 19, 1977: Pre-empted by *The Grammy Awards* special

Feb. 26, 1977: Ben Vereen

Q&A; Tim is helped by Carol in writing a eulogy for their late friend, Charlie, and learns more about him than he expected; Ben performs "If You Believe" with two children in a forest with dancing trees and other costumed creatures; a lawyer eating lunch (Ben) finds himself in the crosshairs between a bickering couple (Carol and Harvey); "As the Stomach Turns" depicts an insurance agent (Tim) looking for Marian's daughter, who he believes has faked her death for the payout; Carol and Ben offer a medley of more than twenty songs written by Harold Arlen.

Comments: Ben Vereen is Carol's first guest star to receive a standing ovation, thanks largely to his Emmy-nominated starring role on the miniseries *Roots* a few weeks earlier. (Laurence Olivier earned one on Oct. 2, 1976, but he was only in the audience.) Carol introduces him after thanking an audience member for congratulating her on a recent win of a People's Choice Award, and she points out Ben's wife and children in the audience.

It is a warm start for a show that oddly works best in the segments without Ben, including the first skit. Encountering writer's block while working on a tribute to his deceased pal, Charlie, Tim recounts to Carol how much his old business partner helped him, beginning with getting him drafted to serve in the war and earn a Purple Heart and a metal plate in his head. He remembers how when he would return home from business trips that Charlie would be at home to meet him, and how much his son with Carol looks like Charlie. As evidence mounts that Carol had an affair with Charlie, the topper arrives when Tim notes how Charlie always gave boxes of candy to his girlfriend, then opens up a closet with a bunch of such boxes swarming out. Finally catching on, Tim announces he knows how to finish his eulogy. Brandishing a gun at Carol, he says "Say hello to Charlie!" as she stares in horror into the camera. This is a rather dark but effective end to a funny sketch.

Wearing a bowler and a hot pink and red outfit, Ben moves well but has to do a sticky song of self-confidence to a boy and girl scared about the animated forest life they see around them. This production never connects as strongly as it could have if the dancers were not in costumes in a juvenile-themed sketch. Stan Mazin notes that whenever a dancing star such as Ben Vereen or Gwen Verdon came on the series, Ernie Flatt tended to favor silly, lightweight dance numbers because he was intimidated and felt this was the best way to showcase them without trying to top serious work they had done with other choreographers such as Bob Fosse. This routine lends justification to that assertion.

Ben is wasted again in the next bit, as he has to join Carol and Harvey at the only free seat in a crowded restaurant and must endure her sniping about Harvey's mother-in-law and his complaints about her attitude. Revealing that he is a divorce lawyer, Ben refuses to be hired by Carol in favor of setting the couple straight. He tells Harvey to get over his obsession with his mother and Carol to lose her insecurity, prompting both to think his advice stinks and leave him alone. Harvey and Carol's complaints are as irritating to hear as they claim, Ben has virtually no humorous rejoinders, and the result is a nag to endure.

Thankfully one of the best "As the Stomach Turns" installments ever follows. The oldest insurance agent in Canoga Falls (Tim) trips on Marian's carpet and falls on top of her chair before telling her he is here to collect $50,000 back from a payout because his company believes Marian's recently deceased daughter is alive. Determined to find her, Tim enters a barn painting on the wall and sticks his head out from the hayloft until a pitchfork pokes him while he searches. Enter Mother Marcus (Harvey), "Canoga Falls' leading yenta," as Marian notes, who pledges to help Marian communicate with her daughter from the great beyond. "I've become a medium," Mother Marcus says. "Really? I would have guessed an extra large!" responds Marian to applause. After ad libbing a lyric from "Somewhere" from *West Side Story* that cracks up Carol, Mother Marcus does prompt the arrival of Marian's daughter (Vicki). She reveals that she had bionic parts but hates having powerful legs so much that she stomps the floor in frustration. This causes Tim to announce the barn is on fire, with eggs falling out from chickens and a miniature horse kicking him on the nose. Suddenly he and Marian's daughter both have amnesia, leading into the "Tune in next time" bit which includes this question about Mother Marcus: "Will she be arrested when it is learned she secretly wears men's clothing?" Harvey's dismayed look and wagging of his finger is just as spot-on and amusing as the rest of this sketch.

The show ends anticlimactically. The finale's hook is Ben loves Harold Arlen's happy songs while Carol wants do the bluesy numbers. Stretched across ten long minutes without much fancy footwork from Ben, it is a drag, especially since the series had featured many Arlen tunes previously. The lack of the dancers hurts a lot, as well as in the closing, where they are nowhere to be seen. But Ben appeared happy and did do the show the next season (see Nov. 19, 1977), so at least he found this installment fulfilling.

March 5, 1977: Hal Linden

Funt and Mundane's play, *A Deadly Affair*, is so popular that they are booked to perform it at the enormous, 25,016-seat Astro Bowl and find they have to yell and exaggerate their movements to compensate; Hal sings "I Won't Last A Day Without You," the Carpenters' 1974 hit, in a brown padded armchair; Harvey is a ship's pilot and Tim is the old man captain who has to take charge as there is an iceberg dead ahead; a two-part parody of *Show Boat* features Hal romancing Carol in the central plot amid much singing and dancing by the other regulars.

Comments: There is no Q&A nor "It's Time to Say So Long" at the end in favor of four rather long (but thankfully not longish, except for the finale) set pieces. The last Funt and Mundane sketch shows them enacting their drama straight and producing headlines in *Variety* about their success. They fail to realize until talking with the stage manager (Don Crichton) that their next performance is on a huge outdoor stage—Dave Powers does an excellent job in conveying this rock concert feeling by showing a proscenium framing them to appear like specks far away in some shots. Funt clomps while moving around before Mundane arrives, and they have to shout their dialogue to each other. They get winded from walking, a jet flying overhead drowns out Funt's speech, and a moth invades Mundane's costume before a windstorm arises and knocks the set and their clothes and wigs off the stage. It is a fittingly overdone scenario for two characters who have comically endured virtually every calamity known to any theatrical performer.

Hal Linden performs the Carpenters' 1974 hit to applause, though one wonders if he could have done better with a Broadway tune, given his New York stage experience. Carol offers afterward to have him do a Q&A with the audience, but she takes up his time describing his background instead. The moment is contrived but tolerably funny.

Bigger laughs are in store when Tim pops up as the Old Man at the helm of a ship with Harvey, his dedicated help who has to tell him that it is a picture of the ocean he is observing and not the sea itself. After repeatedly saluting each other, Tim gets hit in the head when Stan Mazin opens the door to warn of an iceberg. Tim responds first by falling asleep on the telegraph machine, then getting his face stuck in the ship's speaker, which he pulls out and pretends he is an elephant with a trunk, cracking up Harvey. The physical comedy becomes more elaborate as Tim takes over the life-sized wheel from Harvey and spins vertically on it (and wins some applause for his efforts). The radical maneuver saves the ship, but Stan returns to warn that a tidal wave is imminent. Hearing that, Tim opens the door and is knocked off his feet by the torrent of water gushing down on him. Tim has claimed that his fall was real and he had no idea so much water was coming at him. Whatever the case, this is another top drawer Harvey-Tim pairing.

The bright but overextended "Riverboat" musical's high points include good vocalizing by Carol on the "Can't Help Lovin' That Man" takeoff and an elaborate, realistic dockside set. For a spoof on its other famous song, here called "Old Mister Sippi Flows Inexorably," Tim starts off singing it only to be swamped by the backup singers vocally and visually, another great moment. Not making it to air was a duet by Vicki with Hal called "Pretend" where the arpeggio on the piano starting her off began at a higher note than in rehearsal, leading Vicki to trill at the top of her lungs to compensate it and Hal to grimace. They had to redo it, but the blooper did make the 2001 *Show Stoppers* special.

Otherwise, this spotty affair pales mightily compared to the first *Show Boat* parody the series offered on Jan. 15, 1968. As a program where the humor outshone the music, this should have featured Hal's comic acting to better effect.

March 12, 1977: Pre-empted by special *Shirley MacLaine: Where Do We Go From Here?*

March 19, 1977: Neil Sedaka

Q&A; Harvey is a man waiting for an IRS audit who puts the moves on Carol; Neil sings "The Hungry Years"; Carol is a housewife bedeviled by people from TV commercials in her kitchen; the old man (Tim) is a temporary baggage handler who struggles to load suitcases to the chagrin of his impatient boss (Harvey); Carol is the exhausted wife of Harvey, who is trying to make a good impression with his stuffy, elderly boss (Tim) and the latter's spouse (Vicki); the cast and dancers perform different versions of the hit Neil co-wrote, "Love Will Keep Us Together."

Comments: Although he does not sing any recent hits, Neil Sedaka is a welcome presence, offering a fresh face that is game to even act during the commercials spoof in this winning effort. Both Carol and the audience appear enthused for him to be there during the Q&A, where Carol explains the origins of Tudball and Wiggins and agrees with someone says she is twenty-three years old. To a man who wondered if Carol was as sexy as Farrah Fawcett, then starring on *Charlie's Angels* on ABC, she comically scoffs, "Can you look at me and ask that question? Who's Farrah Fawcett?!" Carol reveals she will be doing *Same Time Next Year* in Pasadena next month with Dick Van Dyke and recalls her cameo on *All My Children* a year ago, hilariously accompanied by organ music played spontaneously as she describes her role. She also says Agnes Nixon, who created *All My Children*, is backstage as well, but will not spill any secrets about the upcoming plots. After telling someone Ernie Anderson is still her announcer and that she is willing to appear at the University of Southern California, the cross-town rival of her alma mater, UCLA, Carol ends the Q&A to go into a top skit.

In an IRS office run by Vicki, Harvey turns on the smarm as he makes the moves on her, telling her his name is Artie Bragg, spelled with two G's, like two grand. "And that's what you are—too grand!" he purrs to a disinterested Vicki, who tells him to sit for his appointment. Espying Carol in the waiting room, he uses the same come-on line he did with Vicki and tries to impress her by saying she reminds him of Grace Kelly, "the queen of France." She ignores him until he intrigues her by telling how she can save a few dollars by knowing where to hide her income. Giggling, she has him tell her more, and he boasts of having capital gains schemes, keeping two sets of books and doing phony write-offs. Suddenly Don Crichton tells Carol her break is over, and she learns from Vicki that her next appointment for reviewing an audit is Artie Bragg, with two G's, like two grand. "Well, that's how much it's going to cost you!" she coos to Harvey as he lamely walks behind her, realizing he has been caught dead. This is superbly written and acted.

Neil plays the title cut of his recent album at a piano before saying he has to leave right after the finale, so Carol offers him to sign her guest book now. He just writes his name, which makes Carol prod him to add more until she ends up signing for him and saying that she has a great body too. This bit is a little overextended but pleasant enough.

The advertising send-up by having people bother Carol is a little less effective than in previous installments but still has a few choice moments. Neil shoots her for squeezing tissue paper, Tim gets drunk while cleaning out her sink, Vicki constantly asks her to compare two products and Harvey forces her to call someone. The best joke is the last. Everyone including the dancers sing about looking for the union label, which was a popular campaign at the time, as Neil, Harvey, Tim and Vicki remove Carol's clothes down to her blouse—and Tim even rips off her wig!

The Old Man sketch similarly is not quite the best of its kind but enjoyable nonetheless. Tim first has problems attaching tickets on the tarmac to the luggage, at one point stamping himself as well and proclaiming, "I'm going to Cleveland!" He slowly drags one small bag down from a cart and has difficulty lifting onto the conveyer belt leading up to the plane's belly. The Old Man has the direction wrong one time, sending the suitcase down to land on his foot instead and getting his tie stuck a second time that nearly strangles him as the luggage goes up the ramp. A disgusted Harvey rescues him and tell him he will throw the suitcases to Tim to load them up quickly on the belt. The first case Harvey flips Tim's way knocks Tim over onto going up the ramp along with the bag. Harvey tries to get Tim back down, and Tim tries to scamper up the conveyer belt to avoid his enraged coworker before he accepts his fate and comes down in a crouch like he is about to make a ski jump. Once on the ground, he hears a whistle blow, says it is lunch time and drops a suitcase on Harvey's head, knocking the latter out as he falls onto the ramp as it goes upward. This is a little ragged in execution (even with the sound effects, as the sound of propellers fade in and out), but succeeds overall.

Next, aggravated because it is 2:30 a.m. and Tim continues to spout meandering, low-key stories, Carol loses her will to stay awake. After she passes out on a plate and two hors d'oeuvres on it stick over her eyes, Carol takes matters into her own hands and moves the a grandfather clock close to everyone and alters the time to make it ring 3 o'clock. This does not faze Tim (wearing old age makeup, as is Vicki), nor does Carol singing "The Party's Over" (which Harvey ends by dropping the piano cover on Carol's fingers) and then screaming in the bathroom. At wit's end, she come out in her nightgown, sleeps in Vicki's lap, then pulls out the bed from the sofa. A nervous Harvey pushes the bed back down along with Carol in it and is thrilled Tim finally appreciates him—after which Carol's leg bursts through the sofa and Harvey pretends it is normal. This is pretty good.

The show closes with Neil and Carol doing part of "Love Will Keep Us Together," which Carol incorrectly claims was the Number One song of 1976 (it was actually 1975). She tells Neil that his song was so great, it could have been a hit in the past, even 200 years earlier. This leads us to Vicki singing the tune in a powdered wig, followed by Carol trilling it at a turn-of-the-century bar, with Neil accompanying both on piano. Next up, Harvey offers it as a comic mock flamenco number, followed by Neil and Carol in tux and gown re-envisioning the song as a sultry big band duet. Vicki plays a tambourine with the dancers as a choir backing her as a gospel number. The topper comes with a lip sync of the Captain and Tennille hit, where Carol put on a flip wig to resemble the latter and Tim hilariously portrays the Captain deadpan with a bulldog next to him. After Carol sings the incessant "I will" lyric repeatedly for the chorus, Tim gets a great laugh by interjecting "I won't!" At eight minutes long, this tries one's appreciation for the tune, but it is contemporary with humor, so it's a better-than-average finale overall.

At the closing, Carol tells Neil, "Sign it again" in reference to their earlier dialogue. Incidentally, the Captain and Tennille will guest on the series on Jan. 29, 1978.

March 26, 1977: Ken Berry

Q&A; Mr. Tudball (Tim) instructs Mrs. Wiggins (Carol) on their office fire safety plan in advance of a visit by an insurance representative (Harvey) to renew their contract; Ken and the dancers do a tap routine to "I Got Rhythm"; a military captain (Harvey) tries to convince his lieutenant that a bar he sees in a desert is just a mirage, as is its curvaceous server (Vicki); a spoof of *Babes in Arms* with Carol and Ken in the Judy Garland and Mickey Rooney roles respectively, with Harvey and Vicki as Ken's vaudevillian parents and the dancers as performers.

Comments: The show's first half looks like a winner, but unfortunately the long musical comedy takeoff drains away some enjoyment. The jacked-up Q&A audience even applauds Peter Matz when Carol names him. Showing cleavage, Carol tells a young man she does not show her navel on TV because she lacks one—"I'm from Mars"—and a woman that she refuses to have her daughters appear on the show even if they wanted to do it. When the woman informs her the public would love to see them on the show, Carol jokes that "My old lady didn't have a television show of her own, so let them get theirs!"

Mr. Tudball smokes a stogy and waits for Mrs. Wiggins to come into his office. The slow secretary arrives and says she is tired because she is doing her Christmas shopping now so she will not be worn out come December. A nonplussed Tudball responds, "That makes a lot of sense. That's like eating a jar of jelly in case somebody asks you to the peanut butter prom!" He tells her if they fail to have a fire safety program in place, his insurance premiums will go up. Naturally, he regrets the training as Wiggins gets dizzy blowing a whistle to signal a fire and has a hard time getting down on the floor to crawl out, as her butt sticks up, but he takes it and they return to their work stations. Tudball leaves his cigar in an ashtray in Wiggins' office, and since the smell bothers her, she puts it in a trash can. Harvey appears as the insurance representative, and he thinks he can break Tim with some ad libbed wordplay involving his titles, but Tim shoots him down with a quick "Don't suppose you have any comedy insurance down there!" They discuss their plans when Wiggins sees the trash can is on fire and runs into Tudball's office to blow her whistle and hit the deck. He is confused but sees what is happening and follows suit. Meanwhile, Harvey goes to Wiggins' desk and pours coffee to extinguish the fire. Seeing what could have happened, Harvey cancels Tudball's policy. Wiggins consoles Tudball by singing "Santa Claus is Coming to Town." This is solid humor.

Following a sprightly tap number featuring Ken solo, in duos and with the entire Ernie Flatt crew, "Lost in the Sahara" has Tim finding a bar with a hot blonde cocktail waitress (Vicki) in the desert that Harvey, his fellow explorer, insists is a mirage, despite the fact that Vicki throws drinks at them for their treatment of her, and another man (Brad Trumbull) threatens Tim for getting fresh with Vicki, his wife. When the tables turn and Tim discovers Harvey thinking he sees imaginary rescuers in the distance, Tim shoots Harvey several times as the latter does an elaborate death twirl. He then goes back to enjoy his bar, which turns out to really be a cactus like Harvey had said. Although not the smoothest and strongest of Harvey-Tim collaborations, this still clicks well.

The comic momentum vanishes with "Babes in Barns," a two-part send-up that could have been done ten years earlier—and feels like it. The "hey kids, let's put on a show" genre is easy to mock, and there is little fresh new comedy here in favor of presenting seven so-so songs. Carol presents a good approximation of Judy Garland's quavering vocals, and everyone else is fine too, although Ken's whiny delivery, while accurately Mickey Rooney's style, nonetheless grates. Otherwise, this is better left little discussed.

A memorable blooper occurs here when Carol sings in front of a barn and the horse behind her hears the call of nature and does what comes naturally. Hearing the audience and crew crack up, Carol turns around, sees what the horse is doing and loses it as well. The wrangler comes out to clean up the mess with a bucket and tips his hat with a bow before Carol memorably quips to Dave Powers, "Should we pick it up at Number One or Number Two?" This bit appears frequently in Carol's retrospectives. Too bad it did not make the cut for this show. It was much more entertaining than the rest of "Babes in Barns." Nonetheless, this show does get an Emmy nomination next year for best writing, so somebody liked it.

April 2, 1977: Tenth Anniversary Show

Following showing the opening of the series' debut in 1967, Carol comes out and presents a decade's worth of introducing Jim Nabors as her guest as well as a collection of her Tarzan yells; Harvey, Vicki and Tim join Carol as all sit in directors' chairs to introduce clips of twenty-five memorable moments; the Charwoman waves goodbye to the dancers and regulars and reviews blown-up pictures of her with previous guest stars such as Emmett Kelly in 1970, Jerry Lewis in 1971, Ray Charles in 1972 and Edward Villella in 1973 before singing "It's Time to Say So Long."

Comments: This very enjoyable trip down memory lane has only one bit of new humor, as Carol pretends to be shot midway while doing a Tarzan yell following a compilation of thirteen previous efforts. Otherwise, the regulars (including a pregnant Vicki) recall skits and a few musical numbers mainly focused on them, although Lyle Waggoner pops up five times. He is in the first clip as host of "V.I.P." interviewing Harvey in drag as a King Family singer (Nov. 17, 1969). This is followed by the first commercials spoof (Oct. 2, 1967); a compilation of scenes with Vicki leaving the "Carol & Sis" sketches to visit Marsha; and Eunice, Ed and Mama playing a board game (Nov. 16, 1974).

The second section has the *Mary Hartman, Mary Hartman* takeoff (Sept. 25, 1976); Tim and Harvey's dentist sketch (March 3, 1969); and Carol lip syncing to "The Trolley Song" (Nov. 18, 1968). More fun continues with nine shots of Carol and/or Harvey being hit by the kitchen door to end each "Carol & Sis" shot, followed by one time when Carol did not do that to Harvey. Next comes the nudist sketch (Nov. 6, 1967); Tim cracking up Lyle as a Nazi (Feb. 23, 1974); Tim breaking up during the "clients in love" sketch (Feb. 2, 1974); Don Rickles dancing to the music Carol and Mel make as songwriters (Nov. 11, 1968); the film takeoffs "To Each Her Own Tears" (Feb. 3, 1969), "The Fun Family of Broadway" (Dec. 11, 1967), "When My Baby Laughs at Me" (Feb. 15, 1975) and "The Ballad of Broadway" (Jan. 19, 1972); the Australia show opening and Tim as the world's oldest conductor (Dec. 8, 1973); and Harvey as Mother Marcus (Sept. 29, 1973).

The final segments are Zelda addressing George in prison (Feb. 16, 1970), followed by the movie send-ups "So Proudly We Heal" (Nov. 30, 1970), "Sinful Woman" (Jan. 26, 1972), "Caged Dames" (Nov. 8, 1972), "Lovely Story" (Feb. 1, 1971), "Went With the Wind" (Nov. 13, 1976) and finally the Emmy-nominated choreography (and only really good part) of "43rd Street" (Nov. 17, 1971).

Although exceptionally edited and nicely presented, the show has no clips of such great recurring elements as "As the Stomach Turns," "The Old Folks," Funt and Mundane, Tudball and Wiggins, Nora Desmond or Stella Toddler. It would have been better to have shortened a few bits and drop one or two of the many movie spoofs to make room for them instead. Regardless, it is nice that the bulk of the clips came from the rarely-seen first five seasons.

At the end, Carol says, "As you know, this is Harvey's last show with us. . . . I have mixed emotions. I've been with this—he's the most versatile, talented actor I feel kind of like a parent. You know when your kids get married, you wish for them and pray for them every success and happiness, but you're going to miss them like hell. I love you." He says the same three words back to her as they embrace and the audience applauds, and even Tim is choked up by the emotion of the occasion.

Carol gives Harvey an extended hug as the Charwoman in the traditional season-ending routine, which otherwise is business as usual. The series looks confident as it heads into its next decade without Harvey, but the reality proves to be different than that.

Final Notes for the Season

The finale's optimism belied the fact that although the series won its time slot, it finished at Number Forty-Four for the season, its lowest showing ever. Clearly viewer fatigue was occurring, and more troubling, the series' creative staff seemed little to care, much less to address it.

The series won Emmys for Tim Conway as supporting actor (beating Harvey, among others) and for Dave Powers' direction of the Feb. 12, 1977 show. There were losses for variety series, Vicki as supporting actress (to Rita Moreno for a guest shot on *The Muppet Show*), writing (to *Saturday Night Live*), art direction or scenic design (to *The Mac Davis Show*) and choreography (to the special *America*

Salutes Richard Rodgers: The Sound of His Music). At the Golden Globes, Carol won her fourth statuette as Best Television Actress, Musical or Comedy. Other nominations were for the series, Tim and Vicki.

Overshadowing all these honors was Joe Hamilton's announcement on Feb. 1 that Dick Van Dyke would "equally star" with Carol in 1977-1978. Emphasizing that the actor was not serving as a replacement per se for Harvey, Joe said, "Dick is a major star in his own right. His being on the show will give us a fresh approach to comedy variety."

Although Carol and Dick had worked together in the late 1950s as regular players on *Pantomime Quiz*, Dick told a 1998 seminar of the Museum of Television and Radio that what sparked him to join her series was her guest shot on his ill-fated NBC variety series *Van Dyke and Company* during its short run in the fall of 1976. What was meant to be a short skit turned into 10 minutes of funny ad libbing by the duo, and it made an impression on Carol and Joe to offer Dick to be part of her series when his ended.

It appeared to be a decision made with foresight, as *Van Dyke and Company* was a surprise Emmy winner for outstanding variety series this season over *The Carol Burnett Show* as well as *Saturday Night Live* and *The Muppet Show*. Additionally, to promote their professional working relationship, Carol and Dick appeared on stage in Los Angeles doing *Same Time Next Year* in the summer of 1977 before large, appreciative audiences.

Also during the summer hiatus, Carol acted in the motion picture *A Wedding*, directed by Robert Altman. It was a much better experience for her than *Pete 'n' Tillie* and *The Front Page*, and reviews were favorable when it was released in 1978. The series' summer replacement was *Switch* (1975-1978), a cop drama starring Robert Wagner and previous *Carol Burnett Show* guest Eddie Albert.

But despite these positive developments prior to the star of the eleventh season, Carol and her production team should have heeded what Harvey told reporter Michael J. Hoy in November 1976. "We're starting to repeat ourselves," he said. "We've already run through about fifty writers since the show started ten years ago. . . . The people out there never seemed to get tired of watching us . . . and yet we've sometimes become tired."

As it turns out, the public would lose its enthusiasm for *The Carol Burnett Show* as it became more wearying than perhaps even Korman could imagine. The next season would prove to be the series' last, and sad to say, arguably its worst.

Mrs. Wiggins relaxes on the beach in Hawaii with her stuffy boss, Mr. Tudball, and his wife in a funny skit on the Nov. 19, 1977 episode. Dick Van Dyke is a regular at the start of this season, replacing Harvey, but dissatisfied with his material, he will leave two episodes after this one airs. Amid dropping ratings and sketches that seem to lack freshness, Carol decides to end this series this season. Courtesy of Getty Images.

Chapter 12

1977-1978: Harvey's Gone, and So Is Much of the Magic

"It really is a family."—Carol's comment to a young man congratulating her dancers, noting how many of them and other crew members have been with her since the start of the series and even earlier, from the Nov. 26, 1977 show.

Crew Additions This Season

Writers: Robert Illes, James Stein, Franelle Silver, Larry Siegel.

In 1978, Elias Davis, David Pollock, and Adele and Burt Styler departed the writing staff. Replacing them were the team of James Stein and Robert "Bob" Illes, Franelle Silver and Larry Siegel, who returned after a four-year hiatus without his old partner, Stan Hart.

For Illes and Stein, this was an opportunity to connect back with Joe Hamilton after they wrote for the ill-fated *Smothers Brothers Show* in 1975, where he was executive producer. "But he really wasn't hands on there," Illes notes. "My agent at the time was Mike Ovitz, who was pretty good at packaging shows. And he knew Joe Hamilton."

Illes believes Ed Simmons, the head writer, ultimately signed off on him and Stein. Even so, Illes felt unwelcome by Simmons when he joined the series.

"It was a bit weird at first," Illes recalls. "He regarded us as the young whippersnappers. We were kind of a new wave of people." They were not that new—Illes and Stein had Emmys in 1974 for writing the comedy special *Lily* (starring Lily Tomlin) and Emmy nominations in 1976 for writing *Van Dyke and Company*, the pilot for Dick's series. Despite this, their pedigrees meant little to a skeptical Simmons. (As for the series' executive producer, Illes says, "I never understood the purpose of Joe Hamilton.")

"It took a few weeks before we got into the ground," Illes says. "We would pitch an idea by Monday, and we would do one sketch a week. We kind of did one-off things. There were one or two before they finally had confidence in what we would do to get on air."

Siegel was the writer who most impressed Illes. He called Siegel "An old curmudgeon but great. It was cool to work with him, because I grew up with him on *Mad Magazine*."

Canadian Fran Silver first wrote for a show called *Excuse My French* when she was twenty, followed by the sitcom *King of Kensington*, where she became its story editor, and then the variety series *The David Steinberg Show* (not the 1972 summer replacement series of the same name for *The Carol Burnett Show*). She had a contract to write a sitcom called *Custard Pie* when her agent suggested she send a spec script to *The Carol Burnett Show*.

"I thought, 'There's no way in hell they'll hire me,'" she says of the producers of one of her favorite shows. But they flew her down to Los Angeles for an interview on a Wednesday and hired her two days later. The transition was slightly unnerving for her.

"I was only twenty-four at the time and moving to a different country," Silver says. "I had lived with my family in Florida when I was seven to twelve years old, so it was about the same, except I had to learn how to drive. For us in Toronto, it was subways and buses to get around."

Silver adds that "I was hired as a single, but I ended up working a lot with Roger Beatty accidentally. I had said one of my favorite sketches was Tudball and Wiggins, and Roger had been working on them, and Ed Simmons had me join him on them."

While Illes, Stein and Silver supplied fresh blood and inspiration, many scripts overall this season have a mechanical, stale output. Most sketches from the old staff come off as weak variations of previous efforts or simply fail to click. In his fifth year as head writer, Ed Simmons had run out of inspiration to keep the series compelling viewing, as well as the initiative to take actions to correct its sudden slide into frequent mediocrity.

Part of the initial problem was incorporating Dick Van Dyke as a series regular. As Dick put it in *My Lucky Life in and out of Show Business: A Memoir*, "suddenly I found myself replacing a multi-talented actor who was also the world's greatest second banana." Billed as Carol's equal, Dick was still expected to carry the load that Harvey Korman had handled, plus retain his unique charm and magic. As it turned out, neither happened.

"I was uncomfortable in the skits and unable to find the rhythm among a cast that had been together for a decade," he wrote. He was more frank in a 1998 Museum of Television and Radio seminar: "My mistake was nobody can replace Harvey Korman."

While Carol and Tim offered support, Dick felt the work atmosphere was generally unaccommodating. To showcase his talents, the show featured him an unprecedented five shows without any guests, but it only added pressure to Dick and left him dissatisfied.

"I think we had done five shows, had a hiatus, and he had tried to get out of the show," says

Silver. "Then he made another bunch with a hiatus." After twelve episodes, Van Dyke finally departed the series in December.

Apart from Silver, Dick's departure was sudden and unexpected to many on the series. "He was a very, very quiet guy off stage, very shy," Illes says. "I thought he had some brilliant bits on the show. We were really surprised. Everything seemed to be OK." Illes sympathized with Van Dyke's plight, admitting that he missed Harvey on the series too.

Coincidentally, Dick's son, Barry Van Dyke, was acting opposite the man his dad replaced that same season as a regular on *The Harvey Korman Show*. The wan sitcom had its star playing an actor struggling with his family and career. ABC delayed its planned fall debut until Jan. 31, 1978, while ordering only six shows. Even as producers recast the actress who played Harvey's daughter with future Oscar nominee Christine Lahti, the industry scuttlebutt was that this series stunk.

"Demographically, it was the wrong show," says Fred Silverman, referring to *The Harvey Korman Show* drawing an older audience for what few viewers it had. Silverman was head of ABC programming at the time. "Harvey belonged on CBS. I think Harvey was best used—I hate to use the term—as a second banana."

Silverman did have success with another new ABC series. The network had two highly rated TV-movies in the previous season that served as pilots for what became *The Love Boat*. Fred Silverman slotted the series opposite *The Carol Burnett Show*.

"I thought it would do well," Silverman says. "It was younger than Carol Burnett in terms of appeal." Indeed, once *The Love Boat* debuted in September 1977, it was a top twenty hit, whereas Carol's show slumped badly for three months.

Besides the writing, Van Dyke's dissatisfaction and *The Love Boat*, another factor negatively affecting the series was competing against itself in reruns. *Carol Burnett and Friends* distilled the shows from 1972-1977 into half hours, with the first five seasons omitted because Carol and Joe Hamilton had to share rights with Bob Banner to show them. The repeats ran 30 minutes to meet the needs of TV stations who wanted to run the series five nights a week like old sitcoms. It was an unprecedented tack for any variety series, as conventional wisdom was that no one wanted to see them in repeats.

To meet these demands, *Carol Burnett and Friends* typically omitted the musical numbers including the dancers, not only due to time constraints but to the expensive fees the musical unions charge for public performances by their members. Even under these conditions, the dancers found themselves compensated for their work to an extent.

"We were one of the first dancers to get money," said Randy Doney. "If we were on a show, even if not on camera, we got residuals." Stan Mazin used that money to buy a home and placed a plaque there thanking Carol for allowing him to do so.

Doney credits Harvey Korman for pressuring Joe Hamilton to make this accommodation by threatening to hold a press conference telling performance unions not to support *The Carol Burnett*

Show because of Hamilton's original plans to provide poor residual payments to on-air talent for the reruns. Carol intervened and even extended generosity to the writers. "Every other show has us on as producers, so we received compensation for every other show," notes Bill Angelos. "That's Carol's way of thanking me."

When *Carol Burnett and Friends* appeared in repeats nightly during the fall of 1977, it was a hit. Instead of encouraging viewers to watch the ongoing series, however, it made them realize how lumbering and unsatisfying the current edition was in contrast to earlier installments. *Carol Burnett and Friends* lost some Q&As, had a few sketches edited a little awkwardly and lost Carol saying goodnight at the end, but generally the shows were funnier and better than the new ones airing in 1977-1978.

Amid these pressures in December 1977, CBS moved *The Carol Burnett Show* from five years as its Saturday night closer to the same position on Sunday. It switched slots with *Kojak*, which was failing to keep the large audiences generated by *All in the Family* and *Alice* preceding it. The belief was that Carol's comedy would be a better fit.

UPI reporter Vernon Scott asked Burnett her thoughts about the transition. "I'm pleased with the move because we're being whupped on Saturday," she said. "It's either that or cancellation. This show has gone ten years longer than I thought it would."

Regarding how miniscule ratings for the first three months of 1977-1978 affected morale, Carol told Scott, "When I come to work, I see long faces on the set. But I'm as cheerful as ever. Probably the cast and crew think I'm just putting up a brave front."

In the meantime, Carol had added Joe Blasco as her personal makeup artist. "She was dissatisfied with the makeup being done at CBS, but was fearful to do anything to this makeup artist (Al Schultz), because he was married to Vicki Lawrence," recalls Blasco.

Blasco had been applying makeup for guests being interviewed on camera for Rona Barrett's TV shows for several years in the 1970s. When he performed his work on a very happy Bette Midler, a slender onlooker offered to recommend Blasco to his clients. "I thought he was some kind of agent, but it turns out it was Bob Mackie," Blasco says.

Blasco allowed Mackie to bring Carol to his studio and have a photographer take step-by-step pictures to show his technique on her to Schultz. A week later, apparently dissatisfied by Schultz's efforts to copy Blasco's methods, Carol had Bob and her agent ask Blasco to her makeup every week. He could not do it at CBS Television City initially because he was not a member of the union, so she would come to his office instead.

Eventually Blasco could come on set and use his special yellow highlight to make Carol's face "pop" on screen by increasing its reflectivity with the studio lights. He invented different ways for her to make quick changes while retaining the makeup, and he drew in every eyebrow line to increase her features. "She was just great to work on," he says.

While Carol looked smashing, the producers made few changes concurrent with the time switch beyond more appearances by Ken Berry and Steve Lawrence. Mostly, the show fell on Carol, Tim and Vicki, as indicated by the opening titles. During Dick's tenure, the Charwoman painted on easel where the negative image transforms into his grinning face, followed by the same with Vicki in the spotlight and Tim on a monitor. When Dick left, the animated stage lights open to the faces of Tim and Vicki before fading.

Ratings rose on Sundays but remained below past heights, and the series still looked limp overall. Still, it shocked some when Carol announced on Feb. 6, 1978 that "I want to be free for a while from the demands of a weekly show." CBS Entertainment President Robert A. Daly said he had asked her to reconsider her decision, but Carol remained firm.

"I don't think we were tremendously surprised, because it had been so long," Sande Johnson says of the dancers' reaction to Carol stepping away from the series. "It was tiring, and they wanted to go out on top, without people wanting us to do so."

"I didn't think she thought she would do it so many years," says Gene Merlino, one of the George Becker Singers. He recalls Carol talked several years earlier about ending it.

Illes had a different perspective. "We were pretty thrown, although the ratings were wobbly," he said. "I thought when I joined, well, this should be around a while."

Hints of Carol's desire to leave the series this season occurred with an inordinate amount of references on shows to Hawaii, where Carol often vacationed and relocated afterward for a time. "She wanted to go to Hawaii," asserts Silver, who coincidentally learned about the show ending when she herself was vacationing in the fiftieth state.

So, *The Carol Burnett Show* finally wound down. If it was not the smoothest of exits, at least it was a dignified one. And there were a few good shows left—just not that many.

Sept. 24, 1977: Jim Nabors

Dick and the dancers do "One" from *A Chorus Line*; Q&A; as Eunice copes with a note from Ed saying he has left town with another woman, she receives unsolicited advice on what to do from Mama, Mickey Hart and Dan Fogerty (Dick), an old Army buddy of Ed's who drops by for a visit; Jim performs "After the Lovin'"; Dick and Tim play two carpenters having a dicey time installing a store window; the "All Time Big Star Special" features Jim, the cast and dancers parodying current celebrities.

Comments: The eleventh season opener is an overall success that avoids much of the pitfalls that would plague the series this season, although it surprisingly gives very little for Jim Nabors to do apart from a song and one brief impersonation. The accent is on establishing Dick as Burnett's new featured player and achieves that goal in this outing, beginning with his comic inability to follow the choreography along with the dancers.

The Eunice sketch dealing with Ed's separation avoids being mawkish and uneasy thanks to excellent writing and focused performances. Particularly outstanding is Burnett relating the exact conversation she had with Ed, running the gamut of heartache to anger as he tells Eunice to work with Mickey at the hardware store to support herself. Mama similarly ranges from denial that Ed really was leaving the family to disdain for Dan's words of assurance telling Eunice things will be fine. Even Tim effectively but comically emotes as he cries about losing his boss. The key is Dick, who is pitch perfect in making Dan appear both optimistic and realistic as he listens to Eunice's struggle. One is not surprised when he says he plans to stick around town to see what happens—in fact, one is grateful he will be there to help the hurting heroine in this fine seriocomic segment.

Unfortunately, next comes the start of what would be the worst tendency of the shows during Van Dyke's tenure with the series—the phony, obviously scripted banter prior to the introduction of a production number. Here we have the supposedly hilarious setup of Dick thinking Carol is introducing him instead of Jim, belabored even more by Dick supposedly confessing that he did a bad job in the opening number and thought this would give him a chance to redeem himself. Once this mess ends, Jim finally appears, lip syncing decently to his version of a recent million seller for Engelbert Humperdinck.

Dick fares better in the next bit, pantomiming a number of mishaps he and Tim encounter when installing a piece of glass (faked, not real) on a storefront. Each accidentally breaks three different glass panels before finally nailing in one successfully, only to see the building around the window collapse and Tim accidentally crack the window to boot. Although a little slow at points, this is a winner with several laughs generated.

For the "All Time Big Star Special," Fonzie (Tim) is the host on a motorcycle introducing Polly Darton (Vicki) whose breasts are so big they tend to tip her over, and she falls backward at the end when the male dancers dressed as cowboys miss catching her. Next is Don Denver (Jim), wearing glasses and a blonde shag cut wig as he sings about the environment with images of pollution behind him. Walking and talking slowly, the 7 1/2 Million Dollar Man (Dick) does a slow motion version of the Charleston in real time, eliciting applause, and similarly draws out introducing his wife, Farrah Fawcett (Carol). Posing with a gun and flipping her blonde locks, Farrah reads an open letter to America about why she will not be a Charlie's Angel any more before joining a kick line with everyone. This is amusing but could have been a little sharper.

At the end, Vicki shows off her new infant son. "Is it a bottle baby?" Dick interjects, cracking all on stage. Carol composes herself to put the young one in her arms while singing "It's Time to Say So Long" as a lullaby. It is a sweet finish to a show promising more good times in subsequent episodes—too bad that possibility will be left unfulfilled.

Oct. 1, 1977: Steve Lawrence

Carol enlists the help of a drunk private eye (Tim) to save her from a stalking killer; Steve sings "Every Time I Sing a Love Song," banters with Dick and duets with him on "I Could Never Really Sing"; three blackouts involving TV star holdouts; "The Late Late Show" is a two-part send-up of the 1936 film *San Francisco*, with Dick as a dance hall operator in the early 1900s, Carol as an aspiring talented singer he loves, Tim as a priest who tries to keep both apart, Steve as a rich arts patron and Vicki as Steve's mother.

Comments: The pattern for a lot of what is wrong this season starts here, including the unwise frequency of having no Q&A and a predominance of failed bits. The latter applies to the opening sketch, where twice closets full of empty beer cans spill on Tim as supposed humor—he also steps on piles of them strewn across his office. Still tipsy, he listens as Carol in a blonde wig tells him she believes a murderer is following her. Tim misfires his gun, which leads to the accidental death of the killer (Stan Mazin) before Tim inadvertently shoots himself in the knee. There are some chuckles to be had here thanks to the delivery of Tim and Carol, but this mostly plods along until the end.

Two forgettable tunes appear next, although the first did make the adult contemporary chart in a version by John Davidson in 1976. The contrived part where Dick enters and tells Steve he wishes he had his vocal talents and then gets tutored by the latter is nonsensical. Dick is known for having sung well in *Bye Bye Birdie* and *Mary Poppins*, among other productions, so this portion is just a huge time waster for viewers.

The tedium continues with another dubious premise. Actors leaving TV series for better roles goes back to James Garner from *Maverick* and Pernell Roberts from *Bonanza* in the 1960s. What is worse is that it comes off as a not-too-subtle dig at Harvey for having left the show, and no skit is really funny. Dick threatens to walk off a show run by Tim until he sees the man waiting to audition for his role is his look-alike. Next, Carol and Steve dress fancy at a dinner table to laugh about their replacements before she heads to work as a waitress and he as a cab driver. Finally, Dick leads a table read of a script wherein Vicki, Tim and Carol argue over which one of them deserves more money and perks. This has the only clever ending—it turns out Dick is teaching them how to enact bad behavior—but it is a long way to go for little laughs.

"Fran Sansisco" is the name of Carol's character, and she does a great job mocking the stiffness of Jeanette MacDonald in the original film. Carol is caught between Dick, who has her replace another singer (Sally Donovan) and Steve, who reprises what Carol did in a takeoff of *Anastasia* five years earlier by making his voice sound pinched when has his pince-nez on his nose (see Oct. 25, 1972). For his part, Tim has a sing-song voice he uses to dissuade Carol from kissing Dick. He succeeds, and in Act Two, she is with Steve and his mother when Dick tries to persuade her back to him, but Steve's money impresses her more. Nevertheless, she visits Dick at the saloon, and when they do kiss, an earthquake hits. Effectively staged, this used footage from the original film along with shots of debris falling down in the saloon around Dick and Carol, with Tim coming down as well. Steve arrives and Carol kisses him, which ends the earthquake.

The spoof is as chaotic as the scenario, yet some chuckles can be found. More might have been possible according to Larry Siegel, who wrote the skit and says Steve and Tim switched roles originally set for each other. "I couldn't believe it," he says. "It didn't work."

At the end, Steve sings part of "It's Time to Say So Long" with Carol in his pinched voice, and there is one more earthquake depicted as he signs the guest book. The show needed many more amusing moments like that. As it stands, this is a forgettable entry.

Oct. 8, 1977: Family Show

Q&A; a woman (Carol) is proud about new changes in her appearance, but her husband (Dick) is so obsessed with work that he ignores her totally; Vicki and Carol sing "They Don't Them Like That Anymore"; Tim meet Dick, the unluckiest man in the world, on a park bench; Dick says goodbye to his sister (Carol), brother-in-law (Tim) and niece (Vicki) at an airport, but his flight's delay leads the latter trio to reveal how they really dislike him; Tim bungles several efforts to kill his irritating wife (Carol); Dick performs "Once in Love With Amy" with the dancers.

Comments: The forced comedy and stale numbers here are so bad that one wonders what is bringing down this series' quality. In the long, limp Q&A, a person praises Carol for being great on *The Garry Moore Show* and improving with age. Another talks about being on the same flight with Carol to Honolulu, where the hostess, Tim, a writer and their families went on vacation the previous week. Carol mentions that a recent show of *Concentration* used her name as the answer, plus talks about stage fright, her experience with an earthquake and the location of her star on Hollywood Boulevard. The most interesting conversation has Carol laughing off a suggestion to do a show from the gas station in Plains, Ga., owned by Billy Carter, brother of President Jimmy Carter.

After another *All My Children* recap that emphasizes this Q&As' generally tired and pointless nature, Carol brings out Dick, who after joking about the soap opera's plot delves into a flat scripted bit. Dick demurs doing Q&A with her, saying he would be boring. The hostess protests and tells him to try. She asks him if Dick Van Dyke was his real name. He provides an endless, rambling response whose humor totally goes after fifteen seconds. It's an awkward way to begin the show, and things gets worse as it progresses.

To impress her husband, Carol shows Dick her new looks, but he just grouses about injustices done to him at work. She attempts to shift his focus by showing him his favorite foods, yet he still obsesses on how he wants to be his company's vice president. Carol becomes so desperate for attention that she blurts out lines such as "I sold our cat into white slavery!" while doing things like hanging from a chandelier. Throughout it all, Dick remains oblivious to Carol. Overlong and lacking laughs, this is a loser of a skit.

The musical number with Carol and Vicki at a unisex health club griping about the lack of masculine men while watching Dick and Tim struggle with gym equipment is a contrived lament that could have been done twenty years earlier. Inexplicably, Tim and Dick become proficient in doing exercises, as shown in sped-up video tricks, leading the women to bond with them at the end of a painful four minutes or so.

Unfunny, irritating activities continue with Dick bemoaning to Tim that everything he does backfires. He feeds pigeons that throw food back at him, has lightning strike him when he reads Tim's newspaper, causes a paper delivery boy to be carried away by a hawk and gets rained on no matter where he stands. This is all more odd than humorous. Dick plans to kill himself in frustration, and he gives a ring he got 26 years earlier to Tim before jumping off a ledge. The ring is cursed, as shown by Tim hitting lots of props—the only amusing slapstick in the piece. Tim accidentally knocks into Dick, who takes the ring when he falls to his death. That should end this muddled mess, but then, in another obviously scripted bit portrayed as spontaneous, Carol comes out in a bathrobe laughing at the scene before Dick continues the story he started in the Q&A before Carol summons another burst of rain to fall on him. Like Dick's character, this segment is all wet.

Plodding plotting occurs again as a new tedious sketch has Dick bid farewell to his relatives at a concourse, but his departure is held up, so the quartet awkwardly waits together. They all have nothing new to stay, nor does this skit, where unsurprisingly the deteriorating circumstances lead to Dick's relatives telling him he really got on their nerves during his stay, only to reconcile with him when his plane finally is ready to go. Tim is the best here in being obstinate toward Dick, but this is another loser.

The last comedy bit fails too. Its setup will be repeated in later shows—see the Nov. 26, 1977 entry for more information—but suffice it to say that the supposedly hilarious setup of having Carol accidentally shoot herself while cleaning Tim's gun is tough to endure today given more reports of such events. He also tries to electrocute Carol with a radio in the shower, but the cord is not long enough to reach, so he plugs it in and gets shocked instead. The final encounter has him buying a man-eating plant and of course being the one consumed instead of Carol. Birl Johns plays the plant in a scenario nowhere near as funny when Randy Doney was in the costume in a better skit on the Dec. 6, 1975 show.

The show ends on a sagging note as Dick's clever footwork cannot disguise the boredom of his aping Ray Bolger's presentation of a hit the latter introduced in the stage and film versions of *Where's Charley?* more than 25 years earlier. He even has the audience sing along the way Bolger did on Broadway. Even worse, when Carol comes out at the end to clap, Dick again recites his endless story as the credits roll and Carol ignores him. Amazingly, this horrible episode somehow made the 2014 DVD *Carol's Crack-Ups*.

Oct. 15, 1977: Nancy Dussault

** Eunice has divorced Ed and Mama comes to commiserate with her; Nancy sings "And I Love You So"; Mr. Tudball helps a distraught Ms. Wiggins with the burial of her late canary; a powwow between Indians and the cavalry; Carol and Nancy sing tunes popularized by Mary Martin and Ethel Merman on Broadway.

Comments: It is doubtful most viewers realized that the guest star previously worked with the series' latest regular on *The New Dick Van Dyke Show* from 1971-1973, as that sitcom bombed in reruns after ending a three-year run in 1974. Nancy Dussault was better known at the time as the former co-hostess of *Good Morning America*, ABC's daily wakeup series, from 1975-1977, hardly an incentive to watch this installment. Most of it sounds like a rehash of previous characters and themes, even Nancy and Carol's duet, as it comes nearly 25 years after Merman and Martin sang together as a highlight on the *Ford 50th Anniversary Special* on June 15, 1953.

Oct. 22, 1977: Family Show

Q&A; Carol is a woman disrobing in a hotel room who is stymied by efforts to prevent a man (Dick) from staring at her; Tim endures countless troubles in his attempts to put gas in his car in a self-service lane; Dick complains to an indifferent service representative (Carol) at the electric company about the power being turned off at his house; the regulars play a composition by manipulating their feet; previous trysts by four trapeze artists have consequences for all involved; a finale using "Persons Magazine" as a framework for the dancers and cast to parody current celebrities.

Comments: This episode starts well but falls off dramatically after the fairly sturdy first third of the show, regaining slightly for a wobbly finish. The Q&A has an artificial taste to it as Carol takes the opportunity to invite a sixteen-year-old boy onstage to sit on a stool and hear her sing "How Long Has This Been Going On?" before she hugs and kisses him. Obviously, the approach if not the recipient had been planned in advance by Carol with the orchestra. Less contrived and therefore better is Tim trying to do the same for a female fan invited up by singing (?) "Old Man River" before Carol cuts him off.

Tim reappears in the first skit, where Carol is mortified to see Dick looking at her in an undershirt with an immobile grin from the window of a room opposite hers as she prepares to change clothes. She pulls down the shade but it collapses, and she gets on all fours to try to hide herself before she realizes Dick is a mannequin (the audience gives him deserved applause for being so still and realistic for several minutes as he is carted away). A man dressed as an explorer (Tim) is brought in place of Dick, and a relieved and frisky Carol pretends to flash him, only to be mortified when he starts to clap and pulls out binoculars. This is very good, but even more hysterical was an unaired version where Carol put on a pair of huge falsies when she flashed Tim at one taping, prompting him to crack up before she showed the audience what caused him to break character.

The next bit has Tim envying how a gas station attendant (an unnamed actor) treats Don Crichton's car while Tim's hopes to save money by using the self-service lane causes disasters. The handle comes off the nozzle, the hose leaks gas, and he gets grease on his windshield. He has to plead for help often from the attendant, whose assistance backfires on Tim, causing his car to have its headlights and bumpers knocked off and its hood scratched when the attendant draws a map on it for directions for Tim. Once Tim gets a huge amount of gas accidentally pumped into his crotch, he gives up and pushes his car over to the attendant's side to get the full treatment. (During one taping, the pump did not activate properly in Tim's pants, prompting director Dave Powers to crack on the intercom, "How's it going?") This has guffaws, but not as many as the no-frills airplane sketch from Sept. 20, 1975 that it resembles, and the latter was more focused as well.

Still, the show appears promising until it crawls to a halt with Dick arguing with Carol at the electrical company about his bill. After what seems to be an eternity of useless verbal jousting, Carol finally checks on Dick's claims and tells him he has no power because company records show he is dead. He objects and demands to see Carol's supervisor (Vicki), who agrees with Carol's assessments. Dick vehemently protests that he is alive in such a frenzy that he accidentally falls out a window to his death, which confirms to Carol and Vicki that they were right all along. This is an irritating, ponderous skit.

Next, the quartet dressed in evening attire remove their shoes and socks to make classical music with their toes. Carol's tootsies make the sound of a tuba, while Tim's digits act as a xylophone, cymbals and trombone, and so on. Depending on your perspective, it is either silly or stupid, but it is at least somewhat more effective than the previous sketch.

Following this, the cleverness quotient improves as the four playing two couples cheating on each other who are all trapeze artists. The intricate plot has one of each pair discussing suspicions and worries with each other until one has to leave on a swing to perform. It culminates with all on the high platform confronting each other about infidelities, leading to Vicki pushing Tim off for a fling with Carol, Dick doing the same for Vicki even though Tim was her husband, Carol getting revenge on Dick by making him fall as well and Carol getting knocked out by the swing when it returns to the platform. Although infidelity is a hoary theme on the show by now, the actors give it their all, and the special effects crew lends panache by adding an occasional matte shot from a distance that gives the illusion the actors are indeed off a platform nearly high enough to the top of the tent.

The finale runs the gamut from inspired to insipid. After the dancers dressed in trench coats sing a tune about magazines, Carol and Dick mock the debates columnists Shana Alexander and James J. Kilpatrick did in the newsmagazine *60 Minutes* in the 1970s with the subtlety of a grenade. Arguing over how to fight unemployment, the two engage a slapstick fight that includes Dick squirting a water bottle on Carol and Carol retaliating with spraying foam all over Dick's suit. Dan Aykroyd and Jane Curtin on *Saturday Night Live* sent up this topic much better and quicker than what is presented here. In sharp contrast, Vicki's Rona Barrett after this is a stitch, as she uses her nasal tones to recount recent events in the manner of Noel Coward's song "I Went to a Marvelous Party."

The last portion has Tim as a dead-on, properly fey Truman Capote greeting dancers and extras dressed as Diana Ross, Rep. Bella Abzug and Dolly Parton (leaving his drinking glass on one of her breasts) before encountering Joe Namath (Dick), who sings about the pantyhose he is wearing. Enjoyment of this is diluted since the show already spoofed this on the Feb. 15, 1975 episode, although Dick does his best to sell his character. Tim says hi to a few more guests before encountering Anita

Bryant (Carol, wearing oranges on her left shoulder and dispensing juices from a container). Anita sings a mock gospel number with weak jokes in reference to her campaign against homosexuals (e.g., a woman in a gown walks up to get some juice and Anita complies, saying "I just love queens!") and interacts with Don Crichton as Evel Knievel before this putters to an end.

The mixed returns of this family show should have indicated to the production team that the concept needed to be retired soon. Unfortunately that lesson was not heeded, and two weeks later will be another show without a guest, with similar lackluster results.

Oct. 29, 1977: Ken Berry

Mr. Tudball repaints his office with the dubious help of Mrs. Wiggins; Ken plays a prospector singing about "Girls" with the male dancers and then "Emily" in a song-and-dance with a female; Dick and Carol are an impoverished couple struggling in an apartment who learn that they can collect $50,000 in insurance if one of Dick's hands is broken; "The Late Late Show" presents "Stolen Serenade," featuring Tim as Buzzy Berkeley, Vicki, Ken and Dick as a musical trio auditioning for him, and Carol as the seductress who steals Dick from the group and uses him for her own needs.

Comments: Here's one episode where showing a Q&A in place of anything else would have been more enjoyable than the material presented on air. Even the usually reliable Tudball skit is of lesser quality, although it was the best part of the show. As expected, Wiggins is completely clueless on performing the task at hand, first moving the ladder to the wrong place, making brush strokes without paint and then finally getting some yellow paint that she accidentally puts on Tudball's right hand. When she goes up the ladder, there is a top bit where she wiggles her butt and Tim quips, "From the back, you look like Dolly Parton from the front." She uses a roller that hits him in the face, he gets knocked over spilling lots of paint, and the sketch just kind of peters out from there.

Next is badly forced repartee as Carol tells Dick she needs a crossword answer for a versatile comedy performer, singer and dancer. Dick thinks it he is the answer, but Carol says it is Ken Berry and walks away from Dick, who introduces Ken. It is bland and unfunny as it sounds, and Ken's *Oklahoma*-like number generates few sparks either.

Plodding forward, Carol bawls that she cannot maim Dick's hands even if it will make them rich, but he insists that she do it. She tries to hit his hand with a fire poker but knocks his stomach out instead. He tells her to drop a bowling ball on his hand, but it lands on his feet. Dick crawls hunched over to the apartment door, where she hits him on the head. The obviousness of Carol hurting Dick everywhere but his hands ends when Dick learns he has won a job playing piano in Las Vegas. He celebrates by plunking a few notes, but he sounds so bad that Carol slams the piano cover on his hands for the insurance money. It is an OK end to an unsatisfying skit.

An overlong (it takes the last half of the show) parody of an unspecified 1930s musical has Tim supplying an affected voice as he auditions Vicki, Ken and Dick. The latter impresses Carol, who wants to steal the trio's song for her dance routine and claim Dick as her lover. She does both, and within six months she has reduced Dick to a sot so buzzed that he has trouble placing her on a piano, wherein he has a vision of Vicki and Ken rejoining him. In Act II, he reunites with the twosome, now beggars on the street, and Carol is the one who starts hitting the bottle as Tim decides to feature the trio and not her in his latest musical extravaganza. While the three get rave reviews, Carol winds up in a hospital with a coughing spell (the funniest bit of this piece by far), and Dick visits. She begs his forgiveness, which he gives her—along with a snowball in her face. As she pleads that "My pulse just stopped," the trio performs a song on the saying. Carol ends up dying, her bed levitates and she heads up to the rafters as the sketch ends.

This spoof, like much of the show, lacks warmth and genuine humor. The end is telling. Carol sings "It's Time to Say So Long" with coughing as her bed is lowered back on stage, then Vicki, Tim and Ken try to get in bed with her, but Dick stays underneath the mattress away from them. He is laughing, but one senses he is having difficulty finding his place on the series. The material he has here certainly does not help him.

Nov. 5, 1977: Family Show

* Q&A; Mama and Eunice play Password along with Mickey Hart and Eunice's new boarder, Dan (Dick), a man living in her garage to help her out with house payments who Eunice wants to date; Dick is a host awkwardly trying to fill in for the missing late night movie on his TV station; Vicki and Carol perform "At the Ballet" from *A Chorus Line* with the dancers; a woman planning suicide (Carol) has her plans to jump off a roof complicated by a crook on the lam (Tim); Carol and Dick sing a medley of love songs.

Comments: Just as the series seems like a lost cause, this bubbly installment shines, even during the contrived start when Dick comes in a wig and gown pretending to be Carol (the nonplussed star comes out in a robe to interrupt him). It features a Family sketch with a blooper that many people are more familiar with than the rest of the skit, which is somewhat of a shame given its superior quality.

In that sketch, Mama agrees to play Password with Eunice, Mickey Hart and Dan, even though she thinks the latter is a freeloader. Mama rebuffs Dan telling her the game's rules with "I know, I know, I know! I've been watching *Password* for so many years on TV, I've seen Allen Ludden getting gray right before my very eyes!" Mickey recalls his experiences watching events in theaters as his clues, and that's when the fun escalates.

When Eunice has the password "ridiculous," she gives the clue as "absurd." Mickey responds with "elephant," and it is obvious that Tim is going off on a tangent. During the first taping, which is used on air, he rambles that "See, this elephant had this little dwarf trainer. . . . There was a rumor going around the circus that that dwarf and the elephant were lovers." At this point, Carol, Vicki and Dick are all trying hard to hide their laughter as Tim adds, "They're buried together. Great big tombstone." Somehow they compose themselves and returns to the script, wherein Eunice goes on a rant and calls Dan a "conceited ass" for laughing at the way she and Mickey play the game. A tipsy Dan apologizes and says he was laughing with her and not at her. As he leaves, she tells him to forget the situation—and allows him to continue to live with her without paying any rent as promised. This causes Mama to glare at Eunice, who quietly responds, "Well, it's something, Mama. It's something."

It's a poignant ending, but few remember this in favor of what else that happens during the second taping of this show. Dave Powers gave a note between the shows warning that "Tim's story is going to be different," which irked Vicki, who knew his ad libs will disrupt the flow. "Well, get back at him," said her husband, Al Schultz. And she does.

For the second go-round, Tim unveils a story about "Siamese elephants" at a freak show he saw where a monkey would come out and dance the Merengue under their conjoined trunks. The story destroys everyone with laughter until Carol finally musters the strength to tell Mama it was her turn to play. Vicki shoots back with "You sure that little asshole's finished?" and everyone dies, with Tim falling on the floor in hysterics. Obviously they could not use this version, but it has appeared many times on blooper specials.

Another highlight is Carol as a luckless lady whose ineptitude extends to being unable to write a suicide note properly because her pencil breaks and her pen runs out of ink. She plans to jump off a ledge until a crook (Tim) uses her as a hostage. Carol convinces a disbelieving cop (voice of Dick) that she is real, then argues about philosophy with Tim, which he eventually wins. He thinks he has also convinced her that life is worth living, but she winds up grabbing him as she decides to leap to her death. This is one of the funniest sketches in the final season, thought that is faint praise.

Combined with a nice Vicki-Carol duet and other goodies, this makes a winning show overall. Unfortunately, the next show proves the series still is not fully back on track.

Nov. 12, 1977: Family Show

Q&A; the K-9 Obedience School has three students—Tim with an invisible dog, Vicki with a microscopic one and Dick with a big invisible one; Carol and Dick look at each other in a mirror and get dressed as clowns to dance and sing together to "It All Depends on You"; Carol is an inspector with Accident R Us checking out several malpractice lawsuits at a crowded hospital where Tim is a surgeon; "The Later Late Late Show" features a two-part spoof of the 1945 movie *The Enchanted Cottage*; the cast and dancers portray famous comic strip characters.

Comments: This unsatisfying installment has a promising Q&A, starting with a woman wanting to know the diameter of Carol's mouth and our hostess laughing off the request. However, Carol does fulfill for the first time another woman's suggestion to do the Tarzan yell and displace her hip simultaneously. She generates laughs when interacting with a sixteen-year-old boy with glasses and telling him to slow down as she kisses him on both cheeks, and agrees that she is much more beautiful in person than on the air.

Unfortunately, the show mostly goes downhill from there as Tim, Vicki and Dick pantomime their pets' actions under the direction of an unseen instructor (voiced by Joe Bennett). Dick can barely control his pooch, which eats everything and destroys the classroom when fetching a ball. This is more odd than humorous. Likewise, Dick's routine with Carol emphasizes cuteness over laughter, leaving the show 0-for-2 so far.

The next bit is somewhat better, though still tiresome. Speaking with a Germanic accent, Tim accidentally cuts Carol and claims a living man is dead. Tim is not the only wacky hospital employee, however—another guy runs over Carol's legs, forcing Tim to prop her up and give her crutches that collapse in a truly amusing scene. Replaying what Tim did in the Feb. 22, 1975 show, Tim puts Carol in an electric wheelchair that breaks through a wall and gives her whiplash. It ends flatly with Tim asking a shell-shocked Carol if she would like to join him on the golf course, since it is now 1 p.m. and he is off the clock.

In "The Enchanted Hovel," sporting a unibrow across her entire forehead and buck teeth, Carol is a homely lass applying as a maid at a residence with a blind man (Tim), who first mistakes her for shrubbery. He has some good shtick waving his cane awry while walking before Vicki arrives as the housekeeper talking with a Bavarian accent. Vicki tells Carol a former soldier (Dick) lives in solitude due to wounds he sustained a razor accident in a latrine during the war that he feels makes him ugly. Dick hides his face behind a trench coat until Carol convinces him to show his shaving cuts he has covered with tissue paper. Carol excuses herself to nearly vomit (pretty funny) before a romance begins wherein Carol and Dick become stylish and attractive once they wed—but only when they stay in the enchanted hovel. There are a few comic complications after that, most particularly Tim getting his glasses and being able to see, only to be repelled and nearly falling off a cliff when he sees how Carol and Dick look outside the hovel, but any appreciation for this two-act sketch runs out of gas way beyond its finish.

The show sluggishly tries to rally with Carol telling how she enjoyed "the funnies" in the newspaper as a child and doing a duet with herself at age thirteen on "It Was" about plans to become a cartoonist. After that, thirteen-year-old Carol's fantasies come to life, and she helps Dick as Prince Valiant, Vicki as Little Orphan Annie (with blank eyeholes on her face), and Tim as a muscle-bound Captain Marvel, all of whom fight the dancers playing foes. Carol changes into Sheena, Queen of the Jungle and does her Tarzan yell before the bit ends. It is entertaining but cannot compensate for the wan material preceding it.

No dancers appear at the end. Given the show's quality, that is a smart move by them.

Nov. 19, 1977: Ben Vereen

Mr. and Mrs. Tudball go to Hawaii along with Mrs. Wiggins, who has to keep working while the trio try to relax on the shore; Ben performs a hot Dixieland jazz number with the dancers; a series of nine commercial spoofs features the cast and Ben; Dick attempts to rekindle the magic he had with his divorced wife (Carol) after leaving her for a younger woman after twenty years of marriage; Tim and Dick are ancient baseball players participating in an old-timers reunion game; Carol, Dick and Ben sing and dance to songs about yesterday, today and tomorrow.

Comments: Finally there is another fairly enjoyable installment, despite a loser skit at the midpoint. It starts with a surprising and effective number of ad libs coming from both Vicki as Mrs. Tudball in a huge muumuu and Carol in a typically tight Wiggins outfit to Tim's Mr. Tudball. Mrs. Tudball leaves to shop and Wiggins types a letter for her boss before telling him she feels he uses her. He proclaims that she is essential to him and dares the gods to strike him down with lightning if he is wrong. Naturally, a bolt hits him, capping off a pretty humorous installment.

Ben has fancy footwork as always in his production, but getting there is a chore with another elaborately unfunny scripted introduction. Dick remembers seeing Ben in *Pippin* on Broadway—or was it on *The Mike Douglas Show*? On a Tuesday—or Wednesday? Carol interrupts him to speed along getting to Ben, in a bit that should have been cut.

What is amusing are several of the commercial parodies, starting with Carol showing how her stockings accent her legs only to have Dick and Ben grab the hose to put it over their faces for a robbery. Tim does a great caricature of Ricardo Montalban showing off his open chest in a leisure suit as he attempts to put in a Carol in a fat suit inside a car (her loud burp cracks up Tim in the bit). Ben is proud of how his new pair of underwear prevents unsightly bulges without realizing how it shows up clearly underneath his pants—a rather surprisingly visual joke to see on TV in 1977, even if it just involves seeing the contours of Ben's rump. Carol is so happy with her new bra that she wants to show it to Vicki, but Dick arrests her for public indecency. Finally, in a spin against feminine deodorant spray commercials, Carol tells Vicki of the benefits of eyelash freshener.

The mood sours with a slow, seriocomic episode where Dick wants to prove to Carol he is a new man since the divorce but she tells him she is still the same as she rejects his overtures. Hurting this more during one taping was Carol and Dick noticing a studio light was on fire, prompting a delay and a rare second take. Thankfully, the time wasted here is largely redeemed next by a pantomime by Tim as a pitcher and Dick as a catcher, both past their primes, who valiantly try to play an inning of offense. With radio announcer Tom Kelly calling the really unforced errors, this generates some good guffaws.

Ben, Dick and Carol appear in the finale in colorful shirts, with Carol representing numbers centered on yesterday (including the Beatles hit of the same name), Dick today and Ben tomorrow, with each arguing that his or her time period is the best. Some good grooving moves by Ben and a nice soft shoe routine he does with Dick cannot prevent this spotty affair from leaning more towards being a snooze. Still, apart from no dancers at the end, this concludes as one of the few tolerable episodes overall of this season.

Nov. 26, 1977: Family Show

Q&A; the cast and some dancers appear as TV commercial characters who besiege a woman (Carol) as she wakes up in the morning; Vicki and the dancers present "Sleazy Love" in a tawdry bar dive setting; a hardhat (Tim) plans to murder his dithery wife (Carol), but his three attempts go awry; a salute to MGM pictures includes send-ups of *Gigi*, *Boys Town* and *Dr. Jekyll and Mr. Hyde*, as well as Carol explaining the history behind a hit from *Manhattan Melodrama* and Dick reenacting Gene Kelly's dance routine from the title number in *Singin' in the Rain*.

Comments: Watching this interminable episode, it is easy to speculate this was the breaking point for Dick Van Dyke where he finally determined it was pointless to continue on this series. Everything is pretty much a disappointment outside of the Q&A, even though a great deal of the material covers areas the show usually handles expertly. The Q&A highlights include the hostess telling the audience a few details about her upcoming film *A Wedding* and talking with a woman from Carol's hometown of San Antonio who is celebrating her 55th anniversary. The best is a man who compliments her effusively before adding, "I'm wondering how you've kept going this long. I've been watching you since I was a little baby." "You were doing real fine until the last half," Carol shoots back at him good naturedly. From there, the show sinks quickly.

The first flop is a shocking one, as various TV spokespeople appear in Carol's residence to what usually is gales of laughter but here produces only muted results thanks to weak lines and worn concepts. Among the latter is flushing a guy in the toilet tank once again. Tim, Dick and Vicki pop up often from different locations with little clever to say for the most part, except for the concluding item, where Dick plays a tape machine so loud that he says it can shatter a glass next to it. It does that—along with pretty much everything else in Carol's abode. It is not enough to redeem this from being a miss, however.

In another contrived, trying bit of banter, Tim and Dick mistakenly think Carol is referring to themselves as she mentions a good friend is going to perform before she introduces Vicki. The latter leads a good presentation of a song that sounds a lot like "The Stripper," but it is inconsequential in improving the show's tiresome feel.

Next, as first seen on Oct. 8, 1977, Tim gripes on a girder about wanting to kill his ditzy wife (Carol) to a fellow construction worker (Brad Trumbull), whose newspaper stories suggest ways Tim can achieve his desire. He sprays Carol with chocolate sauce and whipped cream on her outfit to attract a deadly tsetse fly to attack, but he has difficulty opening the container with the deadly insect, and it turns out to be a female who attracts males that sting Tim in retaliation. Tim then bungles an effort to electrocute his wife with a lightning rod attached to an umbrella when she is out during a rainstorm by using an iron pointer to show her where to go that gets hit by a bolt in the process. His final flawed method is to have her dress in red and make a bull attack her, but she goes inside and entices the bull to try to gore Tim as he runs through the wall. This takes ten long minutes compared to shorter Warner Brothers cartoons with Wile E. Coyote and the Road Runner in the 1950s that had more inventive wit and speedy delivery. Even so, the show inexplicably will revive this concept in later episodes.

The series has saluted MGM Pictures several times earlier (twice in 1970-1971 alone), as well as two of the motion spoofed, *Boys Town* (previously done on Dec. 30, 1968) and *Dr. Jekyll and Mr. Hyde* (on Oct. 16, 1967 and Oct. 20, 1973). Not surprisingly, these parodies are pretty pallid. In *Gigi* Carol appears as Vicki's niece and nearly impresses Dick as a cultured young woman until she says she wants to go to the zoo and see the stork so she can learn how to have children (she announces this going from a French accent to Carol's familiar "Shirley Dimple" girl voice). For *Boys Town*, Tim assumes Mickey Rooney's role as a ruffian threatening Dick as Spencer Tracy's Father Flanagan. Dick takes up Tim's challenge to fight him to run the orphanage and ends up getting whipped so badly after repeated fights that he places his collar on Tim and staggers out. *Dr. Jekyll and Mr. Hyde* is the last and least, an overlong and underdone bit where Dick pretends to be the good doctor to his wife (Carol) and a lecher when he meets Vicki. When both women learn the truth about him, Dick attempts to resolve his situation and becomes Tim as the Old Man—the only truly funny and original part of this segment.

Between the last two takeoffs, Carol explains that Richard Rodgers and Lorenz Hart wrote "Make Me a Star" for a Jean Harlow film, but she did not like the tune. The duo rewrote the composition into "Blue Moon," which became a standard after its inclusion in *Manhattan Melodrama*. Carol sings both versions fine, but few people watch her series to hear the history of making of a 40-year-old hit.

Capping the show is Dick's faithful interpretation of Gene Kelly's dancing amid torrents of water on a street setting. It dazzles, but recreating an existing classic without any clever twist seems pointless. Worse yet, after reassuring the audience that all the seven tons of water from the number will be recycled, Carol shows part of what she said Dick did not realize was being taped of him playing with the water. It is neither funny nor enlightening, and the fact that the episode closes with it shows a serious lack of judgment.

Carol, Dick, Vicki and Tim do a kick line with the opening set in the background for the closing. The ending as drab as the rest of the show, one so poor it feels more like a bad knockoff of *The Carol Burnett Show* rather than the real deal. What a shame.

Dec. 3, 1977: Bernadette Peters

Mrs. Wiggins has a cold with complications that is driving Mr. Tudball crazy as they work; Bernadette accompanies the male dancers dressed as construction workers to perform "You Never Done It Like That"; Dick fails to replicate Gene Kelly's skating routine from the 1955 movie *It's Always Fair Weather*; Carol and Dick's plans to savor a fancy meal fall victim to a bottle that refuses to open; three sketches imagine TV commercials for physicians; Bernadette and Vicki vie to show that each is the best friend of Carol's; a mini-musical uses tunes written by Betty Comden and Adolph Green.

Comments: Bernadette Peters impressed writer Bob Illes with this guest shot. "At the run-through, she was wearing a sweat suit pink top thing," he recalls. "Wow!" She injects much-needed life into the series' increasingly moribund presentations here, although this episode is far from classic. It starts with a Wiggins and Tudball skit that gets better as it goes along, though it could have withstood a rewrite to increase the humor content. Wiggins tries to combat her runny nose but ends up getting honey on a letter for Tudball, sneezes loud and opens a window that blows in a lot of wind, all of which infuriate her boss. Laughs finally perk when Wiggins goes to the water cooler to hydrate and it breaks, causing her to attempt to bail out the excess runoff with a spoon. A ticked off Tudball attempts to rectify the situation but ends up getting the cooler to empty all over his pants while Wiggins is on the phone. He apparently slips on the water and falls out the window, leading Wiggins to decide to go home.

After these chuckles comes the most tortured of this season's unfunny introductions. Carol prepares to welcome Bernadette before Dick pleads he should do it, followed by Vicki and Tim, all with flimsy reasons to do so. Amid their arguments, they go backstage to draw straws on who should do the honors, leaving Bernadette to have to introduce herself. How funny. She does fine dressed up and clicking her heels as she does a recent Captain and Tennille hit while flirting with the male dancers. Following this, Dick claims Gene Kelly liked his dance moves from the previous week and tries to emulate them again, only to crash through a wall of fake bricks. The whole setup including the Kelly claim is artificial, but Dick performs it with enough aplomb to make it palatable.

The good vibes vanish in the next offering, however, as Dick and Carol hurt each other as well as damage their furniture while trying to open a stubborn bottle. The slapstick is paced too slow and comes off as nothing new to the show, and the ending, wherein the bottle thrown outdoors knocks on the window and then spouts out its contents on Carol and Dick, is an insult to one's intelligence rather than clever comedy.

Better is "If Doctors Could Advertise," a three-part segment that first finds Tim and Don Crichton undergoing the same operation from different surgeons. As Don recuperates, Vicki waxes to an interviewer (Dick) about how frisky he is now, while Carol blandly recounts how lifeless the slumped-over Tim has become. This so-so effort is surpassed by Dick's amusing take of playing a doctor hawking his cheap procedures like a used car salesman. Somewhere between both of these falls the last bit, where Tim extols the virtues of his wife (Carol), who has been driven insane by all the work he has forced him to do, and praises how her psychiatrist has kept Carol going despite her protests.

Next, Vicki and Bernadette are two friends of Carol's who meet, and Carol insists they will love each other. While Carol nervously laughs at each other's comments, both women appear to be positioning themselves as to which is closer to Carol. Amid this uncomfortable scene, Carol mentions how she thought Vicki and Bernadette would click due to their mutual interest in art. When this topic arises, both women have a heavy discussion and tune out Carol before leaving without her. The latter grimaces and yells at Vicki, "She's not that much fun!" to save face. This is good but long in making its point.

The finale uses about ten Comden-Green compositions to depict Carol and Bernadette as newcomers to Manhattan attempting to find love in the city. That sounds a lot like *On the Town*, and indeed the women sing "Ohio" from that show in reminiscing about their hometown. There is also "New York, New York," "It's Love" (sung by Carol when she sees Dick at first, then to Tim after Dick rejects her), "The Party's Over," "Make Someone Happy" and many more. If not terribly original plot-wise, this is at least well sung by Carol and Bernadette, and it is a pleasant finale.

This was Dick's last time on the series, unbeknown to most. It also ends nearly five years of the program airing on Saturdays—the series moves to Sunday the following week.

Dec. 11, 1977: Rock Hudson

Q&A; Rock meets a barfly (Carol) whose romantic gestures take an unexpected turn; Carol and Tim offer their own interpretation of "Nobody Does It Better"; the president of Vortex Industries (Tim) endures many technical glitches while making a live speech on TV; Rock performs the title tune of *Camelot* and joins Carol in doing "What Do the Simple Folk Do?" from that musical in a skit; Eunice and Mickey Hart help Mama move out of her home; Carol and Vicki alternately challenging each other to come up with tunes based on eight notes, with the dancers accompanying them.

Comments: A new night along with the disappearance of Dick Van Dyke brings the series an opportunity to refresh itself, and it does so considerably, with a marked improvement over recent outings, albeit with some flaws still present. The Q&A is just a guy asking "I'd like to kiss the lips that made the Tarzan yell famous" and Carol shooting back, "OK, but Johnny Weissmuller isn't here!" There is no mention of Dick at all.

In the first skit, a bartender (Brad Trumbull) warns Rock not to make moves on Carol, but he disregards him and finds her receptive, as she fantasizes how they will become lovers. "Until you tell me you're leaving!" she yells, suddenly switching gears and throwing a drink at him as well as hitting him with a bottle. She keeps beating him up repeatedly while spilling details of their imagined affair, prompting great comic reactions by Rock as he fall down each time before scrambling away from her. Tim then arrives and hits Carol while she's leaving, which makes her amorous. Learning his name is Mr. Goodbar, she coos, "I've been looking for you." The wild turns and great timing and presentation of this sketch make it a winner.

There are a few brief laughs in seeing Carol in a rocking chair singing a country version of the Oscar-nominated hit from *The Spy Who Loved Me* to a cross-eyed Tim, but the bit really goes nowhere beyond that description. Better is the next new recurring segment, a KLEV news special with Tim whose microphone fade in and out, prompting a technical crew member's hand (played by Roger Beatty as credited) to take evasive actions like replacing it with a big clunky model in front of Tim and stapling another one to Tim's chest, painfully securing Tim's hand at the same time. The complications are hilarious, and the takes by Tim are on point at all times. This one hums along nicely.

In a mercifully overdue unscripted introduction, Carol mentions how she and Rock performed *I Do I Do* in summer stock and plan to do the same with *Camelot* in 1978 before he does the latter tune in an oversized chair. Half singing and speaking the way Rex Harrison did in *My Fair Lady*, his number is fine enough to watch. It's certainly better than the next one he does with Carol. Dressed as a grungy husband and a ratty housewife, the two prepare for dinner while the song they sing is supposed to be an ironic commentary on their circumstances. It certainly is—and it's not much more than that. This will be the last appearance of Rock on the show until the closing.

Mickey helps pack Mama's belongings as she prepares to go to Oakdale Senior Arms because, as she describes her neighborhood, "Every color in the rainbow is moving in here!" Eunice is delighted even though Mama obsesses about how she still has visions of how her husband Carl died on the toilet in the house. Mama also admits that she has not paid for her new apartment and suggests that they could ride around to find another place that might interest her, or "I could bunk in with you for a night or two." An enraged Eunice shoots down that notion, while Mama tries to sell her on the advantages of the situation. Mama can help raise the kids, for example, while Eunice drinks too much, eats poorly and has no prospects. Eunice retorts that she is glad to be independent, but after some more back and forth, Mama's tears wear her down, and she accepts the new tenant. Immediately, Mama starts critiquing Eunice. This is solid and funny from start to finish.

For the finale, Carol plays the scale on a piano to Vicki and has the latter sing songs based exactly on the notes she hits. These means mainly oldies like "Dinah," "Mammy," "Fly Me to the Moon" and more in a medley that fails to catch fire despite such flourishes as the dancers accompanying the women and Vicki offering a mock operatic voice at one point. At least Carol and Vicki look good in their identical black spangly pantsuits.

Although the ending is weak, this overall is pretty satisfying. The troubling note is how the proceedings were edited from how they were presented during taping—for example, Carol mentions that she and Rock did the "What Do the Simple Folk Do" number in her introduction of his solo, but those two appear in the opposite order during the broadcast. This re-editing will occur at least one more time this season (see Jan. 22, 1978). The fact that a series that used to present its material pretty much in real time in the same order seen by both the studio and home audiences is having to make this kind of change for a supposedly better show indicates the indecision surrounding the production schedule this season. This is not what Carol's series should have to do at this point.

Dec. 18, 1977: Ken Berry, Helen Reddy

Q&A; as Tudball and Wiggins celebrate Christmas by drinking Champagne, the latter becomes tipsy and frets about their working relationship; Helen performs "Blue" dressed as a doll along with the dancers; a couple (Ken and Carol) are confronted by a strict water department inspector (Tim); Ken does "Song and Dance Man" with the dancers; magazine covers serve as introductions for two sketches, one about the Concorde with Vicki and another about a Senate ethics committee with Ken and Tim, and a production of "Strike Up the Band" with everyone except Tim; Carol sings a tune about all the holidays.

Comments: This unremarkable Yuletide-themed edition has little inspired humor or joyful music. Even the Q&A gets short shrift. Carol only responds to what's her New Year's resolution with mock bravado in saying, "Oh, I have none, I'm perfect!" and reveals her middle name of Creighton before the first skit starts. The so-so Tudball-Wiggins routine has the secretary getting on Tudball's nerves by loudly decorating tinsel on her miniature Christmas tree while singing "Deck the Halls." His fears worsen as she gives him a tie with his name painted on it as a gift and he has to kiss her under the mistletoe. Each holds their own noses during the act. Tudball is further dismayed to learn the mistletoe was broccoli. The Champagne celebration is similarly awry—Wiggins cries because Tudball never calls her by her first name, Wanda, and her chipmunk, Henry, has gone. Trying to comfort her, Tudball accidentally rips off her skirt, and she does the same to his pants. Mrs. Tudball (Vicki) arrives to hear her husband tell Wiggins to keep this moment just between themselves and goes after him in response. Although it gets funnier as it goes, the comedy seems rehashed and does not bode well for the rest of the show.

Helen's segment uses $10,000 worth of items donated by the Ideal Toy Company that Carol reveals at the end of the show will be distributed to deserving children. That's more exciting that the presentation itself, where Helen appears as a light blue version of Raggedy Anne with the dancers costumed as dolls for a song that sounds like a bad rewrite of Helen's 1972 hit "I Am Woman."

The tedium worsens when Carol and Ken's happiness as a wife and husband gets tested by Tim, who sports a German accent and threatens them over their water use. He suggests Ken drink water from a washcloth to conserve, then locks their door and pulls down the shade to interrogate them. Carol and Ken alternately accuse each other of being more wasteful before they start choking each other. They then come to their senses, and Ken delivers an impassioned, incoherent mock-patriotic speech in defense of himself and Carol. During this monologue, Tim learns that he has come to the wrong address and leaves, and that's that. This sketch is long and barely amusing.

Vicki and Tim bring out Carol in a costume they supposedly were measuring for her during Carol's introduction of Helen earlier in the show. The hideous kit red and green woolen configuration ill fits her and produces a few chuckles. She introduces Ken, who does his standard tap number in a tan outfit that contrasts with the red and black spangly costumes of the dancers.

The pace and effectiveness pick up a little as the dancers are inexplicably dressed as convicts behind bars reading magazines whose feature stories serve as the basis for the rest of the show's offerings. Vicki is a flight attendant on the Concorde, which flies so quick that by the time she breathlessly finishes her emergency instructions spiel, it has already landed. Better is a congressional hearing during which the witness (Ken) implicates one of the senators (Tim) as the man he paid off recently for favorable votes. Tim is a delight as he expertly tries to hide himself in pantomime. For example, he swallows a cigarette when Ken said his target smoked, and he removes his gold tooth with a gavel when that revelation comes up. The ending is one of the few high spots of the show, as it is revealed that all the other members of the committee including the chairman (Jan Arvan) took gifts as bribes from Ken.

The finale has Carol, Vicki and Helen as Dallas Cowboys-like cheerleaders (their outfits vary mainly in that they use red instead of blue as the primary color) singing and moving to "Strike Up the Band." Ken joins them along with the dancers, who have the same costumes with the addition of large silver capes to move around. It ends with Carol singing an average solo in celebration of all the holidays.

The best thing that can be said about this show is that at least some children got nice toys for Christmas. If it were not for its seasonal references, it is doubtful this dull entry would have been released on DVD in 2013 otherwise. The worst part is that it omits the funniest segment, apparently due to an inability to obtain music rights for it.

In that bit, Vicki's hilarious impersonation of Rona Barrett leads into a very loose Carol sitting down next to Helen to promote the latter's new picture, *Pete's Dragon*. The audience is laughing from the start because technical difficulties screwed up properly superimposing the movie and its logo behind Carol and Helen twice. After the second failure, contained on an outtakes reel at the Paley Center for Media, Carol comically complains about the crew's delay. "They're having problems?! What about my bladder?! I'm going to have to shave again!" When the situation is finally corrected for air, Carol is so animated in her talk with Helen that she even ad libs "Hot damn!" which probably unnerved some of the more staid Disney executives. Finally, Carol and Helen sing "It's Not Easy," a tune from the G-rated movie, with clips appearing behind them on screen.

The segment beats everything else on this show in terms of comedy and humor.

Dec. 25, 1977: Repeat of 1977 show

Jan. 1, 1978: Steve Lawrence

Carol sings "You Light Up My Life" to Tim while bathing him in a tub; Steve performs "We're All Alone"; Steve is a robber perplexed by a grocer (Tim) whose poor grasp of English complicates Steve's crime; Tim is an elderly gentleman on a bench accosted by Carol the pigeon lady and her tales of her previous lives in history; the tables turn as a bartender (Tim) bares his stories of woe to his customer (Carol); a Nazi movie spoof with Tim and Steve; Steve, Carol and Vicki do a medley of top hits of the last eleven years.

Comments: When one of the few interesting aspects of a *Carol Burnett Show* is that the guest star appears in a commercial airing during the episode (in this case, Steve Lawrence hawking toothpaste), you know the installment is in trouble. This show does stand out in highlighting the series' scattershot relationship with contemporary music. By alternately mocking, celebrating and awkwardly paying tribute to songs from 1966-1977, the overall result is confusing at best, with several unfortunate lowlights.

The first variable musical presentation has Carol wailing out that period's omnipresent hit (Debby Boone's "You Light Up My Life" spent ten long weeks at Number One in late 1977) as she soaks Tim in bubbles, who crosses his eyes at the experience. By the last chorus, she joins him in the basin as well, wearing her clothes. This odd number is somewhat amusing, but it is unclear if it is sending up the saccharine sound and message of the song or if it is just occurring because they needed something for Carol to sing.

Doubts continue as Steve vocalizes a straight version of another recent hit. It retains its power as a ballad with his performance (although purists will prefer the more soulful and popular versions done by Boz Scaggs and Rita Coolidge), but it could've just as very well have been spoofed for its pretensions as is implied with the previous routine.

Things fail to improve in a drawn-out sketch that probably would have worked better if Harvey did it instead of Steve. To his credit, Steve does try his best in repeated attempts to steal from Tim, who does things such as confuse Steve saying "gun" with "gum" and offering him to buy a pack. They argue over proper translations and phrasings of items before a policeman arrives, Steve buys an expensive item and scrams to avoid capture. Tim then reveals to the policeman in a normal voice that he is trying his best to speak Rumanian whenever possible. It's a flat kicker to a long bit.

The next segment also needs trimming but is considerably funnier. As a crazed woman, Carol riffs to Tim about her memories of reincarnation while he calls for his nurse who placed him on the bench for relaxation. Recalling her time as Cleopatra, she muses, "Egypt was a little bit like Idaho, except without the mountains and the Winnebagos . . . I had 27 camels." It prompts Tim to yell for his nurse, even though his false teeth are out. Undaunted Carol goes onward and makes Tim grimace into keeping a straight face by mentioning Siamese elephants (see Nov. 5, 1977 for why that amused him). After discussions about Attila the Hun and being Paul Revere's horse, Carol spills hot liquid on Tim's chest. He takes off his shirt, and a visiting cop arrests him for that exposure. As the cop escorts Tim away, Carol notes, "Boy, the weirdoes you meet in a park!"

Tim and Carol shine brighter in the show's best offering, as bartender Tim makes a drink and smokes as he pours out complaints about his wife to an unsuspecting customer. Carol learns she must assume his traditional duties when he even refuses to answer the phone because he does not want to talk to his wife. Alternately defensive and aggressive with Carol, he drinks a beer and asks her if she will cash a check for him before he stumbles out drunk. Carol gives Tim free rein to ham it up here, and he does so expertly.

The goodwill built here comes to a halt with a World War II spy send-up that is generic in virtually every sense. Tim is a bumbling stooge to Steve's confident Nazi leader, both roles that each have played previously and have little new to add here. Invading Carol's residence (Tim breaks down the door thoroughly with the butt of his gun before opening the knob, a nice bit), they attempt to expose her lair as part of the underground resistance. She fools them with a voice from the radio said to be Hitler (vocals by Stan Mazin, who surprisingly counts this as one of his favorite parts on the series) and tricks them into playing "The Fuhrer Says," the Nazi equivalent of "Simon Says," where she gets them to pull out the pins of their grenades but not throw them because she did not say the title phrase first. Naturally they explode and kill them. That is all that should be said about this sluggish and childish waste of time.

To celebrate the series' eleven seasons on the air—and finally give Vicki something to do—snippets of eighteen songs are heard, beginning with Bobby Hebb's "Sunny," which was actually a hit in 1966, before the series debuted. This is a shaky start, and Steve doing the Doors' "Light My Fire" makes one worry it may become an unintentionally campy number. Luckily, Carol, Steve and Vicki fare better in later tunes, sometimes as solos, others as duets and trios, as soft rock songs predominate, such as "Mrs. Robinson," "Aquarius," "Alone Again Naturally" and of course Vicki's hit "The Night the Lights Went Out in Georgia," which generates whistles of appreciation. She follows it with "Tie a Yellow Ribbon Round the Ole Oak Tree" and for some reason runs into the audience, which includes an unidentified Shirley Hemphill, a regular on the ABC sitcom *What's Happening!* at the time. Four more songs follow, including "Feelings," which Carol overdramatizes likes she did as Eunice in the Feb. 12, 1977 show, this time by pretending to hug herself with her back to the camera, as do Vicki and Steve.

They end by all singing "You Light Up My Life" straight, with Tim coming out with a pink towel wrapped around waist to join them and remind everyone of what he did when the song was done earlier in the show. But this just prompted more confusion over whether the show likes current music or not. Anyhow, this concludes one of the season's lesser installments and serves as another indication the series needs to end soon.

Jan. 8, 1978: Roddy McDowall, Ken Berry

Q&A; Carol and Tim do a comic turn to "You Can't Turn Me Off"; Philip (Roddy) has a prize to receive in Raytown, but Mama and Eunice care less about the honor than they do about how they think he treats them; Ken and Tim are competitors at the 1908 world championship pool match who taunt each other; Roddy interrupts Carol's efforts to say goodbye to him; a two-part takeoff of the 1935 film classic *Top Hat* features Ken and Carol in the Fred Astaire and Ginger Rogers roles respectively, joined by the rest of the cast and dancers.

Comments: Every element of this show feels like a warmed-over retread of previous offerings, with the exception of a lively Q&A. "Who do I want to win the Super Bowl? The Lakers," Carol says at the start. "You need a lawyer?" asks one guest as he hands his card to her. "How good are you?" Carol shoots back while keeping the card. A girl from Rhode Island asks for kisses from Carol and Tim, and Carol at least was able to accommodate her. The rest of the show never is as entertaining.

A slovenly Carol singing a recent tune by one-hit wonder girl group High Inergy to Tim in bed while he strips to his long johns and pulls off the mattress with Carol is awfully similar to what the duo did on the previous show to "You Light Up My Life." It is a one-joke premise stretched too long, and Carol sending up a hip, sultry contemporary hit is another sign of how out of touch the series appears to be with the current music scene.

The Eunice segment is better but only ranks as average among the Family sketches. As Eunice's brother Philip (Roddy) prepares to receive an award from his hometown, Mama asks him to take some time with the mayor and tell the later to get rid of stray dogs. Eunice is likewise preoccupied by herself as she requests that he consider her to be his secretary even though she cannot type. After Mama and Eunice argue about what they did to clean and prepare the house for Philip's visit, Eunice wonders why her brother does not visit more often before they head to the ceremony. This is the best skit of the show, but that's not saying much.

Tim mugs some more in a pantomime with Ken (and dancers playing onlookers) in a sketch shot with a brown tint to give it an "old-timey" look. Ken has his cigar placed in his pocket via Tim's cue stick, so he retaliates by putting a bottle on his own cue and breaking it on Tim's head. Other pranks occur, culminating in Ken pushing the pool table through a wall with Tim hanging onto it. This is reminiscent of the Oct. 25, 1975 early twentieth century boxing scene Tim did with Harvey, but where that was original and had a sweet ending, here it just seems like the participants are going through the paces, and the modest result produces a few smiles and no real chuckles.

Things perk up slightly when Carol tells Roddy, her lover, that she must leave him, and he tells her to stop and not move so he can remember her in this moment. That leads to him directing her about how she should look again before departing, and he keeps having her repeat it to the point where she finally pulls off her wig and goes in a huff. Although this gets better as it progresses, the setup is a slender one, and it feels limp in execution.

Déjà vu also permeates what is billed as a 1930s musical homage to Fred and Ginger, "Hi-Hat," which follows the movie for the most part and has precious few highlights. Roddy is in Venice introducing his nephew to Vicki's niece, and they check into a hotel with Tim as the clerk, doing an Italian version of his Tudball voice. Carol and Ken bump into each other at the check-in desk after Roddy and Vicki leave, and the plot's misunderstandings go into place. The meager shining moments include a gondolier paddling by Roddy and Vicki to sing "Putting on the Ritz" in Italian, a great tap routine and parody of Fred Astaire's singing voice by Ken in "Putting on My Top Hat," and Carol doing a solo abetted by humorous sound effects. Otherwise, the numbers presented along with the flat writing make watching this show's second half hour a chore, even with nice overhead shots of the dancers a la Busby Berkeley. Somehow Artie Malvin and Stan Freeman's unmemorable songs win them Emmys. The series desperately needs material better than this fast, even if it is going off the air in two months.

Jan. 15, 1978: Pre-empted by Super Bowl XII

Jan. 22, 1978: Eydie Gorme

Q&A; the nutty bench lady (Carol) perplexes a meek bystander (Tim) again; a construction worker (Tim) has three different inspirations on how to murder his ding-a-ling wife (Carol), yet they all backfire on him; Eydie sings "Come in From the Rain"; Vicki is a writer dictating aloud her story of a housewife (Carol) and her lover (Tim); a KLEV news special features an executive showing how his company's new bottle top prevents tampering—and discovers he cannot open it either; Carol and Eydie perform a medley of 1940s hits, including "A Tisket A Tasket," "Tangerine" and "Sentimental Journey."

Comments: If there was any doubt that this series needs to end soon, this show is Exhibit A. Barren of any new ideas, it rehashes old concepts badly. There is Carol's weird bench lady from Jan. 1, 1978, Tim's hardhat trying to kill Carol from Nov. 26, 1977, the writer changing characters while typing bit that goes back to Oct. 11, 1972, Tim's executive addressing the audience he first did on Dec. 11, 1977, and Carol and Eydie doing a medley with the orchestra on stage, which they first did on Oct. 5, 1970. At least there is the Q&A, where Carol shakes hands with a woman who is celebrating her 70th birthday and receives thanks from a man who works at a convalescent center for providing laughter in his life. After showing off some new heels with socks that she heard are latest trend in France that unimpress her ("Isn't that the stupidest?" she says), she receives greetings from two women from India before the show commences.

The bench lady's non sequiturs include betting Tim $1 that it is raining right now, bringing out a dead bird and imagining a horse race. Fed up and conned out of $20 from her antics, Tim tries to win his money back by pretending a football game is occurring. Carol ignores him, and when a cop (Don Crichton) arrives, she convinces him that Tim is crazy and has him hauled away. This is mostly just odd and long to endure.

Nonetheless, it is better than the tedious trio of supposedly comic setups Tim performs with Carol based on stories in the newspaper told to him by his partner at work (Brad Trumbull). He gets a pet cobra in a basket designed to attack when Carol plays the flute, but the snake escapes and winds up winding around Tim's neck. Carol then comes to another part of the stage and briefly continues to speak in her high-pitched dumbbell voice before taking her wig off and describing Eydie ostentatiously while Vicki translates in yet another irritating guest introduction for this season.

Eydie's number is inconsequential, even though it involves a mild recent hit by the Captain and Tennille (who are next week's guests!). So are the other Tim-Carol bits. He tries to get her to look through a window and instead accidentally gets shot by an assassin again, then has a time bomb he plans to give to her as a gift stuck to his leg, causing an explosion offstage. This last bit is so sloppy even the ticking sound effect stops and starts irregularly on the soundtrack, which is indicative of the shaky level of the comedy.

Between the two last hardhat sketches, Vicki unwittingly manipulates Tim into changing jobs three times and having Carol hit in the knees by milk bottles as Vicki works on a manuscript. Tim and Carol grimace nicely as they pretend they love drinking buttermilk, and in a play on words, the person knocking on the door is a paper boy—literally. Written by Franelle Silver and Roger Beatty, this piece is acceptable but not as funny as the originals done five seasons earlier. Silver says they created it one Wednesday when another bit in rehearsal fell flat—a telling admission of the show's quality by now.

A few more chuckles do abound in Tim's monologue as he and the hand of a hidden assistant (Roger Beatty) attempt to open a stubborn cap on a bottle. The hand bangs it on the desk fruitlessly, hitting Tim in the process, and tries hammering and sawing it noisily offstage, all for naught. An effort to dislodge it with steaming water only gets the latter spread on Tim. It finally ends with the top being blown up offstage and given to Tim, who then opens it and hurts his hand. This is as lively as the show gets.

For the finale, Peter Matz and the band appear behind Carol and Eydie as they trade off doing snippets of "Goody Goody," "Why Don't You Do Right?" "Don't Sit Under the Apple Tree," and at least eight others. Each song inexplicably is met with lots of applause (the women do sound fine, but there are no showstoppers here), and their mock collapse at the end just seems bizarre and unnecessary.

To wind down this wan installment, Vicki summarizes the entire show, supposedly for her Aunt Fran who missed it. Her speedy minute-long recap includes an impression of Eydie singing that cracks up Carol before the latter sings "It's Time to Say So Long." She mentions Carol doing a Tarzan yell that did not make it on the air, and her listing of the order of segments being the typing sketch, the cobra sketch, Eydie singing, the park sketch, the bomb and Tim's bottle routine strongly imply that this show featured heavy post-production editing to try and salvage it unsuccessfully. No dancers appear (lucky for them), and there is no acting for Eydie either, which seems weird given her past success in skits on this series. She does do a fine wide-eyed impression of Vicki's take on how she sings, but it cannot compensate for the many deficiencies on display here.

As final evidence that inspiration had run dry everywhere, even a real commercial during the show featuring Eydie was for the same product her husband pushed on the series three weeks earlier. Cumulatively, it is harder to think of a worse swan song to the series' most frequently seen female guest than what is presented here.

Jan. 29, 1978: Steve Lawrence, Captain and Tennille

Q&A; a meek receptionist (Carol) freaks out over the fear that her boss (Steve) is making sexual advances toward her after work; Steve performs "I'll Go My Way By Myself" in a hotel room beset by guests; Tim plays a man who reconnects with his long-lost sister (Carol) and finds they have little in common; the Captain and Tennille sing "Gentle Stranger"; the regulars and guests participate in a spoof of the year's most unforgettable commercials; an ending medley has the ensemble wear various hats while singing more than ten numbers accompanied by the dancers.

Comments: This is the most extreme up-and-down episode this season, with plenty of incredible highs and deadly lows. The highs start with the Q&A, where the audience screams for the announcement of the Captain and Tennille as guests, followed by a struggling vocalist from Pittsburgh telling Carol he has been wanting to come to her show for four years and wanted to know how to get an agent. Carol responds by having the man join her on stage to sing his tune of choice, "What I Did for Love" from *A Chorus Line*. Tentative in projecting at first, Carol encourages him by saying "Just squeeze your buns!" and he loosens up and sounds fine. Steve Lawrence emerges, acting amazed by what he hears, and the young man put his arm around Steve, who warily regards the overt personal action to the audience's amusement. Carol and Steve accompany the man in harmony for the last verses, and the audience loves it.

From there, it's to two pretty good sketches that could have been even better with some tightening. The first has Steve trying to detain Carol in his office so her colleagues can set up a surprise birthday party in the main room, while she thinks he wants to get romantic instead. Their voiceovers communicate their internal thoughts in their predicament amid some slapstick, such as Steve accidentally tearing off parts of Carol's shirt and skirt and Carol unintentionally swallowing a whistle she planned to use to signal help if Steve became frisky. During her skirt rip, Carol runs out of the office and learns the truth, and she tells everyone she thought Steve was trying to make a pass at her, which cracks him up heartily. His comments about not liking her enrage Carol enough to hit him in the face with her cake, an OK ending for a moderately enjoyable skit.

For Steve's solo spot, it uses the nice approach done previously (see Oct. 4, 1972 for an example) of havoc happening around him as he attempts to croon. Here the dancers and some extras enter his hotel room to clean up and even host a wedding party with guests while he remains unflappable in delivering his tune. It is somewhat funny, but the setup does not really have an ending or much purpose as to why this all is bedeviling Steve.

Next comes a loser skit where Tim is interrupted watching the NBA playoffs by Carol, his kin who he has not seen in 30 years. They recount what has occurred in their lives. Nothing consequential is mentioned—or funny either. This is the most humorless sketch Carol and Tim ever did, going a long way for little laughs, and the payoff where she leaves and he turns on the TV to see he missed the end of the game is pointless.

Mercifully, the Captain and Tennille then both play pianos and do fine for their featured number, even though the banter between Carol and Steve introducing them is weak. Better yet is a hysterical installment of TV commercial takeoffs, where virtually everything scores strongly. Tim is a macho cowboy ordering beer until he gets his spurs on his boots caught and stumbles out of a bar. Steve uses Carol's deodorant meant for women and comes out in drag. Carol mocks Catherine Deneuve's delivery and pretentious commentary for a perfume ad. Best of all, Tim plays Robert Conrad daring someone to knock a battery off his shoulder, and his face repeatedly gets beaten to a pulp over several times during the segment. Also of note is a fragrance ad spoof, not only because it includes the Captain and Tennille providing some choice lines about how awful the room smells, but also because of a memorable blooper Carol created in one taping. As Vicki wrinkles her nose at Carol and asks, "Fish for dinner?" Carol tells her "Get off my ass!" rather than "case," causing Carol to promptly apologize to her amused audience about how easily the word slipped out. Franelle Silver wrote this great segment.

Unfortunately from there comes a finale is tedious to endure—despite relatively quick changes in headwear by participants to match the songs—thanks in part to outdated material (the most recent one is "Up Up and Away" from 1967). Having the dancers painted and acting as mimes does not help. The few highlights include Carol doing her Shirley Temple impression when singing "You Make Me Feel So Young" and Steve mocking Anthony Newley with "What Kind of Fool Am I." But even that was a knockoff of Harvey Korman's Newley impersonation from the Nov. 15, 1975 finale. By the time Tim shows up at the end dressed as the Captain to take over the piano and let the latter join the others up front for a bow, this presentation has become a lost cause.

At the end, Carol pulls down one hat over her face, cracking up Steve, and warmly embraces the Captain and Tennille, who write a lot when they sign her guest book. Glad to see they had a good time despite the overall schizophrenic quality of this show.

Feb. 5, 1978: Ken Berry, Natalie Cole

Q&A; "The Tiff" is a sepia-tinted skit with Carol and Tim arguing in their apartment during the turn of the century; Natalie lip syncs to "Our Love"; Carol and Ken's ennui while eating at a restaurant is interrupted by the arrival of Vicki and Tim; "Tall People" has Ken, Carol, Tim and Vicki standing on their knees to look diminutive while singing a novelty song; Ken lip syncs to a number featuring video tricks with the dancers; thee takeoffs on the effects of TV on people's lives; Carol, Vicki and Natalie present a musical tribute to evil women.

Comments: Natalie Cole doing a contemporary hit, a foreshadowing of Tim's future Dorf character and a decent Q&A are the meager attractions of another disappointment. In the Q&A, a delightfully jittery woman presents Carol with a picture of the latter's mother and her sister when both were nineteen years old in Texas. Carol is touched to see what her parent looked like in 1927 ("Boy, my mom has good legs!"). Amid a few lesser queries, a woman from Missouri claims her brother looks like Tim, and Carol brings Tim out to show a clip from his new movie, *Billion Dollar Hobo*, which gets a few chuckles.

The humor quotient falls off quickly in the opening sketch, an old-timey pantomime with Carol in a ratty robe and Tim sporting a walrus mustache as they wreak revenge on each other. Tim cannot get any coffee, so he makes Carol spill her cup. She does the same with his milk and then hits him hard. Much more uninspired slapstick follows, including Carol putting moving fan blades against Tim's face and filling his crotch with water from their indoor pump, almost a steal from what happened to him in the gas sketch from the Oct. 22, 1977 show. Finally, as he leaves for work, Tim kisses Carol and carries a briefcase that says "Marriage Consultant" on it. It's a long way to go for a little payoff at the end.

Natalie provides the show with its last top ten hit performed by the original artist, something that had not happened more than a year since Glen Campbell did "Southern Nights" on the Jan. 15, 1977 installment. Looking gorgeous in a green gown, the show tries to tart up her silky soul entry by having her look like she is singing to herself, an unnecessary conceit that takes away from an otherwise good musical number.

What follows next is Carol and Ken awkwardly shooting the breeze about food at a restaurant before Vicki and Tim arrive and perk them up by discussing their recent trip to Hawaii. When they leave, Carol and Ken quietly go back to the food, broken up by idle mentions of what's wrong with what they are eating. Whatever the meaning was behind this skit, it collapses horribly both as comedy and drama.

A little better is a send-up of Randy Newman's controversial satire song "Short People," with Ken joining the regulars with shoes on their knees to move around to the tune. Tim will later employ this shtick in home videos in the 1980s and 1990s as Dorf, a dumpy, lumpy comic character. Here it is a serviceable but not stellar bit of comic nonsense to a song that Tim co-wrote with Steve Lawrence, believe it or not.

Another fake bit of chit-chat between Carol and her guest begins Ken's dance number. He tells her she makes him sound too nice and he wants to be tough, swinging, cool, which apparently is supposed to be amusing. The dance itself is allegedly humorous too, with Ken moving before a black screen that allows parts of the dancers to show up and accompany him, but the result is more bizarre than anything else.

Next, after being amazed that Americans average watching six hours and nine minutes of TV every day, Carol announces that this exposure's impact on humans is the basis for a rather unfunny trio of bits. Vicki confesses to her psychiatrist (Ken Berry) about how commercials have affected her by referencing taglines, only for him to tell her she needs to soak her hand in dishwashing liquid, as was promoted in an advertisement at the time. Following that is Carol as a housewife who is drunk to cope with being too engrossed in the storyline of a soap opera—a tiresome conceit. Finally, Ken is a lawyer telling a judge (Don Crichton) and jury that TV violence has no impact on his client (Tim, in a bunny outfit). Tim paint and irons on Ken as part of his tiresome Bugs Bunny-like behavior, which culminates in him giving Ken a stick of dynamite instead of a carrot. Ken runs out and gets blown out offstage, but this sketch already was bombing prior to that event.

The evil women tribute has Carol, Vicki and Natalie performing "Hard Hearted Hannah," "Whatever Lola Wants," "Put the Blame on Mame" and the like in red gowns and black feather boas with dancers acting out parts of the songs. By the time they do a long number on Lizzie Borden, this routine's appeal has run thin. All the show is left with ultimately is that Natalie is the last new musical guest the series introduces with this episode. That's not much of an accomplishment for it.

Feb. 12, 1978: Pre-empted by special showing of 1976 movie *Gator*

Feb. 19, 1978: Ken Berry

** Two Revolutionary War soldiers (Tim and Ken) find themselves trapped in a cabin by Indians; Carol sings "The Shortest Love Song"; a supermarket clerk (Tim) who has difficulty understanding English cannot help a woman asking him for assistance in purchasing an antidote for a poisonous chemical; Ken and Carol duet on "The Singles Bar"; a salute to Warner Brothers movies includes spoofs of *Mr. Skeffington* and *Yankee Doodle Dandy.*

Comments: A rare show from this season not on DVD, the trading circuit or in archive collections, there is little to suggest that this is a missing gem, particularly with Tim recreating his unappealing foreign grocer character from the Jan. 1, 1978 episode and at least the show's third tribute to Warner Brothers (previously done on Jan. 26, 1970 and Dec. 4, 1976). Ken Berry will appear once more on the March 12, 1978 show.

Feb. 26, 1978: Steve Lawrence

Q&A; Mr. Tudball confuses what he overhears Ms. Wiggins say is the problem with her car to think it means she has only a week left to live; a couple (Carol and Steve) en route to their tenth anniversary celebration make unanticipated revelations to each other during a flight emergency; a chauffeur (Tim) protects a veteran stage star (Carol) as she goes to eat at a diner; a live KLEV news special has the head of Vortex Industries (Tim) unveiling a new dog food to calamitous results; Carol and Steve have a distinctive encounter on a crowded elevator car.

Comments: A somewhat better installment than most this season, this last show with one solo guest is odd in several ways. There is no musical number, despite that being Steve's claim to fame. Also, the Q&A runs six and a half minutes, in part because this taping follows Carol's announcement to end the series. "Do you have anything special planned for your last show?" one person asks. She reveals it will be half sketches and half retrospective material. Prior to that, she confirms having cut her hair recently and jokes that her real name is Ben Gazzara (an answer first used on Sept. 18, 1967). Bob Mackie comes out to be kissed by a female fan. Carol does the Tarzan yell and relates her summer stock horror story (see Oct. 9, 1967). She says she consumes soft drinks instead of beer during the Eunice sketches, claims her real-life sister is at home with her husband and children, and gets thanks from a female Marine who says her crew loves her. Amid all this talk, Tim, Vicki and Steve come out to cart her away and commence the show.

The Tudball misunderstanding is typical Burnett farce, meaning it is pleasurable to watch if a little silly and farfetched. Tudball curbs his anger when Wiggins spills coffee on his lap and gets glue on his jacket for the simple fact that he believes she is near death, when in fact it is the body of her vehicle that is falling apart with no hope left for it. The slapstick and the reactions seem somewhat familiar to previous installments, but still this setup generates plenty of chuckles due to expert acting, writing and direction.

Heading to Hawaii, Carol and Steve freak out when they learn their plane is having engine trouble. Steve confesses to have a fling with one of their mutual friends for one and a half years, and Carol tells him she is glad he admitted the truth. But when the crisis passes, she gets angry with him. Another malfunction arises, and this time Carol blurts that she was seeing the husband of the woman Steve was seeing—and that their son is not Steve's. He now is angry, but when they finally land, they both are apologetic. The problem is that Vicki and Tim arrive from the back, and they likewise confessed how they had been cheating on each other with Carol and Steve, prompting fisticuffs among all parties. Despite a clever twist ending, this segment is mostly so-so.

In a sketch that fails to find its rhythm, Carol is an actress in a smash who is surprised when she eats at 3 a.m. that no one at a restaurant recognizes her. While her chauffeur (Tim) consoles her, her waitress (Vicki) and fellow patrons care nothing about her, even when she sings along with a tune playing on a jukebox. This desperate for attention routine while believing you are still famous was done earlier and better with Nora Desmond (see March 10, 1973), and attempts to wring out some new pathos here flop.

However, the show bounces back with Tim's rather uproarious bit of trying to sell some awful new chow for pooches on the air. He winces first when opening the smelly can. It attracts a fly that requires a technician's hand (Roger Beatty) to swat it. That same hand keeps pushing the bowl of food close to Tim as he tries to avoid it. A dachshund placed in front of Tim on the table eats out of another container instead before scampering away to avoid the bowl. In desperation, the technician puts on a hand puppet that resembles a dog, but its head falls off while "eating" the food and gets it on Tim. This is the sort of hysterical material the series has lacked sorely most of this season.

The conclusion is atypically brief. Spying Carol and wanting her regardless of the other passengers going up on an elevator, Steve croons "Be My Love" to an embarrassed Carol, who tries to run away in horror as he pursues her. That's about it, apart from the usual closing and Steve doing a mock strip routine—and once again, no dancers at the finale either. That will change in the next episode, one of the series' all-time best.

March 5, 1978: Steve Martin, Betty White

"As the Stomach Turns" features Marian, her daughter, Canoga Falls' leading interior decorator (Betty) and lineman Richard Dryface (Steve) meeting a mute alien; Steve offers his comedy act designed for four dogs; the pigeon lady (Carol) accosts a meek gentleman (Tim) and tells him to follow her plans; Eunice and Mama surprise Ellen (Betty) with a visit before the latter's anniversary party; a spoof of *Beach Blanket Bingo* with Steve and Carol in the Frankie Avalon and Annette Funicello roles, joined by Vicki as Carol's friend, Betty and Tim as bikers in leather, and the dancers as other bathers.

Comments: This is the series' last great new episode, and even though every segment clicks, it is telling that all the sketches featuring recurring characters. Clearly the search for comedy in new creations has been shot. In any event, "As the Stomach Turns" starts with a visit by Betty, "whose work is known in every bedroom in town," saying she has heard about Marian's missing daughter and offers to redo the upstairs den to console the homeowner. She goes upstairs while Marian's doorbell sounds the five-note movie theme for *Close Encounters of the Third Kind* and leads to the introduction of a hardhat (Steve) who wildly claims that Marian's daughter has been abducted by an alien spacecraft. He throws plants down outside, places down eggs to serve as "landing lights" for the vessel, and then cracks the eggs with a tennis racquet and puts flour on them. As Marian worries about his odd behavior, Steve says his catch phrase "Excuse me!" before red lights appear in the yard. Betty comes downstairs to say Marian's daughter (Vicki) is back, and the latter has a baby with two antennae. Following them is the dramatic entrance of the alien (Tim), appearing to be wearing a puffy purple plastic suit, lavender coloring on its nose and lower lip, and long foam fingers. Steve tries to communicate with the being using hand signals, and both make maneuvers typically seen in Three Stooges shorts. The scene ends with Tim beckoning one of the humans to join him on the ship—but which one? Even for people not familiar with the movie this sends up, this is a fine entry.

Steve keeps the laughs coming by cracking canine-themed jokes in front of four pooches. Two wander off, while another offers him a paw and the remaining one rubs against him. When Steve plays a dog whistle, the two remaining dogs go wild in response. This original, hilarious bit is arguably the best comic monologue ever performed on the show.

The crazy pigeon woman (Carol) this time harasses Tim by talking to imaginary people while taking his watch and ring, among other irritations. When Tim reports her bizarre activity to a cop (Don Crichton), the latter takes Tim away for telling tall tales. This is the weakest element of the show, but still generates a fair share of laughs.

The Family skit finds Ellen peeved that Eunice and Mama have arrived just before she is having guests and wants to hustle them out while she prepares her anniversary party. The gift her sister and mother bring—a cologne box two-for-one deal—irks Ellen, but the other two ignore her. "I'm just pleased that at least one of my daughters was able to keep a marriage together," quips Mama as Eunice glares in response. As Mama goes upstairs to say hello to Ellen's children, Eunice demands her sister share custody of taking care of mother or she will take Ellen to court. Mama overhears the end of the conversation and confronts Ellen. "I have given up my entire life for you!" she yells at Ellen. "Oh, set it to music, Mama!" Ellen says in response (with some applause). As the guests arrive, Ellen dismisses Mama and Eunice's claims about her, and to Eunice's dismay, Mama tells her to respect her sister as they leave. Poignant, pointed and funny, this sketch sizzles.

"The Late Late Movie" presents "Beach Blanket Boo Boo," which opens with the dancers on a beach set that is a real treat who want to see more of their bodies than usual. Most of the females are in bikinis, and all the males except Stan Mazin are shirtless. All look and sound great as Steve enters (with dark hair) and sings with a mike in his hand while Carol ogles him. This is followed by a wonderfully and obviously fake shot of Carol standing on a surf board next to Steve as they sing a love song, during which he invites her to join him on his own board. Their bliss is interrupted on the show by Tim and Betty as bikers who arrive to take over the beach. To settle their dispute over Betty and Carol, Tim and Steve has a surfing competition, with Tim riding the waves with his motorcycle on a board. Vicki, Betty and Carol sing encouragement to both men in the efforts. All ends well, with Steve proposing to Carol so he can see what she looks like with her clothes on. Although beach party movies are an easy target to parody, a lot of energy and dead-on comic moments here make this spoof by Rick Hawkins and Liz Sage a winner.

Carol does not sing "It's Time to Say So Long" before the credits roll, which is a credit to how much is packed into this show. The only downside is this is Steve's only appearance and just the third by Betty, both of whom are perfect guests for the series.

March 12, 1978: Ken Berry, James Garner, George Carlin

Q&A; a doctor (Ken) is distressed that his patients (James, Carol, Vicki and Tim) are regressing to the behaviors that he had eradicated; George does a monologue of a hard-pitching music album salesman on TV; Tim is a husband trying to kill his dense wife (Carol) in a series of blackouts; Ken and Vicki do a vaudeville-style song-and-dance number, "My Cutie's Due at the Two-to-Two Today"; a dental hygienist (Carol) has her ex-husband (George) as a patient; Carol and James are having a hard time ending their relationship; Ken and Carol play kazoos with the dancers in the finale.

Comments: After the highs of last week's show, this is a comedown, even though it has some decent moments. In the Q&A, one girl thanks Carol for making her laugh for eleven years. Quizzed on her future, Carol jokes, "I have no plans. I'll be on the unemployment line in about three weeks." Becoming serious, she notes that she will do a special with Dolly Parton, a TV-movie adaptation of Erma

Bombeck's best-selling book *The Grass is Always Greener Over the Septic Tank* and another motion picture with Robert Altman. There are lighter moments—one gentleman asks if she had any one person in history to spend one with, who would it be, and she tells the men in the director's booth that it would be none of them, as she shows the audience the earpiece that allows her to hear their sometimes off-color comments. Regarding her trio of male guest stars—a first for the show—she says, "They're all backstage, locked up in my dressing room."

The first skit has two of those guest stars, with Ken having led a three-week boot camp to treat Jim for fears about the boogey man, Tim for cross dressing (he appears in a blonde wig, floral print dress and high heels in a great visual gal), Vicki for psychosomatic worries and Carol for a split personality. Those symptoms appear in the order those individuals are described before Ken plans to leave for Hawaii, and he frantically tries to correct them. Ultimately, he gives up and announces to the quartet that "Cure or no cure, I am flying to Hawaii!" He then flaps his arms and exits through a window. This passable sketch could have been great if it was tighter and the behaviors displayed were wilder.

"The wonderful Mr. George Carlin" contributes this show's biggest laughs by far as Carl Closeout, offering viewers a record of the greatest 400,000 songs ever written for just twelve cents a pound or $27,000 total. He has country songs ("A Train Ran Over My Friend"), Latin tunes ("Mexican Corrective Stocking Dance"), symphonies ("Area Code 212") and many more genres. "Try these records in your own home for ten years," he says of the introductory offer, adding that he will throw in rare recordings such as "The sound of Mickey Rooney trying to get out of a garment bag." Carlin's delivery and offbeat material are sharp and focused, something missing in most of the rest of the program.

Next come three blackouts interspersed throughout the show of the now-tired concept of Tim learning ideas about how to kill his wife (Carol) from newspaper items related by a fellow construction worker (Brad Trumbull—three male guest stars plus dancers yet they needed a bit player for this). First Tim tries crushing her head in a trash compactor, then hitting her with a demolition ball and finally putting dynamite in a piano that will ignite when Carol plays "pop" in "Pop Goes the Weasel." Carol does her best by creating a dithering, high-pitched voice that makes you understand how it might get on Tim's nerves, but all three are overdone and unworthy of making the cut on air by this time.

The disappointments continue with Ken and Vicki's unremarkable performance, followed by the obvious gag of Carol wreaking havoc on George's teeth to express her displeasure to him as her ex-husband. To his credit, George does his best to amuse by grimacing while attempting to respond to Carol's inquisition. Similarly, James is much better than the monotonous material he is given of breaking up with Carol amid hassles—she leaves through the wrong door, forgets her glasses and purse, they get interrupted by a phone call. This powerful acting combo is wasted on substandard material.

The finale fails to pull the show out of its slump, with only limited joy generated by Carol and Ken as two bums on a snow-covered street interpolating tunes such as "Put on a Happy Face" via kazoo. It is as unsatisfactory as most of the show itself, which apparently tried too hard to accommodate the visits by Carlin and Garner without having compelling comedy ready to showcase their talents. What a shame, especially near the end of the series' run.

March 19, 1978: Steve Lawrence, Bernadette Peters

Q&A; a writer (Vicki) types a tale set in an emergency room about a nurse (Carol) and her physician lover (Tim); Steve sings "Weekend in New England" and "Here's That Rainy Day"; complications ensue when Tim and Vicki meet Steve and Carol at a restaurant; Bernadette sits on top of a piano played by Don and performs "Jump Shout Boogie" with the dancers; "Off to War" has a doughboy (Tim) awkwardly saying farewell to his girlfriend; facing an office cutback, Carol and Bernadette compete to be the more efficient secretary; a Parisian mini-musical salute to Cole Porter.

Comments: The last hour episode with all original material goes out with more of a whimper than a bang, despite some emotional moments. The sketches are long and have a "been there, done that" look and feel, as do the musical portions. The Q&A does excel, though, as Carol receives a standing ovation and a bouquet of roses from one girl, prompting her to quip, "Have I died?" She cheekily implies the reaction was set up by saying, "That's what I like—a spontaneous standing ovation." Carol complies with a man's request to say hi to his mom in the Queen's voice and accepts a woman's gift of the Burnett Street sign from Brooklyn, New York. "I'm going to put that in my bedroom!" she cracks. After repeating her plans after the series ends, Carol has a touching moment as three children do a kick line, tug on their ears and have Carol sign their guest book in tribute to the star. "Thank you, that's really sweet of you," remarks the humbled star.

As for what follows, there is no need to belabor describing much of the material, as most is just acceptable at best. Don Crichton gets a chance to act with Tim and Carol as their patient during the ER sketch, while Stan Mazin has the honor of being the last person to "kill" another in a Burnett sketch, in this case Steve, the show's last victim. Brad Trumbull plays a bartender in Steve's sketch, while Jan Arvan is the maitre d' there as well as the boss in Carol and Bernadette's competition skit. There, each woman creates mischief to destroy the other one until predictably Jan informs that both can stay, prompting a reconciliation. Like much of the rest of the show, there is a staleness in the presentation. That includes the pointless sepia-tinted excursion of Tim having constant mishaps with his rifle and Carol's purse as he bids goodbye to her to get onto a ship going to World War I.

The finale has Steve the pianist being fought over by Carol, Vicki and Bernadette. After Bernadette does the can-can with the dancers, she leaves with Stan, Vicki goes with Don and Carol ends up with Steve. Then, Carol speaks heartfelt words about Bernadette and Steve's talents and contributions, then brings out Tim and Vicki, who pretend to sulk before joining Carol, Bernadette and Steve in singing "It's Time to Say Goodbye," joined by the dancers. At least they got the closing right for this.

March 29, 1978: "A Special Evening With Carol Burnett"

Carol shows clips of Jim Nabors and the Tarzan yells over the years; introduces highlights with Tim and Vicki between new skits; plays Mrs. Wiggins as she and Mr. Tudball plan to move to new offices, where her bungling makes Tudball reminisce about exactly how and why he hired her in the first place; is surprised by Jimmy Stewart playing the piano and thanking her; portrays Eunice trying to mend her differences with Mama through a counselor (Craig Richard Nelson); and says goodbye to guests, the dancers, her cast and the audience with a special message as the Charwoman.

Comments: Airing on a Wednesday from 8-10 p.m. Eastern and Pacific twelve days after it was taped, this opens with a standing ovation for Carol followed by the hostess thanking a special guest among many friends in the audience—actress Lillian Gish, who was in the movie *A Wedding* with Carol when it was filmed last summer, but neither shared a scene together. The great actress blows a kiss to Carol, who then shows clips from her opening show taped Sept. 1, 1967 and of herself introducing Jim Nabors as her season opener starting from this year going backwards (the last three in the 1960s prompt hysterical laughter with the way Carol looks). Next comes thirteen clips of the Tarzan yell over the years, followed by Carol doing it one more time and getting a mock shot interrupting herself.

After a commercial break, Carol introduces her duets with Liza Minnelli (Sept. 18, 1967), Ella Fitzgerald (Nov. 10, 1969), Perry Como (Jan. 20, 1969), Ray Charles (Nov. 22, 1972), Bing Crosby (Nov. 10, 1969), Rock Hudson (Feb. 15, 1975), Steve Lawrence (Jan. 10, 1976) and Eydie Gorme (Feb. 12, 1977) as well as Burt Reynolds' solo number (Feb. 23, 1972). That leads into Tudball and Wiggins, where it flashes back to her hiring as Mrs. Tudball (Vicki) rejects potential candidates. There is a reference to Hawaii again, and Bernie (Mr. Tudball's first name) calls his wife "Hindenburg" before Wanda Wiggins enters to give her resume, or as she pronounces it, "ree-zoom." She does not take shorthand, and when it comes to filing experience or typing, she says, "I've never tried." Still, Mrs. Tudball favors her, and facing having to continue to work with his wife instead, Bernie picks Wanda to join him, and she promptly messes up his suit with a pen.

This part is hilarious on its own, but during an unaired taped rehearsal, Tim makes an off-color remark about how beautiful the first applicant is and how it proves Father Duffy is full of—well, you can guess. Carol follows by telling Tim she used to work with Father Duffy, which cracks him up, but Vicki beats them all by saying in her exit by calling them a term that rhymes with suckers and announcing plans to see Father Duffy.

Going back to the air show, Tudball returns to the present day and tells Wiggins she is fired. She whimpers at her desk and tells him, "You're the best boss I ever had," which softens him to rehire her after one more problematic conversation using the intercoms. As they head out the door to their new office, Wiggins asks Tudball to get her purse. He does, and she closes the door, locking him in and providing a very satisfying ending.

Incidentally, Franelle Silver had to write this skit without input from her usual collaborator, Roger Beatty, because he was editing the retrospective clips for this show in his role as assistant director. She wanted to explain the back story of how Tudball and Wiggins met. "I thought, 'Why would he hire her?' And it came to me that it probably was the wife who made it happen," she says, explaining her excellent choice here.

The next commercials include a promotion to see the *CBS: On the Air* special recalling Wednesday night highlights coming after this show. The hosts include Danny Kaye, who gave Harvey Korman his first regular series job; Buddy Ebsen, a *Carol Burnett Show* guest in 1975; and Dick Van Dyke, this season's former regular. Those ironies have little time to set in when the show returns and Tim tells Carol a performer who has never done the series wants to appear now. Confused by this unplanned announcement, she screams as she sees Jimmy Stewart playing "Ragtime Cowboy Joe" on the piano delightfully.

"You do not know what this means to me tonight," she tells the audience in tears as Jimmy embraces her after his number. "This man has been my favorite actor for so many years. I've talked about him, I have worshipped him. I can't believe that you. . . ."

Jimmy hugs Carol and says, "I just feel so wonderful to be here and to be a part of these millions of people to thank you, for all the wonderful, wonderful, beautiful times you've given all of us all these eleven years. And frankly, speaking for all of us, all the millions of people (applause), we can't wait to find out what you're going to do next." He concludes with "Thank you for having me on your show, and I love you." They kiss once more.

At this point, Tim re-enters and breaks the emotion by quipping, "You know, speaking of musical numbers." The humor allows Carol to compose herself and introduce with Tim such clips as Harvey doing "They Call the Wind Maria" (April 28, 1969), Carol's mock "The Lady is a Tramp" (Oct. 20, 1973), the "You Light Up My Life" parody (Jan. 1, 1978), and parts of spoofs of *The African Queen* (Oct. 6, 1971), *The Postman Always Rings Twice* (Oct. 6, 1969) and *The Dolly Sisters* (March 29, 1972).

Vicki joins Carol and Tim to show her doing "The Night the Lights Went Out in Georgia" (Feb. 3, 1973) and then falsely jokes that "S-P-L-I-T" from the rural music awards send-up (March 23, 1974) was the song's flip side. There's the Bing Crosby-Bob Hope skit (Nov. 10, 1969), Tim's debut playing a newscaster (Oct. 2, 1967), the *Columbo* bit (Dec. 23, 1972) and even a thankfully brief skit with Dick Van Dyke (Oct. 29, 1977).

Next, Eunice visits Dr. Tate (Craig Richard Nelson), a county psychiatrist trying to help her overcome her situation that she sums up as "I do everything for everybody, and everybody treats me like dirt!" She contends that Mama is her main problems and tenses up talking about her, one of several traits Eunice displays that Tate tries to discourage. He invites Mama to their session but becomes ticked off by their interaction. Tate warns Eunice she will keep having fits as long as Mama is sour with her, prompting the latter to leave in a huff. "Work on your self-esteem!" he urges Eunice. "I never have liked me," she responds. She tells Tate she is OK, but Mama comes back to collect her and berate that "You'll never amount to anything." It is a funny, bittersweet, realistic conclusion.

After reviewing photos of herself with Lucille Ball, Jerry Lewis, Sammy Davis Jr., "the fabulous Mama Cass" Elliot, Gloria Swanson and Emmett Kelly, the audience applauds and Carol gets a little choked up as she presents the Ernie Flatt Dancers. They do the Firebird, a superb number in the style of the movie *The Red Shoes*. Several dancers have said it was the most intricate and exhausting routine they ever did on the show.

Outtakes conclude the rest of the clips, such as Carol accidentally losing her wig during the Rita Hayworth sketch (Feb. 1, 1971), Harvey debuting Mother Marcus (Nov. 10, 1971), Carol overfeeding Vicki (Feb. 14, 1976), Mother Marcus saying she can communicate with the dearly departed and ad libbing, "Wait, wait, I think Lyle Waggoner's coming in," prompting Carol to squeeze one of Harvey's falsies (Feb. 26, 1977), Carol cracking up in "The Little Foxes" sketch (Nov. 1, 1975), a horse doing its business as Carol sings (March 26, 1977) and the "Mary Worthless" skit (Nov. 1, 1972).

For the finale, the Charwoman watches the end of the show and waves goodbye to the dancers plus Bernadette Peters, Jim Nabors, Roddy McDowall, Betty White, Allen Ludden, Craig Richard Nelson and even Harvey Korman, who hugs her. Vicki and Tim sign the guest book, then the Charwoman turns over a sign that says "Closed." She goes downstage, and for the first time, this bit is done before a live audience. Carol doffs her cap and sits on a bucket near the lip of the stage. She did not tell anyone what she would say, only to leave room for her comments.

"This is an evening of mixed emotions for me," she starts. "Like graduation, it's a sad and happy time. It can't be possible that it was 1967 when Harvey, Vicki, Lyle and I stepped on this stage for the first time, because it does seem as if it were only yesterday. Those clichés really have a habit of punching you in the nose, don't they?

"Recently, a lot of people have been running around and expressing their own opinions as to why I decided to quit at the end of this season, and I think I should be the one to tell you, seeing as how I'm the one who really knows. In our eleven years, we have had four different time slots, and we've had our share of being up there in the ratings and being down there in the ratings. And ratings do not have a thing to do with my decision. If they did, I would've called a halt to the proceedings a long time ago, because there've been many, many times when they've been a lot lower than they've been this season.

"Now, I do think it's classier to leave before you're asked to, and the fact that CBS picked up our show for a twelfth year, and was quite adamant about it, is very flattering to all of us here on the show. However, I am adamant too. I'm so proud of our show, and quite simply, I'm no dummy. Now is the time to put it to bed and to go onto other things, because change is growth.

"It's hard, because all of us around here truly did become a second family. We've been through marriages and divorces and deaths and births, and I know the love that we have shared can never be measured by time."

She notes that the first year's director, Clark Jones, was wonderful, and thanks his successor, Dave Powers, as well as producers and technicians present and past. "Our entire creative staff was the best anybody could have," she says to applause.

"No one could feel more grateful than I do tonight for having had the opportunity to work and learn from the brilliant talent of Harvey Korman, who has no creative limits (applause). And we all have watched Vicki Lawrence blossom and grow from a green kid just out of Inglewood High into one of the finest character actresses and comediennes in the industry. I'm so proud of her. (applause)

"Tim Conway defies description. His brain never slows down. Those little wheels are constantly churning out original chunks of genius that amaze us all. I think it is a credit to Tim that some of the giants in comedy today steal from him. Tim would never say that, but I can. And the fact that he is even nicer than he is talented is about the best thing you could know about him. (applause)

"So, on behalf of all of us, I want to thank you here tonight and all of you who've been watching us for making these years possible. You brought us together, and we're so very grateful. I love you." To applause, Carol sings "It's Time to Say So Long" completely, quavering and teary-eyed by the second verse. She exits to a standing ovation and the credits roll, listing all previous writers. The last shot is of a mop and bucket on the floor.

"I'll never forget the last show," says makeup artist Joe Blasco. "It was very emotional. I busted my ass to make her look so beautiful. Her face just popped on that screen."

"I was close enough to reach out and touch her," recalls super fan Kathy Clements of her location during Carol's last words. "And I wouldn't look at her. When she started to cry," Kathy takes a long breath and sighs at the memory. After Carol went past the stage door, according to Kathy, "She went into her dressing room and was a hermit that night."

"It was real emotional for us, but really for the people who'd been there with Carol for a long time," notes Bob Illes, who had written only for the last season. "Really sad." "It was very emotional," concurs fellow last-season writer Franelle Silver.

The finale finished Number Fourteen in the ratings that week and received excellent reviews. "The bits and pieces of scattered remembrances are hilarious," opined John J. O'Connor of *The New York Times*, who assessed that the series overall "has been a consistently outstanding asset on the nation's television schedule."

The day after the taping, Carol showed Aljean Harmetz of *The New York Times* two medallions hanging around her neck. One was a gold and diamond numeral "11," in honor of the series' seasons. The other was from her pal Beverly Sills, who coincidentally had announced her professional retirement from opera. It read, "I did that already."

"Nothing remains the same," Carol told Harmetz. "But a good time was had by all in those eleven years."

Final Notes for the Season

Having ended the season at Number Sixty-Four overall, the show aired Wednesdays from 8-9 p.m. Eastern and Pacific in reruns from June 14 through Aug. 9, 1978, falling just one month shy of officially being eleven years old. Meanwhile, on Aug. 3, 1978, *The Harvey Korman Show* ended on ABC after bouncing around in several slots since the spring. "My father learned really fast that he wasn't a star," Chris Korman says of that experience.

A last hurrah for *The Carol Burnett Show* came on the Emmy Awards on Sept. 19, 1978. Host Alan Alda introduced a tribute by saying, "This spring, a show went off the air after eleven warm and successful years in our living rooms. It was more than a show—it was an institution. And the cornerstone was lovely and vibrant Carol Burnett."

Clips taken from the tenth anniversary played before Carol entered to applause and noted the ceremony's orientation. "I didn't realize that the theme tonight was going to be families and so forth, and I think it's marvelous. We didn't know, and we brought our three girls here with us. They're not old enough to be up here, doing what everyone else has been doing, but they did teeth and potty train during the eleven years of our show. And I'm very proud that they're here tonight.

"And nobody in this business does anything alone. Nobody should try. It was a team effort, and on behalf of all of our staff and the crew, I'd like to thank our peers for recognizing our show tonight, and to pay special tribute to our regulars, Harvey, Lyle, Vicki, Dick, Tim Conway." During this time, there are shots of Vicki and Lyle in the audience. "It was a wonderful, wonderful time for all of us, and we're all out, doing other things, and I'm grateful for what you do for us this evening. Thank you."

More connections to the show occur. Carol's first female writer, Gail Parent, presents the award for best comedy writing. After Carol's speech, a familiar face says, "I'm Harvey Korman. I'm so glad so many of my friends are here tonight to celebrate my return to television. (laughter) I knew they couldn't keep me off. The cameras, the lights, the audience. It's in my blood, I guess. One of the things I'd like to do on my show tonight (laughter) is present the Emmy for the outstanding single performance in variety." He pronounces Tim's name as "Tim Conray" while a laughing Tim motions from his seat for Harvey to speed it up. Tim wins and does a hilarious acceptance speech thanking in jest the absence of his children, who he claims are watching the premiere of *Battlestar Galactica* on ABC while the Emmys run on CBS, his parents, who cannot drive, and his agent and manager, who are coming back from the Los Angeles Rams football game.

While *The Carol Burnett Show* loses Outstanding Variety Series to *The Muppet Show*, presenter Steve Martin does joke while reading the nomination that "Carol Burnett is my closest friend." There are some wins for the series, first for Dave Powers. "What a terrific way to finish!" he says, thanking Joe Hamilton for giving him the opportunity and Carol for supplying her talent before concluding, "I'm so glad we had this time together."

Other Emmy wins come for Tucker Wiard for editing the March 29 finale and for Stan Freeman and Artie Malvin for their special musical material in the Jan. 8 shows. The March 29 finale also earns Emmy nominations for Ernie Flatt for choreography and Paul Barnes, Bob Sansom and Bill Harp for art direction.

The last Emmy won, for best writing, incredibly comes from presenter Dick Van Dyke. He seems a little shocked by the award, which is for the Steve Martin-Betty White episode after he left (and which beat the also-nominated March 26, 1977 episode from the previous season). Ed Simmons is briefly appreciative in his triumphant victory.

Apart from other wins this year (Carol at the Golden Globes, the series' third win as Favorite TV Variety Program in the People's Choice Awards following wins in 1975 and 1977), that was the end of *The Carol Burnett Show*. Or so it seemed at the time.

The last public reunion of the cast of *The Carol Burnett Show* occurs on March 16, 2005, when the TV Land Awards ceremony airs on that cable network as a special. Harvey, Lyle, Carol, Vicki, Tim and Bob Mackie accept their statuettes for the Legend Award during this occasion. Three years later, Harvey would pass away, but the show's legacy grew thanks to subsequent frequent DVD releases of the original shows. Courtesy of Getty Images.

Epilogue:
So Long . . . But Not Goodbye

"God, I miss that show more than anything."—Chita Rivera

The summer of 1979 brought surprising news to those who saw the finale of *The Carol Burnett Show* a year earlier. Carol, Tim and Vicki would return to star in a four-week summer comedy variety series called *Carol Burnett and Company*. Joining them would be *The Carol Burnett Show* veterans Dave Powers as director, Bob Mackie as costume designer, several dancers including Randy Doney and Stan Mazin, and Roger Beatty, Dick Clair, Jenna McMahon, Arnie Kogen, Buz Kohan and Kenny Solms as writers.

During a guest shot on *The Tonight Show* on Aug. 10 to promote the new series, Carol told host Johnny Carson that while "I said goodbye a year and a half ago," she rekindled her interest in returning to television regularly through an offhand conversation. "Not about a month ago, having dinner, Joe and I were with Tim, and Joe says, 'Let's do a summer show.' Click! So we called some people."

"Some people" included two new on-air regulars, Craig Richard Nelson, who had appeared on the 1978 finale, and Kenneth Mars, who had substituted for Harvey on the Nov. 16, 1974 show. Also among the recent arrivals on the writing staff were Bob Arnott, who had been nominated for an Emmy three times earlier for writing *The Sonny and Cher Comedy Hour*, and Ann Elder, a regular on *Rowan and Martin's Laugh-In* from 1970 to 1973 and frequent panelist on *Match Game* during the 1970s who had won two Emmys as a writer for specials starring Lily Tomlin in 1973 and 1975.

Guest stars were new too, all of whom would have been better selections than most of those who appeared in the last season of *The Carol Burnett Show*. They were in order of air date Cheryl Ladd, Alan Arkin, Penny Marshall and Sally Field.

Field's entry nabbed the series its sole Emmy nomination for Outstanding Writing in a Variety or Music Program. It was not deserved, as the presentation tried to pass off broad energy as quality comedy and relied on some trite but true material, including the umpteenth episode of "As the

Stomach Turns." Field did fine with her characterizations, but by and large it was a forgettable enterprise, as were the other three offerings.

There were moments of uproarious comedy in the quartet of shows. Tim shined as a preacher promoting alcohol to deal with life, using the phrase "It don't matter!" as part of his gospel. He and Carol did an effective spoof of the disco hit "Ring My Bell" as a clod who ate pie messily while Carol fed it to him and sang the song in a near-monotone.

However, those occasions were few and far between, making them seem unfortunately more like a continuation of the previous season's sluggish output. CBS, who received the first opportunity to air *Carol Burnett and Company*, wisely rejected this wheezy reprise of one of its premium series of all time, even though it was taped in Studio 33 of CBS's Television City studios like the original.

Carol Burnett and Company ran on ABC Aug. 18 through Sept. 8 Saturdays from 8-9 p.m. Eastern and Pacific, where *CHiPs* on NBC dominated. Replacing the cancelled *Battlestar Galactica*, *Carol Burnett and Company* ranked behind many reruns and even another ABC summer series, *Detective School*, which returned for a failed run midseason in 1979-1980.

Nonetheless, Carol had plans to do another summer series in 1980. However, CBS threw that awry by adding *The Tim Conway Show*, a comedy variety series produced by Joe Hamilton with Harvey Korman as a regular and described by many as being *The Carol Burnett Show* without Carol Burnett (she did guest on one show). Debuting on March 22, 1980 on Saturdays 8-9 p.m. Eastern and Pacific, it not only took the same time slot *Carol Burnett and Company* had held but affected the latter's planned production schedule.

"I'd like to start with four variety shows a year in which we get my gang back together," Carol told *Panorama* in 1980. "We did that last summer for ABC and the network wanted us back again this year, but we couldn't get together. Tim's doing a movie and is also with CBS. But CBS is going to allow Tim to do three guest shots, so next summer, hopefully, I'll do three variety specials—and Mr. Conway will be a guest on all of them."

Those specials failed to occur, even though CBS had cut *The Tim Conway Show* to 30 minutes in the fall of 1980 and canned it later that season, with reruns airing through Aug. 31, 1981. It was probably for the best, as there was little indication anything new could even equal the quality of the original series, particularly as its half-hour reruns as *Carol Burnett and Friends* remained popular on local TV stations in the 1980s.

While successful, *Carol Burnett and Friends* was somewhat problematic for the image of *The Carol Burnett Show* despite keeping the series fresh in the minds of the general public, because some results were bowdlerized even with careful editing in place. It could be confusing to watch, as not only were some sketches shortened due to time, but the series also jumbled elements from different shows. A notorious example is a combination that somehow melded the back-to-back appearances of Sammy Davis Jr. and Cher into one new program.

Nevertheless, demand for the series remained strong in the 1980s, with 25 newly edited episodes joined the 150 ones already in syndication as *Carol Burnett and Friends* in 1987. That devotion created another opportunity for principals of the series.

Mama Returns

In 1980 Dick Clair and Jenna McMahon wrote a funny yet poignant 90-minute special summarizing the trials and tribulations of "The Family." Sold to CBS with Carol, Harvey, Vicki and Betty White returning to their old roles, plus Ken Berry now playing Philip, *Eunice* aired March 15, 1982, and received a huge rating (23.8, bigger than most episodes of *The Carol Burnett Show*) plus an Emmy nomination for Vicki for Outstanding Supporting Actress in a Limited Series or a Special. The acclaim led to a revival of making a series out of "The Family" starring Vicki, and the result was *Mama's Family*.

As with *Carol Burnett and Company*, *Mama's Family* was taped in the same Studio 33 as was *The Carol Burnett Show*, with Vicki even doing a Q&A like Carol did in order to warm up the audience. She was the show's lead, with Ken Berry playing Vint, another son of hers. Carol, Harvey and Betty made occasional appearances as their characters, plus Harvey hosted each episode as "Alistair Quince." Vicki found that the first two shows weren't working because Mama's harsh tones on *The Carol Burnett Show* were not enjoyable in this new setting, so she made Thelma Harper softer with the assistance of Harvey, who helped with the comic staging as well as played Ed occasionally.

Harvey's work in staging harkened back to what he had done on *The Steve Allen Comedy Hour* in 1967 prior to *The Carol Burnett Show*, and his son calls it a unique challenge for him to handle. "He found directing to be like running a day care, because actors by norm are the biggest children in the world," Chris Korman says.

Rejected by CBS even though taped at the network's Television City facility, *Mama's Family* began airing on NBC on Jan. 22, 1983. Although not a ratings blockbuster, it won its time slot most occasions. However, Grant Tinker, who had taken over as president of NBC when the series arrived, disliked it and shifted it into several time slots, hurting its ability to gain a regular audience. It went off on Aug. 17, 1985.

To the surprise of some—including presumably Grant Tinker—*Mama's Family* proved popular in reruns, so it began producing new shows for syndication to local TV stations from 1986 through 1990. It outlasted its co-creator, Dick Clair, who died in 1988 and had his body cryogenically frozen for possible revival in the future. Some cast changes occurred, most notably the defections of Betty White and Rue McClanahan, who played Mama's sister, Fran Crowley, to the hit sitcom *The Golden Girls* (NBC, 1985-1992).

Incidentally, *The Golden Girls* has a strong comic sensibility in line with *The Carol Burnett Show*, probably more so than *Mama's Family* or any other series airing in the 1980s, thanks in part to ex-*Carol Burnett Show* writer Gail Parent being one of its producers. With its wild, bawdy humor and sparkling writing, acting and directing, *The Golden Girls* was very reminiscent of the Burnett brand in all the best senses.

The Burnett influence even affected movies in the 1980s. The 1980 hit *Airplane!* and *The Naked Gun* series of comedies starring Leslie Nielsen later in the decade featured wacky comedy with silly but inventive wordplay and visual gags that would have been right at home on Carol's show. Not surprisingly, ex-Burnett writer Pat Proft contributed to several of the scripts for *The Naked Gun* movies.

Meanwhile, the same decade was tough for comedy variety lovers, as all series in the genre lasted no more than two years except for *The Tracey Ullman Show* (Fox, 1987-1990). As the latter wound down to a close, Carol decided to re-emerge as a regular TV presence and help reclaim her position as a comedy queen in the medium. The problem was that she faced people's memories of her on *The Carol Burnett Show* and would likely compare anything new to that series, and that is a tough task for anyone to follow.

Carol Tries and Tries Again

Besides *Mama's Family*, Carol had spent the 1980s in theatrical features (including a well-received turn as Miss Hannigan in *Annie* in 1982), TV movies, talk shows and a few dramatic guest shots (e.g., *All My Children, Fame* and *Magnum, P.I.*) The routine kept her busy, but Carol wanted more. She proposed a return to series TV with a unique format—a half-hour comedy anthology with new stories told every week featuring a cast of six other regulars playing different principal roles. Most of the latter were little-known talents at the time. CBS and ABC rejected the idea, but NBC gave it a shot.

Carol & Company debuted March 31, 1990, following *The Golden Girls*, then assumed a familiar time slot—Saturdays at 10 p.m. Eastern and Pacific—in April. The series finished in the top twenty several times in its first season due largely to people interested in seeing Carol back in action. For the first time ever since Carol was a regular on *The Garry Moore Show*, Joe Hamilton was not her producer. She had divorced him in 1984 after they had separated two years earlier. (He would die in 1991 at age 62.)

When it came back in the fall of 1990, however, ratings drooped, probably due to the limitations of any anthology format on TV, where some new ideas emerge brilliantly and others bomb badly. The same could happen on *The Carol Burnett Show*, but the duds usually were interspersed with better skits and music, and they never took up a full show was they did on *Carol & Company*.

The series was a bold, audacious concept for Carol to embrace, and she did an excellent job in one notable role as a former quarterback who had transitioned into being female. It won two Emmys (for Swoosie Kurtz as outstanding guest actress in a comedy series and Bob Mackie and Ret Turner for outstanding costume design) and earned two more nominations, one for its main title theme music and the other for its art direction, and Carol snagged another Golden Globe nod too, but the acclaim was for naught. By the spring of 1991 NBC canned the series, with its last episode airing July 20, 1991.

Unwisely thinking that what the audience really wanted was to see her back doing true comedy variety, Carol returned before the end of the year back on CBS with a new *Carol Burnett Show* debuting on Nov. 1, 1991. The hour-long series ran Fridays starting at 9 p.m. Eastern and Pacific for just nine weeks and was a disheartening effort to watch despite some top guest stars such as B.B. King and Carol's finely honed skills.

Besides carrying over Meagan Fay and Richard Kind from *Carol & Company*, the new *Carol Burnett Show* was overstuffed with four other regulars, forcing some of them like Rick Aviles to appear in bit parts with no dialogue in several sketches. For longtime fans, it was tough to adjust and love them the same way they did with Harvey, Vicki, Lyle and Tim, so in terms of comparing the new crew with the veterans, it was no contest that most viewers' affections resided with the originals while looking askance at this bunch.

Even worse, members of the creative team behind the scenes were virtually new to Carol apart from Ken and Mitzie Welch for special musical material, and reportedly Carol clashed with the vision some had about what to do on the series. The bits that did make it to air seem stale and artificial, such as another *Star Trek* spoof more than twenty years after the series had ended and Carol had sent it up on her earlier series in 1967.

In the face of reports about poor ratings, Carol announced she was leaving the series almost as soon as it started. The last episode aired Nov. 27, 1991. For the first time ever since 1967, a series starring Carol Burnett earned no Golden Globe nominations and just three technical Emmy nominations—a sad footnote about what a miss and mess this series was.

Carol endeavored onward with other major projects, though she avoided starring in another TV series, perhaps chastened by this experience. But somewhat oddly and perhaps unexpectedly, the specter of the 1967-1978 *Carol Burnett Show* loomed over what she tried to achieve and eventually wound up dictating much of her career moves into the twenty-first century. Consider this example.

To the Moon, Carol

In September 1995, Carol returned to acting on Broadway for the first time in 30 years in the comedy *Moon Over Broadway*. The role earned her a Tony nomination for best actress in a play, but the experience was bittersweet overall in part because of expectations that stemmed in part from her old series.

"When we started this film, we thought we'd be doing a version of *The Carol Burnett Show*, and everybody would be happy," recalled one of the play's producers wistfully in the DVD commentary for the movie documenting the production, which also was titled *Moon Over Broadway*. Instead, confrontation dominated much of what happened.

For starters, Carol agreed to do the play under the assumption it would be a supporting role, as it was in playwright Ken Ludwig's original draft. But during production, it became obvious that people wanted more of her and of her brand of comedy she did on *The Carol Burnett Show*. Her lines kept changing as more physical humor was added, and it became a challenge for her to keep up with the revisions. Despite reuniting with Jane Connell, her old pal from *Stanley* in the 1950s, Carol felt frustrated rather than ecstatic.

Even so, the documentary captured a wonderful moment during the last dress rehearsal that brings a smile to *Carol Burnett Show* aficionados. When a winch failed to raise a curtain before the last act, Moore convinced Carol to join him before the audience and do a Q&A session that included the Tarzan yell. Bernadette Peters was spotted waving to Carol, and she joined Dom DeLuise backstage in congratulating her after the show. It is a delightful moment in a movie filled with people fretting they had a bomb on their hands.

"I never had people worry so much before," Carol says in assessing her experience in a NPR interview included in the *Moon Over Broadway* DVD commentary track. "If you have fun, the success will come." At 361 performances (it ended in June 1996), the play thrived only when Carol starred. After she left, business dropped off and it closed.

Shortly following *Moon Over Broadway*, Carol decided to embark on a one-woman concert tour featuring herself answering questions from the audience, like she did at the start of *The Carol Burnett Show*. She would continue to do so periodically over the next two decades while involving herself in other projects. It made sense for her to do so because the legacy of *The Carol Burnett Show* had become even bigger as the years rolled on.

Around the same time, TV executives wanted to recapture the appeal of *The Carol Burnett Show*, so Carol and crew found themselves in demand to recall the good old days for several reunion specials. This is not surprising given the virtual deification for the series since it ended in 1978.

Celebrating the Series

Those in the know continued to give accolades to *The Carol Burnett Show* as early as Nov. 25, 1980, when *Thirty Years of TV Comedy's Greatest Hits: To Laughter With Love*, an NBC special, ranked *The Carol Burnett Show* as one of the "Golden Dozen" all-time best comedies on the medium according to a survey of TV critics. Co-hosting the special with Howard Hesseman was Dick Van Dyke, incidentally.

In 1983's *The Book of Lists #3*, Lucille Ball and Phil Silvers both ranked the show as their top ten favorite TV series of all time, and Arthur Godfrey named Burnett as one of the ten best TV performers of all time. The latter was impressive because unlike Ball and Silvers, Godfrey never was a guest on *The Carol Burnett Show*.

The real appreciation for the series' legacy began on television on Jan. 10, 1993, when *The Carol Burnett Show: A Reunion* aired on CBS with clips from the original series. Plans were to include new skits as well, but according to co-writer Kenny Solms, Harvey Korman dismissed doing them, saying they could not match the magic of the originals. Regardless, the special earned good ratings and reviews and two Emmy nominations, for costume design by Bob Mackie and Ret Turner and for editing by Robert Bernstein.

Around the same time (1992-1994), Vicki Lawrence hosted her own syndicated talk show, *Vicki!*, where she reunited with Carol, Harvey and others to reminisce about the old days for a few episodes and see some clips. The same applied when James Lipton talked with Carol on *Inside the Actors Studio* in 1995 and *Biography* profiled her in 1999.

At the turn of the century, the tributes for *The Carol Burnett Show* really began piling up. In 2000, The Paley Center for Media (then known as the Museum of Television and Radio) held a reunion tribute that included Carol, Tim, Vicki and Harvey, director Dave Powers and writers Bill Angelos, Buz Kohan, Mike Marmer, Kenny Solms and Saul Turteltaub. They waited backstage as the clips played on screen before coming out on stage. Harvey's reaction to the classic comic bits was the most effusive he had ever been in public regarding the series, saying "I tell you, it doesn't get better than that, folks."

There were few revelations from the discussion that followed apart from Carol saying she wished the series had booked Lena Horne, Frank Sinatra and Tony Bennett as guests so she could have sung a duet with each of them. It was interesting seeing Marmer, who was fired after the 1971-1972 season, praise the series without rancor despite his dismissal. He said his favorite memories of *The Carol Burnett Show* were "Seeing it grow and seeing what happened with it. . . . This cast was absolutely the most sensational."

That reunion was only a public gathering taped for later viewing at The Paley Center for Media. A bigger forum for the cast occurred in a special for CBS aired on Nov. 26, 2001. *The Carol Burnett Show: Show Stoppers*, highlighted bloopers on the show taken from the 1972-1978 seasons and used no guests except for Dick Van Dyke in the "little asshole" one from 1977 to save costs. As with the Paley Center reunion, Lyle Waggoner was a notable no-show.

Taped before the tragic events of 9/11, the special aired in the series' original time slot (Monday 10-11 p.m. Eastern and Pacific) and attracted a huge audience of 30 million viewers to finish Number One for the week. Viewers were grateful for a chance to laugh amid the depressing circumstances, even if much of the material previously had been released on bootleg compilations of goofs. It received three Emmy nominations, for outstanding technical direction and camerawork, for music and lyrics by Mitzie and Ken Welch in a salute to Bob Mackie by Carol and Vicki, and for outstanding variety, music or comedy special. Its executive producers along with Carol were her former writer Rick Hawkins and her stepson, John Hamilton.

In 2003, Carol was one of five recipients of the Kennedy Center honors for her excellence in the performing arts after having served as a presenter for several years prior. Airing as a special on CBS on Dec. 26, 2003, the highlight of the segment paying tribute to her was several of her peers dressing up in Bob Mackie's outfits to play her characters. Almost all of them originated from *The Carol Burnett Show*.

"I was just the happiest person to do it," Chita Rivera says of her participation. She played Stella Toddler in the classic dowdy costume. "I just looked a mess!" Chita laughs. "The only thing I could've wished for was to have seen her face as we came out." Others who participated was Tim as Mr. Tudball and Harvey as Max (no Vicki or Lyle here, alas).

On May 12, 2004, *The Carol Burnett Show: Let's Bump Up the Lights* brought back Carol, Harvey, Tim, Vicki and Lyle (finally!) for one more CBS special to recount favorite moments from the series' Q&A segments and respond to a few new queries from the studio audience as well. It finished a solid Number Sixteen for the week.

All of them returned less than a year later when the third annual TV Land awards ran on March 16, 2005 and honored the series with its Legend Award. Bob Mackie also turned up for the event, which proved to be unexpectedly bittersweet, as it was the last time the original gang was able to get together.

Harvey: The Final Years

The reunion specials for *The Carol Burnett Show* and personal appearance tours with Tim Conway were the primary activities for Harvey Korman in the early twenty-first century. He soured somewhat from acting on TV after his experiences starring in the short-lived sitcoms *Leo & Liz in Beverly Hills* in 1986 and *The Nutt House* in 1989 and favored doing voiceover work for cartoons predominantly in the 1990s.

Harvey was far from inactive, however. He spent more time helping out with charitable activities in the same period over trying to stay in the spotlight.

"My father was very menschy, very thoughtful," says Chris Korman, pointing out how Harvey and Tim held a golf tournament benefiting people with disabilities. "He always diminished his value to show business. My father never used his fame to say, 'Hey, look at me.'"

Harvey continued his work on a reduced schedule through 2007, when he started having major medical problems. One was a non-cancerous brain tumor, which required surgery in January 2008. According to Chris, Tim made light about his pal's condition to relieve everyone's stress at the time. "How can you tell Harvey Korman with or without a brain tumor? He's always moody!" he proclaimed.

A day after coming home from that surgery, Harvey was readmitted to the hospital for a rupture of an abdominal aortic aneurysm. Given only a few hours to live, he overcame the treatment and returned home to celebrate his 81st birthday a month later. However, complications from the operations on the aneurysm ensued, and Harvey finally succumbed to them and passed away on May 29, 2008.

A few days later, on June 2, 2008, Sen. Barbara Boxer (D-Calif.) put a note in the U.S. Congressional Record honoring Harvey Korman for his career. Carol would include a tribute to him in her one-woman show as well thereafter. But perhaps the most eloquent homage to Harvey and his work on *The Carol Burnett Show* comes from his son.

"My dad's sister, Faye, told me one of his greatest joys was being able to make his mother laugh and one of his greatest sorrows or regrets was not being able to do it professionally," notes Chris Korman. "So making Carol laugh, because she was a strong female influence on him, it filled a void in his life that he never got to experience with his mother. That's why Mother Marcus was a homage to his mother as well.

"He had a love for Carol that was special and timeless, and it was most evident when they played husband and wife on the Carol and Roger sketches. I just wanted you to know that, because it goes to the heart of who my father was as an artist. If you think about it, Wesley, the word 'art' is in 'cathartic,' so making Carol laugh was a way to have closure about his mother."

Contributing to Harvey's memory since 2008 with regard to *The Carol Burnett Show* was the rerelease of the original episodes, a process which began before his death.

Going to DVD

From 2002-2004, Columbia House released 62 full-length episodes of *The Carol Burnett Show* mainly from 1973-1977 on DVD, with commentary on some of them from Carol, Tim and Harvey shot at Studio 33 with Bob Mackie's outfits in the background. Directing them on the familiar location was longtime series director Dave Powers, who would die just a few weeks after Harvey on July 3, 2008.

While the collection was popular, getting music rights cleared was a big obstacle in putting out more of the shows. Still, demand was strong enough that Time-Life announced in 2012 it was issuing several sets of DVDs of the series, the largest being named *The Ultimate Collection*, with new interviews from Carol, Lyle, Vicki and Tim plus Bob Mackie and several guests and fans. Promoted often by an infomercial on the sets on TV, the collection was a jumble of some of the previously released ones on Columbia House that even included the 2004 intros when Harvey was alive, with little explanation in the liner notes.

Nevertheless, reportedly more than 4 million units sold of these shows, and the sketches especially proliferated on YouTube and other video channels on the Internet, showing that demand for Carol remained strong. Indeed, in 2012 a *20/20* poll of TV viewers ranked *The Carol Burnett Show* second among their choices for best variety series. The winner was *Saturday Night Live*, which was still on the air during the survey while Carol's show had ended production nearly 35 years earlier.

The increased exposure and popularity led to more episodes trickling out, but what really made fans happy was the long-awaited release of forty-five 1967-1972 shows in the summer of 2015. Carol claimed in the liner notes that "The truth is, the 'Lost Episodes' weren't missing—they just weren't ready for release. I'll spare you the legal mumbo jumbo and simply say that Time Life is bringing them back for all of us to enjoy again." The real story of *The Lost Episodes* DVD can be found at the Final Notes for the Season section for the 1972-1973 season.

Combine that with many reruns of the half-hour *Carol Burnett and Friends* that began airing on the MeTV channel in 2015, it appears the series will remain with us for a long time. Hopefully more of the first five seasons will come out on DVD, as fans want to see them. In fact, they'd love to have all eleven seasons if possible, but that seems unlikely in the near future, although several bootleg copies do exist of episodes not yet released.

This is all great news, but for the chances of having another series like *The Carol Burnett Show* on television, most observers sadly agree that seems unlikely, for several reasons.

Whither Goes Comedy Variety?

The efforts to restart the moribund comedy variety format in the twenty-first century have been horrible misfires that have lasted just one show each—*Rosie's Variety Show* with Rosie O'Donnell in 2008, *The Osbournes Reloaded* in 2009, *The Maya Rudolph Show* in 2014. Each had its own deficiencies that combined for their individual failures, but several recurring ones have hit those who worked on *The Carol Burnett Show*.

"There were no performers around to do that kind of show," opines Fred Silverman. "As television got older, there was no training ground to do that kind of comedy for performers. They don't know how to do it. I would be hard pressed to find a comedian in today's environment to do a *Carol Burnett Show*. I could count on half a hand who could do one today—maybe Justin Timberlake and Gwen Stefani."

"There's always a 'wink, wink' method," Bill Angelos says of recent variety efforts. "They tell the audience, 'We're smarter than this material.'" Such condescending attitudes detract from the presentation being successful, he believes.

"I think budgets ruined the variety business," opines Ruth Buzzi. "It became too terribly expensive to costume the whole cast like we did back then. . . . The choreography, the songwriters, the comedy writers, the musical conductors and orchestra—all these things became too expensive to do week after week like we once did."

In 2015, Neil Patrick Harris did a comedy variety series in the style of *The Carol Burnett Show* on NBC that unfortunately failed (coincidentally, he was a guest on *Carol & Company*). Many hoped he could have succeeded, just to show that TV humor can be more than stale sitcoms and shows loaded just with sketches and little else, as what currently thrives.

"I really do think television misses it," Silverman says of comedy variety. Perhaps the stories from *The Carol Burnett Show* contained herein will inspire future generations to give the genre a shot.

Closing Comments

For many who participated in *The Carol Burnett Show*, a common refrain of gratitude and happiness about the time appears frequently.

"That was the best experience I ever had," says videotape editor Jerry Davis.

"It was the greatest experience of my life, of course," says Randy Doney.

"That was the best ten and a half years of my life," dancer Stan Mazin says.

"I was very fortunate to have had the privilege of working on *The Carol Burnett Show*," says Lainie Kazan about her sole appearance on the show.

So it was generally as fun to do as to watch. As to why *The Carol Burnett Show* still shines, and still resonates, today, here are some thoughts by those who were there. Most credit its star first and foremost.

"There was no show like Carol's, because there's nobody like Carol," insists Ken Welch.

"There was, and is now, no television personality—man, woman, dog—who can do what she does," says Carl Reiner.

"I think she is one of the most professional women we have on every level," says Pat Carroll. "The lady knows what she is doing. Carol, you are Wonder Woman."

"She is a superior, superior talent," says Charo. "More than A list."

"Carol Burnett made entertainment history over and over," says Ruth Buzzi. "To say she is a legend is almost an understatement. Everybody in America thought she was their next-door neighbor. So likeable, so charming and so real. No one ever knew how much she suffered in her private life. She gave the audience 100 percent and left all her problems in the dressing room."

"Carol is unique, as a person and as a performer," says writer Stan Hart. "Very gracious, and a pleasure to work with."

"She's that rare person you meet that's very grounded, just a wonderful person," Fred Silverman says. "Multitalented. She could do anything. She's that rare artist that can do comedy, singing, anything."

"*The Carol Burnett Show* was unique and the best of its kind because of regular actor-comics who were as talented in their own way as their star they supported, with obvious love," says Michele Lee. "Carol could do everything and had that ability to make her audience feel she was a friend—very difficult to do if you don't have that ability naturally."

"It was all their abilities with the sketches and the characters they did," opines dancer Sande Johnson. "It was that old school of doing it and doing it well. And Carol's a genius. She's brilliant."

"I think Carol's show will always have a place in television history as the best comedy-variety show ever," says Roger Beatty. "Her show is timeless. Good family comedy, amazing production numbers and all the most well-known guest stars in the business. It was a well-oiled machine that ran for an amazing eleven years."

"It was the best show I ever worked on," says Bob Illes, who would write and produce TV series for two decades after *The Carol Burnett Show* ended. "Well produced. Carol was a great person."

"All I can think about *The Carol Burnett Show* was how well it was run," says Barry Levinson. "There was little drama. I think everybody understood what was to be done. From the standpoint of the actors, they worked the material. They really played it. Carol really the worked the lines—the pause, the looks."

"The atmosphere was one of joy, no matter how under the gun you were," says drummer Cubby O'Brien. "It was happiness and love. There was never any tension. She (Carol) wouldn't allow it. It was one of the highlights of my life."

"She had the ability to make you laugh reading the phone book," says composer Dick DeBenedictis. He also credits "The climate of the show—you didn't have the personality conflicts you usually had. I'm sure there were, but none of them affected the flow of the show."

"Carol was determined that her show would be peopled with talented contributors who worked together to produce a show that was above the norm," says writer Gene Perret. "And it was."

Perret adds that "It was a production that we all were proud to be a part of. We writers used to kid that at parties if someone asked what you did for a living, you would not say, 'I'm a television writer.' Why? Because inevitably they'd then ask, 'What show do you write for?' When you told them, they'd say, 'I hate that show.' We were never afraid to say we wrote for *The Carol Burnett Show*. We were always proud to have been part of that creative team."

"It was a great, great show, and it deserved every award it got," says writer Saul Turteltaub.

Indeed, *The Carol Burnett Show* set out to provide viewers quality entertainment, typically met that goal and frequently exceeded it. The series gave the world an estimated 1,500 comedy sketches and 500 musical numbers. It gently mocked American institutions such as classic Hollywood movies, TV series, family life, commercials, popular music and even the First Family. Carol alone portrayed virtually every female pop culture icon of the twentieth century, including but not limited to Cher, Joan Crawford, Bette Davis, Doris Day, Katharine Hepburn, Barbra Streisand—and Minnie Mouse—plus played a robot, an alien, a queen and much more. Quite simply, she and her show did it all.

And it really was the ultimate family show, in every sense of the term, even for participants. "You were part of the Burnett family forever," notes Chris Korman. When he had surgery at age fourteen, half the show's crew visited in the hospital.

For many viewers, watching *The Carol Burnett Show* at its peak gave the impression that being part of a comedy variety series like it was the most fun anyone could have. It created an atmosphere so unique for a TV program that it was one of those rare productions that produced no real imitation. *The Carol Burnett Show* was the real deal in terms of quality entertainment, and it likely will remain a classic now and forever, as long as anyone wants to laugh and feel happy.

And with that, the time comes for this book to say, "So long."

Appendix:

Top Carol Burnett Shows—Author's Choice

Of the nearly 300 installments of *The Carol Burnett Show*, these rank among the top 10 percent as ones that are great to watch from start to finish. These are listed chronologically.

1) Jan. 29, 1968 (Jonathan Winters, Dionne Warwick)

2) Feb. 12, 1968 (Martha Raye, Betty Grable)

3) Feb. 19, 1968 (Nanette Fabray, Art Carney)

4) March 3, 1969 (Ethel Merman, Tim Conway)

5) Nov. 10, 1969 (Bing Crosby, Ella Fitzgerald, Dan Rowan and Dick Martin)

6) Feb. 1, 1971 (Rita Hayworth, Jim Bailey)

7) Oct. 6, 1971 (Steve Lawrence, Carol Channing)

8) Nov. 1, 1972 (Peggy Lee, Anne Meara, Jerry Stiller)

9) Nov. 8, 1972 (Steve Lawrence, Lily Tomlin)

10) Nov. 15, 1972 (Ruth Buzzi, John Davidson)

11) Dec. 23, 1972 (Steve Lawrence, Tim Conway)

12) Jan. 27, 1973 (Kaye Ballard, Tim Conway)

13) Oct. 6, 1973 (John Byner, Helen Reddy)

14) Feb. 16, 1974 (Bernadette Peters, Tim Conway)

15) Nov. 16, 1974 (John Byner, Helen Reddy)

16) Sept. 13, 1975 (Jim Nabors)

17) Oct. 11, 1975 (Bernadette Peters)

18) Nov. 8, 1975 (Helen Reddy)

19) Nov. 15, 1975 (Maggie Smith)

20) Nov. 22, 1975 (Betty White)

21) Nov. 29, 1975 (The Pointer Sisters)

22) Jan. 24, 1976 (Emmett Kelly, the Jackson 5)

23) Oct. 6, 1976 (Madeline Kahn)

24) Oct. 23, 1976 (Steve Lawrence)

25) Nov. 20, 1976 (Ken Berry)

26) Dec. 11, 1976 (Betty White)

27) Jan. 15, 1977 (Glen Campbell)

28) Jan. 29, 1977 (Rock Hudson, Steve Lawrence)

29) Feb. 12, 1977 (Eydie Gorme)

30) March 5, 1978 (Steve Martin, Betty White)

Bibliography

Amory, Cleveland. "*The Carol Burnett Show* Review," *TV Guide*, Dec. 9-15, 1967, p. 28.

Andrews, Peter. "Is Harvey Korman Ripe to Be a Top Banana?" *New York Times*, Oct. 3, 1976, Section II, p. 25.

Archives of American Television website, interviews with Mike Douglas (March 31, 2005) and Bob Schiller (April 4, 2000).

Associated Press, "Carol Burnett show continues to be bright family variety spot," *The Free Lance-Star* (Fredericksburg, VA), Feb. 10, 1972, p. 2.

Ballard, Kaye. *How I Lost 10 Pounds in 53 Years: A Memoir*. New York: Watson-Guptill (Back Stage Books), 2006.

Barthel, Joan. "The Makeup of Carol Burnett," *TV Guide*, Dec. 30, 1967-Jan. 5, 1968, pp. 18-21.

Burnett, Carol. *This Time Together: Laughter and Reflection*. New York: Three Rivers Press, 2011.

"CBS Recipe: Stir With Stars," *Variety*, Oct. 25, 1967, pp. 1 and 32.

Conway, Tim, with Jane Scovell. *What's So Funny?* New York: Simon & Shuster, 2013.

"Dick Van Dyke: A Conversation With" (part of the Museum of Television and Radio Seminar Series), recorded Nov. 12, 1998.

Collette, Buddy with Steven Isoardi. *Jazz Generations: A Life in American Music and Society*. New York: Continuum, 2000.

Farrell, Eileen and Brian Kellow. *Can't Help Singing: The Life of Eileen Farrell*. Boston: Northeastern University Press, 1999.

Fry, William F. and Melanie Allen. *Life Studies of Comedy Writers* (updated edition). New Brunswick, N.J.: Transaction Publishers, 1998.

Gent, George. "TV: Carol Burnett Stars," *The New York Times*, Sept. 12, 1967, p. 93.

Gould, Jack. "TV Review," *The New York Times*, Sept. 15, 1970, p. 95.

Hadleigh, Boze. *Hollywood Gays*. New York: Barricade Books, 1996.

Harmetz, Aljean. "11 Burnett Years at End," *The New York Times*, March 23, 1978, Section III, p. 15.

Hoy, Michael J. "Harvey Korman Leaving Carol Burnett Show," *The Beaver County* (Pa.) *Times*, Nov. 10, 1976, p. D-1.

Hyatt, Wesley. *Emmy Award Winning Nighttime Television Shows, 1948-2004*. Jefferson, N.C.: McFarland & Company, Inc., 2006.

Montgomery, Kathryn C. *Target: Prime Time*. New York: Oxford University Press, 1989.

"Notes on People," *The New York Times*, Feb. 2, 1977, Section III, p. 12.

"Notes on People," *The New York Times*, Feb. 7, 1978, Section III, p. 12.

O'Connor, John J. "TV: Your Choice—Giggle or Snicker," *The New York Times*, March 17, 1971, p. 91.

O'Connor, John J. "TV: Carol Burnett Gives Valedictory," *The New York Times*, March 29, 1978, Section III, p. 27.

"Q&A: Carol Burnett," *Panorama*, August 1980, pp. 18-26.

Scott, Vernon. "Carol Burnett Admits Show In Trouble," *The Nashua* (New Hampshire) *Telegraph*, Dec. 12, 1977, p. 28.

See, Carolyn. "Carol Burnett's Life Style," *TV Guide*, April 11-17, 1970, pp. 30-36.

Suskin, Steven. *Second Act Trouble: Behind the Scenes at Broadway's Biggest Musical Bombs*. New York: Applause, 2006.

Taraborrelli, J. Randy. *Laughing Till It Hurts: The Complete Life and Career of Carol Burnett*. New York: William Morrow & Co., 1988.

"Tip Sheet on Nielsen Quickie," *Variety*, Oct. 4, 1967, p. 27.

Tormé, Mel. *It Wasn't All Velvet*. New York: Viking, 1988.

Van Dyke, Dick. *My Lucky Life in and out of Show Business: A Memoir*. New York: Crown Archetype, 2011.

Whitney, Dwight. "Carol & Joe & Fred & Marge," *TV Guide*, July 1-7, 1972, pp. 10-13.

Index